Directors' Remuneration Handbook

Second edition

Directors' Remuneration Handbook

Second edition

by

Cliff Weight

Bloomsbury Professional

Bloomsbury Professional Ltd, Maxwelton House, 41–43 Boltro Road, Haywards Heath, West Sussex, RH16 1BJ

A CIP Catalogue record for this book is available from the British Library.

ISBN: 978 1 78043 331 8

Typeset by Kerrypress Ltd, Luton, Beds

Printed and bound in Great Britain by CPI Group (UK) Ltd, Croydon, CR0 4YY

'Incentives matter: not because, as some people crudely think, financial rewards are the only human motivation – although there are some people of whom that is true, and many of them are to be found in the financial sector. Most people have more complex goals, but they generally behave in line with the values and aspirations of the environment in which they find themselves. We must create cultures in which business and finance can work together to create high performing companies and earn returns for savers on a sustainable basis.'

Professor John Kay, in the Kay Review Report July 2012

Preface

Directors' remuneration lies at the heart of the debate on effective corporate governance. This is the issue, above all others, in which directors face a conflict of interest.

UK companies are rightly considered to rank among the best in the world in their standards of corporate governance and reporting. However, the recent economic crisis shone a spotlight on all aspects of our regulatory framework including our corporate governance model and forced us to consider where things have gone wrong and why. The broad consensus is that, while the UK model of corporate governance is not essentially flawed, there are areas where we all need to do better – as government, as companies and as shareholders.

Our goal must be to ensure that our companies are clear-sighted and focused on long term success. Disclosing clear, relevant information on these issues in company reporting is necessary if shareholders are to make well informed decisions in their role as company owners. And it is very important that there is a clear link between the company's strategic objectives and the criteria for payments to directors.

In the US, changes have been made by improving the disclosure of executive pay, and by introducing a vote on executive compensation – the 'say-on-pay'.

In the UK, we have avoided a spate of regulation, but we have had significant consultations on the importance of long termism in corporate Britain, on narrative reporting and on the disclosure of directors' remuneration. New legislation was enacted in 2013. Our approach continues to be driven by the concepts that:

(i) it is the shareholders' responsibility to control and approve directors' remuneration.

(ii) it is government's responsibility to ensure that the Companies Act and supporting frameworks enable shareholders to receive information so as to be able to exercise their rights.

How much, when to pay, what to pay for and how to motivate directors are the key questions. Easy questions to ask but good answers require a detailed framework of knowledge. Those interested in the subject of directors' remuneration will find this book most informative and useful. I hope many will read it and that this will lead to a better educated discussion on the complex issue of directors' remuneration and better understanding, from all those involved, of other peoples' opinions and reasons for their points of view.

As the book points out, there is no panacea, but shedding light on what is happening, combined with greater insight, should help the quality of the debate.

Cliff Weight

MM&K Limited

June 2014

Acknowledgements

First and foremost to my wife Joan, who encouraged me to write this book and read and improved all the manuscripts. She supported me throughout and without her help this book would not have been written.

To all my clients, from whom I have learnt so much over my 29 years as a remuneration consultant. Consultancy is a strange business. Clients employ you because of what you know, yet so much of my knowledge has been gathered from the clients I have worked with.

To all my friends and colleagues at MM&K, where since 2006 I have been a director and part owner. Ownership brought a new perspective to my views on directors' remuneration.

Special thanks go to Mike Landon, MM&K's share scheme expert who contributed most of the chapters on the taxation of remuneration and the LSE Listing Rules; to Damien Knight who has criticised and challenged my ideas and provided much positive input; and to my fellow directors and business partners Paul Norris and Nigel Mills. Nigel Mills in particular is the recognised UK guru on private equity remuneration and he has contributed the chapters on private equity and alternative investment remuneration.

To Peter Brown, my old partner at Independent Remuneration Solutions, from whom I learnt so much.

To Sarah Wilson, who campaigns tirelessly for better corporate governance. She and Manifest have been my long term partners in the Executive Directors' Total Remuneration Survey, which continues to shed light on how much directors are paid. The MM&K/Manifest survey has been widely used to provide data and background information in many chapters of this book.

I thank the Institute of Directors, Quoted Companies Alliance, ABI, NAPF, ISS, PIRC, F&C, Hermes and the United Kingdom Listing Authority for allowing me to quote their materials in this book.

Tony Minns contributed a personal view of a Remuneration Committee Chairman. His forthright views provide a bright interlude of beautiful prose in an otherwise rather technical part of this book.

Thanks are also due to Professor Andrew Chambers, who wrote the first Corporate Governance Handbook and for whom I contributed several chapters on Directors' Remuneration from the second edition onwards. He was a strong advocate of the wisdom of taking those chapters and forming a separate book on Directors' Remuneration and encouraged me to do so.

Special thanks go to my new friends at Bloomsbury. To Tom Prince, who edited this book and presented it so well. To Andy Hill who persuaded me to write the book and commissioned it and coached me gently to meet deadlines. And to Jubriel Hanid and Victoria Daniels who handled the marketing programme – a very important role as there is no point writing a book if no-one reads it.

Contents

Table of Statutes

UNITED STATES

Table of Statutory Instruments

List of Figures and Tables

Chapter 1

Chapter 6

Chapter 12

Chapter 13

Chapter 26

Chapter 27

Chapter 28

Chapter 29

Chapter 30

Chapter 31

Chapter 32

Chapter 33

Chapter 34

Chapter 35

Chapter 37

Chapter 38

Chapter 39

Chapter 40

Chapter 47

Chapter 48

Chapter 49

Chapter 51

Chapter 53

Chapter 54

Chapter 57

1 Executive Summary

1.1 CEO pay

It all starts at the top. When the CEO is appointed, a deal is done which involves both a legal contract and a psychological contract.

The psychological contract will run along these lines. 'We want you to come and join our company and do these things. If you do them well and the share price goes up correspondingly we will give you £x million.'

Implicit in this is the agreement that capital will be available for investment and acquisitions; and that if things do not work out the CEO will be asked to leave. Such is the nature of life in the C-suite.

What follows is the determination of how the £x million will be delivered – how much in salary, pension, bonus, incentives and shares; when it will vest; when shares can be sold; what performance conditions and what compensation in the event the CEO leaves. All of this is written into the legal contract.

Each year, and in many cases rather more frequently whenever the opportunity arises, the CEO will negotiate to increase his/her remuneration. This can be via a pay rise or an increase in incentive opportunity, or by making the incentive targets easier.

The CEO also has all the resources of the executive team to help him or her in these negotiations.

The Remuneration Committee (made up of Non-Executive Directors) has the job of setting the CEO's pay and agreeing incentive targets and outcomes. This is not an easy task.

The above is very different to when a mid-level manager is recruited. He or she is offered a pay package with little flexibility to negotiate and has to fit into the company remuneration strategy.

1.2 The Principal Agent problem

At the heart of the problem about executive directors' remuneration is the highly complex dilemma of how to make executive directors think and behave like owners of the business. Executive directors are the agents of shareholders. But, however pure and honest they may be, self-interest may make them behave in ways that maximise their personal rewards and wealth. This may make them take excessive risks. It may make them unduly cautious. They may be tempted to build huge empires, with many minions to look after each and every beck and call, to live and work in glorious ivory towers, transport themselves around the globe in corporate jets and live a life of luxury paid for by their company. Such behaviour may not be in the best interests of the shareholders.

Shareholders are different and have different objectives. Some are long term shareholders. But many trade in and out of shares. Some want long term share price growth. Others are more interested in how the company's share price performs relative to other companies in the same sector. The average time a share is held is six to nine months.

Shareholders elect directors and approve the remuneration report at each AGM, but they operate under conditions of incomplete and asymmetric information. The principal (ie the shareholder) is conscious of the problem of potential moral hazard and conflict of interest in the agent, but has limited tools to affect it.

The UK Corporate Governance Code states that companies should be run by an effective board which is collectively responsible for the long-term success of the company; and remuneration design should promote the long term success of the company.

Companies appoint Remuneration Committees to set the pay of the executive directors and other senior executives. Remuneration Committees are meant to act on behalf of the owners and reflect their interests.

Good examples of when directors' remuneration worked are Apple, where under Steve Jobs shareholders received returns of 20 times their investment, GE under the first three quarters of Jack Welch's reign, and Michael Eisner at Disney. In the UK, Bart Brecht at Reckitt Benckisser, Sir Martin Sorrell at WPP[1] and Sir Terry Leahy at Tesco all produced fabulous returns for long term shareholders. When it works, executives receive huge rewards and shareholders do so as well. But it is not easy. There are few people able to successfully lead, direct, manage and control a large company.

Bad examples in the UK include RBS; BP – 14 years with CEO Lord Browne led to over focus on costs, cost cutting and cutting corners (eg the Houston and Gulf of Mexico disasters lost the shareholders £40bn of shareholder value); and Marconi (formerly GEC) where the agents of shareholders adopted a new high risk strategy, but the risks and rewards were asymmetric. Another example is Shell where the reserves were overstated and the bonuses paid out more than they should have done. There are

[1] In 2012 WPP received much criticism about the rewards offered to its 67 year old CEO, eg http://www.guardian.co.uk/business/2012/jun/13/wpp-martin-sorrell-pay-vote

examples too numerous to list of smaller companies where the management have not acted the way shareholders want.

Solving the principal agent problem requires much wisdom. It is probably one of the most difficult management problems in business today.

1.3 Remuneration strategy

There are five objectives of a remuneration strategy. It must:

(i) **Motivate** executives to achieve a good level of performance and hopefully to exceed it. It should help to provide a focus on key objectives. It must do this within the accepted risk parameters of the company. It should be compatible with risk policies and systems.

(ii) Enable the company to **retain** its key executives. Having chosen the management team it is important that they are retained and not tempted by offers elsewhere. The total remuneration package must therefore be attractive and executives must see a good probability of the targets being achieved and hence that the incentive plans will pay out. If the company has been doing well, the executives should have accumulated deferred bonuses and LTIPs awards which are likely to vest over the coming years. Un-vested, in the money awards act as handcuffs on successful executives, as it makes it more expensive for others to poach the executives.

(iii) Enable the company to **recruit** high-calibre executives from other companies. It may be acceptable to recruit one person on a one-off package. A company should not have to consistently pay higher remuneration to external hires than its own existing executives – this is either evidence that the internal executives' pay should be increased, or questions the competence of the existing management.

(iv) **Exit** executives at a reasonable cost in the event that an executive fails to make the grade or if their performance falls off. It may also be important to have appropriate non-compete and non-poaching clauses in their employment contracts.

(v) **Have total costs that are acceptable** to shareholders. Levels of salary should not be excessive. The costs of bonus and long-term incentives measured as a percentage of profits, cash flow, turnover, increases in shareholder value (and other appropriate metrics relevant to the company's sector), should not be excessive. Benefits and pensions should also not be excessive. (Different stakeholders have different views on what is excessive.)

The remuneration strategy also has to answer the four questions of **what for, how much, when** and **which** proportions of pay (salary, bonus, long term incentives and pension).

- **What** is it that the company wishes to pay for? There are many different views on this and there are many views on how effective alternative approaches are. The choice of performance measures is at the heart of the debate on pay for performance.

- **How much?** The sums involved in directors' remuneration seem huge to the man in the street and to the average journalist. However, this is an area where benchmark remuneration data can confirm what orders of magnitude will be appropriate. Although this may not be a perfect market, the fact that the average tenure of a Chief Executive is about seven years (median five years)[2] means that there is sufficient turnover for supply and demand to drive the levels of remuneration.

- **When** should the remuneration be paid? Obviously salary has to be paid now and pension in an approved pension plan cannot be paid until after retirement. Bonuses can be paid as soon as the accounts have been audited and signed off. However, the growing trend is to defer part of bonus, often into shares, which may not vest for up to three years and so is linked into changes in the share price over this time. Long-term incentive plans typically have a three year performance measurement period so are not really long-term at all. Some are structured as nil cost options, which may have a ten year life. The introduction of share ownership guidelines and share retention rules for shares acquired from bonus and long-term incentive plans can offer remuneration for a longer period. Some companies do not allow the sale of shares (other than to pay for taxes) until retirement or until the executive leaves the company; and some also require the phased sale of shares over a number of years.

- The **mixture** of salary, bonus, long term incentive, pension and other benefits. The reward strategy must specify what proportion of total remuneration should be made up by each of these elements. It needs to be set for target (budget) performance, for stretch (outstanding) performance and also for poor performance.

The following figure shows the percentile rank of length of service by CEOs. The average is hugely influenced by a couple of star CEOs who have 25 plus years of service.

The average tenure in the CEO role is about seven years, whilst the median is five years. The planning horizon for many companies is much longer than this, which highlights one of the problems of alignment of CEOs with long term shareholders.

---

2 This refers to the length of time the CEO has been in the job. Data sourced from Manifest database of quoted companies May 2014.

Figure 1: Length of service of CEOs (Source Manifest database, May 2014)

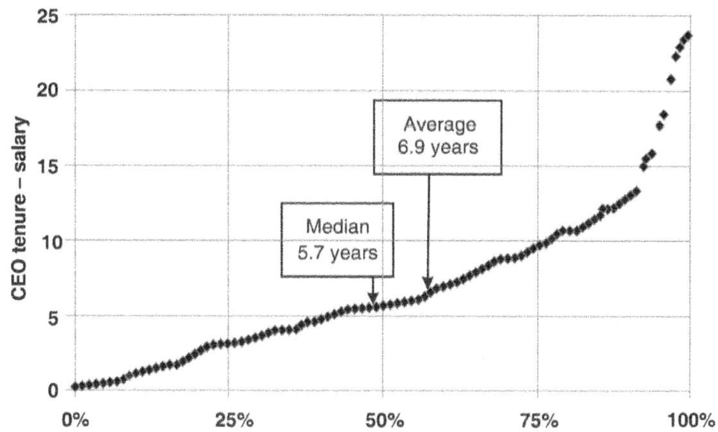

Notably, more than one quarter of CEOs have more than eight years of service in the role. These are by definition successful CEOs, as unsuccessful CEOs will not survive so long. This suggests that starting with an eight year planning horizon could be acceptable for most CEOs.

The author has identified seven basic remuneration strategies, which encompass the vast majority of company situations. These are shown in **Figure 2** below.

Figure 2: The seven remuneration strategies

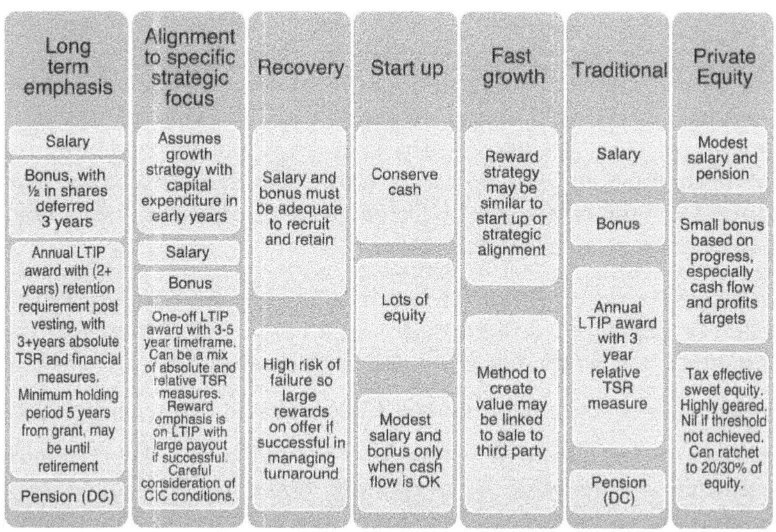

1.4 Definition of Directors' Remuneration

According to the Oxford English Dictionary, 'remuneration' means amounts earned or paid for work.

But the dictionary does not define 'directors' remuneration'. It is one of those phrases that is banded about as if everyone knows what it actually is. The components of directors' remuneration are quite easy to list: salary, bonus, benefits, pension, share options, share schemes, and long term incentive plans (LTIPs) are the main ones. In Part D of this book, each is explained in detail.

The complexity in directors' remuneration is that in any given year:

- some remuneration is paid;
- some is awarded but may not be received until some years later (in the case of pension it might be decades later);
- some is received in the year but might have been awarded some years ago. In some cases the awards made some years ago may have vested some time earlier, and it is only in that year that the executive chooses to exercise them or sells the shares in the awards.

Salary is easy to understand. It is contractual and is paid monthly (usually).

Bonus is the term used to mean annual variable payments or an annual incentive plan. Executive bonuses are usually paid after the end of the financial year based on the results of the financial year. It is normal to pay bonus soon after the results have been audited. Bonus is usually paid in cash, but may be paid partly in shares.

Deferred bonus refers to a bonus awarded for the financial year with payment delayed until sometime in the future. Sometimes the deferred amount is paid in cash but more commonly it is paid in shares, so could be worth more or less when it is actually received than at the award date. Deferred bonus may be paid in two or more stages (the vesting schedule). Typically deferred bonus will not be paid for up to three years after it is awarded and if the executive leaves the company he will not receive any deferred bonus that has not vested. (Typically there are exceptions for good leavers.)

When the deferred bonus is awarded, its value is relatively easy to estimate. The value of the shares in the award would be one way. However, it could be argued that it is worth less than cash, because:

- there is a risk the executive will leave and will not receive the award.
- money in the future is worth less than money today. Therefore the estimated future value of the award should be discounted to today's value. The individual is likely to choose a higher discount rate than a shareholder.

When the award vests it will be worth the number of shares in the award times the share price at the vesting date. This is an easy sum to do. However, the executive may choose to retain the shares and sell them at a later date. In such cases he could receive more, or less, than the award amount. The nature of the award may enable him to choose the date at which he exercises his award and sells his shares. In this case the award may in some cases be classed as remuneration, but it might be better to classify it as part remuneration and part as investment returns.

Long term incentives typically have a three year performance period and often a three to ten year horizon; whilst pension benefits are not paid until after retirement.

Remuneration components can be categorised by the time when the executive receives the reward; see **Figure 3**.

Another categorisation is whether they are performance-linked or not. We should not forget the importance of intrinsic rewards. For some people the need for achievement, self-esteem and power can be just as big a driver as pay. See **Figure 4.**

Figure 3: Timescales of remuneration

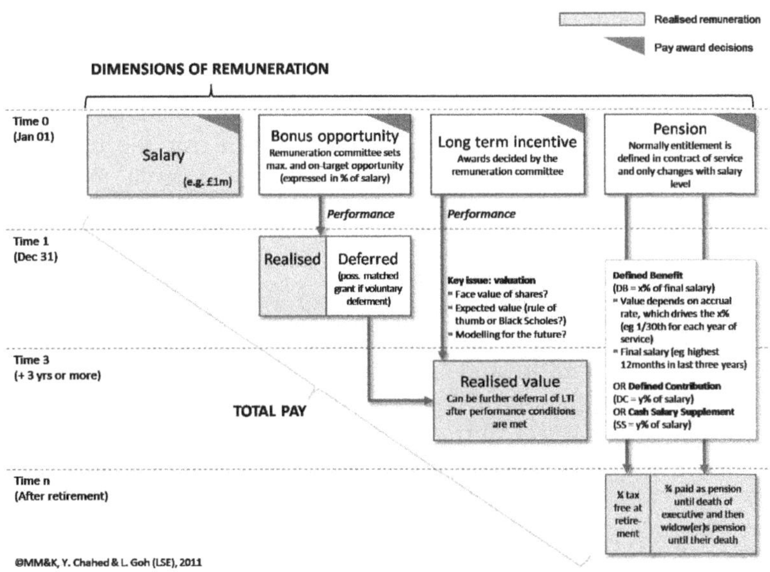

Figure 4: Reward components

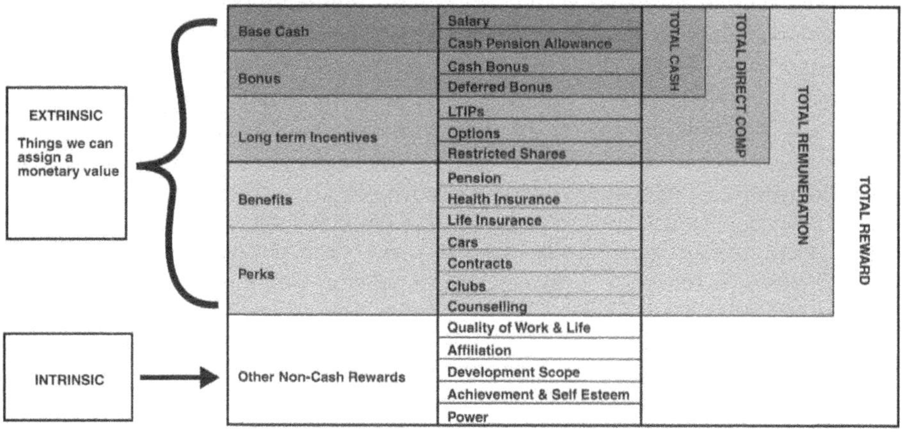

1.5 Motivational impact

The Remuneration Committee and shareholders need to assess the motivational effect of the remuneration strategy and its cost effectiveness.

Executives will value different forms of remuneration differently. To illustrate this point consider the proverb 'a bird in the hand is worth two in the bush'. Thus £1 of salary is worth more than £1 of bonus. How much the £1 of bonus is worth to the executive depends on their estimate of the likelihood of the bonus plan paying out, a discount for the time value of money and a further discount depending on the degree to which the executive feels the events that affect the bonus outcome are beyond their control.

E	=	**O**	x	**T**	x	**C**
Bonus Efficiency (E)	=	Estimated Outcome (O)	x	Discount for Time (T)	x	Controllability Discount (C)

These issues are explored in much greater detail in **Chapter 30** Motivation Theories.

1.6 Pay for performance

First we need to have a good understanding of 'what is performance?' This question must be resolved before effective pay for performance can be considered.

The expectations treadmill[3] is a term used by McKinsey to describe the way the share price has expectations of future growth already built into it. A company with a high p/e ratio is expected to grow faster than one with a lower p/e ratio. The difference in growth required can be modelled using a fairly simple spreadsheet. But should management be rewarded for delivering this higher level of growth? This is not a simple question. Their previous actions may have positioned the company for the growth that is now occurring. Were they rewarded at the time for these strategic moves? Or was the remuneration strategy to wait until the results were evident in the financial figures? At one end of the spectrum there is a danger that managers are not being rewarded for re-organising the business and launching new products. The other end of this spectrum is that managers are being rewarded for achieving strategic goals and then rewarded again when they translate into share price increase – double counting.

But the main point McKinsey makes is that expectations create a treadmill and failure to deliver is then reflected in a major correction in the share price. This fear creates excessive pressure to deliver short term results.

It is far too easy to say that companies should aim to deliver long term sustainable shareholder value and profits should be sustainable. Such words are not enough. More detail is required. The concern is whether the profit growth is sustainable, whether the growth in revenues will lead to long term profitability, whether the cost cuts now will translate into better margins or merely weaken the competitive advantages of the products.

How do we define the value of a company? Nobody has the answer to this question. Different people have different views. Shareholders and fund managers do not have perfect information. This is why share prices vary from day to day and why analysts have such difficulty in agreeing what a share is worth.

Since it is agreed (by some) that directors' remuneration should be linked to value created, we do however have to try and define value. Given this proviso, the reader should recognise that there is no perfect answer and different companies will come to different conclusions. Shareholders will need to assess whether the measures used in the remuneration plans are those that they feel will result in 'value'. If they are comfortable with this then (all other things being equal) they will tend to be buyers of the company's shares.

There is another way to look at this. The CEO and executive directors are asked to set the strategy and then to implement it. If the strategy is successful, then it should result in better TSR relative to comparator companies, share price increasing faster than the cost of capital, a ROCE greater than the cost of capital; or a combination of all of these.

---

[3] See www.mckinseyquarterly.com/The_expectations_treadmill_299

1.7 TSR and other performance measures

It should be noted that:

- The relationship between pay and TSR[4] is long-term. One needs to take care because TSR is not a good short-term measure of management's performance and should not be the sole determinant of incentive pay. Clearly, a company's share price should ultimately reflect both good and bad performance but there is often a lag. An annual comparison of pay and TSR is misleading and potentially dangerous, but long-term trend information is useful. Shareholders should not be overly influenced by an annual comparison, but should focus on the long term as required by the UK Corporate Governance Code, the regulators and other policy makers in the context of executive pay.
- Share prices are driven by many factors. In the list below, only the last two are under the control of management (and many would argue that the market's view of management is somewhat fickle):
  - Interest rates
  - General economic activity and growth forecasts
  - Market sentiment
  - Sector sentiment
  - Existence of a potential buyer of the company
  - Market view of management capability and future strategy
  - Achievement of operational goals and whether management generates sustainable competitive advantage.

As a result share price is frequently out of alignment with the underlying performance of the company – often for substantial periods of time.

Accounting measures are lagging indicators of performance. They measure what happened in the past. They may indicate the future if historic trends continue. But it might be like driving up the motorway and only looking out of the rear view mirror!

Sometimes share prices increase because of factors over which management have little control. (When the tide comes in, all the boats rise. However no-one would suggest that the captains of the boats should be paid a bonus because the tide has risen.) In a bull market most share prices will rise. Companies with high leverage will benefit when interest rates stay low for extended periods. Companies should be managed for the long term. When measuring performance we need to separate out what management have

[4] TSR = Total Shareholder Return = share price change plus dividends.

achieved and what is a result of external factors. Companies which fail to do this may end up with too much focus on financial results and short term share price performance.

Companies cannot manage their share price. It may be possible to manipulate or to massage the share price in the short term, but ultimately the share price will reflect the underlying performance of the company. However, there are numerous examples of where the stock market has failed to value companies correctly and the share price has failed to reflect the underlying value of the company. Such misjudgement (mis-evaluation) can occur over months or even years.

Management should be concerned about both creating value and conserving value:

- A company which aims foremost to conserve value will be cautious about investments in new product development, about moves into new territories, about leverage.

- A start-up company or early stage company will seek to grow quickly. Such companies are risky. A company with a volatility of 50% can expect its share price to decline. It is not easy to explain this statistic to management, who will be fully committed to their plan. Nor to their Non-Executive Directors who have approved the strategy. But it is a statistical fact; that is what happens with log-normal statistical distributions. The reason for this result may not be immediately obvious. However with high volatility, there is a higher probability of high value but low probability events. With 20% volatility there is almost nil chance of the share price increasing by more than 200% in three years; but with 50% volatility the probability is about 13%.

Share prices follow a lognormal distribution. The actual returns over the period 2002 to 2010 were as follows:

Chart 1: FTSE 100 total returns 2002–2010

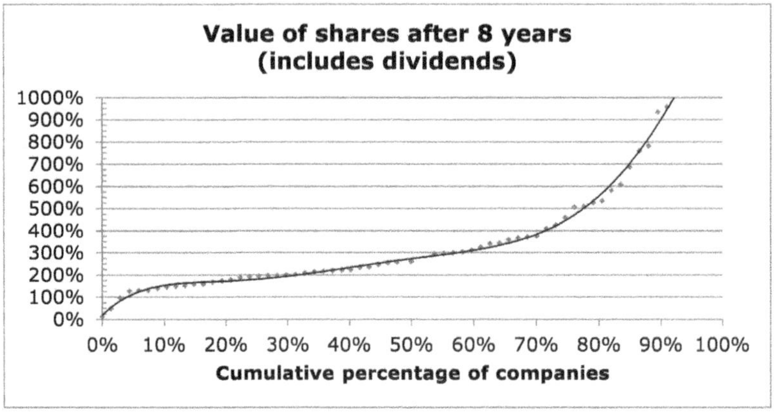

The above is an indicator of the likely distribution of returns over any future eight year period. It shows how much better is the performance of those in the upper quartile. The business strategy will indicate whether attempting to obtain such returns is feasible, high risk, or optimal in its approach.

Companies with high growth potential will have higher p/e ratios. Performance targets for bonus and long term incentives plans for companies with high p/e ratios should be more stretching than for those with average p/e ratios. A company with lower than average p/e ratio may be expecting a profit decrease or have high risk attached to its outlook.

Most mature companies are a mixture of mature and innovation. They need to encourage innovation as otherwise they will decline and die.

Different sectors of business have different issues to face and adopt different strategies, which lead to different Key Performance Indicators (KPIs) and incentive measures. For example:

Sector	**Issues**	**Typical sector KPIs/incentive measures**
Banks	Risk, solvency, liquidity, customer service, short-termism, greed and irresponsibility	RROCE (risk adjusted rate of return on capital employed) Economic profit Company culture

Sector	Issues	Typical sector KPIs/incentive measures
Oil	Large capital investments with long term returns Commodity prices subject to macro-economic events	ROCE Project Milestones Production Targets In Boepd Reserves In Boepd Safety

An easily understood example is easyJet plc, as we are all familiar with the company and the product it offers. Its KPIs, as shown in its 2013 Strategic Report, are:

1. **Safety**
2. **Customer Satisfaction measured by**
   - Satisfaction response as surveyed
   - On-time performance score
   - likely to recommend easyJet to others
3. **Staff turnover**
4. **Network Development**
   - Top 100 airports where easyJet is No 1 or No 2 airline
   - Market share of airports
5. **Financial Strength**
   - Revenue per seat
   - Cost per seat excluding fuel
   - Profit before tax/per seat
   - ROCE
   - Gearing
   - Dividends and basic earnings per share

Once you have understood the above, you will be in a position to develop the remuneration strategy and its incentive plan components. The steps involved are described in **1.09**, but first the impact of tax (and other regulatory issues) must be considered.

1.8 Tax issues

Tax should not be the driver of remuneration strategy. However, it is in both the interests of the executives and the shareholders that, where possible, remuneration is tax effective.

In the UK, in general, UK residents pay income tax and national insurance on their income when it is received. There are several HMRC approved schemes which are tax efficient:

Enterprise Management Incentive (EMI) share options. Gains from EMI share options are subject to capital gains tax. No income tax or national insurance is payable. However, to qualify, numerous qualifications must be met including that the company has less than 250 employees, less than £30 million of gross assets and carries out a qualifying trade. Options over £250,000 of shares are the maximum permitted under current legislation.

CSOP. Gains from Company Share Option Plans (CSOP) are subject to capital gains tax. Like EMI share options no income tax or national insurance is payable. Such plans must meet numerous conditions to qualify. The maximum award permitted is options over £30,000 of shares.

Pension. Under the new HMRC rules which apply from 6 April 2014 to those taxed in the UK, executives can be paid or contribute up to £40,000 per annum into their HMRC approved pension plan, subject to the lifetime allowance figure of £1.25 million.

There are a number of plans (eg growth shares, JSOPs) which are non-controversial with HMRC, who will approve the initial share value and then provide rewards in the form of capital gains. However there are a number of plans which purport to translate income into capital, which are promoted by the tax avoidance industry. HMRC do not like artificial plans and companies should tread with care in this area.

HMRC have attacked 'disguised remuneration'. One of their aims is to stop the use of trusts to defer income. Trust law is a hugely complex. Case law will tell us in time how effective HMRC are in this respect.

1.9 Design process

The Remuneration Committee, a subcommittee of the Board, is usually made up of independent Non-Executive Directors. The Remuneration Committee makes the decisions about the pay of executive directors. The following diagrams illustrate the process that should be followed for:

(i) Remuneration Strategy

(ii) Bonus

(iii) Long term incentives.

Figure 5: Remuneration policy design

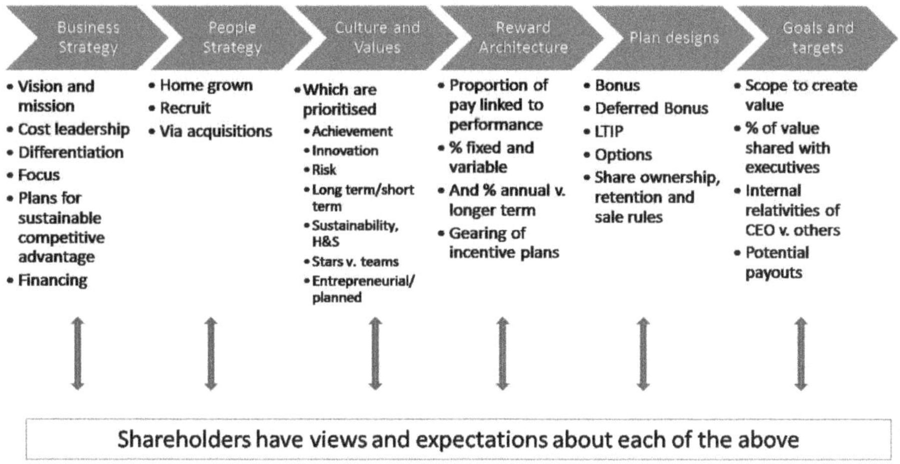

Figure 6: Annual bonus review process and target setting

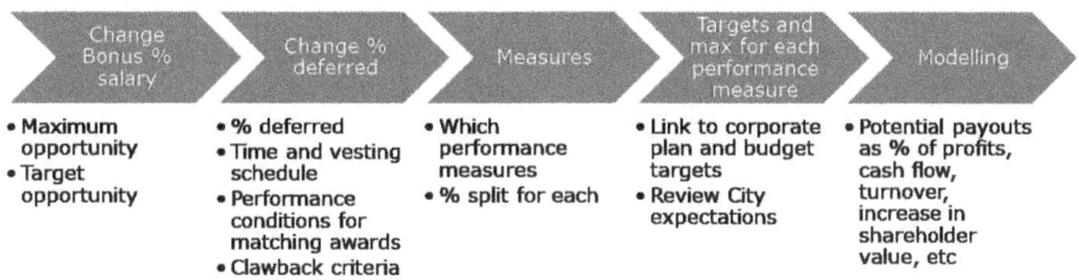

Figure 7: LTIP review process and target setting

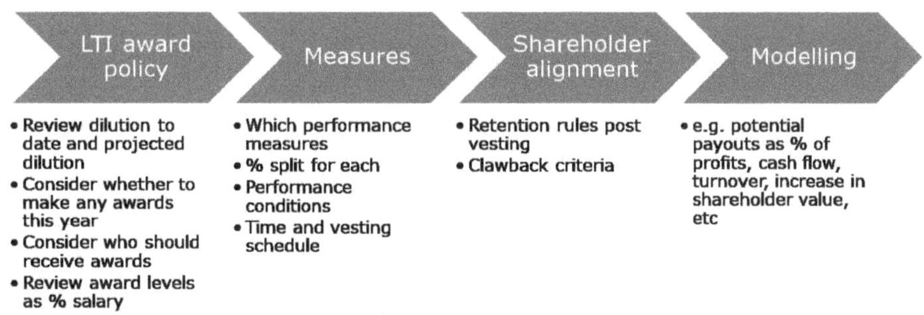

1.10 Chairman

The UK Corporate Governance Code gives no guidance about the remuneration of the Chairman. It is strangely silent on the issue.

The UK Corporate Governance Code distinguishes between a Chairman who is independent on appointment and one who is not. The implication is that after some years as a Chairman the issue of independence is not relevant or the Chairman is no longer independent.

The role

The Chairman must work closely with the CEO and has to establish an effective working relationship. The Chairman must lead the Board and the CEO implements the strategy.

The UK Corporate Governance Code does not distinguish between an Executive and a Non-Executive Chairman.

Some Non-Executive Chairmen undertake the role as similar to a Non-Executive Director, just requiring some extra time to plan and manage the board meetings. The structure of the remuneration of such a role should be similar to that of other Non-Executive Directors.

Other Non-Executive Chairmen are much more heavily involved in the strategy and leadership of the company. For these, the remuneration needs careful consideration. Their remuneration should be set on the initial appointment when the role needs to be clearly defined. If, subsequently, the strategy changes or the executive team changes in a way which impacts on the role of the Chairman, there may be a case for reviewing the Chairman's remuneration.

On appointment there should be a clear understanding of the amount of time that the Chairman is expected to contribute.

Remuneration

The level of pay of the Chairman may reflect:

- His/her track record and ability to command a rate of remuneration in the market place
- How much he/she is paid in their other roles in other companies. This will affect their expectations and what shareholders will see as consistent with the Chairman's pay elsewhere
- The role and contribution he/she is expected to make and the value this will add to the company
- The time commitment
- The amount that the previous Chairman was paid
- The amount the CEO is paid and how this compares on a per day basis with the Chairman
- Shareholders' views about what is acceptable

- Market data for rates of pay for Chairman in similar companies; although it should be noted that there is a wide variation in fees even after controlling for the size of the company.

An Executive Chairman is an executive and will be the most senior executive in the company and should be remunerated like a CEO.

Types of remuneration structure

The most typical practice for quoted companies is that the Chairman is paid a fixed fee and in some cases some of the fee is paid in shares. Sir Derek Higgs, in his Higgs review, recommended that 'innovative' approaches be considered for Chairmen.

The most common types of approach are:

(i) Paid only fees[5]

(ii) Paid a mixture of fees in cash and in shares

(iii) Awarded a number of shares on appointment which vest at a rate of x% per year, plus an annual fee

(iv) Awarded a number of options on appointment plus an annual fee

(v) An annual fee, plus annual awards of options or LTIPs or other types of share awards

(vi) In a turn-round situation a Chairman might be awarded a specific incentive plan as well as his/her annual fees. In such cases the Chairman may become more hands-on.

The use of partly-paid shares could be considered as a tax effective way to remunerate Chairmen and Non-Executive Directors.

1.11 Non-Executive Directors

Non-Executive Directors have the legal duties which pertain to all Directors. In addition they have responsibilities in the areas of strategy, performance, risk and people. See **Sections 2.1** and **2.10**. They are the custodians of the governance process and contribute to the development of strategy. They are not involved in the day to day running of the business.

The remuneration and types of remuneration structure should reflect the time and nature of the desired role and are usually similar to those of the Chairman, ie:

---

5 Annual fees are usually paid monthly.

(i) Paid only fees.[6] In larger companies this will usually reflect a basic fee plus committee fees

(ii) Paid a mixture of fees in cash and in shares

(iii) Awarded a number of shares on appointment which vest at a rate of x% per year, plus an annual fee

(iv) Awarded a number of options on appointment plus an annual fee

(v) An annual fee, plus annual awards of options or LTIPs or other types of share awards.

1.12 How this book is laid out

Part A describes the legal and regulatory framework. It also covers best practice of corporate governance in respect of remuneration and shareholders' views on remuneration.

Part B explains the background of theory and practice. It reviews motivation theory – what works and what does not work. It also provides data on market practice, ie what other companies do.

Part C explains how to develop a remuneration strategy, what to consider and how to evaluate the choices and trade-offs.

Part D explains the detail of how to design the individual components of remuneration – salary, bonus, long term incentives, pensions, etc.

Part E explains how Chairmen and Non-Executive Directors are remunerated.

Part F covers a number of issues not covered elsewhere, including remuneration in private equity, venture capital and hedge funds, a discussion on the merits of the LLP structure versus the plc structure, and a review of developments in executive compensation elsewhere.

---

[6] Annual fees are usually paid monthly.

PART A

LEGAL, REGULATORY AND GOVERNANCE

The current framework for corporate governance of remuneration in the UK is an amalgam of company law, the UK Corporate Governance Code (the 'Code'), the London Stock Exchange Listing Rules, FCA/PCA rules, and the principles, guidance and guidelines of the various UK institutional investors. It is complex, confusing, sometimes contradictory and seemingly forever changing. My challenge in this book is to produce something that is both rigorous and helpful to the reader.

The starting point is to understand the duties and roles of directors and this is covered in **Chapter 2**. **Chapter 3** covers important background on the great governance reports. Next are the legal requirements that are in the Companies Act. The Listing Rules follow. All of these have to be followed if they apply to the Company and there are several potential penalties for any breaches. Next are the FCA Remuneration Code rules, which banks and financial services companies must report on to the FCA. Next is the UK Corporate Governance Code, to which quoted companies must either comply with or explain to their shareholders why that are not complying. **Chapter 13** covers the IFRS 2 requirements of the International Accounting Standards Board about the accounting of share based payments.

Corporate governance can be split between what must be done, what is good practice and what organisations think is good practice. Company law must always be followed. Legal requirements relating to remuneration are described in detail in **Chapter 5.** The UK Corporate Governance Code describes best practice. Institutional investors, their representative bodies and the intermediaries also offer further guidance and guidelines to companies, and their advice is described in some detail in **Chapters 14–26**: Best Practice Guidance.

The Remuneration Committee is a sub-committee of the Board of the company, which has responsibilities for setting remuneration of executives and this is covered in **Chapter 27**. **Chapter 28** covers engaging with shareholders and communicating with them.

2 Role of a Director – what does a director do?

In order to incentivise, or reward fairly, a CEO or director, first one has to understand what the director has to do.

2.1 Legal duties of Directors

The Companies Act 2006 codified the duties of directors. For the purposes of this book, the critical section is s 172(1), duty to promote the success of the company:

> '(1) A director of a company must act in the way he considers, in good faith, would be most likely to promote the success of the company for the benefit of its members as a whole, and in doing so have regard (amongst other matters) to –
>
> (a) the likely consequences of any decision in the long term,
>
> (b) the interests of the company's employees,
>
> (c) the need to foster the company's business relationships with suppliers, customers and others,
>
> (d) the impact of the company's operations on the community and the environment,
>
> (e) the desirability of the company maintaining a reputation for high standards of business conduct, and
>
> (f) the need to act fairly as between members of the company.'

The definition provided in s 172 (1), often described as 'enlightened shareholder value', requires directors to have regard to the long term interests of the company.

The majority of respondents to the Kay Review[1] took the view that this definition gave sufficient emphasis to the success of the company and the promotion of its long term performance.

---

1 http://www.bis.gov.uk/assets/biscore/business-law/docs/k/12–917-kay-review-of-equity-markets-final-report.pdf

2.2 Role of the Chairman

The UK Corporate Governance Code states that the Chairman is responsible for:

- Leadership of the Board, ensuring its effectiveness on all aspects of its role and setting its agenda.
- Ensuring that the directors receive accurate, timely and clear information.
- Ensuring effective communication with shareholders.
- Facilitating the effective contribution of Non-Executive Directors and ensuring constructive relations between executive and Non-Executive Directors.
- Acting on the results of board performance evaluation by recognising the strengths and addressing the weaknesses of the Board and, where appropriate, proposing new members be appointed to the Board or seeking the resignation of directors.

The UK Corporate Governance Code clearly differentiates between the running of the company's business and the running of the Board. The Higgs review saw the Chairman playing a pivotal role in the company, and creating the conditions for overall board and individual Non-Executive Director effectiveness.

The following role descriptions of the Chairman, CEO and Company Secretary are based on information from the ICSA website, www.icsa.org.uk.

The Chairman is responsible for:

(1) Meetings

- Chairing board and general meetings and those of the Nomination Committee.
- Running the Board and ensuring its effectiveness in all aspects of its role, including regularity and frequency of meetings.
- Setting the Board agenda, taking into account the issues and concerns of all board members. The agenda should be forward looking, concentrating on strategic matters.
- Ensuring that there is appropriate delegation of authority from the Board to executive management.
- Ensuring that the directors receive accurate, timely and clear information, including that on the company's current performance, to enable

the Board to take sound decisions, monitor effectively and provide advice to promote the success of the company.

- Managing the Board to allow enough time for discussion of complex or contentious issues. The Chairman should ensure that directors (particularly Non-Executive Directors) have sufficient time to consider critical issues and obtain answers to any questions or concerns they may have and are not faced with unrealistic deadlines for decision making.
- Set the agenda, style and tone of board discussions to promote effective decision making and constructive debate.

(2) Directors

- Facilitating the effective contribution of Non-Executive Directors and encouraging active engagement by all members of the Board.
- Ensuring constructive relations between the executive and Non-Executive Directors.
- Holding meetings with the Non-Executive Directors without the executives present.

(3) Induction, development and performance evaluation

- Ensuring that new directors participate in a full, formal and tailored induction programme, facilitated by the Company Secretary.
- Ensuring that the development needs of directors are identified and, with the Company Secretary having a key role, that these needs are met. The directors should be able to continually update their skills and the knowledge and familiarity with the company required to fulfil their role on the Board and its committees.
- Identifying the development needs of the Board as a whole to enhance its overall effectiveness as a team.
- Ensuring the performance of the Board, its committees and individual directors is evaluated at least once a year and acting on the results of such evaluation by recognising the strengths and addressing the weaknesses of the Board. Where appropriate, through the Nomination Committee, proposing that new members be appointed to the Board or seeking the resignation of others.

(4) Relations with shareholders

- Ensuring effective communication with shareholders.
- Maintaining sufficient contact with major shareholders to understand their issues and concerns, in particular discussing governance, strategy and remuneration with them.
- Ensuring that the views of shareholders are communicated to the Board as a whole so that all directors develop an understanding of their views.

(5) AGM

- Arranging for the Chairmen of board committees to be available to answer questions at the AGM and for all directors to attend.

The Chairman's direct reports are the Chief Executive and the Company Secretary.

2.3 Role of the CEO

The Chief Executive is accountable and reports to the Board and is responsible for running the group's business.

The Chief Executive is responsible for the following, within the authority limits delegated to them by the Board:

(1) Business Strategy and Management

- Developing group objectives and strategy having regard to the group's responsibilities to its shareholders, customers, employees and other stakeholders.
- The successful achievement of objectives and execution of strategy following presentation to, and approval by, the Board.
- Recommending to the Board an annual budget and [5 year] financial plan and ensuring their achievement following board approval.
- Optimising as far as is reasonably possible the use and adequacy of the group's resources.

(2) Investment and Financing

- Examining all trade investments and major capital expenditure proposed by subsidiary companies and the recommendation to the group board of those which, in a group context, are material either by nature or cost.
- Identifying and executing acquisitions and disposals, approving major proposals or bids.
- Leading geographic diversification initiatives.
- Identifying and executing new business opportunities outside the current core activities.

(3) Risk Management and Controls

- Managing the group's risk profile, including the health and safety performance of the business, in line with the extent and categories of risk identified as acceptable by the Board.
- Ensuring appropriate internal controls are in place.

(4) Board Committees

- Making recommendations on remuneration policy, executive remuneration and terms of employment of the senior executive team, including the Company Secretary to the Remuneration Committee.
- Making recommendations to the Nomination Committee on the role and capabilities required in respect of the appointment of executive directors.

(5) Communication

- Providing a means for timely and accurate disclosure of information, including an escalation route for issues.
- Ensuring effective communication with shareholders.

(6) Other

- Setting group HR policies, including management development and succession planning for the senior executive team and approving the appointment and termination of employment of members of that team.

The duties which derive from these responsibilities include:

- Leading the executive directors and the senior executive team in the day to day running of the group's business, including chairing the Executive Committee and communicating its decisions/recommendations to the Board.
- Ensuring effective implementation of board decisions.
- Regularly reviewing the operational performance and strategic direction of the group's business.
- Regularly reviewing the group's organisational structure and recommending changes as appropriate.
- Formalising the roles and responsibilities of the senior executive team, including clear delegation of authorities.
- Supervising the activities of subsidiary companies' most senior executives.
- Developing senior teams within subsidiaries and ensuring succession planning.
- Developing the following policies for board approval and then implementing them:
    - Codes of ethics and business practice;
    - Share dealing code;

  - Health and safety policy, risks and procedures (to be reviewed annually);
  - Communications policy (including procedures for the release of price sensitive information);
  - Investor relations policy;
  - Corporate social responsibility policy (including environmental, employee communications and employee disability);
  - Charitable donations policy.
- Ensuring that all group policies and procedures are followed and conform to the highest standards.
- Together with the Chairman, providing coherent leadership of the company, including, representing the Group to customers, suppliers, government, shareholders, financial institutions, employees, the media, the community and the public.
- Keeping the Chairman informed on all important matters.

2.4 Other Executive Directors

Other executive directors have the normal responsibilities of all directors, plus they will operational responsibilities for their divisions and/or functions.

2.5 Non-Executive Directors

Non-Executive Directors have the normal responsibilities of all directors, plus Non-Executive Directors have responsibilities in the following areas:

- **Strategy:** Non-Executive Directors should constructively challenge and contribute to the development of strategy.
- **Performance:** Non-Executive Directors should scrutinise the performance of management in meeting agreed goals and objectives and monitoring.
- **Risk:** Non-Executive Directors should satisfy themselves that financial information is accurate and that financial controls and systems of risk management are robust and defensible.
- **People:** Non-Executive Directors are responsible for determining appropriate levels of remuneration of executive directors and have a prime role in appointing, and where necessary removing, senior management and in succession planning.

Non-Executive Directors are the custodians of the **governance** process. They are not involved in the day-to-day running of business but monitor the executive activity and contribute to the development of **strategy.**

The Remuneration Committee should consist of some of the Non-Executive Directors and the Chairman.

2.6 Company Secretary

The Company Secretary will usually be the secretary of the Remuneration Committee and has specific responsibilities in relation to directors' remuneration, including:

- Ensuring that the Remuneration Committee is familiar with the Code principles and provisions on remuneration, including the provisions on the design of performance related remuneration set out in Schedule A of the Code.
- Ensuring that grants of share options and other long term incentive awards do not contravene the Code (B.1.2 and B.1.3).
- Ensuring that Non-Executive remuneration is determined in line with Code provisions and within the limits set by the articles of association (B.2.3).
- Ensuring that all new long-term incentive schemes and significant changes to existing schemes are submitted to shareholders for approval, subject to the provisions of the Listing Rules (D2.4) and other scheme rules.
- Contributing to the drafting of the directors' remuneration report and ensuring its compliance with the full range of disclosure requirements.
- Share dealing: communicating and implementing procedures for listed company directors and any other 'person discharging managerial responsibilities' (as defined in s 96B of FSMA) to comply with the Model Code on share dealing annexed to the Listing Rules (LR 9 Annex 1).

The other parts of the Company Secretary role

Over recent years, responsibility for developing and implementing processes to promote and sustain good corporate governance has fallen largely within the remit of the Company Secretary.

Before setting out specific responsibilities of the Company Secretary, it is important to note that the most effective Company Secretary is one who is regarded by the Board as its trusted adviser and who:

- keeps under review legislative, regulatory and governance developments that may impact the company and ensures that the Board is appropriately briefed on them.

- wins the confidence of and acts as a confidential sounding board to the Chairman and other directors on issues of concern.
- provides, where appropriate, a discreet but challenging voice in relation to board deliberations and decision making, drawing in particular on his or her professional experience and historical knowledge of the company.

Code framework

The Corporate Governance Code (the 'Code') gives explicit recognition to the role of the Company Secretary in promoting good corporate governance in listed companies as stated in the principles and supporting provisions quoted below (Code references are shown as applicable):

- 'Under the direction of the chairman, the company secretary's responsibilities include ensuring good information flows within the Board and its committees, between senior management and non-executive directors, as well as facilitating induction and assisting with professional development.' (A.5)
- 'The company secretary should be responsible for advising the Board through the chairman on all governance matters.' (A.5)
- 'All directors should have access to the advice and services of the company secretary who is responsible to the Board for ensuring that Board procedures are complied with.' (A.5.3)

Summarised below are the main responsibilities which should be assumed by the Company Secretary in assisting the Chairman to implement the Code principles and comply with its provisions (Code references are shown as applicable):

(1) Board composition and procedures:

- Establishing a summary of matters reserved for decision by the Board (A.1.1).
- Scheduling meetings, assisting with the preparation of agendas, providing guidance on board paper content, ensuring timely delivery of papers; recording board decisions clearly and accurately, pursuing follow up actions and reporting on matters arising (A.1.1 and A.5).
- Ensuring that appropriate D and O insurance cover is arranged for directors (A.1.5).
- Ensuring board committees are constituted in compliance with the Code and that their membership is regularly reviewed and refreshed (A.3).
- Supporting Board succession planning and overseeing Non-Executive Director rotation (A.4 and A.7).

(2) Board information, development and relationships:

- Building Non-Executive Director induction programmes which provide a full, formal and tailored introduction to the business. (A.5.1).
- Arranging for major shareholders to be offered the opportunity to meet new Non-Executive Directors (A.5.1).
- Facilitating good information flows between board members and fostering effective working between executive and Non-Executive Directors (A.5).
- Establishing and communicating procedures for directors to take independent professional advice at the company's expense if required (A.5.2).
- Developing a proactive relationship with Board members, providing a source of information and advice, and acting as the primary point of contact with Non-Executive Directors (A.5.3).
- Helping develop and support board performance evaluations which are tailored to the company's particular needs (A.6).

(3) Remuneration [*note: this is repeated for completeness and is exactly the same wording as in the first paragraphs of this section* ***2.6***]:

- Ensuring that the Remuneration Committee is familiar with the Code principles and provisions on remuneration, including the provisions on the design of performance related remuneration set out in Schedule A of the Code.
- Ensuring that grants of share options and other long term incentive awards do not contravene the Code (B.1.2 and B.1.3).
- Ensuring that Non-Executive remuneration is determined in line with Code provisions and within the limits set by the articles of association (B.2.3).
- Ensuring that all new long-term incentive schemes and significant changes to existing schemes are submitted to shareholders for approval, subject to the provisions of the Listing Rules (B.2.4) and other scheme rules.
- Contributing to the drafting of the directors' remuneration report and ensuring its compliance with the full range of disclosure requirements (see separate ICSA Guidance Note Directors' Remuneration Report on this topic).

(4) Audit and internal control:

- Having a detailed knowledge of, and advising on the application of, the FRC Guidance on Audit Committees (the Smith guidance) and the

FRC Internal Control: Revised Guidance for Directors on the Combined Code (the Turnbull guidance) as updated from time to time (C.2 and C.3). The Smith and Turnbull guidance are available from the FRC website www.frc.org.uk.

- Ensuring the implementation of and monitoring the effectiveness of the whistle blowing procedures approved by the Audit Committee (C.3.4).

(5) Relationship with shareholders:

- Ensuring the Board keeps in touch with shareholder opinion on a continuing basis (D.1).
- Managing the convening and conduct of the AGM in line with statutory and regulatory requirements and using it as an opportunity to communicate with retail investors (D.2.1 to D.2.4).
- Managing relations with institutional investors on corporate governance issues and board procedures.

(6) Disclosure and reporting:

- Ensuring that the necessary disclosures on corporate governance and the workings of the Board and its committees are included in the annual report (see Schedule C to the Code for a comprehensive checklist).
- Ensuring that the requisite types of governance information (as set out in Schedule C to the Code) are made available, either on the company's website or in documents circulated to shareholders.

Statutory and regulatory compliance

The Company Secretary normally has full responsibility for Companies Act compliance and, where the company is listed, carries much of the responsibility for compliance with the FSA's Listing, Prospectus, and Disclosure and Transparency Rules. For listed companies, there is also the need to make the Board aware of the market abuse provisions of the Financial Services and Markets Act 2000 ('FSMA') including, in particular, the responsibility not to release misleading information about the company's financial performance or trading condition, or to mislead the market by the failure to disclose relevant information.

3 Law, Regulations and Governance Processes

3.1 Background

This section explains the background to the rules, regulations and guidance governing directors' remuneration and explains which are most important.

Remuneration of directors is a key area of corporate governance. Patricia Hewitt, the Secretary of State for Trade and Industry, in her Foreword to the 2001 proposals on directors' remuneration described it thus:

> 'Directors' remuneration lies at the heart of the debate on effective corporate governance. This is the issue, above all others, on which directors face a conflict of interest; it is also one in which there is a real need for non-executive directors to exercise independent judgment. Indeed, some commentators have suggested that non-executive directors who are unable to ensure proper performance linkage in respect of executive directors' remuneration are unlikely to respond effectively to strategic proposals generated by the Chief Executive and management.'

The major corporate governance reports (Cadbury, Greenbury, Hampel, Turnbull, Higgs, Walker, the FRC 2010 review and the Kay Review) have all commented on remuneration. Greenbury was solely concerned with remuneration, as was the 2001-2 DTI consultation on directors' remuneration.

The Cadbury Report (1992) restricted itself to three paragraphs about remuneration. Cadbury reduced the maximum contract length to three years (previously it was five years); required full and clear disclosure of directors' total emoluments, including pension contributions and stock options; and recommended a Remuneration Committee made up wholly or mainly of Non-Executive Directors.

The Greenbury Report was published on 17 July 1995. The backcloth was of large gains from share options in newly privatised companies and the terms of reference to Greenbury referred to unjustified compensation packages in privatised utilities. The Greenbury Report set out three fundamental principles of accountability, transparency and performance linkage. Greenbury developed a detailed Code which has now been superseded by some of the contents of the UK Corporate Governance Code.

The Hampel Report (1998) suggested three broad principles for remuneration (the level and make-up of remuneration, procedure and disclosure) and these were incorporated in the first edition of the Combined Code. With regard to 'the level and make-up of remuneration', Hampel commented:

> 'The wording makes it clear that those responsible should consider the remuneration of each director individually, and should do so against the needs of the particular company for talent at board level at the particular time.'

The 2002 DTI consultation on directors' remuneration concluded that remuneration was a matter for shareholders, but the legal framework could be improved to help the shareholders exert their responsibility. The government enacted the Directors Remuneration Report Regulations 2002, SI 2002/1986, with the aim of improving transparency and accountability. The new Regulations required:

- more and better disclosure of remuneration and its link to performance
- a vote at the AGM on the Remuneration Report.

The Turnbull Report (2003) focused on risk and internal control. Turnbull set some questions for the Board to consider including the following:

> 'Do the company's culture, code of conduct, human resource policies, and performance reward systems support the business objectives and risk management and internal control systems?'

The Higgs Report (2003) made a number of recommendations that affected remuneration:

- Only independent directors should sit on the Remuneration Committee. This meant that the Chairman could not be a member.
- The Remuneration Committee's terms of reference were extended to include the Chairman. Higgs also widened the responsibility of the Remuneration Committee to set the executive directors' and Chairman's remuneration, whereas Hampel had felt that the overall policy should be a matter for the Board as a whole.
- Training of directors and the performance evaluation of the Board, its committees and its individual directors were stressed. A performance appraisal of the Remuneration Committee must be done and how it is conducted must be reported in the annual report.
- The Remuneration Committee should also be responsible for appointing consultants in respect of executive director remuneration. This last point was in response to research which had confirmed the worries of many directors that compensation consultants were often perceived to

be too close to executive management and too ready to encourage companies to position their remuneration policy in the 'upper quartile' of their peer group comparators.

- Notice or contract periods should be set at one year or less and if longer notice or contract periods were needed to recruit new directors from outside these should reduce after the initial period.

The FRC Review of Higgs made minor changes to the wording regarding remuneration, but said:

> 'Remuneration committees should take a robust line on reducing compensation to reflect departing directors' obligations to mitigate loss,'

thus removing the alternative of liquidated damages in contracts.

The FRC reviewed the Combined Code again in 2006 and decided to permit the Chairman to be a member of the Remuneration Committee, if he was independent when appointed.

The Walker Review (2009)

Sir David Walker was asked by the Prime Minister to review corporate governance in UK banks in the light of the experience of critical loss and failure throughout the banking system. The Terms of Reference for the review were to examine corporate governance in the UK banking industry and make recommendations, including in the following areas:

- the effectiveness of risk management at board level, including the incentives in remuneration policy to manage risk effectively
- the balance of skills, experience and independence required on the Boards of UK banking institutions
- the effectiveness of board practices and the performance of Audit, Risk, Remuneration and Nomination Committees
- the role of institutional shareholders in engaging effectively with companies and monitoring of boards
- whether the UK approach was consistent with international practice and how national and international best practice could be promulgated
- identifying where its recommendations were applicable to other financial institutions.

Sir David Walker recommended[1] substantial changes to the way the Boards of banks and big financial institutions function and their corporate governance. The main points of the Walker Review relating to remuneration were:

- More power for Remuneration Committees to scrutinise firm-wide pay
- Remuneration Committee to oversee pay of high-paid executives not on the Board
- Significant deferred element in bonus schemes for all high-paid executives
- Increased public disclosure about pay of high-paid executives
- Chairman of Remuneration Committee to face re-election if report gets less than 75% approval
- Non-Executives to spend up to 50% more time on the job.

FRC Code Reviews in 2009 and 2010

The Walker Report contained a number of recommendations addressed to the FRC, and the FRC agreed to implement those recommendations that it considered should apply to all listed companies. Further details were set out in the FRC's report on its own review of the Combined Code that concluded in December 2009.

Some of the recommendations were implemented through revisions to the Code (now renamed the UK Corporate Governance Code – published in June 2010). Some recommendations have been implemented through the FRC's Guidance on Board Effectiveness, published in March 2010. The Code and Guidance can be found at: http://www.frc.org.uk/corporate/ukcgcode.cfm.

Sir David Walker recommended that the FRC's remit should be extended to cover the development and encouragement of adherence by institutional investors to best practice in stewardship of UK listed companies. The FRC agreed to the Government's request that it should take responsibility for a stewardship code for institutional investors. The Code was published in July 2010. While compliance with the Code is voluntary, all UK authorised asset managers are required to report whether or not they apply the Code. Further details can be found at: http://www.frc.org.uk/corporate/investorgovernance.cfm.

---

1 Sir David Walker's report on the governance of banks and other financial institutions was published in November 2009. The report can be found at: www.hm-treasury.gov.uk/walker_review_information.htm

Sir David asked that the FRC website provide a link to the website of the new Remuneration Consultants Group, which has published a code of conduct for remuneration consultants. Further details of the Group and code of conduct are available at: http://www.remunerationconsultantsgroup.com. A copy of the code is in Appendix 5.

FCA Remuneration Code[2]

The Financial Services Authority's Remuneration Code was first published in August 2009 following the G20 summits in London and Pittsburgh, and the publication of the Financial Stability Board's remuneration principles. The rules came into effect on 1 January 2010, but covered performance in 2009.

The FSA morphed into the FCA and PRA in 2013.

Banks and other financial services organisations have to follow the FCA Remuneration code, with the largest ones (Tier 1) having the most detailed rules, principles and guidance, whilst others have proportionate rules to follow.

A new Remuneration Code came into force on 1 January 2011, covering pay awards made in 2010 and paid in 2011. The Code has been amended to reflect the provisions (approved in July 2010) of the European Union's Capital Requirements Directive (CRD).

These changes bring more than 2,500 firms within the scope of the Code. These include all banks and building societies, asset managers, hedge fund managers, Undertakings for Collective Investment in Transferable Securities (UCITS) investment firms, and some stockbrokers and firms that engage in corporate finance, venture capital and the provision of financial advice.

The Kay Review (2012)

The Kay Review of UK Equity Markets and Long-Term Decision Making Final Report in July 2012[3] urged a rebuilding of trust and confidence in financial intermediation, which he felt were the product of the prevailing culture. The main points of relevance to directors' remuneration were:

- Incentives matter: not because, as some people crudely think, financial rewards are the only human motivation – although there are some people of whom that is true, and many of them are to be found in the financial sector. Most people have more complex goals, but they

---

2 http://www.fsa.gov.uk/pubs/policy/ps10_20.pdf

3 http://www.bis.gov.uk/assets/biscore/business-law/docs/k/12-917-kay-review-of-equity-markets-final-report.pdf

generally behave in line with the values and aspirations of the environment in which they find themselves. We must create cultures in which business and finance can work together to create high performing companies and earn returns for savers on a sustainable basis.

- There is a problem of short-termism, which results in/from a bias for action and hyper-active behaviour by executives.
- Companies should aim to develop relationships with shareholders, rather than with 'the Market'.
- Asset managers should hold more concentrated portfolios with larger stakes in the companies in which they invest.
- Companies should structure directors' remuneration to relate incentives to sustainable long-term business performance. Long-term performance incentives should be provided only in the form of company shares to be held at least until after the executive has retired from the business.
- Therefore, to be consistent with a long approach to decision making:
  - any bonuses should be paid in shares
  - the required holding period of those shares should extend significantly beyond the executive's tenure with the company.

BIS consultations (2009 to 2013)

The Department for Business, Innovation and Skills (BIS) launched a number of consultations on Directors' Remuneration and related issues such as narrative reporting and long-termism in business in the period 2009 to 2013. The conclusion was new legislation requiring additional voting and changes to the disclosure of directors' remuneration for years starting after October 2013. The legislation is covered in **Chapter 10**.

3.2 Shareholders

Ultimately it is the shareholders who approve the remuneration of the directors. Historically it was left to their representative bodies, the Association of British Insurers and the National Association of Pension Funds, to represent institutional shareholders. A number of leading investment houses have issued their own guidelines on remuneration.

Small shareholders can air their views at the AGM and frequently do so at great length. This can be embarrassing to the directors and lead to bad press the next day. However, small shareholders rarely influence the voting results.

3.3 Other interested parties

The list of other interested parties is long: the Institute of Directors, the CBI, the Quoted Companies Alliance, the Investment Management Association (IMA), the government, employees, the TUC and trade unions, PIRC, Manifest, nearly all the major consultants, lawyers, accountants, actuaries, the High Pay Centre and the press. It seems nearly everyone has a view on directors' pay. Directors' pay attracts huge interest in the media and can cause substantial damage to the company's reputation.

The US impacts on UK companies. First, there are lessons to be learnt from best and worst practices. Secondly, the SEC, NYSE and NASDAQ have rules that companies with US listings must follow, most notably Sarbanes Oxley and Dodd Frank.

Corporate governance in Europe became a hot issue in 2004 and the European Commission issued its 'Recommendation on Remuneration of Directors of Listed Companies'. This set a minimum standard for member states to adopt, which is quite a step forward for most, but not for the UK. Implementation has been somewhat variable across member states. The Recommendation was revised in 2009.[4] The EU continues to debate executive remuneration, but to date has had little impact on UK practices. In 2014 new EU rules banned bonuses of more than 100% of fixed pay (or 200% if shareholders gave specific approval to do so) in banks, and this did impact on UK based banks.

---

4 See http://ec.europa.eu/internal_market/company/directors-remun/index_en.htm

4 Principles of Remuneration Governance

4.1 Managing conflicts of interest

No director should be involved in setting his or her own pay. Directors do have a conflict of interest and there is a danger that they may seek excessive remuneration, and do so in ways which are not in the best interests of the company. Where there is a major or controlling shareholder. they may seek to influence remuneration so that their wider interests are maximised. Major shareholders have a legitimate interest in how the directors are remunerated, but they should not be allowed to interfere in the management of the company and should not attempt to micro-manage. Where investors have concerns. they should bring these to the attention of the company. For these reasons, the setting of executive directors' remuneration is best done by a Remuneration Committee made up of independent directors and the Chairman.

The Remuneration Committee should seek the views of the Chairman, the Chief Executive, internal management, shareholders, external advisers and consultants, but ultimately the committee members must make the decisions themselves.

4.2 Disclosure

The UK Corporate Governance Code, company law, London Stock Exchange listing rules and Financial Services Authority (FSA) rules all require the disclosure of how and how much directors are paid. If this information is available to shareholders, then they are in a position to decide if the remuneration is appropriate.

4.3 Transparency and accountability

Transparency and accountability were two of the main Greenbury principles and underpin the Directors' Remuneration Report Regulations. If the remuneration is fully disclosed (in a way that interested parties can see exactly how and how much directors are paid) then those people setting the remuneration can be held accountable for the consequences of their decisions. The additional requirements have added length but not clarity to the disclosures. The Preamble to the 2003 Combined Code did, however, make it quite explicit what is expected:

> 'Para 11: It is important that this [remuneration] report is clear, transparent and understandable to shareholders.'

This laudable goal is currently not being achieved. Remuneration Reports now extend to over 30 pages in some cases. It is very difficult for shareholders to see what is happening. It can take two hours for even an expert to read and understand a long remuneration report. This is clearly an area where greater clarity is required. I have proposed that CEO pay (both awarded and realised) should be disclosed alongside TSR, profit and other KPIs in a table or chart for ten years, so as to show the relationship and how it changes over time.

Accountability is achieved ultimately through the vote at the AGM on the remuneration report and policy resolutions. However, key shareholders will make their views known well before this if they are unhappy with the company's proposals. This is an area where much discussion and negotiation happens behind the scenes.

4.4 Performance linkage and alignment to shareholders

Agency theory says that management are the agents of shareholders and should manage the company in the best interests of shareholders. In order to do so, they need to be incited. The rational economic person will try to maximise his or her wealth with minimum risk. This is, however, totally different to what shareholders want. Therefore agency theory says that the management needs to be incited to manage the company in the best interests of shareholders. Remuneration therefore needs to be linked to shareholders' interests of long-term share price appreciation and dividends. Management will discount any pay that does not pay out until some years ahead and which is dependent on factors which they feel are beyond their control.

4.5 Window on corporate governance

How directors and senior managers are remunerated provides an important window on corporate governance more generally.

- A well-managed process – with a properly constituted Remuneration Committee which operates fully independently, appoints expert, professional, independent remuneration consultants to assist it, listens to shareholders and management and evaluates their inputs – is a good sign that other corporate governance will be effective. If, however, the reverse is true, for example, Remuneration Committee members are seen to be too close to the Chief Executive, consultants are appointed by and are too close to management, shareholder concerns are ignored and excessive remuneration is awarded, then this is a sign that other corporate governance may be poor.

- The choice of performance measures and their relative importance in the delivery of performance-related pay is the second window on corporate governance, as they indicate what is felt to be important in the company. The exclusive use of profit in annual bonus plans is a warning sign. The performance measures that determine the remuneration of the management of the company should include those that drive the future business success, for example, customer satisfaction, customer retention, customer growth, average revenue per customer, employee satisfaction, staff turnover and average length of service, environmental and social responsibility measures, health and safety, effective relationships with regulators etc. If these measures are not part of the incentive plans, then the company may be saying one thing to its shareholders but internally may be behaving quite differently. Hence this is a crucial window on what is happening inside the company.

As Sarah Wilson, CEO at Manifest (an investor lobby group) put it:

> 'Remuneration is the window to the soul of the company. It objectively measures the links between incentives, behaviour, strategy and outcomes.'[1]

I'm not sure about 'objectively' in that context, but remuneration does show the balance between CEO power, behaviour, culture and fairness of rewards.

---

1 FT blog May 2012: http://www.dinamedland.com/apps/blog/categories/show/1071895-investors

5 Companies Act Issues concerning Directors' Remuneration

5.1 At a glance

- The Companies Act 2006 (CA 2006) and The Large and Medium-sized Companies and Groups (Accounts and Reports) Regulations 2008 require detailed disclosures on directors' remuneration to be given in the notes to the accounts.
- Separate disclosure requirements apply for quoted and unquoted companies.
- Additional requirements also apply to listed companies under the Listing Rules that apply to the London Stock Exchange and the UK Corporate Governance Code. Slightly reduced disclosure requirements apply in the case of AIM listed companies.
- Schedule 5 requires all companies (except small companies) to disclose the directors' aggregate emoluments, contributions to defined contribution retirement schemes, share options, amounts payable under long-term incentive schemes and the number of directors accruing benefits under defined benefit retirement schemes.
- Reduced disclosure requirements apply in the case of small companies.
- Schedule 8 applies to listed companies and requires detailed disclosures under the Directors Remuneration Reporting Regulations (DRRR) (see **Chapter 6**).
- The DRRR do not apply to Alternative Investment Market (AIM) companies, but the LSE requirements for AIM companies are similar to the DRRR, although some details can be omitted.
- Amounts paid to or receivable by a person connected with a director must be included in the disclosures.
- Particular difficulties can arise in groups of companies, especially if all directors' remuneration is paid by the holding company.
- The 'cost' of share schemes has to be accounted for and expensed under IFRS 2/FRS 20 (see **Chapter 13**).

5.2 Disclosure under the Companies Act

A company's annual accounts must include detailed information on remuneration paid to or receivable by anyone who was a director during the year. The disclosure requirements cover all amounts receivable by the directors in respect of their services as directors of the company (and, where relevant, of its subsidiaries), regardless of who actually makes the payment. The legislation requires basic disclosures to be given by all companies, and then makes a clear distinction between quoted and unquoted companies in requiring more detailed information to be given.

The Directors' Remuneration Report Regulations (first enacted in 2002, SI 2002/1986), introduced significant changes to the disclosure requirements for quoted companies for accounting periods ending on or after 31 December 2002. For these purposes, a quoted company is defined as a company whose equity share capital is:

- included in the Official List of the London Stock Exchange;
- officially listed in an EEA State; or
- admitted to dealing on the New York Stock Exchange or the Nasdaq Exchange.

Thus, AIM listed companies did not have to report under the Directors' Remuneration Report Regulations, but the London Stock Exchange required AIM companies with effect from 30 March 2010 to disclose the same information as for fully quoted companies with the exception of full details about the performance conditions for share options and other long term share incentive plans.

5.3 Quoted companies

The UK Government (after the banking crisis) launched a number of consultations on executive directors' remuneration, remuneration disclosure, voting, long term-ism and narrative reporting. The outcome is:

- a binding vote on future pay policy, that has to done at least every three years
- an annual advisory vote on how pay policy has been implemented in the previous year
- greater transparency in directors' remuneration reports
- a single figure of total remuneration has to be disclosed
- ten years' history of performance and CEO pay have to be disclosed
- more information on remuneration consultants' conflicts of interest and fees

- changes in the annual report structure, including the Strategic Report, with details of business strategy, model and KPIs.

The DRRR are discussed further in **Chapter 6**.

5.4 AIM companies

Fully listed companies must disclose details of each individual director's remuneration (see **Chapter 6**), including details of performance conditions applying to share options and other long term incentive awards.

AIM notice 36[1] issued in 2010 required all AIM companies for years starting after 30 March 2010 to make additional disclosures regarding directors' remuneration. It said:

> 'The following items for each director of the AIM company are required:
>
> (a) emoluments and compensation, including any cash or non-cash benefits received;
>
> (b) share options and other long term incentive plan details, including information on all outstanding options and/or awards; and
>
> (c) value of any contributions paid by the AIM company to a pension scheme.'

Consequently, unlike fully listed companies, there is no requirement to disclose the details of performance conditions applying to share options and other long term incentive awards.

5.5 Basic accounts disclosures for all companies

The basic requirement in Schedule 5 to The Large and Medium-sized Companies and Groups (Accounts and Reports) Regulations 2008 is that every company should disclose in the notes to the accounts:

> '1(1) …
>
> (a) the aggregate amount of remuneration [ie salary, bonus and benefits, but not pension, or gains from share options exercised or vested share awards] paid to or receivable by directors in respect of qualifying services;
>
> (b) the aggregate of the amount of gains made by directors on the exercise of share options;

1 http://www.londonstockexchange.com/companies-and-advisors/aim/advisers/aim-notices/aim-notice-36.pdf

(b) the aggregate of the amount of money paid to or receivable by directors, and the net value of assets (other than money and share options) received or receivable by directors, under long term incentive schemes in respect of qualifying services; and

(d) the aggregate value of any company contributions—

  (i) paid, or treated as paid, to a pension scheme in respect of directors' qualifying services, and

  (ii) by reference to which the rate or amount of any money purchase benefits that may become payable will be calculated.

(2) There must also be shown the number of directors (if any) to whom retirement benefits are accruing in respect of qualifying services—

(a) under money purchase schemes, and

(b) under defined benefit schemes.

(3) In the case of a company which is not a quoted company and whose equity share capital is not listed on the market known as AIM—

(a) sub-paragraph (1) has effect as if paragraph (b) were omitted and, in paragraph (c), "assets" did not include shares; and

(b) the number of each of the following (if any) must be shown, namely—

  (i) the directors who exercised share options, and

  (ii) the directors in respect of whose qualifying services shares were received or receivable under long term incentive schemes.'

5.6 Unquoted companies

An unquoted company is a company which is not quoted and is not listed on AIM. As well as fulfilling the requirements of **5.5** above, these companies have to disclose under Schedule 5 Part 2 'Provisions applying only to unquoted companies',[2] which states:

'Details of highest paid director's emoluments etc.

2(1) Where the aggregates shown under paragraph 1(1)(a), (b) and (c) total £200,000 or more, there must be shown—

[2] In this context AIM companies are not regarded as quoted. The London Stock Exchange views 'quoted companies' as only those with a full listing. The requirement for AIM companies comes from AIM notice 36 (see 5.6) issued in 2010 which require all AIM companies for years starting after 30 March 2010 to additionally disclose directors' remuneration.

(a) so much of the total of those aggregates as is attributable to the highest paid director, and

(b) so much of the aggregate mentioned in paragraph 1(1)(d) as is so attributable.

(2) Where sub-paragraph (1) applies and the highest paid director has performed qualifying services during the financial year by reference to which the rate or amount of any defined benefits that may become payable will be calculated, there must also be shown—

(a) the amount at the end of the year of his accrued pension, and

(b) where applicable, the amount at the end of the year of his accrued lump sum.

(3) Subject to sub-paragraph (4), where sub-paragraph (1) applies in the case of a company which is not a listed company, there must also be shown—

(a) whether the highest paid director exercised any share options, and

(b) whether any shares were received or receivable by that director in respect of qualifying services under a long term incentive scheme.

5.7 Avoiding duplication

If any of the required details are readily ascertainable from other information included with the accounts, such as a remuneration report, they generally do not have to be disclosed again. The one exception is aggregate gains on the exercise of share options that must always be shown separately in the notes to the accounts. In practice, if the detailed information is included in a separate directors' remuneration report, it is helpful for the notes to the accounts to include a cross-reference.

5.8 Benefits in kind

Emoluments specifically include the estimated money value of benefits in kind received by a director otherwise than in cash. The most common benefits in kind are:

- company car
- free or subsidised accommodation
- insurance for the benefit of the director (eg private health cover, indemnity insurance, personal accident cover)
- loans at preferential interest rates
- relocation costs (unless the relocation is clearly for business purposes).

Some of these may also be disclosable in the annual accounts as loans or transactions with directors. Share options are subject to separate disclosure requirements and are therefore specifically excluded from emoluments for this disclosure purpose. The main difficulty with benefits in kind is establishing an appropriate and realistic money value for the benefit. In most cases, the taxable value or market value will provide the best estimate of money value.

5.9 Bonus payments

Provision should usually be made in the accounts for bonuses in the year in which they are earned. Where a bonus payment to directors requires approval by the shareholders before the directors are entitled to receive it, it is usual to treat the bonus as being receivable by the directors (and therefore disclosable within directors' emoluments) in the year in which shareholder approval is given, even though the bonus may have been charged to the profit and loss account in an earlier period.

5.10 Share options

In addition to the disclosures on share options referred to in **5.4** and **5.5** above, the directors' report (or the notes to the accounts) must give detailed information on directors' interests (including options) in the shares in or debentures of the company or any other body corporate in the same group. Interests include those held by the directors' close family. Certain exemptions apply in the case of wholly owned subsidiaries. In the case of listed companies, extensive disclosures must also be given in the directors' remuneration report (see **Chapter 6** and Checklist in **Chapter 28**).

5.11 Long-term incentive schemes

Amounts payable under long-term incentive schemes are disclosable when they are paid to or receivable by the director. The director must therefore have the right to receive a sum before it becomes disclosable. Amounts should therefore normally be disclosed in the year in which the director becomes entitled to receive payment. In the case of a long-term incentive scheme, the director will not usually be entitled to receive payment until all the specified conditions have been met.

Further disclosures on long-term incentive schemes must be given in the directors' remuneration report (see **Chapter 6**).

5.12 Pension arrangements

For the purposes of The Large and Medium-sized Companies and Groups (Accounts and Reports) Regulations 2008 disclosures referred to in **5.4**, all pension schemes must be classified as either defined contribution or defined benefit schemes. Any death in service benefits are to be disregarded when classifying a pension scheme for disclosure purposes. A pension scheme under which a director will be entitled to receive both defined contribution benefits and defined benefits is classified as a defined benefit scheme for disclosure purposes. Where a scheme provides for the director to receive defined contribution benefits or defined benefits, whichever is the greater, the company is allowed to assume for disclosure purposes that the benefits will be whichever appears more likely at the end of the financial year in question. Listed companies must also give additional details on directors' pension arrangements in the directors' remuneration report.

5.13 Payments to and from other parties

Amounts paid to or receivable by a person connected with a director or a body corporate controlled by him or her are specifically included within the disclosure requirements. Disclosure therefore cannot be avoided by arranging for the payment to be made to a connected party. In the case of payments to a company owned by the director, the emoluments note to the accounts usually includes an explanation that some or all of the payments have been made through the company. Emoluments also include all relevant amounts in respect of a director's services paid by, or receivable from the company, the company's subsidiary undertakings and any other person, unless the director must in turn account to the company or any of its subsidiary undertakings for the amounts received.

5.14 Payments to third parties

The accounts must also disclose the aggregate amount paid to, or receivable by, third parties for making available the services of any person as a director of the company or otherwise in connection with the management of the affairs of the company or group. The most common example of this is an arrangement whereby a substantial investor in a company (eg a bank or venture capital company) has the right to appoint a director to the Board of the investee company and payment for the services of this director is made to the investor rather than to the director himself.

5.15 Disclosure in holding companies

Directors' remuneration in the accounts of the holding company will comprise:

- remuneration paid to directors of the holding company in respect of their services to the company and management of the company and group
- if any holding company directors are also directors of one or more of the subsidiaries, remuneration paid to them for their services in relation to these companies.

Remuneration paid to those who are directors of subsidiaries but who are not directors of the holding company is not disclosable in the accounts of the holding company. The same disclosure requirements apply in the holding company's accounts, regardless of whether some or all of the remuneration costs are recharged to the subsidiaries.

5.16 Disclosure in the accounts of subsidiaries

Where the holding company recharges the subsidiaries with the cost of remunerating their directors, each subsidiary should disclose as directors' remuneration the amount paid to the holding company in respect of directors' services to the company. If the holding company makes a global recharge to the subsidiaries to cover general management costs, including directors' remuneration, and the element for directors' remuneration cannot be separately identified, an appropriate apportionment should be made for disclosure purposes. Where the holding company does not recharge the subsidiaries with the costs of remunerating their directors, the costs borne by the holding company are still disclosable as directors' remuneration in the accounts of the subsidiary – it is not acceptable simply to disclose the fact that the directors have been remunerated by the holding company and not quantify the amount that they have received. However, it may be helpful to explain that this cost has been borne by the holding company and is not charged in the subsidiary's accounts.

Where directors of a subsidiary are also directors or employees of the holding company, it is sometimes argued that the holding company remunerates them only for their services to the holding company and that they receive no remuneration in respect of their services as directors of the subsidiary. The validity of this argument will usually depend on the amount of time that the director or employee devotes to the subsidiary company. If the time is relatively small it may be acceptable that he or she does not receive remuneration for services as a director of the subsidiary. In this case, a brief explanation should be included in the subsidiary's accounts.

5.17 Compensation for loss of office

The aggregate compensation for loss of office paid to, or receivable by, directors and former directors must also be disclosed. Compensation for loss of office constitutes a separate category of payment to directors and should not be included in the figure for directors' emoluments for the period. Where compensation payments include non-cash benefits, these should be included in the disclosures at their estimated money value and the nature of the benefit must be disclosed. Many compensation payments to directors will also require shareholder approval under CA 1985, although this is not usually required for genuine payments in respect of damages for breach of contract or for pensions in respect of past services. If significant non-cash items are included, the compensation payments may also require approval under the provisions on substantial property transactions in The Large and Medium-sized Companies and Groups (Accounts and Reports) Regulations 2008. Where a retired director continues to have an involvement with the company in a part-time or consultancy capacity, any payments in excess of normal market rates for the work performed may well include an element of compensation for loss of office, in which case the details should be disclosed.

5.18 Directors' service contracts – at a glance

- A comprehensive service contract for each executive director can help to prevent misunderstandings
- Each Non-Executive Director will usually have a contract for services
- The Large and Medium-sized Companies and Groups (Accounts and Reports) Regulations 2008 includes provisions on the retention and location of directors' service contracts (see **5.19**)
- Shareholders of the company are entitled to inspect directors' service contracts. Details have to be disclosed in the remuneration report (see **Chapter 6**)
- Shareholder approval is required for any contract giving a director a right of employment for more than two years, unless the company can give unconditional notice at any time
- Drafting issues are covered later in **Chapter 51.**

5.19 Service contracts for executive directors

Where a director has a written contract of service with the company, The Large and Medium-sized Companies and Groups (Accounts and Reports) Regulations 2008 requires the company to retain a copy of the contract at one of the following locations:

- the company's registered office;
- the place where the register of members is kept (if this is not the registered office); or

- the company's principal place of business (provided that this is in the part of Great Britain where the company is registered).

If a director does not have a written contract of service, the company must keep a written memorandum of the terms of his or her appointment. The same rules apply to a variation of a director's contract. A parent company is also required to keep copies of service contracts between its subsidiaries and their directors, or a written memorandum of the terms if these contracts are not in writing. Copies of all contracts and memoranda must be kept in the same place. If they are not kept at the registered office, the company must notify the Registrar of Companies of where they are held and of any changes in location. The Large and Medium-sized Companies and Groups (Accounts and Reports) Regulations 2008 emphasises that these arrangements apply equally in the case of shadow directors. However, there is no formal requirement for a company to retain a copy of a contract, variation or memorandum when the unexpired term is less than 12 months, or where the contract can be terminated by the company within the next 12 months without the payment of compensation.

5.20 Inspection of contracts

Under CA 2006 s 188 and The Large and Medium-sized Companies and Groups (Accounts and Reports) Regulations 2008, any member of the company is entitled to inspect the copies of the directors' contracts of service (or the memoranda where there is no written service contract) without charge. If the company refuses to allow a member to inspect a contract or memorandum, a court can require immediate inspection.

5.21 Director working outside the UK

Where a director of the company, or of one of its subsidiaries, is required under his or her contract to work wholly or mainly outside the UK, the company is not required to keep a copy of the contract, but it must keep a memorandum giving the director's name and the provisions of the contract relating to its duration. In the case of a contract for a director of a subsidiary, the name and place of incorporation of the subsidiary must also be recorded in the memorandum. These memoranda must be kept in the same place as the contracts and memoranda relating to the other directors.

5.22 Shareholder approval for contracts for more than two years

Under CA 2006, s 188 and The Large and Medium-sized Companies and Groups (Accounts and Reports) Regulations 2008, a director cannot be given the right of employment with the company (or, where relevant, with the group) for a period of more than two (previously it was five) years under an agreement which does not allow the company to give unconditional notice at any time, unless this term of the contract has been first approved by the company in general meeting (or, in the case of a private company, by written resolution). Employment is defined as including employment under a contract for services. Where the director is also a director of the company's holding company, prior approval to the arrangement must normally be given by the shareholders of both the subsidiary and the holding company (unless the subsidiary is wholly owned, in which case prior approval of the arrangement by the shareholders of the subsidiary is not required).

A written memorandum setting out the proposed agreement must be available for inspection by the members at the company's registered office for a period of at least 15 days before the meeting and at the meeting itself. In the case of a private company where agreement is to be by written resolution, a copy of the memorandum must be sent to each member before, or at the same time as, the resolution is provided for signature.

A term included in a director's contract in contravention of CA 2006, s 188 is void. The agreement is deemed to include a term entitling the company to terminate the agreement at any time by the giving of reasonable notice.

5.23 Series of agreements

CA 2006, s 188 includes special provisions to prevent a company entering into a series of shorter agreements with the same director in an attempt to avoid the requirement for shareholder approval of a contract that in effect extends for more than two years.

5.24 Claw-back/deferral of bonus

Strictly speaking a claw-back clause will allow bonuses that have already been paid to be clawed back from executives. However, such clauses will always be open to legal dispute. The benefit of deferral is that it is much easier to claw-back that part of bonus that has not already been paid out.

5.25 Summary financial statement

Any summary financial statement has to include the single figure of remuneration table as per the DRRR.

6 Directors Remuneration Report Regulations – Overview

6.1 At a glance

- New legislation was enacted in 2013.
- The directors of a quoted company are required by law to prepare a separate directors' remuneration report. LSE have made almost all of this a requirement for AIM listed companies since 2010.
- Certain elements of the directors' remuneration report are subject to audit.
- The general meeting at which the annual reports and accounts are laid must include resolutions for a binding on the remuneration policy and an advisory vote on the annual remuneration report.
- The content of the directors' remuneration report is specified in the legislation and includes:
  - a summary of the major decisions on and any substantial changes relating to directors' remuneration and the context in which those changes occurred and decisions taken
  - detailed information on the remuneration paid to each individual director
  - a statement on the company's future remuneration policy
  - comparative information on total shareholder return and remuneration for initially the last five years, but this will increase by one year each year until ten years are required.
- The legislation also specifies which elements of the directors' remuneration report should be included in summary financial statements.
- A checklist of disclosure requirements is provided in **Chapter 6.9.**
- Guidance on what to include in the summary statement and how to structure the report is in Chapter **6.6**. Guidance on the detailed contents of the annual remuneration report and the remuneration policy is in Chapter **28**.

- Shareholders have to vote on the directors' remuneration policy (binding vote), the annual report on remuneration (advisory vote) and any new LTI schemes.

6.2 Summary of changes

The 2013 legislation applies to all quoted companies with years starting after 30 September 2013. The 16 tables, two figures and two charts (shown in **Chapter 28**) show the minimum requirement or the typical practice and (suggested) 'best practice'. It should be noted that early adopters may decide that somewhere between the minimum and 'best practice' may be optimum for them at this stage.

The DRRR were enacted by Statutory Instrument and are known as the Large and Medium-sized Companies and Groups (Accounts and Reports) (Amendment) Regulations 2013.

The proposals require:

SUMMARY ANNUAL STATEMENT from the Chairman of the Remuneration Committee.

ANNUAL REPORT ON REMUNERATION of how the policy was implemented in the year, setting out the actual payments and awards made and details of the link between performance and pay.

DIRECTORS' REMUNERATION POLICY description. This is only required when the policy is put to the vote, which must be at least every three years and whenever the policy changes. The policy is forward looking.

The following is a list of the disclosures that will be required. The Table, Figure and Chart numbers refer to tables, figures and the chart later in this Chapter and in **Chapter 28**. A checklist of the requirements of DRRR, LSE, UK Corporate Governance Code, etc is at the end of this Chapter.

Required Remuneration Report contents checklist	Comment/ difference to previous	Example shown in …	Is this subject to audit
1. **SUMMARY ANNUAL STATEMENT** from the Chairman of the Remuneration Committee	Similar to existing best practice		No
2. **REMUNERATION AT A GLANCE** Although this is not required by the legislation, many companies do this and it can be very helpful to shareholders.	Typically 1 page of key facts		No

Required Remuneration Report contents checklist	Comment/ difference to previous	Example shown in …	Is this subject to audit
3. **ANNUAL REPORT ON REMUNERATION** of how the policy was implemented setting out the actual payments and details of the link between performance and pay.			
Items required:			
• Single figure of total remuneration table	New	Table 3	Yes
• Additional requirements in respect of the single figure table	New	Tables 4 and 5	Yes
• Total pension entitlements	Changed	Tables 6, 6a and 6b	Yes
• Scheme interests awarded in the year (and optionally a detailed list of all awards not yet exercised)	Changed	Tables 7, 7a and 7b	Yes
• Payments to past directors	Changed		Yes
• Compensation for loss of office	Changed	Table 8	Yes
• Directors' shareholdings and share interests	Similar	Table 9	Yes
• Line graph comparison of TSR performance and Index over 5(10) years	Similar	Chart 2	
• Table of detailed 5(10) year comparison of CEO Single Total Figure, Bonus as % maximum and LTIP vested %	New	Table 10	
• Percentage change in remuneration of director undertaking the role of CEO	New	Table 11	
• Relative importance of spend on pay	New	Table 12	
• Statement of implementation of remuneration policy in the following financial year	New		
• Consideration by the directors of matters relating to directors' remuneration, including Disclosure of Remuneration Committee advisers and fees	New	Table 13 and 13a	
• Shareholder voting	New	Table 14	
• Dilution	Not required by DRRR. ABI guideline.		

Required Remuneration Report contents checklist	Comment/ difference to previous	Example shown in …	Is this subject to audit
• Requirement of the UK Corporate Governance Code to take account of the views of shareholders	Not required by DRRR.		
• Aggregate Directors' Remuneration	CA requirement. Not required by DRRR.		
• Statement about all employee share plans	Not required by DRRR.		
• Additional data of the history of bonus opportunity and outcomes	Not required by DRRR.	Table 19	
• Additional data of the history of LTI award outcomes as % of maximum award and expected values of extant awards	Not required by DRRR.	Table 20	
4. DIRECTORS' REMUNERATION POLICY description. This is only required when the policy is put to the vote, which must be at least every three years and whenever the policy changes. The policy is forward looking.			
DIRECTORS' REMUNERATION POLICY items required			
• Policy table setting out all elements of remuneration		Table 15	
• Approach to recruitment remuneration	New	Table 16	
• Service contracts		Table 17	
• Scenarios	New	Figures 15 and 15a	
• Policy on payment for loss of office	New	Table 18	
• Statement of consideration of employments conditions elsewhere in the company	New		
• Statement of consideration of shareholders views	New		

What is missing from DRRR?

For shareholders to get a better picture, best practice would be to also disclose:

- dilution (this is a requirement of the ABI guidelines)
- expected value of LTI awards made in the year (this used to be an ABI requirement. It is still requested by the NAPF and some other proxy advisers. Fair values of awards have to be shown separately in the notes to the accounts in share scheme disclosures, but it is more helpful to also show this information here to avoid complex cross referring).
- cross reference to KPIs in the Strategic Report and explanation if and why they do not form part of the incentive plans.
- all outstanding share scheme and option awards (see **Table 7b)**.
- additional data of the history of bonus opportunity and outcomes (see **Table 19)**.
- additional data of the history of LTI award outcomes as % of maximum award and expected values of extant awards (see **Table 20)**.
- how the company met the requirement of the UK Corporate Governance Code to take account of the views of shareholders.

6.3 Requirements of directors in respect of the DRRR

The directors of a quoted company are required to prepare a directors' remuneration report containing the detailed information specified therein. Current directors and those who have served as director in the preceding five years are given a specific duty to disclose relevant information to the company to enable the report to be prepared. The report must be formally approved by the directors and must be signed on behalf of the Board by a director or by the Company Secretary. A signed copy must be delivered to the registrar as part of the company's annual reports and accounts. The auditors are required to report on the auditable part of the report (which is defined as the part covering the detailed disclosures on remuneration received by the directors) and to include any missing information in their audit report, so far as they are reasonably able to do so.

The preparation of a separate directors' remuneration report had been a recommendation under the UK Corporate Governance Code for a number of years and, for listed companies, a requirement of the Listing Rules. The contents of the report required under the Directors' Remuneration Report Regulations (DRRR) are similar to those previously required by the Code and the Listing Rules, but additional requirements include in particular:

- a ten (initially five) year performance graph showing the total shareholder return and supported by a table showing the CEO pay over the same period
- details of the single figure of remuneration for each director, which has to be calculated precisely according to the legislation
- details of the remuneration policy including permitted use of discretion
- disclosure of the names of consultants advising the Remuneration Committee and their fees received, who appointed them, together with details of any other services they provide to the company.

6.4 Shareholder approval

The following votes (requiring the support of a majority of shareholders voting to pass) on remuneration are required under CA 2006:

- **A binding vote on pay policy.** The binding vote will be held annually unless companies choose to leave their remuneration policy unchanged, in which case it will be compulsory at least every three years and in the year following a vote on the annual remuneration report which fails to be approved. Once a policy is approved, companies will not be able to make payments outside its scope. If a company chooses to change its pay policy, it will have to put it before shareholders for re-approval. According to BIS 'this will encourage companies to devise long-term policies and put a brake on annual pay ratcheting'. The policy should clearly set out how pay supports the strategic objectives of the company and include better information on how directors' pay compares to the wider workforce. Investors strongly encourage companies to set a policy for three years and not to come back annually to revise the policy.

  Note re payments which fall outside of the pay policy. As part of their pay policy, companies will have to clearly explain their approach to payments. Companies will not be able to pay directors more than shareholders have agreed. It should be noted that this is not as onerous as it might appear as the GC100 and Investor Group have produced guidance[1] on interpretation of the new DRRR, which allows quite a lot of wiggle room in practice.

- **An advisory vote on the annual remuneration report.** Alongside the binding vote on policy, shareholders will continue to have an annual advisory vote on how pay policy was implemented in the previous year, including actual sums paid to directors. If a company fails the advisory vote, it will be required to put its overall pay policy back to shareholders in a binding vote the following year.

---

1 See http://uk.practicallaw.com/6-540-9731

6.5 Summary financial statements

The provisions of The Companies Act 2006 (Strategic Report and Directors' Report) Regulations 2013 (No. 1970) on summary financial statements are amended to require, in the case of a quoted company, the inclusion of either the whole of the directors' remuneration report or, as a minimum:

- aggregate information on directors' remuneration (see **5.5**)
- that part of the DRRR that sets out the single figure table.

See s426A(2)(e).

6.6 Contents of the remuneration report

The detailed contents required by The Large and Medium-sized Companies and Groups (Accounts and Reports) (Amendment) Regulations 2013 (No 1981) are set out below, in **Chapter 28**, and also in **Chapter 6.9** in the form of a disclosure checklist. The legislation generally requires the detailed information to be given in tabular form and in a way that links the information to each director by name. A limited degree of aggregation is permitted, eg in the disclosure of information on share options.

One of the potential problems here is the considerable amount of detail that may need to be given in the report. In presenting the disclosures, companies need to make a particular effort to ensure that the information that is likely to be of most interest to shareholders does not become obscured by the sheer volume of detail. The Preamble to the 2003 Code referred to this explicitly: '*It is important that this [remuneration] report is clear, transparent and understandable to shareholders.*'

6.7 Summary statement and recommended approach

There is no prescribed format for this.

In order to improve transparency further and make it easier for shareholders to quickly find the key information on pay within a report, the directors' remuneration report must contain a statement by the director who fulfils the role of chair of the Remuneration Committee (or, where there is no such person, by a director nominated by the directors to make the statement) summarising for the relevant financial year:

(a) the major decisions on directors' remuneration;

(b) any substantial changes relating to directors' remuneration made during the year; and

(c) the context in which those changes occurred and decisions have been taken.

In recognition of the fact that the relevant information will vary between companies and from year to year, the Government did not prescribe in the regulations what should be covered.

The Government noted that it was already good practice in many companies for the Remuneration Committee Chairman to write a letter as a preface to the report. As a result, the Government does not envisage this additional requirement will place significant additional burdens on companies.

Companies that have reported to date have adopted one of two approaches,

- to tell the story about remuneration and paint a picture of what is happening. These reports have focussed on remuneration philosophy, KPIs, company performance and remuneration outcomes. I recommend this approach.
- to treat the DRRR as a compliance exercise. These reports have tended to focus on explaining the format of the report, Remuneration Committee membership and activities.

How the summary statement is structured impacts on the decision on how to lay out the rest of the remuneration report. There are three choices for the rest of the report:

- follow the order of the legislation. This makes it easy for shareholders to find things. The main users of the report are shareholders and so it is best to make things easy for them. I recommend this approach.
- report things in the order of importance that you decide. This appears initially attractive, as it appears to help you tell your story. However, shareholders and others reading the report will not be able to find quickly the information they want, and may not want to waste their time wading through 20 odd pages to find what they want. In addition it is less easy to be sure that the report is compliant with the legislation.
- a mixture of the above. This will be confusing to the reader and the worst of both worlds.

Some companies have also introduced another section into their remuneration reports called 'Remuneration at a glance' which shows the key elements. I think this helps the flow of the remuneration report. My recommendation is to include such a section, then to provide the report on remuneration for the year, and then the directors' remuneration policy **in the precise order of the legislation.**

The remuneration report will then consist of four parts:

1. **SUMMARY ANNUAL STATEMENT/LETTER from Remuneration Committee chair**
2. **REMUNERATION AT A GLANCE**

3. ANNUAL REPORT ON REMUNERATION (the implementation report on how much was paid in the year)

4. DIRECTORS' REMUNERATION POLICY

Summary statement/letter from Remuneration Committee chair

This should focus on telling a story about remuneration in the company. It should start with or focus on the pay of the CEO and cover:

- Explanation of company's philosophy of remuneration
  - How pay is linked to performance
  - Demonstrate history of remuneration outcomes (this can cross refer to the tables in 'Remuneration at a glance'), performance and remuneration philosophy (or explain why this was not the case and what changes have been done to improve the linkage)
  - How remuneration is positioned versus the 'market'
- Explain outcomes for the year being reported on
  - Major decisions made by the Committee
  - Performance and other context for decisions made
  - Outcomes for pay
- Explain policy changes for next year
  - Major decisions made by the Committee
  - The context for the changes made
  - Explain performance measures for next year, and targets, if not commercially sensitive
- Short summary of the pay of other directors and senior executives reviewed by the Remuneration Committee.

Two examples illustrate what a company's philosophy of remuneration might be. The first emphasises the motivational aspect of remuneration:

> Our philosophy is to ensure that key management and in particular executive directors:
>
> - Are motivated to accomplish specific strategic millstones, taking due account of risk
> - Have their interests aligned with shareholders over the long-term
> - Are retained and when necessary can be appropriately recruited

- Are not paid excessively and can be exited at a reasonable cost.

The second example has more of an emphasis on rewards and behaviours:

> Our incentive arrangements are critical to the management of the business. Our three key principles are:
>
> - **Reward sustainable growth.** Incentives are designed to promote the achievement of strategic goals and engender the long-term sustainable growth of our business.
> - **Accountability.** Our plans are designed to reward employees for the performance of the business for which they are accountable and can directly influence.
> - **Simplicity and transparency.** We aim for clarity of objectives and relative simplicity of design.

Note that it will be evident (or will rapidly become so) that if the company's TSR has been good, then justifying directors' remuneration will be easy. If TSR has decreased or has done poorly relative to sector peers, then it will be more challenging to justify high pay. If KPIs have not shown good progress, again it will be difficult to justify high pay.

Thus the annual statement/letter is a very powerful process, particularly if the company accepts the task of linking pay to performance over the whole cycle, rather than justifying pay one year at a time. The explanation should focus on the CEO. Most shareholders realise that if the CEO pay is acceptable, then most likely the pay of the other directors will be acceptable too (banks may be an exception to this rule because of the vast numbers of very highly paid executives in banks).

Remuneration at a glance

This should be one or two pages of A4 and should cover KPIs, the single figure of pay for each executive director, CEO five year pay history and TSR, pay policy and measures for bonus and LTIs for the coming year. Ideally it should start with a good rating from Manifest, or other independent rating firm. An example is on the next three pages.

Remuneration at a glance

Manifest Remuneration Assessment					Overall rating		C
Alignment	47/100	Quan-tum	23/120	Contracts	0/20	Dilution & Cost	0/10

Single Figure of total Remuneration – 2013

	M Smith CEO £000	P Brown FD £000
Salary	858	598
Increase with effect 1 April 2014	3%	3%
Bonus (including deferred amounts)	998	510
(Bonus as a % of salary)	(116%)	(85%)
Taxable benefits	37	21
Pension benefits	215	120
LTIP awards vesting in year	0	784
Total remuneration	2,108	2,033

Total Remuneration Policy Summary

The key elements of remuneration for the Executive Directors
M Smith CEO Salary of £858,000; annual bonus opportunity of 100% of salary maximum, 50% of salary on-target, any amount above target deferred into nil cost options for two years; standard LTIP award of 125% of salary vesting in full after five years; pension allowance of 25% of salary; car allowance and family medical insurance.
P Brown FD Salary of £598,000; annual bonus opportunity of 100% of salary maximum, 50% of salary on-target, any amount above target deferred into nil cost options for two years; standard LTIP award of 90% of salary vesting in full after five years; pension allowance of 20% of salary; car allowance and family medical insurance.

Bonus and LTIP metrics

Bonus Measures	As a percentage of maximum bonus opportunity	
	M Smith CEO	**P Brown CFO**
Profit before tax	70%	60%
On-time performance	10%	10%
Customer satisfaction targets	10%	10%

Bonus Measures	As a percentage of maximum bonus opportunity	
Operating costs (excluding fuel) per seat at constant currency	10%	10%
Departmental objectives		10%

The award levels of LTIP Shares for the Executive Directors in the 2014 financial year are 125% of salary for the Chief Executive and 90% of salary for the Chief Financial Officer.

LTIP Measures	**M Smith CEO**	**P Brown CFO**
ROCE	50%	50%
TSR v FTSE 350 Index	50%	50%

Share interests

	M Smith CEO		**P Brown FD**	
	Number 000s	**£000[1]**	**Number 000s**	**£000[1]**
Shares owned	121	£968	25	£200
Vested from incentive plans	289	£2,312	55	£440
Unvested shares in incentive plans:				
– At target or latest estimate of outcome	100	£800	50	£400
– If all plans vest at maximum	350	£2,800	175	£1,400

[1] valued at share price at year end 31.12.13 of £8.24

Remuneration context

KPIs: Corporate performance in 2013	**2013**	**Movement**
Profit before tax	£282m	+10%
Dividend per share	19.2p	+7%
Earnings per share	53.0p	+7%
Share Price	£7.62	+58%

Stock market statistics

Market cap	£2.6bn	**TSR**	**1 yr**	**3 yr**	**5 yr**
P/E at 31.12.13	15.2		+40%	+25%	+95%

Share price at 31.12.13	£7.50	**Highest in year**	£7.83	**Lowest in year**	£4.23
Share Price Volatility	55%	**Beta**	1.05	**Dividend yield**	3.6%

Figure 8: CEO Pay, TSR and KPIs history

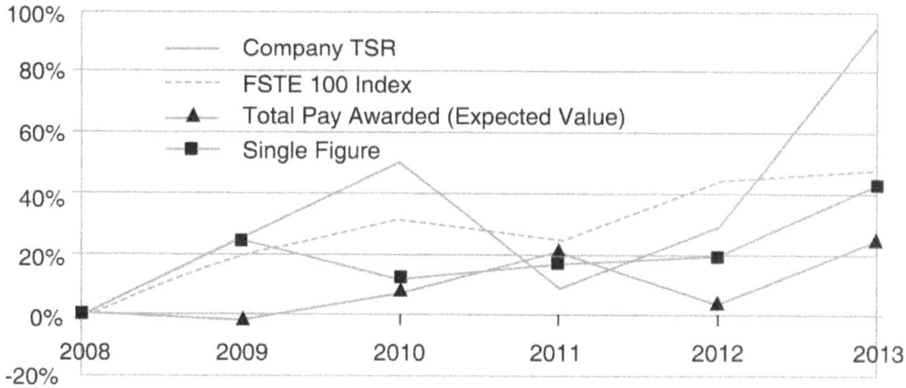

	2008	2009	2010	2011	2012	2013
Single Figure £000		4,569	4,102	4,291	4,374	5,249
Total Pay Awarded (Expected Value)		3,896	4,244	4,771	4,115	4,938
Bonus as % maximum		58%	65%	75%	75%	80%
LTIPs vesting % maximum		0%	25%	0%	75%	100%
Selected KPIs						
Profit (indexed to 100)	100	56	75	100	110	130
Turnover (indexed to 100)	100	91	92	95	96	98
ROCE %		3.6%	6.9%	9.8%	11.3%	17.4%
On-time performance		80	66	79	88	87
Customer satisfaction targets		85	73	79	82	83
Operating costs (excluding fuel) per seat at constant currency £		34.37	36.62	36.62	36.25	38.17
Staff turnover %		6.9%	7.6%	9.7%	7.5%	6.5%

6.8 Annual remuneration report

The Annual Remuneration Report has to show how the policy was implemented setting out the actual payments and details of the link between performance and pay.

A checklist of the contents is in 6.9 and the detailed requirements of the DRRR and examples in relation to policy are in **Chapter 28**.

This part of the report is factual. There is little discretion on how to disclose the data. Most of the requirements are tightly prescribed in the SI. However companies may wish to build on a good Remuneration Committee Chair letter (including its supporting one or two pages Remuneration At A Glance) and also provide additional data such as the history of KPIs, remuneration ratios (as illustrated in **Table 6** in **Chapter 28**) and the linkage with employees' pay.

This part of the report also has to explain how the directors' remuneration policy will be implemented in the current year.

6.9 Directors' remuneration policy

A checklist of the contents is in **6.9** and the detailed requirements of the DRRR and examples in relation to policy are in **Chapter 28**.

In contrast to the annual report on remuneration, there is quite a lot of scope and discretion about choices for policy.

In deciding its policy, the remuneration committee needs to consider at least all of the items in the checklist below.

Key issues – Checklist Overview

- Have each of the requirements in the regulations been met in full?
- When will the policy take effect?
- Is the policy sufficiently flexible to enable it to last for the long term?
- Does the policy cover payments to be made pursuant to existing commitments?
- Are all discretions included in the policy?
- Does the policy include any emergency discretion?
- Are recruitment and leaver policies appropriate for the company's needs?
- Are all policy provisions regarding retirement payments consistent with the company's justification for such provisions?

- Will shareholders approve of what will be included in the policy?
- Does the policy fit together as a whole, and with external documentation?

A company will need to choose the degree of detail it wishes in the policies and the flexibility for discretion.

The illustrations of scenarios make no allowance for share price. Companies will need to consider whether to include additional disclosers showing the impact of share price changes on future rewards and whether such illustrations should include just the latest year's or some or all historic share scheme awards and also shares owned by the director. Some shareholders and fund managers will regard it as positive or very positive if directors' rewards are well aligned with shareholders (some view the lack of such alignment as a reason to sell shares or not to buy them).

6.10 Checklist for the Remuneration Report

The following checklist is based on the requirements of The Directors' Remuneration Report Regulations, the recommendations in the UK Corporate Governance Code, the London Stock Exchange (LSE) Listing Requirements, the Companies Act requirements in respect of remuneration, the ABI guideline regarding dilution and the NAPF guidance on fair value of LTI awards.

LSE have slightly different requirements for companies incorporated overseas who are quoted on the UK LSE.

Additional details may need to be given, depending on the specific circumstances of the company. There are four types of disclosures:

A: Contents subject to audit

B: Contents not subject to audit

C: Items required by the UK Corporate Governance Code or LSE Listing Requirements (LR) for companies on the London Stock Exchange

D: Other items.

A: Contents subject to audit

The following information must be disclosed and is subject to audit.

	SI reference
'The single figure table': A table showing for each director who served during the financial year, the amounts for the financial year and the equivalent amount for the preceding year, of: • Salary and/or fees • The estimated money value of all taxable benefits • Bonuses • Long term incentives that have vested in the year or vest dependent on performance in the year • Pension related benefits • The sum total of all these amounts • Separate tables for executive and non-executives are permitted	Para 4
Additional information to the single figure table: • The types of benefits and where significant their value • For bonus and long term incentives: – Details of performance measures and weightings. – For each performance measure: - the performance targets set at the beginning of the period and the value of the award achievable - details of actual performance relative to targets set and resulting level of award - if discretion used and if so how exercised and how resulting award was determined. • For bonus, if any bonus was deferred, the % deferred, whether it was in cash or shares and if subject to any conditions other than performance measures.	Para 12
For each director who served during the financial year and has rights to defined benefits or cash balance benefits: • Details of those rights (eg accrued pension) and normal retirement date • Additional benefits in the event the director retires early • If director has pension rights (shown in the single figure table) under more than one scheme, separate details of each scheme (eg the % of pension from each type of scheme)	Para 13

	SI reference
Scheme interests (eg LTIPs, options and deferred bonus) ● For each scheme: – Description of the type of interest awarded – Description of the basis on which award made (eg face value of salary) – The face value of the award – The payout at minimum performance as % of the scheme interest awarded – For share options, explanation of any difference between exercise price and price at award – The end date of the performance period – A summary of the performance measures and targets (if not set out elsewhere in the report)	Para 14
Payments to past directors	Para 15
Payments for loss of office ● Total amount paid or receivable, with breakdown by component and explanation of how calculated ● Any other payments paid or receivable, including treatment of outstanding incentive awards that vest on or following termination ● Whether any discretion was exercised, and if so how.	Para 16
Shares and share interests ● Statement of share ownership requirements/guidelines and whether met ● A table showing for each director: – Shares owned – Share interests in the form of shares and share options – Share interests with or without performance conditions – Details of share interests in the form of shares and options which are: - Vested but unexercised - Exercised in the year	Para 17

B: Contents not subject to audit

The following information is required to be disclosed, but is not subject to audit.

	SI reference
Annual statement from the Remuneration Committee Chair summarising the major decisions of the Committee, any substantial changes to remuneration and the context for the decisions and changes	Para 3

	SI reference
Line graph of TSR (for each of the financial years) for the company and a broad equity index for initial five years, but increasing by one year each year until ten years of TSR data is required • Reasons for selecting the index	Para 18
Table showing for the CEO for the same years as the line graph • Single figure of total remuneration • Bonus as % of maximum • LTI shares vested as % maximum	Para 18
The CEO and the average employee percentage change in salary, benefits and bonus (as shown/defined in the single figure table)	Para 19
A graph or table showing: • Remuneration paid or receivable by all employees in the group • Dividends and share buybacks • Any other significant distributions and payment or other uses of profit or cash flow that assist in understanding the relative importance of spend on pay (and why chosen and if different to the previous year an explanation for that change).	Para 20
How the Remuneration Policy will be implemented in the following year: • Performance measures and weightings • Performance targets for the performance measures and how awards will be calculated • Details of any significant changes to the policy for the next year compared to the present year • No need to restate the above if it is included in the remuneration policy	Para 21
Remuneration Committee members and advisers: • Directors who were Committee members in the year • Names of persons who provide advice or services that materially assisted the Committee • For each external adviser: – Nature of the services provided – By whom appointed, and if by the Committee how selected – Whether and how the Committee has satisfied itself the advice was objective and independent – Fees paid for services to the Committee and basis of fees	Para 22
AGM votes on directors' remuneration report and policy showing for each: • % for, % against and number withheld • plus if there was a significant vote against either resolution, a summary of the reasons for those votes and any actions taken in response.	Para 23

	SI reference
Future Remuneration Policy table, showing for Executive Directors for each component: • How it supports the short and long-term strategic objectives of the company • How it operates • Maximum that may be paid • Description of the framework to assess performance, including: – Performance measures and weightings (or an 'indication' of their weightings) – Performance period – Threshold performance payment and details of other performance levels payments set in the policy – Clawback provisions for the recovery of sums paid or the withholding of payment of any sum	Para 26
Supporting notes to the above table setting out: • Explanation of why performance measures were chosen and how targets were set for LTIs • For any bonus or LTI not subject to performance measures, explanation of why there are no such measures • Any changes to the previous policy and why the changes were made • Differences if any of the directors' remuneration policy to those of employees generally and if any, an explanation.	Para 27
Table for non-executive directors' remuneration policy setting out: • Fee payable • Additional fees for any other duties • Other items considered as remuneration	Para 28
Recruitment Remuneration Policy	Para 29
Service Contracts – details of any obligation which could impact on remuneration that is not disclosed elsewhere in the remuneration report	Para 30
Illustration of remuneration of policy (Scenarios) A bar chart showing: • Minimum remuneration (eg salary, fees, benefits and pension) • Remuneration for performance in line with expectations (eg target performance and target payouts) • Maximum remuneration (not allowing for any share price appreciation or dividends) • Each bar must separate minimum remuneration, bonus and LTIs • Each bar must show % of total from each part of the bar and total value of the bar A narrative descriptive of the calculations and assumptions used in the above	Para 34
Policy on payment for loss of office	Para 36

	SI reference
Conditions elsewhere in the group: • How pay and conditions elsewhere in the group were taken into account when setting the policy for directors • Whether and if so how employees were consulted when drawing up the directors remuneration policy • Whether remuneration comparison measures were used when setting the policy and if so how that information was taken into account	Para 38

C: Items required by the UK Corporate Governance Code or LSE Listing Rules (not subject to audit)

	Listing Rules	**Code**
The Annual Report must explain how it applies the principles in the Code, both Main and Supporting Principles, including any special circumstances that have led to a particular approach. (Overseas incorporated companies listed on LSE can follow another code see LR 9.8.7A.)	LR 9.8.6(5) and (6)	yes
The company must comply with the Provisions of the Code or, where it does not, provide an explanation.	yes	yes
• Performance-related elements of remuneration should form a significant proportion of remuneration		D. Main Principle
• Remuneration Committee to be sensitive to pay and employment conditions elsewhere in the group, especially when determining annual salary increases		D. Supporting Principle 3
• Performance related remuneration should follow the provisions of Schedule A to the Code		D.1.1. and Schedule A
• Where an executive director serves as a non-executive director elsewhere, it should be stated whether the director retains such earnings and if so what the remuneration is		D.1.2.
• Contracts should be set at one year or less, with a robust line regarding mitigation. It may be necessary to offer longer periods but this should reduce after the initial period		D.1.4. and D.1.5.

	Listing Rules	Code
• Remuneration Committee should consist of at least three (two if outside FTSE 350) members, who should all be independent directors. Meeting frequency and attendance should be stated		D.2.1. and A.1.2
• Term of reference and delegated authority should be available and should include setting the remuneration for the Chairman and executive directors and the structure and level for senior management		D.2.2.
• Explanation of who sets non-executive directors' remuneration. If options are granted to NEDs, shareholder approval should be sought in advance		D.2.3.
• Significant changes to existing and all new long-term incentives should be approved by shareholders, except as provided in the Listing Rules	yes	D.2.4.
• How performance evaluation of the Remuneration Committee has been conducted	yes	B.6.1.
• The steps the Board has taken to ensure that members of the Board, and in particular the non-executive directors, develop an understanding of the views of major shareholders about their company		D.2. Supporting Principle 2 and E.1.2.
• shares owned by each director, changes in the period and changes after the end of the period and a date not more than one month prior to the date of the notice of the AGM	LR 9.8.6	
• Unexpired term of any director's service contract	LR 9.8.8	

D: Other items that might be included in the Remuneration Report

Item	Source/reference
Dilution	Not required by DRRR. ABI guideline.
Aggregate Directors' Remuneration	CA requirement. Not required by DRRR.
Statement about all employee share plans	Not required by DRRR.
The fair value of awards under any long term incentive scheme	NAPF guideline. Also PIRC and Manifest.

The detailed requirements of the DRRR and examples in relation to policy are described in **Chapter 28**.

7 Taxation of Directors' Remuneration

Taxation is a complex area and is subject to ongoing change. Up to date advice should be sought before implementing new pay arrangements.

Much of the information on share plans in this chapter was kindly provided by Michael Landon, Executive Compensation Director of MM&K.

7.1 Why tax is important in directors' remuneration

The tax regime in the UK has changed quite considerably over the past few decades and has strongly influenced the structure of executive remuneration.

High rates of tax in the past have:

- Led executives to take steps to adopt tax avoidance schemes
- Encouraged executives to swap income into capital
- Reduced the motivation of executives to perform
- Encouraged executives to accept private equity opportunities and Management Buy Outs (MBOs).

Examples of the above are:

- *CGT.* When Capital Gains Tax (CGT) was first introduced in 1965, CGT rates were somewhat lower than income tax rates. From 1988, the CGT rate was the same as the individual's marginal rate of income tax. However, from 2002, the taper relief on business assets meant that only 25% of the gain was chargeable if the assets were held for at least two years – giving an effective CGT rate of only 10% for many higher rate taxpayers. Even today, the CGT rate of 28% for higher and additional rate taxpayers is well below their income tax rate.
- *Pensions.* In the 1960s and 1970s the high rates of tax meant that deferral of pay until after retirement was attractive:
  - Income was generally less after retirement and so the marginal rate of tax that applied was likely to be lower
  - Part of the pension could be paid as a tax free lump sum. The maximum amount was 25% of the value of the fund.

As a result pensions became a very important part of the remuneration package for senior executives. This tax break for directors was viewed as politically acceptable as it encouraged directors to set up pension plans for all employees, which was a political goal of both Labour and Conservatives.

The introduction of caps on the value of tax-advantaged pensions has reduced the attractiveness of rewarding executives in this way.

- *Share Options.* In 1984 the gains on CSOP options were made subject to capital gains tax (then 30%) rather than income tax (then up to 60%). Within one year, 99 out of the 100 largest UK companies had Share Option plans, whereas prior to the tax change only about one third had such plans. After 1995, the maximum value of shares subject to CSOP options was reduced to £30,000, which is one of the reasons for the move away from share options towards conditional and deferred share awards.
- *Carried Interest Plans.* The 2002 Memorandum of Understanding (MOU) between the Inland Revenue[1] and the private equity industry allowed carried interest plans to be viewed as investments that would be subject to CGT and not income tax.
- *Generous benefits and perquisites.* The general rule is that if benefits are provided to executives wholly, exclusively and necessarily for the performance of their duties of employment then the benefits will not be taxable. The Government policy has changed over the years so that the full value of most benefits is taxable and also subject to employers' national insurance.

The Government has gradually been reducing the scope for avoiding income tax and national insurance through the structure of the remuneration package. The tax advantages of paying executives in unit trusts, gold bars and platinum sponge have been removed. There has also been extensive legislation to ensure that remuneration delivered using shares and other securities is subject to income tax and national insurance, as opposed to CGT, except where the executives are exposed to a genuine risk of financial loss.

Most notably, the legislation relating to 'disguised remuneration' in the Finance Act 2011 (see **Section 7.3**) has largely stopped the creation of new 'family benefit trusts', which had been increasingly used to delay or avoid income tax, national insurance and inheritance tax.

---

1 Which is now part of Her Majesty's Revenue and Customs (HMRC).

7.2 How pay is taxed in the UK

The Income Tax (Earnings and Pensions) Act 2003 (ITEPA) legislates for the taxation of remuneration in the UK.

In the UK, in general, directors who are UK tax resident pay income tax and national insurance on their income when it is received. Companies also have to pay employers' national insurance (for tax year 2013–14 it is 13.8%). The main rate of corporation tax on profits, for 2014–15, is 21% and will fall to 20% from April 2015.

For 2014–15 the rates of income tax and national insurance in the UK are shown in the tables below. Income is assessed based on annual earnings. However national insurance is based on weekly or monthly earnings and the rate is based on that.

Income tax allowances

The 'personal allowance' is the amount of income you can earn before you start paying Income Tax.

Income Tax Personal allowance	**2014–15**
Born after 5 April 1948	£10,000
Born between 6 April 1938 and 5 April 1948	£10,500
Born before 6 April 1938	£10,660

The Personal Allowance reduces where the income is above £100,000, by £1 for every £2 of income above the £100,000 limit. This reduction applies irrespective of age or date of birth. This results in an effective marginal income tax rate in 2014–15 of 60% for income between £100,000 and £120,000.

Income tax bands

Tax band	**2014–15**
Starting savings rate*: 10%	£0 – £2880
Basic rate: 20%	£0 – £31,865
Higher rate: 40%	£31,866 – £150,000
Additional rate: 45%	Over £150,000

* The 10% starting rate applies to savings income only. If, after deducting the Personal Allowance from total income liable to income tax, non-savings income is above this limit then the 10% starting rate for savings will not apply. Non-savings income includes income from employment, profits from self-employment, pensions, income from property and taxable benefits.

The rates available for dividends are the 10% ordinary rate, the 32.5% dividend upper rate and the dividend additional rate of 37.5%.

Source: HM Revenue & Customs website (www.hmrc.gov.uk)

National insurance contributions

National insurance contributions – rates and allowances	
£ per week	2014–15
Lower earnings limit, primary Class 1	£111
Upper earnings limit, primary Class 1	£805
Upper accrual point	£770
Primary threshold	£153
Secondary threshold	£153
Employees' primary Class 1 rate between primary threshold and upper earnings limit	12%
Employees' primary Class 1 rate above upper earnings limit	2%
Class 1A rate on employer provided benefits	13.8%
Employees' contracted-out rebate (salary related schemes only)	1.4%
Employers' secondary Class 1 rate above secondary threshold	13.8%
Employers' contracted-out rebate (salary-related schemes only)	3.4%

Source: www.hmrc.gov.uk

For example, for pay above £150,000 rates of tax for 2014–15, the rate of income tax is 45% and in addition there is a 2% rate of employees' national insurance, so the effective individual rate is 47%.

So the net cost to shareholders of each £100 of net pay for high earners is £169.63 (see below) if the company pays corporation tax.

Net Pay	Plus	Employers' National Insurance	Less	Income Tax (45%) and National Insurance (2%)	Less	Corporation Tax not paid	Equals	Gross Cost to Shareholders
£100		x (1+13.8%)		÷ (1–47%)		x (1–21%)	=	**£169.63**

Capital gains tax

There is an Annual Exempt Amount from CGT for individuals of £11,000 for the tax year 2014–15. Above this, the CGT rate is 18% for basic rate taxpayers and 28% for higher and additional rate taxpayers.

A rate of 10% applies for gains qualifying for Entrepreneurs' Relief.

UK Government policy

Nowadays, the HMRC general policy is to treat similarly all forms of income, items and benefits that are received only because the person is an employee. So they are likely to challenge tax avoidance schemes such as those based around shares which are only available to employees.

7.3 Disguised remuneration

The relevant legislation is in ITEPA 2003, Part 7A Employment Income Provided Through Third Parties.

The 'disguised remuneration' legislation, implemented by the UK Government in the Finance Act 2011, was designed to block certain arrangements which use employee benefit trusts (EBTs) to defer or avoid income tax or national insurance contributions. The legislation was mainly targeted at family benefit trusts and some employer-financed retirement benefit schemes (EFRBS).

Income tax (PAYE) and national insurance charges will arise on the value of a sum of money or an asset if a third party (eg an EBT trustee):

- pays or transfers it to an employee, including as a loan;
- makes it available to an employee; or
- 'earmarks' it for an employee, with a view to it being transferred or made available in the future.

It is the 'earmarking' provision which has caused most concern to companies. Many share plans include arrangements for shares to be delivered to employees through an EBT. There is a risk that income tax and national insurance charges will be triggered at the time when the trustees allocate shares which they hold to specific employees in anticipation of the shares being delivered when share awards vest or share options are exercised. Employees may be taxed on the full value of the shares at the time of this 'earmarking', even though they may not become entitled to the shares until many years later – and they may even forfeit their rights in the meantime.

Following representations by MM&K and other share plan practitioners, the Government added a large number of exceptions to the 'earmarking' charge.

The following arrangements are now unlikely to result in tax charges under the 'disguised remuneration' provisions:

- Any plan which involves new shares or treasury shares being issued directly to employees by the employing company (or another group company).
- Any of the tax-advantaged share plans – Share Incentive Plans (SIPs), Savings-Related (SAYE) Share Option Schemes, Company Share Option Plans (CSOPs) and Enterprise Management Incentives (EMI).
- Standard Conditional Share Award and Deferred Share Award Plans, provided that the awards vest on a specified date and the employees become entitled to the shares (and liable to income tax) on the vesting date.
- Awards of Restricted Securities, including under standard Joint Share Ownership Plans (JSOPs).
- Standard Share Options, again if they became exercisable on a specified date and will expire if not exercised within ten years of their date of grant.
- Share Awards and Share Options which vest on the occurrence of an 'exit event', such as flotation on a stock exchange or a change in control of the company.
- 'Phantom' Share Plans which provide cash payments in similar circumstances.
- 'Cashless exercise' arrangements provided that the loan used to exercise Share Options is repaid within 40 days.

The relevant exceptions are, however, detailed and complex. It is therefore recommended that the plan rules and grant documents, for both existing and new share plans, should be reviewed carefully to ensure that they come within one of the exceptions.

Some plans will not be covered by any of the exceptions. These may include:

- Conditional Share Awards where the employee does not become entitled to the shares on a fixed date, but only when the Remuneration Committee or trustee exercises its discretion to release them.
- Share Awards and Share Options where vesting occurs only when specified performance targets are first met.

Where there is some doubt about whether or not a share plan comes within one of the exceptions, some companies have changed their procedures so that the companies themselves, not the EBT trustees, grant the awards. The companies do not give the trustees details of the awards until the shares actually need to be delivered to employees. Guidance issued by HM

Revenue & Customs has confirmed that 'earmarking' will not occur if the trustees only know the total number of shares subject to the awards but do not know how many of those shares have been allocated to particular individuals.

7.4 Tax-advantaged share plans in the UK

There are currently four different types of employee share plans with tax advantages:

- Company Share Option Plans (CSOPs)
- Enterprise Management Incentives (EMI)
- Share Incentive Plans (SIPs)
- Save-As-You-Earn (SAYE) Share Option Schemes.

The limits to the amount of tax relief available make these plans of limited value when remunerating top executives of the largest companies. SIP and SAYE must be offered to all employees (who meet any length of service requirement) and on the same terms. However, the tax reliefs available for all of these share plans can add to the value of the package for senior executives in small and medium-sized companies, middle-ranking executives and, of course, employees generally.

Following a Review of Tax-Advantaged Employee Share Schemes, published by the Office of Tax Simplification in March 2012, the Government has made some significant improvements to the detailed tax legislation for these four plans.

7.5 Company Share Option Plans

A CSOP is a discretionary share option plan which allows the company to select which employees will be granted options and the size of award to be made to each individual.

CSOP options may only be granted to employees of the company setting up the plan or a company which it controls. Directors are only eligible if they normally devote at least 25 hours per week (excluding meal breaks) to their duties.

The maximum value of the shares subject to all CSOP options granted to an individual, which are still capable of exercise, is £30,000 (taking the value at the grant date of each option).

The exercise price of the option must be stated at the time of grant and cannot be less than the market value of the shares at the grant date.

No income tax or national insurance are payable on the grant of a CSOP option or when it is exercised, provided that the exercise date is:

- between the third and tenth anniversaries of the date of grant; or
- before the third anniversary of the date of grant but within six months of the option holder ceasing to be employed because of injury, disability, redundancy, retirement or a TUPE transfer; or
- within 12 months of the participant's death.

On sale of the shares, there is a potential CGT liability on the difference between the sale proceeds and the amount which the employee paid for the shares. It may be possible to reduce or eliminate the chargeable gain through the individual's (and their spouse's) annual CGT exemption (£11,000 in 2014–15).

The employing company can claim a deduction for corporation tax purposes for the difference between the market value of the shares at the exercise date and the amount paid by the employee. If the conditions for income tax relief are met, the employing company is exempt from a national insurance liability.

7.6 Enterprise Management Incentives

EMI schemes are designed to help smaller companies to recruit, retain and incentivise employees. EMI options may only be granted over shares in an independent trading company whose gross assets do not exceed £30 million and which has fewer than 250 employees. The company must not carry out certain excluded activities, which include financial services, software, property development, farming, shipbuilding and producing coal or steel.

An employee of the company or its subsidiary is eligible to be granted an EMI option if the employee is required to spend at least 25 hours per week on the company's business or, if less, 75% of his working time.

The company can select which employees will be granted options and the size of award to be made to each individual, up to a maximum of £250,000 per person.

No income tax or national insurance are payable on the grant of an EMI option or when it is exercised, provided that the exercise price is not set at a discount to the share price at the date of grant. If the exercise price is lower than the share price at the date of grant, there will be an income tax and possibly a national insurance charge on this discount at the time of exercise.

If certain 'disqualifying events' occur, for example the company comes under the control of another company or ceases to carry on a qualifying trading activity, the EMI option must be exercised within 40 days of the event to preserve the favourable tax treatment.

On sale of the shares, there is a potential CGT liability on the difference between the sale proceeds and the amount which the employee paid for the shares (plus any amount which was taxed at exercise). It may be possible to reduce or eliminate the chargeable gain through the individual's annual CGT exemption.

Shares acquired through EMI options exercised on or after 6 April 2012 qualify for Entrepreneurs' Relief, regardless of the number of shares held by the individual. The one-year holding period begins on the date when the EMI option is granted and this new relief can apply to disposals of these shares from 6 April 2013.

The employing company can claim a corporation tax deduction for the difference between the market value of the shares at the exercise date and the amount paid by the employee. The employing company is exempt from employer's national insurance in the same way as the employee.

7.7 Share Incentive Plans

Share Incentive Plans (SIPs) enable employees to acquire and hold shares in their employing company (or parent company) in three ways:

Free Shares	**Partnership Shares**	**Matching Shares**
Up to £3,600 worth of shares (increased from £3,000 on 6 April 2014) can be awarded to employees per year on the same terms.	Employees can contribute up to £1,800 per year (increased from £1,500 on 6 April 2014) to buy shares.	Companies can match each Partnership Share with up to two free Matching Shares.

In addition, cash dividends can be reinvested to buy further Dividend Shares.

All UK-resident employees must be eligible to participate if they have been continuously employed for a qualifying period (of not more than 18 months).

After these shares have been awarded, they are held on behalf of the employees in a trust. Participants must leave their Free Shares and Matching Shares in the plan for a holding period, which must be between three and five years from their award date. The holding period for Dividend Shares is three years. Partnership Shares may be withdrawn from the plan by participants at any time.

Employees are not liable to any income tax or national insurance when Free Shares, Matching Shares or Dividend Shares are awarded to them. Salary deductions to purchase Partnership Shares are made from pre-tax and pre-national insurance earnings.

When shares are withdrawn from the plan or the participants cease to be employed by the company or an associated company, there will be an income tax liability on the following amount:

Timing of withdrawal	**Free Shares or Matching Shares**	**Partnership Shares**	**Dividend Shares**
Within 3 years of award/acquisition	Market value of the shares when they are withdrawn	Market value of the shares when they are withdrawn	The amount of the dividend used to acquire the shares
Between 3–5 years	Lower of market values at award date and at withdrawal	Lower of money used to acquire the shares and the market value at withdrawal	No charge
5 years or longer	No charge	No charge	No charge

These tax charges do not apply if employees leave employment in certain special circumstances, such as injury, disability, redundancy, retirement or a TUPE transfer.

There is no CGT charge in respect of the gains accrued by employees while their shares are held in the plan. The base cost for CGT purposes is the market value at the time when the shares are withdrawn.

7.8 SAYE Schemes

A Sharesave or Save-As-You-Earn share option plan combines a share option with a savings contract, so employees can save the funds to buy shares in their company.

Employees are invited to save a regular amount between £5 and £500 each month (increased from £250 on 6 April 2014) with a bank or building society by deduction from their (after tax) pay for a period of three or five years.

At the time when employees start the savings contract they are granted options over the maximum number of shares which can be bought with the total prospective savings at the end of three or five years. The price to be paid for the shares (the exercise price) must be at least 80% of the share price at the date of grant of the option.

All UK resident employees of participating companies who meet a length of service requirement (not exceeding five years) must be invited to participate in each offer on similar terms.

No income tax is payable on grant of the option or when it is exercised (except in certain exceptional circumstances). There is no national insurance liability.

On disposal of the shares there is a potential CGT liability on the difference between the market value of the shares on disposal and the price paid for the shares. However, for many employees the gain will come within the annual CGT exemption.

The employing company can claim a deduction for corporation tax purposes for the difference between the market value of the shares at the exercise date and the amount paid by the employee.

7.9 Other ways to make gains subject to CGT

By making awards to executives in the form of shares or other securities, the Company can deliver part of the reward in the form of gains chargeable to CGT, instead of income tax and national insurance.

The first £11,000 worth of gains in a tax year is exempt from CGT (2014–15). In some cases, an executive may be able to realise the gain over more than one tax year or to transfer the shares to his/her spouse, so that the spouse's annual exemption can also be used. Higher and additional rate taxpayers are currently charged CGT at 28%. This is noticeably lower than the top income tax and national insurance rates payable by an executive. Employers' national insurance at 13.8% can also be avoided.

	Income tax at 40%	**Income tax at 45%**	**CGT**
Gross payment	£10,000	£10,000	£10,000
Income tax (40% or 45%)	-£4,000	-£4,500	£0
Employees' national insurance (2%)	-£200	-£200	£0
CGT 28% (ignoring annual exemption)	£0	£0	-£2,800
Net of tax amount	**£5,800**	**£5,300**	**£7,200**
Employers' national insurance (13.8%)	-£1,380	-£1,380	£0

Share purchase with a loan

If an executive pays the full market value for the Company's shares, any subsequent increase in value will be subject to CGT on disposal of the shares.

If the Company were to make a loan to the executive, which must be repaid, say, three years later, the tax treatment of any increase in value would be broadly the same as for a CSOP share option. The equivalent of the increase in value of the shares over this period would be subject to CGT, not income tax and national insurance.

Factors to consider are:

- the executive will still need to repay the loan even if the share price falls and will therefore bear the risk of making a loss on the shares.
- if the loan is made by an employee benefit trust (EBT) or other third party, under the 'disguised remuneration' legislation, there may be an upfront income tax charge on the full value of the loan.
- corporation tax deductions will not be available in respect of any gains made by the executives.
- a company may not make a loan to a director exceeding £10,000 without shareholder approval (Companies Act 2006, s 197).
- if the company is a close company and the loan exceeds £15,000, there is likely to be a requirement for the company to make a payment equal to 25% of its amount under the 'loan to participator' provisions (Corporation Tax Act 2010, s 455).

Nil or partly-paid shares

Executives can be invited to acquire shares on a nil or partly-paid basis. The balance of the value of the shares at acquisition is payable at a later date, for example when they wish to dispose of the shares. In this case, any increase in the value of the shares will be subject to CGT.

The executives will be treated for tax purposes as having been given notional loans by the Company and will be taxed on the benefit of the unpaid amounts at the official rate of interest.

Under rule 2.2.4(2) of the Listing Rules, listed companies are not normally permitted to issue shares at a discount (and the alternative of providing the shares through an EBT is likely to be ineffective due to the 'disguised remuneration' legislation).

As in the loan arrangement mentioned above, the executives will still have to pay the balance of the original share value if the share price falls. Again, they will risk making a loss on the shares. Corporation tax deductions will not be available in respect of any gains made by the executives.

Joint Share Ownership Plan (JSOP)

The JSOP is another mechanism for delivering a similar tax effect to a CSOP option, but without the £30,000 limit. Executives are granted joint ownership of a specified number of shares, typically with an EBT being the other joint owner. When the shares are sold in due course, the trust will retain an amount equivalent to the value of the shares at grant (often plus a hurdle increase of, say, 5% per year), while the executives will be entitled to any increase in value of the shares after the grant date (in excess of any hurdle).

The benefit of the increase in value will be subject to CGT, instead of income tax and national insurance.

However, in order to benefit from this CGT treatment, the executive must make a joint election with the Company (under ITEPA 2003, s 431(1)) at the grant date to pay income tax on the value of his interest in the shares at the grant date. Although the intrinsic value of his interest will be zero on the grant date, HMRC will deem it to have a value, calculated in a similar way to the value of a share option.

Therefore, although under this arrangement the executives will not make a loss on the shares if the share price falls, they will have incurred some income tax up front which cannot be recovered.

Corporation tax deductions will only be available in respect of the (small) amount for which the executives are liable for income tax – not for any gain which is subject to CGT.

JSOPs are most likely to be beneficial in a start-up or recovery situation, where there is potential for the share price to increase substantially in value.

Growth Shares

Growth Share (or Flowering Share) arrangements are designed to work in a very similar way to JSOPs. Instead of being granted an interest in shares, the executives are granted a special class of shares, which only have any value if the value of the company as a whole increases.

Growth Shares have broadly the same advantages and disadvantages as JSOPs, except that there will be no need to use an employee trust. However, as they require a new class of shares to be created, they are more likely to be introduced in private companies or in subsidiaries of listed companies. Valuation of the Growth Shares at their acquisition date is also likely to be more difficult.

Using Growth Shares in a subsidiary with significant growth potential could enable executives to participate in tax-effective remuneration arrangements where the incentives and rewards are akin to those offered by private equity companies.

7.10 Deferring remuneration

It has become standard market practice for payment of part of senior executives' annual bonuses to be deferred for a few years. It should be noted, however, that if an EBT (or other third party) is used to hold the cash or shares during the deferral period, there must be a real possibility that the bonus may be subject to forfeiture (eg on leaving employment); otherwise there is likely to be an upfront income tax charge under the recent 'disguised remuneration' legislation.

There could also be benefits from deferring the gross payment over a longer period and investing the deferred amount in the meantime.

In this example, delaying the taxable event until the investment is realised gives a higher net amount than if only the net bonus had been invested.

Option 1: Net bonus invested in shares	
Gross bonus	£50,000
Income tax and national insurance on bonus at start (47%)	-£23,500
Amount invested in shares	£26,500
Value of shares after 3 years (+25%)	£33,125
CGT at sale of shares (ignoring annual exemption)	-£1,855
Net amount received by executive	**£31,270**
Employer's national insurance at start (13.8%)	-£6,900

Option 2: Gross bonus deferred into shares	
Gross bonus invested in shares	£50,000
Value of shares after 3 years (+25%)	£62,500
Income tax and national insurance on share bonus at vesting (47%)	-£29,375
Net amount received by executive	**£33,125**
Employer's national insurance at vesting (13.8%)	-£8,625

8 Financial Conduct Authority Listing Rules

The chapter summarises the main provisions of the Listing Rules, published by the Financial Conduct Authority (FCA), relating to directors' remuneration. **Appendix 1** contains the detailed provisions referred to. If there is any doubt about interpretation of these provisions, the company's brokers should be consulted.

8.1 Shareholder approval of employees' share schemes and long-term incentive plans

Under Listing Rule (LR) 9.4.1R, a listed company that is incorporated in the UK must obtain shareholder approval in general meeting before implementing:

- an **employees' share scheme** under which new shares may be issued or treasury shares transferred; or
- a **long-term incentive scheme** in which any director of the listed company is eligible to participate.

A 'long-term incentive scheme' includes any arrangement for rewarding executives in cash or securities which requires service or performance conditions to be satisfied over more than one financial year. It does not include:

- a retirement benefit plan; or
- a deferred bonus – that is a bonus paid for service and/or performance in a period not exceeding one financial year, even though payment of the bonus may be delayed and depend on continuing employment.

Under LR 9.4.2R, the shareholder approval requirement does not apply to:

- an all-employee share scheme; or
- an arrangement to facilitate the recruitment of a director in unusual circumstances;

unless the arrangement may involve the issue of new shares or transfer of treasury shares.

8.2 Shareholder approval of discounted option arrangements

LR 9.4.4R requires a listed company (wherever incorporated) to obtain prior shareholder approval in general meeting before granting to a director or employee an option to *subscribe for* shares if the exercise price payable is less than the market value of a share at the time of grant.

Exceptions

Under LR 9.4.5R, the above requirement does not apply to an all-employee share scheme, and so offering a 20% discount under an SAYE option scheme would be permitted.

LR 9.4.5R also allows replacement options to be granted, following a take-over or reconstruction, even though the exercise price of the replacement option may be less than the market value of the relevant shares at the time of its grant.

It is generally accepted that LR 9.4.4R does not, in practice, prevent the grant of nil-cost or nominal-cost options under a performance share plan.

However, in all of these cases the scheme itself would have needed prior shareholder approval, under LR 9.4.1R, if it could involve the issue of new shares or transfer of treasury shares.

8.3 Information to be included in a shareholder circular

Under LR 13.8.11R, the shareholder circular for the general meeting seeking approval for an employees' share scheme or a long-term incentive scheme must either contain the full Rules of the scheme or a summary of its main terms. A summary should include:

- whether the scheme involves trustees, and whether the directors of the listed company are trustees or have any interest in the trustees;
- the persons who are eligible to participate;
- overall limits on the number of shares or value of cash or other benefits;
- the maximum entitlement of any individual;
- the basis for determining a participant's entitlement and the terms under which any shares, cash or other benefit will be provided;
- provisions for any adjustment for capital variations;
- whether benefits under the scheme will be pensionable and, if so, the reasons for this.

If the full Rules are not circulated to shareholders in the circular, they must be made available for inspection.

8.4 Amendments to schemes

LR 13.8.11R also requires that any subsequent amendments to the main terms of a scheme to the advantage of participants must also have shareholder approval in general meeting.

There are exceptions for minor amendments:

- to benefit the administration of the scheme;
- to take account of a change in legislation; or
- to obtain or maintain favourable tax, exchange control or regulatory treatments for participants, the company or other group members.

LR 13.8.13R permits the resolution approving the adoption of a scheme to allow the directors to establish similar overseas schemes which are modified to take into account local tax, exchange control or securities law. The shares made available under any modified schemes must count towards the overall and individual participation limits.

8.5 Disclosure of directors' remuneration

Following the implementation of the new BIS Directors' Remuneration Reporting Regulations,[1] to avoid duplication, the FCA has deleted the Listing Rules that relate to directors' remuneration which have the same outcome.

LR 9.8.8R now requires the annual report to contain details of the unexpired term of the service contract of any director proposed for election or re-election.

AIM Rules

The BIS Directors' Reporting Regulations do not apply to AIM companies. However, AIM Rule 19 requires a company's annual account to include details of the remuneration earned in respect of the financial year by each director of the AIM company.

---

1 Schedule 8 of the Large and Medium-sized Companies and Groups (Accounts and Reports) (Amendment) Regulations 2013 (SI 2013/1981).

8.6 Disclosure of corporate governance compliance

Under LR 9.8.6R, a listed company incorporated in the UK must include in its annual report:

- a statement of how the company has applied the Main Principles set out in the UK Corporate Governance Code;
- a statement as to whether the company has complied with all relevant provisions of the Code throughout the accounting period, with an explanation of any non-compliance.

8.7 Directors' dealings

LR 9, Annex 1 contains the Model Code, which restricts directors' dealings on their own account in the company's shares at certain times and governs the approval process as well as the manner and timing of disclosure of such dealings at other times. Through the Model Code, shareholder directors are demonstrating to other shareholders that they will not abuse their position for unfair advantage.

The requirements apply to persons discharging managerial responsibilities (PDMRs), who include not only directors but also senior executives who have regular access to inside information and have power to make managerial decisions affecting the company's future development and business prospects.

PDMRs must have advance clearance before they can deal in the company's securities.

They are also prevented from dealing during a prohibited period. This includes any close period (60 days before the announcement of the company's results) and any other period when there exists any matter which constitutes inside information in relation to the company. This might be a possible take-over offer, a significant share issue or a big contract win or loss.

The term 'dealing' does not just include acquiring and disposing of the company's securities. It can also include the grant and exercise of a share option or grant or vesting of a conditional share award.

The Model Code does not prevent:

- a PDMR from participating in an SAYE option scheme or a share incentive plan (SIP) or similar scheme extended to all or most employees on similar terms;
- a PDMR from transferring shares acquired from one of these all-employee share schemes into a savings scheme investing in the company's securities;

- cancellation or surrender of an option under an employees' share scheme; or
- transfer of securities by an independent trustee of an employees' share scheme to a beneficiary who is not a PDMR.

AIM Rules

Paragraph 21 of the AIM Rules has similar restrictions on dealings by directors and applicable employees. This rule does not apply where an individual has entered into a binding commitment outside a close period.

8.8 Notification of transactions

The FCA's Disclosure Rules and Transparency Rules (DTR) 3.1 require PDMRs and their connected persons to notify the company in writing of all their transactions in the company's shares within four days.

The company must then make a public RIS notification of the transaction before the end of the business day following receipt of the information.

8.9 Disclosure of directors' interests

Under LR 9.8.6, the annual report for a listed company incorporated in the UK must include a statement of each director's interest in the company's shares at the end of the period under review and all changes in the interests over that period and up to a month before the notice of the AGM was issued. This must include the interests of connected persons.

9 UK Corporate Governance Code

9.1 The UK Corporate Governance Code for Remuneration

Section D of Part 1 of the UK Corporate Governance Code sets out the following Main Principles, Supporting Principles and Code Provisions regarding remuneration. Companies must report to their shareholders on how they apply the Main Principles and Supporting Principles and either comply with the Code Provisions or explain why they do not.

Satisfactory engagement between company boards and investors is crucial to the health of the UK's corporate governance regime. Companies and shareholders both have responsibility for ensuring that 'comply or explain' remains an effective alternative to a rules-based system. There are practical and administrative obstacles to improved interaction between boards and shareholders. But certainly there is also scope for an increase in trust which could generate a virtuous upward spiral in attitudes to the Code and in its constructive use.

The UK Corporate Governance Code does not include material in previous Combined Codes on the disclosure of directors' remuneration. This is because The Directors' Remuneration Report Regulations (which superseded the earlier Combined Code Provisions) require the directors of a company to prepare a remuneration report.

The following is taken directly from the UK Corporate Governance Code SECTION D REMUNERATION:

> **'D.1 The Level and Components of Remuneration**
>
> **Main Principle**
>
> Levels of remuneration should be sufficient to attract, retain and motivate directors of the quality required to run the company successfully, but a company should avoid paying more than is necessary for this purpose. A significant proportion of executive directors' remuneration should be structured so as to link rewards to corporate and individual performance.

Supporting Principles

The performance-related elements of executive directors' remuneration should be stretching and designed to promote the long-term success of the company.

The remuneration committee should judge where to position their company relative to other companies. But they should use such comparisons with caution in view of the risk of an upward ratchet of remuneration levels with no corresponding improvement in performance.

They should also be sensitive to pay and employment conditions elsewhere in the group, especially when determining annual salary increases.

Code Provisions

D.1.1 In designing schemes of performance-related remuneration for executive directors, the remuneration committee should follow the provisions in Schedule A to this Code.

D.1.2 Where a company releases an executive director to serve as a non-executive director elsewhere, the remuneration report should include a statement as to whether or not the director will retain such earnings and, if so, what the remuneration is.

D.1.3 Levels of remuneration for non-executive directors should reflect the time commitment and responsibilities of the role. Remuneration for non-executive directors should not include share options or other performance-related elements. If, exceptionally, options are granted, shareholder approval should be sought in advance and any shares acquired by exercise of the options should be held until at least one year (after the non-executive director leaves the board. Holding of share options could be relevant to the determination of a non-executive director's independence (as set out in provision B.1.1)), as required for UK incorporated companies under the Large and Medium-Sized Companies and Groups (Accounts and Reports) Regulations 2008.

D.1.4 The remuneration committee should carefully consider what compensation commitments (including pension contributions and all other elements) their directors' terms of appointment would entail in the event of early termination. The aim should be to avoid rewarding poor performance. They should take a robust line on reducing compensation to reflect departing directors' obligations to mitigate loss.

D.1.5 Notice or contract periods should be set at one year or less. If it is necessary to offer longer notice or contract periods to new directors recruited from outside, such periods should reduce to one year or less after the initial period.

D.2 Procedure

Main Principle

There should be a formal and transparent procedure for developing policy on executive remuneration and for fixing the remuneration packages of individual directors. No director should be involved in deciding his or her own remuneration.

Supporting Principles

The remuneration committee should consult the Chairman and/or Chief Executive about their proposals relating to the remuneration of other executive directors. The remuneration committee should also be responsible for appointing any consultants in respect of executive director remuneration. Where executive directors or senior management are involved in advising or supporting the remuneration committee, care should be taken to recognise and avoid conflicts of interest.

The Chairman of the board should ensure that the company maintains contact as required with its principal shareholders about remuneration.

Code Provisions

D.2.1 The board should establish a remuneration committee of at least three, or in the case of smaller companies[1] two, independent non-executive directors. In addition the company Chairman may also be a member of, but not chair, the committee if he or she was considered independent on appointment as Chairman. The remuneration committee should make available its terms of reference, explaining its role and the authority delegated to it by the board. Where remuneration consultants are appointed, they should be identified in the report and a statement should be made available of whether they have any other connection with the company.

D.2.2 The remuneration committee should have delegated responsibility for setting remuneration for all executive directors and the Chairman, including pension rights and any compensation payments. The committee should also recommend and monitor the level and structure of remuneration for senior management. The definition of "senior management" for this purpose should be determined by the board but should normally include the first layer of management below board level.

D.2.3 The board itself or, where required by the Articles of Association, the shareholders should determine the remuneration of the non-executive directors within the limits set in the Articles of Association.

---

[1] Those outside the FTSE 350.

Where permitted by the Articles, the board may however delegate this responsibility to a committee, which might include the Chief Executive.

D.2.4 Shareholders should be invited specifically to approve all new long-term incentive schemes (as defined in the Listing Rules[2]) and significant changes to existing schemes, save in the circumstances permitted by the Listing Rules.'

The following is taken directly from the UK Corporate Governance Code Schedule A.

'SCHEDULE A THE DESIGN OF PERFORMANCE-RELATED REMUNERATION FOR EXECUTIVE DIRECTORS

i. The remuneration committee should consider whether the directors should be eligible for annual bonuses. If so, performance conditions should be relevant, stretching and designed to promote the long-term success of the company.

ii. Upper limits should be set and disclosed. There may be a case for part payment in shares to be held for a significant period.

iii. The remuneration committee should consider whether the directors should be eligible for benefits under long-term incentive schemes. Traditional share option schemes should be weighed against other kinds of long-term incentive scheme.

vi. Executive share options should not be offered at a discount save as permitted by the relevant provisions of the Listing Rules.

v. In normal circumstances, shares granted or other forms of deferred remuneration should not vest, and options should not be exercisable, in less than three years. Directors should be encouraged to hold their shares for a further period after vesting or exercise, subject to the need to finance any costs of acquisition and associated tax liabilities.

vi. Any new long-term incentive schemes which are proposed should be approved by shareholders and should preferably replace any existing schemes or, at least, form part of a well-considered overall plan incorporating existing schemes.

vii. The total potentially available rewards should not be excessive.

viii. Payouts or grants under all incentive schemes, including new grants under existing share option schemes, should be subject to

---

[2] See Listing Rules LR 9.4

challenging performance criteria reflecting the company's objectives, including non-financial performance metrics where appropriate. Remuneration incentives should be compatible with risk policies and systems.

ix. Grants under executive share option and other long-term incentive schemes should normally be phased rather than awarded in one large block.

x. Consideration should be given to the use of provisions that permit the company to reclaim variable components in exceptional circumstances of misstatement or misconduct.

xi. In general, only basic salary should be pensionable. The remuneration committee should consider the pension consequences and associated costs to the company of basic salary increases and any other changes in pensionable remuneration, especially for directors close to retirement.'

9.2 Link to Listing Rules of the London Stock Exchange

The requirement to report on how the company has applied the Code and whether it has complied or if not to give explanation of reasons for non-compliance is in Listing Rules 9.8.6 R (for UK incorporated companies) and 9.8.6 R(1) (for overseas incorporated companies).

9.3 Disclosure provisions of The UK Corporate Governance Code

In addition to the 'comply or explain' requirement in the Listing Rules, the Code includes specific requirements for disclosure which must be provided in order to comply. These are summarised below with those clearly pertaining to remuneration shown **in bold**.

The annual report should include:

- a statement of how the Board operates, including a high level statement of which types of decisions are to be taken by the Board and which are to be delegated to management (A.1.1).
- the names of the Chairman, the deputy Chairman (where there is one), the Chief Executive, the senior independent director and the Chairmen and members of the Board committees (A.1.2).
- the number of meetings of the Board and **those committees and individual attendance by directors** (A.1.2).

- where a Chief Executive is appointed Chairman, the reasons for their appointment (this only needs to be done in the annual report following the appointment) (A.3.1).
- the names of the Non-Executive Directors whom the Board determines to be independent, with reasons where necessary (B.1.1).
- a separate section describing the work of the Nomination Committee, including the process it has used in relation to board appointments and an explanation if neither external search consultancy nor open advertising has been used in the appointment of a Chairman or a Non-Executive Director (B.2.4).
- any changes to the other significant commitments of the Chairman during the year (B.3.1).
- **a statement of how performance evaluation** of the Board, **its committees** and its directors has been conducted (B.6.1).
- an explanation from the directors of their responsibility for preparing the accounts and a statement by the auditors about their reporting responsibilities (C.1.1).
- an explanation from the directors of the basis on which the company generates or preserves value over the longer term (the business model) and the strategy for delivering the objectives of the company (C.1.2).
- a statement from the directors that the business is a going concern, with supporting assumptions or qualifications as necessary (C.1.3).
- a report that the Board has conducted a review of the effectiveness of the company's risk management and internal controls systems (C.2.1).
- a separate section describing the work of the Audit Committee in discharging its responsibilities (C.3.3).
- where there is no internal audit function, the reasons for the absence of such a function (C.3.5).
- where the Board does not accept the Audit Committee's recommendation on the appointment, reappointment or removal of an external auditor, a statement from the Audit Committee explaining the recommendation and the reasons why the Board has taken a different position (C.3.6).
- an explanation of how, if the auditor provides non-audit services, auditor objectivity and independence is safeguarded (C.3.7).
- a description of the work of the Remuneration Committee as required under the Large and Medium-Sized Companies and Groups (Accounts and Reports) Regulations 2008 including, where an executive director

serves as a Non-Executive Director elsewhere, whether or not the director will retain such earnings and, if so, what the remuneration is (D.1.2).

- the steps the Board has taken to ensure that members of the Board, in particular the Non-Executive Directors, develop an understanding of the views of major shareholders about their company (E.1.2).

The following information should be made available (which may be met by placing the information on a website that is maintained by or on behalf of the company):

- **the terms of reference of the** Nomination, Audit and **Remuneration Committees**, explaining their role and the authority delegated to them by the Board (B.2.1, C.3.3 and D.2.1).
- **the terms and conditions of appointment of Non-Executive Directors (B.3.2).**
- where performance evaluation has been externally facilitated, a statement of whether the facilitator has any other connection with the company (B.6.2).
- **where remuneration consultants are appointed, a statement of whether they have any other connection with the company** (D.2.1).

The board should set out to shareholders in the papers accompanying a resolution to elect or re-elect directors:

- sufficient biographical details to enable shareholders to take an informed decision on their election[3] or re-election (B.7.1).
- why they believe an individual should be elected to a Non-Executive role (B.7.2).
- on re-election of a Non-Executive Director, confirmation from the Chairman that, following formal performance evaluation, the individual's performance continues to be effective and to demonstrate commitment to the role (B.7.2).

Note from UK Corporate Governance Code Provision D.2.1 that a description of the work of the Remuneration Committee should be made available. In order to comply with DTR 7.2.7 R this information will need to be included in the corporate governance statement.

---

[3] Some shareholders will signal their disapproval of the remuneration policy by voting against the reappointment of the Chair of the Remuneration Committee, and in severe cases each of the members.

9.4 Additional guidance

The Turnbull Guidance and FRC Guidance on Audit Committees contain further suggestions as to information that might usefully be disclosed in the internal control statement and the report of the Audit Committee respectively. Both sets of guidance are available on the FRC website at: http://www.frc.org.uk/corporate/ukcgcode.cfm.

The Turnbull Report (2003) focus was on risk and internal control. Turnbull set some questions for the Board to consider including the following which is pertinent to directors' and senior executives' remuneration:

> 'Do the company's culture, code of conduct, human resource policies, and performance reward systems support the business objectives and risk management and internal control systems?'

10 FCA Remuneration Code for Banks and Financial Institutions

10.1 FCA Remuneration Code summary

In 2013, the FSA split into the FCA and the PRA, respectively the Financial Conduct Authority and the Prudential Regulatory Authority.

The Financial Services Authority's Remuneration Code was first published in August 2009 following the G20 summits in London and Pittsburgh, and the publication of the Financial Stability Board's remuneration principles. The rules came into effect on 1 January 2010, but covered performance in 2009.

Banks and other financial services organisations have to follow the FCA Remuneration code, with the largest ones (Tier 1) having the most detailed rules, principles and guidance, whilst for others the rules they have to follow are proportionate.

The FCA Code is a set of principles and guidance and not a set of rigid rules. Companies who have to follow the Code have to submit returns to the FCA, who decide if they are satisfied with the approach adopted. The returns to the FCA are very detailed for large firms (but proportionately less so for Tier 2, 3 and 4 firms). For example the Tier 2 guidance from the FCA for the return is 14 pages of questions and can be downloaded from: http://www.fca.org.uk/firms/markets/international-markets/remuneration-code#. Other parts of the FCA Remuneration Code can be accessed from the FCA site at: http://www.fca.org.uk/firms/markets/international-markets/remuneration-code#

The Remuneration Code came into force on 1 January 2011, covering pay awards made in 2010 and paid in 2011. The Code has been amended to reflect the provisions (approved in July 2010) of the European Union's Capital Requirements Directive (CRD).

These changes bring more than 2,500 firms within the scope of the Code. These include all banks and building societies, asset managers, hedge fund managers, Undertakings for Collective Investment in Transferable Securities

(UCITS) investment firms, and some stockbrokers and firms that engage in corporate finance, venture capital and the provision of financial advice.

The background to the FCA Code was described in Financial Services Authority report 10/20 Revising the Remuneration Code.[1]

Scope of the Code: the FCA has categorised firms into the following tiers:

> '**Tiers one and two** – credit institutions and broker dealers that engage in significant proprietary trading/investment banking activities.
>
> **Tier three** – primarily small banks and building societies and firms that may occasionally take overnight or short-term risk with their balance sheets.
>
> **Tier four** – firms which generate income from agency business without putting their balance sheets at risk.'
>
> 'A proportionate approach will also be applied across the range of firms in each tier, and the aim is to avoid sharp differences between applying the Code to firms at the lower end of one tier and the higher end of the next.'

Firms categorised as tier one and two have to adhere to strict requirements including the need to have a Remuneration Committee, rules on deferral and rules on the proportion of remuneration which must be paid in shares or share equivalents. Small and low risk firms are subject to different requirements.

Application: the FCA has set out examples of key positions in firms that it believes should be subject to the Code: senior management, control functions (audit, risk and compliance) and employees who have an impact on the risk profile of the firm.

Deferral: for tier 1 and 2 firms, at least 40% of variable pay must be deferred over a period of at least three years, and up to five years, for all staff to whom the Code applies. At least 60% must be deferred should variable pay be more than £500,000.

Proportion in shares: at least 50% of any variable remuneration components (both deferred and non-deferred) must be made in shares (or share-linked instruments or other equivalent non-cash instruments of the firm) subject to deferrals and a minimum retention policy.

Retention periods: the Code imposes a requirement that instruments must be subject to an 'appropriate' retention policy to align incentives with the longer-term interests of the firm. The FCA will expect a minimum of six

---

[1] http://www.fca.gov.uk/pubs/policy/ps10_20.pdf

months' retention by the employee after vesting (ie title to the shares or share equivalents has passed from employer to employee).

Performance criteria: the assessment of performance will not simply be in financial terms but will also consider other aspects of an individual's contribution to the firm.

Long-term performance (bonus/malus and claw-back): firms can withhold payment if performance criteria, both financial and non-financial, are not met or there is a misstatement.

Guarantees: firms must not offer guaranteed bonuses of more than one year, and these may only be given in exceptional circumstances to new hires for the first year of service. This can apply to all members of staff.

Strengthening of capital base: firms must ensure that their total variable remuneration does not limit their ability to strengthen their capital base. The FCA signs off distributions (ie dividends to investors and variable pay to employees) to ensure that the firm's capital ratios are sound.

Voiding provisions: a new rule defines instances where breaches of the Code may render a contract void and/or require recovery of payments made.

Severance payments: these should reflect performance over time, and failure must not be rewarded.

Pensions: enhanced discretionary pension benefits should be held for five years in the form of shares or share-like instruments.

10.2 The Code in practice: examples of how it will work

Take, for example, variable pay for the year 2011, to be paid in the spring of 2012:

(i) when the end-of-year accounts books have closed and been processed, the finance department of the bank advises the Board and control functions of any distribution of variable pay to employees.

(ii) The firm's control functions check on adherence to the FCA rules and in-house procedures and the Board's Remuneration Committee reviews the compliance checks and calculations. The review includes non-financial metrics.

(iii) The firm advises the FCA of any distributions approved by the Board, including both dividends to shareholders and bonuses to staff. The FCA checks if the pay-outs are sustainable and do not pose a risk to prudential soundness.

(iv) If the individual pay-out is equal to or less than £500,000, then 100 units of variable pay will typically be delivered as:

30 immediate cash

30 immediate shares, but with a(n employee) retention period of at least six months

20 deferred cash (held by the employer for three years)

20 deferred shares (held by the employer for three years and then held by the employee for at least six months)

(v) if the individual's pay-out is more than £500,000 and/or the employee is categorised as 'Code staff', then 100 units of variable pay will typically be delivered as:

20 immediate cash

20 immediate shares, but with a(n employee) retention period of at least six months

30 deferred cash (held by the employer for five years)

30 deferred shares (held by the employer for five years and then held by the employee for at least six months)

During the vesting period (when the cash and shares are held by the employer), it is possible for the employee to lose his or her entitlement in the case of poor financial performance, misconduct or misstatement.

10.3 EU issues

The FCA policy takes account of EU guidelines on CRD3 prepared by a Committee of European Banking Supervisors (CEBS) working group and the requirements of the European Banking Authority (EBA).

They require that institutions' remuneration policies for staff members whose professional activities have material impact on the institutions' risk profile shall ensure that remuneration is consistent with sound and effective risk management and provides an incentive for prudent and sustainable risk taking. The requirements set out in the Capital Requirements Directive (CRD) are complemented by more detailed Guidelines on Remuneration Policies. Guidelines on Remuneration Policies and Practices were initially published by the Committee of European Banking Supervisors (CEBS). The EBA will review and update those Guidelines in light of the requirements laid down in the revised CRD. The EBA will submit draft regulatory standards to the European Commission as mandated by the CRD, with respect to the criteria for identifying risk takers and additional tier-1, tier-2 and other instruments which can be used for paying variable remuneration.

On 29 November 2013, the EBA published a report on the remuneration of EU bank staff who received one million Euro or more in total in 2012. Figures show that the number of high earners was limited in most Member States and quite significant in some others. The report is part of the EBA's work on bank staff remuneration policies aimed at ensuring prudent and sustainable risk taking in the EU banking sector.

In 2012, the highest values were reported for the United Kingdom (2,714 high earners), Germany (212), France (177), Italy (109) and Spain (100). The figures include staff paid by institutions, including subsidiaries or branches of any EU-parent institution based in another Member State other than the one where the parent company is located, as well as staff in branches of third country institutions.

The report also provides a preliminary analysis of remuneration structures across the EU. Most high earners were found to belong to categories that include functions with responsibilities throughout the whole institution, from the executive board, to risk management, internal audit, information technology, communication, auditing, corporate finance, legal and human resources.

The data in the report will feed into the overall work of the EBA on remuneration in the EU banking sector. As required by the EU Capital Requirements Directive (CRD), this aims at ensuring that institutions' remuneration policies not only allow for sound and effective management, but also provide an incentive for prudent long-term risk taking in the EU banking sector.

10.4 AIFMD

The Alternative Investment Fund Managers Directive (AIFMD) came into effect on 22 July 2013. EU Member States were required to comply with AIFMD by 22 July 2013, subject to transitional provisions for managers who were managing AIFs before that date. 'Managing' under AIFMD means carrying on the activities of portfolio management and risk management for one or more AIFs. Existing AIF managers must be appropriately authorised from 22 July 2014. The FCA has up to six months to determine applications. This means new Applications or Variations of Permission (VoPs) need to be submitted by 22 January 2014 to guarantee they will be dealt with before the deadline. However, on 19 December 2013, HM Treasury announced some relaxation in this timetable.

The AIFMD has a lot to say about remuneration. It focuses on two main areas – disclosure requirements and structures. In terms of structure, AIFMs must ensure that a substantial portion of variable remuneration consists of units or shares in the AIFs concerned (or other instruments depending on the legal form of the AIF). There is also a significant deferral requirement –

variable remuneration must not be paid by an AIFM unless a substantial portion (at least 40%) is deferred over a period that is appropriate to the lifecycle of the fund. This is increased to 60% if variable remuneration is particularly high. AIFMs should also ensure that any variable remuneration vests only if it is sustainable in accordance with the financial position of the AIFM as a whole and is justified in accordance with the performance of the AIF, the individual and the relevant business unit. These rules together are referred to as the pay-out process rules. AIFMs may apply proportionality to these rules and in doing so may dis-apply them. Many Private Equity and Venture Capital firms are taking advantage of the proportionality rules and are arguing that the structure of their carried interest arrangements satisfies all the alignment of interest requirements with investors and avoids incentives for inappropriate risk taking.

Interestingly, in a pulse survey of PE and VC houses that MM&K conducted in 2013, 77% of respondents said that they did not expect that they would have to introduce deferral of any variable pay over and above that which they were already doing (ie through their carry plans).

The disclosure requirements are not avoidable through the proportionality rules and require that the annual report contains:

(1) the total amount of remuneration for the financial year, split into fixed and variable remuneration, paid by the AIFM to its staff, and number of beneficiaries and, where relevant, carried interest paid by the AIF;

(2) the aggregate amount of remuneration broken down by senior management and members of staff of the AIFM whose actions have a material impact on the risk profile of the AIF.

10.5 List of FCA Remuneration Code Principles

Code Principle	**Handbook references (SYSC)**
1: Risk management and risk tolerance	19A.3.7R
2: Supporting business strategy, objectives, values and long term interests of the firm	19A.3.8R
3: Avoiding conflicts of interest	19A.3.9R
4: Governance	19A.3.10R – 19A.3.13G
5: Control functions	19A.3.14R – 19A.3.17G
6: Remuneration and capital	19A.3.18R – 19A.3.19G
7: Exceptional government intervention	19A.3.20R – 19A.3.21G
8: Profit-based measurement and risk adjustment	19A.3.22R – 19A.3.28G
9: Pension policy	19A.3.29R
10: Personal investment strategies	19A.3.30R – 19A.3.31G

Code Principle	**Handbook references (SYSC)**
11: Avoidance of the Remuneration Code	19A.3.32R
12: Remuneration structures	19A.3.33G – 19A.3.53G
13: Effect of breach of the Remuneration Principles (voiding and recovery)	19A.3.54R – 19A.3.55G, SYSC 19A Annex 1

11 Other Regulators

Do OfCom, OfGen, OfWat, Civil Aviation authority (CAA), Office of Rail Regulation (ORR), etc have a remit about directors' remuneration? If they feel that pay is excessive or encourages the wrong types of behaviour and risk, if not enough attention is paid to safety, then they may decide to act.

They may not be able to act directly, but they can signal their discontent. They ultimately have huge power through pricing reviews, making requirements to improve levels of service and the nuclear option of withdrawal of the licence to operate. The impact of remuneration decisions therefore needs careful consideration in a broad business strategic sense.

We live in a regulated environment. Companies are only allowed to do business because they follow the regulations that apply to their industry. In some industries the regulators and regulations that relate to remuneration are clear, eg the FCA with its Remuneration Code; in others the relationships are not at all clear. (For example, in 2012 GSK were fined $3 billion by the FDA. This led to questions about whether claw-back should be applied to directors' remuneration.)

12 Accounting for Share Schemes

12.1 Relevant legislation

IFRS 2 Share-based Payment was issued by the International Accounting Standards Board (IASB) in February 2004 and applies to annual periods beginning on or after 1 January 2005. IFRS 2 sets out the financial reporting of share-based payment transactions. It applies to grants of shares, share options or other equity instruments made after 7 November 2002 that had not yet vested at the effective date of the IFRS. IFRS 2 applies retrospectively to liabilities arising from share-based payment transactions existing at the effective date.

Companies have to follow IFRS 2 or adopt FRS 20 (identical to IFRS 2, but applies to smaller companies) which is effective for periods beginning on or after 1 January 2006. Very small companies are exempt from FRS 20 and IFRS 2.

The Standards state that:

> 'The fair value of an employee share option or similar instrument shall be estimated using an option-pricing model that takes into account as of the grant date the following factors, as a minimum:
>
> (a) the exercise price of the option;
>
> (b) the expected term of the option;
>
> (c) the current price of the underlying share;
>
> (d) the expected volatility of the price of the underlying share;
>
> (e) the expected dividends on the underlying share; and
>
> (f) the risk-free interest rate(s) for the expected term of the option.
>
> The fair value of a share option or similar instrument estimated at the grant date shall not be subsequently remeasured for changes in the price of the underlying share or other pertinent factors incorporated in the estimated fair value of the option at the grant date.'

Market-based conditions (eg total shareholder return (TSR)), shall be taken into account in estimating the fair value of an option.

Non-market-based conditions (eg earnings per share (EPS)) shall not be taken account in estimating the fair value of an option. Instead an estimate of the number of options that will vest is used and this is true-ed up at the end of each year when a better estimate of the likely outcome of the non-market-based condition can be made.

Estimates of leavers also have to be made and these are also true-ed up at the end of each year.

Apart from the delayed implementation for unlisted entities and the exemption for entities applying the Financial Reporting Standard for Smaller Entities (FRSSE), FRS 20 is identical to the IASB's IFRS 2 'Share-based Payment' and therefore has the effect of implementing that IFRS in the UK.

FRS 20, issued April 2004, (like IFRS 2) specifies the accounting treatment to be adopted (including the disclosures to be provided) by entities making share-based payments. In particular, it requires entities to recognise an expense, measured at fair value, in respect of the share-based payments they make. The FRS is mandatory for accounting periods beginning on or after 1 January 2005 for listed entities and 1 January 2006 for unlisted entities (other than those applying the FRSSE). The term 'share-based payments' includes all types of executive share option and share purchase plans and employee share option and share purchase schemes, including Save-As-You-Earn (SAYE) plans and similar arrangements. It also includes arrangements such as share appreciation rights, where a cash payment is made, the amount of which depends on the share price.

However, like the IFRS 2, the FRS 20 does not apply just to transactions with employees; it also applies to transactions with suppliers of goods or non-employee services that involve share-based payments being made in exchange for those goods or services. A 'listed entity' is an entity that has shares or other capital instruments it has issued traded on the London Stock Exchange or any other regulated market of an EU member state.

IFRS 2 (and FRS 20) identifies three types of share-based payment transaction:

- equity-settled share-based payment transactions. These are transactions in which the entity receives goods or services as consideration for equity instruments of the entity.
- cash-settled share-based payment transactions. These are transactions in which the entity acquires goods or services by incurring liabilities to the supplier of those goods or services for amounts that are based on the price (or value) of the entity's equity instruments.
- transactions in which the entity receives or acquires goods or services and the terms of the arrangement provide one or other of the parties to

the transaction with a choice as to whether the transaction is settled in cash or by issuing equity instruments.

The IFRS then sets out the measurement principles and specific requirements that apply to each type of transaction. For equity-settled transactions, entities are required to measure the goods or services received at their fair value, unless that fair value cannot be estimated reliably in which case that fair value should be estimated by reference to the fair value of the equity instruments granted. If a non-employee (or similar) transaction is involved, there should be a rebuttable presumption that the fair value of the goods or services received can be estimated reliably. The relevant measurement date is the date the entity obtains the goods or the counterparty renders service. However, it is typically not possible to estimate reliably the fair value of employee services received so, for transactions with employees and others providing similar services, the entity should use the grant date fair value of the equity instruments granted. That fair value should be based on market prices and should take into account the terms and conditions upon which the instruments were granted.

In the absence of market prices, a valuation technique (such as an option pricing model) will need to be used.

Vesting conditions other than market conditions should not be taken into account when estimating the fair value of the instruments granted. Instead, those conditions should be taken into account by adjusting the number of equity instruments included in the measurement of the transaction amount so that the aggregate amount recognised is based on the number of equity instruments that vest.

The FRS requires, in the case of cash-settled share-based payment transactions, the entity to measure the goods or services acquired and the liability incurred at the fair value of the liability. Until the liability is settled, the entity will remeasure the fair value of the liability at each reporting date and at the date of settlement, and should recognise any changes in value in profit or loss for the period. For share-based payment transactions in which one of the parties to the transaction has a choice of settlement method, the transaction, or the components of that transaction, should be accounted for as a cash-settled share-based payment transaction if, and to the extent that, the entity has incurred a liability to settle in cash (or other assets), or as an equity-settled share based payment transaction if, and to the extent that, no such liability has been incurred.

The IFRS also contains various disclosure requirements designed to enable users of financial statements to understand the nature and extent of share-based payment arrangements, their effect on the period's financial statements, and the methodologies used in arriving at the numbers included in the financial statements.

FRS 20 superseded the existing UK accounting requirements in this area, which were set out mainly in UITF Abstract 17 'Employee share schemes'.

12.2 The debate

There was a great deal of interest and comment about accounting for share options. Of course, the information on awards of options, exercise price, exercise periods and vesting conditions have been available for many years. And yet how and when this appears on the face of the accounts is felt by many commentators to affect the value of the company and the future of remuneration! As the old saying goes 'you cannot fatten the pig by weighing it'; or can you?

How options are accounted for does not affect the cash flow and will not affect the net present value of future cash flows, so will not affect the value of the business. A typical fair value of an option granted at the market price is around 25% to 30% of the value of the underlying share. Values can range from under 10% to over 50%. The main factor that affects this is the volatility of the share price. A high dividend yield reduces the value of the option as will tough performance conditions.

A benchmark UK plc with a p/e ratio of 15, granting options over 0.5% pa of its shares in issue, with a fair value of 25% would have an expense cost equal to 1.3% of profits. Costs are higher in US companies who grant many more options. Standard & Poor's reckoned that if companies expensed all employee options, 2004 earnings across the S&P 500 would be about 6% lower.

Reaction to IFRS 2 has been mixed and there are a number of arguments both for and against the introduction of this standard. Concerns have been raised that the new standard will discourage the use of share-based incentive schemes (particularly all-employee schemes) – because the standard decreases company earnings, it could increase the cost of raising capital. However, it is argued in the alternative that share-based payments are a form of remuneration, a transfer of value from shareholders to employees, and should therefore be treated as an expense. The US corporate sector has never liked the idea of accounting for share options. In 1994 the US standard-setters, the FASB, put forward proposals for showing options as an expense. In response, corporate America put together some $70m as a fighting fund to get the idea overturned.

You can argue all manner of different issues as to the calculation of the value of options. The great investment guru Warren Buffett came up with the definitive comment on stock options over ten years ago. He asked 'If options aren't a form of compensation, what are they?' 'If compensation isn't an expense, what is it?' was his second question. 'And if expenses shouldn't go into the calculation of earnings, where in the world should they go?' was his third. QED, as the Romans used to say.

One of the other problems is that share options were seen as a 'good thing'. It is argued that they make employees feel good throughout the company and increase loyalty and morale. But the reality is that this never happened. There are companies, particularly in the UK, where company-wide share option schemes have worked well, for example, Asda and Tesco. However, significant share options have generally been only given to the few at the top of companies. Figures for the US show that 75% of all options go to people classified as being among the top five executives at their company. The next 50 executives in the pecking order scooped 15%. And the rest of the employees accounted for the final 10%.

Many stock analysts exclude the accounting cost of stock options and other equity incentives and prefer instead to consider their potential dilutive impact on earnings per share, dividends per share and share price. This is an area where companies need to communicate carefully with their shareholders.

12.3 Typical volatilities

Estimating the volatility is a critical part of share option and share scheme valuation. The following table illustrates typical volatilities are around 30%, although there is a high variation.

The sample of 11 companies covers a range of sectors.

Table 1: Typical volatilities

	volatilities based on		**share price change in previous 12 months up to Feb 2012**
	historic data 2003–2012	**previous 12 months up to Feb 2012**	
SSE (Scottish and Southern Electricity)	23%	24%	6%
GSK	26%	20%	22%
Vodafone	28%	22%	-3%
Bunzl	28%	24%	11%
BAe	29%	30%	-7%
M&S	32%	28%	-7%
Compass	32%	24%	1%
BP	38%	30%	1%
Aviva	39%	43%	-20%

Xstrata	51%	55%	-25%
RBS	52%	58%	-36%
Average	**34%**	**33%**	**-5%**
Median	32%	28%	-3%
Q1	28%	24%	-14%
Q3	39%	37%	4%
standard deviation	10%	13%	17%
standard error	3%	4%	5%
kurtosis	-5%	10%	-3%
average excluding highest and lowest	**34%**	**31%**	**-3%**

12.4 Practical guidance on option valuation

A version of this article by Cliff Weight appeared in the August 2011 edition of Executive Compensation Briefing.

> 'If I give you a share option, then it is odds on that it will not pay out, but it's a 20 to 1 outsider that it might pay out a lot, 5 to 1 that the share price will double and 3 to 1 that it will pay out 0.2 times the original exercise price.
>
> The diagram says it all. It's easy to understand and it's roughly right!

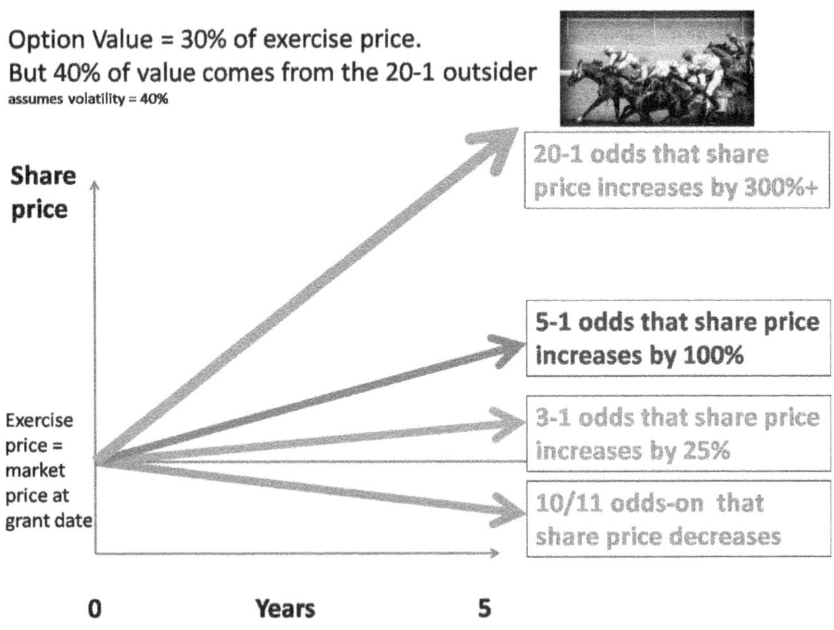

In total, about 40% of the expected value comes from low probability high outcomes or, in our racing analogy, the 20–1 outsider.

The median expected share price growth rate is about 3% to 4% pa.[1] Less than 20% of the expected return from a share option comes from such outcomes. And this is why traditional analysis of outcomes using a single expected value fails miserably to model what is important to shareholders and executives.

Of particular importance, is the fact that much of the value in options comes from the unlikely (low probability) high price gains. To gain the full motivational benefit from incentive pay, the Board needs to understand the strategies that might lead to these gains and the risks attached to them. Such strategies might be:

- New product developments and launches
- Expansion into new geographies
- Financial strategies such as increased leverage
- Acquisitions and/or mergers.

So, I strongly urge Boards and Remuneration Committees to undertake scenario analyses which can reflect the share price outcomes shown in the diagram. Modelling just 4 outcomes usually provides much better insight than single price estimates favoured by accountants and does so without the infinite complexity of Monte Carlo simulations.

I have been worrying about how to value share options for many years, from way back before IFRS 2 forced others to learn about the Black-Scholes theorem, Monte Carlo simulations and Binomial Models.

The problem with the Black-Scholes valuation of options is that is wrong, albeit that it is highly complex and clever piece of mathematics and in many cases produces a result that is roughly right. Many people cast aspersions on Black-Scholes, for example saying its inbuilt assumptions do not reflect reality. It assumes volatility and dividends are constant over time. Executives do not discount future (risky) rewards at the risk free rate; they cannot diversify their risk so as to create a market neutral portfolio; they tend to exercise sub-optimally before the theoretically best time to do so; and most do not understand the maths behind the capital asset pricing model, random walk of share prices and lognormal share price distributions. Concepts such as share price volatility and beta are not part of the accountants' lingua franca. Black-Scholes theory cannot take account of performance conditions.

---

1 Assuming dividends of 3.8%, this gives an expected total shareholder return of 7% to 8% per annum.

The correlation (or lack of it) between performance measures and share price movements can significantly impact on share option values.

Monte Carlo is a lovely place and has a great casino and has given its name to simulations that can value options. Whilst theoretically more correct than Black-Scholes for this purpose, the complexity of a Monte Carlo model (often involving millions of simulations) creates either a black box or diverts attention into the methodologies and assumptions underpinning it. Similar problems exist with Binomial and Lattice models. They can however allow performance measures to be input into the models and can also cater for early option exercise behavioural traits of executives. But their power is also their flaw and all too often just like the other models they become either a black box or divert attention into the methodologies and underpinning assumptions.

Explaining options to executives, so as to get the maximum motivational impact, is an art not a science. Try this simple model and it's odds-on you will do better.'

13 Best Practice Guidance

13.1 Introduction

Chapters 13–25 detail the best practice guidance from investors, their intermediaries and from one Remuneration Committee Chairman, including:

Entity	**Who they are:**
QCA	Representative body of smaller and medium sized quoted companies. Members also include investors and advisers
ISS	Proxy Voting Agency. ISS[1] is owned by PE firm Vestar Capital Partners
NAPF	Representative body of pension funds
PIRC	Proxy Voting Agency. Independent
ABI[2]	Representative body of insurance companies
IVIS	Proxy Voting Agency of the ABI (see footnote 2)
Manifest	Proxy Voting Agency. Independent
Hermes EOS, the National Association of Pension Funds (NAPF), BT Pension Scheme, RPMI Railpen Investments and Universities Superannuation Scheme (USS)	Hermes is a Fund Manager, the NAPF is a representative body of pension pensions and the others are pension funds
F&C	Fund Manager
Fidelity	Fund Manager
IoD	Representative body of Directors
A Remuneration Committee Chairman's personal viewpoint	Tony Minns

1 On 30 April 2014 MSCI Inc (NYSE: MSCI), a leading provider of investment decision support tools worldwide, announced that it has completed the sale of Institutional Shareholder Services Inc ('ISS'), its wholly-owned subsidiary comprising MSCI's Governance segment, to Vestar Capital Partners for total cash consideration of $367 million.

2 In April 2014, the boards of the IMA and ABI agreed in principle to merge the investment activities of the ABI, including the Institutional Voting Information Service (IVIS), with the IMA. The ABI will continue to represent insurers as asset owners.

The QCA (Quoted Companies Alliance) is first in this list because it was written by a combination of company directors, fund managers, remuneration consultants, lawyers and accountants and so represents a consensus view, whereas other guidance is representative of (ie may be biased in favour of) that particular trade association or company.

ISS accounts for about 30% of the votes in most large companies because so many US fund managers follow their advice, so they are second in my list as companies must take account of their advice and the NAPF guidelines upon which ISS base their UK advice.

PIRC is next because their guidelines are so well articulated. They are well argued and there are lots of examples to illustrate why they have a particular point of view. It should be noted that many of their views are not mainstream.

The ABI is next. Traditionally in the UK the ABI guidelines have been regarded as best practice by many companies and advisers and, in their heyday in the 1990's, their members owned over 20% of the UK stock market.

The other proxy adviser in the UK is Manifest, who produces high quality, timely, in depth research and is well respected by their fund management clients. In 2012 they adopted a new methodology to analyse and assess directors' remuneration. My company MM&K collaborate with Manifest to produce the Executive Director Total Remuneration Survey, which is the source of much data in this book.

Institutional Investors share ownership of UK equities has changed significantly in the past 30 years and this has impacted on the relationship of companies with shareholder representatives.

Table 2: Share ownership of UK listed companies as a percentage of total ownership, 1981–2012[3]

	1981	**1989**	**1994**	**2000**	**2004**	**2008**[4]	**2010**[5]	**2011**
Rest of the World	3.6	12.8	16.3	35.7	36.3	41.5	43.4	53.2
Insurance Companies	20.5	18.6	21.9	21.0	17.2	13.4	8.8	6.2
Pension Funds	26.7	30.6	27.8	17.7	15.7	12.8	5.6	4.7

3 Office for National Statistics (2010) Share Ownership Survey, www.ons.gov.uk/ons/ guide-method/ method-quality/specific/econ¬omy/share-ownership/ index.html
The Share Ownership Survey has been conducted at irregular intervals since 1963, which leads to gaps in the time series shown here in tables and figures:

4 The end-2008 survey did not identify any significant shareholdings of quoted shares owned by building societies

5 The change in 2010 partly reflects a change in ONS methodology and is disputed by the ABI and NAPF

	1981	1989	1994	2000	2004	2008[4]	2010[5]	2011
Individuals	28.2	20.6	20.3	16.0	14.1	10.2	10.2	10.7
Unit Trusts	3.6	5.9	6.8	1.1	1.4	1.8	8.8	9.6
Investment Trusts		1.6	2.0	1.3	2.5	1.9	2.1	1.8
Other financial institutions	6.8 [6]	1.1	1.3	2.8	8.2	10.0	12.3	6.6
Charities, etc	2.2	2.3	1.3	1.4	1.1	0.8	0.8	0.6
Private non-financial corporations	5.1	3.8	1.1	1.5	0.6	3.0	2.3	2.3
Public Sector [7]	3	2	0.8		0.1	1.1	3.1	2.5
Banks	0.3	0.7	0.4	1.4	2.7	3.5	2.5	1.9
Total [8]	100	100	100	100	100	100	100	100

The ABI and NAPF, representing the insurance companies and pension funds, accounted for 50% of equities at their peak of influence, but since 1994 this dropped steadily to 26% by 2008 and then has reduced significantly to only 11% by 2012 as solvency rules forced insurance companies to reduce equity holdings, and pension funds reduced their exposure to UK equities.

Figure 9: Percentage holdings of UK equities

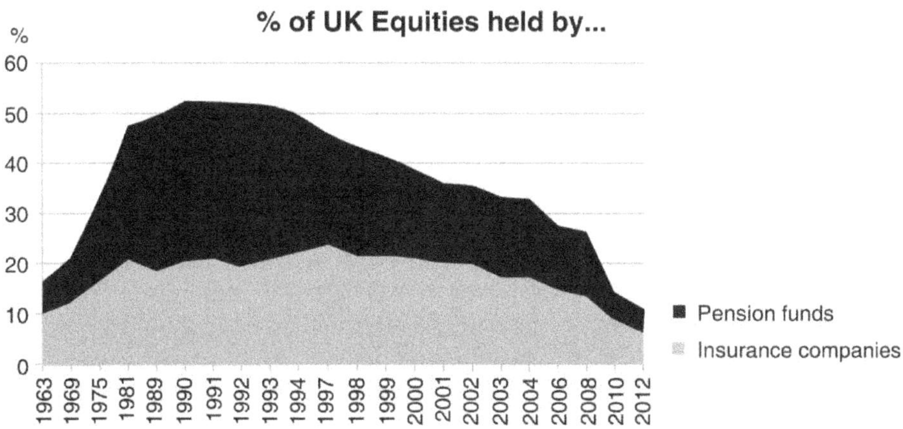

[6] Includes investment trusts

[7] Public sector comprises local government, central government and public corporations

[8] Components may not sum to the total due to rounding.

13.2 The role of the intermediaries

Who are the intermediaries and what do they do?

There are nearly 2,000 listed and AIM companies in the UK and over 200 fund managers. Each company cannot talk to each fund manager about every aspect of corporate governance. They use intermediaries to assist and to make the process manageable. Also, the cost of analysing the remuneration and other corporate governance items is such that it is more efficient for institutional shareholders to subcontract out much of this analysis to the intermediaries.

For a long time, the ABI has provided services to the fund management arms of insurance companies. They provide general guidance on corporate governance and have a separate (for profit) voting issues service, for which clients pay an annual subscription.

The NAPF provides general guidance on corporate governance, mainly to pension funds. PIRC, set up in 1992, provides a range of corporate governance services and its main clients are local authority pension funds. Manifest, set up in 1995, provides a range of corporate governance services to fund managers and other clients. ISS and Glass, Lewis provide similar services but are US-based and have small operations in the UK and Europe. ISS were linked up with NAPF in a commercial arrangement prior to June 2014. ISS is continuing to use the NAPF guidelines to assess the remuneration of UK listed companies.

When a company sends out the remuneration committee report or a proposal for a new remuneration plan to shareholders, the intermediaries will analyse the proposals and report on them to their clients the shareholders. They will flag up areas of concern and may in some cases recommend abstention from or even voting against an AGM/EGM resolution. The press regularly use their reports or quote these intermediaries. It should be noted that most fund managers are extremely reluctant to be quoted as saying anything negative about a company as this may be detrimental to the share price and their personal relationships with directors and senior management. Access to these people is crucial for them to do their job of analysing the company. Thus the intermediaries perform an important role.

When a company wishes to test the reaction of its shareholders to a remuneration proposal, the ABI will organise a subcommittee of (usually three) major shareholders in the company to consider and report back on the proposals on behalf of the ABI. More recently, many companies have started to go directly to their major shareholders rather than via the ABI.

13.3 EU ESMA consultation on conflicts of interest of proxy advisers

The European Commission issued[9] a green paper on corporate governance in April 2011. It not only focused on the need for disclosure of methodology and conflicts of interest but also sought to ban advisers from providing consulting services to companies. While few believe it will lead to regulation soon, no one has ruled this out in the long term.

Central to the conflict of interest debate are those proxy voting agencies that also act as advisers to companies.

Institutional Shareholder Services (ISS), a subsidiary of MSCI and the largest global proxy voting agency with 1,700 clients, has come in for particular scrutiny.

Jean-Nicolas Caprasse, head of business at ISS, said it had a 'robust policy in place to govern any conflicts', which included the imposition of a firewall separating the two sides of the business.

On 28 October 2013, the Drafting Committee of the Best Practice Principles for Governance Research Providers launched a public consultation on the draft Principles which concern activities associated with the provision of shareholder voting and analytical services.

The Committee – which is independent from the European Securities and Markets Authority (ESMA) – has drafted the Principles following ESMA's 19 February 2013 Final Report which states that the proxy advisory industry would benefit from increased disclosure and transparency regarding how it operates.

The draft Principles can be found on the website of the Committee.[10]

---

9 www.esma.europa.eu/system/files/2012–212.pdf

10 http://bppgrp.info/wp-content/uploads/2013/11/BPP-Group-Principles-Consultation.pdf

14 QCA

14.1 Introduction

The Quoted Companies Alliance (QCA) is an independent not-for-profit trade organisation that works for small and mid-cap quoted companies in the UK, including those listed on AIM and PLUS markets, and Europe to promote and maintain vibrant, healthy and liquid capital markets.

The QCA was founded in 1992 (originally known as CISCO), and is funded by its membership. Its membership consists of small and mid-cap quoted companies, their advisors, investors, companies seeking admission to a UK equity market and other market participants.

The small and mid-cap quoted sector is vital to the UK economy – there are nearly 2,000 such companies, representing 85% of all quoted companies.

For more information, contact The Quoted Companies Alliance, 6 Kinghorn Street, London EC1A 7HW.

Tel: 020 7600 3745

Email: mail@theqca.com

Website: www.theqca.com

Twitter: @quotedcompanies

14.2 The QCA Remuneration Committee Guide

The QCA published the Remuneration Committee Guide for Smaller Quoted Companies in February 2012. Companies are recommended to consider using the QCA guide to avoid the over-burdensome rules and regulations of other bodies.

The QCA guide is particularly more suitable for smaller companies. It avoids the rather lengthy principles and guidelines of the ABI and others, which are focussed more towards the very largest companies.

Cliff Weight was a member of the QCA working group who produced the guide. The working group consisted of a cross-section of interested parties including company directors, fund manager executives, remuneration consultants, accountants and lawyers.

The QCA have declined permission for large extracts from their Remuneration Committee Guide to be reproduced in this book. However, copies of the guide can be purchased from the QCA for the modest price of £20.

14.3 Summary of the QCA Guide

The **key points** to note are the emphasis on:

- Aligning rewards with long term success
- Share ownership and share retention
- Communications with shareholders
- Motivation and alignment of interests of executives[1] (see objectives below).

The **overarching objectives** of the remuneration committee should be to ensure that key management, and in particular executive directors:

- Are motivated to accomplish specific strategic milestones, taking due account of risk
- Have their interests aligned with shareholders' interests over the long-term
- Are retained and when necessary, can be appropriately recruited
- Are not paid excessively when individuals leave or join.

14.4 Best Practice

Much of the QCA guide replicates the best practice of the UK Corporate Governance Code and the ABI/NAPF guidelines. Points where the QCA guide differs **and in my opinion is better** are as follows.

No remuneration scheme will be suitable for all companies, at all stages of development. Every company is unique and is evolving constantly. Therefore, what constitutes good remuneration practice is linked to a company's size and stage of development.

The pay of the chief executive is the most high profile and critical decision the remuneration committee makes. The chief executive's pay is often the most challenging to set. This can be for a variety of reasons,

---

[1] This is a significant difference to the UK Corporate Governance Code, whose Main Principle says 'Levels of remuneration should be sufficient to attract, retain and motivate directors ...'. The QCA guide has as its first objective motivation, whereas the Code has attraction as its first objective and its second objective as retention. The achievement of Code's first two goals is likely to create the wrong mind-set and most likely will be inflationary. The QCA guide addressees the cost issue with practical guidance: it notes that full consideration should be given to what is an appropriate proportion of cash, revenue and profit to expend on key executives' pay and what degree of dilution is acceptable.

including the influence of the chief executive's pay on other pay schemes in the company, the advantageous bargaining position that the chief executive may have (particularly if succession plans are not sufficiently developed), or his influence as a significant shareholder.

Succession planning is a vital task for boards. The board should have plans in place for the permanent or prolonged absence from work of the executive directors and other important senior managers. Such plans will also provide comfort to the remuneration committee that no member of the board or staff is indispensable.

In terms of Performance Linked Pay, the QCA guide notes that full consideration should be given to what is an appropriate proportion of cash, revenue and profit to expend on key executives' pay and what degree of dilution is acceptable.[2] The QCA guide notes that it may be more appropriate for smaller quoted companies to set a different level to the normal 10% and engage with their investors on this.

In terms of Annual Bonus, the QCA guide notes that the remuneration committee should consider the deferral of annual bonuses and establish what proportions should vest at which times.

In terms of Long-Term Incentives (LTIs), the QCA guide notes that awards should be phased so that a regular award policy is operated (ie annual awards granted after a company's final results announcement each year) as opposed to ad-hoc awards. **However, importantly, the QCA guide notes that this is not always the best approach:**

> 'Exceptionally, one-off equity awards may be appropriate occasionally, but will require robust justification and stretching performance targets.'

Share Ownership. The QCA guide is particularly strong on this point. It says:

> 'The principles and culture of long-term share ownership should be encouraged for executive directors, senior management and elsewhere, through establishing share ownership guidelines and other means. This leads to directors and senior managers building their shareholding during their time at the company.
>
> There should be a formal policy on how share sales may be conducted, including:
>
> – compliance with the company's share dealing code;

[2] The Association of British Insurers' Principles of Executive Remuneration note that potential dilution arising from all share plan awards should be limited to a maximum 10% of the company's issued share capital in any ten year period (exercised awards plus outstanding awards).

- at a minimum, an agreement that no share sales should be permitted until executive directors have built a meaningful shareholding in the company; and
- ideally, an agreement that shares should not normally be sold while directors maintain tenure at the company, except to fund tax obligations relating to awards.

A long-term focus is achieved through deferral of part of the annual bonus into shares and operating performance periods beyond three years.

Consideration should be given to the introduction of clawback provisions in the exceptional events of misstatement and/or misconduct or if a director's employment terminates within three years of an award.

Remuneration policy can encourage retention of executives through:

- retention periods being set for vested share awards beyond their normal vesting dates;
- long-term incentive awards being granted subject to stretching but realistic targets; and
- a performance culture where apt rewards can be earned through the achievement of transparent but stretching targets.'

14.5 Communicating with shareholders

The QCA guide is particularly good in its explanation of communications between companies and shareholders.

For example, it says institutional investors tend to hold more significant stakes in smaller quoted companies, and, as a result, would be expected to have a strong understanding of the business, its value drivers as well as having a good relationship with management. In particular, it may be easier for such investors to assess the appropriateness of performance measures as smaller quoted companies tend to have more transparent business models, and so key performance indicators for success should be clearly definable.

Institutional investors are likely to wish to participate actively in remuneration consultations and it should be noted that usually such investors will account for a significant proportion of voting rights at shareholder meetings. Investors and their advisers tend to show more flexibility in relation to smaller quoted companies when bespoke and appropriate explanations are provided for the rationale of remuneration policy and practice and the quantum of remuneration.

Remuneration committees should provide meaningful disclosure – in particular, why the remuneration practice at the company appropriately motivates the executives to achieve strategic milestones and aligns them to the interests of shareholders over the long-term.

The company will also benefit from a clear expression of shareholders' views through the result of any vote, which will help the remuneration committee's future activity.

A voluntary vote[3] demonstrates that the company is striving to engage with its investors in a meaningful way, which sends an important message about corporate governance at the company.

---

3 AIM companies are not required to put the same resolutions to the vote that fully listed companies are.

15 ISS

ISS is the leading provider of corporate governance solutions to the global financial community. More than 1,700 clients rely on ISS' expertise to help them make more informed investment decisions on behalf of the owners of companies. ISS' services include objective governance research and analysis, end-to-end proxy voting and distribution solutions, turnkey securities class-action claims management, and reliable governance data and modelling tools.

Its team of more than 600 research, technology and client service professionals are located in financial centres worldwide. Investors, regulators and media regularly turn to ISS experts for insight and data on trends in corporate governance, proxy voting operations and mechanics, and securities litigation.

ISS was a subsidiary of MSCI Inc, a leading provider of investment decision support tools to investors globally, but on 30 April 2014 MSCI Inc announced that it has completed the sale of Institutional Shareholder Services Inc ('ISS'), its wholly-owned subsidiary comprising MSCI's Governance segment, to Vestar Capital Partners for total cash consideration of $367 million.

ISS and the NAPF have had various agreements whereby ISS would use the NAPF guidelines when they produced their reports and voting recommendation on UK listed companies.

As so many US fund managers and investors follow ISS recommendations (effectively voting about 30% of the shares of typical UK companies), this made the NAPF guidelines very important.

On June 11, 2003, through its wholly owned subsidiary, ISS RREV, Inc, ISS executed a joint venture agreement with the National Association of Pension Funds (NAPF). The joint venture, RREV, provided corporate governance analysis and electronic voting services to institutional investors and fund managers in the United Kingdom. The RREV service offering was first introduced January 1, 2004 and was equally owned by ISS and the NAPF.

On June 29, 2006, ISS acquired the outstanding minority interest in RREV from the joint venture partner for approximately $5.8 million, of which $1.6 million will be paid over the license agreement of seven years.[1]

In connection with the RREV acquisition, ISS entered into an agreement with its former joint venture partner to license certain proprietary corporate governance policies and other rights for a period of seven years.

On 9 October 2013, ISS and the NAPF announced that this agreement would end in June 2014 and would not be renewed, but ISS would continue to use the NAPF guidelines to assess directors' remuneration of UK listed companies.

ISS' approach of using the NAPF principles to assess UK listed companies had provoked some criticism, most notably from WPP who argued that as it is a global company ISS should use the same methodology it applies to WPP's US competitors.

---

1 Source: http://apps.shareholder.com/sec/viewerContent.aspx?companyid=MSCI&docid=5575360&print=yes

16 NAPF

16.1 Introduction

The NAPF (National Association of Pension Funds) was established in 1923. It represents all types of schemes including defined benefit, defined contribution, group personal pensions and statutory schemes such as those in Local Government. Between them, its members:

- Provide retirement income to nearly 16 million people
- Operate almost 1,300 separate pension schemes
- Have combined assets of nearly £900bn, about one-sixth of the UK stock market.

The NAPF mission is: 'Securing the future of pensions'. It objective is to influence the direction of retirement provision. It seeks to influence the outcome of, and pro-actively shape, UK pension policy to achieve a viable and sustainable workplace pensions sector that instils public confidence. This means for a fair and affordable pensions system and an environment that encourages good workplace pensions. It also places members at the heart of everything it does. The NAPF exists to serve its members' needs.

> 'We work hard to ensure we stay in touch with our members and their concerns, including through the provision of valued services and policy solutions that help raise standards and improve understanding.'

Its membership also includes a wide range of over 400 providers of essential advice and services to the pensions sector. This includes accounting firms, solicitors, fund managers, consultants and actuaries.

16.2 Corporate governance approach

The NAPF has been at the forefront of promoting good corporate governance for over 20 years, and as representatives of major institutional investors has a real interest in seeing high standards achieved and maintained. The NAPF:

- regularly engage with the companies in which pension funds invest on issues including board structures and executive remuneration.
- help members by organising Case Committees through which specific company problems can be addressed directly with Boards on a confidential basis.

- provides, through its Corporate Governance and Voting Policy, guidance to investors and companies on corporate governance matters.
- via its Corporate Governance PensionsConnection offers access and key information on corporate governance and is a forum for members to exchange information and ideas.
- has produced guidance on the Stewardship Code, including Stewardship Made Simple and a Stewardship Code Implementation Checklist to help pension funds discharge their stewardship responsibilities.

In the wake of the financial crisis, pension funds, other investors, government and the EU have been reviewing the effectiveness of corporate governance. This has led to a number of changes to the application of corporate governance policies. The NAPF has been heavily involved in shaping the debate to protect the interests of NAPF members.

The NAPF stresses its commitment to the UK Corporate Governance Code and the 'comply or explain' regime. The NAPF policy guidelines follow the same structure as the Code and this makes it much easier for users, unlike some other codes which fail to cross reference back to the Code.

On 9 October 2013, ISS and the NAPF announced that their agreement would end in June 2014. Joanne Segars, NAPF Chief Executive said 'Despite the ending of the agreement both the NAPF and ISS will continue to work together when appropriate for the benefit of NAPF members and all other interested market constituents.'

'ISS' standard benchmark policy for the UK will continue to refer to the best practice principles established by the NAPF' said Stephen Harvey, Head of ISS. 'The end of the agreement will provide further clarity to market constituents over the different roles of the NAPF and ISS respectively, especially with regard to company engagement meetings.'

For further information and to find out more about the NAPF's corporate governance work, please contact will.pomroy@napf.co.uk

16.3 NAPF views on directors' remuneration

The Corporate Governance Policy of the NAPF was introduced with effect from 1 January 2004 and reviewed and updated regularly since then. The latest revision was in November 2013, and it would appear that the NAPF is no longer so closely aligned with the ABI and has chosen to set out its own stance in relation to remuneration.[1]

In the introduction to the November 2013 Guidelines, the NAPF state:

> 'This year sees significant reforms being introduced in the area of executive remuneration, with changes to the way it is to be reported by companies and the introduction of a binding vote alongside an advisory vote on remuneration. The NAPF and Hermes EOS with the BT Pension Scheme, RPMI Railpen Investments and Universities Superannuation Scheme have published "Remuneration principles for building and reinforcing long-term business success" – we expect companies to be able to articulate how their pay policies meet these principles in a manner which is most appropriate for their company. As the new reforms settle in over the next 12 months, we encourage appropriate and constructive dialogue between issuers and their shareholders.
>
> The main purpose of the NAPF Corporate Governance Policy and Voting Guidelines is to assist investors and their proxy voting agents in their interpretation of the provisions of the Code when assessing a company's compliance with it. While it is particularly focussed on what voting sanctions may be applied at a company meeting, a decision to vote against management can only be taken after proper consideration of the company's explanation for non-compliance and in the light of the particular circumstances at that company.'

NAPF Voting Policy

Remuneration practices which would most likely cause concern and may trigger a voting sanction **in the absence of sufficient explanation** include:

- Increases in base salary in excess of inflation or that awarded to the rest of the workforce;
- Layering of new share award schemes on top of existing schemes;
- Insufficient alignment with shareholders, eg a shareholding requirement of less than 2x salary.
- Inappropriate use (or lack of use) of discretion;

---

1 For example, the latest guidance is silent about the ABI Principles of Remuneration, whereas their November 2011 guidance, in its Section D.1.2 stated: 'In the UK, good practice in remuneration has been set out by the Association of British Insurers (ABI) in its "ABI Principles of Remuneration". The NAPF anticipates that most institutional investors and issuers will use the ABI Principles as a guide to remuneration policies and has therefore chosen not to reinterpret them in detail here. However it is important that companies tailor their policies to their own particular circumstances and do not slavishly follow established guidelines.'

- An awarding of a 'sign-on' bonus without the inclusion of any conditionality and which pays for awards not already vested at previous employer;
- Insufficient disclosure on the scope of annual bonuses and performance conditions (retrospective disclosure *can* be acceptable).

Remuneration practices which would likely cause concern and may trigger a voting sanction **regardless** of any explanation given include:

- Over frequent re-benchmarking
- Insufficiently demanding or inappropriate performance targets;
- Guaranteed, pensionable, discretionary or 'one-off' annual bonuses;
- Any provision for re-testing of performance conditions;
- Ex-gratia and other non-contractual payments;
- Change in control provisions triggering earlier and/or larger payments and rewards;
- The absence of service contracts for executive directors.

Remuneration Levels and Structure

In respect of remuneration levels and structure, the NAPF Guidelines say:

> D.1.1. The NAPF believes that remuneration should be proportionate and aligned with shareholder interests and long-term sustainable value creation.
>
> D.1.2. The Principles for Executive Remuneration – set out below – are intended to provide high-level guidance to companies about investor expectations of their remuneration structures and practices. The Principles deliberately avoid prescribing any specific structures or measures; however, we do expect companies to be able to articulate how their pay policies meet these Principles in a manner which is most appropriate for their company.
>
> **1. Remuneration committees should expect executive management make a material long-term investment in shares of the businesses they manage**
>
> - The best form of alignment between executives and shareholders is the ownership of shares over the long-term, with ownership obligations increasing with seniority.
> - To the extent this is feasible and appropriate the bulk of variable rewards should flow over time from the benefits of being an equity owner.

2. Pay should be aligned to long-term strategy and the desired corporate culture throughout the organisation

- We encourage remuneration committees to design rewards that encourage the specific behaviours required to drive long-term strategic success. A starting point should be the company's strategic plan and key performance indicators (KPIs).

3. Pay schemes should be clear, understandable for both investors and executives, and ensure that executive rewards reflect returns to long-term shareholders

- Firms should avoid operating multiple long-term schemes – we do not believe that a multiplicity of awards, with varying performance conditions helps to motivate executives.

4. Remuneration committees should use the discretion afforded them by shareholders to ensure that awards properly reflect business performance

- Remuneration committees should exercise their judgement about the overall performance of the company when determining awards. In particular, the committee should consider how the results have been achieved, not just what was achieved.

5. Companies and investors should have appropriately regular discussions on strategy and long-term performance.

- Dialogue should be initiated at an early stage of the decision making process and include those investors who are committed to stewardship.

D.1.3. Just as the remuneration committee should adopt a holistic approach when designing and assessing packages, so investors should evaluate remuneration arrangements in their entirety. Shareholders will seek reassurance that there is a clear link between strategy, performance and reward. Total remuneration should be structured to reflect the ambitions and risks inherent in the business. Performance pay should motivate management to deliver results which are both stretching and sustainable.

Voting

In respect of Voting, the NAPF Guidelines say:

Remuneration policy is seen by many investors as a litmus test for wider corporate governance practices, it for example encompasses board effectiveness, oversight, strategy and risk management. Shareholders will therefore continue to examine remuneration policies critically, with a view to ensuring that they are closely aligned with their interests.

We expect companies to be able to articulate how their pay policies meet our Principles in a manner which is most appropriate for their company. With the introduction of the new binding vote on remuneration policy shareholders now have several mechanisms through which to express their view on a firm's approach to remuneration; these include:

- A binding vote on remuneration policy
- A binding vote on new share plans
- An advisory vote on the policy's implementation
- A binding vote on the re-election of related directors.

Companies can expect investors to utilise these rights in different manners and as such there will be an onus on investors to communicate their rationale for dissent. On the whole:

- If investors judge that the firm's remuneration policy fails to meet the Principles then they may decide to vote against the policy and potentially the chairman and members of the remuneration committee.
- If investors subsequently judge that the policy has been implemented inappropriately, or the remuneration committee has used its discretion inappropriately then they may decide to vote against the implementation report.
- Additionally, if investors judge that discretion has been used egregiously or consistently inappropriately; or they believe that the policy remains or has become wholly inappropriate for the business they may decide to vote against the remuneration committee chair or even the board chairman.
- Voting sanctions will normally focus on the implementation report and new share scheme proposals, but may from time to time extend to or be escalated to the chairman and members of the remuneration committee.

Remuneration reporting

In respect of remuneration reporting, the NAPF Guidelines say:

D.2.1. The NAPF supports the recent reforms to the reporting of executive remuneration introduced by the Government. These reforms give shareholders a binding vote on a company's remuneration policy and require companies to communicate clearly how their policies are being implemented – best practice will evolve over time. The guidance produced by the GC100 and Investor Working Group should assist companies and their investors to implement them successfully and has particular regard for the practical aspects of implementing the directors' remuneration reporting requirements.

D.2.2. Companies should pay close heed to the GC100 Investor Working Group guidance which provides a framework for the reporting of executive remuneration within the Remuneration Report. Companies should avoid boilerplate language and strive to provide meaningful and preferably concise disclosures relevant to the company and its particular circumstances. The report should include a statement from the Remuneration Committee Chairman reflecting the Committee's decisions in that year, including a summary of any discretion applied and stakeholder engagement.

D.2.3. The statement of implementation of remuneration policy should include details on material changes to the remuneration structure (within the pre-approved remuneration policy) and specific details on performance measures and targets for the current financial year (subject to commercial sensitivity), which may not have been determined when the remuneration policy was originally approved. In addition, companies should include a summary of engagement activity with investors during the year, including any significant concerns raised and where appropriate how they've been responded to.

Consultants to the Remuneration Committee

In respect of Consultants to the Remuneration Committee, the NAPF Guidelines say:

D.2.4. Consultants to the Remuneration Committee should be appointed by the committee and be independent of the company's management. Potential conflicts of interest should be scrupulously and demonstrably addressed.

D.2.5. The remuneration committee is exclusively responsible for the selection and appointment of its advisors.

D.2.6. The remuneration committee should disclose whether the Remuneration Consultants Group's 'Code of Conduct' has been taken into consideration when selecting its consultants.

D.2.7. Companies are encouraged to consider submitting the remuneration consultant function to periodic tender and disclose their policy on this matter, including when the consultant was last subject to tender.

D.2.8. If any services are provided by the same remuneration consultants to the company:

- They should be fully disclosed to the remuneration committee and to shareholders.
- The chairman of the remuneration committee should explain to shareholders why it is appropriate for the committee to appoint the same consultants as the company, notwithstanding this conflict of interest.

The NAPF are leading other institutions in the way they are demonstrating their concerns about remuneration advisers.

Contracts

The NAPF issued in December 2002 a joint statement with the ABI regarding executive directors' contracts. It is still current and is in Appendix 5.

16.4 Joint NAPF and LAPFF policy on pensions' disclosure

The NAPF and LAPFF,[2] in 2010, called for greater transparency[3] on:

1. Accrual rates in defined benefit pensions, which include 'final salary' schemes. Some directors benefit from a rapid accrual rate, such as 1/30th, when other employees may typically be on a rate of 1/60th or 1/80th.
2. Company contributions to defined contribution pension schemes. Recent studies have shown that directors' contributions are often far higher than those made to other staff.
3. Payments in lieu of pensions. An increasing number of firms offer cash payments instead of a pension contribution. These can be sizeable – in some cases over 50% of salary.
4. The retirement ages of directors. The reasons for any differences between the boardroom and other employees should be explained.
5. Special early retirement provisions. Firms should make it clear that an unreduced pension on early retirement is usually inappropriate.

---

[2] Local Authority Pension Fund Forum.

[3] For full details see http://www.napf.co.uk/PressCentre/Press_releases/~/media/Press%20Documents/PressReleases/0024_061510_Investors_want_greater_transparency_on_%20boardroom_%20pensions_0610.ashx

Currently a company's remuneration report, which shareholders have to approve, carries a mixture of mandatory disclosures under the Directors Remuneration Reporting Regulations (DRRR) and further voluntary reporting.

Some of the enhanced provisions available to directors raised in the joint NAPF/LAPFF letter (which they sent to all listed companies) are not captured by the mandatory disclosure requirements, and so a number of companies do not make them explicit.

16.5 NAPF Corporate Governance Policy and Voting Guidelines

As noted above, the Corporate Governance Policy and Voting Guidelines were revised in November 2013. The NAPF have kindly consented for these to be reproduced in this book.

Those parts that are relevant to remuneration are in **Appendix 2**.

Other documents produced by the NAPF that are related to remuneration include:

Remuneration principles for building and reinforcing long-term business success
18 November 2013

The NAPF and Hermes EOS, in conjunction with RPMI Railpen, the BT Pension Scheme and USS Investment Management, have published the Remuneration principles for building and reinforcing long-term business success.[4] The key points are included in para D.1.2 of the NAPF Guidelines (see **16.3** above).

NAPF Responsible Investment guide 2013[5]
21 May 2013

This guide updates the NAPF's Responsible Investment Guidance, last published in 2009 and aims to:

- summarise the case for why pension fund investors should be seeking to incorporate extra-financial risks – including governance and material environmental and social risks, within their investment decisions in an effort to protect against value destruction, to potentially enhance risk adjusted returns and ultimately support better member outcomes.

---

4 http://napf.co.uk/PolicyandResearch/DocumentLibrary/0351_remuneration_principles_for_building_and_reinforcing%20_longterm_business_success_nov2013.aspx

5 http://napf.co.uk/PolicyandResearch/DocumentLibrary/0308_NAPF_Responsible_Investment_guide_2013.aspx

- Set out how pension funds can, in keeping with their fiduciary duty, move the market towards one where responsible investment is considered the norm.

NAPF Stewardship Policy 2012[6]

22 November 2012

The NAPF's first ever Stewardship Policy sets out best practice for pension fund trustees and simply explains how funds should fulfil their stewardship responsibility. The NAPF believes that 'signing up' to the Code demonstrates that a pension fund believes companies should adhere to the highest standards of governance and that their managers should integrate the Code's Principles into their investment processes. A greater weight of pension fund signatories to the Code will further influence behavioural changes that lead to better stewardship by asset managers and companies.

---

6 http://napf.co.uk/PolicyandResearch/DocumentLibrary/0272_Stewardship_policy_NAPF_2012.aspx

17 PIRC

Pensions & Investment Research Consultants Ltd (PIRC) have kindly allowed the reproduction of those parts of their guidelines that related to remuneration and they are included below and in **Appendix 3**.

17.1 Introduction

PIRC is the UK's leading independent research and advisory consultancy providing services to institutional investors on corporate governance and corporate social responsibility.

Since 1986, it has been the pioneer and champion of good corporate governance within the UK. PIRC has a wide spectrum of clients ranging from pension funds, faith-based investors, trade unions to banks and asset managers.

Its Corporate Governance Service is an authoritative and vital resource for active investors, whilst its widely-read Shareowner Voting Guidelines provide a market-wide benchmark for investors and forms part of the movement for corporate governance reform and long-term wealth creation strategies for responsible investors. For more information about PIRC visit their website www.pirc.co.uk or call PIRC on 0207 247 2323.

PIRC acts on behalf of institutional shareowners when raising governance concerns with investee companies. PIRC engages with every UK company it reports on, but declines any paid consultancy as this would create an unacceptable conflict of interest.

Its clients manage worldwide assets of several trillion pounds, but PIRC itself is not an investing institution.

PIRC's analysis is based on its experience in dealing with sustainability issues, whether environmental, social or governance (ESG).

PIRC's primary goals are to encourage boards of listed companies to:

- Adopt clear values and standards in business dealings throughout the organisation
- Be able to account for shareowner capital and achieve an appropriate return on it

- Develop a culture of transparency and accountability
- Focus on strategic issues and the quality of the business rather than simply short term numbers
- Develop appropriate checks and balances to deal with conflicts of interests
- Maintain effective systems of financial control and risk management
- Create fair remuneration structures that reward the achievement of business objectives at all levels and
- Recognise and manage impacts on all stakeholders.

These goals are intended to assist companies in making effective business choices so as to maximise the wealth and welfare of all affected by its operation.

PIRC's UK shareholder voting guidelines 2013 were subtitled 'Promoting high standards of business and wealth creation'. This document represents PIRC's independent judgement of good corporate practice. This is the seventeenth edition of PIRC's Shareowner Voting Guidelines, first issued in 1993. It replaces the version published in Spring 2012. Since PIRC launched its Corporate Governance Service in 1991, it has sought continually to update and improve its policies and this document represents the latest expression of PIRC's independent judgement of good corporate practice in accordance with the law.

17.2 Key points from 2013 guidelines

PIRC provide a detailed analysis of current problems in corporate governance (including remuneration). These are well argued and, although their views are not mainstream, a detailed reading of their guidelines is recommended. Their key concerns are:

- A debate is needed on the future of comply or explain;
- Problems with accounting standards and auditors who are 'too few to fail' and conflicted in some of the advice they give;
- Mergers and acquisitions, where many do not add value and those involved are conflicted;
- Share buy backs;
- Remuneration concerns including:
  - market failure in executive pay has been passing-off under unsound assertions;

- fundamental flaws in the basis of remuneration design which are underpinned by myths concerning attraction, retention, motivation and alignment of interest with shareholders;
- incomprehensibility;
- the binding shareholder approval model of the law – has been circumvented by other means;
- vested interests of remuneration consultants.

17.3 PIRC's voting policy on management proposals

In 2012, PIRC recommended support for 77% of company proposals for which we issued advice in the UK, and 12% received an oppose recommendation.

In respect of remuneration reports, recommendations in favour were 30%, opposed 44% and abstention 26% (inclusive of votes at investment trusts). This clearly demonstrates a systemic problem on the matter of pay. PIRC considers the following in coming to voting recommendations:

- PIRC's shareowner voting guidelines;
- The Board's explanation for the proposal including any departure from good practice;
- Board assurances on positive changes;
- Potential impact of oppose votes on corporate structure (and likelihood of occurrence);
- The materiality of any concern and timescales involved;
- Opportunities for further votes in the future on the issue;
- Market implications from any precedent created.

PIRC's role is to provide advice in the best interests of our clients. In assessing where these interests lie, we assume our clients are long-term equity investors who value high standards of business conduct, the creation of wealth within legitimate boundaries and the importance of good relations with other stakeholders as key factors in the ongoing success of the companies in which they invest. PIRC will always apply its judgment and experience to the individual circumstances of companies, which may lead to different outcomes.

17.4 Reasons for opposing, abstaining from, or voting for a remuneration report vote

Source: PIRC and Railpen Say on Pay report Sept 2009.

The points below indicate the typical factors that are taken into account when deciding how to vote on remuneration reports.

Voting against: A variety of different issues that cause concern:	**Voting to abstain:**	**Voting in support:**
• Performance conditions have been changed which causes them to be easier to meet.	• No evidence of excess and a good level of disclosure; but salaries have been increased year on year and there is no justifiable reason as to why.	• Clear disclosure of the main aspects of remuneration (ie, performance criteria, maximum awards, any departures from normal practices/scheme details).
• High levels of pay and there is no real link to the performance achieved, or to be achieved.	• Overall, there are no structural issues but there is a general lack of disclosure and there is scope for more information to be disclosed and for the company to be more transparent.	• No evidence of excess.
• Annual bonuses continue to rise and salaries continue to increase, perhaps double digit salary increases become a pattern.		• Clear link between pay levels and performance.
• Structural issues and overall lack of performance linkage.		• Clear alignment of the interests of shareholders and directors through robust remuneration practices.
• Performance targets do not align with the long-term strategy of the company.		• Remuneration committee demonstrates behaviours that protect the interests of shareholders whilst offering pay packages and remuneration policies which allow incentivisation and retention.

Voting against: A variety of different issues that cause concern:	**Voting to abstain:**	**Voting in support:**
		• Performance targets for the long-term incentive plans support the long-term strategic plan of the company.

17.5 PIRC Remuneration guidelines

PIRC have kindly consented for their guidelines that relate to remuneration to be reproduced in this book. These are included in **Appendix 3.**

18 ABI (and IVIS)

18.1 Introduction

The Association of British Insurers (ABI) is the trade association for authorised insurance companies operating in the UK. The ABI's role is to be the voice of the UK insurance industry, leading debate and speaking up for insurers. It has over 300 members, which together account for around 90% of premiums in the UK domestic market and who, as institutional investors, have some £1.5 trillion of funds under management including around £800 billion or 12% of all UK equities[1] (compared to one quarter in 1999).

After the UK Corporate Governance Code, Company Law and the Listing Rules, the ABI principles and guidelines are viewed by most people involved in directors' remuneration as probably the most important. The ABI have kindly consented for these to be reproduced in this book, in full. The (November 2013) ABI Principles of Remuneration are in **Appendix 4.**

18.2 ABI Principles of Remuneration

In September 2011, the ABI significantly revised its Principles of Remuneration. They were the latest update to ABI guidance which has evolved over thirty years. They addressed investors' renewed concern on executive pay. ABI members believe that non-executive directors have a key role to play in determining the appropriate remuneration and shareholders should be actively involved without micromanaging companies.

When the ABI revised its old guidelines and replaced them with its new set of principles, it did however retain most of its old guidelines as an appendix to its new principles.

The document is designed in a format of over-arching Principles, general Guidance and additional Appendices, containing further helpful guidance on the operation of incentive schemes. The document is predominantly for companies with a main market listing, but is useful for companies on other public markets and for other entities too.

---

1 This is according to a 2011 CityAM article both the ABI and NAPF members represents about 12% each of the UK market. Retail investors own a share, as do other kinds of UK-based institutions. Another 15 to 20% of the UK market is managed by UK institutions for overseas investors. The rest is owned by overseas investors. See http://www.cityam.com/news-and-analysis/the-pensions-chief-who-says-investors-are-no-longer-soft-touch

Key principles of the guidance are that company boards should:

- Support appropriate reward for exceptional performance
- Strongly resist any payment for failure
- Understand that excessive or undeserved remuneration undermines the efficient operation of the company, adversely affects its reputation and is not aligned with shareholder interests
- Not engage in crude benchmarking when seeking to justify increases.

On 5 November 2013, the ABI wrote to the Remuneration Committee Chairman of all FTSE 350 companies, to outline the main revisions to the ABI's Principles of Remuneration and how the ABI's Institutional Voting Information Service ('IVIS') will approach the new voting and reporting regime. The ABI wrote:

> 'The ABI's Principles of Remuneration are reviewed annually. Last year, we made significant revisions to the content and structure of the guidance. Given this, we have made only minor amendments and clarifications in 2013. The main changes relate to:
>
> - Performance Adjustment/Malus and Clawback – we provide a clearer definition of performance adjustment and clawback and ask Committees to disclose the circumstances in which performance adjustment or clawback could be used.
> - Executive shareholdings – This has been updated to clarify which shares would qualify as meeting the guideline.
> - Performance on grant schemes – Whilst many members still retain significant reservations over the use of performance-on-grant schemes, the update provides the conditions shareholders expect these schemes to meet, such as genuinely long holding periods, significant shareholding requirements, lower overall amounts and the disclosure of targets/performance achieved.
> - The new Reporting and Voting Regime – Appendix 1 outlines ABI views on various practical aspects of the new reporting arrangements.
>
> With the introduction of the Reporting Regulations and Voting Legislation, the coming year will see significant changes in the way companies report, and shareholders vote, on pay. The Principles should be viewed in conjunction with the guidance on the new reporting regulations produced by the GC 100 and Investor Group. The ABI supports this guidance and encourages companies to adopt the best practice within it.
>
> Under the new voting and reporting regime, IVIS will continue its current approach of assessing companies. IVIS does not issue direct

voting recommendations. Instead, in the spirit of comply-or-explain, we highlight key issues and non-compliance with best practice through our Colour Coding system. This gives us flexibility in our dealings with companies and the ability to consider well-reasoned arguments.

When companies seek approval for the Policy Report, IVIS will produce a separate conclusion and status for each of the Policy Report and the Annual Remuneration Report.

The two votes will be colour coded separately. Under our colour coding system, a Blue Top indicates no areas of major concern. The colour showing the strongest concern is Red, followed by Amber.

IVIS's analysis of a company's Policy Report is likely to highlight the following issues on a Red or Amber top:

- Remuneration structures not aligned to the ABI Principles of Remuneration (including the guidance and appendix) – As is our current practice, IVIS will highlight remuneration policies or structures which are not in accordance with the ABI Principles of Remuneration.
- Lack of detail in the Policy Report – IVIS will highlight where companies fail to provide sufficient detail in the policy report to allow shareholders to make an informed voting decision. ABI members recommend that companies consider the guidance issued by the GC 100 and Investor Group to ensure that they provide sufficient detail in the Policy Report.
- Use of wide ranging discretion – Discretion will be an important aspect of the Policy Report, as it will allow Remuneration Committees to ensure their policies will be appropriate over their life. However, IVIS will highlight where policies are drafted with overarching or widely-ranging discretion provisions, particularly without any clear explanation.

If you need any further details on the Principles of Remuneration or IVIS's approach to the forthcoming AGM season, please do not hesitate to contact our Head of Corporate Governance, Andrew Ninian (andrew.ninian@abi.org.uk, 020 7216 7671), or one of the IVIS team (www.ivis.co.uk/contact.aspx).'

18.3 IVIS

The Institutional Voting Information Service (IVIS) is produced by the ABI. IVIS is a subsidiary of the ABI.

First published in January 1993, the service has been developed to advise Association members on aspects of corporate governance of UK companies in which they invest. Through consultation with members it seeks to represent the consensus view of UK insurance companies on these matters.

In 2012, the ABI reviewed its Principles, and issued new Principles just as this book went to press. These latest (November 2012) ABI Principles of Remuneration are in **Appendix 4**, together with an introduction explaining the changes and themes for 2013.

What does IVIS do?

IVIS reviews UK company annual reports and accounts and company meeting notices for compliance with corporate governance best practice. The service has developed from the low-key, proactive but non-confrontational approach to corporate governance adopted by the ABI.

Its benefits are fourfold. It:

- does the essential groundwork in the review of reports and accounts and meeting notices
- identifies matters of concern, particularly to insurers, and seek resolutions prior to voting at meetings
- provides the relevant information in a focused way and in a standardised user-friendly format and
- contributes to the audit trail on voting policy.

IVIS covers all the companies which comprise the UK FTSE All Share Index. Other companies are monitored on an ad hoc basis when requested by members. The ABI guidelines and the Stock Exchange Combined Code provide the basis for the monitoring service. Matters of concern are dealt with in liaison with ABI members who tend to be major shareholders in the companies they monitor.

19 Manifest

Note: Manifest and MM&K work together to jointly produce The Executive Director Total Remuneration Survey. Much of the survey data in this book comes from the Manifest/MM&K survey.

For further information about Manifest:

Contact: Paul Hewitt, Business Development Manager

Tel: +44 (0)1376 503500

Email: paul.hewitt@manifest.co.uk

Manifest is an independent corporate governance and proxy voting specialist. Since 1996 Manifest has delivered timely, accurate and impartial governance support services to institutional investors, consultants and quoted companies. Manifest offers a range of conflict-free, global proxy governance support services through its innovative web platform.

Manifest places particular emphasis on independence and impartiality to ensure that all users of its services can benefit from the widest range of issues analysis.

With over 6,000 global companies under review, and global 'say on pay' experience, this vast wealth of information helps clients avoid problem situations with investee companies by helping you understand their governance strengths and weaknesses, not wasting time sourcing, collating and analysing raw data.

Manifest has over a 15 years of in-depth experience of gathering some of the most complex financial data available in the market. The data is independent, impartial and conflict free. It is logically organised but easy to use and includes a data export facility for manipulation in statistical packages. It's no surprise then that many of the UK's institutional investors and compensation consultants use Manifest as their primary source of executive compensation data.

Manifest produces a detailed pre-meeting research report on each company for clients which includes peer group comparisons of remuneration levels. Voting clients are provided with customised guidance which reflects their voting policy rather than 'house' voting recommendations.

The Manifest database – with data on UK stocks going back to 1996 – can also be used for detailed analysis of issues such as remuneration trends.

The key issues Manifest considers in relation to remuneration are if:

- the remuneration committee is not considered to be independent.
- the remuneration policy does not demonstrate an alignment with the company's objectives and key performance indicators.
- a director's notice period may be greater than 12 months or provide for payments on termination in excess of 12 months' fixed remuneration.
- a proposed new option or share scheme does not contain an overall 10% dilution limit in ten years.
- a proposed new incentive scheme:
  - has maximum annual participation which provides for significant levels of individual participation, given the company's circumstances
  - allows bailing out of underwater options
  - has no performance targets, or targets that do not include a comparator group or relative benchmark (such as RPI or WACC)
  - allows the non-executive directors to participate
  - allows preferential vesting of awards in the event of a change in control.

Manifest Total Remuneration Assessment

The Manifest Total Remuneration Assessment (MTRA) provides a practical, objective and quantitative evaluation of the key components of executive remuneration. The MTRA delivers a report on the state of both the current and historic structures of reward, alignment and achievement.

Evidence to date shows that the Manifest rating is a good predictor of voting outcomes on remuneration resolutions.

Manifest analyse each company's remuneration under four key areas – Alignment, Quantum, Contracts and Dilution & Cost – and then provide an overall score and rating of A = Very Good to F = Very Bad.

Remuneration Benchmark	% Score Weight	Maxi-mum 'Worst Case'	Actual Score Total
Alignment	**40**	**100**	
Link to Strategy	12	30	
Short Term Incentive – Performance Measures	8	20	
Long Term Incentive – Performance Measures	16	40	
Director Shareholdings	4	10	
Quantum	**48**	**120**	
Total Remuneration	12	30	
Salary	12	30	
Pensions & Other Benefits	4	10	
Short Term Incentive	10	25	
Long Term Incentive	10	25	
Contracts	**8**	**20**	
Dilution & Cost	**4**	**10**	
Overall Assessment Score	**100**	**250**	
Grade Assigned	**A–F**		

Scoring	0–25	26–50	51–75	76–100	101–125	126+
Rating	A	B	C	D	E	F

Methodology

Full details of the scoring matrix are available from Manifest on request.

20 Hermes, NAPF, BT, Railpen and USS

20.1 Remuneration principles for building and reinforcing long-term business success

These principles have been jointly produced by Hermes EOS, the National Association of Pension Funds (NAPF), BT Pension Scheme, RPMI Railpen Investments and Universities Superannuation Scheme (USS). They have kindly given permission for this document to be reproduced in this book.

The Principles are intended to provide high-level guidance to companies about our expectations of their remuneration structures and practices.

The Principles deliberately avoid prescribing any specific structures or measures; instead we expect companies to articulate clearly to shareholders how their pay policies meet these principles in a manner which is most appropriate for their specific situation.

The Principles

1. **Remuneration committees should expect executive management to make a material long-term investment in shares of the businesses they manage.**
2. **Pay should be aligned to long-term success and the desired corporate culture throughout the organisation.**
3. **Pay schemes should be clear, understandable for both investors and executives, and ensure that executive rewards reflect long-term returns to shareholders.**
4. **Remuneration committees should use the discretion afforded them by shareholders to ensure that awards properly reflect business performance.**
5. **Companies and investors should have regular discussions on strategy and long-term performance.**

Introduction

At the beginning of 2013, Hermes EOS and the NAPF, in conjunction with RPMI Railpen Investments, the BT Pension Scheme and USS Investment

Management, the wholly owned investment management subsidiary of USS, published 'Remuneration Principles for building and reinforcing long-term business success'. Since then, we have held discussions with the chairs and remuneration committee chairs of almost half of FTSE 100 companies, along with executives responsible for reward, remuneration consultants and other institutional investors. We are encouraged by the willingness of many to rethink fundamentally current practices. The principles within this final document reflect the feedback we have received. We believe that these principles provide a sound framework for remuneration committees to use when thinking through, devising and implementing their remuneration policies.

Each company is unique and as such faces different challenges and opportunities. While we hope that our principles will provide a useful framework, it is for boards to determine which specific pay structures will work best for their company's executives and to communicate intelligently their reasoning to investors. We seek neither to prescribe a particular structure, nor to micro-manage pay, but rather to start a healthier and more constructive on-going conversation than often occurs today.

We firmly believe that there is a significant appetite for change and urge companies to consider how they might align pay more closely with the interests of their long-term owners in order to position themselves best for future success. We look forward to supporting those companies who share our desire for change.

We firmly believe that there is a significant appetite for change and urge companies to consider how they might align pay more closely with the interests of their long-term owners in order to position themselves best for future success.

The Principles

1 Remuneration committees should expect executive management to make a material long-term investment in shares of the businesses they manage.

We consider that the best form of alignment between executives and shareholders is the ownership of shares over the long-term, with ownership obligations increasing with seniority. While we recognise that flexibility is needed to ensure that effective executives are appropriately remunerated, remuneration committees should strive to ensure that, to the extent this is feasible and appropriate, the bulk of their variable rewards flows over time from the benefits of being an equity owner.

The meaning of 'long-term' will differ from company to company but three years, the most commonly used time period for long- term awards, is often not long enough. In many situations it may be appropriate for a material proportion of shares granted to be held for a longer period, the length of time would be aligned to the business cycle and strategy of the company and take account of the demographic of the executives.

Wherever possible, we believe that remuneration committees should foster a culture in which executives are encouraged to invest in the shares of the company they manage. It is important, of course, that the board monitors and guards against the possible unintended consequences of long-term ownership such as overly aggressive dividend policies, encouraging takeovers to crystalise awards and overly risk-averse strategies intended to preserve, rather than increase, the value of shares. In particular, as executives approach retirement they may wish to ensure their investments are appropriately diversified, however, they should continue to maintain a material holding. Having 'skin in the game' is an important motivator and one that we believe is under-used.

Companies should also consider ensuring that executives are exposed to some tail risk for an appropriate length of time once they leave a company, for example, by requiring that any sale of shares be staggered over time, notwithstanding competitive or regulatory barriers to continued share ownership. In practice, many long- serving executives have significant holdings in the company, but this kind of commitment can help to encourage longer-term thinking to continue right through to the end of a career. While clawback is one way of aligning executives and shareholders it does not necessarily encourage a CEO actively to develop a new generation of talent to succeed the current executive directors. At the same time, it is recognised that outgoing executives cannot be held responsible for the actions of their successors and so remuneration committees must strike an appropriate balance.

2 Pay should be aligned to long-term strategy and the desired corporate culture throughout the organisation.

We encourage remuneration committees to design rewards that encourage the specific behaviours required to drive long-term strategic success. Too much of the debate between companies and owners has focused on the minutiae of short to medium term performance conditions. This is exacerbated when the ultimate owners of companies delegate their oversight responsibilities to agents who themselves operate according to short-time horizons. As a result, certain performance measures, such as earnings per share (EPS) and total shareholder return (TSR) have been over-emphasised, with little regard for the company's specific strategy or the timeframe over which that strategy should be achieved. Rather, we believe remuneration committees should take as a starting point the company's strategic plan and key performance indicators (KPIs) and ensure there is a strong read across from the company's strategy to the drivers of executives' remuneration.

While we do not believe that well-structured remuneration is a panacea we do believe that it is a vital indication of and contributor to the desired culture, values and ethos of a company. We therefore encourage a coherent remuneration philosophy which is cascaded down the organisation. For example, it is not always clear why some executive directors receive pay increases that are greater than those awarded elsewhere in the organisation, and which feed through to the bonus and long term incentive plan (LTIP) to widen the pay differentials within the company, or enjoy preferential tax treatment or far more generous pension arrangements – or cash in lieu – than less senior colleagues. Remuneration committees should consider whether they are able credibly to justify any such differentials.

The nominations committee and the remuneration committee must also work closely together, particularly in agreeing the parameters around the remuneration for new appointees to the board. The remuneration committee should ideally be involved at a sufficiently early stage of succession planning to be able to agree the acceptable parameters for pay with the nominations committee during the initial stages of recruitment, rather than waiting until a preferred candidate has been selected.

3 Pay schemes should be clear, understandable for both investors and executives, and ensure that executive rewards reflect returns to long-term shareholders

The desire of some investors to encourage improved company performance by focusing on metrics and targets rather than behaviour and outcomes is at least in part responsible for the increased complexity we have seen in remuneration schemes in recent years. So too is the feeling among executives and non-executives that the outcome of long-term incentive schemes is unsatisfactory, frequently being described as a "lottery".

As a result of these and other factors, many companies now operate multiple long-term schemes because one or more has been deemed not to have worked well and executives often have outstanding awards under a number of them. There may also be a deferred bonus scheme, or a share matching scheme on top of the short and long-term awards. We wonder therefore whether this multiplicity of awards, with varying performance conditions really helps to motivate executives to give them a clear line of sight over what they need to achieve.

Setting a long-term course and measuring, explaining and incentivising progress annually may be a more effective way to encourage long-term value creation than the current prevailing system. For example, in some circumstances it may be better to have a single bonus scheme – with no long-term incentive plan – using a single balanced scorecard of metrics based on KPIs, over which the remuneration committee may use its discretion, and which pays out predominantly in shares which must be held for the long term. The significant component of the reward is accrued over time through being a share owner. This type of award might be more highly valued by executives than traditional LTIPs due to the increased certainty of outcome. A number of companies have adopted this approach recently and we applaud their desire to ensure that rewards better reflect individual and company performance.

4 Remuneration committees should use the discretion afforded them by shareholders to ensure that awards properly reflect business performance

Running companies is far more complicated than even the best designed remuneration policies can ever hope to reflect. To distil complex company performance into a few metrics is an oversimplification that can sometimes lead to awards that are not reflective of actual performance, eroding trust and increasing reputational risk.

We wish to see remuneration committees taking greater ownership of, and being accountable for, both the remuneration policy and its outcomes. Remuneration committees consist of experienced individuals; they can, and we believe should, exercise their judgement about the overall performance of the company when determining awards. In particular, the committee should consider how the results have been achieved, not just what was achieved. For instance, if targets have been met by employing aggressive accounting policies, by deferring important investments in the business or by unnecessarily increasing leverage, then the remuneration committee should consider scaling back payments. Similarly, if the executives have hit their performance targets but the company has had serious reputational issues or has underperformed the market or peer group, there are strong arguments for making lower awards.

We support committees that take a holistic approach to performance rather than applying simplistic mechanistic formulae to determine awards to executives. We recognise that shareholders will require additional explanation to be included in the remuneration report when judgement and discretion is exercised by the committee. Committees should ensure their considerations and judgements are thoroughly explained and appropriately justified; this will be of particular importance if the committee exercises upward discretion. Such an approach will allow investors to have greater confidence that the remuneration committee is acting in their best interests.

5 Companies and investors should have appropriately regular discussions on strategy and long-term performance.

While much of the focus of the debate around remuneration has been on companies, we believe it is also vitally important that investors are aware of their responsibilities under the Stewardship Code to engage with companies on a full range of issues. Our preference would be for this dialogue to take place throughout the year, rather than compressed into the period leading up to the shareholder meeting.

We recognise that trust between some companies and investors has diminished over time and believe that both parties have a role to play in helping to rebuild this relationship. Investors should inform themselves properly ahead of meeting a company and ensure that they are able to have intelligent, holistic conversations about the business, its strategy and how remuneration structures support that strategy. Likewise, companies should consider how they might identify and engage with those investors who are committed to stewardship. These should include investors who are outside of their top ten shareholders and asset owners such as those we represent.

As investors, and investor representatives, we encourage remuneration committees to be more innovative in designing pay schemes that drive the behaviours required of executives to deliver long-term business performance. We urge them to be less mechanistic in determining awards. To enable this to happen we recognise that we need to give the companies in which we invest sufficient space to innovate and we must take time to consider carefully new proposals with an open mind.

Time for change

We strongly believe that the time is right for companies and investors to fundamentally rethink their approach to executive remuneration.

We are confident that there is a significant appetite for change among many to consider how they may more closely align pay with the interests of their long-term owners in order to position themselves best for future success.

The above principles do not seek to prescribe any particular structure or model of remuneration. Instead we encourage companies to innovate and come forward with proposals which are most appropriate to their own business model. We stand ready to support this change which we believe is in the interests of both companies and their investors.

Hermes Equity Ownership Services

Hermes Equity Ownership Services (HEOS) enables institutional shareholders around the world to meet their fiduciary responsibilities and become active owners of public companies. HEOS is based on the premise that companies with informed and involved shareholders are more likely to achieve superior long-term performance than those without.

National Association of Pension Funds

The National Association of Pension Funds (NAPF) has been at the forefront of promoting good corporate governance for over 20 years, and as representatives of major institutional investors we have a real interest in seeing high standards achieved and maintained.

We regularly engage with the companies in which pension funds invest on issues including board structures and executive remuneration.

Our Corporate Governance and Voting Policy provides guidance to investors and companies on a wide range of corporate governance matters, including remuneration.

Contact Information Hermes Equity		
Jennifer Walmsley, Director National Association of Pension Funds	+44 (0)20 7680 3777	j.walmsley@hermes.co.uk
Will Pomroy, Policy Lead: Corporate Governance BT Pension Scheme	+44 (0)20 7601 1719	will.pomroy@napf.co.uk
Daniel Ingram, Head of Policy RPMI Railpen	+44 (0)20 7680 2368	d.ingram@btps.co.uk
Deborah Gilshan, Corporate Governance Counsel USS Investment Management Ltd	+44 (0)20 7220 5012	deborah.gilshan@rpmi.co.uk
Dr Daniel Summerfield, Co-head Responsible Investment	+44 (0)20 7972 0300	d.summerfield@uss.co.uk

This communication is directed at professional recipients only.

The activities referred to in this document are not regulated activities under the Financial Services and Markets Act. This document is for information purposes only. It pays no regard to any specific investment objectives, financial situation or particular needs of any specific recipient. No action should be taken or omitted to be taken in reliance upon information in this document. Any opinions expressed may change. This document may include a list of Hermes Equity Ownership Services Limited ('HEOS') clients. Please note that inclusion on this list should not be construed as an endorsement of HEOS' services. HEOS has its registered office at Lloyds Chambers, 1 Portsoken Street, London, E1 8HZ.

20.2 Feedback from 2012 Seminar

On 27th February 2012, Hermes EOS and the National Association of Pension Funds (NAPF) hosted a meeting with representatives from 44 FTSE 100 companies and 42 occupational pension funds to consider solutions to the problems associated with executive pay. The discussion focused on how long-term investors can best support companies in improving remuneration practices through engagement and considered use of their voting powers.

Observations from the seminar:[1]

> 'It was very useful for remuneration committee members, often for the first time, to be exposed to the views and concerns of pension fund representatives in relation to executive remuneration. Pension funds' voices are often not heard sufficiently clearly or directly and this needs to change. Improving stewardship by funds will also involve greater accountability of their fund managers on matters such as pay.
>
> The growing complexity of remuneration actually encouraged the trend of de-linking pay from performance and reduced the incentive effect of remuneration structures. This phenomenon could also be one of the causes of the increases in pay, as complexity encouraged discounting of the value of awards by executives.
>
> The typical three-year vesting period of long-term incentive plans (LTIPs) was considered insufficient.
>
> Alignment with long-term owners and companies' employees – achieving long-term success lies in the responsibility of company boards to drive the right culture and behaviours through the organisations.'

---

1 See http://www.hermes.co.uk/NewsEvents/DisplayPostsbyCategory/tabid/637/PostID/237/language/en-US/Default.aspx for more information.

21 F&C

21.1 Introduction

F&C has kindly allowed the publication of its remuneration guidance in this book.

F&C Asset Management is a leading diversified multi-specialist investment management group with a heritage spanning more than 140 years to the launch of the world's first collective investment – the Foreign & Colonial Investment Trust.

With over 25 years' experience, F&C are at the forefront of ethical investing. It has one of the largest dedicated teams in Europe and an ethical fund range containing UK equity, global equity and fixed income options.

F&C has approximately £100 billion of assets under management.

The excerpts below are from the general corporate governance guidelines and guidelines for the UK. They both contain a section on remuneration, which outlines F&C's approach to this matter. The reader may also find of interest two other papers: its 2011 viewpoint on Credit Quality as Bonus Underpin[1] aimed at the banking sector as well as this year's (2012) viewpoint on bank pay.[2]

F&C approaches the issue of quantum on a case-by-case basis. The starting point is the remuneration committee's ability to justify the quantum of remuneration they propose to pay top executives to shareholders, as well as other stakeholders in the company. F&C is reviewing whether its current policy on quantum needs to be taken further.

For further information please contact:

Eugenia Jackson
Senior Analyst, Governance & Sustainable Investment

Tel: +44 (0) 20 7011 4284

Eugenia.jackson@fandc.com

---

1 http://www.fandc.com/FundNets_FileLibrary/file/co_GSI_reo_viewpoint_February_2011.pdf
2 http://www.fandc.com/FundNets_FileLibrary/file/Bank_Pay.pdf

21.2 Voting on remuneration

'F&C will consider all votes relating to remuneration on their merits, and vote against a policy or individual schemes where it considers that these are not in the best interests of the company and its shareholders. F&C strongly welcomes dialogue with companies on remuneration issues.

F&C will vote against schemes that could lead to excessive dilution, unless there are extenuating circumstances.

Where substantial awards can be made under a scheme, and are not backed up by appropriate disclosure, F&C will usually vote against.

If F&C considers the overall award package excessive, and no acceptable justification is provided, F&C will vote against.

F&C may oppose the re-election of the chairman or members of the remuneration committee if the company lacks a far-reaching clawback policy despite recent material restatements.

F&C may oppose the re-election of the chairman or members of the remuneration committee if the company had a significant vote against the remuneration plan in the prior year, yet had not made material adjustments to its remuneration structures.'

21.3 Remuneration Guidance

In F&C's general corporate governance guidelines, its Chapter 5 covers remuneration. They state:

'Remuneration

Levels of remuneration and other incentives should be adequate to recruit, incentivise and retain appropriate staff, reflecting the work carried out and the executives' contribution to the company. No director should be involved in setting his own remuneration. F&C expects companies to demonstrate the alignment of their remuneration policy with their overall business strategy and planning. F&C sees no useful purpose in setting guidelines for levels of cash remuneration beyond the principles mentioned below. However, given the strong upward trend in total remuneration, F&C expects greater disclosure and justification of benchmarks and performance targets. F&C expects justification of base pay levels awarded, and that a significant proportion of total remuneration should be subject to performance conditions. F&C supports the ABI's Principles of Remuneration, which were released in September 2011. These remuneration principles underscore the importance of linking remuneration to strategy and risk, and also place emphasis on remuneration committees having the greatest accountability to ensure that remuneration systems are responsible and fair.

Relationship to strategy and risk

F&C expects companies to demonstrate the alignment of their remuneration policy with their overall business strategy and planning. Performance metrics should relate to the company's articulated strategy and risk tolerance. Targets should be constructed to align executive incentives to the interests of long-term shareholders, and should not create incentives for executives to undertake short-term risks that might imperil longer-term performance. F&C advocates the introduction of risk-related underpins – or preconditions – to bonus awards, to ensure that inappropriate incentive payments are not awarded in the event the company's financial strength or credit quality might deteriorate.[18]

Disclosure

F&C seeks appropriately detailed disclosure of board and management remuneration packages. The purpose of the remuneration report should be to enlighten and enhance understanding; it should not be used simply as a compliance document. The annual remuneration report should disclose the total amount of remuneration including cash, options, stock and benefits that executives may receive under different performance scenarios. Pension arrangements for executives and employees should be disclosed in detail, including expected funding and pay-out scenarios.

Where consideration of commercial confidentiality may prevent fuller disclosure of specific short-term targets at the start of the performance period, F&C expects companies to disclose these targets retrospectively. Following the award of the bonus or vesting of the equity incentive awards, companies should provide a meaningful analysis in the remuneration report of the extent to which the relevant targets were actually met. Companies should also include details on how, and in which cases, the remuneration committee might exercise its authority to withhold or reclaim all or part of non-base pay from executives. The remuneration report should be written in plain English and include the tax implications for the company. The company should not compensate management for changes in national tax regulations. Where tax efficient schemes are designed for the benefit of executives, F&C would expect the net result to be cost-neutral to the company.

At a minimum, the remuneration of all directors, including all non-executive and executive directors, should be disclosed individually, and there should be banded disclosure of those individuals at sub-board level who make a significant contribution to the group. This enables shareholders better to understand the company's remuneration strategy, including succession planning and where incentive-related risks might lie.

Executive contracts

Executive contracts should not be for more than 12 months, except in unusual cases, for example, where an initial 24-month period is required for recruitment. In such cases, the notice period should reduce month by month until the agreed period of no more than 12 months is attained. F&C also believes that, prior to agreeing employment contracts, companies should actively consider the potential rewards on severance in the event of inadequate performance, and clarify the performance conditions under which such severance benefits are to be payable. F&C expects companies to seek mitigation in case a director has taken up employment elsewhere and to adjust the length and size of any payments accordingly. F&C considers it best practice that the maximum amount does not exceed one year's base pay and pension entitlements.

Share schemes & dilution

F&C believes that strict guidelines should be observed with regard to the issue, or potential issue, of shares for incentive schemes, both as to the proportion of shares issued and to the rate at which these are issued each year. Normally, F&C would expect no more than a total of 10% of a company's equity to be used for all share schemes within a 10-year period, with no more than 5% being available for discretionary schemes during this period. Treasury shares should be included within these limits. Best practice is to include all shares used, whether market purchased or newly issued, within these limits. F&C will deviate from these limits where it is convinced that the commercial drivers outweigh the dilution impacts. If the company is insufficiently transparent regarding the details of such schemes, F&C may abstain or even vote against them.

Equity Incentive Plans

F&C supports the principle of motivating and rewarding executives through the granting of equity incentives. Schemes should be structured to reward long-term growth in shareholder value, and be subject to performance-vesting.

Performance targets for equity incentive schemes should be clearly disclosed and challenging. F&C believes that the remuneration committee is in the best position to determine the most appropriate performance metrics for driving the long-term business strategy.

However, overall remuneration packages should reflect a range of performance targets and should not rely too heavily on the achievement of a single performance metric. In cases where a relative performance measure, such as total shareholder return, is employed, use of an absolute performance metric should serve as an underpin to ensure that rewards are scaled back if the company's overall performance suffers. Generally, F&C believes executive pay plans should reflect a balance of financial, operational, and relative performance targets.

F&C opposes fixed caps on pay and strongly believes that exceptional performance over a significant period merits an exceptional level of remuneration. The length of the performance period should, to the extent possible, reflect the strategic time horizon of the company's business and risk profile to ensure that management rewards reflect sustainable long-term value creation. It is ultimately the responsibility of the remuneration committee to justify the quantum of incentive rewards paid to executive management.

F&C will consider one-off equity awards on a case-by-case basis in light of justification provided by the company. However, frequent use of exceptional awards raises questions over the adequacy of the overall remuneration strategy. F&C will take particular care when reviewing equity awards granted for the purposes of retention when such awards are not linked to stretching performance targets. Barring exceptional circumstances, F&C will not support the award of free shares to executives that were overlooked for the position of chief executive.

F&C encourages the inclusion of social, environmental and other non-financial goals for performance-related payments, where these factors have a significant impact on the company's performance. F&C also expects a discussion of the process undertaken by the company to identify such factors and an explanation as to why it considers these factors to be relevant. If the company chooses not to include any such factors in an industry where they are significant contributors to business success, the company should explain the reasons for this.

Holding periods, vesting and "Clawback" policies

Bonus payment and long-term incentive schemes should be structured to reward long-term growth in shareholder value, and be subject to performance-vesting conditions. F&C encourages a portion of the short-term bonus to be satisfied in deferred shares. Longer-term incentive plans should be share-based, and vesting periods should extend from three to five years.

The remuneration committee should maintain authority to withhold or reclaim (ie "claw back") all or part of performance-based pay from executives in cases where it deems it appropriate.[3] This might occur following a significant restatement of accounts, where previously granted awards were paid on the basis of inaccurate figures or where the long-term outcomes of a specific strategy result in significant value destruction for shareholders.

In particular, where representations that executives made to the audit committee about the integrity of controls have been revealed to be inaccurate, or where executives have failed to exercise due caution in the discharge of their duties, the company should consider seeking the reclamation of performance awards.

Clawback policies may also be supplemented with extended deferral periods for share and bonus plans.

Ex-gratia and transaction payments

F&C expects that any ex-gratia and transaction payments be subject to prior shareholder approval. F&C would not normally support transaction bonuses which are not linked to a measurement of value creation over time.

Employee ownership

Widespread employee ownership can positively contribute to shareholder value, as it further aligns employees' interests with those of shareholders. Such devices should not, however, be instituted as anti-takeover devices, and should be included within company-wide dilution limits. While F&C generally supports broad-based stock option plans, employee discounts should not exceed 20% on a fixed date, the company should not extend loans to purchase options, and options should not be re-priced without shareholder approval. Non-executive directors should not be entitled to options and therefore should not be included in any such schemes.

Remuneration Committee

The remuneration committee is responsible for setting the remuneration of executive directors and senior executives, and should co-ordinate with the Group Human Resources function to develop a coherent and effective remuneration strategy throughout the company. It should consist exclusively of independent non-executive directors, at least three in number. While F&C recognises that the UK Corporate Governance Code suggests that an independent chairman may be a

---

3 F&C's 2005 Annual Voting & Governance Report and 2006 Corporate Governance guidelines asked for the remuneration committee to use its discretion to claw back bonus payments where these had been based on misstated accounts and/or misleading representations as to the effectiveness of internal controls http://www.fandc.com/uploadFiles/co_gsri_annual_voting_governance_report_2005.pdf

member of, though not chair, the remuneration committee, F&C strongly prefers that he attend by invitation only.

F&C encourages remuneration committees to engage in direct dialogue with their largest institutional shareholders so as to seek support prior to the formal adoption of remuneration policies.

The remuneration committee must consult with other board functions to ensure that pay mechanisms are well aligned with strategic goals and the corporation's appetite for risk. In particular it must work with the board to determine the appropriate balance in the allocation of profits to employees as incentive payment, to shareholders as dividends and for retention or reinvestment in the business itself. The committee's fiduciary duty is also to ensure that the quantum of payment to management is fair and appropriate. Finally, the committee should be attentive to compensation across the corporation to assure itself that management is driving risk and strategy properly and addressing other important issues linked to pay such as discrimination and glass ceilings.'

F&C also publishes a separate paper F&C Position on Remuneration which largely replicate the above but contains additional commentary on variable pay. This notes in particular:

'Variable Pay and Equity Incentive Plans

F&C supports the principle of motivating and rewarding executives through the granting of variable pay. Annual bonuses serve the purpose of rewarding executive performance in terms of implementing the company's strategy. Such bonuses are typically comprised of key performance indicators, both financial and operational, that reflect the company's strategy – often in a balanced scorecard context. As noted above, these metrics should be clearly disclosed and the company should ensure that the rationale behind bonus awards is clearly explained and justified. While F&C has no specific guidelines as to bonus limits, it expects annual bonus opportunities to be capped at a reasonable percentage of salary, and will challenge annual bonus payments for years in which the company has experienced weaknesses in performance that are not fully captured by the defined performance metrics. In this context F&C expects remuneration committees to exercise appropriate discretion in the granting of incentive awards to ensure that rewards are a fair reflection of overall company performance.

Long-term share-based schemes should be structured to reward long-term growth in shareholder value, and be subject to performance-vesting. Performance targets for equity incentive schemes should be clearly disclosed and challenging and the company should not soften pre-agreed performance metrics to allow for bonus payments that otherwise would not have been made. F&C believes that the remuneration committee is in the best position to determine the most appropriate performance metrics for driving the long-term business strategy. However, overall remuneration packages should reflect a range of performance targets and should not rely on the achievement of a single performance metric. In cases where a relative performance measure, such as total shareholder return, is employed, use of an absolute performance metric can serve as an underpin to ensure that rewards are scaled back when the company's overall performance suffers. Generally, F&C believes executive pay plans should reflect a balance of financial, operational, and relative performance targets.

F&C believes that exceptional performance over a significant period merits an exceptional level of remuneration. The length of the performance period should, to the extent possible, reflect the strategic time horizon of the company's business and risk profile to ensure that management rewards reflect sustainable long-term value creation. It is ultimately the responsibility of the remuneration committee to justify the quantum of incentive rewards paid to executive management.

F&C will consider one-off equity awards on a case-by-case basis in light of justification provided by the company. However, frequent use of exceptional awards raises questions over the adequacy of the overall remuneration strategy. F&C will take particular care when reviewing equity awards granted for the purposes of retention when such awards are not linked to stretching performance targets. Barring exceptional circumstances, F&C will not support the award of free shares to executives that were overlooked for the position of chief executive.

F&C encourages the inclusion of social, environmental and other non-financial goals for performance-related payments, where these factors have a significant impact on the company's performance.'

Other Useful F&C Publications

F&C's voting record and guidelines for voting:

http://www.fandc.com/new/Institutional/Default.aspx?ID=80958

F&C Responsible Investment Report 2011:

http://www.fandc.com/FundNets_FileLibrary/file/398_7252_RIM_Ann_Report_WEB.pdf

22 Fidelity

22.1 Introduction

Fidelity has kindly allowed the publication of its remuneration guidance in this book, which is reproduced below.

One area where Fidelity is different to others is in regard to the length of long term incentive schemes, where it favours at least either a five year performance period, or a three year performance period and a minimum further two years holding, so making the incentive over five years in total. Their guidelines say 'The period for performance measurement and vesting should be at least three years in duration but there should be a period of at least five years between the date of grant of the award and any sale of shares. Ideally at least a portion of these shares should be career shares which must be retained until the termination of employment or retirement.'

> 'Fidelity is one of the UK's largest investment fund managers with over 660,000 customers in the UK. We look after assets worth £162.5 billion and are dedicated to achieving the best possible returns for our investors.
>
> **Our philosophy**
>
> Since Fidelity Worldwide Investment was established in 1969, we have been committed to creating funds that help our clients make wise investment choices.
>
> **Corporate Governance**
>
> At Fidelity we believe in making sure we know that the companies we invest in are managed legally and responsibly. We see this as a key element of our commitment to act in the best interests of our clients at all times.
>
> The excerpts below are from the Fidelity website https://www.fidelity.co.uk/investor/about/corporate-governance/default.page
>
> For further information please contact: Trelawny Williams, Trelawny.Williams@fil.com

22.2 Voting on remuneration

Remuneration Policy

It is in the interest of shareholders that boards should have the ability to attract and retain the highest quality of executive directors. In our view setting appropriate remuneration levels is primarily the responsibility of the remuneration committee of the board and will be a market-based judgement although all remuneration arrangements should be aligned with the interests of the shareholders and be proportionate to the contribution of the individuals concerned. Companies should also seek to achieve an appropriate balance between the rewards to management and the returns to shareholders.

We support the concept of variable remuneration and believe that properly crafted incentive schemes play a role in aligning the interests of management and owners. We encourage management ownership of shares and over time we expect executive directors to build a shareholding in the company which is material in relation to their remuneration such that over time dividend income can become a meaningful component of their remuneration.

The remuneration committee should play a key role in ensuring the correct balance between the potential rewards for management and the dilution of shareholders' interests. Incentive schemes should be voted on by shareholders and should be designed to ensure that the rewards reflect genuine outperformance and the creation of additional shareholder wealth by the executives. All relevant information should be disclosed to enable shareholders to reach an informed decision on the likely costs and benefits of a proposal and unnecessary complexity should be avoided. Once a scheme has been approved by shareholders and brought into operation, there should be continuing disclosure of how it is working in practice relative to its original benchmarks.

We strongly support the use of performance driven vesting criteria and believe that these should incorporate a combination of absolute and relative return targets and a direct linkage with share price performance. There should also be a period of mandatory retention once a share award has vested.

Boards should not sanction rewards for failure and should seek to mitigate termination costs. Ex-gratia payments to directors should always be the subject of a specific vote of approval from shareholders and as a generality we do not support rolling service contracts for executive directors of more than twelve months in duration. For additional detail on our approach to incentive schemes for the senior executives at UK and European listed companies, please refer to the Appendix.

22.3 Appendix

Guidelines on remuneration plans for senior executives at UK and European listed companies

A. Terms and provisions of share incentive plans and share option plans:

1. The dilution effect of the new shares authorised under the plan plus the shares reserved to be issued under all other stock option plans should not be greater than 10% in any rolling 10-year period.
2. The Board should not be able materially to alter the plan without shareholder approval.
3. There should not be a performance retesting period for grants of new shares. If performance targets for a given year are not met then awards for that year should be foregone.
4. The period for performance measurement and vesting should be at least three years in duration but there should be a period of at least five years between the date of grant of the award and any sale of shares. Ideally at least a portion of these shares should be career shares which must be retained until the termination of employment or retirement.
5. The offering price of options must be at least 100% of fair market value at the date of grant.
6. The terms of share plans should not permit the re-pricing of options.

B. The use of performance criteria:

1. For plans that grant awards whose vesting conditions are based in whole or in part upon the company's performance relative to a comparator group, FIL will generally vote against such plans if they allow for any portion of the award to vest for below median performance.

   We also encourage the use of a comparator group comprised of a reasonable number of constituent companies whose business profiles are broadly similar to that of the subject company.

2. For plans that grant awards whose vesting conditions are based in whole or in part upon attainment of internal measures of performance such as earnings per share:

   a. FIL will have regard to consensus expectations in evaluating whether the proposed targets are sufficiently challenging; and

   b. To the extent such internal measures are intended to encourage a company's organic growth, the performance hurdles should be adjusted to account for the impact of subsequent corporate actions such as mergers and/or acquisitions.

3. We encourage the use of sliding scales which correlate the reward potential with a performance scale. In the event of a change of control, performance conditions should not be waived and awards should also be determined on a time pro-rated basis.

C. Voting:

In those instances where the terms of proposed share incentive schemes and option plans are not consistent with FIL's guidelines we will consider voting against a Remuneration Report. On occasion we may accompany this vote with a vote against the re-election of the Chairman of the Remuneration Committee in question.

Other Useful Fidelity Publications

For these and other information visit https://www.fidelity.co.uk/investor/about/corporate-governance/default.page

23 IoD

The IoD (Institute of Directors) was founded in 1903 and obtained a Royal Charter in 1906. The IoD is a non-party political organisation with upwards of 45,000 members in the United Kingdom and overseas. Membership includes directors from right across the business spectrum. See www.iod.com for more information about the IoD.

Together with the ecoDa[1] it published the Corporate Governance Guidance and Principles for Unlisted Companies in the UK (First edition: November 2010) and has kindly agreed for the following excerpts to be reproduced in this book.

The main parts relating to remuneration are the key concept number (vii) aligning incentives and Principle 5. The following comments extracted from the full guidance which runs to 55 pages help to put the remuneration comments into context. The IoD have kindly agreed to these extracts being reproduced in this book.

23.1 Introduction

> 'This initiative has been made possible thanks to the pioneering work of ecoDa, which developed the original European text from which this UK edition has been adapted.
>
> Of the UK's 2.6 million registered companies, most are not listed or quoted on tradable equity markets. The overwhelming majority are SMEs or start-up companies that remain under the ownership and control of the founder or founding family.
>
> Such unlisted enterprises are the backbone of the UK economy. They account for a significant proportion of its GDP and employment. Furthermore, they are a key source of dynamism and entrepreneurial spirit.

1 ecoDa, the European Confederation of Directors' Associations, is a not-for-profit association acting as the European voice of board directors, active since March 2005 and based in Brussels. On behalf of its ten national institutes of directors, ecoDa ensures that their views on corporate governance are clearly communicated to policymakers in the EU institutions. ecoDa acts as a high-level forum for debate and for the exchange of experiences to promote high standards for directors in Europe. It acts as a standing body where national experiences are shared and discussed in detail. www.ecoda.org

The principles provide a governance roadmap for family owners or founder-entrepreneurs as they plan the development of their companies over the corporate life cycle. These principles may be relevant for subsidiary companies and joint ventures as well. Even state-owned companies or social enterprise organisations can be inspired by the best practices laid down here.

According to the OECD,[2] a corporate governance framework consists of three main elements:

- A set of relationships between a company's management, its board, its shareholders and other stakeholders.
- A structure through which the objectives of the company are set and the means of attaining those objectives and monitoring performance are determined.
- Proper incentives for the board and management to pursue objectives that are in the interests of the company and its shareholders.'

23.2 Foundations of good governance – key concept (vii) Aligning incentives

'The incentives of directors and employees are primarily (although not entirely) shaped by the firm's remuneration policy. Remuneration is an issue that frequently attracts the attention of the media. Indeed, an impression may be gained from the public discourse that corporate governance is almost entirely about remuneration, which is of course a gross distortion.

Unlisted companies benefit from the fact that they are not subject to the same degree of public scrutiny and mandatory transparency regarding remuneration as publicly listed companies. However, unlisted companies have an equal need to ensure that remuneration policy is incentivising behaviour from directors, managers and employees in a way that is consistent with the long-term interests of the enterprise.

Furthermore, a credible and transparent remuneration policy can help win the commitment and loyalty of company stakeholders (eg employees, suppliers, providers of finance, the media, and the local community) to the company's objectives.

Some important issues of remuneration policy include the following:

- What are the relevant benchmarks and performance criteria in the remuneration process?

---

2 OECD Principles of Corporate Governance (2004), page 11.

- Who makes the decisions about remuneration?
- How much information regarding remuneration issues should be disclosed?'

23.3 Principle 5: Levels of remuneration

'Levels of remuneration should be sufficient to attract, retain, and motivate executives and non-executives of the quality required to run the company successfully.

Key points

A clear distinction must be made between the remuneration of executives and non-executives. The former are full-time employees of the company, and are responsible for its operational activities. In contrast, non-executives are "office holders" rather than company employees, and dedicate their time to the company on a part-time basis. Remuneration structure should reflect these differing roles.

Members of the board are ultimately accountable to shareholders for their remuneration. However, in practice, many boards will themselves define and propose to the shareholders' meeting any change in their annual remuneration.

Levels of remuneration for non-executive directors should reflect the time commitment and responsibilities of the role.

Caution should be exercised when linking non-executive remuneration to company performance.

The board should develop a formal executive remuneration policy and a transparent procedure for implementing the policy, eg in terms of fixing the remuneration packages of individual executives and non-executives.

No one should be involved in deciding on his or her own remuneration.

Boards should compare the remuneration of their executives and non-executives with that of other relevant companies. But they should use such comparisons with caution, in view of the risk of an upward ratchet of remuneration levels with no corresponding improvement in performance.

Boards should be sensitive to pay and employment conditions elsewhere in the company, especially when determining annual salary increases.

A significant proportion of executive remuneration should be structured so as to link rewards to corporate and individual performance. They should be designed to align their interests with those of shareholders and other key stakeholders, and give these executives incentives to perform at the highest levels.

The board should consider the financial implications of early termination of executives' terms of office. In addition, careful thought should be given to notice or contract periods. The aim should be to avoid rewarding poor performance.

Practical considerations for unlisted companies

Although board remuneration is ultimately a matter for shareholders, initial responsibility over this area is often delegated to the board (through the firm's articles of association, although board decisions may still require approval from shareholders).

In contrast to executives, non-executive directors are normally remunerated on a fixed-fee basis. This is to ensure that non-executives retain an objective and independent perspective on the activities of the company. For this reason, share options would not normally form part of a non-executive's remuneration framework.

Shareholders and boards may consider the rewarding of non-executives through stock. However, although stock ownership may increase the alignment of directors' interests with those of shareholders, the board should be aware that equity holdings may affect external perceptions of independence (see IOD guidelines, principle 11). The compatibility of stock-based remuneration with non-executive duties is ultimately a matter for shareholders.

Although care should be exercised in linking non-executive remuneration to performance, there should exist a relationship between compensation and the attention and effort required of the individual director. Directors should receive higher remuneration for a greater time commitment, eg arising from participation on board committees.

The board should ensure that executive remuneration (particularly that of the chief executive) is reasonable and aligned with the performance of the company. The performance of the company should be measured not only in terms of the achievement of short-term financial targets, but also on the basis of a qualitative assessment of the extent to which a company is fulfilling its longer-term objectives.

In an increasing number of companies, boards develop and disclose a remuneration policy statement covering board members and key executives. Such policy statements specify the relationship between remuneration and performance, and include criteria that emphasise the longer-run interests of the organisation over short-term considerations.

For unlisted companies this external transparency may initially be a bridge too far, but open governance information can be a step on the road to a higher degree of professionalism and transparency (certainly for Phase II companies).[3]

Good practice in executive remuneration is likely to consider the following elements in its design:

- A balance between fixed and variable pay, and the linkage of variable pay to pre-determined performance criteria
- Deferment of some proportion of variable pay
- In cases where shares are granted, a minimum vesting period. A requirement to retain some proportion of those shares until the conclusion of employment
- The reclaim of variable pay paid on the basis of data which subsequently proves to be manifestly misstated ("clawback")
- A limit on severance pay, and non-payment of severance pay in case of poor performance.

It is important that both executive and non-executive compensation is as transparent and straightforward as possible. It is helpful to canvas what other similar companies pay to ensure that compensation is not out of line, and many boards turn to external experts for this information.

However, boards should exercise caution in their use of remuneration consultants or head-hunters in defining pay levels. In particular, they should pay attention to consultants' potential conflicts of interest (eg in advising both executives and non-executives from the same company). The board needs to develop its own pay philosophy, and should avoid just going along with the crowd.'

[3] Phase 2 companies are defined by the IOD as those who have gone past the initial start-up phase.

24 Others

Chapters 14 to **23** have shown a wide range of views of those who have an interest in directors' remuneration. There are many others who impact on directors' remuneration. Some of these are discussed below.

24.1 Fund Managers

Fund managers are intermediaries in the chain between the ultimate investor and the company. Fund managers compete to manage the assets of investors. They have different views on executive compensation. Some use their view of remuneration as a source of competitive advantage and differentiation.

The views of Hermes, F&C and Fidelity are shown in **Chapters 20, 21** and **22**.

Two other fund managers' views worthy of note are those of Threadneedle and Old Mutual, which are given below.

24.2 Threadneedle

Iain Richards is Head of Governance and Responsible Investment at Threadneedle Investments. Thread-needle is a leading active investment manager and the international investment management arm of Ameriprise Financial, one of the 40 largest asset management firms globally.

The following article is reproduced from MM&K's December 2013 Board Walk briefing for remuneration committees and reflects Threadneedle's views.

> *Iain Richards of Threadneedle Investments describes how he looks at executive remuneration and the new remuneration disclosure rules*
>
> When we consider a company's remuneration arrangements, we will generally focus on the six questions in the panel [below].
>
> When companies draw up their extensive remuneration reports they don't always consider the time constraints shareholders may have when it comes to reviewing them. At its worst, I have had as many as 14 report & accounts to look at on a particular day and the remuneration

report is just one small bit of them. The only practical way of managing that is to screen and speed-read them, to decide which need a more in-depth review.

So simplicity, relevance and clarity of the key messages is really important to me. Where the person drafting the report has thought about the reader's perspective and has, say, made intelligent use of graphs and tables, it really makes a difference.

Threadneedle questions for reviewing remuneration reports

1. Are they clear, simple and understandable? – we hope companies will avoid complex, overlapping or over-engineered arrangements
2. Is the package and its elements balanced and proportionate? – that is for example, in relation to other employees, competitors and the marketplace?
3. Is remuneration aligned with strategy? – We look for a clear linkage to the strategic KPIs; consistency across what a company is telling us is important
4. Are payments subject to stretching performance conditions? – for LTIs, we look to see three-year forward looking measures, plus two further years of deferral with risk of malus (limiting that to material misstatement won't impress). We're not particularly keen on EPS as a measure. Despite the problems with its operation, institutional shareholders do like to see some linkage to TSR – after all it's the basis on which they themselves are rewarded
5. Do the policies mitigate the risk of rewards for failure? We attach particular importance to remuneration committees having an overriding discretion to ensure outcomes are appropriate
   and

Most importantly of all, do the arrangements deliver outcomes that reflect the outcomes for our clients? Over the crisis and subsequent downturn this has often not been the case. Banks do spring to mind here, but it's certainly not just them.

A good example of that is likely to be the new ten-year performance graph and associated pay and performance table. Whether or not we feel we need to do an in-depth review, it is something I expect to look at. However, companies will need to add a bit more information to the prescribed minimum if they want to tell their story effectively.

The final new disclosure rules require companies to provide a statement for the coming year which will describe how they are intending to implement the approved future remuneration policy. This will be an important source of information to use in assessing the merits of policies. We have already seen some good examples of detailed but flexible policies in draft. A good one should, for example, provide the company with enabling rights (for example the discretion to add deferral to awards vesting from LTIPs where that is not current practice), allow for exceptional circumstances and enable reasonable flexibility to ensure outcomes are sensible.

We do not want to tie companies in knots as they adapt to the new legally binding regime, so we will generally look to be flexible with companies where we don't have concerns about how they are approaching pay in practice. That said, where a policy has been framed in rather general terms, we will certainly look to see more detailed explanations about the standards and approach that will be applied (a blank cheque approach won't impress!). Companies need practical flexibility, but we need to understand their focus and the boundaries they intend to operate within.

Generally we do not want to micro-manage companies or stop them applying common sense. Our real problem in this area, often has more to do with companies paying excessively for going sideways or even going backwards. We have little issue with real value creation being rewarded. There is one thing I would flag though: gold-plated executive pensions are almost certain to feature on the investor agenda now! Given the way the rest of the executive package has developed, the preferential arrangements that are seen in many cases simply can't be justified. It really is time for contribution rates to come into line with those for other employees.

Overall, I personally don't think that the blanket approach of the regulations will really add much (other than cost) – shareholders already had the tools required to intervene where it was needed, if they had wanted to. If the public commitments that led to this had been taken forward in a more focused and considered way, it might have been a different story.'

24.3 Old Mutual

This policy applies to Old Mutual Investment Group South Africa, and should not be seen as a global Old Mutual Plc position on executive pay.

'Remuneration of Directors

3.3.1 General principles

- Old Mutual Investment Group expects the Board to maintain a Remuneration Committee that is responsible for the direction and oversight of the company's executive remuneration programme and for regularly evaluating the performance of senior management. In order to be effective and avoid conflicts of interest, this committee must be made up entirely of independent directors with company executives attending by invitation as required. Directors who are chief executive officers of other companies should not sit on the committee. Members of this committee should not be nominated or selected by management.

- Remuneration of executives and senior management should be guided by a remuneration policy which should be tabled for a non-binding shareholder vote on an annual basis.
- Remuneration paid to each executive director and non-executive director must be fully disclosed. Such disclosure should include details of base pay, bonuses, share-based payments, granting of options or rights, restraint payments and all other benefits. Disclosure of the maximum and expected potential dilution that may result from incentive awards granted in the current year is also required. In addition, this information must also be disclosed for the three most highly-paid employees who are not directors in the company.

3.3.2 Remuneration Policy

- Director remuneration should be sufficient and appropriate to incentivise and retain excellence on the Boards of companies Old Mutual Investment Group invests in. Remuneration should be structured to ensure the creation of value for the company and shareholders over the long term. While it is difficult to define set remuneration parameters Old Mutual Investment Group will make use of comparative peer analysis to gauge the appropriateness of remuneration packages.
- Executive remuneration must enjoy independent and objective oversight. Consequently, all members of the Remuneration Committee must be non-executive directors and the majority of the members as well as the chairperson must be independent non-executive directors. Executives may attend on invitation, but must excuse themselves when their remuneration is under consideration. Contrary proposals from issuers will not be supported.
- Where a company releases an executive director to serve as a non-executive director in another company, the remuneration report (or such other disclosure to shareholders where a report is not produced) must state whether the director is permitted to retain any remuneration, including share options.

3.3.3 Base Pay and Bonuses

3.3.3.1 Executive Remuneration

- The majority[1] of executive remuneration should be "at risk" and be linked to both business targets as a whole, and the performance targets of the executive concerned.
- The personal performance targets for executives must include a combination of financial and non-financial targets.
- Business performance objectives may be benchmarked against industry and appropriate competitor performance, as well as fixed or absolute targets; the reasons for setting such targets should be disclosed to shareholders.
- Old Mutual Investment Group will not consider supporting a short-term incentive scheme where the maximum incentive is uncapped unless a clear motivation and full disclosure on the performance requirement is presented in the remuneration report. Upper limits of such schemes should be capped as a percentage of basic remuneration.

3.3.3.2 Non-executive remuneration

- Non-executive remuneration should be merit based, determined by the issuer according to performance standards, and each director should therefore receive an appropriate rate that may be different from other non-executive directors. Remuneration should be directly linked to the time, commitment and expertise of the non-executive director. Old Mutual Investment Group will not typically enquire into the reasonability of the performance standards or the reasons for the differentials but will require confirmation regarding measurements that are defined and objectively based.
- Fees for non-executive directors should be proposed to shareholders for their approval on an annual basis. Explanations for the resolutions provided in the notice of the meeting should clearly indicate the quantum of fees proposed for the Chairman, the Deputy Chairman, Lead Independent director, the Chairman of the Board committees, members of the committees and directors.
- Old Mutual Investment Group will support non-executive directors being paid an attendance fee and will support individual director's fees reflecting attendance levels, as well as participation on board committees.

---

1 'The majority' is a much more useful term than 'a significant proportion' in the Code.

- Share options for non-executives will not be supported as Old Mutual Investment Group is of the view that it compromises their independence.

Old Mutual Investment Group will, however, support a proposal where a portion of director fees is paid in shares, subject to vesting conditions.

- In exceptional circumstances, and only once alternate strategies have been explored and rejected, Old Mutual Investment Group will consider a one-off share option grant to non-executive directors as a specific empowerment strategy and for justifiable commercial reasons, subject to the following:
  - full disclosure of quantum, strike price, time of issue and assumptions on valuation.
  - the grant is linked to business and personal performance targets.
  - the grant has a vesting period of at least three years.
  - the grant is made at market or mid-market price with no discounting.
  - the scheme rules require the non-executive director to retain the options for one year after termination of the director's contract.
  - the Board is sufficiently independent (by number of people) after issuing the shares to non-executive BEE candidates.

3.3.4 Employment contracts, severance and retirement benefits

- Exit provisions must be monitored to ensure the absence of provisions such as "poison pills" or inappropriately generous "golden parachutes".

  Specifically, there should be no waiver of financial performance targets should there be a change in control of the company or where subsisting options and awards are "rolled over" in the event of a capital restructuring and/or early termination of a participant's employment – short-term and long-term incentives may, however, be paid on a pro rata basis.

- Pension entitlements often represent a significant and costly item of director remuneration. A company should make informative disclosures identifying incremental value accruing to pension scheme participation, or from any other superannuation arrangements, relating to service during the year in question. This should include the cost to the company, the extent to which liabilities are funded, and aggregate outstanding unfunded liabilities.

3.3.5 Share-based and other long-term incentives

- Old Mutual Investment Group will generally not support repricing or "surrender and re-grant" of underwater share options.
- Old Mutual Investment Group will not support share option schemes where the vesting periods are less than three years and the directors have unrestricted discretion with regards the shortening of vesting periods. Vesting periods may only be shortened in respect of retirement, retrenchment, death or change of control of the company. In the event that the share scheme rules do not provide for a limit on the director discretion, this must be confirmed in writing by the issuing company.
- Old Mutual Investment Group will not support options and grants issued at a discount to the market price – pricing should be set at the market price.
- Old Mutual Investment Group will generally not support share grants priced at a discount to net asset value per share.
- Old Mutual Investment Group will only support proposals where the quantum, strike price, time of issue and assumptions regarding valuation of options and grants have been disclosed.
- The potential dilution of shareholder funds or equity should be limited and the maximum possible dilution (ie face value) should be disclosed.
- The group aggregated dilution from a new issue of shares should be limited to 10% of issued share capital in any rolling ten-year period (as adjusted for scrip/bonus and rights issues).
- Old Mutual Investment Group discourages the use of derivative instruments by option participants prior to end of the vesting period.

3.3.6 Remuneration disclosure

Old Mutual Investment Group supports companies that enhance their disclosure. In line with best practice, remuneration disclosure should contain details on the following:

- disclosure of directors' interests, including a director who has resigned during the reporting period.
- disclosure of individual directors' remuneration and benefits, including those of any director who has resigned during the reporting period.
- basic salary, bonuses and performance – related payments and sums paid by way of expense allowance

- charts comprising company performance and CEO pay.
- any other material benefits received, with an explanation as to what this includes.
- contributions paid under any pension scheme.
- any commission, gain or profit-sharing arrangements.
- detail regarding share options including assumptions made in calculations.
- detail regarding remuneration consultants and fees paid.
- composition of the Remuneration Committee.
- a statement in relation to votes cast in relation to remuneration at the last AGM. This statement should include reasons for substantial votes against and actions taken in response.'

24.4 Institutional Investors

An institutional investor is a non-bank person or organisation that trades securities in large enough share quantities or dollar amounts that they qualify for preferential treatment and lower commissions. Institutional investors face fewer protective regulations because it is assumed that they are more knowledgeable and better able to protect themselves.

Some examples of institutional investors are pension funds and life insurance companies.

Larger institutions such as USS, Railpen and BT Pension Fund have strong views on directors' remuneration (see **Chapter 20**).

24.5 High Pay Centre

The High Pay Centre is an independent non-party think tank established to monitor pay at the top of the income distribution and set out a road map towards better business and economic success.

They state:

> 'We aim to produce high quality research and develop a greater understanding of top rewards, company accountability and business performance. We will communicate evidence for change to policymakers, companies and other interested parties to build a consensus for business renewal.
>
> The High Pay Centre is resolutely independent and strictly non-partisan. It is increasingly clear that there has been a policy and market failure in relation to pay at the top of companies and the structures of

business over a period of years under all governments. It is now essential to persuade all parties that there is a better way.'

For more information see http://www.highpaycentre.org/about. The author, Cliff Weight, is a member of the Advisory Board of the High Pay Centre.

24.6 CBI

The CBI is the UK's top business lobbying organisation. It says it has unmatched influence with government, policymakers and legislators.

Its views on directors' remuneration were summarised in its April 2012 submission on the director pay consultation:[2]

'i. Executive remuneration must always be squarely linked to performance. High pay is only ever justified by outstanding performance. High rewards for mediocre performance are unacceptable. And failure should never be rewarded.

ii. The link between pay and performance must be strong, clear and stand up to scrutiny. This has not always been the case. This link needs to be strengthened and its operation clearly demonstrated in every public company.

iii. The corporate governance framework is the right context in which to address this challenge. The UK's corporate governance model is held in high regard. Operated correctly, and with rigour, it enables shareholders to hold Boards to account for their actions, including setting executive pay. It is important that shareholders have the right information and powers to enable them to perform this role effectively, but that they are not encumbered with duties that they lack the time or resource to adequately perform. Transparency and disclosure play a critical part here.'

24.7 TUC

The Trades Union Congress (TUC) frequently comment on directors' remuneration and lobby against high levels of pay. For example on June 20th 2012 following Vince Cable's announcement, TUC General Secretary Brendan Barber said:

'Shareholders have shown increasing unease recently at the mammoth pay and bonus packages enjoyed by those at the top despite, in many cases, poor company performance.

---

2 See http://www.cbi.org.uk/media/1469003/cbi_response_to_bis_consultation_on_shareholder_voting_rights.pdf

> Binding annual votes – or even binding votes every third year if the company chooses that option – where shareholders get to vote on real numbers on pay and actual remuneration packages could mean a new era of more sensible pay setting for those at the top.
>
> But if all shareholders are being asked to do is vote on a vague notion of a company's pay policy little will change and directors' pay will continue to rise at rates ordinary workers can only dream about.
>
> Giving employees a voice in discussions about pay at the top of their organisations is the one reform that would see an immediate reining in of corporate pay excess. Employees who have seen their pay held down or frozen as austerity bites would inject a similar dose of economic reality to the pay of those in the boardroom.
>
> Those with the most to lose from executive pay reform have already persuaded ministers against the 75 per cent approval rating for pay packages – a move which would've given these proposals real bite. Ministers must not allow the business lobby to water down any more government moves to curb executive excess.'

The TUC's website contains many reports about directors' remuneration and corporate governance; see http://www.tuc.org.uk/economy/index.cfm?mins=90&minors=3&majorsubjectID=4.

24.8 EU and G20

The EU continues to debate executive remuneration, but to date has had little impact on UK practices.

CEBS[3] has impacted quite strongly on pay in the financial sector with the FSA/FCA keen to be in line with the G20 proposals and the EU.

[3] Committee of European Banking Supervisors: a former independent advisory group on banking supervision in the European Union.

25 A Remuneration Committee Chairman's View

The preceding chapters have covered the views of the institutional shareholders and their representatives. This chapter (written in 2012) provides an alternative viewpoint from a remuneration committee chairman. Anthony Minns has kindly written the following contribution to this book in which he argues for significant changes to the current orthodoxy on remuneration and governance.

Anthony Minns is Chairman of the Remuneration Committee of Antares Managing Agency Limited, a Lloyd's of London Insurance Syndicate. During his extensive business career he has been a chairman and director of numerous companies.

The views expressed below are his personal opinions and are not necessarily those of either Antares or any other person or entity.

Directors' pay – Does the 'Investor's Spring' mean that directors' pay is at last under control?

MPs foolishly remained in denial about their excessive expense claims and failed to grasp just how angry the public was about the issue. As a result when Nemesis arrived, some had to leave the House of Commons and a few, sadly, ended up the wrong side of a criminal prosecution. Directors have been equally foolish about their large pay packages, choosing to believe the 'Because you are worth it' punch line of an expensive cosmetics advert. Corporate Remuneration Committees too, have failed to grasp the uncomfortable nettle and so have lost control of the issue.

In October 2011, the Financial Times reported that the average pay of the directors of FTSE 100 companies had increased by 49% over the previous period of 12 months. During this same period the average pay of workforces in these companies had increased by only 2.9% and shareholders had seen the average value of their shares increase by only 3.5%. So this huge pay increase could scarcely be described as a reward for superlative performance. Moreover in the prior 12 month period 2009/10, the average pay of the directors of FTSE 100 companies increased by 50%.

The directors' pay issue festered quietly over Autumn/Winter 2011. The Press by then had its teeth into the issue and a high profile was given to the multi-million pound pay awards arising from the 2011 year-end bonus season. Although Remuneration Committees tightened their oversight of these awards and some encouraged directors to forgo salary increases or part of their bonuses, the actual amounts paid out were still so large that the public outcry against 'Boardroom excesses' increased.

Finally, in Spring 2012, institutional investors, fearing a backlash from their pension fund and unit trust customers against their supine approach to directors' pay, lost patience with the inability of Remuneration Committees to control directors' pay and began to use their voting power to oppose the pay policies of the companies in which they had invested. As a result, a number of companies met with serious shareholder revolts. In May 2012, 58.6% of votes cast at the Aviva Annual General Meeting opposed its pay policies. Barclays Bank, Inmarsat, Premier Foods, Reckitt Benckiser, Unilever, William Hill, WPP also faced adverse shareholder reaction. The Chief Executives at Astra Zeneca, Aviva, 3i and Trinity Mirror paid with their jobs for poor corporate performance despite their high personal pay packages. But the wooden spoon award was reserved for the directors and senior managers of Xstrata who decided that in addition to all their usual salary, bonus and long term incentive award payments, they would take £163 million as 'retention awards' plus £44.5 million 'demotion' payments for those who would no longer have the same seniority following the merger with Glencore. Since the annual savings from the proposed merger were only just over £500 million, this proposal attracted an avalanche of criticism. As folk group Peter, Paul and Mary sang 50 years ago 'Oh, when will they ever learn?'

So what are the current control mechanisms on directors' pay and how did we get here?

The seemingly inexorable rise in executive pay started with the Thatcher Government's reduction in the top rate of income tax to 40% in 1988. Whilst this had many welcome effects in boosting both UK economic performance and tax revenues, it also had side effects and one of these was create a surge in executives' pay (and in City of London bonuses!). From 1988 on, it became worth receiving large sums of money. This was certainly not the case earlier when the top rate of income tax was 83% (and 'non-earned' income, such as interest and dividends, was taxed at an additional 15%).

As directors' pay levels surged in the aftermath to low income tax rates, this became a political issue. A series of reports by the 'Great and Good' were published starting with the Cadbury Report in 1995 followed by Greenbury, Higgs and Walker. These Reports were earnest attempts to resolve the issue of how to control directors' pay. All come to broadly the same recommendations that:

- NEDs (Non-Executive Directors) should 'referee' pay awards internally;
- Full, indeed exhaustive, disclosure of directors' pay should be made on a company's annual report and accounts; and
- Directors' pay should be subject to shareholder votes but these would be non-binding on the company.

And all have largely failed!

Why?

They have failed for three fundamental reasons:

First, they overestimate the effective power of NEDs. The principal 'weapon' possessed by an NED is to resign if he disagrees with a Board decision but examples of NEDs of major plcs who have resigned over the issue of directors' pay are scarcer than 'hens' teeth'.

Second, the belief that publishing full details of directors' pay in the company's annual report and accounts will in some way 'embarrass' senior directors into being less greedy has proved ineffective. So many issues now require full disclosure 'ad absurdum' that the average length of large UK plc accounts is now 140 pages. No wonder the Financial Reporting Council is campaigning for the 'de-cluttering' of company accounts. In fact as Chairman of a Remuneration Committee, I now find that these extensive disclosures are used against me. As soon as a competitor publishes an annual report that discloses higher pay levels than ours, 'for information' photocopies appear in my in-tray – with the higher pay numbers highlighted just in case I should miss them. I do note though that the lower numbers are never highlighted!

Third, companies have ruthlessly used the non-binding nature of shareholder votes on director's pay to ignore them.

Most important of all, until the recent 'Investors' Spring', those who should be responsible for dealing with controlling directors' pay, the shareholders, have ducked the issue.

The delicate balance between untrammelled capitalism and 'fairness' is under challenge

Protests outside St Paul's Cathedral in the City of London and elsewhere have highlighted the issue of the apparent greed of the privileged few. It is perhaps rather surprising that during the 13 years of office of a 'New Labour' Government, the gap in our society between the 'haves and the have-nots' has widened considerably.

This is not, however, a new problem. Towards the end of the Roman Republic, Cato identified 'publice egestas, privatim opulenta' (public poverty in the midst of private opulence) as a major factor in the decline of the republic.

American economist, J K Galbraith, author of 'The Affluent Society' wrote in 1978 that:

> 'The salary of the chief executive of the large corporation is not a market reward for achievement. It is frequently in the nature of a warm personal gesture by the individual to himself'.

Although the concept that there is an informal 'social contract' between the haves and the have-nots has been widely discredited, there is considerable public distaste for the huge pay increases received over the past two decades by the privileged few as contrasted with the modest pay rises awarded to the majority. NEDs should be aware of public sensitivities and take them into account when setting directors' pay levels. It is after all in the best commercial interest of companies that the societies in which they operate should be both economically and politically stable.

The role of NEDs in controlling directors' pay

NEDs can play a significant role in controlling directors' pay but it is wholly unrealistic to expect that they can achieve this in isolation and unsupported. There has to be some constituency which the NED represents and upon which he or she can call for support if needs be. Ultimately this constituency has to be the owners of the business, the shareholders.

NEDs can have an effective role only if they have more authority than that provided by the threat of resignation.

In my view there are four ways in which NEDS could be made more effective in playing their part in controlling directors' pay. These are:

1. Require NEDs to ensure that alternative candidates are put up regularly at directors' elections;
2. Limit the amount of legal damages that are payable when directors (and for that matter, the highest paid employees are dismissed);
3. Ensure that NEDs don't 'go native' by limiting their maximum tenure of office to five years; and
4. Compel institutional shareholders either to disclose how they have voted their shareholdings or to allow their investors or policy holders to have a say in the voting process.

Contested elections

In recent years, the UK has sent its armed forces to Afghanistan, the Balkans, Iraq and Libya to ensure that the benefits of democracy are available to the populations of those territories. How can we reconcile that with our major corporates which are run by executives who once appointed, seldom, if ever, have to face a contested election? It is unsurprising therefore that to the public at large our companies and banks appear to be run by self-perpetuating cliques with the freedom to pay themselves whatever they will.

It is reasonable to require that companies should display the democratic characteristics of the society in which they operate. Therefore, companies which have their shares listed on The London Stock Exchange should be required to hold contested elections for their directors every three or five years. This could be achieved by a change to the Listing Agreement entered into by companies when listing their shares in London. It should be a major role of NEDs to supervise these elections and to ensure that there are alternative candidates for each directorship position.

If an executive team is really that good and the company has been performing well under their stewardship, then they should deservedly win the election. If on the other hand, they have been paid over-generously for mediocre performance or worse, then why not allow other executives who think that they can do a better job for less money to have a turn?

It has been argued that it would be disastrous for a major company to face the risk of losing all its senior executives in one election. My answers to this objection are as follows:

First, the UK often loses all its Ministers at one time, following a General Election and the country doesn't come to a halt. Of course, the civil service acts as bridge between the old and the new government and they act as a 'backstop' until the new Ministers are settled in. The middle management layer at corporates can fill the same role.

Second, there is the outstanding example of Eurotunnel Group which changed its entire Board of Directors at a shareholder meeting held in June 2005. Dissident shareholders had put up an alternative team of their own and won the elections. Since then Jacques Gounon and his new team have steered Eurotunnel away from bankruptcy, rescued it from the deathly hands of the banker and hedge funds, returned the business to profits, started paying dividends to shareholders and rewarding its employees appropriately. So a complete change of management can be healthy.

Third, to avoid losing all senior executives in a single election, elections for each directorship role could be staggered across a three year cycle, rather similar to UK local government elections. I am incidentally involved in local politics in a modest way and I am always encouraged to note the return of humility to local Councillors in the months preceding elections.

Limit the amount of compensation payable on loss of office

The Companies Acts should set limits on the amounts of compensation that can be awarded to departing directors. Compensation of no more than 12 months base pay plus pension contributions subject to an overall cap of, say, £500,000 should be more than sufficient.

It is regularly argued by politicians that the UK needs to shake itself out of its 'compensation culture'. This would be a significant step in that direction. The public gets particularly upset at news coverage of multi-million pound payments made to 'failed directors'. We can all remember the public outcry over the termination package paid to Sir Fred Goodwin at RBS.

At present NEDs can be deterred from dismissing non-performing directors because of the huge sums of compensation that the lawyers advise would have to be paid upon termination. This impediment to management change must go.

This is particularly so now that age discrimination legislation means that senior directors as well as other employees may have an expectation of continuing in office after what was previously 'normal retirement age'. Of course, they are likely to want to hold on to their million pound pay packages. This is fine if their companies also wish to retain their services but not so good if a change of manager would be in the company's best interests. Even worse, companies may lose their next generation of talented managers if the existing team remain in place blocking promotion opportunities.

Limited tenure for NEDs

This issue has already been identified and tentative recommendations made that NEDs should hold office for only 3 to 5 years. In my view, three years is too short as it can take a year or so for a new NED to grasp fully the fundamentals of the business. If they are to leave mandatorily at the end of three years, this would mean that they are at their most productive for the Company for only two years. I would suggest that the position of each NED be reviewed thoroughly at the end of three years and that, following the review, the Company may or may not choose to extend the engagement for another two years.

This could be 'policed' by making it part of The London Stock Exchange Listing Agreement.

Institutional Shareholder voting should be transparent

The public suspects that institutional shareholders are reticent about exercising ownership control over directors' pay because the fund managers don't want to draw attention to their own pay and bonus packages and there is probably some truth underlying that suspicion.

At the very least, institutional shareholders should be required to vote and to publish the manner in which their votes are exercised. This could be 'policed' by the FSA under its 'best practice' rules.

It would be even better if the underlying private investors were to be given the chance of a say. A sad side-effect of the changes to the Companies Acts which permit companies to provide shareholder documentation and information electronically has been to make private shareholders even more remote from the corporate governance arena as they no longer automatically receive full shareholder documents through the post. It would be a big step towards the 'democratisation' of corporate Britain if institutional shareholders were to permit their private investors whether they be unit trust holders, ISA investors or life insurance policy holders to have an input into the way shareholdings are voted. Some ISA providers already provide this service electronically.

Conclusions

I don't delude myself that all these proposals are likely to be put in place any time soon. The weight of the status quo is hard to shift. If the momentum from the Investors' Spring is to be maintained, major changes in the manner in which directors' pay is 'policed' are required. We need to bring the 'fresh air' of democracy into UK corporate governance. I really look forward to another Eurotunnel style AGM at which an incumbent management team are challenged by an alternative energetic team with refreshing new views on how the business could be run. Boy, that meeting was well attended and so I believe would be future AGMs of the UK's major corporates at which a 'real' voting process was on offer.

26 The Role of the Remuneration Committee

26.1 Introduction

The Remuneration Committee has to interface with many different stakeholders as illustrated in the diagram below.

Figure 10: Remuneration Committee relationships

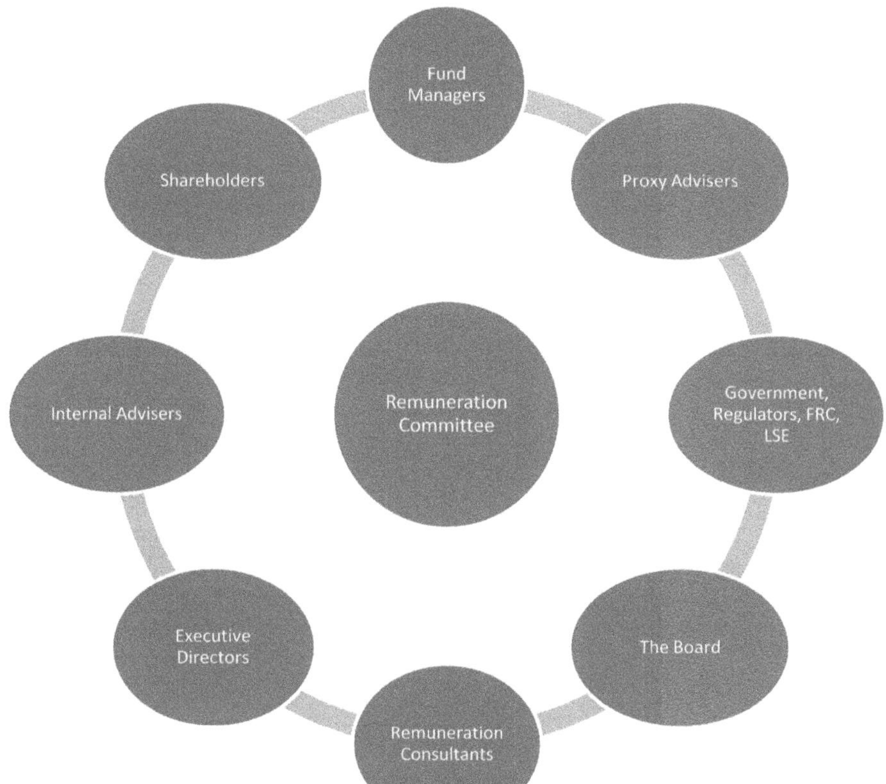

26.2 Terms of reference

The main board will usually delegate to the Remuneration Committee authority with regard to the remuneration of the executive directors, the Chairman and usually some senior executives. The Remuneration Committee will propose its terms of reference which will be approved by the Board. The terms of reference will be summarised in the annual report to shareholders and posted on the company's website.

The UK Corporate Governance Code (the Code) states that:

> 'There should be a formal and transparent procedure for developing policy on executive remuneration and for fixing the remuneration packages of individual directors.'[1]

It goes on to state that:

> 'The Board should establish a remuneration committee … [which] should make available its terms of reference, explaining its role and the authority delegated to it by the Board.'[2]

As with most aspects of corporate governance, the above Principles make it clear that, not only should companies go through a formal process of considering executive remuneration, but they must be seen to be doing so in a fair and thorough manner. It is, therefore, essential that the Remuneration Committee is properly constituted with a clear remit and identified authority.

The Code recommends the committee be made up of at least three independent Non-Executive Directors (although two is permissible for smaller companies).[3]

Although not a Provision in the Code, the Higgs Review states as good practice in its Non-Code Recommendations that the Company Secretary (or their designee) should act as secretary to the committee. It is the Company Secretary's responsibility to ensure that the Board and its committees are properly constituted and advised. There also needs to be a clear co-ordination between the main board and the various committees where the Company Secretary would normally act as a valued intermediary.

The frequency with which the committee needs to meet will vary from company to company and may change from time to time. It is, however, clear that it must meet close to the year end; to review the remuneration report which is required to be prepared under the Directors' Remuneration Report Regulations and be submitted to shareholders with or as part of the

---

1 UK Corporate Governance Code D2
2 UK Corporate Governance Code D2.1
3 UK Corporate Governance Code D2.1

company's annual report for their approval at the AGM. The committee should meet at least twice a year in order to discharge its responsibilities properly.

The list of duties the Institute of Company Secretaries and Administrators (ICSA) has proposed are those contained within the Summary of Principle Duties of the Remuneration Committee which ICSA helped compile for the Higgs Review and which are now appended to the Code. Some companies may wish to add to this list and some smaller companies may need to modify it in other ways. The Code also states that the Chairman of the committee should attend the AGM prepared to respond to any questions that may be raised by shareholders on matters within the committee's area of responsibility.

There is clearly a need for a guiding document for the effective operation of the Remuneration Committee. This has led the ICSA to produce a Guidance Note proposing model terms of reference for a Remuneration Committee. The document draws on the experience of senior company secretaries and best practice as carried out in some of the country's leading companies.

The Code also requires that the terms of reference of the Remuneration Committee, explaining its role and the authority delegated to it by the Board, be made available on request and placed on the company's website.[4]

The model terms of reference were first published in October 2003 and can be downloaded free from www.icsa.org.uk along with much other useful information.

Model Terms of Reference for the Remuneration Committee from ICSA (2010)

'Note: square brackets contain recommendations which are in line with best practice but which may need to be changed to suit the circumstances of the particular organisation.

1. Membership

   The committee shall comprise at least [three] members, all of whom shall be independent non-executive directors. The chairman of the board may also serve on the committee as an additional member if he or she was considered independent on appointment as chairman. Members of the committee shall be appointed by the board, on the recommendation of the nomination committee and in consultation with the chairman of the remuneration committee.

[4] UK Corporate Governance Code D2.1

Only members of the committee have the right to attend committee meetings. However, other individuals such as the chief executive, the head of human resources and external advisers may be invited to attend for all or part of any meeting, as and when appropriate and necessary.

Appointments to the committee are made by the board and shall be for a period of up to three years, which may be extended for further periods of up to three years, provided the director still meets the criteria for membership of the committee.

The board shall appoint the committee chairman who shall be an independent non-executive director. In the absence of the committee chairman and/or an appointed deputy, the remaining members present shall elect one of themselves to chair the meeting who would qualify under these terms of reference to be appointed to that position by the board. The chairman of the board shall not be chairman of the committee.

2. Secretary

The company secretary or his or her nominee shall act as the secretary of the committee.

3. Quorum

The quorum necessary for the transaction of business shall be [two]. A duly convened meeting of the committee at which a quorum is present shall be competent to exercise all or any of the authorities, powers and discretions vested in or exercisable by the committee.

4. Meetings

The committee shall meet at least [twice] a year and otherwise as required.[5]

5. Notice of meetings

5.1 Meetings of the committee shall be called by the secretary of the committee at the request of the committee chairman.

5.2 Unless otherwise agreed, notice of each meeting confirming the venue, time and date together with an agenda of items to be discussed, shall be forwarded to each member of the committee, any other person required to attend and all other non-executive directors, no later than [five] working days before the date of the meeting. Supporting papers shall be sent to committee members and to other attendees, as appropriate, at the same time.

---

[5] The frequency and timing of meetings will differ according to the needs of the company. Meetings should be organised so that attendance is maximised (for example by timetabling them to coincide with board meetings).

6. Minutes of meetings

6.1 The secretary shall minute the proceedings and resolutions of all committee meetings, including the names of those present and in attendance.

6.2 Draft minutes of committee meetings shall be circulated promptly to all members of the committee. Once approved, minutes should be circulated to all other members of the board unless it would be inappropriate to do so.

7. Annual general meeting

The committee chairman should attend the annual general meeting to answer any shareholder questions on the committee's activities.

8. Duties

The committee should carry out the duties below for the parent company, major subsidiary undertakings and the group as a whole, as appropriate.

The committee shall

8.1 determine and agree with the board the framework or broad policy for the remuneration of the company's chairman, chief executive, the executive directors, the company secretary and such other members of the executive management as it is designated to consider.[6] The remuneration of non-executive directors shall be a matter for the chairman and the executive members of the board.[7] No director or manager shall be involved in any decisions as to their own remuneration.[8]

8.2 in determining such policy, take into account all factors which it deems necessary including relevant legal and regulatory requirements, the provisions and recommendations of the UK Corporate Governance Code and associated guidance. The objective of such policy shall be to ensure that members of the executive management of the company are provided with appropriate incentives to encourage enhanced performance and are, in a fair and responsible manner, rewarded for their individual contributions to the success of the company.[9]

---

6 The Code, D.2 and Schedule A, and D.2.2. Recommendations 29–34 of the final report of the Walker review [...] states the remit of remuneration committees of Banks or other Financial Institutions should cover 'high end' employees. The Walker report is available separately from HM Treasury website at www.hm-treasury.gov.uk/walker_review_information.htm.

7 The Code, D.2.3

8 The Code, D.2

9 The Code D.1 Recommendation 35 of the Walker review, November 2009: remuneration committees of Banks or other Financial Institutions should seek advice from the board risk committee on specific risk adjustments to be applied to performance objectives.

8.3 when setting remuneration policy for directors, review and have regard to the remuneration trends across the company or group.[10]

8.4 review the ongoing appropriateness and relevance of the remuneration policy.[11]

8.5 within the terms of the agreed policy and in consultation with the chairman and/or chief executive, as appropriate, determine the total individual remuneration package of the chairman, each executive director, company secretary and other designated senior executives including bonuses, incentive payments and share options or other share awards.[12]

8.6 obtain reliable, up-to-date information about remuneration in other companies.[13] To help it fulfil its obligations the committee shall have full authority to appoint remuneration consultants[14] and to commission or purchase any reports, surveys or information which it deems necessary, within any budgetary restraints imposed by the board

8.7 be exclusively responsible for establishing the selection criteria, selecting, appointing and setting the terms of reference for any remuneration consultants who advise the committee

8.8 approve the design of, and determine targets for, any performance related pay schemes operated by the company and approve the total annual payments made under such schemes

8.9 review the design of all share incentive plans for approval by the board and shareholders. For any such plans, determine each year whether awards will be made, and if so, the overall amount of such awards,

8.10 the individual awards to executive directors, company secretary and other designated senior executives and the performance targets to be used[15]

8.11 determine the policy for, and scope of, pension arrangements for each executive director and other designated senior executives[16]

---

10 The Code, D.1

11 Taking account of the principles in Code, D.1. Recommendation 28 of the Walker review, November 2009: for Banks and Other Financial Institutions this should include responsibility for setting the over-arching principles and parameters of remuneration policy on a firm-wide basis.

12 The Code, D.2

13 The Code, D.1

14 The Code, D.2.1

15 Recommendation 34 of the Walker review, November 2009: remuneration committees of Banks or other Financial Institutions should note the requirements for "high end" employees to maintain a shareholding.

16 The Code, D.2.2

8.12 ensure that contractual terms on termination, and any payments made, are fair to the individual, and the company, that failure is not rewarded and that the duty to mitigate loss is fully recognised[17]

8.13 oversee any major changes in employee benefits structures throughout the company or group

8.14 agree the policy for authorising claims for expenses from the directors

9. Reporting responsibilities

9.1 The committee chairman shall report to the board on its proceedings after each meeting on all matters within its duties and responsibilities.

9.2 The committee shall make whatever recommendations to the board it deems appropriate on any area within its remit where action or improvement is needed.

9.3 The committee shall produce a report of the company's remuneration policy and practices to be included in the company's annual report and ensure each year that it is put to shareholders for approval at the AGM.

10. Other matters

The committee shall

10.1 have access to sufficient resources in order to carry out its duties, including access to the company secretariat for assistance as required

10.2 be provided with appropriate and timely training, both in the form of an induction programme for new members and on an ongoing basis for all members

10.3 give due consideration to laws and regulations, the provisions of the Code and the requirements of the

10.4 UK Listing Authority's Listing, Prospectus and Disclosure and Transparency Rules and any other applicable Rules, as appropriate

10.5 arrange for periodic reviews of its own performance and, at least annually, review its constitution and terms of reference to ensure it is operating at maximum effectiveness and recommend any changes it considers necessary to the board for approval.'

---

[17] The Code, D.1.4 and D.1.5 Recommendation 37 of the Walker review, November 2009 sets out disclosure requirements for remuneration committees of Banks and other Financial Institutions in relation to any additional enhanced benefits for executive directors or other "high end" employees

26.3 Membership and skills

The Remuneration Committee should be comprised of independent directors. The Combined Code was changed in 2006 to permit a Chairman if he or she were independent on appointment to be a member of, but not chair, the Remuneration Committee.

The Chief Executive and the Chairman (if not a member of the committee) will usually be invited to attend Remuneration Committee meetings (in a non-voting capacity) and withdraw when their own pay is discussed.

Committee members require considerable background knowledge and skills with regard to remuneration, including:

- statistics to interpret market data
- business acumen regarding performance measures, including but not limited to accounting knowledge and the potential behaviours and motivations of participants in incentive schemes
- financial theory to understand option valuation and risk
- pensions and actuarial knowledge
- tax, both personal and company tax that is pertinent to remuneration issues
- trust law
- employment law.

A good working knowledge of the above is essential in order to be able to participate in the Remuneration Committee debate. Expert skills are not needed if the Remuneration Committee has access to independent expert advice.

Members also require the ability to read and digest long complex reports.

26.4 Advisers

There is always a danger that a Remuneration Committee is merely asked to rubber-stamp management's proposals. Executive directors have huge internal resources and pay large fees to their consultants to prepare and justify their case for more money, bigger bonuses, increased incentives and better benefits. The scales are not evenly balanced. Remuneration Committees need to take the lead and appoint their own independent advisers who can comment objectively on management's proposals.

The Company Secretary (or an external independent adviser) should be the secretary of the Remuneration Committee. The HR director should not perform this role as he or she works for the CEO and is conflicted.

As noted above, the Chairman works closely with the CEO and is best placed to assess the CEO's performance, his or her current motivation and the risk that they may be lured elsewhere and hence the remuneration required to retain the CEO's services and motivate him or her to achieve tough performance goals and high standards of performance. It is therefore vital that the Chairman attends the Remuneration Committee, but withdraws when his or her own remuneration is discussed.

Similarly the CEO is best placed to provide input on the executives who report to him or her and should also attend Remuneration Committee meetings, but withdraw when his or her own remuneration is discussed. Both the Chairman and the CEO provide valuable input to the committee on the performance of individuals, the risk of them leaving and how easily they could be replaced either internally through normal succession plans or by external recruitment.

The HR director and/or the remuneration and benefits director may be invited to Remuneration Committee meetings. Their input about remuneration elsewhere in the group is particularly valuable. They may also have considerable knowledge of the history of directors' remuneration and of practices in other companies. The HR director or remuneration and benefits director often will also be involved in preparing papers for the committee. Such papers may reflect the views of the Chief Executive and the other executive directors. Few HR or remuneration and benefits directors are prepared to disagree with or disappoint their CEO. There will, however, be times when the Remuneration Committee wishes to discuss items without internal management present.

External consultants are used to provide market data, commentary on trends, latest best practice, to design new incentive arrangements, both short and long-term, and to provide legal, tax and accounting advice. Most of the large accountancy firms have executive compensation consulting arms. For them this is a natural extension of their work in tax, share schemes, HR and audit. Most of the large actuarial firms also have executive compensation consulting arms. In their case it is a natural extension of their work in pensions, benefits and HR consulting. There are also a small number of specialist executive remuneration firms.

The Remuneration Committee must disclose the names of their advisers, who appointed them and what other services they provide to the company, and from October 2013, their fees for advice to the Remuneration Committee.

As noted above, the Remuneration Committee should appoint its own independent remuneration consultants. This is an essential prerequisite for promoting transparency and accountability to shareholders regarding directors' remuneration. Shareholders and other interested parties will continue to be concerned if companies seek advice from consultants who are dependent on executive management for fees for other services to the company. The Enron debacle is only one example of the conflict of interests when advisers are not independent.

Consultants often call themselves 'management consultants', and all too often act as management's consultants! Almost all consultants predicate their business strategy on developing good relationships with executive directors and senior executives and then cross-selling their other consulting services. It is worth noting that the fees for other consulting services will generally dwarf the fees for Remuneration Committee consultancy. Remuneration Committees should ask to see these breakdowns of fees.

Figure 11: Criteria to choose remuneration advisers:

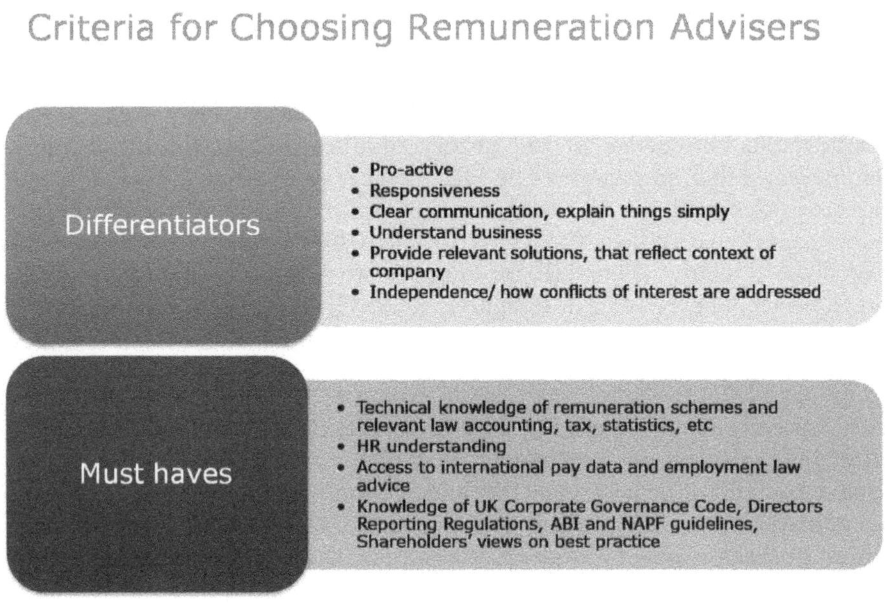

Most remuneration consultants are members of the Remuneration Consultants Group,[18] which has produced its own code of ethics, reproduced in Appendix 6.

26.5 The remuneration setting process

Companies have boards of directors who delegate the remuneration setting process for directors and usually some senior executives to the Remuneration Committee, made up wholly of independent Non-Executive Directors.

18 See http://www.remunerationconsultantsgroup.com/ for further information.

The Chairman of the Remuneration Committee sets the agenda and dates of the meetings, having consulted with the secretary of the committee, the company Chairman, CEO, HR director/remuneration and benefits director, and the committee's adviser. The committee Chairman commissions research and position papers relevant to the agenda items. He briefs other committee members of any contentious issues prior to the meetings and obtains their views.

As noted above, the Chief Executive and the Chairman (if not a member of the committee) will usually attend Remuneration Committee meetings (in a non-voting capacity) and withdraw when their own pay is discussed. They provide valuable input to the committee on the performance of individuals, the risk of them leaving and how easily they could be replaced either internally through normal succession plans or by external recruitment.

The HR director or remuneration and benefits director often will also attend the Remuneration Committee and/or be involved in preparing papers for the committee.

External consultants may also be used to provide data and advice across a range of remuneration issues.

Using all of this advice and assistance, the Remuneration Committee will set the remuneration strategy for the executive directors and senior executives. Typically this will include:

- selection of appropriate comparator group of companies
- identification of desired pay market position and linkage to performance
- mix of fixed and variable compensation
- alignment to shareholders' interests.

Consultants perform another role in this process: they are aware of what is and is not acceptable to shareholders. Some consultants will talk to shareholders and their representatives on behalf of their clients, explain the new remuneration proposals and gain their acceptance. In some cases a negotiation ensues and a compromise deal is done. In some companies the Chairman of the Remuneration Committee or the Chairman will talk to the key shareholders.

Finally, the company will vote in general meeting on new long-term incentive plans and the Remuneration Committee report. Some shareholders may vote against the appointment of individual directors because of remuneration issues.

26.6 US practice regarding CEO pay and performance

The terms of reference of Compensation Committees in the USA tend to be similar to those of UK companies, with the notable exception that in the US the requirements regarding the CEO are usually explicit and imply an assessment of performance, which should link into the CEO compensation.

The New York Stock Exchange's regulations regarding Compensation Committees are as follows

The NYSE Listed Company Manual Section 303A (amended: November 25, 2009 (NYSE-2009–89); January 11, 2013 (NYSE-2012–49)) requires specific duties of the Compensation Committee.

303A.05 Compensation Committee

(a) Listed companies must have a compensation committee composed entirely of independent directors. Compensation committee members must satisfy the additional independence requirements specific to compensation committee membership set forth in Section 303A.02(a)(ii).

(b) The compensation committee must have a written charter that addresses:

   (i) the committee's purpose and responsibilities – which, at minimum, must be to have direct responsibility to:

      (A) review and approve corporate goals and objectives relevant to CEO compensation, evaluate the CEO's performance in light of those goals and objectives, and, either as a committee or together with the other independent directors (as directed by the board), determine and approve the CEO's compensation level based on this evaluation;

      (B) make recommendations to the board with respect to non-CEO executive officer compensation, and incentive-compensation and equity-based plans that are subject to board approval; and

      (C) prepare the disclosure required by Item 407(e)(5) of Regulation S-K;

   (ii) an annual performance evaluation of the compensation committee.

   (iii) The rights and responsibilities of the compensation committee set forth in Section 303A.05(c).

Commentary: In determining the long-term incentive component of CEO compensation, the committee should consider the listed company's performance and relative shareholder return, the value of similar incentive awards to CEOs at comparable companies, and the awards given to the listed company's CEO in past years. To avoid confusion, note that the compensation committee is not precluded from approving awards (with or without ratification of the board) as may be required to comply with applicable tax laws (i.e., Rule 162(m)). Note also that nothing in Section 303A.05(b)(i)(B) is intended to preclude the board from delegating its authority over such matters to the compensation committee.

The compensation committee charter should also address the following items: committee member qualifications; committee member appointment and removal; committee structure and operations (including authority to delegate to subcommittees); and committee reporting to the board.

Boards may allocate the responsibilities of the compensation committee to committees of their own denomination, provided that the committees are composed entirely of independent directors. Any such committee must have a committee charter.

Nothing in this provision should be construed as precluding discussion of CEO compensation with the board generally, as it is not the intent of this standard to impair communication among members of the board.

Website Posting Requirement: A listed company must make its compensation committee charter available on or through its website. If any function of the compensation committee has been delegated to another committee, the charter of that committee must also be made available on or through the listed company's website.

Disclosure Requirements: A listed company must disclose in its annual proxy statement or, if it does not file an annual proxy statement, in its annual report on Form 10-K filed with the SEC that its compensation committee charter is available on or through its website and provide the website address.

(c)

(i) The compensation committee may, in its sole discretion, retain or obtain the advice of a compensation consultant, independent legal counsel or other adviser.

(ii) The compensation committee shall be directly responsible for the appointment, compensation and oversight of the work of any compensation consultant, independent legal counsel or other adviser retained by the compensation committee.

(iii) The listed company must provide for appropriate funding, as determined by the compensation committee, for payment of reasonable compensation to a compensation consultant, independent legal counsel or any other adviser retained by the compensation committee.

(iv) The compensation committee may select a compensation consultant, legal counsel or other adviser to the compensation committee only after taking into consideration, all factors relevant to that person's independence from management, including the following:

(A) The provision of other services to the listed company by the person that employs the compensation consultant, legal counsel or other adviser;

(B) The amount of fees received from the listed company by the person that employs the compensation consultant, legal counsel or other adviser, as a percentage of the total revenue of the person that employs the compensation consultant, legal counsel or other adviser;

(C) The policies and procedures of the person that employs the compensation consultant, legal counsel or other adviser that are designed to prevent conflicts of interest;

(D) Any business or personal relationship of the compensation consultant, legal counsel or other adviser with a member of the compensation committee;

(E) Any stock of the listed company owned by the compensation consultant, legal counsel or other adviser; and

(F) Any business or personal relationship of the compensation consultant, legal counsel, other adviser or the person employing the adviser with an executive officer of the listed company.

Commentary: Nothing in this Section 303A.05(c) shall be construed: (A) to require the compensation committee to implement or act consistently with the advice or recommendations of the compensation consultant, independent legal counsel or other adviser to the compensation committee; or (B) to affect the ability or obligation of the compensation committee to exercise its own judgment in fulfillment of the duties of the compensation committee.

The compensation committee is required to conduct the independence assessment outlined in Section 303A.05(c)(iv) with respect to any compensation consultant, legal counsel or other adviser that provides advice to the compensation committee, other than (i) in-house legal counsel; and (ii) any compensation consultant, legal counsel or other adviser whose role is limited to the following activities for which no disclosure would be required under Item 407(e)(3)(iii) of Regulation S-K: consulting on any broad-based plan that does not discriminate in scope, terms, or operation, in favor of executive officers or directors of the listed company, and that is available generally to all salaried employees; or providing information that either is not customized for a particular company or that is customized based on parameters that are not developed by the compensation consultant, and about which the compensation consultant does not provide.

Nothing in this Section 303A.05(c) requires a compensation consultant, legal counsel or other compensation adviser to be independent, only that the compensation committee consider the enumerated independence factors before selecting or receiving advice from a compensation adviser. The compensation committee may select or receive advice from any compensation adviser they prefer including ones that are not independent, after considering the six independence factors outlined in Section 303A.05(c)(iv)(A)—(F).

The rules for compensation consultants' disclosure changed in July 2012. Under Item 407(e)(3)(iii), registrants will continue to be required to disclose 'any role of compensation consultants in determining or recommending the amount or form of executive and director compensation.' Specifically, registrants are required to:

- identify the consultants.
- state whether such consultants were engaged directly by the compensation committee or any other person.
- describe the nature and scope of the consultant's assignment and the material elements of any instructions given to the consultants under the engagement.
- disclose the aggregate fees paid to a consultant for advice or recommendations on the amount or form of executive and director compensation and the aggregate fees for additional services if the consultant provided both and the fees for the additional services exceeded $120,000 during the fiscal year.

The US Conference Board in a 2011 survey[19] found the following, which is pertinent to the above rule change:

[19] http://www.conference-board.org

'Disclosed Fees Paid to Compensation Consultants

Fees paid to the consultants for compensation-related services ranged from approximately $100,000 to $440,000.

Fees paid to the consultants for additional services ranged from approximately $2.4 million to $4.9 million, with one outlier at approximately $14.9 million. Very few companies voluntarily disclosed the fees paid to their compensation consultant when not required to do so pursuant to Item 407(e)(3)(iii).'

26.7 Survey data

Independent Remuneration Solutions (IRS), (which is now a subsidiary of MM&K), in association with Hanson Green, surveyed the views of Non-Executive Directors regarding fees, board practices and Remuneration Committees. The survey was conducted in November/December 2006. The sample covered individual directors holding 750 separate appointments.

IRS asked some special questions on the data collection form to provide an insight into aspects of independent directorship that readers may find particularly interesting. The results related to Remuneration Committees were as follows. Questions were aimed at directors who were Chairmen or members of a Remuneration Committee. IRS received replies from 240 directors responding to the Remuneration Committee questionnaire, who sat on 480 Remuneration Committees.

	2004[20]		2007	
Consultant and Committee Issues	Yes (%)	No (%)	Yes (%)	No (%)
Are you happy with the objectivity of your consultants?	78	22	94	6
Are remuneration decisions very influenced by submissions from the CEO/Director of Human Resources or other executives?	76	24	82	18
Are the advisers part of a larger professional services firm offering other fee-based advice to the group?	85	15	22	78
In such cases do you feel the advice given is sufficiently objective and free from executive influence?	80	20	92	8
Is any strategic/remuneration training available for committee members?	28	72	24	76

[20] This refers to the IRS survey of 2003/4, when comparable questions were asked.

	2004[20]		2007	
Does the committee plan to assess its effectiveness over time?	66	34	82	18
Would the committee probably use an outside consultant or facilitator to help it?	58	42	35	65

Committee papers

On the same tack IRS asked whether or not Remuneration Committee papers are properly prepared for the Chairman and members.

There is a very marked difference between effective and ineffective committees as on less effective committees it is quite clear that the papers are not properly presented, which may be a reason for their underperformance. Looking at the overall figures, this is an area in which committee Chairmen need to become more active in insisting their proper papers and briefing notes are prepared. A score of only 72% for most effective committees does not look adequate for such a crucial part of the committee's modus operandi.

How much time is spent on [remuneration] committee meetings each year?

IRS gave a breakdown of the time spent on committees by the 283 directorships analysed. On average the Chairman was spending eight to nine days a year on this responsibility and members between four and five. The principal time driver is the number of committee meetings.

How many days per year do you spend on committee work?		
Formal meeting days	Chairman	Member
1	5	23
2	41	27
3	17	13
4	17	19
5+	20	18
Informal contact meetings/phone calls between members	Chairman	Member
1	16	40
2	33	22
3	18	14
4+	33	24

How many days per year do you spend on committee work?		
Preparing for meetings	Chairman	Member
1	36	50
2	31	35
3	13	7
4+	20	8

The committee should have one meeting in which there are no specific items on the agenda, when members can discuss the strategic development of remuneration within the senior ranks of the company and possibly have a presentation from consultants on what is going on in the outside world. Two or three formal meetings each year are fully occupied in deciding on annual salary reviews, allocating options, the agreement of executive bonuses and other items that do not allow for a general strategic discussion.

There was general satisfaction with the terms of appointment under which members serve, which is probably the best criteria for accepting that the current system was working well.

How many directors are on the Remuneration Committee?

With the London Stock Exchange recommending that quoted companies should have three[21] independent directors, it is not so surprising that this is a most popular number. The size of the committee to some extent reflects the size of the company as very major groups are likely to have committees of five or six. Most of the respondents felt that the make-up was approximately correct. A small percentage see the size of some less effective Remuneration Committees as one of their problems, with 4% indicating they have too many members.

Are they all independent or Non-Executive Directors?

It is interesting that on the most effective Remuneration Committees 20% of the members were not independent directors with the number rising to 42% on less effective groups.

Training

There has been intense interest in the training of independent directors. IRS highlighted the issue as 93% of members of effective and 96% of less effective Remuneration Committees (RemCos) do not receive any training to help them undertake their duties.

[21] But only two for those companies outside the FTSE 350.

IRS was aware that there was a resistance from experienced executives who sit on other boards accepting that they might need some high-level training for their independent director responsibilities. This is reflected in the figures below which show about the same number of independent directors who feel they might benefit from further training as those that do not.

	Most effective RemCo (%)	Least effective RemCo (%)
Does the company offer training to RemCo members?		
Yes	7	4
No	93	96
Do you think they would benefit if it were available?		
Yes	27	34
No	32	30
Maybe	41	36

In IRS' experience Remuneration Committee meetings were usually run on fairly tight timescales on a day where there are several other meetings to be slotted into the Board schedule. This can lead to a less than full examination of all the issues. IRS felt that directors might think that additional members would simply slow down the agenda. IRS did question whether the attitude shown by the respondents to this survey to training and committee membership is adequate in a situation where remuneration, and particularly directors' remuneration, is seen as a touchstone of good corporate governance.

Perhaps the most interesting finding in the tables below is that a third of the most effective committees used more than one consultant.

Does the Remuneration Committee use more than one consultant?

IRS noted that the second consultant might often be an option or a pension specialist, but there is no doubt that the use of two specialist consultants for main board directors' remuneration is an increasingly favoured option. Remuneration Committee Chairmen clearly want an alternative opinion on the increasingly complex issue of balancing the interest of shareholders and their executive cadre.

There is relatively little difference between the appointment procedures, length of service and re-appointment system for consultants of the most effective and the least effective Remuneration Committees.

Independent consultants – what kind?	Most effective RemCo (%)	Least effective RemCo (%)
Use traditional consultants who have serviced the company for years	17	19
Use consultants linked to accountants, actuaries, solicitors or other professional adviser	10	12
Recommended consultants by committee members	40	32
Independent consultants not associated with other professional advisers	33	37

Perhaps the fact that the most effective committees use the same consultant for three years or more shows a consistency of remuneration strategy that is likely to bring benefits to the shareholders.

	Most effective RemCo (%)	Least effective RemCo (%)
Consider formally appointing new consultants every:		
1 year	10	33
2 years	20	33
3 years	70	34

By contrast, a third of consultants servicing less effective committees only last a year, suggesting there is a fair amount of dissention between the consultants and members or between the members of the committee itself.

	Most effective RemCo (%)	Least effective RemCo (%)
If appointing new consultants we would carry out a 'beauty parade'		
Yes	75	65
No	25	35
We take out references with consultants' current clients		
Yes	66	52
No	33	48

How dependent is the committee on consultants' advice?

One of the areas in which there is a significant difference between most and least effective committees is the dependency of the committee on the consultant's advice. The figures for the most effective committee, showing 13% very dependent and 83%, as you would expect, quite dependent, reflecting the experience and skill of the members of the committee who ultimately determine the director's remuneration package. The comparator figures for least effective committees are quite interesting as they show both excessive dependence at 28% and 19% deriving very little benefit from outside advice.

The percentages for the length of appointment and the dependency on the consultant's report suggests that in some less effective committees outside consultants are used as a necessary evil as their input is not seen as particularly relevant to what may be entrenched attitudes.

How often have you seen consultants' reports challenged and significantly changed for the better by the Remuneration Committee's input?

In terms of challenging consultants' reports, the figures are extremely interesting. The most effective Remuneration Committee pattern with 21% often challenged, 23% seldom challenged and 56% never challenged probably indicates that consultants have been fully briefed so that their report does cover the ground required. On the other hand, when the percentage of reports that are never challenged goes to 80%, it seems the Remuneration Committee does not feel confident enough to debate any of these suggestions with the consultants or, alternatively, that they plan to ignore the report, any challenge is pointless.

Do you feel consultants are often too close to executive directors to be able to give really objective independent advice?

The final question assesses the relationship between consultants and executive directors and whether this could lead to less than fully objective reports has not been posed in any other survey. 47% of respondents think that there is or may be too close a relationship. This is concerning. Nowadays Remuneration Committees are urged to appoint consultants who are totally independent of the executive team.

Finally, who writes the Remuneration Committee report? The full committee should always approve the draft. This only seems to happen in 50% of companies.

Who writes the Remuneration Committee's report in the annual accounts?	**Most effective RemCo (%)**	**Least effective RemCo (%)**
Committee Chairman	40	36
Chief executive	8	6
HR director	7	8
Committee secretary or other	45	50
Is it approved by:		
Committee Chairman?	43	50
Whole committee?	57	50

Summing up

1. The choice of Remuneration Committee Chairman is critical if the committee is going to be fully effective.
2. There is some reluctance among Remuneration Committee members, most of who will be widely experienced, to accept that training or additional members of the committee would increase its competence.
3. It is of some concern that a high percentage of Remuneration Committee members feel that their consultants, who are meant to be completely independent, are or could be too close to the executive team.

27 Engagement and Reporting to Shareholders

27.1 The annual remuneration report to shareholders

Each year the company has to report to shareholders on directors' remuneration and details of the information that must be contained in the report are described in **Chapters 6 and 10**.

The requirements are different for:

- UK quoted companies on the LSE, ie where the company is located in UK
- Overseas quoted companies on the LSE, ie where the company is located overseas
- AIM listed companies

This guidance relates to the disclosures required by Schedule 8 to the Large and Medium-sized Companies and Groups (Accounts and Reports) Amendment) Regulations 2013 (the 'Regulations'), which first apply to UK quoted companies in their financial years ending on or after 30 September 2013 and to the remuneration policy that will be required to be submitted to shareholders for approval for the first time at the AGM in the following financial year.

27.2 Items requiring shareholder approval

Companies quoted on the LSE have to have their remuneration policy voted on by shareholders at least every three years.

The implementation report must be voted on by shareholders every year, but the vote is only advisory.

New long term incentive plans for fully quoted companies must be approved by shareholders. See **9.1**.

Individual directors also have to be re-elected every year. So shareholders who object to remuneration can signal disapproval by voting against the Chair of the Remuneration Committee, its members, or the executive(s) whose pay is an issue.

27.3 Who to talk to, when and what to engage upon

It is impractical to talk to all shareholders, so if a contentious item about directors' pay has arisen, or better still if one is likely to arise, then it is best practice to talk to key shareholders and/or their representatives.

For a very large company it might be necessary to talk to ten or even 20 shareholders. For a small company with two or three shareholders with large stakes this might be all that is necessary.

In order to decide what to talk to shareholders about, companies need to know their shareholders' views and track record of voting on contentious remuneration issues. They can then evaluate the likely reaction to proposals and shape their communications in light of this. These issues are explored in more detail in the next section.

27.4 Communicating Directors' pay

Introduction

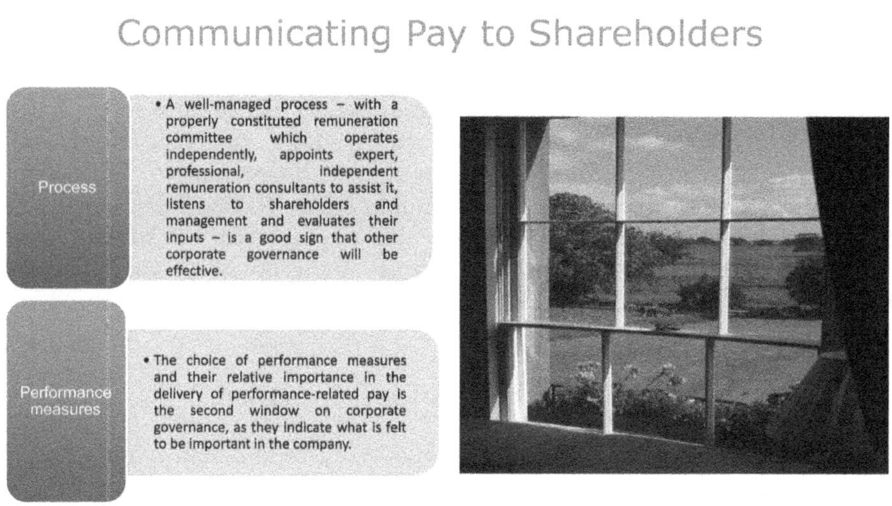

How directors and senior managers are remunerated provides an important window on corporate governance more generally.

Seventy-eight per cent of people believe directors of large companies are overpaid, according to a UK MORI poll commissioned by the *Financial Times* (30 June 2003), and 80% think that top company directors cannot be trusted to tell the truth. Public opinion polls in the US provide similar results. For example, in a Gallop poll in July 2002, 79% of people, when asked if corporate executives take improper actions to benefit themselves at the expense of their corporation, responded that this practice was very or somewhat widespread. 73% thought that CEOs of large corporations could not be trusted.

Only 1% of the general public think the average FTSE 100 Company CEO should be paid more than £4 million, according to the research for the High Pay Commission carried out by ICM Research in 20–22 January 2012. This showed in answer to the question 'how much should a CEO of a FTSE 100 company be paid' that the respondents (2003 of them) said:

- Mean £532k (standard deviation £777k, standard error £20K)
- Mode – the range £51,000 to £150,000
- Median – about £250k
- Just 1% said > £4million
- 27% said don't know.
- Women had a mean answer of £448k versus men who had a mean of £608k.

It is well worth looking at the research. The link is http://www.icmresearch.com/wp-content/blogs.dir/1/files/2012/01/High-Pay-Centre-Executive-Pay-Jan-2012.pdf

£4.2 million was the comparable figure in 2010 for the average FTSE CEO pay (total remuneration awarded), according to the MM&K/Manifest survey.

Chairmen and Non-Executive Directors (who are the people who sit on Remuneration Committees and decide on pay levels) think that executive directors pay is about right (source 2011 MM&K Chairman and Non-Executive Director survey).

Figure 12: Is executive directors' remuneration too high/too low?

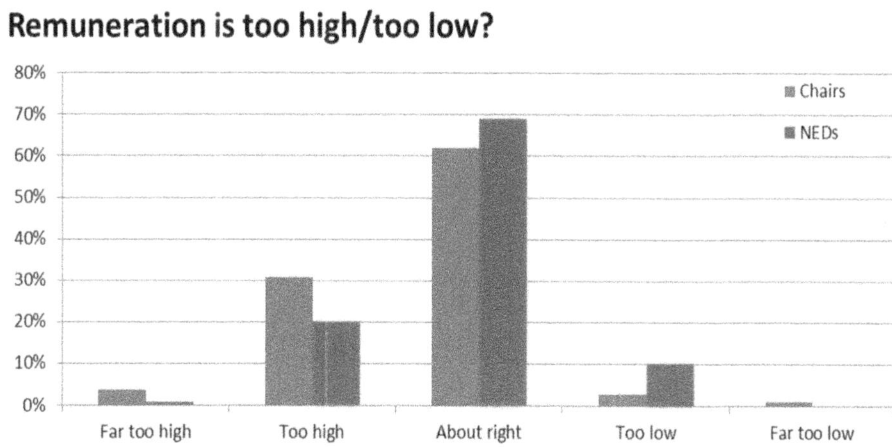

This is a stark contrast to what the general public think.

So, is it worth trying to communicate CEO pay to the man/woman in the street?

Does it matter what the general public think about directors' pay? It does, because the issue is in the political arena. When UK companies failed to clean up their act by 2013, the UK government felt it had no choice but to legislate, and it will continue to monitor developments to see if further action is required.

In addition there is research which shows that excessive pay and poor ethics impact on customers' views of brands.

Do people believe directors are overpaid because they are, or because of the way pay is communicated? Directors' pay is complex and traditionally it has not been transparent. Its communication suggests there is something to hide.

There is, however, a systemic problem here. If a company communicates more clearly than anyone else, it will be easier for journalists to write about that company and they may draw unwelcome and unwarranted attention to themselves. Thus no one company wants to be leading in this respect.

Historically, a major problem has been that the press have not reported directors' remuneration in a balanced responsible manner. Instead they have sought out the easy story and looked for controversy. Many organisations in the remuneration arena have an agenda and have sought publicity for their views. Consequently the best approach for most companies has been to adopt a low profile and disclose as little as possible. Less information means less ammunition.

27.5 Communications issues

Remuneration attracts publicity. It is an easy story and nearly always negative. The PR and investor relations could be managed better.

Remuneration is high profile and increasingly high risk. Examples in this millennium include GlaxoSmithKline, Vodafone, Jarvis, Marconi, Sainsbury, Prudential, RBS, and more recently Aviva, Barclays and Trinity Mirror. In some cases it is potentially damaging to the brand as well as to investor relations. Companies and individuals who attract negative PR on pay issues often find their shareholders less willing to support them on other issues.

The government's 2013 Regulations mean all companies have to put their remuneration to a vote at their AGM and also require better, more transparent Remuneration Committee reports. Consequently remuneration will continue to attract much publicity.

The 2013 Regulations require graphs of total shareholder return (TSR) over the past ten[1] years have to be included in the remuneration report, together with explanations of the variations in CEO pay over the same period. The shareholders can now easily see the pay linkage (or lack thereof), thus improving accountability.

TSR comparisons have in some cases been against a general index, whereas companies say they are comparing their remuneration against a specific market sector. Many companies in other parts of their annual report comment on measures of performance other than TSR, but do not include such data in the remuneration report, although early signs are this is beginning to change. Since they link remuneration to more than just TSR, it would be logical to report on the other measures and such explanation would help justify changes in remuneration levels.

The new strategic report requires a clear explanation of the business model and the KPIs. This should link into the remuneration report and it may be appropriate to cross refer or to repeat the information.

Remuneration is complex. This is one area where the saying 'the devil is in the detail' is true. For example, problems often arise many years in the future because of seemingly innocuous small print.

In order to manage the PR of directors' remuneration, detailed analysis is required, underpinned by up-to-date knowledge of the various stakeholder views.

It is not only the high-profile cases which need help. All companies would benefit from a risk assessment and analysis of the strengths and weaknesses of their remuneration arrangements – from a shareholder perspective.

---

1 Initially five years but an extra year of data will be required each year until ten years are reported.

27.6 How to communicate with shareholders

This is emerging as increasingly important. Most Remuneration Committee reports are impenetrable. Is this what companies and shareholders want? Remuneration Committees must decide.

Figure 13: Communications impact assessment process

Impact Assessment – Directors' Remuneration Report Regulations

Analysis	**Report**	**Actions**
Process Committee membership Report	Executive summary Draft Remuneration Report in new format	Compliance issues Re-Draft Remuneration Report in new format Adopt new policies where non-compliant
Practice (pay history)	Areas where non-compliant	
Policy (for the future)	Shareholder voting assessment	Remuneration Policy Review Redesign
Perceptions PR Investors	Remuneration issues needing review	Communications Explain your case to press and shareholders
	Implications for future years	

The history of alignment of pay and performance should be tested. Since a ten-year performance graph will be required, it is essential that the last ten years of remuneration awarded and paid out should be reviewed by the Remuneration Committee. This analysis will reveal how successful the Remuneration Committee has been in:

- implementing its stated policy
- linking pay and performance.

It also needs good graphics to explain complex ideas simply. There should be more than the bare minimum covered in the DRRR. For example **Figure 14** shows how performance measures have changed over time and the outcome against the maximum.

Companies have to convince their shareholders to vote at their AGM for the remuneration report resolution and for any new share schemes. Companies who are open and fully transparent will receive a better reception from their major shareholders than those who only partially disclose or try to pull the wool over the eyes of their shareholders. MM&K research shows that

Figure 14: Communicating and measuring performance

2008

	Max	Actual
Profit Growth (Absolute)	20	5
Profit v. Budget	20	15
Profit Growth/Sales (Relative)	30	20
Key Strategic Goals	20	10
Effort	10	10
Total	100	60

2009

	Max	Actual
Profit Growth (Absolute)	10	5
Profit v. Budget	20	15
Profit Growth/Sales (Relative)	30	25
Key Strategic Goals	30	10
Effort	10	10
Total	100	65

2010

	Max	Actual
Profit Growth (Absolute)	10	5
Profit v. Budget	20	15
Profit Growth/Sales (Relative)	30	25
Key Strategic Goals	30	30
Effort	10	10
Total	100	85

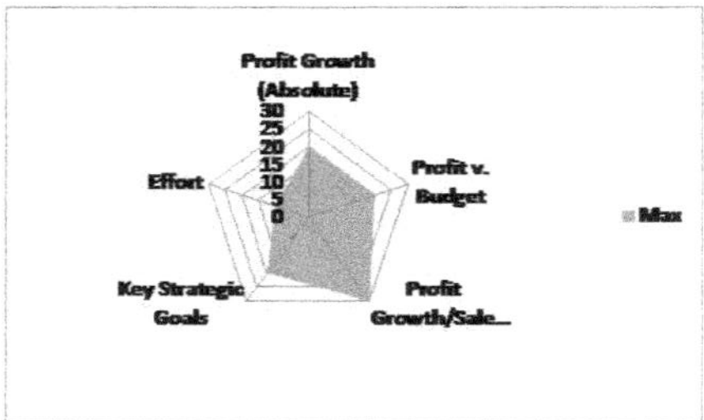

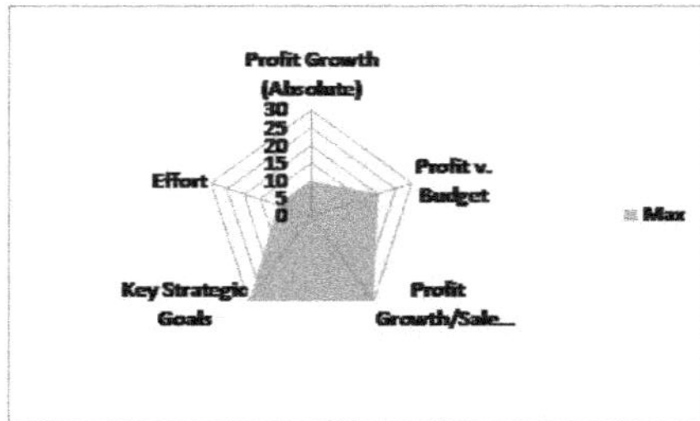

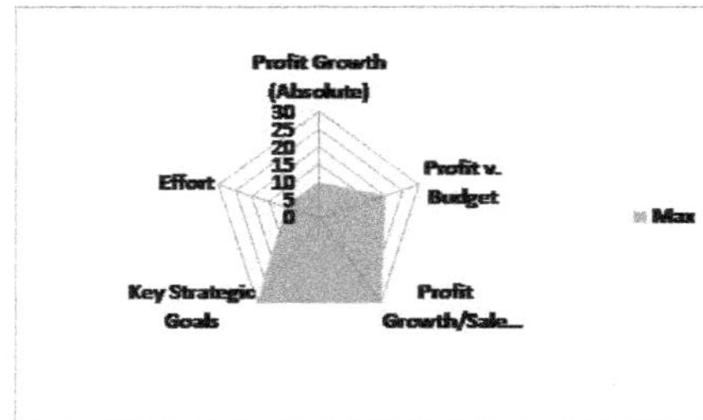

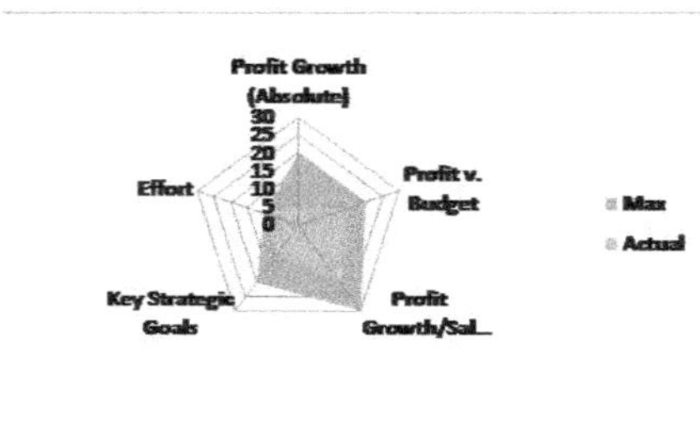

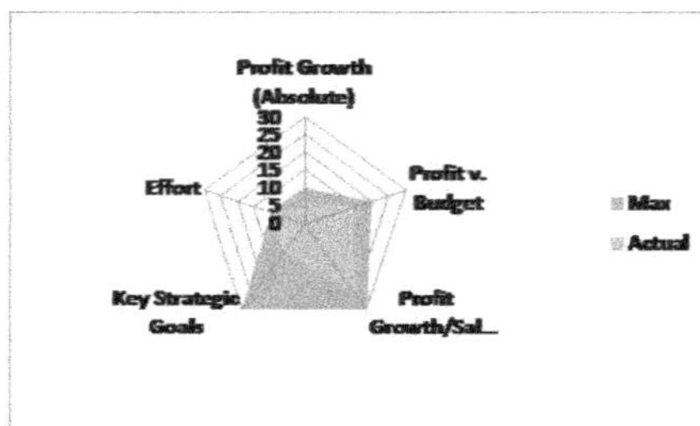

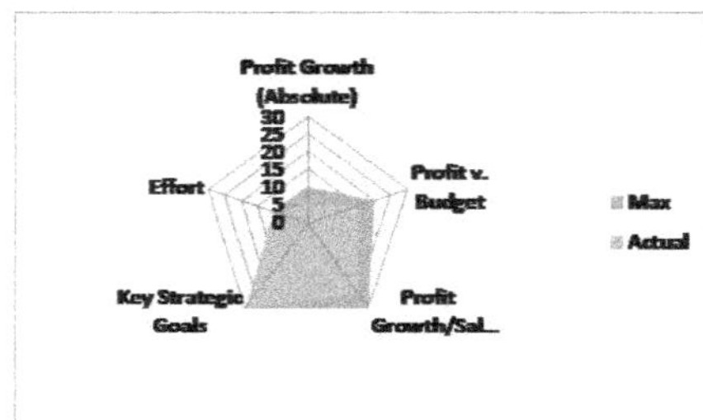

shareholders want to have collaboration with companies about pay. They want constructive dialogue. They do not want public spats all over the newspapers.

Some companies' proposals are like a red rag to a bull. A number of the institutions have their own agenda and the company should not feed them ammunition for them to publicise their agenda. If the minutiae have not been addressed, the company is always going to be on, in cricketing terms, a sticky wicket.

The mantra should be 'collaboration not conflict' with shareholders. To do so requires a better understanding of each other's points of views. The checklist at the end of this chapter is a good starting point.

27.7 The communication process

Step 1: Assess where you are. MM&K have developed a 180-item questionnaire to undertake a detailed assessment of a company's current arrangements to identify their strengths and weaknesses. In particular it considers the impact of the directors' remuneration report regulations.

Part of this assessment should include detailed scenario analyses which:

- illustrate a range of possible outcomes
- consider *all* elements of remuneration
- consider *all* historic awards of medium- and long-term incentives as well as the current proposals
- consider share ownership and rules about selling and holding shares.

Companies should also review their voting results at the AGM for the past five years to identify any trends and concerns about remuneration, the vote on the remuneration report, votes on new long term incentive plans and the voting for the reappointment of directors involved in remuneration.

Step 2: Develop a communication plan, for example:

- plan what you want to say
- assess the likely reaction
- modify your strategy and if necessary change your remuneration policy
- test your proposal with informal discussions
- understand the likely objections and arguments and decide how to address them
- decide what are 'must-haves' and where you can be flexible if you have to be
- refine your messages

- decide who should communicate to whom and in what order, and
- be flexible. Once you have started to communicate you must expect feedback and you need to evaluate the feedback and decide if a change of plan is necessary. If you go into the process with the objective of persuading key shareholders that your remuneration plan is right, do not be surprised if shareholders and their representatives say that you are stubborn and out of touch.

Step 3: Consult with major shareholders, listen and react.

Step 4: The Remuneration Committee report needs to be drafted so that it meets the regulations and achieves the optimum impact with shareholders and other target audiences. Best practice is to include a letter from the Remuneration Committee Chairman to shareholders, summarising key actions in the year and giving an explanation of remuneration policy. Full details of the required content are in **Chapter 10**.

Step 5: Once the above steps have been completed, the company has to publish its remuneration report and share plan proposals. These will be analysed by the intermediaries, the ABI, NAPF (RREV/ISS), Manifest, PIRC etc. They may already have been consulted as part of your communication plan. At this stage it may be necessary to give them some questions and answers to provide further explanation and background data on top of what is in the remuneration report and shareholders' circular. Some intermediaries will send the company copies of their report in draft form to ask for confirmation it is factually correct. This is another opportunity for the company to explain itself.

Through this process there may be leaks to the press. When the intermediaries issue their reports and voting guidance they may also comment to the press.

Step 6: Companies need to prepare thoroughly for the AGM with questions and answers for their Chairman and/or Chairman of the Remuneration Committee, so they can answer accurately and confidently.

Companies should expect some shareholders to vote against their proposals. They need to take a view about what is acceptable and manage either their remuneration policy or communication strategy accordingly, or preferably both together.

27.8 The press and how to work with them

Most companies fail to educate the press, most of whom are very busy, but not very knowledgeable about these issues. The companies with problems generally need to be much more open and more detailed in what is communicated.

To communicate with the press successfully needs good initial assessments of the likely reactions to the company's proposals.

27.9 How to communicate directors' pay to employees

It is not just shareholders who have a view about directors' pay. It can be highly demotivational and bad for morale if the CEO and directors are getting large bonuses, pay rises and awards of options and LTIPs when staff are being made redundant and asked to work harder. Before pay decisions are made, Remuneration Committees should consider how those decisions can be explained to employees and their likely reactions.

A review of the ratio of CEO pay to average pay is an essential pre-requisite to this process.

27.10 Example of good practice regarding KPIs

The following is an example of how to use KPIs in a business and communicate them to shareholders, taken from the 2010 Tesco Annual report.

Key performance indicators (KPIs)*

We operate a balanced scorecard approach to managing the business that is known internally within the Group as our 'Steering Wheel'. This unites the Group's resources and in particular focuses the efforts of our staff around our customers, people, operations, finance and the community. Its prime focus is as a management tool for the Company so that there is appropriate balance in the trade-offs that need to be made between the main levers of management – such as operations measures, financial measures or delivery of customer metrics.

It therefore enables the business to be operated and monitored on a balanced basis with due regard to the needs of all stakeholders. For the owners of the business, it is simply based around the philosophy that if we look after customers and staff well and operate efficiently and effectively then shareholders' interests will always be best served by the inevitable outputs of those – growth in sales, profits and returns.

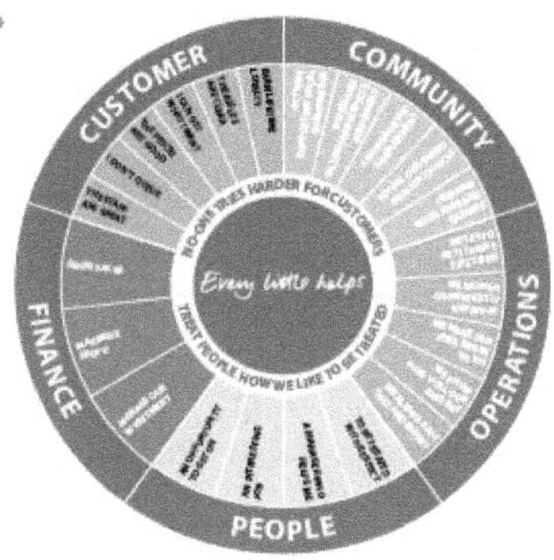

	2010	2009	2008
Sales growth			
Change in Group sales over the year (including value added tax)	6.8%	15.1%	11.1%
UK sales growth	4.2%	9.5%	6.7%
International sales growth	8.8%	30.6%	25.3%
International sales growth (at constant exchange rates)	6.6%	13.6%	22.5%
Retailing Services sales growth	4.2%	11%	–
Profit before tax	£3,176m	£2,917m**	£2,803m
Underlying profit before tax	£3,395m	£3,124m**	£2,846m

Trading margin			
UK trading margin	6.2%	6.2%	5.9%
International trading margin (excluding the United States)	5.3%	5.3%	5.6%
Trading margin is calculated from the trading profit expressed as a percentage of Group revenue (sales excluding value added tax) and excluding the impact of IFRIC 13. It is a measure of profit generation from sales and is a comparable performance measure with other companies. This is how much we made from trade in our stores, taking account of the cost of the products sold, wages and salaries, expenses associated with running the stores, depots and head office, and the cost of depreciation of the assets used to generate the profits. Trading profit is stated after adjusting operating profit for the impact of IAS 19, IAS 32 and IAS 39 (principally pension costs and the marking to market of financial instruments). It also excludes the non-cash elements of IAS 17 'Leases', relating to the impact of annual uplifts in rents and rent-free periods, and the IFRS 3 amortisation charge on intangible assets arising on the acquisition of Tesco Personal Finance (TPF).			
Net cash (outflow)/inflow	£(739)m	£1,601m	£801m
Net cash (outflow)/inflow is the cash received less cash spent during the financial period, after financing activities			
Capital expenditure	£3.1bn	£4.7bn	£3.9bn
This is the amount invested in purchasing fixed assets			
UK	£1.5bn	£2.6bn	£2.3bn
International	£1.5bn	£2.1bn	£1.6bn
Tesco Bank	£0.1bn	–	–
Net borrowings and gearing			
Net borrowings	£7.9bn	£9.6bn	£6.2bn
Gearing	54%	74%	52%
Return on capital employed (ROCE)	12.1%	12.8%**	12.9%‡
ROCE is calculated as profit before interest less tax divided by the average of net assets plus net debt plus dividend creditor less net assets held for sale. ROCE is a relative profit measurement that not only incorporates the funds shareholders have invested, but also funds invested by banks and other lenders, and therefore shows the productivity of the assets of the Group.			
Underlying diluted earnings per share	31.66p§	28.87p**	27.02p
Underlying diluted earnings per share is the calculation of profit after tax and minority interest divided by the diluted weighted average number of shares in issue during the year. It is the amount which could be paid out on each share if the Company decided to distribute all its profits as dividends instead of retaining some for future expansion.			

* All KPIs are for 52 weeks ended 27 February 2010, 53 weeks ended 28 February 2009 and 52 weeks ended 23 February 2008 unless otherwise stated.
** Restated for IFRS 2 and IFRIC 13.
‡ Using 'normalised' tax rate before start-up costs in the US and Tesco Direct, and excludes the impact of foreign exchange in equity and our acquisition of a majority share of Dobbies.
§ Underlying diluted earnings per share grew by 9.7% on a statutory basis.

27.11 Checklist for communicating directors' remuneration

Note: this is a list of questions to be asked before developing a communications strategy. The list contains many of the items required by the DRRR.

1. Process

1.1. Remuneration Committee

- Does the Remuneration Committee make a report to shareholders and is it signed off by a member of the committee?
- Are all members independent?
- Are terms of reference defined, clear and in line with the UK Corporate Governance Code?
- Are the Remuneration Committee advisers independent:
  - — what other services do they provide; and
  - — what are their fees for Remuneration Committee advice and other work?
- Is the Chairman a member of the Remuneration Committee?
- Do the Chairman and CEO attend the Remuneration Committee and withdraw when their own pay is discussed?
- Is the Remuneration Committee secretary the Company Secretary or HR director?

1.2.	Is the Remuneration Committee report put to the vote at the AGM: ● Are there separate votes for forward looking policy and on the actual practice and payments for the previous year? ● Are substantive changes in remuneration policy explained to shareholders and voted upon at the AGM? ● Are all new share schemes and incentives over more than one year put to a vote?	
2. Remuneration Policy		
2.1.	Is there a remuneration policy?	
2.2.	Is it stated in the remuneration report?	
2.3.	Does the remuneration policy cover these key elements: i. Selection of appropriate comparator companies: — types of executives required — importance of individual executives to delivery of business strategy — size of talent pool — comparator companies location UK, Europe, Global — comparator companies size – sales, market cap, employees, assets, profits etc ii. Identify pay market position(s) and linkage of pay market position to performance. iii. Mix of performance related and not-performance related elements. iv. Alignment to shareholders' interests: — upside alignment — downside alignment: – contracts – LTIPs/options v. Share ownership guidelines vi. Alignment to business strategy vii. Performance measures: — are KPIs included? — can they be massaged in the short term? — is there a good mix of leading and lagging indicators?	
2.4.	Detailed remuneration policy issues: ● Is there a graph/table to show total remuneration at different performance levels? ● Relativities of CEO to other executive directors – are they justifiable/sensible? ● Is there flexibility to adjust the remuneration policy in special circumstances:	

- — to retain those who have been offered jobs elsewhere?
  - — to attract key hires?
  - — to adjust future award levels if market practice changes?
  - — adjust performance targets if special circumstances arise?
- Annual bonus:
  - — Target and maximum annual bonus?
  - — Are the annual bonus performance measures drivers of long term shareholder value or short term focused?
  - — Bonus deferral and matching:
    - – performance condition for minimum match
    - – performance condition for maximum match
    - – are expected value and potential value disclosed?
- Options:
  - — Are face value and expected value disclosed?
  - — Are potential gains disclosed?
  - — Are performance conditions sufficiently stretching? Is there retesting?
  - — Are higher awards subject to tougher performance conditions?
  - — Are higher awards part of a cohesive integrated reward strategy?
  - — Can options vest for below median/RPI performance?
  - — Is exercise subject to an underlying improvement in financial performance?
  - — Is a holding period required post exercise?
  - — What are the length of time until vesting and performance period length?
- LTIPs (restricted share plans):
  - — Are face value and expected value disclosed?
  - — Are potential gains disclosed?
  - — Are performance conditions sufficiently stretching? Is there retesting?
  - — Are higher awards subject to tougher performance conditions?
  - — Are higher awards part of a cohesive, integrated reward strategy?
  - — Can LTIPs vest for below median/RPI performance?
  - — Is exercise subject to an underlying improvement in financial performance?
  - — Threshold performance for payment?
  - — of award paid at threshold?
  - — Award at Q3 performance?

- — Maximum performance level?
- — Award at maximum performance level?
- — Length of performance period and subsequent holding period?
- Combined long term incentive plans (bonus matching, options and LTIPs):
  - — Are Combined Face Value and Expected Value disclosed?
  - — Are Combined potential gains disclosed?
  - — Are the Combined schemes excessive?
  - — Are the Combined schemes part of a cohesive integrated reward strategy?
- Share ownership guidelines:
  - — Is the policy disclosed?
  - — Level?
  - — Years to achievement?
  - — Which shares are included?
  - — Penalties for non-achievement?
  - — Share retention policy for shares acquired from incentive schemes?
  - — Policy for phased sales of shares?
  - — Career shares?

2.5. Does directors' remuneration take account of pay conditions within the company:

- Is there information on employee remuneration policy?
- Is pay elsewhere in the company considered in determining directors' pay?
- Do all employees benefit from business success?

3. Remuneration Practice, ie how much was paid/awarded for the previous year

3.1. Are all remuneration figures clearly disclosed:

- Full table(s) of option and share awards – not average issue price
- Pension
- Salary increase and new salary for present year
- Is the total remuneration awarded and received disclosed?
- Is performance basis for all incentives clearly set out?

3.2. Salary:

- Level
- Position v comparators
- Relativities – ie internally
- increase on previous year

	• Alignment of performance and salary % increase
3.3.	Pension: • Level of benefits • Transfer value £, as % salary • Treatment of pay above the cap • Definition of final salary – is only basic salary pensionable? • Early leaver provisions? • For DB plans, age, service, accrual rate, special terms different to normal employees
3.4.	Other benefits: • Benefits disclosed £, as % salary • Housing allowance • Access to exotic benefits such as planes, yacht, company mansion, loans to directors from third parties on preferential terms, etc
3.5.	Contracts: • Notice period – is the policy for one year or less? Have you considered maximum termination payments of six months' salary or less? • If notice periods are greater than one year are they satisfactorily explained? • Mitigation (including statement of policy) or liquidated damages • 'Pay as you go' or lump sum • Treatment of bonuses and incentives including guarantees and early vesting • Enhanced pension provision
3.6.	Annual bonus (including special one off bonuses): • Actual amount £, as % of salary? • Performance measures – are they what the City looks at? • Bonus matching and deferral • Alignment of performance and bonus paid – are targets stretching?
3.7.	Options: • Level of award £, % salary • Are Face Value and Expected Value disclosed? • Are potential gains disclosed? • Are (paper) gains to date shown? • Performance measures: — Is the expected probability of performance measures disclosed? — Is it transparent how the measures align to shareholder value? — Threshold for grants above 1x salary per annum — Degree of stretch for maximum award

	— Can options vest for below median/RPI performance — Is exercise subject to an underlying improvement in financial performance? • Holding period required post exercise? • dilution • Number of shares over which options awarded each year including those bought in the market – % total • P&L impact disclosed (as per IFRS 2) • of all options granted that are granted to CEO • of all options granted that are granted to top five executives • Is the full history of awards and performance achievement and expected payout disclosed?
3.8.	LTIPs • Level of award £, % salary • Are face value and expected value disclosed? • Are potential gains disclosed? • Performance measures: — Is the expected probability of performance measures disclosed? — Is it transparent how the measures align to shareholder value? — Threshold for grants above 1x salary per annum — Degree of stretch for maximum award — Can options vest for below median/RPI performance? — Is exercise subject to an underlying improvement in financial performance? • Holding period required post exercise? • dilution • Number of shares over which LTIPs awarded each year including those bought in the market – % total • P&L impact (as per IFRS 2) • of all LTIPs granted that are granted to CEO • of all LTIPs granted that are granted to top five executives • Is the full history of awards and performance achievement and expected payout disclosed?
3.9.	Mix of remuneration: • Is the mix of remuneration disclosed? • Is pension included? • Does the mix of remuneration contain too much or too little performance-related? • Mix of remuneration:

3.10. Total remuneration: • Is the total remuneration disclosed for the single figure and the expected value of awards? • Is it possible to calculate the total remuneration from the disclosed data: — Total of actual cash pay and benefits received plus the expected value of long term incentives — Total of actual cash pay and benefits received plus the paper gains of awards that vested in the year from the long term incentives — Total of actual cash pay and benefits received plus the amounts realised from the exercise of long term incentives — The gains on actual shares owned
3.11. Share ownership • How big are the directors' shareholdings? • Was the share ownership policy achieved? • Does level of share ownership (plus other remuneration) provide alignment with shareholders?
• Are there rules for retaining and selling shares?
4. PR and investor relations perceptions
4.1. Transparency of Remuneration Committee report
4.2. Sensitivity of Remuneration Committee report: • Are remunerations levels high? • Alignment of remuneration and performance • Previous history and sensitivity to pay issues • Company performance this year, last three years and last five years: — TSR – absolute – versus comparators – versus FTSE 100 — EPS – absolute – versus comparators – versus FTSE 100 – versus inflation — Other KPIs
4.3. Media views: • On the company • On remuneration in the company

4.4. Fund managers views: • On the company • On remuneration in the company
• Shareholder voting record on remuneration issues for past five/ten years
4.5. Compliance with corporate governance guidance on remuneration: • UK Corporate Governance Code • ABI • NAPF • PIRC • Manifest • [three] largest institutional shareholders

28 Directors Remuneration Report Regulations – annual report contents

28.1 Introduction

Readers are advised to read **Chapter 6** (DRRR Overview) before reading this chapter.

As noted in **Chapter 6**, the remuneration report is recommended to consist of four parts:

1. **SUMMARY STATEMENT/LETTER FROM REMUNERATION COMMITTEE CHAIR**
2. **REMUNERATION AT A GLANCE (an optional one page summary of key facts and figures)**
3. **ANNUAL REPORT ON REMUNERATION (the implementation report on how much was paid in the year)**
4. **DIRECTORS' REMUNERATION POLICY**

Chapter 6.6 covered the contents of the first two items above: the summary statement and the one page remuneration at a glance. These should describe the philosophy of the way the company pays the way it does and provide key facts on remuneration policy, measures and payments. This chapter covers the detailed contents of the rest of the remuneration report.

28.2 Annual Report on Remuneration

Part 3 of the Large and Medium-sized Companies and Groups (Accounts and Reports) Regulations 2008 ('the SI') as amended by the 2013 (Amendment) Regulations specifies the information required in the Annual Report on Remuneration.

This is confusingly titled, as it is only part of the Remuneration Report, which must also cover the summary statement and the remuneration Policy.

This part of the report is factual. There is little discretion on how to disclose the data. Most of the requirements are tightly prescribed in the SI. However companies may wish to build on a good Remuneration Committee Chair letter (with its supporting one page remuneration at a glance page) and provide additional data such as the history of KPIs and remuneration ratios (as illustrated in **Table 6** below) and the linkage with employees pay.

Potential areas for discretion in terms of additional disclosures are:

Item	**Possible extra disclosures**
Single figure of total remuneration table	Extra years of data Extra columns to help explain data
Additional requirements in respect of the single figure table	Targets disclosed
Total pension entitlements	Follow NAPF/LAPFF guidance
Scheme interests awarded in the year	Detailed list of all awards not yet exercised
Payments to past directors	More explanation
Compensation for loss of office	More explanation
Directors' shareholdings and share interests	Include historic awards by date of award and estimates of value of interests
Line graph comparison of TSR performance and Index over 5(10) years	Extra years of TSR and Index Include CEO pay on chart
Table of detailed 5(10) year comparison of CEO Single Total Figure, Bonus as % maximum and LTIP vested %	Extra years of data Include TSR data points in table; and Add extra KPIs to table
Percentage change in remuneration of director undertaking the role of CEO	Extra years of data Include total remuneration single figure and expected value
Relative importance of spend on pay	Extra years of data Include total remuneration of all directors
Statement of implementation of remuneration policy in the following financial year	Include targets for each measure
Consideration by the directors of matters relating to directors' remuneration, including Disclosure of Remuneration Committee advisers and fees	Add fees for other remuneration services provided to management, other fees to the company and to the pension funds
Shareholder voting	Include history for several years
Dilution	Include this ABI requirement
Fair Value or expected value of LTI awards	
Requirement of the UK Corporate Governance Code to take account of the views of shareholders	
Aggregate Directors' Remuneration	Companies Act Requirement. Can also include it here or cross refer to it.
Statement about all employee share plans	
Additional data of the history of bonus opportunity and outcomes	Show five or ten years of this
Additional data of the history of LTI award outcomes as % of maximum award and expected values of extant awards	Show five or ten years of this

This part of the chapter is structured to follow exactly the same order as the legislation. For each part of the legislation, the structure is to show:

- First the legislation
- Then some commentary
- Then some examples of minimum or typical and then the author's view of what might become or best practice.

Single total figure of remuneration for each director

(The following is an extract from the SI)

4.(1) The directors' remuneration report must, for the relevant financial year, for each person who has served as a director of the company at any time during that year, set out in a table in the form set out in paragraph 5 ('the single total figure table') the information prescribed by paragraphs 6 and 7 below.

(2) The report may set out in separate tables the information to be supplied in respect of directors who perform executive functions and those who do not.

(3) Unless otherwise indicated the sums set out in the table are those in respect of the relevant financial year and relate to the director's performance of, or agreement to perform, qualifying services.

5.(1) The form of the table required by paragraph 4 is—

Single Total Figure Table						
	a	**b**	**c**	**d**	**e**	**Total**
Director 1	xxx	xxx	xxx	xxx	xxx	xxx
Director 2	xxx	xxx	xxx	xxx	xxx	xxx

(2) The directors may choose to display the table using an alternative orientation, in which case references in this Schedule to columns are to be read as references to rows.

6.(1) In addition to the columns described in paragraph 7, columns—

(a) must be included to set out any other items in the nature of remuneration (other than items required to be disclosed under paragraph 15) which are not set out in the columns headed '(a)' to '(e)'; and

(b) may be included if there are any sub-totals or other items which the directors consider necessary in order to assist the understanding of the table.

(2) Any additional columns must be inserted before the column marked 'Total'.

7.(1) Subject to paragraph 9, in the single total figure table, the sums that are required to be set out in the columns are—

(a) in the column headed 'a', the total amount of salary and fees;

(b) in the column headed 'b', all taxable benefits;

(c) in the column headed 'c', money or other assets received or receivable for the relevant financial year as a result of the achievement of performance measures and targets relating to a period ending in that financial year other than—

(i) those which result from awards made in a previous financial year and where final vesting is determined as a result of the achievement of performance measures or targets relating to a period ending in the relevant financial year; or

(ii) those receivable subject to the achievement of performance measures or targets in a future financial year;

(d) in the column headed 'd', money or other assets received or receivable for periods of more than one financial year where final vesting—

(i) is determined as a result of the achievement of performance measures or targets relating to a period ending in the relevant financial year; and

(ii) is not subject to the achievement of performance measures or targets in a future financial year;

(e) in the column headed 'e', all pension related benefits including—

(i) payments (whether in cash or otherwise) in lieu of retirement benefits;

(ii) all benefits in year from participating in pension schemes;

(f) in the column headed 'Total', the total amount of the sums set out in the previous columns.

(2) Where it is necessary to assist the understanding of the table by the creation of sub-totals the columns headed 'a' to 'e' may be set out in an order other than the one set out in paragraph 5.

8.(1) In respect of any items in paragraph 7(1)(c) or (d) where the performance measures or targets are substantially (but not fully) completed by the end of the relevant financial year—

(a) the sum given in the table may include sums which relate to the following financial year; but

(b) where such sums are included, those sums must not be included in the corresponding column of the single total figure table prepared for that following financial year; and

(c) a note to the table must explain the basis of the calculation.

(2) Where any money or other assets reported in the single total figure table in the directors' remuneration report prepared in respect of any previous financial year are the subject of a recovery of sums paid or the withholding of any sum for any reason in the relevant financial year—

(a) the recovery or withholding so attributable must be shown in a separate column in the table as a negative value and deducted from the column headed "Total"; and

(b) an explanation for the recovery or withholding and the basis of the calculation must be given in a note to the table.

(3) Where the calculations in accordance with paragraph 10 (other than in respect of a recovery or withholding) result in a negative value, the result must be expressed as zero in the relevant column in the table.

9.(1) Each column in the single total figure table must contain, in such manner as to permit comparison, two sums as follows—

(a) the sum set out in the corresponding column in the report prepared in respect of the financial year preceding the relevant financial year; and

(b) the sum for the relevant financial year.

(2) When, in the single total figure table, a sum is given in the column which relates to the preceding financial year and that sum, when set out in the report for that preceding year was given as an estimated sum, then in the relevant financial year—

(a) it must be given as an actual sum;

(b) the amount representing the difference between the estimate and the actual must not be included in the column relating to the relevant financial year; and

(c) details of the calculation of the revised sum must be given in a note to the table.

10.(1) The methods to be used to calculate the sums required to be set out in the single total figure table are—

(a) for the column headed 'a', cash paid to or receivable by the person in respect of the relevant financial year;

(b) for the column headed 'b', the gross value before payment of tax;

(c) for column 'c', the total cash equivalent including any amount deferred, other than where the deferral is subject to the achievement of further performance measures or targets in a future financial year;

(d) for column 'd'—

(i) the cash value of any monetary award;

(ii) the value of any shares or share options awarded, calculated by—

(aa) multiplying the original number of shares granted by the proportion that vest (or an estimate);

(bb) multiplying the total arrived at in (aa) by the market price of shares at the date on which the shares vest; and

(iii) the value of any additional cash or shares receivable in respect of dividends accrued (actually or notionally);

(e) for the column headed 'e',—

(i) for the item in paragraph 7(1)(e)(i), the cash value;

(ii) for the item in paragraph 7(1)(e)(ii), what the aggregate pension input amount would be across all the pension schemes of the company or group in which the director accrues benefits, calculated using the method set out in section 229 of the Finance Act 2004(1) where—

(aa) references to 'pension input period' are to be read as references to the company's financial year, or where a person becomes a director during the financial year, the period starting on the date the person became a director and ending at the end of the financial year;

(bb) all pension schemes of the company or group which provide relevant benefits to the director are deemed to be registered schemes;

(cc) all pension contributions paid by the director during the pension input period are deducted from the pension input amount;

(dd) in the application of section 234 of that Act, the figure 20 is substituted for the figure 16 each time it appears;

(ee) subsections 229(3) and (4) do not apply; and

(ff) section 277 of that Act is read as follows—

'277. Valuation assumptions

For the purposes of this Part the valuation assumptions in relation to a person, benefits and a date are—

(a) if the person has not left the employment to which the arrangement relates on or before the date, that the person left that employment on the date with a prospective right to benefits under the arrangement,

(b) if the person has not reached such age (if any) as must have been reached to avoid any reduction in the benefits on account of age, that on the date the person is entitled to receive the benefits without any reduction on account of age, and

(c) that the person's right to receive the benefits had not been occasioned by physical or mental impairment.'.

(2) For the item in paragraph 7(1)(e)(ii) where there has not been a company contribution to the pension scheme in respect of the director, but if such a contribution had been made it would have been measured for pension input purposes under section 233(1)(b) of the Finance Act 2004, when calculating the pension input amount for the purposes of sub-paragraph (1)(e)(ii) it should be calculated as if the cash value of any contribution notionally allocated to the scheme in respect of the person by or on behalf of the company including any adjustment made for any notional investment return achieved during the relevant financial year were a contribution paid by the employer in respect of the individual for the purposes of section 233(1)(b) of the Finance Act 2004.

(3) For the purposes of the calculation in sub-paragraph (1)(d)(ii)—

(a) where the market price of shares at the date on which the shares vest is not ascertainable by the date on which the remuneration report is approved by the directors, an estimate of the market price of the shares shall be calculated on the basis of an average market value over the last quarter of the relevant financial year; and

(b) where the award was an award of shares or share options, the cash amount the individual was or will be required to pay to acquire the share must be deducted from the total.

Definitions applicable to the single total figure table

11.(1) In paragraph 7(1)(b) 'taxable benefits' includes—

(a) sums paid by way of expenses allowance that are—

(i) chargeable to United Kingdom income tax (or would be if the person were an individual, or would be if the person were resident in the United Kingdom for tax purposes), and

(ii) paid to or receivable by the person in respect of qualifying services; and

(b) any benefits received by the person, other than salary, (whether or not in cash) that—

(i) are emoluments of the person, and

(ii) are received by the person in respect of qualifying services.

(2) A payment or other benefit received in advance of a director commencing qualifying services, but in anticipation of performing qualifying services, is to be treated as if received on the first day of performance of the qualifying services.

Commentary

The minimum requirement is as in paragraph (5), supplemented by notes.

Table 3 shows a typical layout (taken from the easyJet 2013 remuneration report)

Table 3: What did the Directors earn in relation to the 2013 financial year?
We have set out the amount earned by the Directors in the table below (£000) (Audited):

	2013						2012					
£ 000	**Fees and Salary**	**Benefits**[3]	**Bonus**[4]	**LTIP**[5]	**Pension**[6]	**Total**	**Fees and Salary**	**Benefits**	**Bonus**	**LTIP**	**Pension**	**Total**
Executive												
Carolyn McCall OBE	665	5	1,153	4,565	47	6,435	665	5	1,274	1,703	47	3,694
Chris Kennedy	410	5	533	2,746	30	3,724	400	5	373	1,024	29	1,831
Non-Executive												
John Barton[1]	125					125						
Sir Michael Rake[2]	175					175	300					300
Charles Gurassa	90					90	85					85
David Bennett	75					75	65					65
Rigas Doganis	63					63	55					55
John Browett	55					55	55					55
Keith Hamill OBE	55					55	60					60
Adele Anderson	55					55	55					55
Andy Martin	55					55	55					55
Total	1,823	10	1,686	7,311	77	10,907	1,795	10	1,647	2,727	76	6,255

1 Appointed to the Board on 1 May 2013.
2 Retired from the Board on 1 May 2013.
3 Benefits relates to the cost to the Company of personal accident and life assurance cover and the value of free and matching shares during the year under the Company's Share Incentive Plan.
4 One third of the bonus will be compulsorily deferred in shares for three years and subject to forfeiture. Carolyn McCall chose to defer the maximum 50% of her bonus and Chris Kennedy chose to defer the maximum one third of his bonus.
5 This relates to the 2011 LTIP awards which vests in March 2014 based on performance measured to 30 September 2013. For the purposes of this table, the award has been valued using the average share price over the three months to 30 September 2013 of £13,254.This compares to £3,379 at grant.
6 Chris Kennedy received £1,315 in exchange for sacrificing salary into the pension scheme, in line with easyJet's SMART pension arrangements. Carolyn McCall has reached her lifetime pension limit and receives a cash alternative (of £47,000) in lieu of pension contributions.

The valuation assumptions are laid out in the legislation. In case of doubt, the GC100 and Investor Group guidance should be considered.

Best practice

Best practice is **Table 3a**, showing five years of data for the CEO with variable pay colour coded and additional columns showing the fair value (expected value) of LTIs and total remuneration awarded.

Table 3a: Suggested best practice format to show five years of CEO and two (or possibly three) years of other Directors (Audited)
[Show the executive directors in a separate table from the Chairman and NEDs, and show sub totals at the bottom of each.]

					PAY FOR PERFORMANCE							
	Salary	**Benefits**	**Pension**	**sub-total**	**Bonus**		**FIXED PAY + Bonus**	**LTI Received**	**sub-total Bonus + LTI**	**Total Received**	**LTI Awarded EV**	**Total Remuneration Awarded**
Notes*	a	b	f		c	% deferred		d		f		
CEO 2012 (current year)	xxx	xxx	xxx	xxx	xxx	50%(S)		xxx	xxx	xxx	xxx	xxx
CEO 2011 (previous year)												
CEO 2010												
CEO 2009												
CEO 2008												
Director 2												
2012												
2011												
2010												
Director 3												
2012												
2011												
2010												
etc.												

sub totals executives directors													
2012													
2011													
2010													
sub totals Non-Executive Directors (state if including or excluding Chairman)												not applicable as no LTIs for NEDs	
2012													
2011													
2010													
Total of all directors													
2012													
2011													
2010													

Note regarding Bonus % deferred: this is a requirement of paragraph 12(4) and it seems sensible to put it in here. Enter C or S to show whether deferred in cash (C) or shares (S).

Separate tables for Chairman and NEDs are permitted. For example:

Table 3b: Chairman and NEDs (Audited)

An example of typical disclosure is:

Name	2014			2013		
	Fees	Other	Total	Fees	Other	Total
Chairman	105	20	125	100	20	120
NED1	42	0	42	40	0	40
NED2	42	0	42	40	0	40
NED3	42	0	42	40	0	40
Total	231	20	251	220	20	240

Additional requirements in respect of the single total figure table

These additional disclosures relate to notes about the benefits, bonus, and LTIs.

(The following is an extract from the SI)

12.(1) In respect of the sum required to be set out by paragraph 7(1)(b), there must be set out after the table a summary identifying—

(a) the types of benefits the value of which is included in the sum set out in the column headed 'b'; and

(b) the value (where significant).

(2) For every component the value of which is included in the sums required to be set out in the columns headed 'c' and 'd' of the table by paragraphs 7(1)(c) and (d), there must be set out after the table the relevant details.

(3) In sub-paragraph (2) 'the relevant details' means—

(a) details of any performance measures and the relative weighting of each;

(b) within each performance measure, the performance targets set at the beginning of the performance period and corresponding value of the award achievable;

(c) for each performance measure, details of actual performance relative to the targets set and measured over the relevant reporting period, and the resulting level of award; and

(d) where any discretion has been exercised in respect of the award, particulars must be given of how the discretion was exercised and how the resulting level of award was determined.

(4) For each component the value of which is included in the sum set out in the column headed 'c' of the table, the report must state if any amount was deferred, the percentage deferred, whether it was deferred

in cash or shares, if relevant, and whether the deferral was subject to any conditions other than performance measures.

(5) Where additional columns are included in accordance with paragraph 6(1)(a), there must be set out in a note to the table the basis on which the sums in the column were calculated, and other such details as are necessary for an understanding of the sums set out in the column, including any performance measures relating to that component of remuneration or if there are none, an explanation of why not.

Typical practice

Minimum disclosure is the single figure table, together with a written explanation covering the points above. A typical disclosure might be:

Table 4: Annual report on remuneration: bonus measures (Audited)

The Bonus is split into three categories and weighted appropriately to the role of the executive. The following illustrates performance against targets for the profit measures:

Measure	*weighting*	*Below target*	*Threshold = 0%*	*Target = 100%*	*Maximum = 200%*	*Outcome %*
Profit	50%				×	167%
Cash Flow	20%			×		110%
Strategic goals	30%				×	150%
Overall					×	151%

The above table does not disclose the performance targets. This is permissible under the get-out clause concerning commercial sensitivity – see paras 2(5) and (6) of the SI (reproduced in footnote[1]). However the fact that the targets (ie threshold, target and maximum performance levels) have not been disclosed at this stage should be stated together with an indication of when they will be disclosed.

A similar table could be used for the LTI performance measures. Or they could be combined into one table, as shown below.

Best practice

As well as notes to the single figure table, the following table is recommended.

---

[1] (5) Any requirement of this Schedule to provide information in respect of performance measures or targets does not require the disclosure of information which, in the opinion of the directors, is commercially sensitive in respect of the company.
(6) Where information that would otherwise be required to be in the report is not included in reliance on sub-paragraph (5), particulars of, and the reasons for, the omission must be given in the report and an indication given of when (if at all) the information is to be reported to the members of the company.

Table 4a: Annual report on remuneration: variable pay additional disclosure of performance conditions and outcomes for latest year (Audited)

Variable Pay	Details of performance conditions (and weightings)	Targets set	Award achievable	Performance achieved	State if discretion used and is so: How exercised? How resulting award determined?
Bonus	Profit growth (50%)	Threshold = +10% Target = +15% Maximum = +25%	Nil 50% 100%	75%	Discretion not exercised
	ROCE (20%)	Threshold = 10% Target = +11% Maximum = +13%	Nil 50% 100%	50%	Discretion not exercised
	New Product launches and sales progress (15%)	Threshold, Target and Maximum Set by rem com and judgment/discretionary assessment at year end	Nil 50% 100%	25%	Discretion not exercised
	International Expansion (15%)	Threshold, Target and Maximum Set by rem com and judgment/discretionary assessment at year end	Nil 50% 100%	100%	Discretion not exercised
	Overall			**56.5%**	
LTI	TSR relative to comparator group (50%)	Median Q3	25% 50% 100%	50%	Discretion not exercised
	EPS growth over three years (50%)	Threshold = RPI + 3% pa Maximum = RPI + 10% pa	25% 100%	30%	Discretion not exercised
	Overall			**40%**	

Where different directors have different goals and/or weightings the above table would have additional rows for each director.

The above table shows the precise targets for profit growth and ROCE. Arguably, the DRRR would require the disclosure of precise targets for the other two bonus measures. However, early signs are that companies are not disclosing such precise targets and auditors are willing to sign off reports without detailed targets.

Arguably, the best practice would be to also include the history of outcomes, after **Table 3 or 4.** The information to show would be as in suggested additional **Tables 19 and 20**, either here in the report or to cross refer to them elsewhere.

Bonus deferral – para 12(4)

Minimum disclosure is a set of notes or a simple table like this.

Table 5: Bonus deferral

	Bonus	**Bonus deferred in**
	deferred	Cash or shares
Director 1	xxx	xxx
Director 2	xxx	xxx
etc		

Best practice

Best practice disclosure is to include this information in **Table 3a**. Whilst this adds clutter, it saves the need to cross refer.

Total pension entitlements

(The following is an extract from the SI)

13.(1) The directors' remuneration report must, for each person who has served as a director of the company at any time during the relevant financial year, and who has a prospective entitlement to defined benefits or cash balance benefits (or to benefits under a hybrid arrangement which includes such benefits) in respect of qualifying services, contain the following information in respect of pensions—

(a) details of those rights as at the end of that year, including the person's normal retirement date;

(b) a description of any additional benefit that will become receivable by a director in the event that that director retires early; and

(c) where a person has rights under more than one type of pension benefit identified in column headed 'e' of the single total figure table, separate details relating to each type of pension benefit.

(2) For the purposes of this paragraph, 'defined benefits', 'cash balance benefits' and 'hybrid arrangement' have the same meaning as in section 152 of the Finance Act 2004.

(3) 'Normal retirement date' means an age specified in the pension scheme rules (or otherwise determined) as the earliest age at which, while the individual continues to accrue benefits under the pension scheme, entitlement to a benefit arises—

(a) without consent (whether of an employer, the trustees or managers of the scheme or otherwise), and

(b) without an actuarial reduction,

but disregarding any special provision as to early repayment on grounds of ill health, redundancy or dismissal.

Minimum disclosure

If the company does not operate a defined benefit scheme the following table is not required.

Table 6: Total pension entitlement

Annual report on remuneration table x: Executive Directors' accrued entitlements under the xyz plc Senior Executives' Pension Fund – Audited

The Group operates a ... [description] ... defined benefit scheme for senior employees. It is the Company's policy that annual bonuses, payments under the Executive Bonus Scheme and benefits in kind are not pensionable.
No Executive Directors are now accruing further pension in the xyz Senior Executives' Pension Fund. The normal retirement age under the Fund for this group is 60.

	Defined Benefit: Accrued annual benefit values at 30 September 2013 based on normal retirement age	**Defined Benefit: Normal retirement date**	**Defined Benefit: Additional value of benefits if early retirement taken**	**Weighting of pension benefit shown in single figure table**
CEO name	£75,000	3 Feb 2005	–	Cash allowance: 100%
Dir 1 name	£84,000	16 Aug 2016	n/a	Cash allowance: 100%
Dir 2 name	£652,000	14 Nov 2008	n/a	n/a

Or alternatively if there is no DB scheme, or more than one type of scheme:

Table 6a

	Defined Benefit: accrued benefits	**Defined Benefit: Normal retire-ment date**	**Additional value if retires early (note only required if such a benefit exists and will need a note explaining it if so)**	**Weighting of Pension**		
				Cash allowance	**Money purchase**	**Defined Benefit**
CEO name						
Dir 1 name						
Dir 2 name						

Best practice

Best practice is **Table 6b** and **6c.**

Table 6b: Pension components

Name	**Total Pension Benefit £00 as shown in Table 6/6a**	**Cash in lieu of pension**		**Money purchase scheme benefit achieved in year**		**Defined benefit scheme benefit achieved in year**		**Defined benefit scheme additional value if retires early**
		£000	**of total pension**	**£000**	**of total pension**	**£000**	**of total pension**	
CEO								
Director 2								
Director 3								

Table 6c: Additional defined benefit disclosures

Name	Retirement age	Age	Length of service	Accrual rate	Individual's contribution to DB plan	Accrued Pension as % of final pensionable salary	Accrued pension at end of year	Increase in accrued pension in the year	Increase in accrued pension net of inflation	Transfer value of accrued pension at start of year	Transfer value of accrued pension at end of year	Increase in transfer value of accrued pension net of individual's contributions	Benefit achieved in year from participating in a defined benefit scheme (HMRC value of 20x increase in accrued benefit)
CEO													
Director 2													
Director 3													

Notes:

If retirement age is different for any director and other employees the reasons for any differences should be explained.

Personal pension contributions to company pension plans should be disclosed. The reasons for any differences to other employees should be explained.

Tables 9a and **9b** also include the items required by the NAPF/LAPFF policy on pension disclosure.

Although not a legal requirement, it should be noted that in 2010 the NAPF and LAPFF[2] called for greater transparency in disclosures on:

- Accrual rates in defined benefit pensions, which include 'final salary' schemes. Some directors benefit from a rapid accrual rate, such as 1/30th, when other employees may typically be on a rate of 1/60th or 1/80th.
- Company contributions to defined contribution pension schemes. Recent studies have shown that contributions for directors are often far higher than those made for other staff.
- Payments in lieu of pensions. An increasing number of firms offer cash payments instead of a pension contribution. These can be sizeable – in some cases over 50% of salary.
- The retirement ages of directors. The reasons for any differences between the boardroom and other employees should be explained.
- Special early retirement provisions. Firms should make it clear that an unreduced pension on early retirement is usually inappropriate.

Scheme interests awarded during the financial year

This will include LTIP and option awards, deferred bonus awards and matching bonus awards but not cash bonus paid out in respect the financial year

(The following is an extract from the SI)

14.(1) The directors' remuneration report must for each person who has served as a director of the company at any time during the relevant financial year contain a table setting out—

(a) details of the scheme interests awarded to the person during the relevant financial year; and

(b) for each scheme interest—

(i) a description of the type of interest awarded;

(ii) a description of the basis on which the award is made;

(iii) the face value of the award;

(iv) the percentage of scheme interests that would be receivable if the minimum performance was achieved;

(v) for a scheme interest that is a share option, an explanation of any difference between the exercise price per share and the price specified under paragraph 14(3);

---

[2] Local Authority Pension Fund Forum.

(vi) the end of the period over which the performance measures and targets for that interest have to be achieved (or if there are different periods for different measures and targets, the end of whichever of those periods ends last); and

(vii) a summary of the performance measures and targets if not set out elsewhere in the report.

(2) In respect of a scheme interest relating to shares or share options, 'face value' means the maximum number of shares that would vest if all performance measures and targets are met multiplied by either—

(a) the share price at date of grant or

(b) the average share price used to determine the number of shares awarded.

(3) Where the report sets out the face value of an award in respect of a scheme interest relating to shares or share options, the report must specify—

(a) whether the face value has been calculated using the share price at date of grant or the average share price;

(b) where the share price at date of grant is used, the amount of that share price and the date of grant;

(c) where the average share price is used, what that price was and the period used for calculating the average.

Minimum disclosure

Table 7: Scheme interests awarded during the financial year – Audited

Name	**Scheme**	**Type of interest**[1]	**Basis of award made**[2]	**Face value of award**[3]	**receivable if minimum vesting**	**Date award vests**[4]	**Summary of perform-ance criteria**[5]
CEO	2008 LTIP	Nil cost option	133% of salary	£500,000	25%	15 Nov 2017	See page xx
etc.							

1 eg conditional share award, nil cost option, etc.
2 eg as multiple of salary, set number of shares or value of shares
3 'face value' means the maximum number of shares that would vest if all performance measures and targets are met multiplied by either the share price at date of grant or the average share price used to determine the number of shares awarded.
4 the end of the period over which the performance measures and targets have to be achieved (or if there are different periods for different measures and targets, the end of whichever of those periods ends last);
5 or reference to where this is shown elsewhere in the report

A typical practice example is shown below.

What LTIP awards were granted to Directors in the year?

Performance and Matching Share Awards were made in the year under the LTIP scheme. Details of the awards made to the Executive Directors are summarised below, with further details given in the table on outstanding share interests on page 85.

Table 7a

	Award	Type	Shares – Number	Face Value[1]	of salary	Perform-ance condition	Perform-ance period	Perform-ance threshold
CEO	Perform-ance	Nil cost option	180,461	£1,443,688	200%	50% TSR v FTSE 100 index 50% ROCE[4]	3 years plus 2 years minimum retention	25%
	Matching	Nil cost option	86,438	£691,504	81%	None	3 years	100%
CFO	Perform-ance	Nil cost option	180,461	£1,329,998	150%	50% TSR v FTSE 100 index 50% ROCE[4]	3 years plus 2 years minimum retention	25%
	Matching	Nil cost option	45,226	£361,800	72%	None	3 years	100%

1 Face value calculated based on the grant date share price of 737p on 18 December 2012.
2 [...]
3 Matching awards are granted over an equal number of shares as the Executive Directors voluntary defer bonus (pre-tax).
4 ROCE (including operating lease adjustments) 12% threshold to 16% maximum.
5 In addition, the TSR awards will not vest unless there has been positive TSR over the performance period.

Best practice

See **Table 7b**.

Table 7b: Scheme interests awarded during the financial year

Name	Scheme	Type of interest [1]	Basis of award made [2]	Number of shares in award	Share price at date of award	Face value of award[3]	Exercise price	receivable if minimum vesting	Date of award	Date award vests[4]	Last date award may be exercised	Summary of performance criteria[5]
CEO	2008 LTIP	Nil cost option	133% of salary	100,000	£5	£500,000	£5	25%	15 Nov 2014	15 Nov 2017	14 Nov 2024	See page xx

1 eg conditional share award, nil cost option, etc.
2 eg as multiple of salary, set number of shares or value of shares
3 "face value" means the maximum number of shares that would vest if all performance measures and targets are met multiplied by either the share price at date of grant or the average share price used to determine the number of shares awarded.
4 the end of the period over which the performance measures and targets have to be achieved (or if there are different periods for different measures and targets, the end of whichever of those periods ends last);
5 or reference to where this is shown elsewhere in the report

The DRRR do not require companies to give full disclosure of historic awards. However it is strongly recommended that such awards are disclosed in full either here or at the end of the report on remuneration in Table 19.

Payments to past directors

(The following is an extract from the SI)

15. The directors' remuneration report must, for the relevant financial year, contain details of any payments of money or other assets to any person who was not a director of the company at the time the payment was made, but who had been a director of the company before that time, excluding—

(a) any payments falling within paragraph 16;

(b) any payments which are shown in the single total figure table;

(c) any payments which have been disclosed in a previous directors' remuneration report of the company;

(d) any payments which are below a *de minimis* threshold set by the company and stated in the report;

(e) payments by way of regular pension benefits commenced in a previous year or dividend payments in respect of scheme interests retained after leaving office; and

(f) payments in respect of employment with or any other contractual service performed for the company other than as a director.

Minimum disclosure

Even if there were no payments it is best practice to state this as this will confirm to readers that no payments were made. Without such a statement in a logical place, the proxy voting agencies will need to undertake a search of all the report to confirm that no payments were made. An example of wording is:

> **Payments to past Directors**
>
> There were no payments made to past Directors during the year.

Payments for loss of office

(The following is an extract from the SI)

16. The directors' remuneration report must for the relevant financial year set out, for each person who has served as a director of the company at any time during that year, or any previous year, excluding payments which are below a *de minimis* threshold set by the company and stated in the report—

(a) the total amount of any payment for loss of office paid to or receivable by the person in respect of that financial year, broken down into each component comprised in that payment and the value of each component;

(b) an explanation of how each component was calculated;

(c) any other payments paid to or receivable by the person in connection with the termination of qualifying services, whether by way of compensation for loss of office or otherwise, including the treatment of outstanding incentive awards that vest on or following termination; and

(d) where any discretion was exercised in respect of the payment, an explanation of how it was exercised.

Minimum disclosure

Even if there were no payments it is best practice to state this as this will confirm to readers that no payments were made. Without such a statement in a logical place, the proxy voting agencies will need to undertake a search of all the report to confirm that no payments were made. An example of wording is:

Payments for loss of office

There were no payments made to any Directors relating to loss of office during the year.

If payments have been made then users may find a table may be easier than a narrative description, to ensure that the disclosure follows the same format as the single figure table, eg:

Table 8: Payments for loss of office

Name	Salary	Benefits	Bonus	LTI	Pension	Other	Total	Explanation of how payment was calculated

Note: also required is an explanation of how each component was calculated, any other payments received, the treatment of outstanding incentive awards, and if and how discretion was exercised (this should cross reference to how it was allowed for within the policy on payments for loss of office and how discretion was exercised)

Best practice

Best practice is the same as the minimum disclosure.

Statement of directors' shareholding and share interests

(The following is an extract from the SI)

17. The directors' remuneration report for the relevant financial year must contain, for each person who has served as a director of the company at any time during that year—

    (a) a statement of any requirements or guidelines for the director to own shares in the company and state whether or not those requirements or guidelines have been met;

    (b) in tabular form or forms—

        (i) the total number of interests in shares in the company of the director including interests of connected persons (as defined for the purposes of section 96B(2) of the Financial Services and Markets Act 2000(2));

        (ii) total number of scheme interests differentiating between—

            (aa) shares and share options; and

            (bb) those with or without performance measures;

        (iii) details of those scheme interests (which may exclude any details included elsewhere in the report); and

        (iv) details of share options which are—

            (aa) vested but unexercised; and

            (bb) exercised in the relevant financial year.

Minimum disclosure

The following table would meet the minimum, although it would be possible to have fewer columns, supplemented by footnotes and some details may be excluded here if included elsewhere in the report.

Table 9: Directors' shareholdings

Name	Requirement to own shares	Whether requirement met	Shares owned	Deferred shares without performance conditions	Deferred shares subject to performance conditions	Options without performance conditions	Options subject to performance conditions	Options exercised in the year
CEO								
Dir 2								
Dir 3								
etc								

A typical example is that of easyJet.

> **What are the shareholding guidelines for Directors?**
>
> Executive Directors are required to build up a shareholding of 175% of salary, to be built up over 5 years from the adoption of the policy (27 September 2012) or their appointment (if later). It is expected that this guideline will be achieved within five years of appointment. Until the guideline is met, they are required to retain 50% of net vested shares from the LTIP. Other senior executives have a 100% of salary shareholding requirement.
>
> The Non-Executive Directors, including the Chairman, are required to build up a shareholding of 100% of annual fees, to be built up over 3 years from the adopt ion of the policy or their appointment (if later).

What are the Directors' current shareholdings?

The following table provides details on the Directors' shareholdings, as at 30 September 2013 (Audited):

	Beneficially shareholding owned[3] shares – Number	guideline achieved[4]	Interests in Shares			
			SAYE	LTIP[5]	SIP	Total
Carolyn McCall OBE	100,916	100%	3,133	1,256,501	2,485	1,262,119
Chris Kennedy	58,091	100%	3,133	622,054	2,509	627,696
John Barton[1]	20,000	85%				
Sir Michael Rake[2]						
Charles Gurassa	18,198	100%				
Adele Anderson	5,114	100%				
David Bennett	9,166	100%				
John Browett	4,312	100%				
Professor Rigas Doganis	12,467	100%				
Keith Hamill OBE	1,960	45%				
Andy Martin	7,000	100%				

1 Appointed to the Board on 1 May 2013.
2 Retired from the Board on 1 May 2013.
3 Includes any shares owned by connected persons.
4 Shares counting towards achievement of the guideline include beneficially owned shares.
5 LTIP are granted in the form of nil cost options subject to performance.

Note: Changes to the position above since 30 September 2013 can be found at our corporate website.

Best practice

Table 9a: Directors' shareholdings

Name	Salary	Share ownership guideline (as multiple of salary or as number of shares)	Shares owned at year end, including vested awards	Value as multiple of salary	Whether requirement met	Shares owned	Deferred shares without performance conditions		Deferred shares subject to performance conditions		Options without performance conditions		Options subject to performance conditions		Options exercised in the year
							Vested	Un-vested	Vested	Un-vested	Vested	Un-vested	Vested	Un-vested	
CEO Number £ value[1] Increase in value in the year[2]	£750,000	5 x salary	800,000 £2,400,000 £500,000	2.0	No	400,000 £1,200,000 £250,000	100,000 £300,000 £62,500	50,000 £150,000 £31,250	100,000 £300,000 £62,500	50,000 £150,000 £31,250	100,000 £300,000 £62,500	50,000 £150,000 £31,250	100,000 £300,000 £62,500	50,000 £150,000 £31,250	20,000 £60,000
Dir 2 etc.															

1 Value is at end of the last financial year. For options it is the notional gain if the option were exercised at the end of the last financial year.
2 If any shares have been sold during the year then this should be explained in notes to the above table.

There should be a cross reference to performance conditions or a description of them, including the latest estimate of their outcome, unless judged commercially sensitive, but if so a note of when such information will be disclosed.

Ideally there should also be a list of all awards that have yet to be exercised as in **Table 9b** below.

Table 9b: Outstanding share scheme and option awards

Name	Share plan	Date of award	Length of performance period in years	Date vesting	Last date for exercise	Maximum number of shares in award	Share price at award date	Face value of award	Expected value of award as % of maximum	Latest estimate of outcome as % of maximum	Vested	Estimated gain based on share price at year end (example assumes share price £7.50)
CEO	LTIP	23/02/2012	5	22/02/2017	22/02/2022	100,000	£5.00	£500,000	50%	75%		562,500
		22/02/2011	5	23/02/2016	22/02/2021	100,000	£4.50	£450,000	50%	75%		562,500
		22/02/2010	5	22/02/2015	23/02/2020	100,000	£4.00	£400,000	50%	75%		562,500
		22/02/2009	5	22/02/2014	22/02/2019	100,000	£3.50	£350,000	50%	75%		562,500
		23/02/2008	5	22/02/2013	22/02/2018	100,000	£3.00	£300,000	50%	75%		562,500
		22/02/2007	5	23/02/2012	22/02/2017	100,000	£2.50	£250,000	50%	100%	vested	750,000
		22/02/2006	5	22/02/2011	23/02/2016	100,000	£2.00	£200,000	50%	50%	vested	375,000
		22/02/2005	5	22/02/2010	22/02/2015	100,000	£4.00	£400,000	50%	25%	vested	187,500
		23/02/2004	5	22/02/2009	22/02/2014	100,000	£3.50	£350,000	50%	100%	vested	750,000
		22/02/2003	5	23/02/2008	22/02/2013	100,000	£3.00	£300,000	50%	90%	vested	675,000
		22/02/2002	5	22/02/2007	23/02/2012	100,000	£2.50	£250,000	50%	75%	vested	562,500
	Options	23/02/2012	3	22/02/2015	22/02/2022	100,000	£5.00	£500,000	50%	75%		562,500
		22/02/2011	3	22/02/2014	22/02/2021	100,000	£4.50	£450,000	50%	75%		562,500
		22/02/2010	3	22/02/2013	23/02/2020	100,000	£4.00	£400,000	50%	75%		562,500
		22/02/2009	3	23/02/2012	22/02/2019	100,000	£3.50	£350,000	50%	100%	vested	750,000
		23/02/2008	3	22/02/2011	22/02/2018	100,000	£3.00	£300,000	50%	100%	vested	750,000
		22/02/2007	3	22/02/2010	22/02/2017	100,000	£2.50	£250,000	50%	100%	vested	750,000
		22/02/2006	3	22/02/2009	23/02/2016	100,000	£2.00	£200,000	50%	50%	vested	375,000
		22/02/2005	3	23/02/2008	22/02/2015	100,000	£4.00	£400,000	50%	25%	vested	187,500
		23/02/2004	3	22/02/2007	22/02/2014	100,000	£3.50	£350,000	50%	100%	vested	750,000
		22/02/2003	3	22/02/2006	22/02/2013	100,000	£3.00	£300,000	50%	90%	vested	675,000
		22/02/2002	3	22/02/2005	23/02/2012	100,000	£2.50	£250,000	50%	75%	vested	562,500
	subtotal vested awards					£1,400,000		£4,150,000				£8,100,000
	subtotal unvested awards					£800,000		£3,350,000				£4,500,000
	total					**£2,200,000**		**£7,500,000**				**£12,600,000**
Dir 2 etc.												

Comparison of overall performance and pay

(The following is an extract from the SI)

Performance graph and table

18.(1) The directors' remuneration report must—

(a) contain a line graph that shows for each of—

(i) a holding of shares of that class of the company's equity share capital whose listing, or admission to dealing, has resulted in the company falling within the definition of 'quoted company', and

(ii) a hypothetical holding of shares made up of shares of the same kinds and number as those by reference to which a broad equity market index is calculated,

a line drawn by joining up points plotted to represent, for each of the financial years in the relevant period, the total shareholder return on that holding; and

(b) state the name of the index selected for the purposes of the graph and set out the reasons for selecting that index.

(2) The report must also set out in tabular form the following information for each of the financial years in the relevant period in respect of the director undertaking the role of chief executive officer—

(a) total remuneration as set out in the single total figure table;

(b) the sum set out in the table in column headed 'c' in the single total figure table expressed as a percentage of the maximum that could have been paid in respect of that component in the financial year; and

(c) the sum set out in column headed 'd' in the single total figure table restated as a percentage of the number of shares vesting against the maximum number of shares that could have been received, or, where paid in money and other assets, as a percentage of the maximum that could have been paid in respect of that component in the financial year.

(3) For the purposes of sub-paragraphs (1), (2) and (6), 'relevant period' means the specified period of financial years of which the last is the relevant financial year.

(4) Where the relevant financial year—

(a) is the company's first financial year for which the performance graph is prepared in accordance with this paragraph, 'specified' in sub-paragraph (3) means 'five';

(b) is the company's 'second', 'third', 'fourth', 'fifth' financial year in which the report is prepared in accordance with this Schedule, "specified" in sub-paragraph (3) means 'six', 'seven', 'eight', 'nine' as the case may be; and

(c) is any financial year after the fifth financial year in which the report is prepared in accordance with this Schedule, 'specified' means 'ten'.

(5) Sub-paragraph (2) may be complied with by use of either—

(a) a sum based on the information supplied in the directors' remuneration reports for those previous years, or,

(b) where no such report has been compiled, a suitable corresponding sum.

(6) For the purposes of sub-paragraph (1), the 'total shareholder return' for a relevant period on a holding of shares must be calculated using a fair method that—

(a) takes as its starting point the percentage change over the period in the market price of the holding;

(b) involves making—

(i) the assumptions specified in sub-paragraph (7) as to reinvestment of income, and

(ii) the assumption specified in sub-paragraph (9) as to the funding of liabilities; and

(c) makes provision for any replacement of shares in the holding by shares of a different description;

and the same method must be used for each of the holdings mentioned in sub-paragraph (1).

(7) The assumptions as to reinvestment of income are—

(a) that any benefit in the form of shares of the same kind as those in the holding is added to the holding at the time the benefit becomes receivable; and

(b) that any benefit in cash, and an amount equal to the value of any benefit not in cash and not falling within paragraph (a), is applied at the time the benefit becomes receivable in the purchase at their market price of shares of the same kind as those in the holding and that the shares purchased are added to the holding at that time.

(8) In sub-paragraph (7) 'benefit' means any benefit (including, in particular, any dividend) receivable in respect of any shares in the holding by the holder from the company of whose share capital the shares form part.

(9) The assumption as to the funding of liabilities is that, where the holder has a liability to the company of whose capital the shares in the holding form part, shares are sold from the holding—

(a) immediately before the time by which the liability is due to be satisfied, and

(b) in such numbers that, at the time of the sale, the market price of the shares sold equals the amount of the liability in respect of the shares in the holding that are not being sold.

(10) In sub-paragraph (9) 'liability' means a liability arising in respect of any shares in the holding or from the exercise of a right attached to any of those shares.

Minimum disclosure

The minimum disclosure is **Chart 2**, the performance graph below, and **Table 10,** the supporting table of the Single Total Figure Bonus payout and LTIP vesting over five years (initially, but this will increase by one year each year until ten years are shown).

Chart 2: Comparison of TSR for last ten years (five years initially)

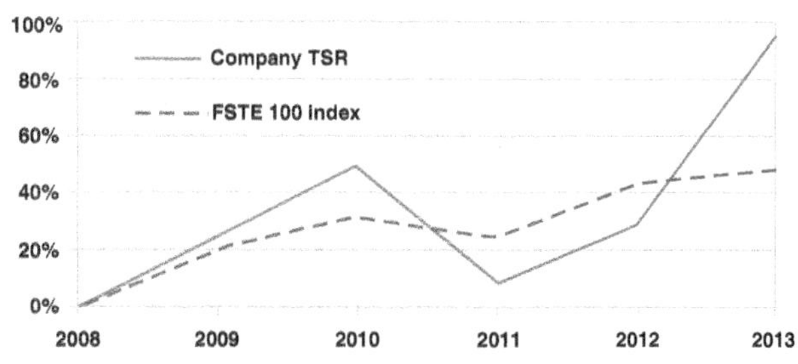

	2009	2010	2011	2012	2013
Single Figure £000	4,569	4,102	4,291	4,374	5,249
Bonus as % maximum	58%	65%	75%	75%	80%
LTIPs vesting % maximum	0%	25%	0%	75%	100%

Typical practice

This an area where best and typical practice will emerge over time. Initial reports under the new regime suggest most companies are being very conservative in their approach and merely providing the minimum disclosure. There is a strong argument for also disclosing the expected value of awards, as well as the single figure which will be highly volatile and, because it does not report LTIs until they pay out, will understate the real level of remuneration and may lead to surprises for shareholders in the future (if the expected value and high quality commentary are not also made).

Companies may find the following approach useful.

Chart 2a: Comparison of TSR and CEO pay for last ten years (five years initially)

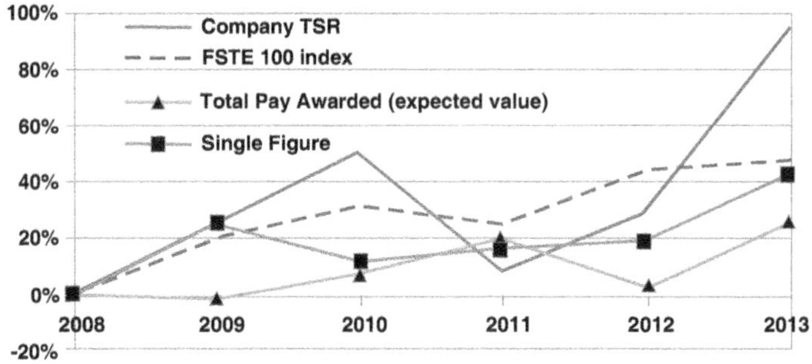

	2009	2010	2011	2012	2013
Single Figure £000	4,569	4,102	4,291	4,374	5,249
Total Pay Awarded (Expected Value)	3,896	4,244	4,771	4,115	4,938
Bonus as % maximum	58%	65%	75%	75%	80%
LTIPs vesting % maximum	0%	25%	0%	75%	100%
Selected KPIs					
TSR	25%	50%	9%	29%	95%
Profit % increase	8%	10%	10%	-4%	1%
Turnover % increase	-2%	-3%	-11%	0%	0%
ROCE %	3.6%	6.9%	9.8%	11.3%	17.4%
On-time performance	80	66	79	88	87
Customer satisfaction targets	85	73	79	82	83
Operating costs (excluding fuel) per seat at constant currency £	34.37	36.62	36.62	6.25	38.17

Best practice

This chart will seem to some readers the most logical place to start when explaining the linkage of pay and performance. It is recommended that a summary version is included in the 'Remuneration at a Glance' section of the report, with reference to it in the summary statement, to explain the historic linkage of pay and performance or reasons why this was not the case. The commentary would explain why the Remuneration Committee had adopted the remuneration policy and why it had paid out the amounts it had, noting the performance of the company and the linkage of pay and performance and other material factors.

Best practice would be to include as well as the graph above, the index of the components of pay and the actual amounts in a table (see **Table 10**). In addition, the requirements of paragraph 24 could usefully be included in this table.

Table 10: Detailed comparison of company performance and CEO pay and profit, dividends and overall compensation costs[3]

Year	**-10**	**-9**	**-8**	**-7**	**-6**	**-5**	**-4**	**-3**	**-2**	**-1**	**0**
TSR	**100**	**77**	**86**	**93**	**109**	**121**	**123**	**87**	**105**	**115**	**109**
Total Pay	**100**	**144**	**154**	**171**	**183**	**183**	**215**	**219**	**216**	**235**	**264**
Salary	100	118	125	128	136	135	144	154	156	157	162
Other Benefits	100	91	102	105	110	110	120	90	111	95	116
Pension	100	123	142	145	155	154	163	135	185	144	168
sub-total not performance related	**100**	**118**	**130**	**132**	**141**	**140**	**149**	**142**	**163**	**147**	**160**
Bonus	100	154	191	231	248	266	317	303	316	362	429
LTI	100	189	175	202	217	205	266	309	243	312	344
sub-total performance related pay	**100**	**174**	**182**	**214**	**230**	**232**	**288**	**306**	**275**	**334**	**381**
KPIs											
TSR	100	77	86	93	109	121	123	87	105	115	109
Turnover	100	100	107	109	117	138	108	151	157	163	221
Profit	100	100	107	109	117	138	108	151	157	163	221
ROCE	100	135	131	118	122	116	97	122	140	141	175
ARPU	100	101	75	104	82	95	86	87	90	95	100
Dividends	100	100	113	115	129	164	164	234	245	256	351
Overall expenditure on pay	100	100	107	109	117	138	108	151	157	163	221
Average employee pay	100	100	102	107	113	128	106	128	135	141	142

[3] **Table 10** in this example has been populated with the average FTSE 100 CEO remuneration, TSR, turnover and profits data. Other data on KPIs, dividends and employee compensation was not readily available and is not the average FTSE 100.

Year	**-10**	**-9**	**-8**	**-7**	**-6**	**-5**	**-4**	**-3**	**-2**	**-1**	**0**
CEO remuneration in £000											
Salary	525	620	659	672	716	711	755	810	818	825	850
Other Benefits	83	75	84	87	91	91	99	74	92	78	96
Pension	347	427	494	504	537	534	566	467	642	499	581
sub-total not performance related	**954**	**1,122**	**1,237**	**1,262**	**1,344**	**1,336**	**1,421**	**1,351**	**1,552**	**1,402**	**1,527**
Bonus	372	573	708	859	922	990	1,178	1,127	1,177	1,345	1,597
LTI	479	904	841	966	1,038	983	1,278	1,480	1,167	1,497	1,647
sub-total performance related pay	**851**	**1,477**	**1,549**	**1,825**	**1,960**	**1,973**	**2,456**	**2,607**	**2,344**	**2,842**	**3,244**
Total Pay	**1,806**	**2,600**	**2,786**	**3,087**	**3,305**	**3,309**	**3,877**	**3,958**	**3,896**	**4,244**	**4,771**
Annual % change (profit, dividends and overall expenditure on pay are required by Para 24).											
Profit	11%	0%	8%	1%	8%	18%	-22%	39%	4%	4%	*35%
Dividends	5%	0%	8%	1%	8%	18%	-22%	39%	4%	4%	*35%
TSR	-15%	-23%	12%	7%	17%	11%	2%	-29%	21%	9%	*-5%
Overall expenditure on pay	3%	35%	-3%	-10%	3%	-5%	-16%	25%	15%	1%	*24%
Average employee pay	0%	0%	2%	5%	5%	13%	-17%	21%	5%	5%	*1%
Total Pay	**29%**	**44%**	**7%**	**11%**	**7%**	**0%**	**17%**	**2%**	**-2%**	**9%**	***12%**

*Note minimum disclosure is only latest year.

Other possible KPIs and remuneration figures:

(Note these are examples. Each company should choose its own KPIs.)

CEO Pay – Total expected value of awards
CEO Pay – Total received
Total Shareholder Return – absolute value
Total Shareholder Return – relative to an index eg FTSE 100, 250, All Share etc. and/or comparator index or group of companies
Share price growth (as the make-up of TSR is useful to see)
Dividends – yield as % share price
Market Capitalisation (Note: it is suggested this is included as well as TSR and share price. It is not quite the same as share price as, by issuing new shares, a company might increase market cap but reduce the price per share. Pay is correlated to size of company so this is an important piece of background)
Net Debt
Enterprise Value
Turnover
Profit (EBITDA)

Profit margin
Profit growth/Turnover relative to peers
Cash flow
ROCE
WACC
Debt/EBITDA
EPS
P/E ratio (share price/EPS)
Other KPIs Eg ARPU (average revenue per user), key strategic goals, Customer satisfaction, staff effectiveness, Health and Safety, CSR measures
CEO Salary
CEO Bonus
CEO shares and options – expected value of awards made in the year
CEO share awards and options realised – total of gains from options exercised in the year and restricted shares that vested in the year
Pension – transfer value of increase in accrued benefits
Benefits – taxable value of benefits received
Average Remuneration of employees
Ratio of CEO (expected/realised) pay to average employee

Percentage change in remuneration of director undertaking the role of chief executive officer

(The following is an extract from the SI)

19.(1)The directors' remuneration report must set out (in a manner which permits comparison) in relation to each of the kinds of remuneration required to be set out in each of the columns headed 'a', 'b' and 'c' of the single total figure table the following information—

(a) the percentage change from the financial year preceding the relevant financial year in respect of the director undertaking the role of the chief executive officer; and

(b) the average percentage change from the financial year preceding the relevant financial year in respect of the employees of the company taken as a whole.

(2) Where for the purposes of sub-paragraph (1)(b), a comparator group comprising the employees taken as a whole is considered by the company as an inappropriate comparator group of employees, the

company may use such other comparator group of employees as the company identifies, provided the report contains a statement setting out why that group was chosen.

(3) Where the company is a parent company, the statement must relate to the group and not the company, and the director reported on is the director undertaking the role of chief executive officer of the parent company, and the employees are the employees of the group.

Minimum disclosure:

Table 11: Percentage change in remuneration of CEO

	(a) Salary	(b) Benefits	(c) Bonus	Total of Salary, benefits and bonus
CEO	+3%	+2%	-10%	-5%
Average of all employees	+3%	+3%	+0%	+3%

Best practice

Best practice will to disclose this information for a number of years in **Table 10**. And to put a paragraph in the report here, to cross refer to the table.

Relative importance of spend on pay

(The following is an extract from the SI)

20.(1)The directors' remuneration report must set out in a graphical or tabular form that shows in respect of the relevant financial year and the immediately preceding financial year the actual expenditure of the company, and the difference in spend between those years, on—

(a) remuneration paid to or receivable by all employees of the group;

(b) distributions to shareholders by way of dividend and share buyback; and

(c) any other significant distributions and payments or other uses of profit or cash-flow deemed by the directors to assist in understanding the relative importance of spend on pay.

(2) There must be set out in a note to the report an explanation in respect of sub-paragraph (1)(c) why the particular matters were chosen by the directors and how the amounts were calculated.

(3) Where the matters chosen for the report in respect of sub-paragraph (1)(c) in the relevant financial year are not the same as the other items set out in the report for previous years, an explanation for that change must be given.

Minimum disclosure

Table 12: Relative importance of spend on pay (example)

	2014	**2013**	**change in the reporting period compared to previous year**
Remuneration paid or receivable by all employees in the group	577	476	21%
Dividends (including share buyback)	85	308	-72%

EasyJet discloses more than most companies in this part of the report.

How much does easyJet spend on employee pay each year?

The table below shows the total pay for all of easyJet's employees compared to other key financial indicators.

	Year ended 30 September 2012	**Year ended 30 September 2013**	**change**
Employee costs (£m)	476	517	8%
Ordinary dividend (£m)	85	133	56%
Special dividend (£m)		175	
Average number of employees	8,206	8,343	2%
Revenues (£m)	3,854	4,258	10%
Profit before tax (£m)	317	478	51%

Additional information on the number of employees, total revenues and profit has been provided for context. The majority of easyJet's employees (around 85%) perform flight and ground operations, with the rest performing administrative and managerial roles.

Best practice

Best practice is to also include the total remuneration paid to directors, and to show all of this data for five or ten years as is shown in **Table 10**; which will also include TSR, KPIs and a full breakdown of CEO pay.

Statement of implementation of remuneration policy in the following financial year

(The following is an extract from the SI)

21.(1)The directors' remuneration report must contain a statement describing how the company intends to implement the approved directors' remuneration policy in the financial year following the relevant financial year.

(2) The statement must include, where applicable, the—

(a) performance measures and relative weightings for each; and

(b) performance targets determined for the performance measures and how awards will be calculated.

(3) Where this is not the first year of the approved remuneration policy, the statement should detail any significant changes in the way that the remuneration policy will be implemented in the next financial year compared to how it was implemented in the relevant financial year.

(4) This statement need not include information that is elsewhere in the report, including any disclosed in the directors' remuneration policy.

Also of relevance to the above are para 2(5) and (6) of the SI.

(5) Any requirement of this Schedule to provide information in respect of performance measures or targets does not require the disclosure of information which, in the opinion of the directors, is commercially sensitive in respect of the company.

(6) Where information that would otherwise be required to be in the report is not included in reliance on sub-paragraph (5), particulars of, and the reasons for, the omission must be given in the report and an indication given of when (if at all) the information is to be reported to the members of the company.

Typical disclosure

Although para 21 above is quite specific, para 2(5) and (6) of the SI provides that companies do not have to disclose commercially sensitive targets.

Typical wording might be:

The targets themselves, as they relate to the 2014 financial year, are deemed to be commercially sensitive. However, retrospective disclosure of the targets and performance against them will be provided in next year's remuneration report to the extent that they do not remain commercially sensitive at that time.

EasyJet example

How will the Remuneration Policy be applied for the 2014 financial year?

What are the Executive Directors' current salaries? The Executive Directors' salaries for the 2014 financial year are as follows:

	1 Jan 2014	1 July 2012	Change
CEO	£681,600	£665,000	2.50%
CFO	£420,250	£410,000	2.50%

[1] To ensure consistency across the Group, salary increases are effective from 1January from 2014 onwards. This is now the policy on an on-going basis.

How will annual performance be rewarded for performance in the 2014 financial year?

The annual bonus for the 2014 financial year will operate on the same basis as for 2013 financial year and will be consistent with the policy detailed in the Remuneration policy section of this report in terms of the maximum bonus opportunity, deferral and clawback provisions. The measures have been selected to reflect a range of financial and operational goals that support the key strategic objectives of the Company.

The performance measures and weightings will be as follows:

Measure	CEO	CFO
Profit before tax	70%	60%
On-time performance	10%	10%
Customer satisfaction targets	10%	10%
Operating costs (excluding fuel) per seat at constant currency	10%	10%
Departmental objectives		10%

The proposed target levels for 2014 have been set to be challenging relative to the 2014 business plan.

The targets themselves, as they relate to the 2014 financial year, are deemed to be commercially sensitive. However, retrospective disclosure of the targets and performance against them will be provided in next year's remuneration report to the extent that they do not remain commercially sensitive at that time. The safety of our customers and people underpins all of the operational activities of the Group and the bonus plan includes an underpin that enables the Remuneration Committee to scale back the bonus earned in the event that there is a safety event that occurs that it considers warrants the use of such discretion.

How will the LTIP be operated in relation to the 2014 financial year awards?

The award levels of Performance Shares for the Executive Directors in the 2014 financial year are 200% of salary for the Chief Executive and 150% of salary for the Chief Financial Officer.

If Executive Directors elect to voluntarily defer more of their bonus into shares beyond the compulsory deferred element. Matching Share Awards may be granted. The amount they voluntarily defer may be eligible for a 1:1 match dependent on the delivery of performance goals, with awards vesting over a three year period. The CEO may voluntarily defer up to 50% of the annual bonus earned and the CFO may defer up to 33% of the bonus earned. The CEO and CFO both deferred the maximum amount of their 2013 financial year bonus and will be eligible for Matching Awards on these amounts (including operating lease adjustments) over the three year performance period (being three financial years from 1 October 2013). The TSR targets are based on relative TSR compared to companies ranked FTSE 51–150 at the date of grant, where the average share price is calculated over three months at the start and end of the period. In addition in order for the TSR awards to vest, easyJet must have achieved positive absolute TSR performance over the performance period. The Executive Directors have confirmed that they will retain the after tax value of shares for a minimum of six months from the vesting of this award.

These targets will require management to deliver strong, sustainable performance over the period.

The 2014 financial year LTIP awards (Performance and Matching Share Awards) will be subject to the following performance conditions:

	Below Threshold (0% vesting)	Threshold (25% vesting)	Maximum (100% vesting)
TSR (50% of total award)	< median	median	upper quartile

As a percentage of maximum bonus opportunity:

	Below Threshold (0% vesting)	Threshold (25% vesting)	On-target (40% vesting)	Maximum (100% vesting)
ROCE (50% of total award)	15.0%	15.0%	18.5%	20.0%

Awards vest on a straight line basis between these points. As with the awards granted in the 2013 financial year the ROCE targets are based on average ROCE.

How will the Non-Executive Directors be paid in the 2014 financial year?

The fees for the Chairman and Non-Executive Directors will be as follows:

	FY 2014	FY 2013
Chairman	£300,000	£300,000
Basic fee for other Non-Executive Directors	£60,000	£55,000
Fees for Deputy Chairman and SID Role	£25,000	£25,000
Chairmen of the Audit, Safety and Remuneration Committees	£15,000	£10,000
Chairman of the Finance Committee	£10,000	£10,000

Basic fees were reviewed and increased on 1October 2013; the previous rates had been in place since October 2010. Fees for the Chairmen of the Audit, Safety and Remuneration Committees were also increased at this time to reflect the increasing workload of these Commit tees.

Consideration by the directors of matters relating to directors' remuneration

(The following is an extract from the SI)

22.(1)If a committee of the company's directors has considered matters relating to the directors' remuneration for the relevant financial year, the directors' remuneration report must—

(a) name each director who was a member of the committee at any time when the committee was considering any such matter;

(b) state whether any person provided to the committee advice, or services, that materially assisted the committee in their consideration of any such matter and name any person that has done so;

(c) in the case of any person named under paragraph (b), who is not a director of the company (other than a person who provided legal advice on compliance with any relevant legislation), state—

(i) the nature of any other services that that person has provided to the company during the relevant financial year;

(ii) by whom that person was appointed, whether or not by the committee and how they were selected;

(iii) whether and how the remuneration committee has satisfied itself that the advice received was objective and independent; and

(iv) the amount of fee or other charge paid by the company to that person for the provision of the advice or services referred to in paragraph (b) and the basis on which it was charged.

(2) In sub-paragraph (1)(b) 'person' includes (in particular) any director of the company who does not fall within sub-paragraph (1)(a).

(3) Sub-paragraph (1)(c) does not apply where the person was, at the time of the provision of the advice or service, an employee of the company.

(4) This paragraph also applies to a committee which considers remuneration issues during the consideration of an individual's nomination as a director.

Minimum disclosure

There should be written paragraphs covering the details required, possibly including a table of remuneration consultants and fees.

Table 13: Disclosure of Remuneration Committee advisers and fees

Name	**Fees for advice to the committee which materially assisted the committee**
MM&K	£60,000
Big 4 accountant firm	£25,000
Large Actuarial firm	£25,000

Best practice

Full disclosure of the basic information such as in the table below will help shareholders see the scale of the potential conflicts of interests. The background data will then enable the shareholders to review the supporting statement requited by the SI to demonstrate the conflicts have been managed and the degree of independence in the advice given to the Committee.

Table 13a: Disclosure of Remuneration Committee advisers and fees

Name	**Whether appointed by Remuneration Committee**	**How selected**	**Fees for advice to the Committee which materially assisted the Committee**	**Fees for other remuneration related services**	**Fees for other services to the company**	**Fees for services to the company's Pension fund**
MM&K	Yes	First appointed in 2004. Subject to annual review.	£60,000	£20,000		
Big 4 accountant firm	Yes	Committee reviewed who was best suited to do this work	£25,000	£200,000	£3,300,000	
Large Actuarial firm	Yes	Committee reviewed who was best suited to do this work	£25,000	£25,000	£75,000	£2,000,000

Statement of voting at general meeting

(The following is an extract from the SI)

23. The directors' remuneration report must contain a statement setting out in respect of the last general meeting at which a resolution of the following kind was moved by the company—

(a) in respect of a resolution to approve the directors' remuneration report, the percentage of votes cast for and against and the number of votes withheld;

(b) in respect of a resolution to approve the directors' remuneration policy, the percentage of votes cast for and against and the number of votes withheld; and,

(c) where there was a significant percentage of votes against either such resolution, a summary of the reasons for those votes, as far as known to the directors, and any actions taken by the directors in response to those concerns.

Minimum disclosure

Table 14: Shareholder voting

Resolution	Votes for	Votes against	Number of Votes withheld
Remuneration report on the previous year	90%	10%	100,000
Remuneration Policy	95%	5%	100,000

There should be written paragraphs covering the details required including where in either (a) or (b) there were substantial shareholder votes against the resolution, where known to the company, the reasons for that vote and any actions taken by the directors in response to that.

Best practice

There should be a history of previous votes on remuneration policy and the resolution to approve the report on the previous year and previous votes on the Remuneration Report and resolutions to approve new share plans and changes to share plans.

Note for years where the previous DRRR applied, the resolution on the remuneration report could be included in the previous years' data in rows 2 to 5 of the above table.

Table 14a: Shareholder voting

Resolution	Votes cast	of shares voted	Votes for number	Votes for – percentage of total votes cast including abstentions	Votes against	Abstentions
Remuneration report on the previous year	10,000,000	76%	9,000,000	90%	900,000	100,000
Previous year -1	10,000,000	76%	9,000,000	90%	900,000	100,000
Previous year -2	10,000,000	76%	9,000,000	90%	900,000	100,000
Previous year -3	10,000,000	76%	9,000,000	90%	900,000	100,000
Previous year -4	10,000,000	76%	9,000,000	90%	900,000	100,000
Remuneration Policy Previous year	10,000,000	76%	9,000,000	90%	900,000	100,000
Previous year -1	10,000,000	76%	9,000,000	90%	900,000	100,000
Previous year -2	10,000,000	76%	9,000,000	90%	900,000	100,000
Previous year -3	10,000,000	76%	9,000,000	90%	900,000	100,000
Previous year -4	10,000,000	76%	9,000,000	90%	900,000	100,000
New LTIP 2009	10,000,000	76%	9,000,000	90%	900,000	100,000
New SIP 2011	10,000,000	76%	9,000,000	90%	900,000	100,000
Votes on exit payments	etc.					

Other items that could be included in the report

Dilution

This is not a requirement of the DRRR, but there is an important 10% ABI guideline, against which companies should reported shareholders. A typical disclosure from the easyJet report is below:

> **Position against dilution limits**
>
> easyJet complies with the ABI Principles of Executive Remuneration. These principles require that commitments under all of the Company's share ownership schemes must not exceed 10% of the issued share capital in any rolling 10 year period. The requirement for shares under all current share incentive schemes, (LTIP. Deferred Annual Bonus Plan, Save As you Earn and Share Incentive Plan) will be satisfied with share purchases on the market. The remaining 0.8 million options under the Discretionary Share Option Schemes, when or if exercised, will continue to be settled by the issue of new shares. The Company's current position against its dilution limit is therefore under the maximum 10% limit.

Employee Share Plans

This is not a requirement of the DRRR, but many shareholders regard such plans as good things to have. High take up will be a sign of good employee engagement. A typical disclosure, taken from the easyJet report, is below:

> **Employee share plan participation**
>
> easyJet encourages share ownership throughout the Company by the use of Performance (Free) Shares and Matching shares within a Share Incentive Plan and a Save As You Earn. Take up of the schemes remains high with over 91% of eligible staff participating in one or more of the plans during the year. Executive Directors may also participate in these plans on the same terms as other eligible staff. They are summarised in the Corporate Responsibility section on page 50.

UK Corporate Governance Code Items

Section D.1 Supporting Principle Three says 'They should also be sensitive to pay and employment conditions elsewhere in the group, especially when determining annual salary increases.'

Section D.2 Supporting Principle Two says 'The Chairman of the board should ensure that the company maintains contact as required with its principle shareholders about remuneration.'

In Schedule A, paragraph 8, the last sentence says 'Remuneration incentives should be compatible with risk policies and systems.'

Section B.6.1 requires an evaluation of the performance of the remuneration committee.

The following wording may convey the necessary messages to shareholders (noting that the Code does not have to be complied with and that explanations may be the more appropriate response to the Code).

> Remuneration is reviewed annually for the following year taking into account contractual agreements, general economic and market conditions and the level of increases made across the Group as a whole. Base salary increases elsewhere in the Group are set at a business level, taking into account economic factors, competitive market rates, roles, skills, experience and individual performance. The change in wages and salaries for the Company as a whole is reported in chart 2 on page 59.
>
> The Committee seeks the views of its main Shareholders on matters of remuneration that it thinks Shareholders are interested in. The Committee considers the 98% vote in favour of the Remuneration Report in 2012 (table 17 on page 70) to demonstrate strong Shareholder support for the Group's remuneration arrangements.

Risk and reward: During the year, the Committee reviewed and confirmed that the plans in operation throughout the Group did not incentivise excessive risk and, in particular, that the remuneration incentives in the Company are compatible with its risk policies and systems.

In September 2013, the Committee conducted a formal review of its effectiveness and concluded that it had fulfilled its remit and had been effective in the year.

28.3 Directors' Remuneration Policy

The remuneration policy disclosure needs to reflect what is said in the summary statement from the remuneration committee chairman.

A checklist of the contents of the remuneration policy is in **Chapter 6.9** and the detailed requirements of the DRRR and examples in relation to policy are shown below.

In contrast to the annual report on remuneration, there is quite a lot of scope and discretion about choices for policy.

In relation to the disclosure the remuneration committee needs to consider at least all of the items in the checklist below.

Key issues – Checklist Overview

(i) Have each of the requirements in the regulations been met in full?

(ii) When will the policy take effect?

(iii) Is the policy sufficiently flexible to enable it to last for the long term?

(iv) Does the policy cover payments to be made pursuant to existing commitments?

(v) Are all discretions included in the policy?

(vi) Does the policy include any emergency discretion?

(vii) Are recruitment and leaver policies appropriate for the company's needs?

(viii) Are all policy provisions regarding retirement payments consistent with the company's justification for such provisions?

(ix) Will shareholders approve of what will be included in the policy?

(x) Does the policy fit together as a whole, and with external documentation?

Companies will need to choose the degree of detail it wishes in the policies and the flexibility for discretion.

The illustrations of scenarios make no allowance for share price. Companies will need to consider whether to include additional disclosers showing the impact of share price changes on future rewards and whether such illustrations should include just the latest year's or some or all historic share scheme awards and also shares owned by the director. Some shareholders and fund managers will regard it as positive or very positive if directors' rewards are well aligned with shareholders (some view the lack of such alignment as a reason to sell shares or not to buy them).

This part of the chapter is structured to follow exactly the same order as the legislation. For each part of the legislation, the structure is to show:

- First the legislation
- Then some commentary
- Then some examples of minimum or typical and then the author's view of what might become or best practice.

PART 4 of the SI specifies the information required.

Remuneration policy

(The following is an extract from the SI)

24.(1)The information required to be included in the directors' remuneration report by the provisions of this Part must be set out in a separate part of the report and constitutes the directors' remuneration policy of the company.

(2) Where a company intends to move a resolution at a meeting of the company to approve a directors' remuneration policy and it is intended that some or all of the provisions of the last approved directors' remuneration policy are to continue to apply after the resolution is approved, this fact must be stated in the policy which is the subject of the resolution and it must be made clear which provisions of the last approved policy are to continue to apply and for what period of time it is intended that they shall apply.

(3) Notwithstanding the requirements of this Part, the directors' remuneration policy part of the report must set out all those matters for which the company requires approval for the purposes of Chapter 4A of Part 10 of the 2006 Act(3).

(4) Where any provision of the directors' remuneration policy provides for the exercise by the directors of a discretion on any aspect of the policy, the policy must clearly set out the extent of that discretion in respect of any such variation, change or amendment.

(5) The directors' remuneration policy (or revised directors' remuneration policy) of a company in respect of which a company moves a resolution for approval in accordance with section 439A of the 2006 Act must, on the first occasion that such a resolution is moved after 1st October 2013 set out the date from which it is intended by the company that that policy is to take effect.

Future policy table

25.(1)The directors' remuneration report must contain in tabular form a description of each of the components of the remuneration package for the directors of the company which are comprised in the directors' remuneration policy of the company.

(2) Where the report complies with sub-paragraph (1) by reference to provisions which apply generally to all directors, the table must also include any particular arrangements which are specific to any director individually.

(3) References in this Part to 'component parts of the remuneration package' include, but are not limited to, all those items which are relevant for the purposes of the single total figure table.

26. In respect of each of the components described in the table there must be set out the following information—

(a) how that component supports the short and long-term strategic objectives of the company (or, where the company is a parent company, the group);

(b) an explanation of how that component of the remuneration package operates;

(c) the maximum that may be paid in respect of that component (which may be expressed in monetary terms, or otherwise);

(d) where applicable, a description of the framework used to assess performance including—

(i) a description of any performance measures which apply and, where more than one performance measure applies, an indication of the weighting of the performance measure or group of performance measures;

(ii) details of any performance period; and

(iii) the amount (which may be expressed in monetary terms or otherwise) that may be paid in respect of —

(aa) the minimum level of performance that results in any payment under the policy, and (bb) any further levels of performance set in accordance with the policy;

(e) an explanation as to whether there are any provisions for the recovery of sums paid or the withholding of the payment of any sum.

27. There must accompany the table notes which set out—

(a) in respect of any component falling within paragraph 26(d)(i)–(iii), an explanation of why any performance measures were chosen and how any performance targets are set;

(b) in respect of any component (other than salary, fees, benefits or pension) which is not subject to performance measures, an explanation of why there are no such measures;

(c) if any component did not form part of the remuneration package in the last approved directors' remuneration policy, why that component is now contained in the remuneration package;

(d) in respect of any component which did form a part of such a package, what changes have been made to it and why; and

(e) an explanation of the differences (if any) in the company's policy on the remuneration of directors from the policy on the remuneration of employees generally (within the company, or where the company is a parent company, the group).

28. The information required by paragraph 25 may, in respect of directors not performing an executive function, be set out in a separate table and there must be set out in that table the approach of the company to the determination of—

(a) the fee payable to such directors;

(b) any additional fees payable for any other duties to the company;

(c) such other items as are to be considered in the nature of remuneration.

Minimum disclosure

In the case of paragraphs 25 to 28, there is quite a bit of discretion for companies to interpret how to describe their policy. The following table (taken from the June 2012 BIS Consultation on revised remuneration reporting regulations Annex B, because it is a good example and well laid out) would appear to be the minimum requirement.

It should be prefaced with a statement along these lines:

Executive Directors' remuneration policy

Introduction

In accordance with the Large and Medium-sized Companies and Groups (Accounts and Reports) Regulations 2013, Shareholders are provided with the opportunity to endorse the Company's remuneration policy through a binding vote. The first binding vote on our intended Directors' remuneration policy will be put to Shareholders at the AGM on xxxx 2014 (see page 39) and the policy will be operated, as described, from that date [or state other date].

After the table below, there should be an explanation of why measures were chosen (and if none for bonus and long term incentive schemes, and an explanation of why none were chosen), and explanation of differences to terms for employees generally in the group.

Table 15: Policy table setting out all elements of remuneration

Key elements of Remuneration					
	Purpose and link to strategy	Operation	Opportunity and maximum	Performance measures and framework (covers 26. (d) and (e))	Changes in year
Base salary	*Help recruit and retain employees. Reflects individual experience and role.*	*Reviewed annually and fixed for 12 months commencing 1 April. Decision influenced by:* *– role, experience and performance;* *– average change in broader workforce salary;* *– total organisational salary budgets.* *Salaries are benchmarked against the FTSE 100.*[4]	*Maximum annual increase of 10%.*	*None*	*Directors salaries increased by 2%.*
Benefits	*Help recruit and retain employees.*	*Directors are entitled to healthcare, car and life assurance.*	*Full cost of annual policy c. £40,000*	*None*	*None*

[4] This is the BIS example. Obviously, FTSE 100 would not be the best benchmark for most companies.

Key elements of Remuneration					
Pension	*Rewards sustained contribution.*	*Company X operates a defined contribution pension scheme. Benefits are accrued according to length of service up to retirement. Company X does not provide cash in lieu of pensions or a top up scheme.* *Company X has closed its DB scheme but Director1 is still a member. 2/3 final salary scheme, accrual rate 1/60; no service requirement, retirement age 60; no additional benefits on early retirement.*	*New executives receive 15% base salary (they contribute 5%).*	*None.*	*None*
Annual bonus	*Rewards the achievement of annual financial and strategic business targets and delivery of personal objectives.* *Deferred element encourages long-term shareholding and discourages excessive risk taking.*	*Targets are renewed annually and relate to areas of the business over which the executive has particular control.* *Bonus level is determined by the Committee after the year end, based on performance against targets.* *Individuals may choose to defer up to 50% of any bonus earned over three years. The deferred element is subject to forfeiture if the performance which led to its being paid is found to be incorrect or in the event of misconduct.*	*Target % of salary: 125%* *Maximum % of salary: 200%*	*The majority of the bonus is based on achievement of challenging financial objectives:* *– 75% judged by performance of Group operating profit* *– 25% judged on Group profit before interest and tax* *– Adjusted to reflect individual performance in achieving global sales and restructuring the group.* *The deferred element of the bonus is subject to the same performance measures as the LTIP.* *Clawback of vested and unvested awards is possible in the event of material misstatement of information or misconduct.*	*No change has been made to measures or weighting.*

Key elements of Remuneration					
Long Term Incentive Plan	*Incentivises Directors to achieve returns for shareholders over a longer time frame.*	*Company X has one LTIP which was agreed by shareholders on XX. Awards of conditional shares are made annually with vesting dependent on the achievement of performance conditions over the three subsequent years.* *The committee reviews the quantum of awards annually to ensure that they are in line with market rates.*	*Maximum % of salary: 600%* *Working maximum: 400%*	*Awards vest at end of three year performance period based on three equally weighted performance measures:* *– Business diversification performance* *– Adjusted free cash flow* *– Relative TSR* *25% vests at threshold, rising to 100% for stretching performance exceeding the set threshold by a specified margin.* *Against comparator group comprising ten other companies, 30% vests at median with 100% vesting for upper quartile performance.* *Clawback of vested and unvested awards is possible in the event of material misstatement of information or misconduct.*	*A new measure of business diversification has been added to reflect feedback from shareholders following the advisory vote on our remuneration report at last year's AGM.*

Colour coding the table, to show fixed pay, annual variable pay and long term variable pay, will also help the reader.

Best practice

Best practice will be the minimum requirement plus any specific company disclosures that assist shareholders in understanding the policy.

It might be appropriate to note here that the reason for the policy of exit payments and contracts is to reward long term loyalty and treat employees fairly but not excessively. Such policies also help to attract and retain the right type of employees. A separate table for NEDs is the simplest way of showing the remuneration policy, as their policy will have different philosophy and components. The easyJet example shows how to fulfil the requirements of para 28 in a simple, transparent way.

> **How are the Non-Executive Directors paid?** The Chairman, Deputy Chairman and Non-Executive Directors receive an annual fee (paid in monthly instalments). The fee for the Chairman is set by the

Remuneration Committee and the fees for the NonExecutive Directors are approved by the Board, on the recommendation of the Chairman and Chief Executive.

Element	Purpose and link to strategy	Operation (including maximum levels)
Fees	To attract and retain a high-calibre Chairman, Deputy Chairman and Non-Executive Directors by offering market competitive fee levels.	The Chairman is paid an all-inclusive fee for all Board responsibilities. The other Non-Executive Directors receive a basic Board fee, with supplementary fees payable for additional Board responsibilities.
		The Non-Executive Directors do not participate in any of the Company's incentive arrangements.
		The fee levels are reviewed on a periodic basis, and may be increased taking into account factors such as the time commitment of the role and market levels in companies of comparable size and complexity.
		Flexibility is retained to go above the current fee levels if necessary to do so to appoint a new Chairman or Non-Executive Director of an appropriate calibre.
		No benefits or other remuneration are provided to Non-Executive Directors. Fee levels for current incumbents for 2013/14 are as follows:
		• Non-Executive Chairman: £300,000;
		• Non-Executive Director Base Fee: £60,000;
		• Supplementary fee for Deputy Chairman and Senior Independent Director (SID) role: £25,000; and
		• Supplementary fee for Chairmen of the Audit, Remuneration and Safety Committees £15,000. Finance Committee Chairman £10,000.

Approach to recruitment remuneration

(The following is an extract from the SI)

29.(1)The directors' remuneration policy must contain a statement of the principles which would be applied by the company when agreeing the components of a remuneration package for the appointment of directors.

(2) The statement must set out the various components which would be considered for inclusion in that package and the approach to be adopted by the company in respect of each component.

(3) The statement must, subject to sub-paragraph (4), set out the maximum level of variable remuneration which may be granted (which can be expressed in monetary terms or otherwise).

(4) Remuneration which constitutes compensation for the forfeit of any award under variable remuneration arrangements entered into with a previous employer is not included within sub-paragraph (3) of this paragraph, but is subject to the requirements of sub-paragraphs (1) and (2).

Typical practice

A typical policy which creates flexibility in the case of unforeseen or exceptional circumstances is:

Table 16: recruitment policy

Policy report table x: Executive Director's recruitment policy	
Principles	When appointing or recruiting Directors, the Company will normally aim to set remuneration at a level which is consistent with the remuneration policy in place for other Directors and the previous incumbent of the role.
Details	The main components of remuneration will be salary, bonus, long-term incentives, pension (or cash pension allowance), benefits (which may include those relating to relocation such as: flights; immigration costs; relocation allowance; shipping and storage; temporary living accommodation; housing allowances; annual leave travel; international medical insurance cover; legal and tax services; school fees; school search; movement of pets; termination of car leases and costs of replacement goods) and compensation for loss of earnings from his/her previous employment that are forfeited in order to take up the role. The approach for each component will be to try to set each in line with the remuneration policy for Directors, except that the approach in respect of compensation for forfeit of remuneration in respect of a previous employer will be considered on a case by case basis taking into account all relevant factors such as performance achieved or likely to be achieved, the proportion of the performance period remaining and the form of the award.
Maximum	In order to secure the best candidate for the role, the Company may need to pay more than its existing Directors. The maximum level of variable remuneration that may be granted will be 200% of salary under the bonus plan and 300% under the LTIP (these limits already apply to the existing bonus and LTIP plans). Pre-existing contractual agreements for internal candidates may be maintained on recruitment to an Executive Director role.

Service contracts

(The following is an extract from the SI)

Service contracts

30. The directors' remuneration policy must contain a description of any obligation on the company which—

    (a) is contained in all directors' service contracts;

    (b) is contained in the service contracts of any one or more existing directors (not being covered by paragraph (a)); or

    (c) it is proposed would be contained in directors' service contracts to be entered into by the company

    and which could give rise to, or impact on, remuneration payments or payments for loss of office but which is not disclosed elsewhere in this report.

31. Where the directors' service contracts are not kept available for inspection at the company's registered office, the report must give details of where the contracts are kept, and if the contracts are available on a website, a link to that website.

32. The provisions of paragraphs 30 and 31 relating to directors' service contracts apply in like manner to the terms of letters of appointment of directors.

Typical practice

Typical practice is a set of paragraphs to meet the above. Para 36 requires additional disclosures on the policy for payments for loss of office.

Best practice

Best practice is a table which clearly identifies how the policy applies to each element of remuneration, including past awards. (It will need to cross refer to tables which disclose the requirements of para 36.) See **Table 17** below.

Table 17: Example table of exit payment policy

<table>
<tr><th>Name</th><th>Contract duration</th><th>Notice Period</th><th colspan="10">Termination Payments</th></tr>
<tr><th></th><th></th><th></th><th></th><th>Salary</th><th>Benefits</th><th>Pension</th><th>Bonus</th><th>Deferred bonus awards</th><th>LTIP awards –unvested</th><th>LTIP awards vested</th><th>Options unvested</th><th>Options vested</th></tr>
<tr><td rowspan="3">CEO</td><td rowspan="3">12 months rolling</td><td rowspan="3">12 months</td><td>how each element of the payment will be calculated</td><td colspan="3">12 months</td><td>Pro-rate to service in year</td><td>Vests on normal date, but award must be exercised within six months</td><td colspan="4">Vests on normal date, but award must be exercised within six months</td></tr>
<tr><td>whether the company will distinguish between–
(i) types of leaver; or
(ii) the circumstances under which a director left</td><td colspan="3">No differentiation</td><td>Only good leavers receive bonus.</td><td>Only good leavers receive bonus</td><td>Only good leavers can exercise awards; others lapse awards on leaving.</td><td></td><td></td><td></td></tr>
<tr><td>how performance will be taken into account</td><td colspan="3">Not applicable</td><td>Yes according to the scheme rules</td><td>Not applicable</td><td>Pro rate for performance in the performance period and pro-rate for proportion of performance period served.</td><td>Not applicable</td><td>Pro rate for performance in the performance period and pro-rate for proportion of performance period served.</td><td>Not applicable</td></tr>
</table>

Name	Contract duration	Notice Period	Termination Payments									
			any contractual provision agreed prior to the commencement of these regulations that could impact on the quantum of the payment.									
Dir 2 etc.												

Example of note to follow the above table: 'employees who are terminated for gross misconduct are not entitled to any payment. Claw-back provisions apply to all bonus and LTIP awards made after [xxx].'

In addition any policy on the use of discretion should be noted, either here or after the table to satisfy paras 36 and 37.

Illustrations of application of remuneration policy (Scenarios)

(The following is an extract from the SI)

33. The directors' remuneration report must, in respect of each person who is a director (other than a director who is not performing an executive function), set out in the form of a bar chart an indication of the level of remuneration that would be received by the director in accordance with the directors' remuneration policy in the first year to which the policy applies.

34.(1)The bar chart must contain separate bars representing—

(a) minimum remuneration receivable, that is to say, including, but not limited to, salary, fees, benefits and pension;

(b) the remuneration receivable if the director was, in respect of any performance measures or targets, performing in line with the company's expectation;

(c) maximum remuneration receivable (not allowing for any share price appreciation).

(2) Each bar of the chart must contain separate parts which represent—

(a) salary, fees, benefits, pension and any other item falling within sub-paragraph 34(1)(a);

(b) remuneration where performance measures or targets relate to one financial year;

(c) remuneration where performance measures or targets relate to more than one financial year.

(3) Each bar must show—

(a) percentage of the total comprised by each of the parts; and

(b) total value of remuneration expected for each bar.

35.(1)A narrative description of the basis of calculation and assumptions used to compile the bar chart must be set out to enable an understanding of the charts presented.

(2) In complying with sub-paragraph (1) it is not necessary for any matter to be included in the narrative description which has been set out in the future policy table required by paragraph 25.

It should be noted that the legislation is flawed in concept, as it takes no account of previous years' awards, shareholdings nor the scenarios for future share price outcomes (these issues are discussed in **Chapter 40.2** on modelling tools). The legislation only requires part of remuneration to be modelled and takes no account of the crucial variable of future share prices.

Typical practice

The following is an example of typical practice, to satisfy Paras 33–35.

Figure 15: Illustrations of application of remuneration policy – Pay scenarios

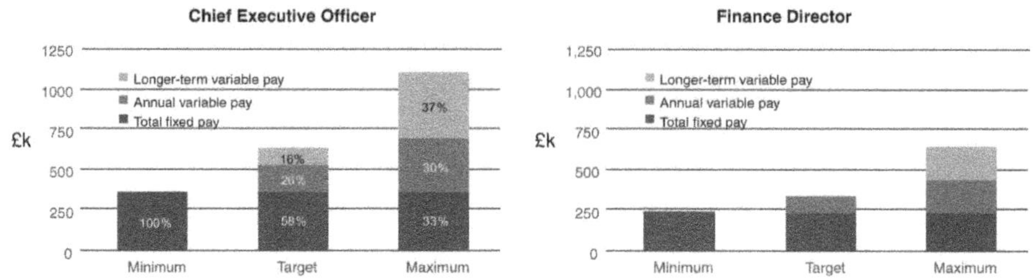

How much could the Executive Directors earn under the remuneration policy?

A significant proportion of remuneration is linked to performance, particularly at maximum performance levels. The charts on page 79 show how much the CEO and CFO could earn under easyJet's remuneration policy (as detailed above) under different performance scenarios (based on their salaries as at 1 October 2013). The following assumptions have been made:

- **Minimum (performance below threshold)** – Fixed pay only with no vesting under any of easyJet's incentive plans.
- **In line with expectations** – Fixed pay plus c bonus at the mid-point of the range (giving 50% of the maximum opportunity and assuming half of the maximum voluntary deferral) and vesting of one third of the maximum under the Performance and Matching Share elements of the LTIP.
- **Maximum (performance meets or exceeds maximum)** – Fixed pay plus maximum bonus (with maximum voluntary deferral) and maximum vesting under the Performance and Matching Shares elements of the LTIP.

Fixed pay comprises:

- salaries – salary effective as at 1 October 2013;
- benefits – amount received by each Executive Director in the 2013 financial year:
- pension – amount received by each Executive Director in the 2013 financial year: and
- Free and Matching Shares under the all employee share incentive plan.

The scenarios do not include any share price growth or dividend assumptions.

It should be noted that since the analysis above shows what could be earned by the Executive Directors based on the 2014 financial year remuneration policy described above (ignoring the potential impact of share price growth), the numbers will be different to the values included in the table on page 83 detailing what was actually earned by the Executive Directors in relation to the financial year ended 30 September 2013, since these values are based on the actual levels of performance achieved to 30 September 2013 and include the impact of share price growth in relation to share awards.

Best practice

Best practice would be, in addition to the requirements of the legislation, to also include an illustration of the impact of share price movements. The following example for the CEO could be used in place of the graph above:

> The legislation requires that the graph below should be constructed with no adjustment for share price potential changes. However it does permit additional information to be shown and we have included the potential impact on the maximum payout if the share price were to double or treble. These illustrate very good and exceptional performance and potential payments and hopefully will ensure shareholders are not surprised in several years' time if such exceptional payments arise. The legislation also requires the percentages shown in the graph to be % of total pay assuming no change in share price. We hope shareholders will find this graph a more useful illustration of potential outcomes than what most companies currently disclose.
>
> **What is our policy when an Executive Director leaves or there is a takeover?**
>
> The rules of both schemes (LTIP and Deferred Share Bonus Plan) set out what happens to awards if a participant ceases to be an employee or Director of easyJet before the end of the vesting period. Generally, any outstanding share awards will lapse on such cessation. except in certain circumstances.
>
> If the Executive Director ceases to be an employee or Director of easyJet as a result of death. injury, retirement, the sale of the business or company that employs the individual or any other reason at the discretion of the Committee then they will be treated as a 'good leaver' under the plan rules.

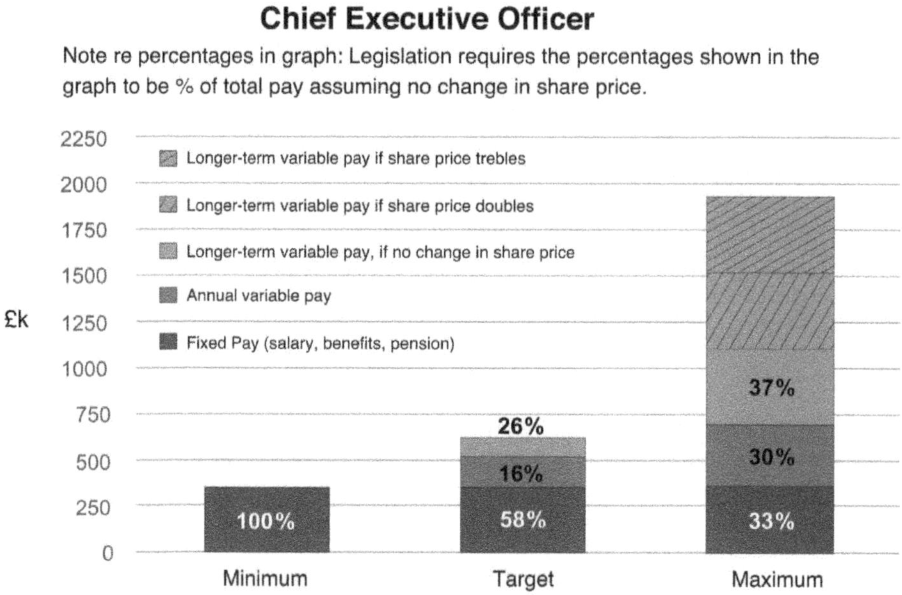

Policy on payment for loss of office

(The following is an extract from the SI)

36. The directors' remuneration policy must set out the company's policy on the setting of notice periods under directors' service contracts.

37. The directors' remuneration policy must also set out the principles on which the determination of payments for loss of office will be approached including—

    (a) an indication of how each component of the payment will be calculated;

    (b) whether, and if so how, the circumstances of the director's loss of office and performance during the period of qualifying service are relevant to any exercise of discretion; and

    (c) any contractual provision agreed prior to 27th June 2012 that could impact on the quantum of the payment.

Typical practice:

Table 18: Payment for loss of office

Policy report table x: Executive Director's policy on payment for loss of office	
Policy on setting of notice periods	The Company normally sets the notice period of Executive Directors as 12 months, but may decide to vary this in circumstances it deems appropriate.
How termination payments are determined	On termination, the Company will normally make a payment in lieu of notice (PILON) which is equal to the aggregate of: the basic salary at the date of termination for the applicable notice period; the pension allowance over the relevant period; the cost to the Company of providing all other benefits (excluding pension allowance and bonus) or a sum equal to the amount of benefits as specified in the Company's most recent Annual Report and a bonus payment calculated in accordance with the service contract of the Director. The treatment of the Long-Term Incentive Plan on termination will be in accordance with the rules of the Plan and, where appropriate at the discretion of the Committee. The Company may pay the PILON either as a lump sum or in equal monthly instalments from the date on which the employment terminates until the end of the Relevant Period. If alternative employment (paid above a pre-agreed rate) is commenced, for each month that instalments of the PILON remain payable, the amounts, in aggregate (excluding the pension payment), may be reduced by half of one month's basic salary in excess of the pre-agreed rate. All leavers have to exit SharePurchase+ and either sell or transfer their Shares. If identified as a 'Good Leaver', under the rules of SharePurchase+, no tax or NICs are paid.
Discretion	If identified as a 'Good Leaver', for the purposes of the bonus, the Committee may determine that the leaver's contribution was significant in early or high achievement of targets, in which case, it may decide to make a payment which is equivalent of up to a full year bonus. If identified as a 'Good Leaver' under the deferred bonus Plan rules (including those identified at the discretion of the Committee), outstanding awards shall vest in full on the normal vesting date or on such earlier date as the Committee may determine. If identified as a 'Good Leaver' under the LTIP rules, (including those identified at the discretion of the Committee), outstanding awards may be exercised, either on the normal vesting date or on such earlier date as the Committee may determine, to the extent that they have vested. If, in the judgement of the Committee, greater progress towards achievement of targets has been made as a result of the performance of the Leaver, it may, at its absolute discretion, decide to vest up to 100% of the outstanding award. The Committee may also agree to make payments in respect of statutory employment claims, legal fees, outplacement and accrued holiday or sick leave.

Statement of consideration of employment conditions elsewhere in company

(The following is an extract from the SI)

38. The directors' remuneration policy must contain a statement of how pay and employment conditions of employees (other than directors) of the company and, where the company is a parent company, of the group of other undertakings within the same group as the company, were taken into account when setting the policy for directors' remuneration.

39. The statement must also set out—

    (a) whether, and if so, how, the company consulted with employees when drawing up the directors' remuneration policy set out in this part of the report;

    (b) whether any remuneration comparison measurements were used and if so, what they were, and how that information was taken into account.

Minimum disclosure

Minimum disclosure is a number of paragraphs commenting on the above requirement.

Best Practice

Best practice disclosure is to include the data as shown in **Table 10**, ie to show this data for five or ten years and also to include profit, dividends and overall expenditure on pay (as required by Para 30) and other KPIs.

Few companies will want to disclose this much information. An example of a company which discloses quite a lot of information is easyJet (see above) but in relation to policy it merely states:

> **How does the executive pay policy differ from that for other easyJet employees?**
>
> The remuneration policy for the Executive Directors is more heavily weighted towards variable pay than for other employees to make a greater part of their pay conditional on the successful delivery of business strategy. This aims to create a clear link between the value created for shareholders and the remuneration received by the Executive Directors. However, in line with the Company's strategy to keep remuneration simple and consistent, the benefit and pension arrangements for the current Executive Directors are on the same terms as those offered to eligible employees below the Board.

Although it is OK to be silent if the company has not consulted employees, WPP is an example of a company which addresses this point head on and says 'The Committee did not consult employees when drawing up this Executive Remuneration Policy.'

Statement of consideration of shareholder views

(The following is an extract from the SI)

Statement of consideration of shareholder views

40. The directors' remuneration policy must contain a statement of whether, and if so how, any views in respect of directors' remuneration expressed to the company by shareholders (whether at a general meeting or otherwise) have been taken into account in the formulation of the directors' remuneration policy.

Minimum disclosure

Minimum disclosure is a paragraph(s) describing this.

Best Practice

Best practice would be to cross refer to **Table 14a:** Best Practice Shareholder voting and then to add paragraphs such as this:

> **Policy report Table x: Consideration of Shareholder views**
>
> The Committee receives annual updates on the views and best practices of Shareholders and their representative bodies and takes these into account. The Committee seeks the views of Shareholders on matters of remuneration that it thinks Shareholders are interested in. A good example of this was the adoption of the 2012 Long-Term Incentive Plan, where Shareholders were consulted. The Committee considers the xx% vote in favour of the Remuneration Report in 2013 (table xx on page 70) to demonstrate strong Shareholder support for the Group's remuneration arrangements.
>
> Where individual shareholders have voted against our policy, the Committee has sought to engage with them to understand their concerns as part of determining remuneration policy.

28.4 Additional Information

The following appear not to be covered in the draft legislation.

- Requirement to show history of bonus opportunity and outcomes.

- Requirement to show all outstanding share scheme and option awards.
- Requirement to show history of LTI award outcomes as % of maximum award and expected values of extant awards.

The following suggested additional tables to cover these items should be regarded as best practice and are as follows.

Table 19: Requirement to show history of bonus opportunity and outcomes

Bonus Year	**Maximum bonus opportunity % salary**	**Target Bonus % salary**	**Actual outcome % salary**	**Deferred into shares**	**Share price at date of award of deferred shares**	**Value of deferred shares at last year end as % salary**	**Total value of award (based on latest share price) as % salary**
2012	250%	125%	125%	50%	£6.00	78%	141%
2011	200%	100%	150%	50%	£5.00	113%	188%
2010	200%	100%	175%	50%	£4.00	164%	252%
2009	175%	88%	50%	50%	£2.00	94%	119%
2008	150%	75%	50%	50%	£3.00	63%	88%
average of above	195%	98%	110%	50%	£4.00	102%	157%

Table 20: History of LTI award outcomes as % of maximum award and expected values of extant awards

Share plan	**Date of award**	**Length of performance period in years**	**Date vesting**	**Last date for exercise**	**Maximum shares in award as % salary**	**Expected value of award as % of maximum**	**Actual outcome or latest estimate of outcome as % of maximum**	**Vested**	**Share price at award date**	**Estimated gain based on share price at year end as % salary**
LTIP	23/02/2012	5	22/02/2017	22/02/2022	150%	50%	75%		£5.00	169%
	22/02/2011	5	23/02/2016	22/02/2021	150%	50%	75%		£4.50	188%
	22/02/2010	5	22/02/2015	23/02/2020	150%	50%	75%		£4.00	211%
	22/02/2009	5	22/02/2014	22/02/2019	150%	50%	75%		£3.50	241%
	23/02/2008	5	22/02/2013	22/02/2018	150%	50%	75%		£3.00	281%
	22/02/2007	5	23/02/2012	22/02/2017	100%	50%	100%	vested	£2.50	300%
	22/02/2006	5	22/02/2011	23/02/2016	100%	50%	50%	vested	£2.00	188%
	22/02/2005	5	22/02/2010	22/02/2015	100%	50%	25%	vested	£4.00	47%
	23/02/2004	5	22/02/2009	22/02/2014	100%	50%	100%	vested	£3.50	214%
	22/02/2003	5	23/02/2008	22/02/2013	100%	50%	90%	vested	£3.00	225%
	22/02/2002	5	22/02/2007	23/02/2012	100%	50%	75%	vested	£2.50	225%
	average of above						**74%**			**208%**

Share plan	Date of award	Length of performance period in years	Date vesting	Last date for exercise	Maximum shares in award as % salary	Expected value of award as % of maximum	Actual outcome or latest estimate of outcome as % of maximum	Vested	Share price at award date	Estimated gain based on share price at year end as % salary
Options	23/02/2012	3	22/02/2015	22/02/2022	200%	50%	75%		£5.00	225%
	22/02/2011	3	22/02/2014	22/02/2021	200%	50%	75%		£4.50	250%
	22/02/2010	3	22/02/2013	23/02/2020	200%	50%	75%		£4.00	281%
	22/02/2009	3	23/02/2012	22/02/2019	200%	50%	100%	vested	£3.50	429%
	23/02/2008	3	22/02/2011	22/02/2018	150%	50%	100%	vested	£3.00	375%
	22/02/2007	3	22/02/2010	22/02/2017	150%	50%	100%	vested	£2.50	450%
	22/02/2006	3	22/02/2009	23/02/2016	150%	50%	50%	vested	£2.00	281%
	22/02/2005	3	23/02/2008	22/02/2015	150%	50%	25%	vested	£4.00	70%
	23/02/2004	3	22/02/2007	22/02/2014	100%	50%	100%	vested	£3.50	214%
	22/02/2003	3	22/02/2006	22/02/2013	100%	50%	90%	vested	£3.00	225%
	22/02/2002	3	22/02/2005	23/02/2012	100%	50%	75%	vested	£2.50	225%
	average of above						**79%**			**275%**

PART B

THEORY AND PRACTICE

This part of the book explains both the theory underpinning directors' remuneration and the market practice. It starts by reviewing the history of directors' remuneration since 1970, in **Chapter 29**. This describes the mega-trends that have occurred and their impact – globalisation of business, tax biases and changes, regulations and politics, the diffusion of shareholder power as shareholders have become more remote and diverse, and the growth of Private Equity, Hedge Funds and Sovereign Wealth Funds.

Chapter 30 reviews motivational theories and provides a sound basis to consider the impact of remuneration on management behaviour.

Chapter 31 reviews academic analyses and their conclusions with respect to directors' remuneration.

Chapter 32 provides details of market practice in terms of directors' remuneration.

29 A short history of remuneration 1970–2012

History helps us to understand why we have got to where we are today and how we got there. So it helps in making informed decisions for the future.

29.1 1970s

The 1970s are remembered for the three-day week, power cuts, 83% rate of income tax and a stock market low of 146 for the FT 30 Index and 62 for the All Share. There was a banking crisis and the Chancellor had to ask the International Monetary Fund for a loan. Unions were strong and managers' jobs were difficult. It was also a time of pay freezes applying to all employees, including directors. High inflation and stock losses destroyed profits and bonus plans did not pay out. The highest rate of tax of 83% was a big disincentive, but only applied to the top slice of income. Below that there were a series of lower rates which applied to different layers of income. Creative minds spent their time devising ways to avoid tax rather than improve business performance. Consequently pension plans were extremely popular, as executives could expect a lower rate of taxation after they retired. There was brief flurry of interest in options under Ted Heath's government between 1970 and 1974, but for most of the decade the tax environment was not favourable. Some company perks were not taxed as income, so some companies went to great lengths to provide employee benefits, for example, free suits. Performance-related pay dropped off the agenda.

The Conservatives, under Margaret Thatcher, were elected in 1979 and this was the start of change.

29.2 1980s

The 1980s saw the Thatcher revolution, which transformed the business landscape. Union power was curtailed. Uncompetitive practices were changed. Unemployment rose to three million. Much of UK manufacturing moved overseas, where products could be made for less cost and often better. The stock market took off, with the All Share rising to 1238 on 16 July 1987, four-and-a-half times its level on 4 May 1979 when Margaret Thatcher took power and some twenty times its 1974 low of 62.

The top rate of tax was reduced to 60%. Incentive plans to motivate top management were introduced. Salary differentials between directors and employees which had shrunk in the 1960s and 1970s widened again.

The biggest change came in 1984 with the removal of income tax on share options. Gains were subjected to capital gains tax at the then highest rate of 30%. This was a huge tax bias in favour of share options over cash remuneration. A £100 gain from share options netted the executive £70, whereas £100 of cash pay would deliver only £40 net of tax. The same £100 share option gain would cost shareholders £100 through dilution (but have no profit impact and result in a cash inflow equal to the exercise price), whereas the £100 cash would cost the company £110, as National Insurance contributions were payable on cash remuneration but not on share options. As the bill went through Parliament, one Labour MP, who saw the potential bonanza, proposed a limit on the amount of share options that could be awarded. This limit was set at four times remuneration face value of options, ie the number of shares under option times the exercise price, which would be the market price at the date of grant. As all too frequently happens when politicians intervene, things did not go as planned. Companies and their executives realised that:

- if these new options were such a good thing that there had to be a maximum award, then they had to have a scheme as soon as possible
- if there was a limit then they better fill their boots with them quickly, so most companies granted the maximum at the earliest opportunity.

99% of FT 100 companies adopted executive share option plans within one year of Royal Assent to the Finance Act 1984.

There were factors which conspired against share options. To receive the favourable capital gains tax treatment, options could not be exercised until three years after the date of grant and not until three years after the previous grant. This meant that executives tended to exercise as soon as the three years were up and then expected the company to grant them another set of options. This problem, like the four times remuneration limit, could have been avoided by better design.

The 1980s was a rampant bull market. Many directors and executives had large gains (some had realised them, whilst for others they were only on paper). In 1987 the stock market crashed and 30% of the value was wiped off stocks in a few days in October. Directors and executives who had exercised and sold their shares had made considerable sums. Those who had not were most unhappy. Many people started to say that options were a lottery.

In 1988 income tax was reduced to 40% and capital gains tax increased to 40% (a disastrous change enacted by those who had little knowledge of entrepreneurs and the risks they take, for which they deserve a tax incentive). So the huge tax bias in favour of share options largely evaporated

– there still remained a small bias as options were still treated as a benefit and not subject to National Insurance – and they still had no profit impact under the accounting rules.

The Finance Act 1988 introduced a limit on the amount of pension that could be provided through an approved scheme. The limit for the final pensionable salary was set at £60,000, and would increase with RPI. The limit by 2006 was £108,600. Indexing the limit in line with RPI meant that more and more people would be affected over time. Most companies reacted by pretending the new law did not exist, ie they gave executives subject to the cap the same benefits as those who were not. Some did this via a promise, by what came to be known as an Unfunded Unapproved Retirement Benefit Scheme (UURBS). Others set money aside to guarantee the benefit using Funded Unapproved Retirement Benefit Scheme (FURBS). Although the pension cap was not a large problem initially, it was slowly and inevitably going to become a much bigger one.

Companies became more global. Many UK companies made acquisitions in the US. US pay levels, which were much higher than the UK, began to be cited as justification for increases in UK remuneration. Dick Giordano, an American, was appointed CEO of BOC, with a US-style package and this set a new level for other UK plcs to aspire to.

The ABI published its first set of guidance on remuneration, but this was limited to share schemes and mainly focused on dilution. The dilution limit for executive share options set by the ABI was 5% over ten years and most companies followed this limit. This meant that the maximum a prudent company would grant was an average of 0.5% a year.

To judge from the press at the time, one would have thought UK pay was surging ahead. However, there were three factors which held back executive directors' remuneration:

- the conservatism of Non-Executive Directors
- the limit on executive share options of four times remuneration
- the dilution limit for executive share options set by the ABI and NAPF of 5% over ten years.

29.3 1990s

The FTSE 100 more than tripled, from 2,000 to almost 7,000 between 1990 and 1999. The 17-year bull market up to 2000 led to enormous wealth creation. This was particularly the case in the US where executive compensation reached levels which many commentators called obscene. Wall Street compensation levels reflected profits and both were high.

Chart 3: FTSE 100 since 1985 and Dow Jones since 1930

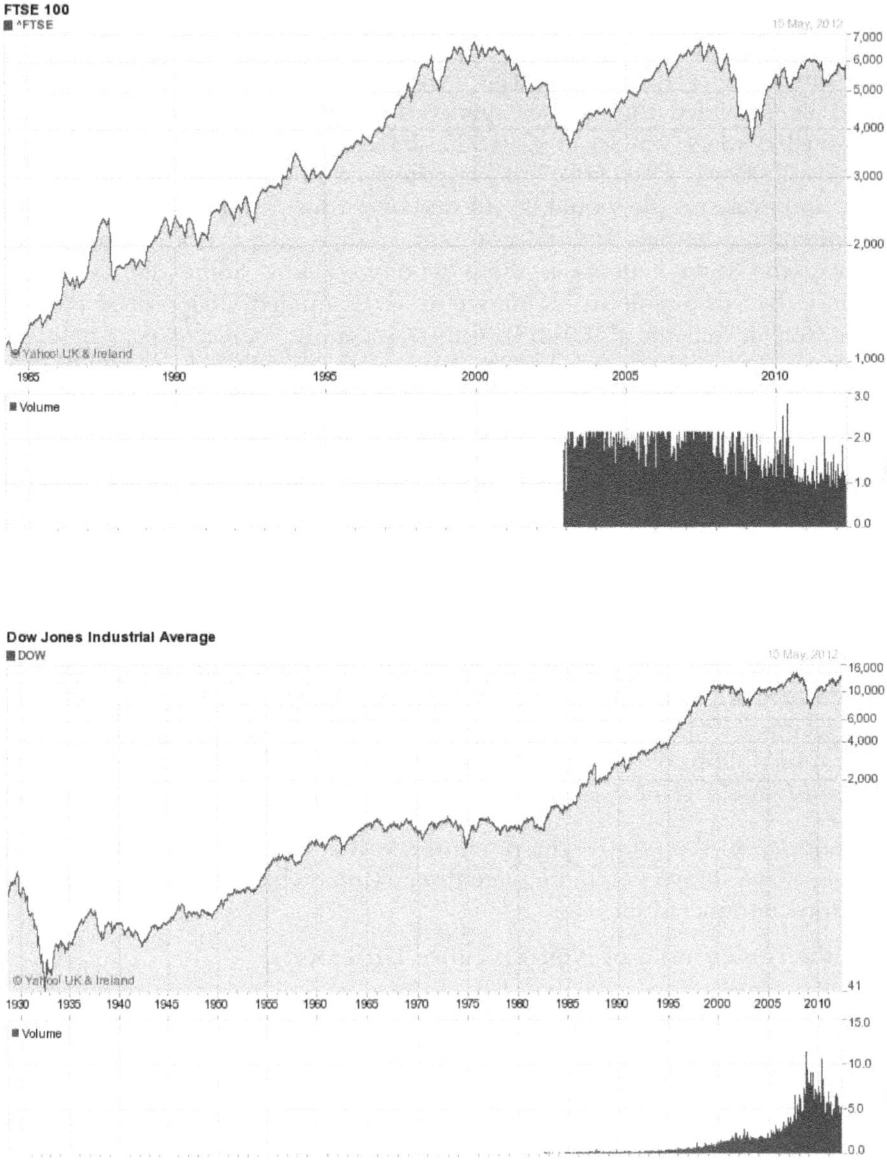

Over in the USA, these levels of expectation flowed into most other areas of business. US corporations, who had always been keen on granting share options, now fell in love with them. S&P data show that 79% of the increase in median CEO compensation from 1992 to 2000 was due to growth in long-term incentives, primarily stock options. In 1992 options were 27% of median CEO compensation, whereas by 2000 options were 60% of median CEO compensation. A proposal to account for stock options in the profit and loss account was strongly resisted and the eventual compromise was that the cost of options had to be shown in a footnote to the accounts. Leading US companies were granting options over as much as 2% or even 3% of their shares each year. Appointing a good CEO led to a huge surge in the share price and a poor choice could negatively impact the share price. Thus CEOs had huge leverage when asking for higher compensation. The US passed a law, S162, intending to curtail pay – any pay above $1 million, unless it was performance related, was non-deductible for tax. As often happens when governments intervene in executive pay, there were unexpected consequences. A $1 million salary became the norm for a CEO of a large US company and there was a huge surge in the options awarded.

As globalisation of business continued, pressure increased on UK companies to pay similar rates. Although few UK executives went to the US to head up US corporations, a number of UK FTSE plcs recruited US and other nationals to lead their companies. These executives expected remuneration commensurate with what they would receive in their home country. This further increased the expectations of the UK nationals.

UK directors were caricatured as 'fat cats' smoking cigars and licking the cream. There was particular concern about newly privatised industries. These were state regulated and therefore the future share price was dependent on a beneficial regime operated by the regulator. There were, however, gross inefficiencies in the utilities and (with the benefit of hindsight, it is clear that) they were sold too cheaply. Share options were granted at privatisation. The rationale was that executive directors and senior managers now had to think and act like the private sector. It was believed that options would help. Salaries were increased as executives from the private sector were recruited and it was felt divisive if existing employees were not paid at a similar level. Annual bonus plans were introduced. Share prices roared ahead. Water and electricity companies share prices trebled, which was rather surprising as they were privatised with high yields and low risk and modest expectations of share price growth. (They were meant to be safe 'granny shares'). Executive directors became rich beyond their wildest dreams. Public sector managers of utilities – who were perfectly happy earning £40,000 plus a good pension in the public sector – became millionaires leading large quoted companies, and were then courted by their advisers to expand overseas. After all, how else were they going to get the share price to grow in the future? The excesses of remuneration led to political action and the Greenbury Report. The growth strategies led to many dubious acquisitions, investments and higher risk.

The Greenbury Report[1] criticised the use of share options and proposed in their place awards of shares contingent on other performance measures such as total shareholder return (TSR) compared to a comparator index or group of companies. The Conservative government removed capital gains tax relief on executive share options on awards of shares above £30,000, thereby reversing its policy of 1984 where it had granted favourable tax treatment to options.

Many companies had already found the limit of options that any single executive could receive, of four times remuneration, somewhat restrictive. A number had used super options which were allowed under the ABI guidelines. Super options were a further four times remuneration of options, but exercise of this was contingent on being in the top 25% of companies over a five-year period. No thought was given to the incentives this created – steady growth at below the upper quartile level received no super option payouts; high risk strategies suddenly had increased rewards, but with no corresponding downside penalty the incentives were asymmetric to those of shareholders.

Companies realised that by switching to use restricted shares in place of options they could avoid the four times limit of options. Annual awards of options at the level of one times salary of options had become typical practice. A similar limit of one times salary of restricted shares each year rapidly became the norm. Even with a discount for the performance conditions, of say 40%, the restricted share award was probably worth twice as much as the option award.[2]

The result was that in the UK, options fell out of favour and restricted shares became the hot form of long-term incentive, gaining a new name – long-term incentive plans (LTIPs). Whether it was convenience or careful planning or luck one can only guess.

In 1997 a Labour government was elected, the first since 1979. One of their first acts was a windfall tax on privatised electricity and water companies. Their share prices declined and executives' option gains disappeared. Most of these companies had (with the government's encouragement) strongly encouraged their employees to buy shares via SAYE share option plans and Inland Revenue-approved Profit Sharing Plans. Employees now began to realise the truth in the statement that share prices can go down as well as up.

---

1 The first major corporate governance report was Cadbury, published in December 1992, which recommended a 'Code of Best Practice'. The Greenbury report (1995) sought to identify good practice in determining Directors' remuneration. This was followed by the Hampel Committee Report 1998 which recommended the 'Principles of Good Governance'.

2 The option had an expected value of approximately 30% of the share price at the award date, whereas the expected value of the performance restricted share was about 60%.

The Labour government also removed the tax credit on dividends. Relatively little criticism was made at the time. But as the impact became more apparent, more and more criticism was levied and it became known as the pension tax. (The tax was about £5 billion per annum or an annuity value of c £100 billion). It levelled the field in terms of dividends or capital growth. Dividends which were particularly attractive to some shareholders now lost their favourable tax bias. Dividends in the UK had always been higher than in the US, but had always been partly driven by the dividend tax credit.

US companies continued granting options. As the 1990's came to a close, there was resurgence in the granting of options in the UK, due mainly to the continued perceived pressure from the US for comparable remuneration.

29.4 2000s

The 2000s started with the dot.com boom and bust. Looking back, with the benefit of hindsight, we wonder why all those fabulous growth projections were accepted and why the stock market ratings of technology shares were so high. As companies announced bigger and bigger losses, their share prices seemed to go higher and higher as this was viewed by analysts as a signal of investment for the future. Hi-tech companies paid low salaries, few benefits and compensated with lots of options. There was an exodus of bright young people from traditional companies to dot.com start-ups where they hoped to make their millions. The traditional companies made attempts to retain staff by themselves offering more and more options. Dilution and overhang in large technology companies grew and grew; for example, Microsoft issued options over 30% dilution.

The dot.com boom became a bubble and burst. The outcome resembled the Dutch tulip bulb bubble (1637), the South Sea bubble (1711) and the stock market crash of 1929. The Nasdaq (which was heavily biased towards technology stocks) went from a high of 5000 to a low of 1200, losing over 70% of its value. As the stock market fell, many companies' options went underwater. They were left with the choice of granting more or letting their employees leave and get buckets of options from their new employer. They chose to grant more options and many cancelled options and re-loaded. The above is primarily a US story. It did filter through to the UK, but what occurred was much more extreme in the US than in the UK.

Then came 9/11. Some people in the UK do not recognise its significance. The US psyche was forever changed. It changed the political landscape and led to the Iraq war, the War on Terror and the Afghanistan War, which changed the world's political landscape and had a huge economic impact.

The scandals at Enron, WorldCom, Tyco and elsewhere led to a decline in stock markets worldwide. Excessive executive compensation and greed were cited as causes. Compensation consultants were often too close to management and had not worked in the best interests of the company. They had in all too many cases colluded with management to design and recommend schemes whereby executives got rich at the expense of the company. This was a low point in business morality. The US enacted the Sarbanes-Oxley Act 2002, which was far reaching. In addition, the Conference Board of America formed the Commission on Public Trust and Private Enterprise. They noted that the general public felt they could trust CEOs less than used car salesmen. They said that CEO compensation and the use of stock options had become out of control and made proposals to improve the situation.

In response to the continued highly critical press coverage of directors' remuneration the UK government announced a consultation exercise in July 2001. This resulted in the Directors' Remuneration Report Regulations 2002 (SI 2002/1986) which came into effect for any company year ends on or after 31 December 2002.

The 2003 reporting season led to massive publicity about pay and shareholder rebellions at many leading plcs including voting down of remuneration report at GlaxoSmithKline. PIRC analysed the results of proxy votes from each of the companies on which they report. To the end of June 2003, it reported the results of 58 AGMs held by FTSE 100 companies. Thirty-two companies received positive support of 85% or less on the required vote on its remuneration report, ie over 15% opposition. For comparison, in a survey PIRC carried out in 2002 average opposition recorded against remuneration reports at All Share Companies (not just the FTSE 100) was around 4%.

In 2003, the DTI announced another consultation exercise – this time into directors' contracts and severance packages. In December 2003 the ABI and NAPF issued a joint statement on this issue, including detailed guidance on what they would find acceptable. They publicly opposed companies who did not fall in line. Most companies did fall in line and in 2005 the government announced that following consultation it would not legislate for the present and left market forces to resolve the problem. The ABI updated its guideline in respect of change in control clauses (in December 2004) – this appears to a veiled response to Carlton, where Michael Green received £15 million following the takeover by ITV.

On 7 November 2002, the International Accounting Standards Board (IASB) announced their intention that the cost of options should be an expense shown on the face of the accounts. In 2004 the IASB and Federal Accounting Standards Board (FASB) published proposals to expense options that apply to all accounting years starting on or after 1 January 2005 (see **Chapter 13**). It was widely predicted that the new accounting rules would cause companies to reappraise whether to continue to use options. In August 2003, Microsoft announced it was stopping granting employee options. In place it would issue restricted stock. It also announced a plan to buy out existing options, partly to ensure employees understood the value of their options. Subsequently, many other US companies changed their policy.

The Enron/WorldCom malaise proved to be part of a deeper-seated problem. The New York Stock Exchange, Hollander and Fannie Mae are other US problem cases. Citigroup and other banks settled their case with Elliot Spitzer for $1.4 billion, without admitting guilt. In 2004 Spitzer started to pursue the insurance industry and the CEO of Marsh & McLennan had to resign. Elsewhere in the world there was Ahold, Parmalat and China Aviation.

It is an important distinction that the UK's corporate governance crises were of poor strategy or implementation (eg Marconi, Jarvis, Northern Rock and RBS), whereas the US cases covered fraudulent accounting, illegal business practices and/or excessive compensation.

On 6 April 2006, the new UK pensions regime came into effect and limited the maximum pension pot to £1.5 million (see **49.5** for details). Pensions require long-term planning, so it is unfair that the government keeps changing the rules. The consequences may be a switch to more performance-related pay to offset lower pensions, higher salaries or cash supplements in lieu of pension. The ABI in December 2004 warned companies not to compensate executives for changes in the pensions' tax regime. There were several further changes in subsequent years and the annual limit for pension contributions to HMRC approved schemes from 2011 was £50,000 and for 2014 is £40,000.

2007 saw the collapse of Bear Stearns, Lehman and Northern Rock. The 2007/08 banking and liquidity crisis saw the destruction of $2 trillion of shareholder value in banks. The Dow went from 13,000 down to 8,000 and the FTSE 100 went from a high of 7,000 to a low point of 3,500, but has since recovered to around 5,600 at April 2012, when the first edition of this book was written, and 6,700 at 31 December 2013 when the second edition of this book was written. There was a danger that the banking system might collapse. We looked over the abyss.

There were cries for change, and in particular for the three R's:

- Retribution
- Regulation
- Remuneration Reform

Remuneration was not felt to be the cause of the crisis, but it was a contributory factor. President Obama in his Inaugural Speech in 2009 criticised 'greed, short-termism and irresponsibility'.

In the UK, the Walker report led to the FSA's remuneration guidelines. The G20 Financial Stability Group recommendations on bankers' compensation similarly identify the key issues – risk alignment of bonuses, the measurement of true profit, short-termism, and a need for bonus deferral and clawback mechanisms.

The income tax rate was increased in 2011 from 40% to 50% for income above £150,000. Individuals also had to pay 2% NI on top of this and NIC is payable by the company.

Both the FSA and FSG recommended a vastly increased role for the Remuneration Committee. Companies are going to struggle to find Non-Executives with the expertise and time willing to serve on Remuneration Committees to do this work.

In recent years the longer-term emphasis in incentive pay has switched from ten years to three years. Previously, share options, with a ten-year life, were the main type of long-term incentive. This gave the executives an interest in the long-term share price performance: it was particularly strong when the share price had increased and the options were significantly in the money.

Following the 1995 Greenbury Report there was been a shift away from share options towards performance shares, and this gained momentum with the introduction of the accounting charge for options. The use of performance shares was encouraged by The Combined Code[3] which talks of relative performance. The result was the introduction of three-year relative TSR plans, with no payout for below median performance, and maximum payout usually for 75th percentile performance.

Students of gaming theory will realise that, to maximise their income from such relative TSR plans, many executives will be tempted to increase the volatility of the share price rather than aim for steady growth. One way to increase the volatility of the share price is by making an acquisition. Another is to increase gearing by taking on more debt and paying back cash to shareholders. Remuneration Committees have also encouraged an acquisition culture by linking salary to company size: hence the inherent incentives in the remuneration system have encouraged growth by acquisition and merger. (Note too that the advisers to companies who so strongly encourage acquisitions, mergers and higher debt all receive their fees for advice at the time of the deal.) A whole edifice has arisen which encourages short-termist behaviour.[4]

---

3 In 1998, the 1992 'Code of Best Practice', Greenbury report (1995) and 1998 'principles of good Governance' were combined and 'The Combined Code' was formally incorporated into the listing rules of the London Stock Exchange.

4 This was brilliantly explained by Professor John Kay in the Kay Review, published in July 2012, see http://www.bis.gov.uk/assets/biscore/business-law/docs/k/12–917-kay-review-of-equity-markets-final-report.pdf

So the FRC in 2010 changed The Combined Code (which it renamed the UK Corporate Governance Code[5]) to encourage:

- Consideration of risk
- Long-term performance (rather than the previous guidance of 'keen incentives to perform' which inevitably led to a short-term focus).

Banks deserve special mention.

First and foremost, there was the blind faith of almost all of today's bankers in their banking system. Executive compensation did not cause the recent financial crisis, either. Capital adequacy and liquidity, excessive money supply, the rating agencies and auditors who failed to warn of the danger all played their part. So too did greed, irresponsibility and short-termism. These factors led to opportunism on the part of traders at banks and a culture of risk-taking. Poor remuneration design allowed the crisis to happen but it was chicken and egg. There was almost unfettered power of many bank CEOs. Emperor-like, they ruled over independent Non-Executive Directors who often had little prior banking experience.

The banks caused the banking crisis, yet bankers got rich and the general public had to suffer and pay for the consequences. The general public felt executive pay was too high. The politicians responded and lashed out. As a stop gap measure in the UK, from April 2010 the income tax rate was increased from 40% to 50% for income above £150,000. Although aimed at the bankers' bonuses, it also hit companies in all other sectors.

There was also a special bankers' bonus tax. In his Pre-Budget statement on 9 December 2009 the then Chancellor, Alistair Darling, announced a new bank payroll tax: 'a special one-off levy of 50 per cent on any individual discretionary bonus above £25,000' to 'be paid by the bank, not the bank employee.' Mr Darling anticipated that the levy would apply from the date of his statement to the end of the tax year – 5 April 2010 – and raise 'just over £500m'. In the March 2010 Budget the Labour Government confirmed that the payroll tax would not be extended, though its yield has proved far higher than initially forecast: £3.5 billion in gross terms. The Coalition Government set out its priorities for taxation in its agreement, published in May 2010, and as part of this stated that it would 'introduce a banking levy and seek a detailed agreement on implementation.' In his first Budget speech on 22 June 2010 the Chancellor George Osborne announced that a new levy would be introduced from January 2011 to 'apply to the

[5] The Higgs Committee Report provided a further review of corporate governance including Non-Executives in 2003. In 2010 The Combined Code was revised and renamed The UK Corporate Governance Code.

balance sheets of UK banks and building societies, and to the UK operations of banks from abroad' which would 'generate over £2 billion of annual revenues.'

There were different approaches in the US, Britain and continental Europe. The UK Government launched a number of consultations on executive directors' remuneration, remuneration disclosure, voting, long term-ism and narrative reporting.

In the US, the Federal Reserve Board position was described in a press release dated October 22, 2009:

- 'Compensation practices at some banking organisations have led to misaligned incentives and excessive risk-taking, contributing to bank losses and financial instability,' Federal Reserve Chairman Ben S. Bernanke said. 'The Federal Reserve is working to ensure that compensation packages appropriately tie rewards to longer-term performance and do not create undue risk for the firm or the financial system.
- 'Flaws in incentive compensation practices were one of many factors contributing to the financial crisis. Inappropriate bonus or other compensation practices can incentivise senior executives or lower level employees, such as traders or mortgage officers, to take imprudent risks that significantly and adversely affect the firm. With that in mind, the Federal Reserve's guidance and supervisory reviews cover all employees who have the ability to materially affect the risk profile of an organisation, either individually, or as part of a group.'

During the crisis the banks lost huge amounts of shareholders' money. Regulators insisted on increased capital requirements. This combination has made trading and other parts of investment banking less profitable, particularly after the cost of capital is deducted. Bank pay has reduced, but the distribution of dividends and compensation has continued to favour the employees over the shareholders.

Those who wish to read more on the banks and the cultural problems and challenges they created and now face are advised to read the Kay Review and the Salz Review. Professor John Kay, in the Kay Review Report July 2012 summed it up well:

> 'Incentives matter: not because, as some people crudely think, financial rewards are the only human motivation – although there are some people of whom that is true, and many of them are to be found in the financial sector. Most people have more complex goals, but they generally behave in line with the values and aspirations of the environment in which they find themselves. We must create cultures in which business and finance can work together to create high performing companies and earn returns for savers on a sustainable basis.'

In 2013, Barclays published its internal assessment of the bank by its independent non-executive director Sir Anthony Salz,[6] which provides a fascinating insight into the complexities and challenges faced by a large global bank, and the importance of culture.

Private Equity and Hedge Funds

There have been two other important developments that impact directors' remuneration. The rapid growth of private equity as an alternative to the quoted company markets has created much public debate. Private equity has a number of advantages. Private Equity owned companies usually have higher leverage and the interest on debt is tax deductible, thus reducing their tax bills relative to quoted companies. Directors and senior managers invest in their company, usually in shares with an initially low value but with an opportunity for large gains that are taxed as capital (at 10% if entrepreneurs' relief applies, but otherwise 28%), whereas executives in quoted companies have relatively modest incentives and have to pay 50% income tax plus 2% NI and the company has to pay 13.8% NIC on top of this. A number of private equity owners and their managers (who as a result of a Memorandum Of Understanding with the Inland Revenue in 2003 are also able to have their gains treated as capital gains) have become very rich and powerful, by buying quoted companies and improving their performance. The availability of these large incentives creates further pressure on quoted companies to respond in ways that incentivise, reward and motivate their managers.

The second development has been that of the hedge funds. They have been able to attract very large amounts of funds under management and now form a very significant proportion of the daily trading on the Stock Exchange. Their typical fee structure of 2% of funds under management plus a 20% performance fee means that many hedge fund managers are very highly rewarded. They also have a powerful influence on companies in which they invest as they are usually more active and interventionist than traditional 'long only' fund managers.

29.5 2010's

The 2010's have seen further consultations on directors' remuneration and continued high profile media coverage. The consultations resulted in new legislation and increased disclosures which are described in **Chapters 6** and **28**.

There has also been a slight moderation in the rate of growth of directors' remuneration and the expected value of awards of total remuneration has decreased slightly.

---

6 http://www.euromoney.com/downloads/2013/Barclays-Salz-review.pdf

2012 saw a number of shareholder revolts and what the media proclaimed was a shareholder spring. It is unclear if any significant change has occurred. However companies do now spend more time on communicating and 'engaging' with shareholders.

29.6 The future?

There has been a huge surge in corporate governance activity and I expect this to continue. However, it has not had much if any impact in controlling the level of directors' remuneration.

Power still resides with the executive management. Non-Executives have to balance the risk that executives may leave or be demotivated against shareholders views and most shareholders are much more interested in the performance of the share price than they are about executive pay.

Dr Cable's admirable efforts to redress this balance are worthy. He and his department are working to ensure there is more transparency about directors' remuneration, its linkage to performance, improvements in narrative reporting and additional voting rights for shareholders with respect to directors' remuneration.

Shareholders are beginning to realise that there is a leakage in shareholders' funds to those who promote excessive numbers of acquisitions and mergers. The fees for these are enormous and there is very little in the way of competitive pricing for these services. Those who benefit are the big investment banks, lawyers and accountancy firms who do the supporting work related to acquisitions and mergers. These are the same people who have benefited from encouraging companies to take on excessive leverage and drive the tax avoidance industry.

Since 2007/8 there has been huge public furore about executive compensation, and this has moderated pay levels in the US and slowed the rate of increase in the UK.

The UK remains behind the US in terms of pay levels and the standard of living that US pay can provide. The other factors at work here in the UK are the high levels of pay available in private equity industry in hedge funds and in investment banks, legal partnerships and accountancy firms. For these reasons, I predict that directors' remuneration in the UK will stay high and will continue to increase at a higher rate than that of the average UK employee.

30 Motivation Theories

'It is difficult to overstate the extent to which most managers believe in the redemptive power of rewards.' – Alfie Kohn

30.1 Does pay motivate CEOs and leaders?

Most of the psychologists' research about motivation and pay is about employees. In this book we are specifically interested in CEOs and top executives, so must consider carefully whether results for general employees can be extrapolated to CEOs.

The seminal piece of research was by Jensen and Murphy, published in the Harvard Business Review 1989 article 'Performance pay and top management incentives'. They concluded that CEOs' remuneration was not sufficiently aligned with shareholders.

As a result, they argued, CEOs were inadequately rewarded for increasing the returns to shareholders, and instead ran organisations as if they were their own empire. This was ground-breaking stuff and was seized upon by many CEOs, who took it as an opportunity to significantly increase their equity incentives, principally via share options.

It is difficult to overstate the extent to which most managers – and the people who advise them – believe in the redemptive power of rewards. So argued Alfie Kohn in 'Why incentive plans cannot work' in the Harvard Business Review in September 1993. He found that, by and large, incentive rewards succeed in securing one thing only: temporary compliance. They do not create an enduring commitment to any values or actions. They merely and temporarily change what we do. According to Kohn, such rewards:

- do not motivate
- punish
- rupture relationships
- ignore legitimate reasons for missing targets
- discourage risk-taking, and
- undermine interest.

Kohn said that incentives (or bribes) simply cannot work in the workplace.

Alfie Kohn's paper produced much debate. Bennett Stewart, the senior partner of Stern Stewart commented:

> 'A world without A's, praise, and gold stars or incentives? No thank you, Mr. Kohn. Communism was tried and it didn't work.'

Another guru said:

> 'Money is the outcome of high performance. Satisfaction and respect are incentives to it.'

and Dennis Kozlowski, the Chairman and CEO of Tyco, wrote his response:

> 'I'll accept that elephants cannot fly and that fish cannot walk, but Kohn's argument that incentive plans cannot work defies the laws of nature at Tyco.'[1]

Kohn concluded that he thought it useful to think in terms of three Cs: choice, collaboration and content. Choice means that employees should be able to participate in making decisions about what they do every day. Collaboration denotes the need to structure teams in order to facilitate an exchange of ideas and a climate of support. Content refers to what people are asked to do: as Frederick Hertzberg said:

> 'If you want people motivated to do a good job, give them a good job to do.'

Kohn believed innovation and excellence are the results of helping people experience intrinsic motivation.

Motivation is complex. I reviewed the literature in preparing this book and identified at least 15 different theories.

Robert Owen, a 19th century Scottish mill owner, thought people should be looked after, cared for and maintained well; and if so they (like his machines) will perform efficiently, reliably and lastingly.

In contrast, Bentham's carrot and stick approach is used by many managers.

Maslow's hierarchy of needs sounds plausible but has little research to validate it.

Herzberg refined Maslow's ideas into those items that are satisfiers (but not motivators) and other factors the absence of which leads to demotivation.

---

1 At the time Mr Kozlowski's views held great sway. Subsequently, however, Mr Kozlowski was found guilty in June 2005 on 22 of 23 counts, including grand larceny, conspiracy and securities fraud, stemming from giant bonuses and other improper compensation he got as Tyco's CEO. He received a sentence of between eight years four months (minimum) and 25 years (maximum), compared with 25 years for former WorldCom CEO Bernard J Ebbers and 24 for former Enron President Jeffrey Skilling. In seeking the maximum sentence, Assistant District Attorney Owen Heimer called Mr Kozlowski's crimes 'unprecedented' and said he made Tyco a 'symbol of kleptocratic management.' Source http://online.wsj.com/article/SB10001424052970203752604576643093882076826.html

Figure 16: Maslow's hierarchy of needs

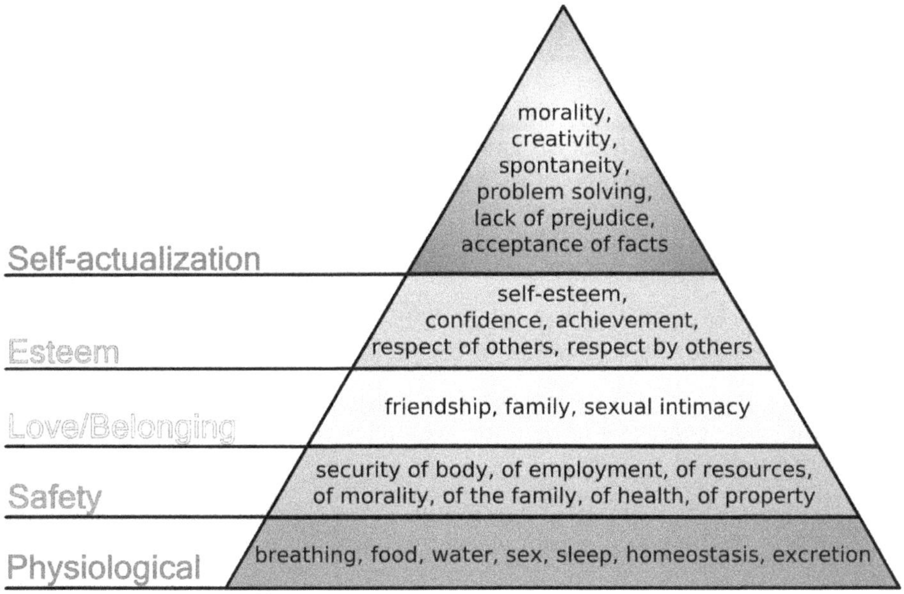

McGregor thought you could separate employees into Theory X, those who do not like work and only do what they have to, and Theory Y, those who are self-directed and try to do their best.

The Hawthorne effect noted that when lighting was changed, performance increased, ie attention and interest from management leads to improved performance.

Victor Vroom (I love the name) propounded the most widely accepted theory: **motivation = expectancy x value of rewards**. Porter and Lawler refined his theory.

The expectancy theory, as proposed by Victor Vroom of Yale School of Management in 1964, stresses and focuses on outcomes, and not on needs, unlike Maslow and Herzberg. The theory states that the intensity of a tendency to perform in a particular manner is dependent on the intensity of an expectation that the performance will be followed by a definite outcome and on the appeal of the outcome to the individual.

Expectancy theory states that an employee's motivation is an outcome of how much an individual wants a reward (Valence), the assessment that the likelihood that the effort will lead to expected performance (Expectancy) and the belief that the performance will lead to reward (Instrumentality). In short, **Valence** is the significance associated by an individual with the expected outcome. It is the expected and not the actual satisfaction that an employee expects to receive after achieving the goals. **Expectancy** is the faith that better efforts will result in better performance. Expectancy is influenced by factors such as possession of appropriate skills for performing the job, availability of right resources, availability of crucial information and getting the required support for completing the job.

Instrumentality is the faith that if you perform well, then a valid outcome will be there. Instrumentality is affected by factors such as trust in the people who decide who receives what outcome, the simplicity of the process deciding who gets what outcome, and clarity of relationship between performance and outcomes. Thus, the expectancy theory concentrates on the following three relationships:

- Effort-performance relationship: What is the likelihood that the individual's effort be recognised in his performance appraisal?
- Performance-reward relationship: It talks about the extent to which the employee believes that getting a good performance appraisal leads to organisational rewards.
- Rewards-personal goals relationship: It is all about the attractiveness or appeal of the potential reward to the individual.

Vroom was of view that employees consciously decide whether to perform or not at the job. This decision solely depended on the employee's motivation level which in turn depends on three factors of expectancy, valence and instrumentality.

Edwin Locke's Goal Setting theory said that setting specific, clear pronounced objectives helped motivation, but vague objectives demotivate. Underpinning this is people's belief they can achieve a hard task. Their 'self-efficacy' drives them to perform. Locke's goal setting theory is widely acknowledged as correct and useful for motivating employees. However it may be less useful in respect of predicting the behaviour of CEOs.

David McClelland's theory is particularly pertinent to CEOs and says people have needs for Power, Affiliation and Achievement. This theory says that there are three main needs – the power, in which the main motivation is the chance to manage others; the affiliation, in which the motivation is the cooperative and harmonious environment; and the achievement, in which the motivation is the challenge and feedback.

In 2003, McClelland and Burnham in the Harvard Business Review article 'Power is the Great Motivator' concluded

> 'when it comes to managing big companies, the desire for power – that is a manager's desire to have an impact, to be strong and influential – is more important than the need to get things done or the wish to be liked.'

Figure 17: McClelland distribution of need behaviours

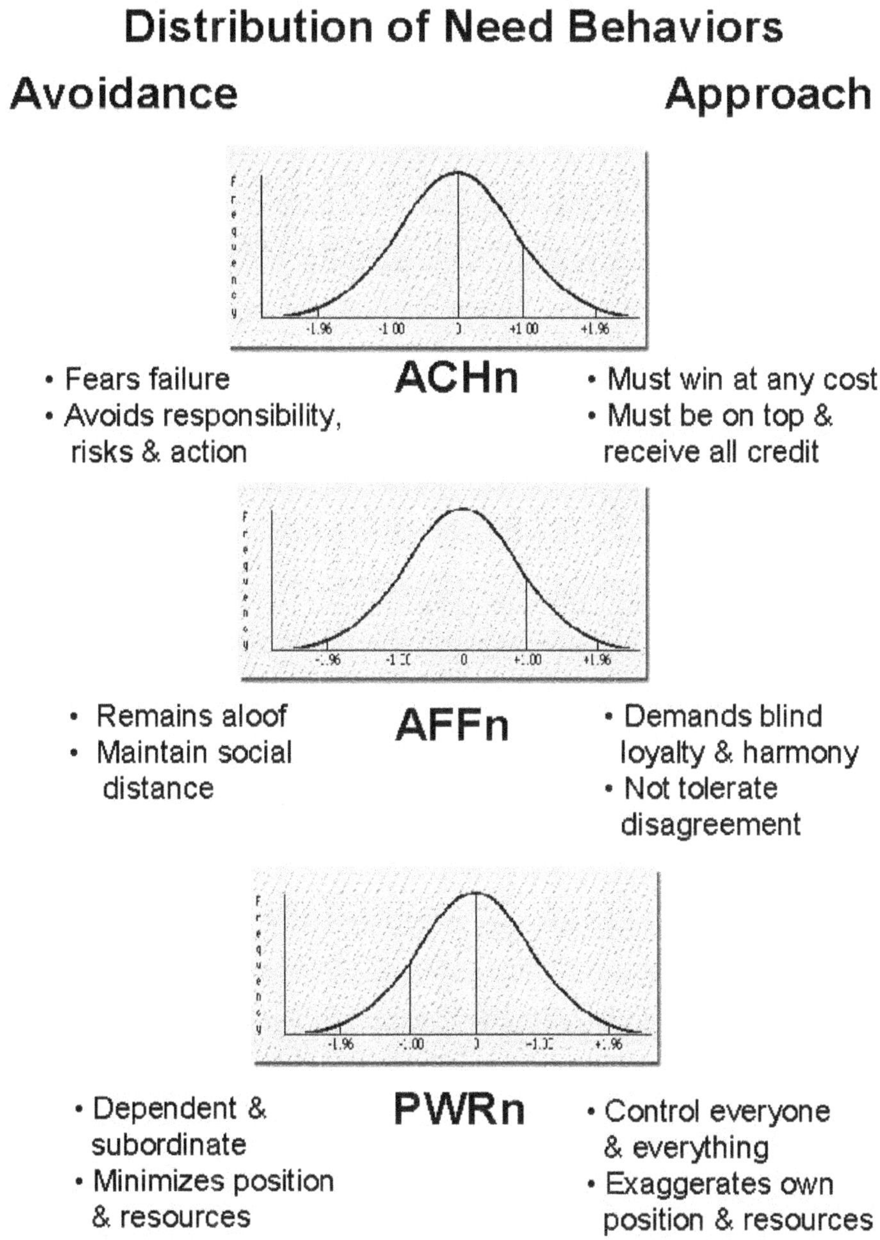

Image taken from http://faculty.css.edu/dswenson/web/LEAD/McClelland.html

The One Minute Manager (1982), by Kenneth Blanchard and Spencer Johnson is also worthy of mention. Time voted it one of the 25 Most Influential Business Management Books. This slim volume, with its simple (critics argued, simple-minded) business homilies, immediately became a worldwide publishing phenomenon, and spent more than two years on the New York Times bestsellers list. In it, would-be effective managers are advised to 'catch an employee doing something right,' and to reinforce that good behaviour with a One Minute Praising. Bad deeds are similarly to be pointed out and punished with a One Minute Reprimand. The authors themselves were accused of a bad deed by the Wall Street Journal – plagiarism, to be exact – which they denied. But by that time, the tiny tome was ubiquitous, having been distributed by FORTUNE 500 companies everywhere. The book also advocated 'different strokes for different folks', which is particularly relevant to the point of director motivation and rewards.

A 2011 study by PwC[2] in conjunction with the London School of Economics into the psychology of incentives called 'Making executive pay work' concluded that:

- Executives are risk-averse
- Complexity and ambiguity destroy value
- The longer you have to wait, the less it's worth
- It's all relative – fairness is fundamental
- People don't just work for money
- The key motivation of a long term incentive programme is recognition

and made these design recommendations:

- Performance pay has a cost – be sure you're getting value
- Keep it short, sweet and simple
- One size does not fit all – know your people and pay them accordingly
- Money is only part of the deal – and recognition matters as much as financial incentives
- Be realistic about how variable pay can be from year to year.

FUSE[3] by Jim Finkelstein with Mary Gavin is a book about combining the knowledge, experience and perseverance of 20th century workplaces with the speed, digital intelligence and global view of 21st century workforces, to

---

2 The study was predominantly of executives below the Board (median pay was about £200,000), so its results cannot be extrapolated to CEOs and other executive directors. However their survey provides important contextual background. See http://www.pwc.com/en_GX/gx/hr-management-services/publications/assets/making-executive-pay-work.pdf

3 See http://www.fusethebook.com/about-the-book/. I was asked if this is a good reference and given this alternative view. The book is about motivation of junior staff against middle managers. It appears to state that money is less important to the younger generation whereas I am arguing that it is very important to the CEOs/top execs. (It might be a better reference in 20–30 years' time if these younger employees reach the top positions!) Furthermore the 'crunch' question may not be relevant. These

ignite a high-productivity and profitable future for our organisations. It poses the crunch question about motivation and money. If you won the lottery tomorrow, would you still carry on working in your current job? The honest answer for almost everyone is no! So we have to recognise that people go to work for the money. They are motivated by their desire for money. They will do things so as to get more money. So we must make sure that the reward systems reward people for doing the right things.

Money is not the only motivator, nor for most people the main motivator. Professor John Kay, in the Kay Review Report July 2012 summarised it well:

> 'Incentives matter: not because, as some people crudely think, financial rewards are the only human motivation – although there are some people of whom that is true, and many of them are to be found in the financial sector. Most people have more complex goals, but they generally behave in line with the values and aspirations of the environment in which they find themselves. We must create cultures in which business and finance can work together to create high performing companies and earn returns for savers on a sustainable basis.'

The issue of culture is discussed further in **Chapter 37.2**.

30.2 Motivational Impact

The Remuneration Committee and its shareholders need to assess the motivational effect of the remuneration strategy and its cost effectiveness.

Executives will value different forms of remuneration differently. To illustrate this point consider the proverb 'a bird in the hand is worth two in the bush'. Thus a £1 of salary is worth more than a £1 of bonus. How much the £1 of bonus is worth to the executive depends on their estimate of the likelihood of the bonus plan paying out, a discount for the time value of money and a further discount depending on the degree to which the executive feels the events that affect the bonus outcome are beyond their control.

E = O x T x C

Incentive Efficiency(E) = Estimated Outcome (O) x Discount for Time (T) x Controllability Discount (C)

CEOs do win the lottery and get millions – but they don't stop working; they carry on to try to get even more – especially those in private equity. These CEOs mix with other like-minded and rich/powerful people. The lottery winner by contrast is suddenly forced out of his depth in his social group – the wealth contrast is too great for them to be able to work or socialise with their former colleagues.

30.3 Conclusions

Motivation is complex:

- people are different and
- different approaches work best with different people.

Since organisations consist of different people, we have to recognise that no remuneration system will be perfect. The best approach is to have a motivation and pay system that:

- fits the company style and culture
- keeps most of the people happy
- helps the CEO and divisional chief executives reinforce their management style(s).

Companies should:

- recognise that pay is only one of the levers to motivate people
- set themselves a goal to create a framework which will enable people to succeed
- learn from Locke to set clear, specific measures so people know what to strive for and when they have achieved success.

30.4 Motivation Checklist

Companies should test themselves against these four questions to see if they are optimising the impact of their reward systems:

(i) Satisfiers OK? People are demotivated if there is not a minimum level of these satisfiers.

(ii) Provision of opportunity for self-esteem and self-actualisation? Does the company provide people with the opportunity to grow and have a sense of fulfilment?

(iii) Pay fairness (equity) is important. People can be demotivated if they see others getting paid more than them for reasons which they do not regard as fair. Does the company pass this test?

(iv) Does the company change its pay systems too frequently? Has the company been tinkering with its pay system, such that it becomes a source of friction or too complex/opaque and thus demotivational?

31 Academic Research on Directors' Remuneration

31.1 US Research

There is much research in the US.

As noted earlier in this book, the seminal piece of research was by Jensen and Murphy, published in the Harvard Business Review 1989 article 'Performance pay and top management incentives'. They found that for every $1,000 change in shareholder wealth, the performance pay of the CEO only changes by $3.25. They concluded that CEOs' remuneration was not sufficiently aligned with shareholders. This was a message that (not surprisingly) CEOs were in agreement with and led to very large increases in performance related pay, particularly in the form of grants of stock options.

Lucien Bebchuk[1] and Jesse Fried,[2] two Harvard professors, have done extensive research into executive compensation in the US. Their books and research are well worth reading. Some of the points they make are:

- It is not just a few rotten apples. The problems of executive compensation are widespread, persistent and systemic.
- Arm's length bargaining approach inadequately explains CEO pay practice. Instead, pay practice can only be understood once one accepts the managerial power model.
- Executive compensation is not designed to tightly link pay and performance.
- The pay of the top five executives accounted for 7.5% of profits last year.[3] This is less than the 10% peak in the period 1998–2002, but remains a significant cost for shareholders.
- The executives' ability to unwind equity positions provides incentives for executives to make short term profits from their shareholdings, which are not available to shareholders. (They are not saying executives trade on inside information – that would be illegal. However executives are better informed than most shareholders about markets, customers

1 Bebchuck and Spamman 'Regulating Bankers' Pay', May 2010
2 Fried and Jackson 'Pay Without Performance – the unfulfilled promise of executive compensation', Executive Pensions HBR Discussion Paper 507, March 2005
3 At the time they were referring to 2009.

and trends: as a result they can come to a decision to reduce their exposure to their company shares earlier than others might do.)

- Non-Executive Directors as not operating as independents. The gift of their continued role is heavily influence-able by the CEO and it is usually better not to upset the apple cart by disagreeing about executive compensation issues.
- Pay is not unlimited. But only at a certain level does the outrage factor come into play.
- Companies routinely camouflage their disclosure of executive compensation so as to make if difficult or impossible for readers of the annual reports to see how much executives have been paid and how much they might receive in the future.
- Companies use pay practices that make less transparent the total amount of executive compensation and the extent to which managers' compensation is de-coupled from their own performance.
- The devil is in the detail, particularly with equity pay and pensions.[4] Executives are often able to persuade their compensation committees to exercise discretion in respect of performance conditions in their favour. Executives are able to sell shares when they get wind of information that has not yet been formally assessed or announced to the Board or the market.[5]

Academic theories break down into three camps. Otten, in 'Theories on executive pay: a literature overview and critical assessment' (January 2008),[6] provides an overview of 16 theories that have been used in the literature to explain the phenomenon. The theories can be classified into three types of approaches:

(i) the value approach

(ii) the agency approach and

(iii) the symbolic approach.

A critical assessment of the theories shows that the dominant use in the literature of the perfect contracting approach of agency theory neglects:

(i) the socially determined symbolic value that executive pay could represent, and

---

4 See Executive Pensions Discussion Paper 507, March 2005, Harvard Law School. This paper identified that the median pension value as of total compensation was 34%; and because public firms are not required to disclose the monetary value of pension plans, financial economists and the media alike have generally excluded pension from their pay analyses causing significant distortions in comparison among executive compensation packages and overestimates of the extent to which executive pay is linked to performance.

5 Please note I am not suggesting this is insider trading, but it doesn't seem very ethical!

6 http://mpra.ub.uni-muenchen.de/6969/

(ii) the contextual conditions under which executive pay is set.

A more conclusive understanding of executive pay would be based on considering executive pay as an outcome of socially constructed corporate governance arrangements in which the actors involved have considerable discretion to influence the outcomes.

These theories overlap:

Figure 18: Agency, symbolic approaches and value theories of executive pay

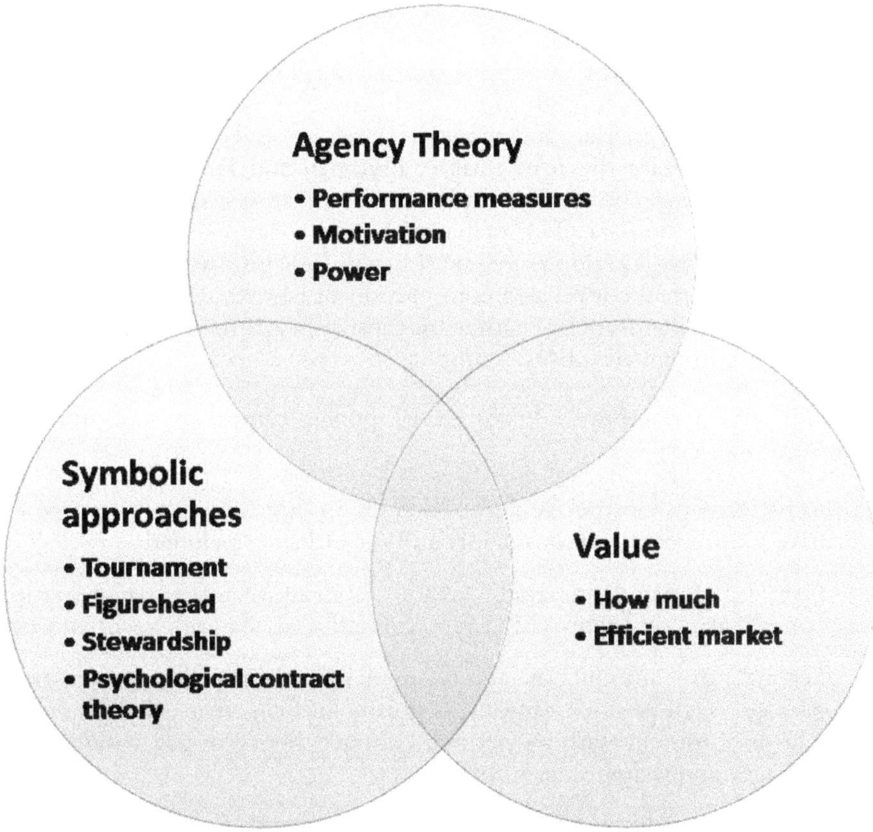

Kevin Murphy in 'Executive Compensation: Where We Are, and How We Got There' (April 2012), concludes:[7]

> 'In this study, I summarise the current state of executive compensation, discuss measurement and incentive issues, document recent trends in

[7] See http://ssrn.com/abstract=2041679

executive pay in both U.S. and international firms, and analyse the evolution of executive pay over the past century. Most recent analyses of executive compensation have focused on efficient contracting or managerial-power rationales for pay, while ignoring or downplaying the causes and consequences of disclosure requirements, tax policies, accounting rules, legislation, and the general political climate. A major theme of this study is that government intervention has been both a response to and a major driver of time trends in executive compensation over the past century, and that any explanation for pay that ignores political factors is critically incomplete.'

Frydman and Jenter (2010)[8] explain that the academic literature focused on explaining the pay trends is roughly divided into two camps: the 'efficient contracting' camp and the 'managerial power' camp. The efficient-contracting camp – rooted in optimal contracting theory – maintains that the observed level and composition of compensation reflects a competitive equilibrium in the market for managerial talent, and that incentives are structured to optimise the firm's value. Frydman and Jenter conclude that neither camp offers convincing explanations for cross-sectional and time-series patterns in the data. The managerial-power camp – exemplified in a series of papers by David Yermack, Lucian Bebchuk and Jesse Fried – maintains that both the level and composition of pay are determined not by competitive market forces but rather by captive board members catering to rent-seeking entrenched CEOs.

The efficient-contracting and managerial power camps are not mutually exclusive.

Martin J Conyon, of the Wharton School in his May 2008[9] paper on Executive Compensation Consultants and CEO Pay concluded:

- First, CEO pay is generally greater in firms that use compensation consultants, consistent with a rent-extraction theory of executive pay.
- Second, the amount of equity used in the overall compensation package, such as stock options, is greater in firms that use consultants. This is consistent with an optimal contract theory of pay which aligns manager and shareholder interests.
- Third, there is little evidence that consultants with potential conflicts of interest, such as supplying other business to client firms, leads to greater CEO pay or the adverse design of pay contracts.

Consultants are controversial, however, and are frequently blamed for contributing to excessive pay. The core criticism is that consultants are not

---

8 http://www.nber.org/papers/w16585.pdf

9 http://www.vanderbiltlawreview.org/2011/03/executive-compensation-consultants-and-ceo-pay/

sufficiently independent or impartial and this leads to pay packages that are not optimal from the shareholders' perspective.

The Waxman Committee[10] inquiry argued that consultant independence and impartiality might be compromised, leading consultants to give biased advice to clients. Specifically, the Committee was concerned about conflicts arising from the cross selling of business services.

Corporate consultants can have a financial conflict of interest if they provide both executive compensation advice and other services to the same company. According to experts on corporate governance, consultants hired by corporate executives to administer employee benefit plans or to provide other services to a company may not be able to provide objective advice about the compensation of the executives who hire them.

The Waxman inquiry also found that compensation consultants of Fortune 250 firms were paid almost eleven times more for providing other services than they were paid for providing executive compensation advice. The mean payment was about $2.3 million for other services and $220,000 for executive compensation advice.

The relative importance of other work questions the consultant's impartiality when offering executive compensation advice. In general, the fees consultants received for executive compensation advice and for other services were not voluntarily reported by U.S. firms (but will be since Dodd Frank[11]). The Waxman Committee had unique access to proprietary information. However, Canadian firms do report this data. Murphy and Sandino[12] report that the ratio of fees for other Non-Executive pay services to fees for executive compensation advice is approximately one to thirteen.

Another thread of research is the issue of overconfident CEOs and overpaid CEOs. Overconfident CEOs have a tendency to make acquisitions which, whilst grand, tend to destroy value. Ulrike Malmendiera and Geoffrey Tateb of University of California, Berkeley, and University of California at Los Angeles,[13] concluded in 2006 that overconfident CEOs over-estimate their ability to generate returns. As a result, they overpay for target companies and undertake value-destroying acquisitions, The effects are strongest if they have access to internal financing. Michael Cooper, Huseyin Gulen and P Raghavendra Rau in 2013, using a big data set (of S&P 1500 firms) over a long time span (1994–2011), found a negative association between high compensation and a firm's future stock performance. Looking at the CEOs whose compensation placed them in the top 10%, the authors were surprised to see

---

10 http://www.erieri.com/PDF/Executive-Consultant-Conflicts.pdf

11 http://www.sec.gov/about/laws/wallstreetreform-cpa.pdf sections 951–957

12 http://www.nd.edu/~carecob/Workshops/08–09%20Workshops/Sandino%20Paper.pdf

13 http://eml.berkeley.edu/~ulrike/Papers/OCmergers_Final_JFEformat_20feb2008.pdf

that, over the next one to three years, their firms underperformed the market – by 5 to 10%. That's a huge loss of shareholder wealth, said one of the lead authors.[14]

31.2 UK Research

There is less research in the UK, although this is an area where there is has been significantly more interest in recent years.

The Walker[15] Report was published in 2009. In respect its terms of reference Walker said:

> 'In February I was asked by the Prime Minister to review corporate governance in UK banks in the light of the experience of critical loss and failure throughout the banking system (the Review). The terms of reference are as follows: To examine corporate governance in the UK banking industry and make recommendations, including in the following areas: the effectiveness of risk management at board level, including the incentives in remuneration policy to manage risk effectively; the balance of skills, experience and independence required on the boards of UK banking institutions; the effectiveness of board practices and the performance of Audit, Risk, Remuneration and Nomination Committees; the role of institutional shareholders in engaging effectively with companies and monitoring of boards; and whether the UK approach is consistent with international practice and how national and international best practice can be promulgated.'

Walker concluded that remuneration and incentives were not the reason for the financial disasters, but that they were a contributing factor. (The US came to similar conclusions as did the G20 Financial Stability Group.)

There have been a number of studies which attempted to show a relationship (or lack of it) between pay and performance. A number of these research studies were flawed, but it would be invidious of this author to list those studies here, except to point out the reasons why some research is flawed:

- Between 1998 and 2010 there has been a huge growth in the amount of performance related pay that has been awarded. This has been in response to the desires of shareholders and their representatives (the ABI, NAPF, FSA and the FRC via UK Corporate Governance Code)
  - Bonus has increased from 44% salary to 207% salary (FTSE 100 average CEO 'bonus' is part cash and part deferred)

---

14 http://papers.ssrn.com/sol3/papers.cfm?abstract_id=1572085

15 http://webarchive.nationalarchives.gov.uk/+/http:/www.hm-treasury.gov.uk/d/walker_review_261109.pdf

  - LTI expected value of awards has increased from 35% to 181% of salary
  - Total of performance related pay has increased from 80% of salary to nearly 350% of salary.
- Changes in the amount of performance pay will be partly because of changes in performance and partly because of the growth in performance related pay. It is not easy to separate out these factors and many studies fail to attempt to do so.
- Not all elements of pay are included
  - Some studies only use cash pay
  - Some exclude pension
  - Some use the expected value of long term incentive awards and compare with performance over a different period to the performance period in the long term incentive plan (a better comparison would be the amounts that vest in an LTIP and a comparison with the performance over the comparable period).
- The payouts in many LTIPS are based on relative TSR, so researchers who look for a correlation of absolute TSR and pay should not be surprised when they do not find one. (In contrast, researchers in the US have traditionally expected and found such a relationship, which is to be expected because of the greater prevalence of share options in the US companies.)
- Too many studies look for links of performance and pay over a one year period. Many pay strategies reward the achievement of internal targets (other than the metrics used by the researchers) in the year.
- Business cycles drive many metrics, eg profit margins, ROCE. Most researchers fail to allow for the impact of the business cycle.
- Sectors move in different ways. Some sectors influence the overall results, eg technology and mobile telecoms in 1998–2003, mining in the 2000s (they boomed, dropped back in the 2007/08 crash and then recovered), banks (they boomed up to 2006, slumped in 2007/08, then raised lots of capital and have been in the doldrums ever since).
- Consequently there is a lot of what statisticians call heteroschedasticity in the data and most analyses fail to appreciate this point and so produce flawed analyses.

Dr Ruth Bender of Cranfield Business School has done much research into remuneration in the UK. In a November 2008 paper 'Paying For Advice: The Role of the Remuneration Consultant in UK Listed Companies' she concluded:

- The use of remuneration consultants to advise on executive pay is ubiquitous amongst larger listed companies, and has attracted academics to consider how their work impacts upon the structure of pay plans. This paper adds to that literature, extending it by taking a qualitative approach and providing a rich context to the interaction between consultants, executives and Remuneration Committees.
- It finds that they have several functions, both explicit and implicit. Acting as experts, they provide advice and recommendations in an increasingly technical area; model the implications of suggested plans; implement the chosen plans; provide an education in remuneration-related matters to committee members; and liaise on their behalf with institutional investors. Additionally, they provide proprietary survey data on pay in comparator companies, on which the Remuneration Committee can base its decisions. In doing so, they influence the choice of comparators, and thus the level of pay.
- Another function of the consultant is to legitimise the committee's decisions in an area which is often contentious. However, this ability to legitimise relies to some extent on the consultants' independence from the board and the committee. This can be at odds with a growing public belief that they are influenced by company executives, and not totally independent. This is one reason why companies employ several different consultants.
- The use of impression management techniques by remuneration consultants is also considered, as this impacts upon the work they obtain, and the way in which their value is perceived.

Her 2011[16] study of remuneration consultants concluded:

- The industry is dominated by a few large firms, of which most are multi-business organisations earning fees from other activities in addition to advice on executive compensation. The main factor determining a firm's ability to attract executive compensation assignments is its reputation, enhanced by expertise and proprietary knowledge. However, reputation may be damaged due to two potential conflicts of interest: the consultants' desire to retain an assignment in future years, and their wish to cross-sell other services. Investors and regulators perceive that these conflicts of interest can lead to the firms shaping their advice to favour the client's executives, which is damaging the reputation of the industry.
- These operational matters give a context to the final part of the chapter, in which we review research on the impact that the use of consultants has had on the level and structure of executive compensation in the USA, UK and Canada, the three main jurisdictions in which studies

---

[16] http://papers.ssrn.com/sol3/papers.cfm?abstract_id=1788322

have been undertaken. This research demonstrates that companies using consultants have higher pay levels and more equity-based compensation than do others. However, the reasons for these differences are unclear.

- Furthermore, contrary to common perceptions, research is equivocal as to whether there is evidence that pay structures do indeed reflect a conflict of interest between the firms and their clients.

Brian Main has done a lot of research into holding shares[17] and concludes that executives holding shares for a long time, including up to and beyond retirement, is a good idea. He also recommends phased sales over at least two years.

[17] For example Gregory and Main in 2012, see http://www.homepages.ed.ac.uk/mainbg/images/JMS%20version%20for%20WEB_05-07-2012.pdf

32 Market Data – Total Remuneration

32.1 Typical packages

The table below summarises typical market practice in FTSE 100, 250 and Small Cap companies for Chief Executives and other executive directors

Table 21: Typical remuneration packages for FTSE 100, 250 and Small Cap companies

	FTSE 100		FTSE 250		Small Cap	
	Chief Executive	**Other Executive Directors**	**Chief Executive**	**Other Executive Directors**	**Chief Executive**	**Other Executive Directors**
Salary increase (median 2012/13)	2.5%	2.5%	3.0%	32.9%	2.6%	2.3%
Salary (£000s) (median 2012/3)	851	501	470	305	352	232
Pension	**Defined contribution and/or cash allowance**					
Value of Pension as % salary (median)	30%	29%	20%	16%	14%	12%
ANNUAL BONUS						
Maximum bonus (percentage of salary)	180%	150%	110%	100%	100%	90%
Target Bonus (percentage of salary)	90%	75%	55%	50%	50%	45%
Most common performance measure	Individual performance/profit					
Deferred bonus (no matching)						
Companies with plan	60%	60%	40%	40%	20%	20%
Deferred (most common)	50%	50%	50%	50%	50%	50%
Deferral period (most common)	3 years	3 years	3 years	3 years	3 years	3 years
Deferred bonus with matching						
Companies with plan	25%	25%	15%	15%	5%	5%
Maximum permitted deferral (percentage of annual bonus)	50%	50%	50%	50%	50%	50%
Typical matching ratio, if applicable	1:1 / 2:1	1:1 / 2:1	1:1 / 2:1	1:1 / 2:1	1:1 / 2:1	1:1 / 2:1
Deferral period (most common)	3 years	3 years	3 years	3 years	3 years	3 years
Most common performance measure on matching shares	EPS* growth					

	FTSE 100		FTSE 250		Small Cap	
Performance share plans (LTIPs)						
Companies with this type of plan	95%	95%	90%	90%	60%	60%
Maximum award (percentage of salary)[1]	200%	200%	150%	150%	150%	150%
Actual award (percentage of salary) [1]	204%	202%	124%	114%	114%	96%
Most common performance measure	TSR** relative to comparator group and EPS growth					
Share option plans						
Companies using this type of plan for executive directors	20%	20%	25%	25%	50%	50%
Actual grant (percentage of salary) [1]	350%	200%	200%	133%	150%	100%
Most common performance measure	EPS growth					
Estimated value of total remuneration (£000s)[2]	**3,520**	**2,015**	**1,440**	**864**	**786**	**497**

* Earnings Per Share.

** Total Shareholder Return.

1 Face Value, ie number of shares times share price at award date.

2 Includes pension and other benefits, total bonus and estimated value of LTIP and share options awarded in the year.

Table 22: Excerpt from September 2013 MM&K/Manifest Total Remuneration Survey – CEO

Turnover £m	<30			31-100			101-300			301-1,000			1,001-3,000			3,001-10,000			>10,001		
Remuneration in £000	Q1	**Median**	Q3	Q1	**Median**	Q3	Q1	**Median**	Q3	Q1	**Median**	Q3	Q1	**Median**	Q3	Q1	**Median**	Q3	Q1	**Median**	Q3
Total Remuneration Awarded	180	**296**	607	313	**506**	761	522	**813**	1,112	863	**1,200**	1,945	1,247	**1,897**	2,427	2,169	**2,597**	3,373	3,157	**4,173**	6,200
Salary	150	**199**	294	202	**252**	331	289	**345**	428	373	**425**	520	460	**549**	670	606	**730**	845	868	**949**	1,063
Total Pension (Cash+DC+DB)	0	**2**	25	0	**22**	36	1	**39**	63	38	**78**	126	74	**143**	214	113	**209**	312	246	**349**	817
Benefits	0	**2**	10	2	**9**	21	4	**16**	32	11	**19**	28	19	**27**	46	20	**31**	54	25	**44**	124
Cash Bonus	0	**0**	74	0	**54**	186	51	**133**	285	82	**249**	449	226	**398**	643	156	**394**	791	0	**498**	840
Deferred Bonus	0	**0**	0	0	**0**	0	0	**0**	0	0	**0**	0	0	**0**	280	0	**7**	515	0	**217**	783
LTIPs, Options and other LTI awards	0	**0**	120	0	**50**	219	0	**169**	291	2	**258**	455	225	**440**	724	576	**828**	1,170	1,004	**1,345**	2,428
Total Cash (Salary + Cash Bonus)	160	**225**	341	250	**340**	495	354	**493**	721	515	**672**	923	722	**972**	1,264	844	**1,171**	1,537	1,188	**1,483**	1,827
% increases over previous year	Q1	**Median**	Q3	Q1	**Median**	Q3	Q1	**Median**	Q3	Q1	**Median**	Q3	Q1	**Median**	Q3	Q1	**Median**	Q3	Q1	**Median**	Q3
Total Remuneration Awarded	-15%	**3%**	25%	-9%	**2%**	34%	-14%	**2%**	15%	-15%	**0%**	14%	-17%	**0%**	15%	-9%	**-1%**	16%	-17%	**-2%**	5%
Salary	0%	**2%**	11%	0%	**3%**	8%	2%	**5%**	10%	0%	**3%**	5%	0%	**3%**	3%	0%	**2%**	3%	0%	**2%**	3%
Total Pension (Cash+DC+DB)	0%	**0%**	2%	0%	**0%**	7%	0%	**0%**	15%	-8%	**2%**	10%	0%	**2%**	5%	-1%	**2%**	11%	-1%	**2%**	7%
Benefits	0%	**0%**	4%	-8%	**0%**	13%	0%	**4%**	25%	-9%	**0%**	8%	-5%	**2%**	6%	-14%	**0%**	21%	-0%	**6%**	41%
Cash Bonus	-11%	**0%**	21%	-21%	**0%**	34%	-39%	**-6%**	4%	-26%	**0%**	30%	-28%	**0%**	41%	-27%	**0%**	13%	-39%	**-7%**	13%
Deferred Bonus	0%	**0%**	0%	0%	**0%**	0%	0%	**0%**	0%	0%	**0%**	0%	-3%	**0%**	4%	-16%	**0%**	18%	-14%	**0%**	0%
LTIPs, Options and other LTI awards	0%	**0%**	29%	-2%	**0%**	33%	0%	**2%**	8%	-3%	**0%**	7%	-4%	**3%**	7%	-1%	**1%**	5%	-2%	**1%**	8%
Total Cash (Salary + Cash Bonus)	-10%	**2%**	21%	-5%	**7%**	20%	-13%	**1%**	12%	-8%	**0%**	12%	-12%	**0%**	15%	-10%	**0%**	9%	-15%	**-4%**	6%
Total Remuneration "Realised"	173	**260**	470	290	**416**	667	445	**724**	1,161	675	**1,128**	2,138	1,191	**1,620**	2,677	1,697	**2,243**	4,557	2,292	**4,306**	6,631
LTIPs, Options and Deferred Bonuses "Realised"	0	**0**	0	0	**0**	0	0	**0**	319	0	**50**	897	0	**363**	1,401	0	**503**	2,532	447	**1,863**	3,958

Market Capitalisation £m	<30			31-100			101-300			301-1,000			1,001-3,000			3,001-10,000			>10,001		
Remuneration in £000	Q1	**Median**	Q3	Q1	**Median**	Q3	Q1	**Median**	Q3	Q1	**Median**	Q3	Q1	**Median**	Q3	Q1	**Median**	Q3	Q1	**Median**	Q3
Total Remuneration Awarded	178	**247**	326	271	**425**	813	514	**679**	923	787	**1,127**	1,445	1,234	**1,945**	2,418	2,290	**3,047**	3,678	3,734	**5,203**	6,643
Salary	150	**190**	225	198	**274**	327	250	**332**	405	351	**410**	472	418	**523**	617	650	**758**	851	925	**1,010**	1,113
Total Pension (Cash+DC+DB)	0	**0**	20	0	**25**	53	0	**34**	60	25	**51**	118	51	**113**	190	105	**219**	309	238	**373**	1,205
Benefits	0	**2**	13	2	**11**	26	4	**15**	29	4	**16**	29	13	**22**	33	20	**31**	47	31	**56**	145
Cash Bonus	0	**0**	2	0	**38**	115	0	**103**	238	91	**255**	371	175	**374**	619	306	**490**	786	0	**581**	886
Deferred Bonus	0	**0**	0	0	**0**	0	0	**0**	0	0	**0**	0	0	**0**	200	0	**239**	584	0	**112**	1,042
LTIPs, Options and other LTI awards	0	**0**	22	0	**26**	163	0	**147**	236	137	**276**	440	192	**536**	806	485	**880**	1,177	1,102	**2,017**	3,111
Total Cash (Salary + Cash Bonus)	150	**205**	264	222	**317**	494	340	**463**	601	467	**661**	832	672	**910**	1,174	968	**1,254**	1,527	1,208	**1,614**	1,971
% increases over previous year	Q1	**Median**	Q3	Q1	**Median**	Q3	Q1	**Median**	Q3	Q1	**Median**	Q3	Q1	Median	Q3	Q1	**Median**	Q3	Q1	**Median**	Q3
Total Remuneration Awarded	-16%	**-2%**	9%	-11%	**2%**	9%	-20%	**0%**	22%	-8%	**6%**	28%	-15%	**-2%**	11%	-16%	**-1%**	5%	-14%	**2%**	20%
Salary	0%	**3%**	11%	0%	**3%**	7%	0%	**3%**	8%	1%	**4%**	7%	0%	**3%**	4%	0%	**2%**	3%	0%	**3%**	5%
Total Pension (Cash+DC+DB)	0%	**0%**	0%	0%	**0%**	5%	-1%	**0%**	5%	0%	**4%**	22%	0%	**0%**	7%	-3%	**0%**	3%	-1%	**3%**	25%
Benefits	0%	**0%**	4%	-6%	**0%**	20%	-4%	**0%**	10%	-6%	**0%**	16%	-4%	**0%**	12%	-7%	**0%**	6%	3%	**11%**	45%
Cash bonus	-28%	**0%**	0%	-14%	**0%**	22%	-40%	**0%**	50%	-34%	**0%**	14%	-23%	**0%**	22%	-30%	**-4%**	13%	-22%	**-5%**	5%
Deferred bonus	0%	**0%**	0%	0%	**0%**	0%	0%	**0%**	0%	0%	**0%**	0%	-2%	**0%**	0%	-4%	**0%**	26%	-18%	**0%**	0%
LTIPs, Options and other LTI awards	0%	**0%**	0%	-11%	**0%**	7%	-3%	**0%**	10%	0%	**4%**	12%	-8%	**1%**	8%	-2%	**0%**	6%	-2%	**3%**	8%
Total Cash (Salary + Cash Bonus)	-9%	**0%**	11%	-6%	**4%**	9%	-15%	**2%**	22%	-10%	**1%**	17%	-9%	**1%**	13%	-13%	**-1%**	6%	-11%	**-3%**	6%
Total Remuneration "Realised"	162	**214**	278	264	**363**	606	429	**605**	873	725	**1,100**	1,728	1,073	**1,570**	2,623	1,815	**2,567**	4,531	3,553	**5,362**	7,686
LTIPs, Options and Deferred Bonuses "Realised"	0	**0**	0	0	**0**	0	0	**0**	117	0	**102**	596	0	**298**	1,266	0	**1,012**	2,751	1,060	**2,863**	4,540

Notes

Total remuneration awarded includes the fair value of long term incentive awards, including share options. The amounts that are actually paid out will not be known for several years. The LTIPs, Options and Deferred Bonuses "Realised" figure refers to earlier awards that have vested in the latest year, or for share options the gains made at the date of exercise. Total Remuneration "Realised" is the total of salary, benefits, bonus and the "paid out" figures for LTIPs, Options, deferred bonuses, other long term incentives and pension.

32.2 How Company Size Affects Pay

In terms of pay, size matters. Bigger companies pay bigger salaries, bigger bonuses, much bigger long term incentives and bigger pensions. Added together this gives them far larger total remuneration.

Remuneration increases in line with the logarithm of turnover or market capitalisation. For smaller companies this is a straight line relationship. For larger companies, executive directors are on a curve to infinity. **Chart 4** and **Table 22** highlight the very different make-up of the package of the largest companies.

In small companies, directors' remuneration packages are a significant cost, which limits the scope to pay more and acts as a control mechanism on the potential total remuneration. In large companies, directors' remuneration is a small proportion of total costs and profits and no such internal constraint exists.

Chart 4: Size matters

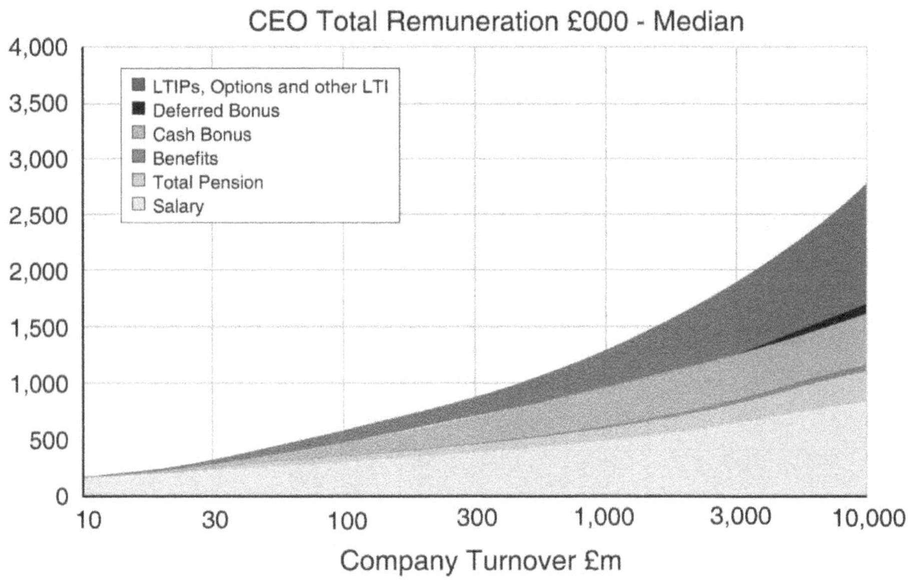

Source: MM&K/Manifest Executive Director Total Remuneration Survey, September 2013

32.3 How Company Sector Affects Pay

Some sectors pay their executive directors higher than others. The following figures show the average sector differences on a turnover and market capitalisation basis.

Figure 19: CEO sector pay differences (for companies with similar market capitalisation)

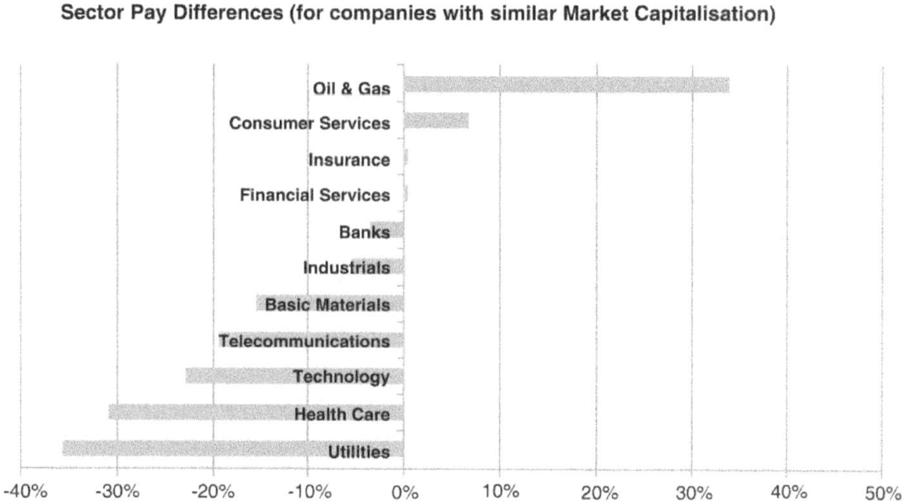

Source: MM&K/Manifest Executive Director Total Remuneration Survey, 2013

The differences by sector are different if the comparison is done on a turnover basis:

Figure 20: CEO sector pay differences (for companies with similar turnover)

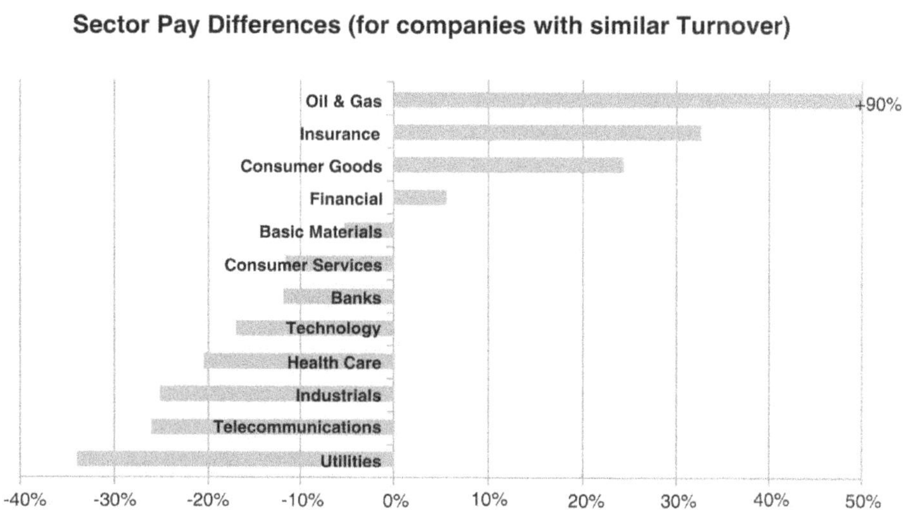

Source: MM&K/Manifest Executive Director Total Remuneration Survey, 2012

In most sectors, the major determinant of market capitalisation, the current perceived value of the business, is based on current turnover, profits and future growth which are reflected in its p/e ratio. This is also true for established (producing) companies, but for companies where the focus is on exploration, a company's market capitalisation is often made up principally by its perceived future value of income, which might not arise until many years into the future. As a result, a comparison of the remuneration of CEOs based on market capitalisation would be unfair, as other sectors would comprise larger, more developed, more complex companies with greater turnover.

Thus, when looking at this type of analysis, it is important to use the most reflective measure of business 'size' for that industry.

Utilities pay lower total remuneration than other companies. They operate in a highly regulated environment and to pay too much would risk a negative reaction from their regulator.

Many of the sector differences vary for different size companies. For example small start-up fast growth telecoms companies pay much less than similar sized other companies, but mature telecoms companies pay similar rates to most other large companies.

Cautionary notes about using survey data:

- The MM&K/Manifest survey provides a good estimate of the remuneration market and excellent background data. It complements, rather than being a substitute for, detailed individual company benchmarking data.

- It should be noted that sector differentials can be highly influenced by small sample sizes. It is recommended that the user considers carefully if there is a logical reason why the sector is paying above or below the market. If so, then the differential can be added or subtracted from the turnover category figures above.

- The same differential should be applied to the CEO as to the other executive directors, with the possible exception of very large companies. In all cases judgement is required.

- Although sector can be a key driver of pay, the degree of internationalism, the complexity of the business and many other factors impact on pay levels. Consequently the differentials above should not be blindly followed in the design of future awards for executives.

32.4 Pay Differentials

In the larger companies, the CEO is generally paid 60% more than the second highest paid director, but in one quarter of companies the CEO is paid twice as much as the second highest paid director. If this is a true reflection of the added value of the CEO vis-à-vis other directors, it highlights the gap between these roles and a potential problem of internal succession.

In smaller companies, the differentials between the CEO and other executive directors are lower – the second highest paid director is paid at 75% of the rate of the CEO. This means that the CEO, whilst the boss, is paid only one third more than the others and suggests he/she is more likely to support a team approach.

32.5 Total Remuneration Awarded

Total Remuneration Awarded is the sum of salary, bonus, the expected value of deferred bonus awards, share options and other long term incentive awards made in the year, plus benefits and the value of pension.

CEO Total Remuneration increases have bounced back above the historic averages, following the slowdown observed in 2009. The median figures are as follows:

Table 23: CEO – median increases in total remuneration awarded

Turnover £millions	**<30**	**31–100**	**101–300**	**301–1,000**	**1,001–3,000**	**3,001–10,000**	**>10,000**
Latest data 2012/13[3]	**3%**	**2%**	**2%**	**0%**	**0%**	**-1%**	**-2%**
2012	**3%**	**3%**	**5%**	**0%**	**5%**	**-3%**	**1%**
2011	3%	6%	6%	8%	5%	3%	7%
2010	7%	8%	10%	12%	14%	16%	13%
2009	0%	-4%	0%	-1%	7%	7%	1%
2008	8%	2%	3%	5%	6%	1%	9%
2007	7%	10%	14%	12%	19%	13%	33%
2006	4%	10%	12%	14%	8%	9%	7%
2005	12%	10%	7%	4%	6%	6%	14%
2004	10%	8%	6%	11%	17%	13%	0%
2003	6%	5%	7%	10%	4%	16%	11%
Average 2003–2012	6%	6%	7%	8%	9%	8%	10%

There was a wide range of practice in terms of increases in total remuneration.

---

[3] This latest data is a mix of annual reports of companies with year ends March 2013 and December 2012. 2012 refers to the results from the MM&K/Manifest June 2013 report, which contains most 2012 year end data.

Chart 5: % increases in total remuneration awarded to CEOs (2011)

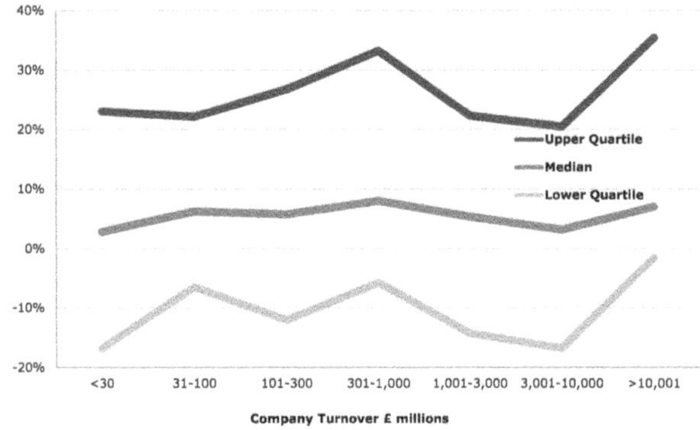

The ten year analysis of average FTSE 100 CEO pay shows that the increases have primarily been in the form of performance-related pay.

32.6 Total Remuneration Growth

Total remuneration has grown fastest in the largest companies. The biggest growth has been in long term incentive awards, with many companies now using two or sometimes three plans, eg options, LTIPs and bonus deferral/matching plans. Bonus opportunities and payments have also increased significantly.

Since 1998, FTSE 100 average CEO remuneration has grown rapidly, whilst the FTSE 100 index at 31 December 2010 was at the same level as 1998. The comparison with the long term trend of TSR shows how average Total Remuneration Awarded has increased from £1 million to £4.8 million when the FTSE 100 index has not increased, except for dividends.

Chart 6: Average total remuneration awarded to FTSE 100 CEOs and FTSE 100 Index

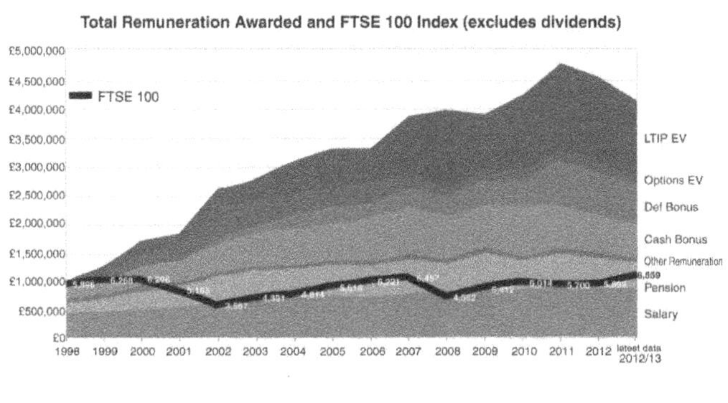

Table 24: Cumulative growth rates for FTSE 100 average CEOs' remuneration and indices

Element	growth 1998–2012 cumulative	growth 1998–2012 average per annum
Salaries	103%	5%
Bonus (excl Deferred Bonus)	243%	9%
Deferred Bonus	1039%[4]	28%
Options	112%	6%
LTIPs	2254%	25%
Sub-total of Options & LTIPs	1000%	19%
Pension	198%	8%
Total Remuneration	352%	8%
Average UK earnings	67%	4%
RPI	51%	3%
FTSE 100 (excl dividends)	0%	0%
FTSE 250 (excl dividends)	172%	7%

MM&K do not have comparative data for FTSE 250 remuneration over the same period, but I believe that pay has not increased at such a fast rate as for the FTSE 100 companies. The performance over the last 14 years of the mid 250 is very much better than the FTSE 100. The FTSE 250 has more than doubled whilst the FTSE 100 index has not increased. The indices exclude dividends, so shareholders have had a positive return, albeit a small one.[5]

Salaries

From 1998 to the end of 2012, average FTSE 100 CEO salaries rose 5% per annum compound; whilst Total Remuneration zoomed up by 8% per annum. In the same period average UK earnings went up 4% per annum, retail prices by 3% per annum and the FTSE 100 index did not grow at all.[6] Directors did significantly better than shareholders and employees.

Executive directors' salaries increased more rapidly for than other employees. This could be due to:

- Salary increases of 5% per annum not attracting shareholder criticism to the same extent as contract length and design features of incentive

[4] Growth since 2002. Date on deferred bonus is not available for earlier periods. Deferred bonus was rare and small in those days.

[5] At April 2012 the FTSE 100 index average yield was 3.8%.

[6] If dividends are included, shareholders returns were similar to retail price inflation.

plans. Salary increases can usually be explained by changes in the role, increased scope of the company's operations and the need to pay competitively.

- Many institutions have traditionally focused on incentive plan award quantums as a multiple of salary, rather than looking at the amount in £ terms. They had neither the methodology nor the expertise to review total remuneration.
- The knock-on effect to the value of pension. Many of the largest companies still have defined benefit (DB) pension arrangements for directors, often with 30th accrual rates. This makes the benefit very valuable – for the average FTSE 100 CEO, who is in a DB plan, the transfer value of the increase in pension accrued was about 80% of salary.

Bonuses

Bonus – or more properly, Short Term Incentive – opportunities are now much larger than ten years ago. It is therefore easier to achieve a bigger award for the same performance or the same award for less performance than ten years ago, particularly in the larger companies.

The transition from a low bonus culture to a high bonus culture has increased costs. There is no evidence of improved performance from bigger bonuses. However there is anecdotal evidence that larger bonuses have led to more attention being paid to their design and to the assessment of performance outcomes.

Long Term Incentives

Options have been much criticised – mostly unfairly[7] – and some companies have abandoned them in favour of LTIPs. The introduction of multiple long term incentive plans is common. Most large companies have two or even three forms of long term incentives and this trend, like many others, is beginning to trickle down to smaller companies. The effect of multiple plans is to increase the likelihood of payments – See Section D47.4 which shows that long term incentives have paid out in most very large companies, in relatively few £100–1,000 million turnover companies and rarely in the

---

[7] The best research the author has is Professor Kees Cools' study (May 2005) of why companies do 'bad' things 'The dilemma of the successful CEO'. He identified CEOs of 25 major frauds and identified as the major causes Huge Stock Option grants (8 times), Large Press Profile (3 times) and High Growth Targets (6 times). Although huge stock options grants can lead to fraudulent behaviour, it is illogical to extrapolate that normal size option grants are a bad thing. Grants of sensibly sized options can create a long term incentive in increasing the share price of the company and that this helps to create an identity of interest with shareholders.

smallest companies. As companies become aware that multiple plans are more likely to pay out, more are switching to this approach.

2009 saw the first reduction in the average Long Term Incentive Award for FTSE 100 Chief Executives since MM&K/Manifest analysed the data. It appears that those companies who reduced Long Term Incentives may have increased Short Term Incentives.

32.7 Total Remuneration Mix

In developing a remuneration strategy a key decision is the proportion of remuneration that is performance related and, within that, the proportion that is linked to annual and longer term incentives. The MM&K/Manifest survey[8] shows the proportions of remuneration that are risk at target or expected performance. For CEOs the split is:

Figure 21: CEO mix of remuneration (2012 data)

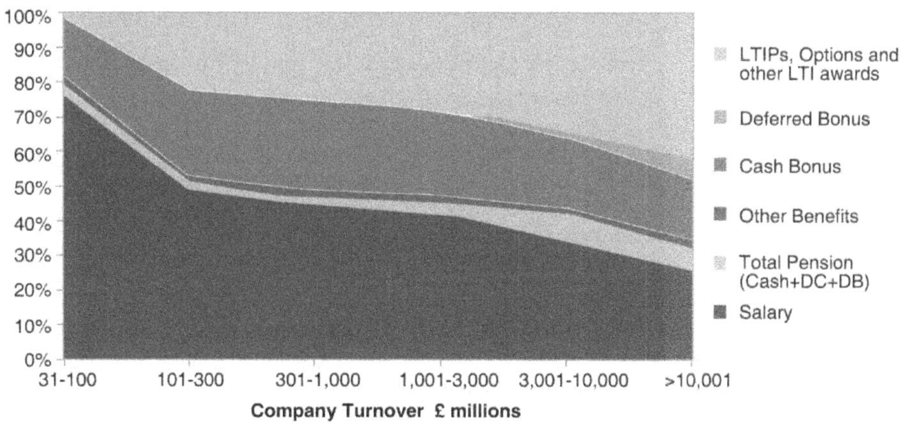

[8] MM&K/Manifest Executive Director Total Remuneration Survey, May 2013 (for the first figure above) and September 2013 (for the diagrams decomposed by indice – SmallCap, FTSE 250 and FTSE 100).

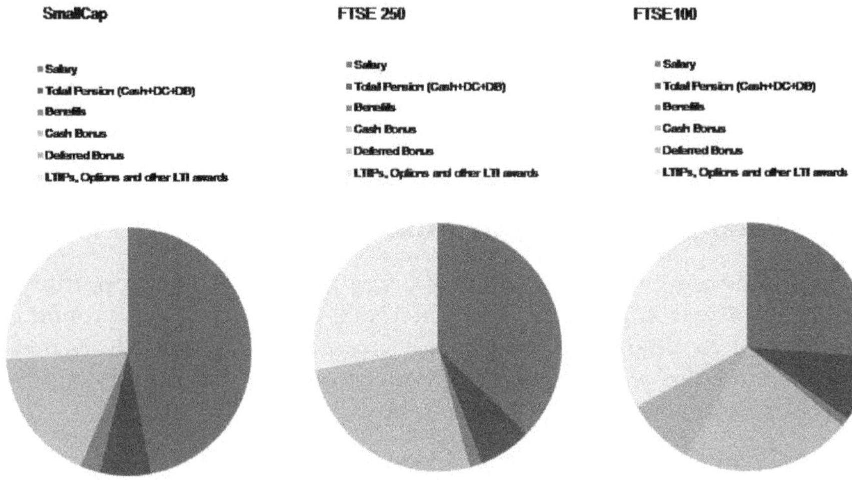

The challenge for each company is to decide what types of incentive it wants and how much to pay for each type of performance.

Performance matters

In 2012, MM&K and Manifest[9] researched the pay of chief executives in the FTSE 100, using data in annual reports up to October 2011. The main finding was that the pay realised by these executives went up by a median 10% in the last reported year. The research also looked at the movement over the past eight years, comparing the latest remuneration with that in 2002 (for the 66 of the current FTSE 100 members which were listed at the time). It found that the expected value of remuneration granted went up 120% over the period (10% per annum) and that of actual remuneration realised (after performance hurdles were applied) by 96% (9% per annum).

The individual company comparisons of growth in chief executive earnings with total shareholder return are in **Chart 7**. This shows a fairly good correlation between total realised remuneration increases (cumulative) and shareholder return over the eight years. But, since there is an expectation of some shareholder return without any increase in pay, it could be concluded that many Remuneration Committees have probably been over-generous in the increases they have granted.

Tullow Oil came top – with the top TSR of 39% per annum and also the top remuneration increase of 50% per annum.

---

9 See www.cityam.com/forum/the-real-story-high-pay-how-manipulated-statistics-misled-the-national-debate.

Chart 7: FTSE 100 CEO pay increases vs total shareholder return 2002–2010

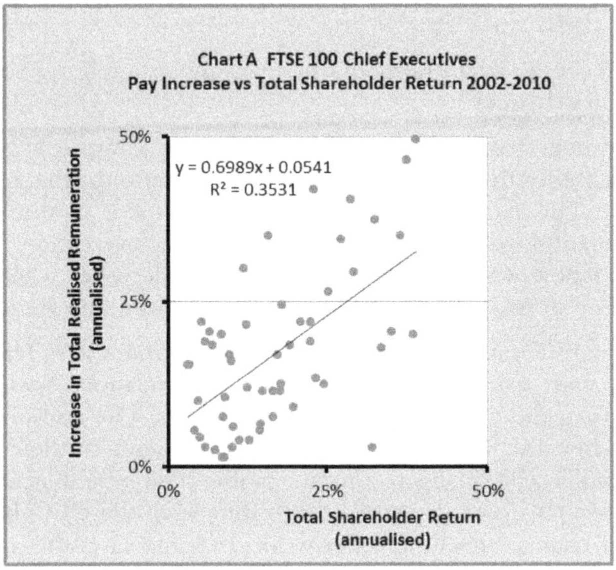

Negative TSR and pay reduction cases excluded

32.8 Conclusions

Larger companies continue to lead the way in increasing pay. Around the year 2000, GlaxoSmithKline, Vodafone and BP led the way – they were the bellwethers. Other companies followed in their footsteps.

Factors influencing pay trends:

- Globalisation led to executive demands to be paid closer to US norms.
- Acquisitions of US businesses came with US executives on US style pay packages. In order to retain US executives, everyone's pay tended to average up to US levels.
- Private equity offers much larger rewards, often for running simpler businesses.
- Many lawyers, accountants, consultants, investment bankers, hedge fund and long only fund managers are paid more than the executive directors of trading companies.

This led to remuneration inflation. There was little to restrain it:

- Institutional investors set overall dilution limits for share schemes. They focused on excessive rewards for failure and argued for reduced contract lengths. They also focused on increasing the proportion of performance-related pay. They tried to set individual limits as a % of salary for share schemes, but were ignored by many companies who argued theirs was a special case.

- Until recently, institutions did not pay much attention to salary levels and pension issues.
- Government action was intended to increase transparency and increase accountability through the annual advisory vote on the Remuneration Report. This failed as there was no requirement to disclose the total remuneration, so companies spread the data over many pages of the annual report. Only a very few experts can decipher what is hidden in the 16 or so pages of the Remuneration Committee Report.
- Many consultants suffer from a conflict of interest.[10] They work too closely with management – their recommendations favour executives rather than the company and its shareholders. The consultants' fees are large. They also sell other consulting assignments to their clients. They are unwilling to make recommendations that might upset the CEOs and other buyers of their services. If they keep the CEO happy, there is a better chance of selling other work. In some cases the group auditors were also the remuneration consultants. Many people believe that such remuneration consultants ratchet up pay.

All this rapid change has meant some companies have fallen inevitably behind. To catch up they have, of necessity, made well above average awards for some elements of the remuneration package in some years. This is reflected in the upper quartile data in the annual MM&K/Manifest survey. For example, of those companies with over £1 billion turnover, one quarter increased CEO Total Remuneration by 33% or more. One quarter increased the value of long term incentive awards by over 50% (2012 MM&K/Manifest survey data).

Total remuneration in smaller companies has not grown as fast as in the largest companies. There is, however, a trickledown effect as smaller companies review their remuneration arrangements to ensure they remain competitive, both in amount and structure. The proportion of remuneration that is performance related is noticeably less in smaller companies.

The number of quoted companies is reducing. Private equity offers bigger incentives than small quoted companies. To retain and motivate executive directors, smaller quoted companies will have to rely on other ways of motivating their directors or increase the amount of performance related pay.

---

[10] See the 2002 US Conference Board report on 'Public Trust and Private Enterprise' and the Higgs Report 2003 which commented on the need for independent remuneration consultants.

PART C

REWARD STRATEGY AND ARCHITECTURE

This part of the book explains how to develop a reward strategy and the make up of remuneration in terms of its component parts. The detailed design of each of the component parts (eg salary, bonus, pension, etc) is covered in Part D of this book.

The focus throughout is on how to link pay to business strategy in a way that supports and reinforces the actions required to achieve that strategy.

33 Linking Pay to Business Strategy

Before we can discuss how to develop a reward strategy, it is useful to give some examples of different reward strategies, so that the reader can understand what a reward strategy looks like.

33.1 The Seven Reward Strategies

The author has identified seven reward strategies as shown in the diagram below.

Figure 22: The seven reward strategies

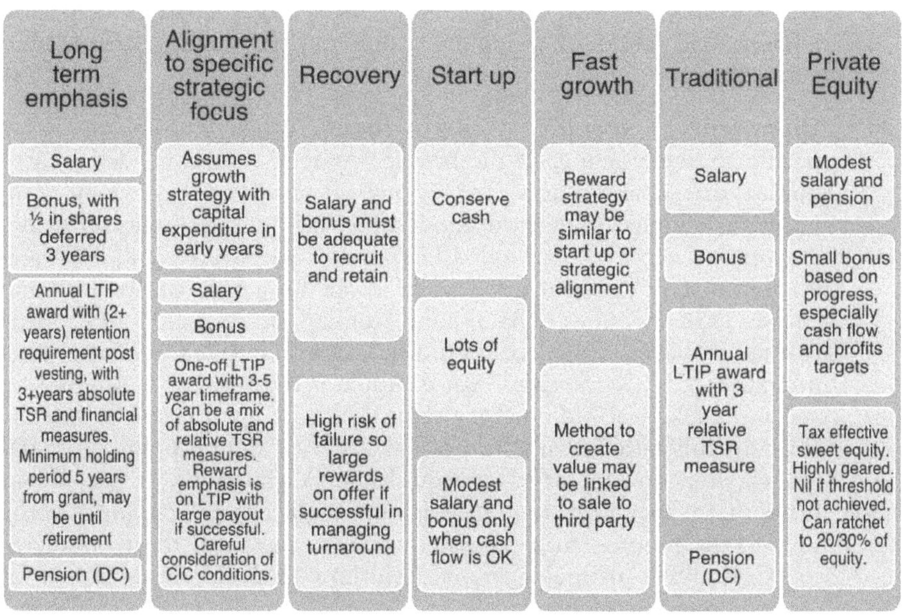

- **Start-up:** In the traditional start up there is little income as the products are often still being developed. Hence there is usually a need to conserve cash. Even if a company has raised cash, it will not want to burn up its investment capital with high remuneration costs. Its preference will be have a reward strategy consisting of low salaries, low bonus and lots of equity. Such reward structures will not be attractive to some executives. Others will however be attracted by the combination of the opportunity of being part of a start up with future growth potential and the very real possibility of significant gains from equity based incentive plans.

- **Fast growth:** Companies can have a strategy of fast growth for a number of reasons. A company may have developed a new product and wish to exploit it as fast as possible before others can copy it or develop something similar. A company that is successful in one geography may wish to grow quickly in other geographies. Usually the fast growth will require some investment before profits are achieved. Also there is usually some risk that the projected sales growth will not be achieved. Hence a reward strategy similar to the start-up situation may be appropriate as it keeps costs down. The strategic alignment reward strategy may also be appropriate in this case, particularly if key strategic goals can be identified. To achieve fast growth requires a culture of quick decision making and sharing of information throughout the company. A good reward strategy can reinforce the desired culture.

  On occasion, successful start-up companies transform to the fast growth stage and may need to recruit one or more key executives who have different skill sets. It may require a different pay package in order to recruit them.

- **Alignment to specific strategic focus:** When a company has a specific strategic goal then the rewards strategy should be designed to support that goal. In this case, a one-off award of large long term incentives coupled with more modest salary, bonus and pension would be appropriate. The one-off LTIP award would have a 3–5 year timeframe. The performance measures can be a mix of absolute and relative TSR measures. The reward emphasis is on LTIPs with large payouts, if successful. There should be careful consideration of change in control (CIC) conditions. For example if the strategy is progressing well and a takeover bid emerges, then it may be appropriate to vest the LTIPs in full rather than the normal pro-rata approach for time and performance up the date of acquisition. Alternatively, if the Board thinks that it may take some time for the market to fully appreciate the value of the progress made to date, it may request that the Remuneration Committee maintains discretion in how to decide what happens if a change in control occurs.

- **Traditional quoted plc:** The traditional and most popular reward strategy was to have a market related salary, an annual bonus (usually measured by profits or EPS versus budget), an annual award of LTIPs with a relative TSR performance condition measured over a three year period and a DC or DB pension. This approach is losing favour as more and more people have realised the potential problems with this approach – it is too short term, it encourages volatility and not enough of the reward is linked to equity or the long term success of the company.

- **Long term emphasis:** This could also be referred to as the 'steady as she goes strategy', as it is analogous to a super-tanker whose stopping distance is measured in miles and can only change direction slowly compared to the nimble manoeuvrings and directional changes of a wind-surfer. Large companies which are run for the benefit of long term shareholders and make large capital expenditure investments that may involve long timescales fall into this category. For example the investment in a new oil production field or a mineral mine, construction of an oil refinery, coal mine, electricity power station or water waste treatment plant: each may require several years to build and then income may be received for decades. Such companies must build, reinforce and maintain an effective company culture that supports operational excellence and sustainable long term performance. The long term emphasis reward strategy is well suited to such companies. Much of the reward comes from the ownership of shares over the long term. The long term incentive plan has annual awards with the requirement that shares acquired must be held post vesting (net of any requirement to pay taxes). LTI vesting conditions can involve absolute TSR levels and financial measures such as return on capital employed and economic profit (profit in excess of the cost of capital). Annual bonus can be linked to annual operational targets, but with half of awards deferred into shares and contingent on future performance: this ensures that the achievement of operational goals is worth more to executives, when that is then translated into future share price growth, compared to when the reverse happens.

The long term emphasis reward strategy helps to create and support a culture of long term-ism in the company's employees. It makes executives think of the long term effect of their actions. It helps to create loyalty to the firm and rewards long service.

In the past, companies used defined benefit pension plans to reward long service and such plans were well suited to the long term emphasis reward strategy. The HMRC annual allowance limit of £40,000 to approved pensions means such an approach is no longer tax effective. The long term emphasis reward strategy is now more likely to have a defined contribution pension arrangement.

For many companies the business strategy, corporate plan and annual budget can be reduced to a series of operational goals that have to be achieved in the short term. The intention and belief is that if these are achieved, the company will do better than its competitors and this will ultimately lead to long term success.

If a Remuneration Committee buys into the logic of such a plan, then its reward strategy might be as shown in the diagram below.

Figure 23: A pay reward structure

Do these operational things in the short term	Beat the competitors in the medium term	Share price growth in the long term
Rewarded by	**Rewarded by**	**Rewarded by**
Annual bonus, bonus deferral and bonus matching	LTIPs and bonus matching (using Relative TSR)	Options and share ownership

- **Recovery:** A company that has had a difficult trading period, finds itself with a large amount of debt compared to equity, or has seen its share price drop substantially will need a change of strategy in order to ensure its recovery. It may need to achieve operational goals such as cost savings or quality improvements and improved cash flow, the sale of non-core parts of the business, etc. It may need to hire new executives. Often, in such cases, shareholders demand or encourage a change of the executive team. New hires will need new incentive packages. Existing executives, who are required for the recovery phase, will often find that their existing long term incentives plans are unlikely to pay out, share options are massively underwater, the annual bonus plans reflect the old strategy, and the shares they have previously acquired are now worth much less than previously. Consequently a new reward strategy is required. Cash is likely to be in short supply and shareholders will not be willing to see high salaries and bonuses. New hires will want the opportunity of making significant amounts, but will also want guaranteed compensation if the company situation turns out worse than expected, or if their skills do not turn out to as useful as expected. Such situations occur often with no blame due on the executive or the company. As such cases occur quite regularly, executives will demand and receive guarantees. It is a necessary cost of the turnaround that such guarantees are given. It should be recognised that part of the reason the company got into trouble in the first place may be because the previous management were not good enough to solve the company's problems. Therefore the new management team will expect higher remuneration. However there is usually some trade-off between fixed pay and incentive pay. Higher amounts of equity incentive can usually be offered to create appropriate incentives. When designing incentives plans for such cases, detailed modelling is required, as it may be possible for the share price to increase by a factor of five or even ten times if the turnaround is successful.

- **Private equity:** This reward strategy is made up of tax effective sweet equity, a relatively modest salary and pension, and a small bonus based on progress, especially cash flow and profits targets. The equity is highly geared as most private equity (PE) deals are structured so that the equity is highly leveraged with several layers of debt. So the equity incentives pay out nothing if the threshold is not achieved. However the executives can ratchet up to 20/30% of equity if they hit their targets. There is a lot more risk in this type of package. PE owners will closely monitor management performance and underperformers will be exited and replaced. This produces a strong performance based culture with a focus on results. It is attractive to high performers and provides bigger rewards than comparable quoted companies' remuneration packages.

  It could be argued that there are two additional private equity reward strategies. The first happens when a private equity company has significantly failed to meet its targets, and hence the likelihood of any payment from the equity arrangements is nil or very small. In this case, the owners will often re-incentivise the management. However, first, they will evaluate the performance of the business and the team who've been running it, to assess whether the failure to achieve targets is because of the team or because of other extenuating circumstances. Such evaluations are done with much rigour and frequently lead to members of the top team leaving the business. Where gaps in capability have been identified, the private equity owners will insist that new competent managers are recruited. It will then be appropriate to re-incentivise the management team, by reloading them with equity, starting from a new base case position.

  The second potential additional private equity reward strategy occurs after a management team has successfully completed a management buyout and the business has either been floated or sold on to a third party. The management team will have received significant capital gains. They will also have established their credibility and private equity owners will often look for another opportunity for the management team to manage on their behalf. In this case, the remuneration structure which will be offered will have to be much more generous than their first one. For example, someone who has made £0.5 million from their first management buyout will be looking for an incentive package of two to ten times that amount from their second management buyout, as otherwise it will not be worth the effort involved. Similarly, someone who has made £5 million from a successful management buyout will be looking for an incentive package of two to ten times that amount from their next management buyout opportunity. The scaling is the same but the amounts are much larger.

It could also be argued that Profit Sharing is another reward strategy. The nature of profit sharing is that the payout goes up or down in line with changes in profits. Hence the term profit share, as it is a sharing of the profit between employees and owners. Another nature of profit sharing is that participants share in the success of the company. If the economy is buoyant and the company is doing well, then the participants' profit shares go up. If times are tough and profits drop, then so do the profit share payments. Profit sharing is a reward for success, not a reward for management achieving specific goals. Splitting bonus into its component parts of sharing in success and incentives to achieve specific targets can greatly add to clarity of what the reward strategy is trying to achieve. Viewed this way, Profit Sharing is a reward mechanism and merely a type of bonus plan, rather than a reward strategy. Profit Sharing is discussed further in **46.15.**

33.2 Reward Strategy Objectives

How do you recognise a good remuneration strategy? What does a successful remuneration policy look like?

There are five objectives of a remuneration strategy. It must:

- **Motivate executives to achieve a good level of performance and hopefully to exceed it**. It must do this within the accepted risk parameters of the company. It should be compatible with risk policies and systems. Some people might argue it should motivate executives to achieve outstanding performance. This may be the goal, but it needs a good debate, as often 'outstanding' performance brings 'tail-risk' along with it.

- Enable the company to **retain** its key executives. Having chosen the management team it is important that they are retained and not tempted by offers elsewhere. The total remuneration package must therefore be attractive and executives must see a good probability of the targets being achieved and hence that the incentive plans will pay out. If the company has been doing well, the executives should have accumulated deferred bonuses and LTIPs awards which are likely to vest over the coming years. Un-vested, in the money awards act as handcuffs on successful executives, as it makes it more expensive for others to poach them.

- Enable the company to **attract** high-calibre executives from other companies. Whilst it may be acceptable to recruit one person on a one-off package, if a company finds it consistently has to pay higher remuneration to external hires than its own existing executives this is evidence that, either the internal executives' pay should be increased, or questions the competence of the existing management.

- **Exit** executives at a reasonable cost in the event that an executive fails to make the grade or if their performance falls off. It may also be important to have appropriate non-compete and non-poaching clauses in their employment contracts.

- **The total costs should be acceptable to shareholders**. Levels of salary should not be excessive. The costs of bonus and long-term incentives measured as a percentage of profits, cash flow, turnover, increases in shareholder value (and other appropriate metrics relevant to the companies sector) should not be excessive. Benefits and pensions should also not be excessive. (Different stakeholders have different views on what is excessive.)

The remuneration strategy also has to answer the four questions of what for, how much and when and which proportions of pay (salary, bonus, long term incentives and pension).

- **What** is it that the company wishes to pay for? There are many different views on this and there are many views on how effective alternative approaches are. The choice of performance measures is at the heart of the debate on pay for performance.
- **How much?** The sums involved in directors' remuneration seem huge to the man in the street and to the average journalist. However, this is an area where benchmark remuneration data can confirm what orders of magnitude will be appropriate. Although this may not be a perfect market, the fact that the average tenure of a chief executive is about 6.9 years (median 5.7 years)[1] means that there is sufficient turnover for the laws of supply and demand to drive the levels of remuneration.
- **When** should the remuneration be paid? Obviously salary has to be paid now and pension in an approved pension plan cannot be paid until after retirement. Bonuses can be paid as soon as the accounts have been audited and signed off. However, the growing trend is to defer part of bonus, often into shares, which may not vest for up to three years and so is linked into changes in the share price over this time. Long-term incentive plans typically have a three year performance measurement period so are not really long-term at all. Some are structured as nil cost options, which have a ten year life. The introduction of share ownership guidelines and share retention rules for shares acquired from bonus and long-term incentive plans can offer remuneration for a longer period. Some companies do not allow the sale of shares (other than to pay for taxes) until retirement or until the executive leaves the company; and some also require the phased sale of shares over a number of years.
- **The mixture** of salary, bonus, deferred bonus, long term incentive, pension and other benefits. The reward strategy must specify what

---

[1] This refers to the length of time the CEO has been in the job. He will expect to serve longer than this. One quarter of CEOs serve more than eight years as CEO and many will have had prior service in the company.

proportion of total remuneration should be comprised of each of these elements. It needs to be set for target (budget) performance and for stretch (outstanding) performance and also for poor performance. A bar chart will however show the variation in total amounts of remuneration as well as the proportions. See **Figures 30, 31** and **32** in **Chapters 38** and **39**.

33.3 Checklist for a good remuneration strategy

This checklist is in **Chapter 43**.

34 Developing Remuneration Strategy and Policy

34.1 Introduction

The Remuneration Committee, a subcommittee of the Board, is usually made up of independent non-executive directors. The Remuneration Committee makes the decisions about the executive directors' remuneration strategy and policy.

The UK Corporate Governance Code is a good starting point. It states the following:

Main Principles (Section D: Remuneration)

> 'Levels of remuneration should be sufficient to attract, retain and motivate directors of the quality required to run the company successfully, but a company should avoid paying more than is necessary for this purpose. A significant proportion of executive directors' remuneration should be structured so as to link rewards to corporate and individual performance.
>
> There should be a formal and transparent procedure for developing policy on executive remuneration and for fixing the remuneration packages of individual directors. No director should be involved in deciding his or her own remuneration.'

Supporting Principles

> 'The performance-related elements of executive directors' remuneration should be stretching and designed to promote the long-term success of the company.
>
> The remuneration committee should judge where to position their company relative to other companies. But they should use such comparisons with caution in view of the risk of an upward ratchet of remuneration levels with no corresponding improvement in performance.
>
> They should also be sensitive to pay and employment conditions elsewhere in the group, especially when determining annual salary increases.'

More detail is given in Schedule A. The design of performance-related remuneration for executive directors. Most of Schedule A concerns the design of remuneration components (which are discussed in Section D). One sentence of particular relevance to reward strategy is in para 6 of Schedule A:

> 'Remuneration incentives should be compatible with risk policies and systems.'

Schedule A also encourages payment of bonuses in shares:

> 'There may be a case for part payment in shares to be held for a significant period.'

Schedule A also encourages long term incentives to be longer than three years and shares acquired from such schemes should be held for longer:

> 'In normal circumstances, shares granted or other forms of deferred remuneration should not vest, and options should not be exercisable, in less than three years. Directors should be encouraged to hold their shares for a further period after vesting or exercise, subject to the need to finance any costs of acquisition and associated tax liabilities.'

34.2 The Principal Agent issue

I think that the Code does not give sufficient weight to the principal agent issue.

Agency theory says that management are the agents of shareholders and should manage the company in the best interests of shareholders. The rational economic person will try to maximise his or her wealth with minimum risk. This may be, however, totally different to what shareholders want. Therefore agency theory says that management need to be incited to manage the company in the best interests of shareholders. Remuneration therefore needs to be linked to shareholders' interests of long-term share price appreciation and dividends. Management will discount any pay will does not pay out until some years ahead and is dependent on factors many of which they feel are beyond their control.

34.3 Remuneration Strategy – elements

The objective of the reward strategy is to enable the company to motivate, retain and recruit suitably competent executives, who can direct and deliver the business strategy, but not at excessive cost.

Consequently a remuneration policy should reflect the above issues and should therefore cover four key elements.

Table 25: The 4 key elements of remuneration policy

1.	**The selection of appropriate comparator companies should reflect:** • types of executives required • importance of individual executives to the delivery of the business strategy • size of talent pool • comparator companies location – UK, Europe and global • comparator companies size – sales, market cap, employees, assets, profits etc.
2.	**Pay market position(s) and linkage of pay market position to performance:** • at target payout, outstanding payout, and scenarios analyses of other performance levels • pay as % of share value created; profits; cash flow, dilution etc.
3.	**Mix of performance-related and not-performance-related elements:** • % performance related • % paid now; in 1 year, 3 years, 5 years, etc • % paid in cash; % paid in equity • Claw-back and malus rules.
4.	**Alignment to shareholders' interests. Issues to be covered include:** • performance measures • upside and downside alignment • share ownership guidelines and • alignment to business strategy.

34.4 Remuneration Strategy inputs

In order to develop a remuneration strategy and policy, Remuneration Committees need to take account of a wider range of issues than those mentioned in the Code.

The next diagram summarises the key inputs.

Figure 24: Inputs to remuneration strategy and policy

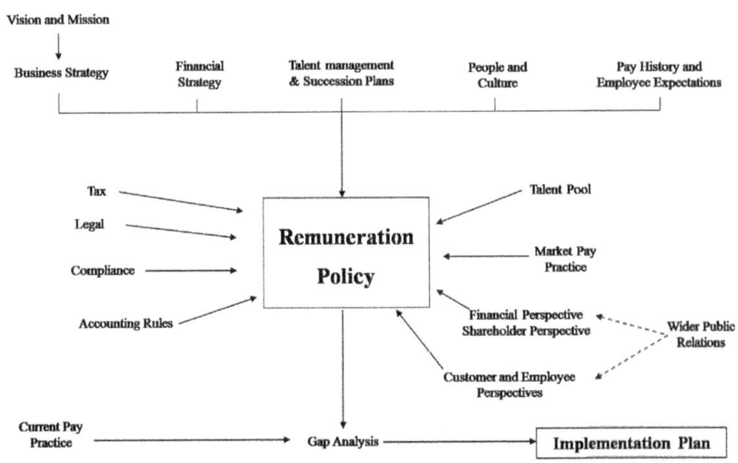

Business strategy and financial strategy are discussed in **Chapter 35** and **Chapter 36** below and HR strategy (which includes talent management and succession plans; people and culture; people performance management and remuneration history and expectations) is discussed in **Chapter 37** below. Motivation Theory was reviewed in **Chapter 30**.

Part A of this book has reviewed in detail the tax, legal, compliance (including regulatory issues and best practice guidance from various bodies) and the accounting rules. **Part A** has also reviewed the shareholder perspective in terms of preferences in respect of remuneration.

Chapter 32 has given detail on market practice in terms of levels of directors' remuneration and the mix and make-up of total remuneration.

Chapter 27 (Engagement and Reporting to Shareholders) has reviewed what information has to be communicated to shareholders.

The communication of directors' remuneration can require wider consideration, because of the potential impact on different aspects of the business.

There are more stakeholders than simply shareholders that need to be considered – for example, debt holders. Mostly the interests of debt holders are aligned with shareholders as when the share price increases the holders of debt are reassured that they will, in due course, be paid their debt in full and in the interim all interest payments will be made. However, when there is a risk or increased risk of default on the interest or the principal debt payments, the remuneration strategy needs to take account of the interests of debt-holders. Awards of excessive cash bonuses and guarantees may help to retain key executives, but may be unpalatable to debt-holders. Equally, awards of options or other equity based long (or mid) term incentive plans may overly align executives with shareholders and lead to executives making decisions that favour shareholders over debt holders.

Lavish payouts to senior executives at a time when employees generally are being given low or nil salary increases can be difficult to justify. If employees are being made redundant this will also impact on the remuneration decisions that the Remuneration Committee has to make.

And it is not just employees. Suppliers who are being asked to moderate their price increases and accept demands for higher quality and better service levels will not like it if they see their hardships end up in the pockets of their clients' senior executives. There needs to be moderation and any payouts need to be justified.

The reward strategy needs to consider all of the above.

34.5 Simplified Process for Remuneration Strategy

If the above model is felt to be too complex to follow, then the following flowchart can be used to develop a reward strategy suitable to the company's needs.

Figure 25: Remuneration strategy design (simplified approach)

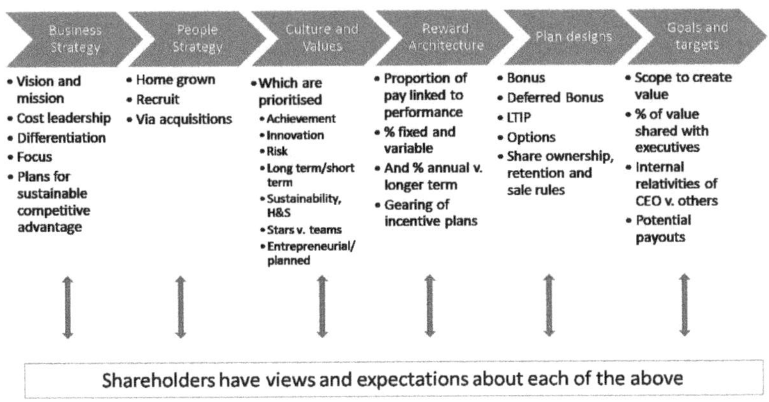

Following the above should result in an aligned remuneration strategy that incentivises and motivates management, as is reflected in the diagram below:

Figure 26: Aligning remuneration strategy

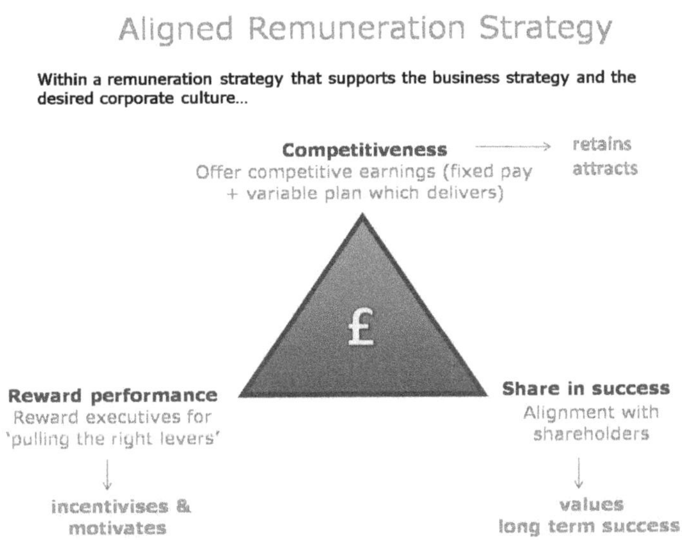

35 Business Strategies

Remuneration strategy should reflect and reinforce business strategy. Therefore it is important that this book summarises the typical business strategies.

Three basic business strategies were identified by Porter:[1]

- Low cost, or cost leadership
- Differentiation
- Focus, or niche.

In each of these, the company seeks to achieve and maintain sustainable competitive advantage.

Michael Porter argued that a firm's strengths ultimately fall into one of two headings: cost advantage and differentiation. By applying these strengths in either a broad or narrow scope, three generic strategies result: cost leadership, differentiation, and focus.

35.1 Cost Leadership Strategy

This strategy involves the firm winning market share by appealing to cost-conscious or price-sensitive customers. It is achieved by having the lowest prices in the target market segment, or at least the lowest price to value ratio (price compared to what customers receive). To succeed at offering the lowest price while still achieving profitability and a high return on investment, the firm must be able to operate at a lower cost than its rivals.

There are three main ways to achieve this.

The first way is achieving a high asset turnover. In service industries, this may mean for example a restaurant that turns tables around very quickly, or an airline that turns around flights very fast. In manufacturing, it will involve production of high volumes of output. These approaches mean fixed costs are spread over a larger number of units of the product or service, resulting in a lower unit cost, ie the firm hopes to take advantage of economies of scale and experience curve effects. For industrial firms, mass production

---

1 ME Porter, *Competitive Strategy* (Free Press, New York, 1980). The book was voted the ninth most influential management book of the 20th century in a poll of the Fellows of the Academy of Management.

becomes both a strategy and an end in itself. Higher levels of output both require and result in high market share, and create an entry barrier to potential competitors, who may be unable to achieve the scale necessary to match the firm's low costs and prices.

The second way is achieving low direct and indirect operating costs. This is achieved by offering high volumes of standardised products, offering basic no-frills products and limiting customisation and personalisation of service. Production costs are kept low by using fewer components, using standard components, and limiting the number of models produced to ensure larger production runs. Overheads are kept low by paying low wages, locating premises in low rent areas, establishing a cost-conscious culture, etc. Maintaining this strategy requires a continuous search for cost reductions in all aspects of the business. This will include outsourcing, controlling production costs, increasing asset capacity utilisation, and minimizing other costs including distribution, R&D and advertising. The associated distribution strategy is to obtain the most extensive distribution possible. Promotional strategy often involves trying to make a virtue out of low cost product features.

The third way is control over the supply/procurement chain to ensure low costs. This could be achieved by bulk buying to enjoy quantity discounts, squeezing suppliers on price, instituting competitive bidding for contracts, working with vendors to keep inventories low using methods such as Just-in-Time purchasing or Vendor-Managed Inventory. Wal-Mart, Tesco and other supermarkets are famous for squeezing their suppliers to ensure low prices for its goods. Dell Computer initially achieved market share by keeping inventories low and only building computers to order. Other procurement advantages could come from preferential access to raw materials, or backward integration.

Some writers posit that cost leadership strategies are only viable for large firms with the opportunity to enjoy economies of scale and large production volumes. However, this takes a limited industrial view of strategy. Small businesses can also be cost leaders if they enjoy any advantages conducive to low costs. For example, a local restaurant in a low rent location can attract price-sensitive customers if it offers a limited menu, rapid table turnover and employs staff on minimum wage. Innovation of products or processes may also enable a start-up or small company to offer a cheaper product or service where incumbents' costs and prices have become too high. An example is the success of low-cost budget airlines who despite having fewer planes than the major airlines, were able to recruit staff at lower pay than the majors and achieve market share growth by offering cheap, no-frills services at prices much cheaper than those of the larger incumbents.

A cost leadership strategy may have the disadvantage of lower customer loyalty, as price-sensitive customers will switch once a lower-priced substitute is available. A reputation as a cost leader may also result in a reputation for low quality, which may make it difficult for a firm to rebrand itself or its products if it chooses to shift to a differentiation strategy in future.

The Cost Leadership Strategy calls for being the low cost producer in an industry for a given level of quality. The firm sells its products either at average industry prices to earn a profit higher than that of rivals, or below the average industry prices to gain market share. In the event of a price war, the firm can maintain some profitability while the competition suffers losses. Even without a price war, as the industry matures and prices decline, the firms that can produce more cheaply will remain profitable for a longer period of time. The cost leadership strategy usually targets a broad market.

Some of the ways that firms acquire cost advantages are by improving process efficiencies, gaining unique access to a large source of lower cost materials, making optimal outsourcing and vertical integration decisions, or avoiding some costs altogether. If competing firms are unable to lower their costs by a similar amount, the firm may be able to sustain a competitive advantage based on cost leadership.

This strategy has its risks. For example, other firms may be able to lower their costs as well. As technology improves, the competition may be able to leapfrog the production capabilities, thus eliminating the competitive advantage. Additionally, several firms following a focus strategy and targeting various narrow markets may be able to achieve an even lower cost within their segments and as a group gain significant market share.

35.2 Differentiation Strategy

In this strategy the company differentiates the products in some way in order to compete successfully. Examples of the successful use of a differentiation strategy are Rolls Royce motor cars, Orange mobile phones (before it was taken over by France Telecom), Marks and Spencer, ARM, Coutts Bank, Daily Mail, Nike athletic shoes, Perstorp BioProducts, Apple Computer, and Mercedes-Benz automobiles.

A differentiation strategy is appropriate where the target customer segment is not price-sensitive, the market is competitive or saturated, customers have very specific needs which are possibly under-served, and the firm has unique resources and capabilities which enable it to satisfy these needs in ways that are difficult to copy. These could include patents or other intellectual property (IP), unique technical expertise (eg Apple's design skills or Pixar's animation prowess), talented personnel (eg a sports team's star players or a brokerage firm's star traders), or innovative processes. Successful brand management also results in perceived uniqueness even when the physical product is the same as competitors. This way, Pret a Manger was able to brand sandwiches, Starbucks could brand coffee, and Nike could brand sneakers. Fashion brands rely heavily on this form of image differentiation.

A differentiation strategy calls for the development of a product or service that offers unique attributes that are valued by customers and that customers perceive to be better than or different from the products of the competition. The value added by the uniqueness of the product may allow the firm to charge a premium price for it. The firm hopes that the higher price will more than cover the extra costs incurred in offering the unique product. Because of the product's unique attributes, if suppliers increase their prices the firm may be able to pass along the costs to its customers who cannot find substitute products easily.

Firms that succeed in a differentiation strategy often have:

- access to leading scientific research
- highly skilled and creative product development teams
- strong sales team with the ability to successfully communicate the perceived strengths of the product
- a strong brand image.

The risks associated with a differentiation strategy include imitation by competitors and changes in customer tastes. Additionally, various firms pursuing focus strategies may be able to achieve even greater differentiation in their market segments.

Variants on the Differentiation Strategy

The **shareholder value model** holds that the timing of the use of specialised knowledge can create a differentiation advantage as long as the knowledge remains unique. This model suggests that customers buy products or services from an organisation to have access to its unique knowledge. The advantage is static, rather than dynamic, because the purchase is a one-time event.

The **unlimited resources model** utilises a large base of resources that allows an organisation to outlast competitors by practicing a differentiation strategy. An organisation with greater resources can manage risk and sustain profits more easily than one with fewer resources. This provides a short-term advantage only. If a firm lacks the capacity for continual innovation, it will not sustain its competitive position over time.

35.3 Focus or Strategic Scope

This dimension is not a separate strategy per se, but describes the scope over which the company should compete based on cost leadership or differentiation. The firm can choose to compete in the mass market (like Wal-Mart) with a broad scope, or in a defined, focused market segment with a narrow scope. In either case, the basis of competition will still be either cost leadership or differentiation.

In adopting a narrow focus, the company ideally focuses on a few target markets (also called a segmentation strategy or niche strategy). These should be distinct groups with specialised needs. The choice of offering low prices or differentiated products/services should depend on the needs of the selected segment and the resources and capabilities of the firm. It is hoped that by focusing your marketing efforts on one or two narrow market segments and tailoring your marketing mix to these specialised markets, you can better meet the needs of that target market. The firm typically looks to gain a competitive advantage through product innovation and/or brand marketing rather than efficiency. It is most suitable for relatively small firms but can be used by any company. A focused strategy should target market segments that are less vulnerable to substitutes or where a competition is weakest to earn above-average return on investment.

Examples of firms using a focus strategy include Easyjet and Ryanair. They provide short-haul point-to-point flights in contrast to the hub-and-spoke model of mainstream carriers.

In adopting a broad focus scope, the principle is the same: the firm must ascertain the needs and wants of the mass market, and compete either on price (low cost) or differentiation (quality, brand and customisation) depending on its resources and capabilities. Wal Mart has a broad scope and adopts a cost leadership strategy in the mass market. Pixar also targets the mass market with its movies, but adopts a differentiation strategy, using its unique capabilities in story-telling and animation to produce signature animated movies that are hard to copy, and for which customers are willing to pay to see and own. Apple also targets the mass market with its iPad, iPhone and iPod products, but combines this broad scope with a differentiation strategy based on design, branding and user experience that enables it to charge a price premium due to the perceived unavailability of close substitutes.

The focus strategy concentrates on a narrow segment and within that segment attempts to achieve either a cost advantage or differentiation. The premise is that the needs of the group can be better serviced by focusing entirely on it. A firm using a focus strategy often enjoys a high degree of customer loyalty, and this entrenched loyalty discourages other firms from competing directly.

Because of their narrow market focus, firms pursuing a focus strategy have lower volumes and therefore less bargaining power with their suppliers. However, firms pursuing a differentiation-focused strategy may be able to pass higher costs on to customers since close substitute products do not exist.

Some risks of focus strategies include imitation and changes in the target segments. Furthermore, it may be fairly easy for a broad-market cost leader to adapt its product in order to compete directly. Finally, other focusers may be able to carve out sub-segments that they can serve even better.

35.4 A Combination of Generic Strategies – Stuck in the Middle?

These generic strategies are not necessarily compatible with one another. If a firm attempts to achieve an advantage on all fronts, it may achieve no advantage at all. For example, if a firm differentiates itself by supplying very high quality products, it risks undermining that quality if it seeks to become a cost leader. Even if the quality did not suffer, the firm would risk projecting a confusing image. For this reason, Michael Porter argued that to be successful over the long-term, a firm must select only one of these three generic strategies. Otherwise, with more than one single generic strategy the firm will be 'stuck in the middle' and will not achieve a competitive advantage.

Porter argued that firms that are able to succeed at multiple strategies often do so by creating separate business units for each strategy. By separating the strategies into different units having different policies and even different cultures, a corporation is less likely to become 'stuck in the middle'.

However, there exists a viewpoint that a single generic strategy is not always best because within the same product customers often seek multi-dimensional satisfactions such as a combination of quality, style, convenience, and price. There have been cases in which high quality producers faithfully followed a single strategy and then suffered greatly when another firm entered the market with a lower-quality product that better met the overall needs of the customers.

35.5 Regulated Industry Strategy

I think that there is another strategy, which is where there is a natural monopoly – for example, in the supply of water. Once one company has built the infrastructure to deliver water to a house, it is extremely expensive for another to compete. On the Monopoly board there were just two utility companies, water and electric. In real life, the ability of monopolies to charge customers is heavily regulated. Prices are set for five years at a time (eg they can increase at RPI +/- x% per annum). The negotiation and agreement of such agreements is crucial to the success of the company and the long term returns to shareholders. Regulators also look to the quality of service provided. In the extreme case they can remove the licence or licences to operate and allocate it to some other body.

Strategic success comes from being able to influence the regulator and keeping costs down and quality to an acceptable level. (In most regulated industries there is no opportunity to premium price for providing the service at a higher than the minimum quality standard.) There may be opportunities to develop property or expand the services into related areas. But, in the main, the strategy is 'steady as she goes' and the long term emphasis reward strategy is appropriate.

Increasingly, as society has developed and become more complex, many industries are impacted by the regulator(s).

Some are semi regulated rather than fully regulated industries/sectors. Drugs are an interesting example. New drugs have to undergo many years of testing to prove they are safe. They are then licensed for use, often at high prices/margins, for many years until patents run out and generic alternatives can be produced. Often the treatment of a particular condition can be undertaken with a number of alternative drugs.

Another example is telecommunications. The traditional fixed line telephone appeared to be a natural monopoly, particularly in the 'final mile' from the exchange to the household door. In the UK, the telephone company was owned by the state. Then it was privatised as British Telecom (later renamed as BT), but the prices it was allowed to charge were closely monitored by its regulator OFCOM. The growth of cable TV produced competition for BT, as the cable could also be used to provide telephone services. Wireless telephony (mobile phones) further encroached on BT. Mobile phone companies bought licensed bandwidth from the government. Originally they paid little and charged lots and provided a service that many wanted and were able to afford; so they made large profits and their share prices shot through the roof. The government decided to auction the next generation of 3G licenses in 2001 and used a cunning auction process which made the mobile companies bid £22bn for the licences, which was much higher than most peopled expected and led to a huge transfer of wealth from shareholders to the government coffers. The point of this long example is that management, fund managers and shareholders had failed to understand that the industry was semi regulated and that they could not expect to make super-normal profits for ever.

35.6 High Level, Mid-Level and Implementation Level Strategies

Strategies should also be considered at high level, mid-level and implementation level.

High level strategies address the fundamental issues of mission and values and, long term economic and social trends. It is about positioning the company for long term success. It involves long term decisions such as major investments to produce new products or to increase manufacturing capacity or to move into new geographic markets. Such investments may be capital expenditure or acquisitions. Decisions at this level will determine how the company performs over the next decade. Those who make the decisions are often no longer around when the benefits of their strategic choices become apparent. Some examples may help illustrate this: IBM's decision not to compete in the pc market; GEC's decision to focus on telecommunications and rename itself Marconi; BP's move into Russia in the 2000's and before that its 1990 acquisitions of US oil companies Amoco and Arco; Vodafone's acquisition of Mannesmann to give it global coverage; HSBC's strategic focus on Asia; RBS's expansion of its retail banking via the acquisition of NatWest and their attempted expansion into global investment banking via its acquisition of ABN Amro were all high-level decisions.

If high level strategy is like looking down from 30,000 feet, where you can see buildings but cannot spot individual people, then **mid-level strategy** is like looking down from 15,000 feet. Porter's Value Chain is a good tool to use for mid-level strategy.

Figure 27: Porter's value chain

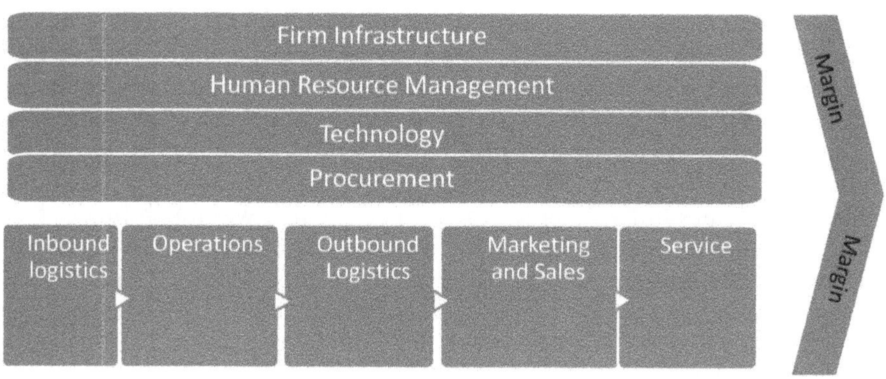

Typically here, we are thinking of a three to five year timeframe. Companies need to understand which parts of the value chain they need to work on, where the biggest changes are needed, what the impact will be on the value of the firm if successful and the risks if they are not.

A simple questionnaire along these lines will enable the company to assess where it needs action:

Table 26: Value Chain Assessment Tool

Value Chain item	**current score** (1–5)	**desired score** (1–5)	**Potential impact on the business** (1–5)
Supply Chain/ Inbound Logistics	1	2	1
Operations/ manufacturing	1	1	1
Outbound Logistics/ Distribution	1	2	1
Marketing	1	2	2
Sales	1	4	4
Customer Service	4	4	4
Quality	3	4	3
Human Capital	2	4	5
R&D	1	2	3
Technology/ Engineering/ Design	1	1	1
Product Development	1	4	5
Purchasing	1	1	1
IT	1	2	1
Financial	1	1	1
Legal	1	1	1

Implementation or specific business strategies

If the value chain is at 15,000 feet then the implementation or specific business strategy can be thought of as 5,000 feet. You can see the ground and details from this level and you can see individuals running around on the ground. Strategy at this level is below the general business strategic. Examples of specific business strategies might be:

- Grow market share
- Grow from within
- Grow though merger
- Use joint ventures

- Retain market share
- Build better customer relationships
- Differentiate products/services
- Increase cash flow
- Optimise margins
- Expand sales geographically
- Expand operations geographically
- Re-engineer costs/operations
- Become more global
- Maximise profit not market share
- Price product to acquire more market share and deter competitors
- Product development: reduce time to produce and launch new products
- Hold price/margin
- Six Sigma quality improvement
- Reduce production capacity
- Bring online new factory and reduce production costs.

These specific strategies will be unique to the specific time, maturity or phase of the overall business strategy.

36 Financial Strategy

Whilst the business strategy defines what the company wishes to achieve, the financial strategy addresses the issue of how the business strategy will be financed. It analyses the future cash flows under a range of scenarios and identifies how much debt and equity will need to be raised, when this will need to be done and when debt will need to be repaid.

It also considers tax and tax planning opportunities.

Maintaining appropriate debt to equity and debt to EBITDA ratios are important. The company's cost of debt will depend on these and the lenders views about the future security of their debt and the company's future performance.

The financial strategy will identify the company's WACC (the weighted average cost of capital) and the required return on equity. To be successful in the long term requires profits to be higher than the cost of capital.

The issue of risk and, in particular, tail risk (ie the risk of low probability high impact events, eg the Tsunami and earthquake in Japan, BP's Gulf platform Deepwater Horizon oil spill, mortgage backed CDOs in the financial services industry) is now given the due consideration that previously it was not (in too many companies). The transfer of risk to tail risk which boosts short term profits (and short term incentive rewards) is now a much more widely recognised problem and will take considerable Remuneration Committee time when it develops a new reward strategy.

The financial strategy also covers the issue of dividend policy and share buybacks. Earnings per share (EPS) is often a key measure in incentive plans and the impact of dividends, share buybacks, rights issues, capital raisings and debt repurchases all impact on EPS in both the short and long term.

Clarity on the financial strategy makes it easier to design incentives. It also helps in the drafting of the small print of the rules and in future interpretation of those rules. Without such clarity at the outset, there will always be pressure from executives to interpret the small print of the incentive plan rules in their favour.

Funding Remuneration

Remuneration can either be paid as a cash item or through equity which will dilute shareholders.

For mature companies which have good profit margins the costs of remuneration will usually be small, and the dilution from share schemes will usually be acceptable to shareholders.

In the UK the established dilution limits are 10% over ten years, which averages out at 1% per annum.

For companies that are in start-up mode and are trying to conserve cash, investors will usually accept a higher dilution, but in return will expect that cash remuneration is not excessive and preferably is modest. A package that is weighted in favour of equity over cash will generally be viewed positively.

Share schemes will have an accounting charge under IFRS 2 on the profits and balance sheet. They are however a non-cash item if new issue shares are used to fund the payment of awards when they are exercised or realised. From a financial strategy point of view, it is important to model the impact of cash flows and dilution of shareholders under a variety of scenarios.

37 HR Strategies

HR Strategy needs to cover talent management, culture, performance management and reward strategy.

37.1 Talent Management

Each company should have assessed its top management and developed a talent plan to ensure it has enough high calibre managers at the necessary levels, in order to implement its business strategy.

If the strategy involves a series of acquisitions then new management will be acquired as a result of the strategy and it may be possible to retain them in the new enlarged company. However they may not be a cultural fit. Very often entrepreneurs do not feel comfortable in a large organisation.

The company must assess how many managers it has and how many it expects to grow from within. Then it needs to go back to its business strategy and work out how many managers it will need in the future.

The result is a gap analysis. The company then knows how many managers it is going to need to recruit externally. This is a crucial component of executive remuneration strategy. A company that has to recruit significant numbers of managers will have to set its remuneration at a high level in order to attract the necessary recruits. It should also place great emphasis on retaining its good people: fairly obviously the more people that leave, the more external recruits are needed.

This has a further knock on effect as the existing management team is the corporate memory. Creating and maintaining the culture and spreading the winning culture amongst new recruits is crucial to a successful HR strategy (and hence to a successful business strategy).

Succession planning is important. The succession plan involves identifying for each current and planned top job, which are the likely candidates and how much extra time and skills they will require to take on the new role. But talent management is wider than just succession planning.

We have seen over the past decades the growing importance of talented management groups. This is the so called 'war for talent'. This has led to shortages across different industries, technologies and geographies, which has driven up remuneration as talent in short supply demands higher pay. Planning for talent is a key part of a remuneration strategy.

37.2 Culture

This chapter is about matching pay to business strategy and how people are motivated. Culture is of critical importance to this, but is often ignored or only paid lip-service to.

Organisational culture is the collective behaviour of people that are part of an organisation. It is formed by the organisation values, visions, norms, working language, systems, and symbols, and it includes beliefs and habits. It is also the pattern of such collective behaviours and assumptions that are taught to new organisational members as a way of perceiving, and even thinking and feeling. Organisational culture affects the way people and groups interact with each other, with clients, and with stakeholders.

Organisational culture is reflected in the way people perform tasks, set objectives, and administer the necessary resources to achieve objectives. Culture affects the way individuals make decisions, feel, and act in response to the opportunities and threats affecting the organisation.

A 2003 Harvard Business School study[1] reported that culture has a significant impact on an organisation's long-term economic performance. The study examined the management practices at 160 organisations over ten years and found that culture can enhance performance or prove detrimental to performance. Organisations with strong performance-oriented cultures witnessed far better financial growth. Additionally, a 2002 HR Executive forum study entitled 'Corporate Leadership Council' found that cultural traits such as risk taking, internal communications, and flexibility are some of the most important drivers of performance, and may impact individual performance. Furthermore, innovativeness, productivity through people, and the other cultural factors cited by Peters and Waterman[2] (1982) also have positive economic consequences.

Denison, Haaland, and Goelzer [3](2004) found that culture contributes to the success of the organisation, but not all dimensions contribute the same. It was found that the impacts of these dimensions differ by global regions, which

1 Nitin Nohria, William Joyce, Bruce Roberson 'What Really Works', Harvard Business Review, 1 July 2003.
2 *In Search of Excellence* (Harper & Row, 1982).
3 Daniel R. Denison, Stephanie Haaland, Paulo Goelzer 'Corporate culture and organizational effectiveness: Is Asia different from the rest of the world?' Organizational Dynamics, Vol 33(1), 2004, pp 98–109. Doi: 10.1016/j.orgdyn.2003.11.008

suggests that organisational culture is impacted by national culture. Additionally, Clarke (2006)[4] found that a safety climate is related to an organisation's safety record.

Ravasi and Schultz[5] (2006) state that organisational culture is a set of shared mental assumptions that guide interpretation and action in organisations by defining appropriate behaviour for various situations. At the same time although a company may have its 'own unique culture', in larger organisations, there are diverse and sometimes conflicting cultures that co-exist due to different characteristics of the management team. The organisational culture may also have negative and positive aspects.

A HBS Working Paper No: 12–035 May 9, 2012 by Robert G Eccles, Ioannis Ioannou and George Serafeim 'The Impact of a Corporate Culture of Sustainability on Corporate Behavior and Performance' found, using a matched sample of 180 companies, that corporations that voluntarily adopted environmental and social policies by 1993 – termed as High Sustainability companies – exhibited fundamentally different characteristics from a matched sample of firms that adopted almost none of these policies – termed as Low Sustainability companies. In particular, the boards of directors of these companies were more likely to be responsible for sustainability and top executive incentives were more likely to be a function of sustainability metrics. Moreover, they were more likely to have organised procedures for stakeholder engagement, to be more long-term oriented, and to exhibit more measurement and disclosure of nonfinancial information. They provided evidence that High Sustainability companies significantly outperform their counterparts over the long-term, both in terms of stock market and accounting performance. The outperformance is stronger in sectors where the customers are individual consumers, companies compete on the basis of brands and reputation, and in sectors where companies' products significantly depend upon extracting large amounts of natural resources.

Schein[6] (2009), Deal & Kennedy[7] (2000), Kotter[8] (1992) and many others state that organisations often have very differing cultures as well as subcultures.

4 Sharon Clarke 'Safety climate in an automobile manufacturing plant: The effects of work environment, job communication and safety attitudes on accidents and unsafe behaviour', Personnel Review, Vol. 35 Issue 4, 2006, pp.413–430

5 D Ravasi and M Schultz 'Responding to organizational identity threats: Exploring the role of organizational culture', Academy of Management Journal, 2006.

6 Edgar H Schein, 'Organizational Culture and Leadership' (The Jossey-Bass Business & Management Series)

7 Terrence E Deal, Allan A Kennedy, *Corporate Cultures* (Perseus, 2000)

8 John Kotter, *Corporate Culture and Performance* (Free Press, 7 April 1992), ISBN 0-02-918467-3

Kim Cameron and Robert Quinn[9] (1999) carried out research on organisational effectiveness and success. Based on the Competing Values Framework, they developed the Organisational Culture Assessment Instrument that distinguishes four culture types. Competing values produce polarities like flexibility vs. stability and internal vs. external focus – these two polarities were found to be most important in defining organisational success. The polarities construct a quadrant with four types of culture:

- **Clan** culture (internal focus and flexible) – A friendly workplace where leaders act like father figures.
- **Adhocracy** culture (external focus and flexible) – A dynamic workplace with leaders that stimulate innovation.
- **Market** culture (external focus and controlled) – A competitive workplace with leaders who are hard drivers
- **Hierarchy** culture (internal focus and controlled) – A structured and formalised workplace where leaders act like coordinators.

Cameron & Quinn designated six key aspects that will form organisational culture which can be assessed in the Organisational Culture Assessment Instrument (OCAI) thus producing a mix of the four archetypes of culture. Each organisation or team will have its unique mix of culture types.

Clan cultures are most strongly associated with positive employee attitudes and product and service quality, whereas market cultures are most strongly related with innovation and financial effectiveness criteria. The primary belief in market cultures is that clear goals and contingent rewards motivate employees to aggressively perform and meet stakeholders' expectations; a core belief in clan cultures is that the organisation's trust in and commitment to employees facilitates open communication and employee involvement. These differing results suggest that it is important for executive leaders to consider the match between strategic initiatives and organisational culture when determining how to embed a culture that produces competitive advantage. By assessing the current organisational culture as well as the preferred situation, the gap and direction to change can be made visible as a first step to changing organisational culture.

Constructive cultures

Constructive cultures are where people are encouraged to be in communication with their co-workers, and work as teams, rather than only as individuals. In positions where people do a complex job, rather than something simple like a mechanic one, this sort of culture is an efficient one. Four constructive cultures are typically recognised by experts in this field:

---

[9] Kim S Cameron, and Robert E Quinn, *Diagnosing and Changing Organizational Culture* (Addison-Wesley, New York, 1999).

- **Achievement:** completing a task successfully, typically by effort, courage, or skill (for example pursue a standard of excellence or explore alternatives before acting).
- **Self-Actualizing:** realisation or fulfilment of one's talents and potentialities – considered as a drive or need present in everyone. People with this style demonstrate a strong desire to learn and experience things, creative yet realistic thinking and a balanced concern for people and tasks.
- **Humanistic-Encouraging:** help others to grow and develop (resolve conflicts constructively). People high in this style devote energy to coaching and counselling others, are thoughtful and considerate and provide people with support and encouragement.
- **Affiliative:** treat people as more valuable than things (cooperate with others). This style reflects an interest in developing and sustaining pleasant relationships. People high in this style share their thoughts and feelings, are friendly and cooperative and make others feel a part of things.

Organisations with constructive cultures encourage members to work to their full potential, resulting in high levels of motivation, satisfaction, teamwork, service quality, and sales growth. Constructive norms are evident in environments where quality is valued over quantity, creativity is valued over conformity, cooperation is believed to lead to better results than competition, and effectiveness is judged at the system level rather than the component level. These types of cultural norms are consistent with (and supportive of) the objectives behind empowerment, total quality management, transformational leadership, continuous improvement, re-engineering, and learning organisations.

The use of power can be constructive or destructive. For example, the ability to use power to positively coerce staff to things and speed the implementation of a new strategy. Or in the military the coercive power to order their soldiers to attack the enemy. In some situations there is no time for socialising ideas.

In most of today's companies employees have choices and will react negatively to any senior executive who misuses the power of his or her position.

Stephen McGuire[10] (2003) defined and validated a model of organisational culture that predicts revenue from new sources. An Entrepreneurial Organisational Culture (EOC) is a system of shared values, beliefs and norms of

[10] Stephen JJ McGuire 'Entrepreneurial Organizational Culture: Construct Definition and Instrument Development and Validation' (2003), PhD Dissertation, The George Washington University, Washington, DC

members of an organisation, including valuing creativity and tolerance of creative people, believing that innovating and seizing market opportunities are appropriate behaviours to deal with problems of survival and prosperity, environmental uncertainty, and competitors' threats, and expecting organisational members to behave accordingly.

A checklist of elements that may impact on/determine the company culture

1. People and empowerment focus
2. Power
3. Value creation through innovation and change
4. Attention to the basics
5. Hands-on management
6. Doing the right thing
7. Freedom to grow and to fail
8. Commitment and personal responsibility
9. Emphasis on the future
10. Risk and reward, or risk aversion?
11. Freedom to make mistakes
12. Focus on performance outcomes versus inputs
13. Blame culture
14. Willingness to tolerate poor performers
15. Paternalistic
16. Meritocracy
17. Poor performers are fired/exited
18. Under-performers are fired/exited/managed out quite quickly; versus organisations where it takes a very long time to identify and manage out under performers; versus organisations where underperformers are tolerated
19. The problems of the banking culture – greed is good, short termism and irresponsibility
20. Silo mentality
21. Over focus on short term profits? Balance of long term and short term?
22. Performance measures. What is the balance of lagging versus leading indicators; and financial versus non-financial drivers of long term value?

23. Immediate investment versus profits and cash flow
24. The negative impact of quarterly reporting
25. The importance of the annual budget
26. Working together in teams versus individual emphasis
27. Stars are celebrated and rewarded and regarded as role models for others
28. Recognition that star performers rely on the contribution of many others and the brand power of the company
29. Importance that is given to Health and Safety
30. Importance that is given to corporate sustainability issues

Culture and values

The Remuneration Committee should be clear about the culture of the company, both the desired culture and where it is now.

By culture I mean 'the way we do things around here'. The Remuneration Committee needs to ask:

- What sorts of culture are there?
- What do we value?
- What behaviours should we encourage and reward?

The most useful culture consulting tool I use is my pen, which I hold up as a pendulum and ask my clients to say where in the swing from right to left[11] is the item of culture under consideration. Having assessed where the culture item is, I then ask in which way the culture should be moved and at what speed? Gently or be given a great big shove?

A more formalised approach is to select the culture items which you think may be relevant for your company and then to score where you think the culture currently is and what is the desired culture. The culture tool below can be used.

Note that a low score is not necessarily bad. In the nuclear power industry, being cautious and following procedures and processes is a good thing.

---

11 For example, more focus on short term goals where too little might be on the left and too much might be on the right. Or there may be two mutually exclusive items, for example emphasis on stars on the left and emphasis on teams on the right.

Table 27: Culture assessment tool for senior executive reward strategy design

Item		1	2	3	4	5	6	7	8	9	
Achievement orientation	Emphasis on process										Emphasis on results
Innovation	Cautious and keen to follow existing procedures and processes										Very strong emphasis on new products and new ideas
Risk taking v risk aversion	Strong risk aversion										Company thrives on taking risks. Willing to roll the dice.
Planning processes	Very short term										Very long term
Sustainability issues, H&S, CO_2, H_2O, etc	These items given a very low priority										These items given a very high priority
Stars v. teams	Emphasis on teams										Emphasis on stars
Planning	Actions are carefully planned										Decisions are made on the hoof! Very reactive.
Performance focus	Under-performance tolerated										Anything less than top performance is not tolerated.
Money orientation	Rewards are adequate, but not high priority										High focus on monetary rewards

In 2013, Barclays published its internal assessment of the bank by its independent non-executive director Sir Anthony Salz,[12] which provides a fascinating insight into the complexities and challenges faced by a large global bank and the importance of culture.

[12] online.wsj.com/public/resources/documents/SalzReview04032013.pdf

37.3 Performance management

As the following diagram illustrates, goal setting, performance planning, performance monitoring, feedback and coaching is on-going and supports the creation of the performance appraisal, which in turn supports processes related to rewards, learning and development. Performance monitoring, feedback and coaching creates a separate feedback loop within the larger loop which should take place more often, allowing for necessary adjustments to performance planning as conditions dictate.

Figure 28: Performance management process

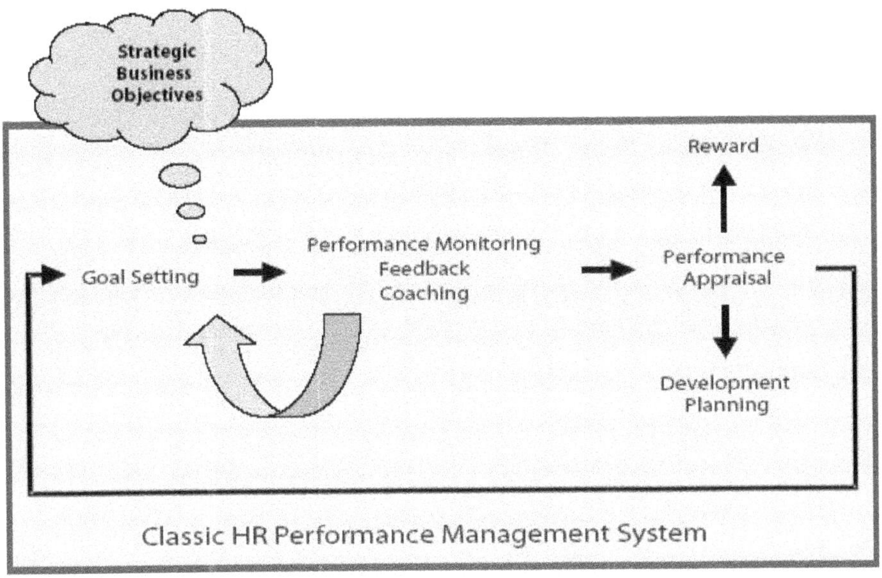

The reward strategy should ideally be integrated with the performance management system. In too many companies they become detached and lip service is paid to performance management.

Employees recognise that what is important in the organisation is what is rewarded. This creates or supports the culture of the organisation.

'What gets measured is what gets done' is a useful rule to remember.

38 Reward Strategy – Level

As noted in Section 33.2 the reward strategy needs to cover five objectives. It must:

- **Motivate**
- **Retain**
- **Attract**
- Enable **Exit** of executives at a reasonable cost
- The **Total Costs** should be acceptable

The remuneration strategy also has to answer the four questions of:

(i) How much will be paid.

(ii) For what (ie what performance measures and what the targets are).

(iii) When it will be paid, including requirements to hold shares and claw-back provisions.

(iv) The mix of salary, bonus, deferred bonus, LTIPs, options pensions and other benefits, including key contractual terms.

This Chapter focuses on point (i), the level of remuneration.

38.1 Target level of total remuneration

The guidance from the UK Corporate Governance Code about target levels of remuneration is:

> **'D.1 The Level and Components of Remuneration**
>
> Main Principle
>
> Levels of remuneration should be sufficient to attract, retain and motivate directors of the quality required to run the company successfully, but a company should avoid paying more than is necessary for this purpose.
>
> A significant proportion of executive directors' remuneration should be structured so as to link rewards to corporate and individual performance.'

And the seventh paragraph of Schedule A says

> 'The total potentially available rewards should not be excessive.'

The first step for the company is to decide what its target level of total remuneration should be. It will need to consider market data, but not necessarily be religiously influenced by it. In so doing it needs to consider what comparator groups/companies it should look at. It also needs to decide the reward for different levels of performance.

Motivation, retention and recruitment are key goals of remuneration policy. To achieve these goals, remuneration must be competitive with appropriate comparator companies, ie companies of similar size and complexity, operating, probably, in similar sectors or environment. Companies should not compare themselves with larger companies as this is inflationary, but should look to those companies and countries to which they lose their best talent or from which they recruit.

Remuneration Committees should ask themselves:

(i) How much would it cost the company if the executive left?

(ii) How long would it take to find a replacement?

(iii) Are there good internal successors?

(iv) If not, how much extra would they have to pay to attract a high calibre replacement?

(v) What is the minimum they can pay the incumbent executive and expect to keep him or her motivated?

(vi) How much more than the above minimum is needed to be sure to keep him or her?

(vii) Is it worth the risk of paying less than this?

As well as deciding the target level of remuneration, the Remuneration Committee should consider detailed scenario analyses of remuneration proposals, which:

- illustrate a range of possible outcomes
- consider all elements of remuneration
- consider all historic awards of medium and long-term incentives as well as the current proposals. (See the CEO lifetime rewards analysis tool (**Sections 40.2** and **42.2**) for an example of how this can be done.)

All of the above should be presented in an easily understood format. Examples of clear formats are given in **Figures 30, 31 32** and **43** and **Table 32.**

Such analyses will also enable the Remuneration Committee to decide the mix of fixed and variable performance linked pay.

In the text that follows, reference is made to tiers in the organisations, as illustrated in the diagram below. For example someone in tier 4 reports to his/her manager who is in tier 3 who reports to a tier 2 person who reports to the CEO.

Figure 29: The organisation tier structure for pay

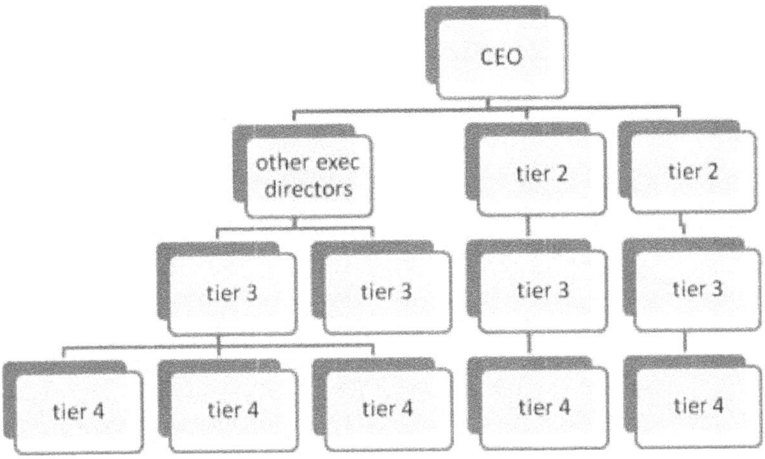

Figure 30: Reward strategy – target and outstanding – internal comparisons

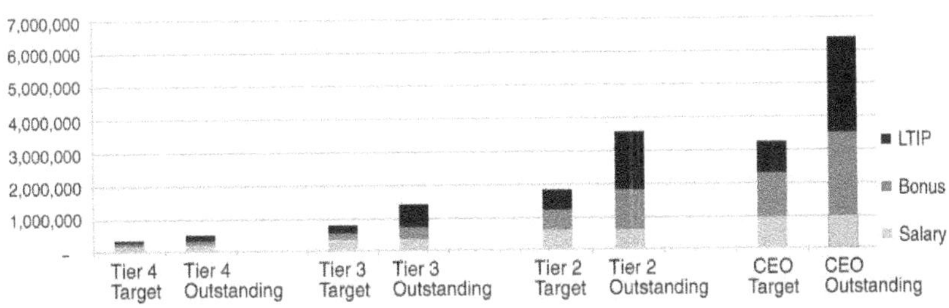

	Target Tier 4	Outstanding Tier 4	Target Tier 3	Outstanding Tier 3	Target Tier 2	Outstanding Tier 2	Target CEO	Outstanding CEO
Salary	200,000	200,000	350,000	350,000	600,000	600,000	1,000,000	1,000,000
Bonus Target as % salary	25.0%	50%	50%	100%	100%	200%	125%	250%
LTIP award % salary	50%	50%	100%	100%	150%	150%	200%	200%
Total Remuneration	316,550	495,313	757,925	1,383,594	1,798,950	3,557,813	3,248,250	6,429,688
Salary As % CEO	20%	20%	35%	35%	60%	60%		
Total Pay As % CEO	10%	8%	23%	22%	55%	55%		

For LTIPs, target assumes 50% vesting and 10% p.a. TSR; outstanding assumes 100% vesting and 25% p.a. TSR Assumes Deferred bonus paid in shares and assumes vesting in 3 years and for target grows at 10% p.a. TSR and for outstanding 25% p.a. TSR.

Figure 31: Comparison of potential earnings versus market rates

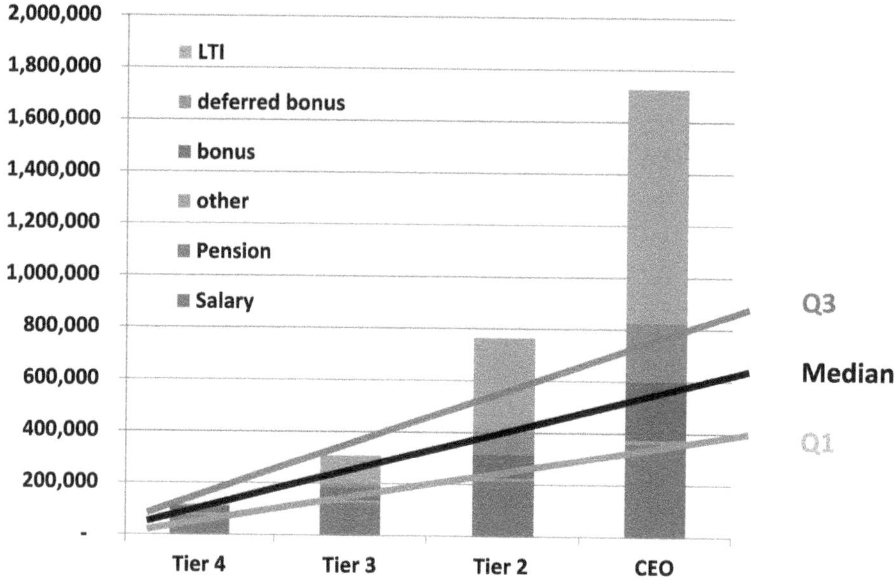

Figure 32: Comparison of fixed pay, target and potential earnings versus market rates

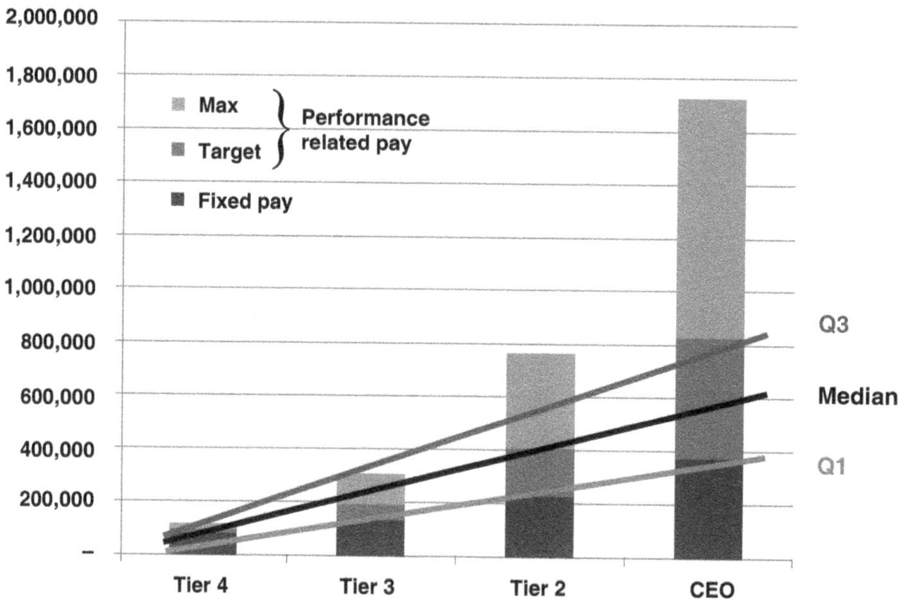

39 Reward Architecture – Reward Mix

Reward architecture it the term normally used to refer to the mix or make-up of the different components of the reward package.

39.1 Code Guidance

Main Principle D.1 of the UK Corporate Governance Code says:

> 'A significant proportion of executive directors' remuneration should be structured so as to link rewards to corporate and individual performance.'

However, no guidance is given on what is significant.

39.2 Market Data

For example for a large company the mix of the different elements of a typical large UK plc is as follows:

Figure 33: Typical remuneration mix (large company)

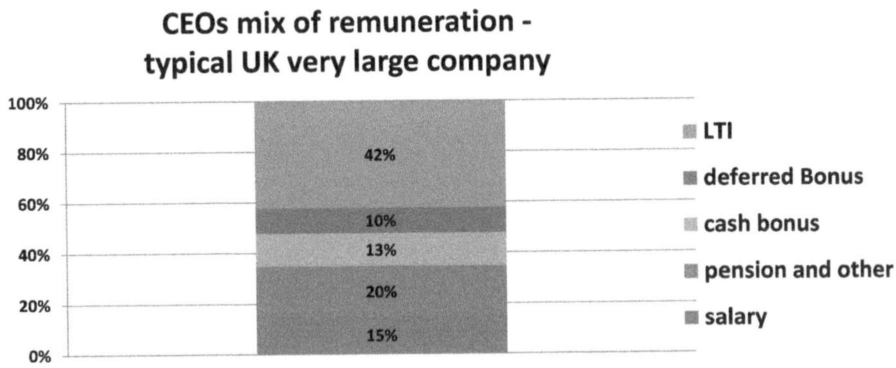

Salaries make up on average only 15% of the total remuneration of the CEOs of the largest companies quoted in the UK. The ten largest companies comprise about one-quarter of the UK stock market capitalisation, are highly visible and tend to set trends for other companies to follow.

The above analyses total remuneration awarded: this is the total value of salary, benefits, the transfer value of the increase in accrued pension, annual bonus and the expected value of long-term incentives, shares and share options awarded during the year.

Other findings of the analysis of very large companies were as follows.

- It is not immediately clear how much CEOs are actually paid. Although companies have to disclose the single figure of total remuneration, and each of the elements of remuneration, they spread the data over numerous pages of the Remuneration Committee report. Some do not include the expected value of long-term incentives.
- Pension makes up 19% of total remuneration (other benefits average 1% of total remuneration) as illustrated in **Figure 33**.
- The lack of data on the expected value and potential value of share options and share plans makes it difficult to understand most companies' remuneration plans. The author had to make estimates of the expected value in order to calculate total remuneration awarded in several cases.
- Companies have very different proportions of the various elements of remuneration.

Table 28: Examples of large companies' remuneration practices. Most are based on 2011 annual reports, ie data pertaining to 2011.

Company	**HSBC**	**Shell**	**BP**	**GSK**	**BAT**	**Vodafone**	**Rio Tinto**	**SABMiller**	**L&G**	**Average**	**Total**
CEO	**Stuart Gulliver**	**Peter Voser**	**Bob Dudley**	**Sir Andrew Witty**	**Nico Durante**	**Vittorio Colao**	**Tom Albanese**	**Graham McKay**	**Tim Breedon**		
market cap (Apr. 2012) £bn	**98**	**115**	**84**	**71**	**61**	**84**	**49**	**40**	**7.2**	**68**	**609**
Salary	1,250,000	1,348,163	1,062,500	1,000,000	1,348,163	1,099,000	1,030,000	1,192,000	808,000	1,126,425	10,137,826
Pension DC or cash	527,000	-	-	-	-	330,000	-	357,600	178,000	524,900	2,099,600
Pension increase in TV of DB plan		1,123,478	3,067,500	3,269,000	1,123,478		2,924,000	-	567,000	2,012,409	12,074,457
Pension 20 x increase in accrued pension of DB plan		750,000	3,050,000	330,000	750,000	681,250	1,620,000	-	240,000	1,236,875	7,421,250
Total pension (DC/cash + increase in TV of DB plan)	527,000	1,123,478	3,067,500	3,269,000	1,123,478	330,000	2,924,000	357,600	745,000	1,574,895	14,174,057
Other benefits	266,000	36,000	41,250	36,000	36,000	569,000	269,000	110,602	20,000	153,761	1,383,852
Bonus (target) (cash and deferred)	1,875,000	2,022,245	2,656,250	1,250,000	2,022,245	1,039,000	1,236,000	1,043,000	606,000	1,527,749	13,749,739
Bonus (cash)	862,000	1,521,739	531,250	1,300,000	1,521,739	1,039,000	-	1,775,000	502,000	1,005,859	9,052,728
Bonus (deferred award EV)	1,156,000	1,521,739	2,125,000	1,050,000	1,521,739	-	-	-	302,000	852,942	7,676,478

Company	HSBC	Shell	BP	GSK	BAT	Vodafone	Rio Tinto	SABMiller	L&G	Average	Total
Bonus (previous deferred awards vesting in the year)	3,696,000	1,087,826	-	-	1,087,826	-	334,375	-	246,000	716,892	6,452,027
LTIP awarded (EV)	*3,750,000*	3,629,490	3,863,284	2,499,999	3,629,490	5,058,750	1,957,000	3,663,250	808,000	3,206,585	28,859,261
LTIP vesting in the year	98,000	5,221,739	506,640	3,738,000	5,221,739	9,308,829	-	215,540	245,000	2,728,388	24,555,488
Options award (EV)	-	-	-	-	-	-	1,042,500	1,219,375	-	251,319	2,261,875
Options vesting in the year	-	-	-	-	-	-	-	1,219,375	-	135,486	1,219,375
Options exercised in the year	-	143,000	-	143,000	143,000	-	-	1,603,411	-	225,823	2,032,411
SAYE	-	-	-	-	-	-	-	-	-	-	-
SIP	-	-	-	5,000	-	-	-	-	-	556	5,000
Other	-	-	-	-	-	-	-	-	-	-	-
Total awarded (EV) (uses increase in transfer value of pension)	7,811,000	9,180,609	10,690,784	9,154,998	9,180,609	12,547,750	7,222,500	8,317,827	3,185,000	8,587,897	77,291,077
Total received (using higher of increase in TV and 20x increase in accrued pension)	6,699,000	10,481,946	5,209,140	9,486,000	10,481,946	16,797,829	4,557,375	5,254,153	2,566,000	7,948,154	71,533,389

Company	HSBC	Shell	BP	GSK	BAT	Vodafone	Rio Tinto	SABMiller	L&G	Average	Total
Total receivable	6,699,000	10,338,946	5,209,140	9,343,000	10,338,946	16,797,829	4,557,375	4,870,117	2,566,000	7,857,817	70,720,353
mix of pay awarded:											
Salary	16%	15%	10%	11%	15%	9%	14%	14%	25%	14%	129%
Pension and other	10%	13%	29%	36%	13%	43%	44%	6%	24%	24%	217%
Cash bonus	11%	17%	5%	14%	17%	8%	0%	21%	16%	12%	109%
Deferred Bonus	15%	17%	20%	11%	17%	0%	0%	0%	9%	10%	89%
LTI	48%	40%	36%	27%	40%	40%	42%	59%	25%	40%	356%

Note: companies differ in their interpretation of best practice and disclosure requirements. Some companies will present information in their annual reports in different formats to the above and so it is difficult to be able to present consistent data. Allocation of rewards between fiscal years is one particularly difficult area to have consistency. The author acknowledges that some companies may not agree with his interpretation of their data.

These very large companies are not typical of most quoted companies.

It should be noted that smaller companies in general set salaries that comprise a higher proportion of total remuneration.

Smaller companies tend to have less pension and less performance related pay, as is illustrated in the diagram below, which shows the proportions of pay for target/expected values of total remuneration awarded:

Figure 34: Typical remuneration mix (smaller company)

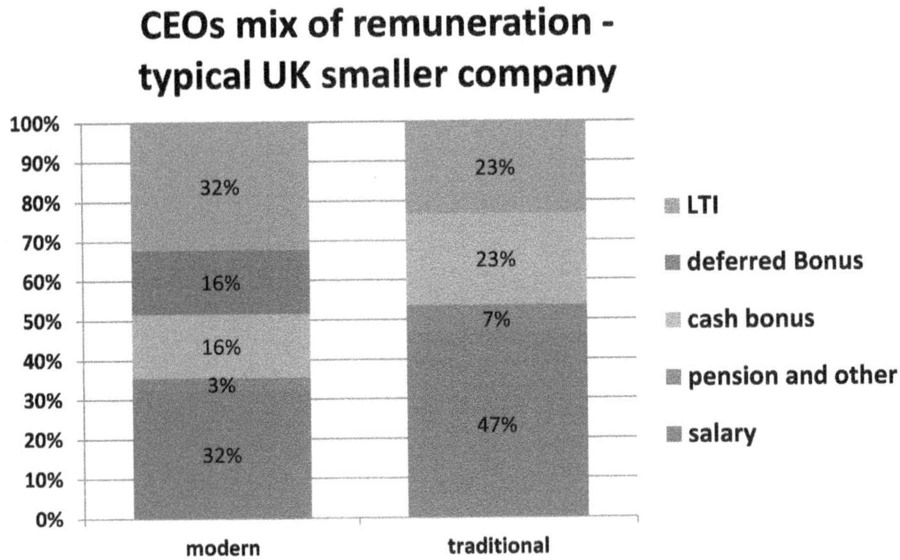

39.3 Mix of fixed pay versus variable performance linked pay

The MM&K/Manifest survey[1] shows the CEOs of the largest UK companies have an average of 65% of total remuneration that is performance related.

Example: if we take the example of a CEO with a salary of £1 million per annum, the proportions of pay at target and outstanding performance might be as follows:

[1] MM&K/Manifest Total Remuneration Survey 2011

Figure 35: Proportion of performance related pay

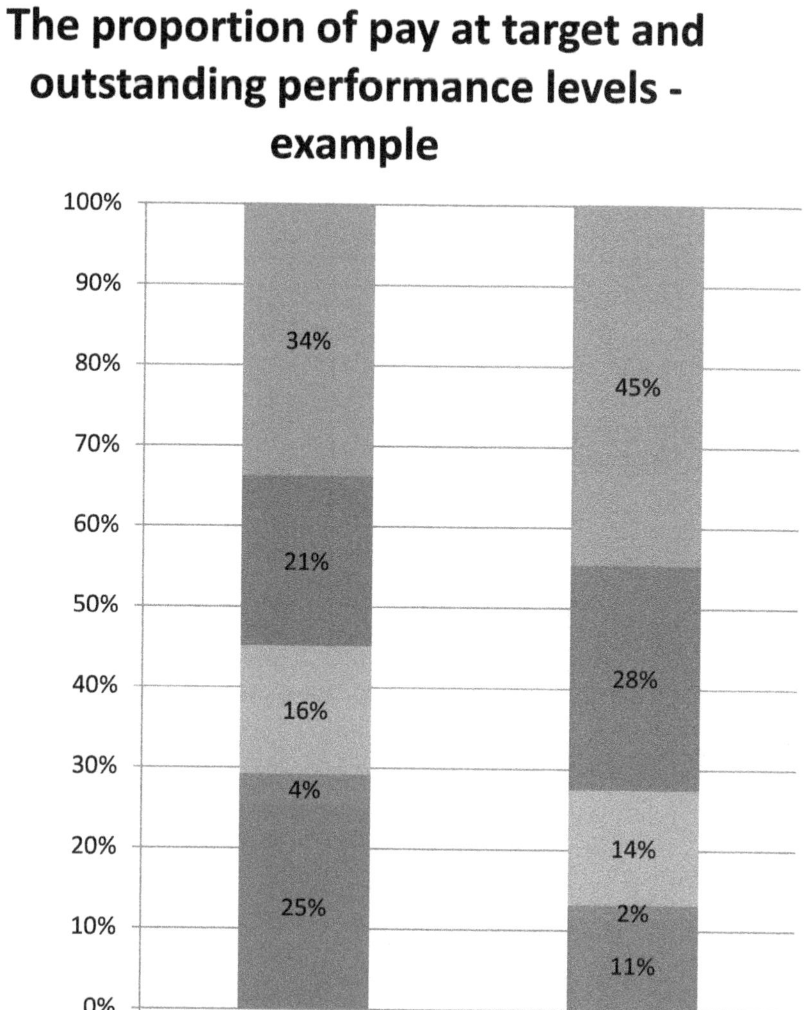

	target £	outstanding £
LTIP	34%	45%
Deferred Bonus	21%	28%
Bonus	16%	14%
Pension	4%	2%
Salary	25%	11%

	Target		**Outstanding**	
	£	**of total**	**£**	**of total**
Salary	1,000,000	25%	1,000,000	11%
Pension	150,000	4%	150,000	2%
Bonus	625,000	16%	1,250,000	14%
Deferred Bonus	831,875	21%	2,441,406	28%
LTIP	1,331,000	34%	3,906,250	45%
Performance pay	2,787,875	71%	7,597,656	87%
Total Remuneration	3,937,875		8,747,656	

Another way to look at this is to consider the performance-related elements opportunity value as a percentage of salary. Using our same example as before this would be:

Bonus (including deferred bonus) maximum opportunity	250% of salary
LTIP maximum award that will vest	200% of salary
Total performance related pay	450% of salary

The reader will notice that the 450% takes no account of the change in the share price between the award date and the payout. Using the assumption that outstanding performance results in 25% per annum TSR, the performance related awards when they vest in full would be worth £7,597,656 or 760% of salary.

The 450% is the figure that is more generally used in discussions of performance related pay award levels.

It is worth noting that PIRC suggest that the performance related elements should not be more than 200% of salary.

The 2011 MM&K/Manifest Total Remuneration Survey shows that the average FTSE 100 CEO's proportion of performance-related remuneration increased to 67% in 2006 from only 33% in 1998. And the average performance related payments have increased from 80% to nearly 350% of salary over the same period.

Many commentators ignore pensions (which is simpler, BUT incorrect) and look at the proportions of salary, bonus and long term incentives. A company which has a bonus opportunity of 100% of salary and an LTIP of 100% of salary would then have a remuneration model of 40/20/40 of salary/bonus/LTI.

The FTSE 100 average model is 33/32/35, if pension and other benefits are included with salary as fixed pay (but 22/37/41 of fixed/bonus/LTI if pension and other benefits are excluded). In 2011 Average CEO pay in FTSE 100 companies was £4.8 million in 2011.[2]

Whilst some companies have adopted the 10/10/80 or even 5/5/90, others may find that the traditional 40/20/40 model may be more appropriate. Also shown below is a 30/15/65 model where the bonus maximum is 200% of salary (target is half this), but as half of bonus is deferred into shares which have to be kept until retirement, the deferred bonus is classified as LTI.

If pension is included with salary in fixed pay then these examples translate into the following examples in £ terms.

Future values	**33/32/35**	**05/05/90**	**10/10/80**	**40/20/40**	**30/15/65**
Fixed Pay (salary, pension and other benefits)	1,584,000	240,000	480,000	1,920,000	1,440,000
Bonus (including deferred bonus)	1,536,000	240,000	480,000	960,000	720,000
LTI	1,680,000	4,320,000	3,840,000	1,920,000	3,120,000
Total Remuneration	4,800,000	4,800,000	4,800,000	4,800,000	4,800,000

The examples show each package equal in terms of total remuneration. Economists believe that there is a trade-off for risk, so those packages with more risk for the CEO, ie those with more performance related pay, would normally have a higher expected total remuneration that those with less risk.

The amount to discount future risk is subjective and depends on the individual's perception of risk, their accumulated wealth to date and their degree of diversification of their assets. With this proviso **Table 29** illustrates the potential trade-off and additional rewards required under each reward architecture.

Table 29: Reward architecture – adjusted for risk

	Reward Architecture (Reward Mix)				
	33/32/35	**05/05/90**	**10/10/80**	**40/20/40**	**30/15/65**
Adjustment for risk					
risk discount factor per annum.	10%	30%	25%	10%	20%
after 3 years	33%	120%	95%	33%	73%

2 Average total remuneration awarded (including the expected value of long term incentives) had reduced to £4.1 million in 2013.

Future values	Reward Architecture (Reward Mix)				
Fixed Pay (salary, pension and other benefits)	1,584,000	425,866	719,568	1,923,319	1,588,666
Bonus (including deferred bonus)	1,536,000	425,866	719,568	961,659	794,333
LTI	1,680,000	7,665,590	5,756,543	1,923,319	3,442,110
Total Remuneration	4,800,000	8,517,322	7,195,679	4,808,297	5,295,554
Present values					
Fixed Pay (salary, pension and other benefits)	1,584,000	425,866	719,568	1,923,319	1,588,666
Bonus (including deferred bonus)	1,396,364	327,589	575,654	874,236	661,944
LTI	1,262,209	3,489,117	2,947,350	1,445,018	1,991,962
Total Remuneration	4,242,573	4,242,573	4,242,573	4,242,573	4,242,573

39.4 Share ownership guidelines and share retention rules

Share ownership guidelines are usually set as a % of salary or number of shares or a monetary amount of shares that must be held.

Share retention rules refer to shares acquired from bonus and long term incentive schemes. For example executives might have to retain all or a fixed percentage (eg 75%) of shares received from bonus or long term incentive plans, net of any taxes that they have to pay.

Such arrangements can result in executives building up significant amounts of value of shares in their company. Thus when the company's share price goes up they will financially benefit. If it goes down they will suffer a loss. Such arrangements increase the alignment of executives with long term shareholders.

They can also significantly impact on the bonus and long term incentives as they increase the leverage of the outcomes versus the movement in the share price of the company over the long term.

39.5 Best Practice

The choice of reward architecture will depend on the reward strategy and a number of other factors. **Table 30** illustrates best practice.

Table 30: Reward Strategy and Reward Architecture

Reward strategy	**suggested mix**	**note re other factors that may influence choice**
Traditional	**33/23/35**	Culture, need to retain and attract, history of rewards in the organisation and any regulatory issues.
Long term emphasis Bonus, with ½ in shares deferred 3 years. Annual LTIP award with retention requirement post vesting, with absolute TSR and financial measures.	**30/15/65**	
Alignment to specific strategic focus One-off LTIP award with 3–5 year timeframe. Can be a mix of absolute and relative TSR measures. Reward emphasis is on LTIP with large payout if successful. Careful consideration of CIC conditions.	**10/10/80**	
Recovery Salary and bonus must be adequate to recruit and retain. High risk of failure so large rewards on offer if successful in managing turnaround.	**30/15/65**	High risk so rewards have to attractive even in the vent the recovery does not succeed. So a good salary is required, plus a very large reward if successful.
Start up Conserve cash Lots of equity Modest salary and bonus only when cash flow is OK	**10/5/85**	
Fast growth Reward strategy may be similar to start up or strategic alignment	**30/15/65** or 5/5/90	Depends on specific circumstances. Sector issues may influence the choice.
Private Equity Modest salary and pension Small bonus based on progress, especially cash flow and profits targets. Tax effective sweet equity. Highly geared. Nil if threshold not achieved. Can ratchet to 20/30% of equity.	**10/5/85**	

39.6 Funding Remuneration

Remuneration can either be paid as a cash item or through equity which will dilute shareholders.

For mature companies who make have good profit margins the costs of remuneration will usually be small and the dilution from share schemes will usually be acceptable to shareholders.

In the UK the established dilution limits are 10% over ten years which averages out at 1% per annum.

For companies that are in start-up mode and are trying to conserve cash, investors will usually accept a higher dilution, but in return will expect that cash remuneration is not excessive and preferably is modest. A package that is weighted in favour of equity over cash will generally be viewed positively.

40 Performance Related Pay – what for?

How much, **what for** and **when** should it be paid? These are the three key questions in respect to performance related pay.

The **how much** question (including the proportion of performance related pay) was discussed above in **Chapter 38**. One additional point is worthy of note: the UK Corporate Governance Code warns, as regards pay levels, about the upward ratchet of pay levels with no corresponding improvement in performance.

> 'The remuneration committee should judge where to position their company relative to other companies. But they should use such comparisons with caution in view of the risk of an upward ratchet of remuneration levels with no corresponding improvement in performance.' (Supporting Principle D.1)

The **what for** question (ie performance measures) is discussed below and the **when** question in **Chapter 41**.

40.1 Code Guidance

The UK Corporate Governance Code is more conservative in approach than the old Combined Code. It recommends that

> 'Performance related pay should be stretching and designed to promote the long term success of the company.' (D.1 Supporting principle)

And in the Schedule A to the UK Corporate Governance Code, it says:

> '[In respect of annual bonuses] performance conditions should be relevant, stretching and designed to promote the long-term success of the company.
>
> There may be a case for part payment [of bonus] in shares to be held for a significant period.
>
> Payouts or grants under all incentive schemes, including new grants under existing share option schemes, should be subject to challenging performance criteria reflecting the company's objectives, including non-financial performance metrics where appropriate.
>
> Remuneration incentives should be compatible with risk policies and systems.

In normal circumstances, shares granted or other forms of deferred remuneration should not vest, and options should not be exercisable, in less than three years. Directors should be encouraged to hold their shares for a further period after vesting or exercise, subject to the need to finance any costs of acquisition and associated tax liabilities.

Grants under executive share option and other long-term incentive schemes should normally be phased rather than awarded in one large block.

Consideration should be given to the use of provisions that permit the company to reclaim variable components in exceptional circumstances of misstatement or misconduct.'

In the light of the 2007/08 banking crisis and ensuing credit/liquidity crisis and slowdown in world economic activity, it is with the benefit of hindsight that I criticise the old Combined Code which recommended 'keen incentives to perform at the highest levels' for executive directors. The new wording is much more focused on the long term success of the company and compatibility with risk management, policies and systems.

Greenbury referred to incentive plans as being part of a 'cohesive, integrated reward strategy'. Those words are no longer part of the Code, although whether this is by design or by chance is not clear. Schedule A, para 4 to the Code merely states that:

'any new long term incentive plan should form part of a well-considered overall plan'.

Institutional shareholders and their intermediaries give plenty of guidance about individual plans but little or none on the interaction of plans.

40.2 Modelling Tools

The design of good performance related pay arrangements require a good understanding of the inter-relationships of complex variables. This will need to be modelled using spreadsheets and the results summarised in clear graphics and tables.

Some examples of modelling techniques and tools have already been shown in the preceding chapters.

Figure 30: Reward Strategy – Target and Outstanding – Internal Comparisons

Figure 31: Comparison of potential earnings versus market rates

Figure 32: Comparison of fixed pay, target and potential earnings versus market rates

Table 29: Reward architecture – adjusted for risk

Table 30: Reward Strategy and Reward Architecture

Below are three further models.

Figure 36 and **Table 31**: Modelling Performance Pay linkage.

This model looks at the key factors that drive long term value and considers ranges of outcomes for these variables. In this case the key factors are the sales growth, margin improvements and the impact of acquisitions as allowed by the financial strategy.

Figure 37: Compensation Trade-off Tool to show impact of relative and absolute performance on remuneration received.

This allows the consideration of a large number of scenarios. In particular it enables Remuneration Committee members and executives to see the outcome of low probability events. Such scenario analysis is essential to no-surprises in the future.

This model can also be used to model the trade-off of any two variables.

Table 32: Lifetime earnings model.

This considers all existing and probable future awards and estimates the total earnings over the working lifetime of the executive.

Figure 36: Modelling performance pay linkage

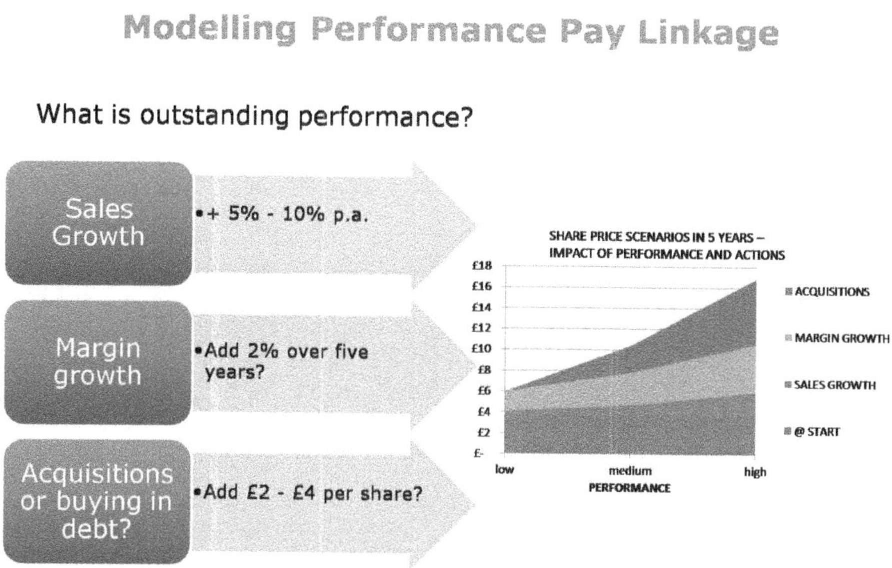

Table 31: Modelling performance pay linkage

EXAMPLE COMPANY ZYZ plc												
Financial overview and potential business growth targets												
									5yr growth assumptions			
Year ended: 31 March		2006	2007	2008	2009	2010	today		low	medium	high	
Turnover	£m	257	164.5	159.5	165.4	181.6			201	232	292	
% growth			-36%	-3%	4%	10%			2%	5%	10%	
Operating Margin	%	3.77	3.46	5.14	0.06	-0.94			7%	8%	9%	
Operating Profit	£m	8.4	3.7	2.6	-32.6	-6.3			14.04	18.54	26.32	
Market Cap at B/S date	£m	93.78	105.28	43.19	25.1	42.63		100	160.63	210.42	284.08	
Total Debt	£m	23.4	17.3	10	8.7	3.4		3.4	26.92	36.65	53.46	minus
Market Cap + debt		117.18	122.58	53.19	33.8	46.03		103.4	133.72	173.77	230.62	
EV / Profit		13.95	33.13	20.46	1.04	7.31			12	14	16	
							(= Profit over period (assumes 3 x profit to allow for profit build up over time and capex excluding acquisitions) less tax at 28%)					
Cash Flow									30.32	40.05	56.86	
share price		3.14	5.81	1.73	0.95	1.58			5.96	7.81	10.55	
shares in issue		29.84	18.12	25.00	26.33	26.94			26.94	26.94	26.94	
Impact of Acquisitions												
Cost of Acquisitions									50	50	50	
Turnover							cost = 1x turnover		50	50	50	
Cost savings achieved as % turnover									1%	2%	3%	
Cost savings achieved									0.5	1	1.5	
Profit margin pre cost savings									6%	8%	10%	
Profit									3.50	5.00	6.50	
Profit Margin									7.0%	10.0%	13.0%	
ROCE									7.0%	10.0%	13.0%	
WACC									8%	8%	8%	
Value added									-6.00	14.00	40.00	
group value (market cap)									154.63	224.42	324.08	
share price									5.74	8.33	12.03	range to model
delta share price to base case of low										2.59	6.29	
discount rate									15%	15%	15%	
NPV of future share price									2.85	4.14	5.98	
share price at 22 June 2011								3.10				
Compensation analysis and ratios												
Number of top executives						5			5.00	5.00	5.00	
Salary: Total						900,000			900,000	900,000	900,000	
Average Bonus % salary									25%	50%	100%	
Average LTIP payout % salary									0%	50%	100%	
Average pension and other benefits % salary									0%	52%	104%	
Total Remuneration Received (TRR)									20%	20%	20%	
Average TRR per exec									6.53%	9.97	14.59	
CEO analysis												
Salary						300,000						
Average Bonus % salary									25%	50%	100%	
Average LTIP % vesting as % salary									0%	50%	100%	
LTIP payout allowing for change in share price and dividends									0%	117%	293%	
Average pension and other benefits % salary									20%	20%	20%	
Total Remuneration £ million									2.18	4.30	7.69	
Top Executives share of the value added												
Delta Comp									0%	3.45	8.06	
Delta Comp as % delta cash flow										35%	30%	
Delta Comp as % delta profit before tax										31%	26%	
Delta Comp as % delta shareholder value										5%	5%	

Figure 37: Compensation trade-off tool to show impact of relative and absolute performance on remuneration received

remuneration is in £millions

		absolute performance					gearing
		poor	ok	good	very good	excellent	
relative performance	poor	£ 0.88	£ 1.09	£ 1.64	£ 2.87	£ 5.74	0
	ok	£ 1.31	£ 1.64	£ 2.46	£ 4.31	£ 8.61	0.25
	good	£ 1.75	£ 2.19	£ 3.28	£ 5.74	£ 11.48	0.5
	very good	£ 2.19	£ 2.73	£ 4.10	£ 7.18	£ 14.36	0.75
	excellent	£ 2.63	£ 3.28	£ 4.92	£ 8.61	£ 17.23	1
gearing		-	0.5	1.0	1.5	2.0	

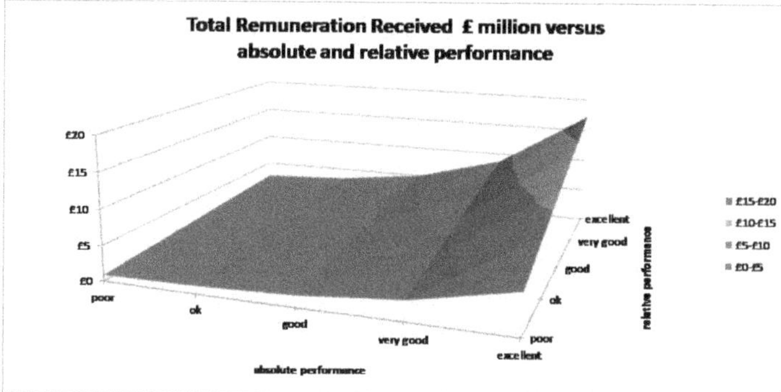

This can be used to model the trade off of any two variables, eg (i) TSR versus financial metrics
(ii) relative TSR and operating profits
(iii) relative EBITDA growth versus share price in absolute terms.

Table 32: Lifetime earnings model

	Salary	Cash Bonus	Deferred Bonus	Medium Term Incentive Plan	Long Term Incentive Plan	Investment Shares	Matching Shares	Share Options	Pension (n.b. 25% cash lump sum and annual pension)	Total Received	Shares Owned (including investment shares pledged)
2011	300	75				(150)				225	450
2012	309	77								386	495
2013	318	80								398	545
2014	328	82	100	399						909	1,098
2015	338	84	103	411						936	1,722
2016	348	87	106	424	483	242	725			2,414	3,632
2017	358	90	109	436	498					1,491	5,038
2018	369	92	112	449	513					1,536	6,616
2019	380	95	116	463	528					1,582	8,384
2020	391	98	119	477	544					1,629	10,362
2021			123	491	560			3,684	1,500	6,359	16,257
2022			126	506	577				196	1,405	19,092
2023			130	521	594				196	1,441	22,246
2024									196	196	24,471
2025									196	196	26,918
2026									196	196	29,610
2027									196	196	32,571
2028									196	196	35,828
2029									196	196	39,410
2030									196	196	43,351
2031									196	196	47,687
2032									196	196	52,455
2033									196	196	57,701
2034									196	196	63,471
2035									196	196	69,818
2036									196	196	76,800
Total	3,439	860	1,144	4,578	4,296	92	725	3,684	4,436	23,254	
				Indexed to share price							
								note - phased sale rules for shares are recommended			

ASSUMPTIONS AND MODEL INPUT PARAMETERS

Age	50							
Normal Retirement Date	60	**MTIP award level**	100%	salary	**Options as % salary**	200%	**pension TV multiple**	20
Salary Inflation	3%	**MTIP vests after x years**	3	years	**Investment Shares**	50%	**Shares ownership guideline as % salary**	150%
Bonus Target % salary	50%	**Bonus Matching shares multiple - Target**	3		**LTIP award level**	100%	salary	
Bonus maximum % salary	100%	**Bonus Matching shares vest after**	5	years	**LTIP vests after x years**	5	years	
% of bonus deferred	50%				**Share price growth incl Dividends**	10%	**dividends yield**	2%

40.3 Performance measures

Understanding performance measures is key to a well-designed, cohesive integrated reward strategy.

First we need to have a good understanding of 'what is performance'? This question must be resolved before effective pay for performance can be considered.

The expectations treadmill[1] is a term used by McKinsey to describe the way the share price has already built into it, expectations of future growth. A company with a high p/e ratio is expected to grow faster than one with a lower p/e ratio. The difference required can be modelled using a fairly simple spreadsheet. But should management be rewarded for delivering this higher level of growth? This is not a simple question. Their previous actions may have positioned the company for the growth that is now occurring. Were they rewarded at the time for these strategic moves? Or was the remuneration strategy to wait until the results were evident in the financial figures? At one end of the spectrum there is a danger that managers are not being rewarded for re-organising the business and launching new products. The other end of this spectrum is that managers are being rewarded for achieving strategic goals and then rewarded again when they translate into share price increase – double counting.

But the main point McKinsey made is that expectations create a treadmill and failure to deliver is then reflected in a major correction in the share price. This fear creates excessive pressure to deliver short term results.

It is far too easy to say that companies should aim to deliver long term sustainable shareholder value and profits should be sustainable. Such words are not enough. More detail is required. The concern is whether the profit growth is sustainable, whether the growth in revenues will lead to long term profitability, whether the cost cuts now will translate into better margins or merely weaken the competitive advantages of the products.

How do we define the value of a company? Nobody has the answer to this question. This is why share prices vary from day to day and why analysts have such difficulty in agreeing what a share is worth.

Since it is agreed (by most people) that directors' remuneration should be linked to value created, we do however have to try and define value. Given this proviso, the reader should recognise that there is no perfect answer and different companies will come to different conclusions. Shareholders will need to assess whether the measures used in the remuneration plans are those that they feel will result in 'value'. If they are comfortable with this then (all other things being equal) they will tend to be buyers of the company's shares.

---

1 See www.mckinseyquarterly.com/The_expectations_treadmill_299

40.4 TSR

It should be noted that:

- The relationship between performance and TSR[2] is long-term. One needs to take care because TSR is not a good short-term measure of management's performance and should not be the sole determinant of incentive pay. Clearly, a company's share price should ultimately reflect both good and bad performance but there is often a lag. An annual comparison of pay and TSR is misleading and potentially dangerous, but long-term trend information would be useful. Shareholders should not be overly influenced by an annual comparison, but should focus on the long term as required by the new UK Corporate Governance Code, by the regulators and other policy makers in the context of executive pay.
- Share prices are driven by many factors. In the list below, only the last two are under the control of management, eg:

  (i) Interest rates

  (ii) General economic activity and growth forecasts

  (iii) Market sentiment

  (iv) Sector sentiment

  (v) Market view of management capability and future strategy

  (vi) Achievement of operational goals and whether management generates sustainable competitive advantage.

As a result share price is frequently out of alignment with the underlying performance of the company, often for substantial periods of time.

As noted above, items (i) to (iv) are not under the control of management.

Only item (vi) is truly under the control of management.

Item (v), the market's view of company management, can be particularly capricious. Someone judged to be a hero one year can quickly be relegated to a 'dunce'. Jack Welch was for 15 years a hero at GE. John Browne was heralded as the 'Sun King', made a Lord and then disaster struck at a refinery in Houston and then in the Gulf of Mexico[3].

---

2 TSR = Total Shareholder Return = share price change plus dividends.

3 In 2000 the transnational oil giant BP Amoco rebranded itself as 'bp: beyond petroleum.' The rebranding was part of an effort to portray BP as an energy company, not just an oil company: one that incorporated solar energy in its portfolio and was willing to move away from oil. BP replaced its logo with a vibrant green-white-and-yellow sunburst named after Helios, the ancient Greek sun god. The logo was meant to connote 'commitment to the environment and solar power' and promote the new bp 'as the supermajor of choice for the environmentally-aware motorist.' The lower-case letters were

The reader who understands the following diagram is well positioned to understand the difference between rewards for being lucky and in the right place it the right time; and rewards for achieving things by their direct actions. History, of course, teaches us that great leaders are very good at taking credit for good things that happen on their watch even though they may have done little or nothing to make it happen.

Figure 38: How the stock market values companies

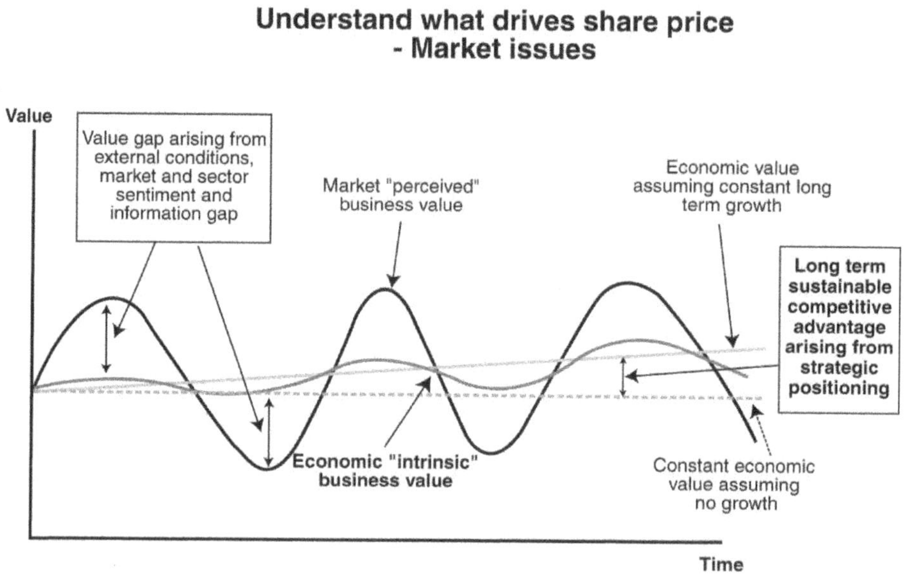

A company can be performing well but this might not be reflected in the share price, in the short term. Over the long term the company's performance will drive the share price, but how do we design incentive plans that motivate in the short and medium term?

One problem is that internal performance measures may be achieved but this may not translate to the share price performance. Companies should nevertheless choose performance measures for annual bonus plans that if achieved should translate into long-term share price performance. It is up to the Remuneration Committee to justify annual bonus payments in the remuneration report to shareholders. The Committee is accountable to

chosen 'because focus groups say bp is friendlier than the old imperialistic BP,' which stood for British Petroleum. See for example William Maclean, 'BP Goes Greener with "Beyond Petroleum" Rebrand' Planet Ark, July 25, 2000 (www.planetark.org/dailynewsstory.cfm?newsid=7577) and Brian Hale, 'BP Goes Green, Solar, Connected' Sydney Morning Herald, July 26, 2000, pp. 25–6

shareholders and if it approves large annual bonuses for a number of years that do not translate into share price performance it can expect criticism from shareholders.

Another problem is that the share price already discounts future performance. It expects a certain amount of performance and if that is not achieved then the share price will decline (subject to any concomitant changes in interest rates, market and sector sentiment).

There should be a balance of incentive between annual and long-term incentives to reflect that no one can be sure that the annual performance measures will translate into long-term performance. So some incentive should be linked directly to TSR performance.

If we knew for sure what the measures of annual performance should be in the annual bonus plan then we would not need to have long-term incentives. From a governance viewpoint, some would say that long-term incentives developed because shareholders were not satisfied with the way annual bonus plans were operating, for example, they were paying out year after year with no improvement in the share price.

Implementation of strategy (and the rewards for its success) may take several years to be reflected in the share price. However, the Remuneration Committee should ensure the executives are rewarded for the successful implementation of the strategic goals and milestones. This is best done through the annual bonus plan. Bonus deferral/bonus matching can provide a kicker when the strategy results in subsequent increases in shareholder value.

Another problem is that most long-term incentive plans are not long term at all – they are usually three-year, medium-term incentive plans.

Although the board as a whole is collectively responsible for strategy, it is appropriate that a considerable part of total remuneration package for the CEO and senior executives is linked to the share price performance, either through LTIPs or options, or both.

Share price will grow over the long term if the profits generated are higher than the cost of capital. There is a danger of incentivising executives to beat the competition – they can achieve this but the share price may reduce. It may have been a better strategic decision to refrain from investing rather than compete.

Sometimes share prices increase because of factors over which management have little control. (When the tide comes in, all the boats rise. However no-one would suggest that the captains of the boats should be paid a bonus because the tide has risen.) In a bull market most share prices will rise. Companies with high leverage will benefit when interest rates stay low for extended periods. Companies should be managed for the long term. When measuring performance we need to separate out what management have achieved and what is a result of external factors.

Companies which fail to do this may end up with too much focus on financial results and short term share price performance.

Companies cannot manage their share price. It may be possible to manipulate or massage the share price in the short term, but ultimately the share price will reflect the underlying performance of the company. However there are numerous examples of where the stock market has failed to value companies correctly and the share price has failed to reflect the underlying value of the company. Such misjudgement (mis-evaluation) can occur over months or even years.

More about Total Shareholder Return (TSR)

In the long term, shareholders want Total Shareholder Return (ie share price appreciation and dividends). However, share price movements can be capricious. Share prices can be driven by fear and greed, particularly in the short term.

As noted above the expectations treadmill is a term used by McKinsey to describe the way the share price has already built into it, expectations of future growth.

It is far too easy to say that companies should aim to deliver long term sustainable shareholder value and profits should be sustainable.

Most fund managers measure themselves on relative performance, as they market their services to clients as being better than their competitors. To sell retail funds requires top decile or even top three performance. The wholesale funds market is more sophisticated and recognises that beating the median over the long term is a significant achievement. However, below median performance is unacceptable. As most fund managers' personal bonus depends on relative performance this has become inbred in their culture and they tend to be in favour of such approaches for the executive directors of the companies in which they invest.

There is also a great danger in using relative TSR as a measure of management's performance and/or as the only measure in incentive plans. It is very difficult to find good competitors as few are of the same size, have the same debt/equity ratios, are in the same point in the business cycle and face the same competitive pressures. A company which is more highly leveraged than its competitors will usually beat its competitors if the general economy grows faster than expected, so relative TSR looks good. Acquisitions can also impact on TSR and can lead to favourable relative TSR results but usually incur higher risk. They may also increase tail risk.

Relative TSR has its place as a performance measure, but it should be looked at in combination with absolute movements in the company's share price as well as the risk being taken.

Volatility[4] may also influence share prices.

It should be noted that when shares vest the share retention rules and ownership guidelines will (or perhaps one should say can) increase the alignment of executives with total shareholder return. When choosing performance measures the impact of such rules needs to be considered.

40.5 Profit growth and p/e ratio

Management should be concerned about both creating value and conserving value.

- A company which aims foremost to conserve value will be cautious about investments in new product development, about moves into new territories and about leverage.

- A start-up company or early stage company will seek to grow quickly. However, such companies are risky. Statistical theory tell us that a company with a volatility of 40% can expect its share price to decline. It is not easy to explain this statistic to management, who will be fully committed to their plan. Nor to their non-executive directors who have approved the strategy. But it is a statistical fact.

The diagram below shows approximately what profit growth might be expected.

Most mature companies are a mixture of mature and innovation. They need to encourage innovation as otherwise they will decline and die. Once this has been understood, you will be in a position to develop the remuneration strategy and its incentive plan components.

---

[4] **Volatility – an explanation:**
Mathematically, volatility is the standard deviation of share prices expressed as an annual % figure. Thus we expect that the share price of a company with a 30% volatility (and Beta of 1) will be within 30% of the mean market change with probability 32%; and within 60% with probability 95%.
Companies with high Beta will have share prices which change faster than the market average. Volatility, in theory, should not affect the share price over the medium to long term, but option theory tells us that an option over a volatile share is worth more than one over a less volatile share.

Figure 39: Theoretical relationship of P/E ratio and expected future growth rate

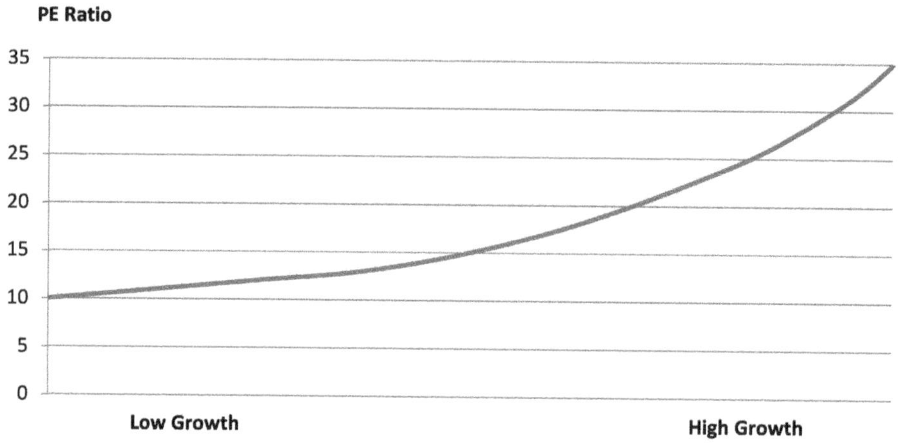

40.6 Accounting and other measures

When measuring performance, a distinction should be made between measures of operational performance and measures of financial performance. Both are important. Line management are tasked with managing the operational performance (growing sales, making pricing decisions, brand and product development, improving productivity, discovering new reserves and bringing them on-stream). There are a variety of ways to increase value of the company as illustrated in the diagram below.

The finance function, the chief executive and the board make the key financial decisions such as raising debt or equity finance, setting dividends, managing treasury, tax and risk hedging strategies. Finance decisions are often difficult to evaluate in the short term, as there may be fat tails and or long tails associated with them and future economic circumstances are always uncertain. There are numerous examples of companies who have boosted short term profits by increasing risk.

Lagging and leading indicators of performance

Accounting measures are lagging indicators of performance. They measure what happened in history. They may indicate the future if historic trends continue. But it might be like driving up the motorway and only looking out of the rear view mirror.

Profit is a lagging indicator of performance. It measures how well the company has done in the accounting period. It gives information neither about whether profits will grow or decline in the future, nor about the risks in the business model.

Figure 40: Ways to drive shareholder value

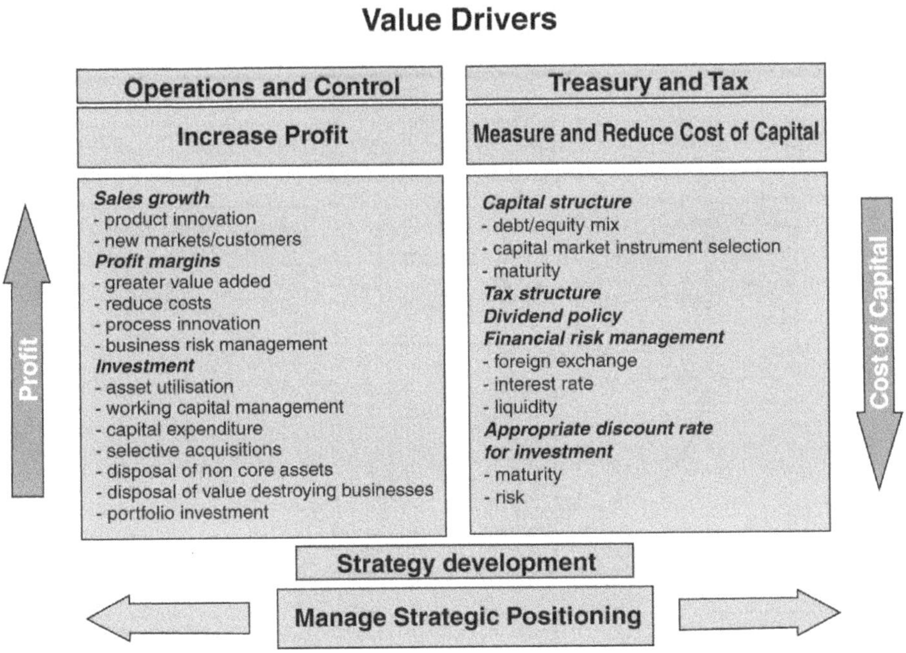

40.7 Balanced scorecard approach

Many people now favour the balanced scorecard as it contains a range of measures. A company may measure itself with, say, a 50% weighting of profits, but it also needs to measure key indicators of future success, eg sales growth, customer satisfaction, customer retention and new product pipeline.

The balanced scorecard is a strategic planning and management system that is used extensively in business and industry, government, and non-profit organisations worldwide to align business activities to the vision and strategy of the organisation, improve internal and external communications, and monitor organisation performance against strategic goals. It was originated by Drs Robert Kaplan (Harvard Business School) and David Norton as a performance measurement framework that added strategic non-financial performance measures to traditional financial metrics to give managers and executives a more 'balanced' view of organisational performance. While the phrase balanced scorecard was coined in the early 1990s, the roots of the this type of approach are deep, and include the pioneering work of General Electric on performance measurement reporting in the 1950's and the work of French process engineers (who created the *Tableau de Bord* – literally, a 'dashboard' of performance measures) in the early part of the 20th century.

Figure 41: The balanced scorecard

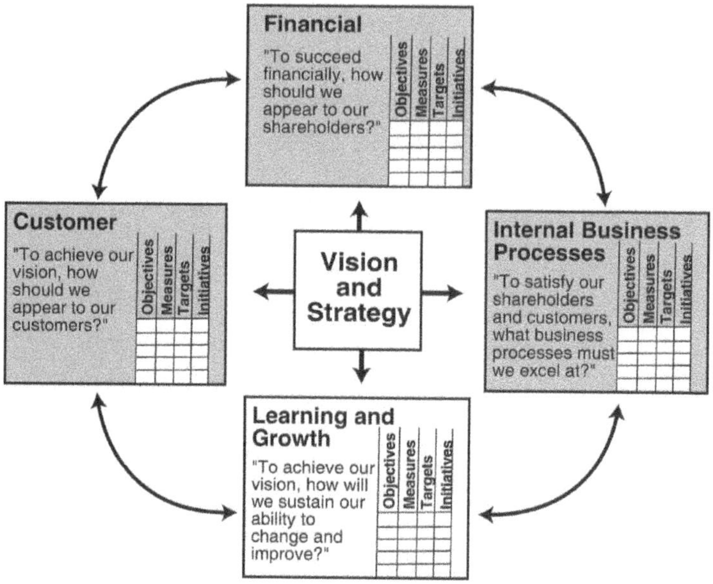

40.8 Sector Issues

Different sectors of business have different issues to face and adopt different strategies, which lead to different KPIs and incentive measures.

An easily understood example is easyJet plc as we are all familiar with the company and the product it offers. Its KPIs, as shown in its 2013 Strategic Report are:

1. **Safety**
2. **Customer Satisfaction measured by**
   - Satisfaction response as surveyed
   - On-time performance score
   - likely to recommend easyJet to others
3. **Staff turnover**
4. **Network Development**
   - Top 100 airports where easyJet is No 1 or No 2 airline
   - Market share of airports
5. **Financial Strength**
   - Revenue per seat

- Cost per seat excluding fuel
- Profit before tax/per seat
- ROCE
- Gearing
- Dividends and basic earnings per share

The following illustrate some typical measures for different sectors. Of course, the KPIs for a company should reflect its strategy and desired culture. Copying other companies without stopping to think about what is best for one's own company, is a recipe for disaster.

Table 33: Typical KPIs/incentive measures by sector

Sector	**Issues**	**Typical sector KPIs/incentive measures**
Banks	Risk, solvency, liquidity, customer service, short-termism, greed and irresponsibility	RROCE (risk adjusted rate of return on capital employed) Economic profit Company culture
Mining	Large capital investments with long term returns Commodity prices subject to macro-economic events	ROCE Project milestones Production targets in tonnes Reserves
Oil	Large capital investments with long term returns Commodity prices subject to macro-economic events	ROCE Project milestones Production targets in boepd Reserves in boepd Safety
Utilities	Regulator impact Customer service	Customer satisfaction Profit Relationships with regulators
Retail	Rapidly changing fashions Sustainability Fickle customers	Profit/EPS Like for like sales growth Profit margin ARPU (average revenue per unit or per customer) Customer churn Staff turnover
Manufacturing	Costs Quality and Service Product differentiation Product development Large capital investments with long term returns	Profit margin ROCE Customer satisfaction Market share
Hi Tech, IT, Media	Rapidly emerging/changing technologies Product development R&D effectiveness	Sales growth Market share ARPU

Sector	Issues	Typical sector KPIs/incentive measures
Pharmaceuticals	R&D effectiveness Patent life New products	Profits sales from new products Product development pipeline
Services	Costs Quality and Service Product differentiation Product development	Profit growth Profit margin Customer satisfaction Market share
Building and Construction	Buying land at the right time in the cycle Costs and quality of product Building efficiencies Ability to win obtain favourable planning decisions	Landbank Profits Average sale price per unit Profit margin
Luxury Goods	Image Brand Product differentiation Product development Rapidly changing fashions Sustainability Fickle customers	Market share Sales growth Profit
Insurance	Solvency Risk Investment returns Customer satisfaction	Profit Balance sheet measures Customer satisfaction Premium revenue growth increase in reserve for claims underwriting ratio reserve adequacy level increase in investment returns liquidity level frequency of complaints

40.9 Performance metrics may change over time

At different stages of a company's strategic development, it should change the focus and weighting of its performance metrics. Performance radar charts enable companies to keep track of changes in measures and performance against different measures. Good graphical presentation helps readers to assimilate a lot of information quickly.

In **Figure 42** the darker polygon represents the maximum bonus for each measure. If it is close to the centre, the performance measure has a low weighting; and the closer it is to the perimeter of the pentagram, the bigger the weighting for that performance measure.

The lighter polygon represents the actual result. Where the two coincide the maximum performance has been achieved. If the inner polygon stretches to two thirds of the outer then the performance is at 67% of target. In the diagram below the amount of the inner polygon in 2010 is much larger than 2009 and 2008, showing that performance has been improving.

Figure 42: Measuring performance

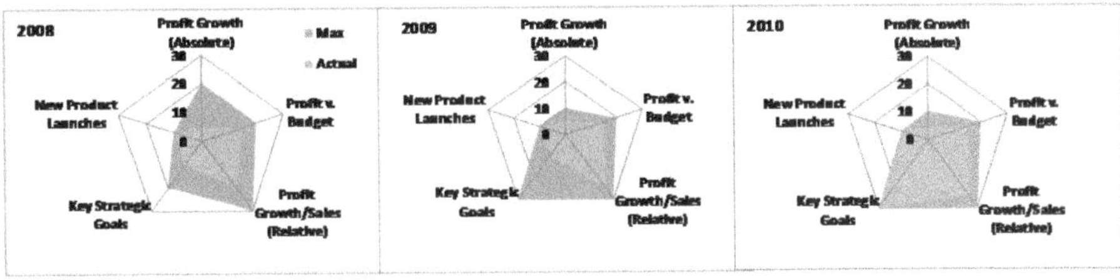

Tesco is a much admired company which uses the balanced scorecard throughout the organisation to explain what it thinks is important. The extract from the 2010 Tesco annual report pages 50–51 is shown in **Chapter 27** of this book.

40.10 Understand the impact of acquisitions

Acquisitions can be a key part of a company's growth strategy. It is often useful to distinguish between small acquisitions and large ones.

Small acquisitions are usually in related business areas and offer natural synergies. For example exploiting the existing client base to increase sales by selling a wider product range, cost savings of moving production to fewer sites, provision of additional resources to speed up the acquired company's growth and exploit its growth opportunities.

Large acquisitions often do not work. The academics tell us that 60% to 70% fail to achieve their objectives. Not all fail. Sometimes they are essential, for example to create global reach or to add product and enable cost savings (eg Smith Kline and Beecham; Glaxo and Welcome; Marsh and Sedgwick, which was a brilliant example of a purchase of an underperforming company where the acquiring company was able to raise the performance of the acquired company up towards its own standards where sales/employee were two to three times higher).

Some large acquisitions fall into the 'bet the shop' or 'bet the bank' category. The RBS acquisitions of NatWest and later ABN Amro illustrate this.

Large acquisitions require a huge increase in debt and/or the issue of additional equity. They also offer the chance to arbitrage tax, through the structuring of the location of debt. By increasing the financial gearing, the future profits will increase (but at the cost of increased foreseeable and unforeseeable risk, ie a potential fat tail). These are important aspects of measuring financial performance.

In all acquisitions there are dangers that expected synergies will not be realised and/or differences in cultures will lead to a drop off in operational performance.

40.11 Measure operational performance relative to peers

Profits rise in most companies when the economic backcloth is favourable!

Hermann Stern (the CEO of Obermatt[5]) came up with the ground-breaking idea that you can best measure management's performance when you take out the effect of the business cycle. You can do this by comparing performance with a group of companies that follow the same business cycle. For example:

Chart 8: Impact of the business cycle

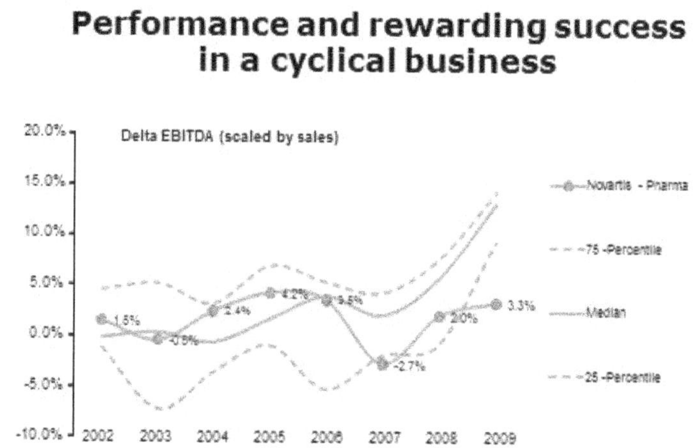

This approach is not suitable for all company circumstances, because:

- Annual results can depend on where a company is in the cycle. If it has just had a bad year then the bounce back can mean it is easy to come towards the top relative rank the following year.

[5] MM&K is the UK representative of Obermatt. www.obermatt.com provides more information on the Obermatt Bonus Index.

- Capital expenditure and investments may take some time to pay back and will not show through into profit for some time. All financial metrics are backwards looking. A balanced scorecard may be needed to cover all the key measures that executives must manage.
- Company gearing affects the extent to which the relative performance measurement approach takes out the cycle effects.

40.12 Motivational Impact

The Remuneration Committee and shareholders need to assess the motivational effect of the remuneration strategy and its cost effectiveness.

Executives will value different forms of remuneration differently. To illustrate this point consider the proverb 'a bird in the hand is worth two in the bush'. Thus £1 of salary is worth more than £1 of bonus. How much the £1 of bonus is worth to the executive depends on their estimate of the likelihood of the bonus plan paying out, a discount for the time value of money and a further discount depending on the degree to which the executive feels the events that affect the bonus outcome are beyond their control.

E	=	**O**	**x**	**T**	**x**	**C**
Bonus Efficiency (E)	=	Estimated Outcome (O)	x	Discount for Time (T)	x	Controllability Discount (C)

40.13 Incentive Gearing

Consider two plans. Both pay out 50% of maximum at target performance. Plan A starts to pay out at 50% of target and pays the maximum at 150% of target. This is a low geared plan.

Plan B starts to pay out at 90% of target and pays the maximum at 100% of target. This is a highly geared plan.

Both plans could have the same expected value.

Some people will argue B has the bigger motivational effect as the reward for each additional 1% above target is higher, as is the penalty for under-achievement. However as noted above, the motivational effect will depend on the degree to which the performance measures are viewed by those in the incentive plans as under their control.

Plan B also provides large rewards to executives who manage to negotiate soft targets. In the longer term, Plan B can be quite dysfunctional, unless the target setting process is robust.

Chart 9: Incentive gearing

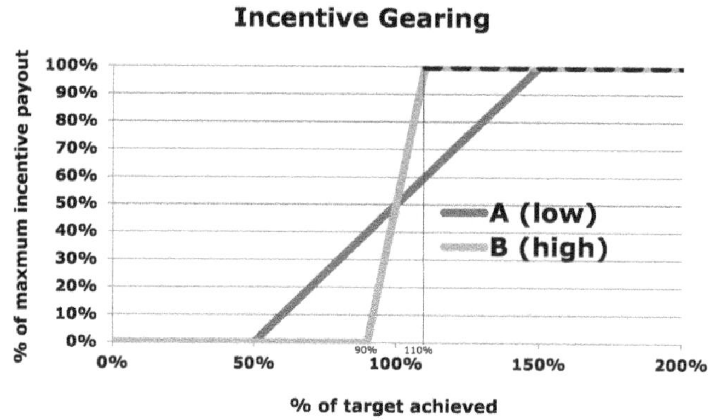

Plan B can be very de-motivating to executives if they see the targets are unachievable. It can promote short term behaviour.

The ABI/NAPF and others providing guidance on LTIP performance targets recommend that no payment should be for below median performance. The predominant performance metric has been relative TSR. This has led to the following typical scale with maximum LTIP payout at Upper Quartile (75 percentile) performance.

Chart 10: Incentive gearing and LTIPs

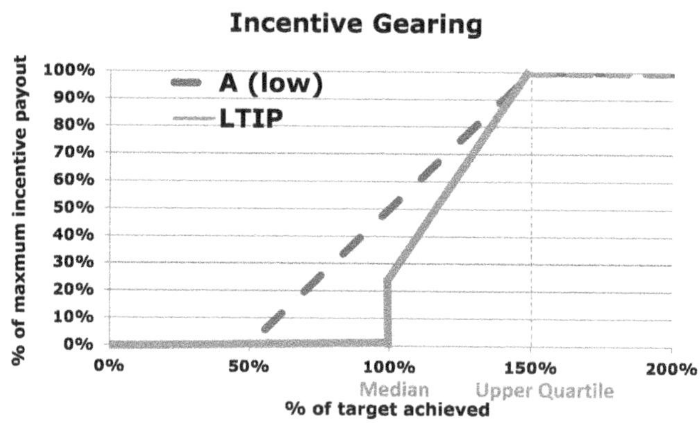

Given the capricious nature of share prices, this leads to incentive payouts that are highly geared and which many executives feel are largely beyond their control.

There is a strong argument for LTIP awards with Plan A type gearing (perhaps with a lower award level so as to provide the same Net Present

Value of the award). Indeed HSBC introduced a plan with no gearing in 2012 (the vesting was subject to clawback if performance was subsequently viewed as not warranting such a large payment as the plan would otherwise deliver).

40.14 Conclusions re Performance Measures

A variety of measures is usually the best approach, with some scope for judgment and interpretation by the Remuneration Committee and ideally the use of clawback/malus and non-payment of deferred bonus.

The choice of reward strategy as outlined in **Chapter 34** will influence the choice of performance measures.

An annual comparison of pay and TSR, or indeed any other single measure, is particularly misleading and potentially dangerous in assessing the justification of remuneration, but long-term trend information is useful. Shareholders should not be overly influenced by an annual comparison, but should focus on the long term as required by the new UK Corporate Governance Code, by regulators and other policy makers in the context of executive pay.

The private equity model is simpler and arguably works better. It consists of large amounts of heavily geared share incentives, modest salaries and annual bonuses linked to cash flow and other key targets. The focus is on meeting the bank debt covenants and liquidity events which enable investors to realise capital and managers to receive their rewards very tax-effectively. The share incentives are based on absolute growth, with a single large initial award at the time of the MBO. This should be contrasted with the typical quoted company which measures performance on a relative basis and has annual grants of incentives.

41 Performance Related Pay – Timing

Chapters 38 and **40** discussed the first two of the three key questions of 'how much', 'what for' and now it is time to discuss **when**.

This issue is inter-related to the other two because, as has been explained above, it is not always straightforward to assess whether performance is as good as it initially appears and whether it will be sustained in a way that leads to long term shareholder value.

41.1 The choices

The choice of when to pay remuneration is illustrated in the diagram below:

Pay now	**Pay next year**	**Pay in 3 years**	**Pay in 5 to 10 years**	**Pay after retire**
Salary				
Benefits				
				Pension
	Bonus (but not deferred bonus)			
		Deferred bonus		
		LTIPs		
		Share options	Share options	
			Share ownership guidelines and share retention rules	

Broadly speaking the company and its shareholders will prefer remuneration to be paid later, when everyone is sure that the performance has truly been delivered and has proved to be sustainable. In addition the ability to contractually tie people in and make it financially punishing for them to leave or expensive for competitors to buy out their deferred contingent pay is also of value to the company and its shareholders.

Executives will typically:

- discount future rewards[1]
- need access to cash now to spend
- wish to diversify their wealth and de-risk their portfolio of investments
- desire to have a share in the upside if the company is successful in the medium and long term.

41.2 How to decide

The Remuneration Committee must decide on one of the following or a combination of these:

- Follow market practice on the typical size of bonus, deferral and LTIP awards and share ownership guidelines and share retention rules. Doing this saves the need to think through this issue at all.
- Work out the Net Present Value of alternatives and discuss with management which they would prefer.
- Identify trends in best practice and become an early adopter of emerging best practice.
- Follow the analytical approach adopted in this book and identify the reward strategy most appropriate to the company. This will identify if there is a need to be different to market practice and provide a rationale to discuss with the executives and gain their commitment to the proposal.

There will be a negotiation with executives. If there is a danger that executives will leave if they do not get their way, and if there are no good internal successors if executives leave, the Remuneration Committee will have difficulty in negotiating an outcome that is in the best interests of the company in the long term.

1 PWC research indicates executives apply a discount rate of 30% per annum. See www.pwc.com/en_GX/gx/hr-management-services/publications/assets/making-executive-pay-work.pdf

42 Special Considerations

42.1 Introduction

The goals of remuneration policy are different for CEOs and other senior executives:

For the CEO

- Satisfy his personal desires for wealth, power, personal esteem and other priorities
- Motivate
- Retain
- Align with shareholders
- Be fair to CEO and to shareholders.

For CEO reports

- Enable good people to accumulate wealth over time
- Be attractive, so as to retain good people
- Assist CEO to manage his team
- Motivate
- Differential to CEO must be fair and logical to his reports
- Offer opportunities for career progression (not all will expect further promotion)
- Assist succession planning.

42.2 CEO pay

The CEO is the most visible executive in the company to the outside world. Thus the CEO's pay is open to particular scrutiny.

The nature of the role is such that there can be great scope to create or destroy value. This is reflected in the differentials in the pay of the CEO against that of other directors.

There is, however, a problem of short tenure. The average CEO is in the role for six years, so there is a significant probability that the CEO will last less than two, three or four years; but most boards think that 'of course that won't happen to us'. Whilst taking all steps to ensure that the appointment is the right one, the Remuneration Committee must consider all scenarios and ensure that the CEO package is skewed in the best interests of the company and not one-sided in favour of the CEO.

CEOs do not think and act like owners, because their pay creates and supports a culture of short termism, high risk taking and incentivises asymmetric risks.

Those are some of the problems. I think the CEO pay problem is not insoluble. The ten steps to success are:

- Plan for the long term when you can. One quarter of CEOs serve eight or more years in the role. Most if not all CEOs will expect to be successful, so design remuneration plans with an eight year horizon whenever you can.
- Succession planning. If there are lots of other good internal people who can fill vacant slots, companies will not have to recruit externally and pay top dollar.
- Keep data on the internal relativities of CEO pay versus the number two and the average of the top tier and the average of the next tier, over the last ten years. Review this each year and ensure that the relativities and changes in them are sensible and justifiable to shareholders.
- Emphasise teams and recognise leadership rather than superstars.
- Make sure the Remuneration Committee is made up of independent directors, capable of standing up to the CEO's demands. Ensure the Remuneration Committee appoints its own remuneration advisers, who are independent. Critically evaluate input from advisers who also receive fees from management for other consultancy work.
- Make sure the Remuneration and Nominations Committees work together and are aware of key executives' desires, motivations, ambitions, career plans, lifestyle goals, wealth and appetite for risk.
- Beware of risk and volatility. Do scenario analysis and consider, in particular, tail risk. Take more account of risk when setting incentive targets and the level and timing of payments.
- Be open with shareholders about the CEO's pay – how it is paid and why. Explain the link to performance and show this over a ten year period. Consult the shareholders to find out what they want. The UK Corporate Governance Code permits companies to explain why they do not wish to comply with the standard approach.

- Create an ownership culture. Make CEOs think about creating long term value.
- Use the lifetime earnings consulting tool to assess the long term value of the package to the CEO and to facilitate discussion of time horizons.

The CEO lifetime earnings model is a powerful executive remuneration tool which illustrates how a CEO might accumulate pay over time and computes his/her potential personal wealth over a number of years. The nature of CEO remuneration is complex as it is made up of several components and the timing of when the awards are made, when they vest and when they can be realised depends on detailed rules. The model (see **Table 32** in **Chapter 40** and **Figure 43** below) shows the following:

- Salary which is assumed to increase at x% per annum. A high flyer might achieve a higher % increase than average.
- Bonus is paid annually after the end of the year, but part may be a deferred bonus.
- The deferred bonus shows the amount which vests in the year. However depending on rules for sale of shares and share retention rules the executive may not be able to sell the shares at that time. He/she may also choose to hold on to the shares. In the model shown this is assumed and so the shares owned increases each time deferred bonus vests. The same assumption applies for shares received from LTIPs and options.
- Pension is not paid until after the executive retires.

One reason the model is powerful is that it shows how much the CEO might earn over his/her career if they stay with the company and it continues to grow. It forces a long term perspective rather than a get rich quick approach.

Figure 43: CEO lifetime earnings model and implications

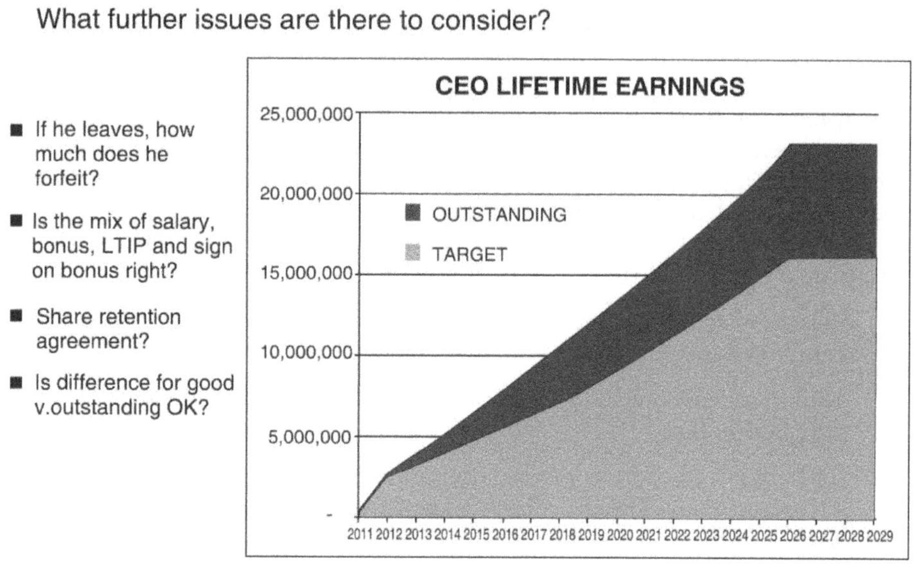

42.3 Other Executives

For senior executives below the CEO level, the remuneration may be aligned to a mix of measures based on the company, division, business unit and individual performance. The weighting attached to each will usually be different for each executive.

The reason for these differences is that their focus and is different and therefore their rewards should reflect this.

The process to set the reward strategy and remuneration policy should follow similar steps to that described above in **34.3**.

It is important to consider:

- The proportions of annual bonus and LTI that are linked to group, division or business unit and individual performance.
- The differential with the CEO at target and exceptional performance levels.

These two questions are interlinked. The outcome is a matrix such as shown in **Table 34**:

Table 34: Other executives' performance related pay as % salary

Tier	**Bonus**						**LTI**						**Total performance related pay**	
	Group	Div	Business Unit	Indi-vidual	Target % salary	Maximum % salary	Group	Div	Business Unit	Indi-vidual	Target % salary	Maximum % salary	Target % salary	Maxi-mum % salary
CEO	75%	-	-	25%	100%	200%	100%	-	-	-	100%	300%	200%	500%
2 FD	75%	-	-	25%	100%	200%	100%	-	-	-	100%	300%	200%	500%
2 Line	0	75%		25%	100%	200%	50%	50%	-	-	100%	300%	200%	500%
3	0	25%	50%	25%	50%	100%	50%	50%	-	-	25%	75%	75%	175%
4	0	0	75%	25%	30%	60%	100%		-	-	10%	30%	40%	90%

42.4 Special situations

Special arrangements for recruitment

It may not be possible to follow the normal remuneration practice when recruiting a new director, particularly a new CEO. In order to persuade an established director to move company he or she will usually need to be offered more than he or she currently receives. Moving company entails additional risk and risk requires additional compensation. In addition, he or she may have unvested long-term incentives and be giving up the time value of options. The recruiting company has two alternatives, either to buy out these options and incentives or to recruit someone who is cheaper!

If the recruiting company buys out the 'oldco' incentives, it needs to decide the form in which to compensate. This might be in the form of a guaranteed bonus, a payment of deferred shares or an additional option award. One creative approach is to persuade the recruit to buy some shares in 'newco' and award a matching number, some contingent only on service and some performance linked.

Special considerations for large global companies

Global companies have to compete globally for customers and employees. They will need to pay rates that are locally competitive, not necessarily at the top of the market, but not at the bottom. The issue is not just about salary, but about the structure of the package. For example, if the company has operations in the US and all its competitors issue a lot of options then granting small amounts of LTIPs is not competitive and may breed dissatisfaction in local employees unless the company can communicate very clearly why it wishes to pay differently to everyone else.

42.5 Banks

Banks have particular problems in relation to remuneration and attract much attention. Therefore a separate section on banks is below.

Banks have to follow the FCA Remuneration Code (see **Chapter 11**).

How Bank CEOs Should Be Paid

First consider some of the problems.

Part of the problem is that the US model of CEO compensation is broken. It has been for years. Enron, WorldCom, Tyco and Hollander are examples of the CEO having too much influence in setting their own pay. This is still the case as is shown by the large payoffs to the CEOs of companies such as NYSE, Citigroup and Merrill Lynch. Their Remuneration Committees approved the awards. Why?

Too many CEOs in the US have the combined Chairman and CEO role. They strongly influence the choice of their non-executive directors and ensure the Remuneration Committee consists of people minded to continue to vote through excessive pay awards. Sarbannes Oxley does not address this problem. Laws and regulations about caps on pay will not work. There is bad precedent in the law of unintended consequences, eg s 162 of the US Tax Code which limited pay to $1m per annum unless it was performance related, which led to a huge increase in the use of options and rises in previously sub-$1m salaries up to the $1m restriction.

Analysts contribute to the excessive pay levels of CEOs. Shares surge on the appointment of a big name CEO. Usually such CEOs command much higher compensation packages than lesser known internal appointments. To justify themselves, new CEOs have to do something. They adopt new strategies, which entail more risk. More risk = higher share price volatility = more chance of a large payout if successful. New hires, not unreasonably, negotiate safety nets[1], in case things don't work out as planned. But they win both ways. The poor shareholder has to suffer the burden and cost of an asymmetric reward package.

Academic research (performed by people who do not have a conflict of interest) is conclusive: 70% of acquisitions and mergers do not add value. Nevertheless, CEOs are strongly urged to do deals by investment bankers, strategy consultants, accountants and lawyers, whose fees are paid when the deal is done, irrespective of whether the deal generates superior shareholder returns in the long term. An example is RBS whose incentives strongly encouraged its CEO to buy ABN Amro – his odds of achieving the maximum incentive payments were much higher by doing the deal than if he had not.

Banking crises occurred in 1973, 1987/88, 1991/92, 1998, 2001/02 and 2007/08 – on average every six or seven years. But most long term incentive plans have a three year performance period, so allowing CEOs to maximise their expected income by adopting risky business strategies. The cycles are out of synch.

Too often banks pay CEOs as superstar entrepreneurs rather than as excellent administrators. The role of CEO is neither entrepreneur nor administrator, but somewhere in between.

---

[1] It is not the existence of the parachute that is the problem – it is the circumstances in which it can be opened. Once an executive has been in post for three years, surely six months' pay on leaving is adequate – if he is a good performer he will be able to find a new job within six months.

The ABI and others mean well, but their guidelines are too prescriptive and have:

- produced boilerplate remuneration schemes not suited to individual company circumstances; and
- allowed executives to maximise their personal wealth by following strategies that are not in the best interests of long term shareholders.

Bank CEOs do not think and act like owners, because their pay creates and supports a culture of short termism, high risk taking and incentivises asymmetric risks.

Those are some of the problems. The CEO pay problem is not insoluble. My ten steps to success (see **42.2**) are equally applicable to Bank CEOs.

Bankers' Pay

The way bankers are paid does not work. However to change bankers' pay will require leadership from the very top. I believe this will not occur until banks change the way their CEOs are paid.

The way bankers are paid does not work in a number of ways. In most cases the expected value of an executive's pay package will increase if his actions increase tail risk, tracking error and share price volatility. Executives receive asymmetric returns: they are not aligned with shareholders.

Most banks operate a simple rule that no more than 50% of net revenue should be paid out as pay. This is fine in theory, but most banks break their rule when income does not meet expectations.

Another typical rule is that a team/unit will share 20% of the profits between the team. The exact percentage will vary between the type of business, the particular skills of the team and their leverage in negotiation.

The banking pay problem is complex. A good start is to consider these ten issues:[2]

- Not enough bonus is deferred. The lack of handcuffs means that executives can move elsewhere and have too much leverage in their pay negotiations.
- No 'claw-back' if losses occur next year. Deferred pay should be contingent on future profits. A particularly case is when bonus is paid on 'paper' profits, which may not recur in future years, or which fail to generate cash. (Compare this with private equity companies, whose executives receive their incentive pay based on 'cash on cash' returns –

---

[2] These problems were prevalent before the Financial Crisis. The FCA Remuneration Code has addressed deferral, claw-back and risk.

so aligning their interests with investors. Their incentives are also usually based on whole fund returns, rather than on a share of each investment, thus if one project fails the others need to make up for it before the executives receive any incentive pay.)

- No link to risk. 'Profits' are not worth so much if there is a higher risk of losses.
- No cost of capital. If a team/unit needs capital (or trades off the parent bank's credit rating) then the cost of capital (risk adjusted) should be charged prior to sharing profits.[3]
- It is also very difficult in some areas to identify whether the financials have been due to good performance or to luck. Some will argue that it does not matter. It is a question of culture whether you pay for financial measures, behavioural measures under the control of management, or take account of both. The affordability argument drives companies to link rewards to financial measures. Making pay a variable cost rather than a fixed cost makes strategic sense when it is a large part of the cost base. But when guaranteed bonuses are awarded, the 'variable' cost becomes semi-fixed and the company loses both ways. Employees whose pay is based on financial measures may perceive higher levels of personal risk and demand a higher expected value of pay to compensate.
- Does Tiger Woods' manager get paid more than Tiger? Of course not. Not by a long way. Yet many banks assume the manager has to be paid more than those in his/her team. I am not saying the star culture is wrong, just remember that the team manager is not (always) the 'star'.
- Banking is a people business. Banks cannot grow without the people. If banks see an opportunity and wish to exploit it, they have to redeploy existing people or recruit externally. External recruits demand guaranteed bonuses. Hiring people is risky – at least 25% of senior recruits fail. Banks' HR strategy should be to recruit very few senior people, and instead to grow their own. Banks need to be tremendously effective in hiring high quality graduates/MBAs and growing them into partners/directors. Goldman Sachs do this very well.
- The pay problem starts at the top. As noted above, the US model of CEO pay is broken. Nevertheless, US pay levels and practices have influenced executives' expectations in the UK.
- Executives do not think and act like owners, because their pay does not encourage them to.
- The Turnbull Report asked Boards to consider: 'Do the company's culture, code of conduct, human resource policies, and performance

[3] Banks have started to change and many now do try to do this.

reward systems support the business objectives and risk management and internal control systems?' Did the Boards of Northern Rock, HBOS, Citigroup, Merrill Lynch and UBS consider this question? Boards need to pay more attention to Turnbull and establish ways to check that the incentives and pay arrangements support the culture the company wants.

Will things change? Will they get better?

There are four stages in change.

1. DENIAL>>> 2. ACCEPTANCE>>> 3. PLANNING>>> 4. IMPLEMENTATION.

Most bankers are just about moving from Denial to Acceptance. Many are still in denial mode. Shareholders are finding it difficult to exert influence. As a result change will be reluctant and slow.

Note to the second edition of this book. The section above on banks has not been changed from what was written in the first edition in September 2012. Writing now in January 2014 I see some shoots and acorns of change, but suspect that for most banks the challenge of changing their culture and their remuneration will be long, difficult and fraught with dangers.

43 Checklist for a remuneration strategy

Has the reward strategy achieved these objectives over the past few years and is the company confident the reward strategy is currently doing so?

Objective	Has it worked historically?	Is it currently working?
Motivates		
Retains good executives		
Alignment with long term success		
Promotes a culture focussed on long term success		
Enables recruitment of high quality executives		
Costs are not excessive if someone leaves		
Defensible to employees, customers and suppliers		
Fair split between executives and shareholders		
Meets the appropriate corporate governance standards and keeps shareholders happy		
Clearly explains: • How much will be paid • For what (ie what performance measures and what the targets are) • When it will be paid, including requirements to old shares and claw-back provisions • Mix of salary, bonus, deferred bonus, LTIPs, options pensions and other benefits, including key contractual terms		

A remuneration strategy should cover these four key elements:

1.	**The selection of appropriate comparator companies should reflect:** • types of executives required • importance of individual executives to delivery of business strategy • size of talent pool • comparator companies location – UK, Europe, global and • comparator companies size – sales, market cap, employees, assets, profits etc.

2.	**Pay market position(s) and linkage of pay market position to performance:** • at target payout, outstanding payout; and scenarios analyses of other performance levels • pay as % of share value created; profits; cash flow, dilution etc.
3.	**Mix of performance-related and not-performance-related elements:** • % performance related • % paid now, in one year, three years, five years, etc • % paid in cash; % paid in equity • Clawback and malus rules. • Use of discretion rules.
4.	**Alignment to shareholders' interests. Issues to be covered include:** • performance measures • upside and downside alignment • share ownership guidelines and • alignment to business strategy.

PART D

REMUNERATION DESIGN

In Part D we consider the design of each of the individual elements of remuneration:

- Salary
- Bonus
- Deferred Bonus
- Matching Bonus Plans
- Long term Incentive Plans (LTIPs)
- Share Options
- Share Ownership Guidelines and Retention Rules
- Pensions
- Other Benefits
- Contracts

The context within which this should be done has already been established in **Part C** which explained how to develop the remuneration strategy, including:

(i) how much will be paid

(ii) what for (ie what performance measures and what the targets are)

(iii) when it will be paid, including requirements to hold shares and claw-back provisions

(iv) the mix of salary, bonus, deferred bonus, LTIPs, options pensions and other benefits, including key contractual terms.

This section also covers how the overall package and performance should be benchmarked.

44 Benchmarking – when and how to do it

Companies should benchmark their remuneration when:

(i) they are worried that executives might leave by being attracted to a different remuneration package elsewhere.

(ii) they are recruiting or considering external recruitment and wish to know what other companies are paying.

(iii) the remuneration package is not generating the desired motivation, culture and behaviours.

The fact that executives might wish to be paid more is not a sound reason to benchmark remuneration.

44.1 Code and best practice guidance

The UK Corporate Governance Code says:

D.1 The Level and Components of Remuneration

> **'Supporting Principles**
>
> The remuneration committee should judge where to position their company relative to other companies. But they should use such comparisons with caution in view of the risk of an upward ratchet of remuneration levels with no corresponding improvement in performance.
>
> They should also be sensitive to pay and employment conditions elsewhere in the group, especially when determining annual salary increases.'

Best practice

The NAPF guidance says:

> 'Remuneration practices which would most likely cause concern and may trigger a voting sanction in the absence of sufficient explanation include:
>
> Over frequent re-benchmarking (NAPF suggests 3 – 5 year intervals)'.

'The NAPF will continue to press for prudence in executive pay and to oppose the use of peer benchmarking, unless it is applied infrequently (we suggest 3 – 5 yearly intervals) and then only as one part of the committee's assessment of remuneration policy.'

The ABI guidance says:

'Where Remuneration Committees seek to increase base pay the reasons should be fully disclosed and justified. Salary decisions should not be taken purely on the basis of simple benchmarking against peer companies. If benchmarking is used, the aim should not solely be to match the "median" but to provide a point of reference for determining the appropriate salary for the specific job. The constant chasing of a perceived median has been a major contributor to the spiralling levels of pay.

Remuneration Committees should also be aware of the multiplier effect that increases in base pay have on the overall quantum of remuneration.'

'The Remuneration Committee should seek specific points of reference against which the appropriateness of quantum can be judged. Useful reference points, which should help avoid unnecessary disagreements with shareholders, include:

- A stated policy that links aggregate remuneration to overall corporate performance. High pay for exceptional performance is consistent with this approach.
- The remuneration policy of the company as a whole. Remuneration Committees should assess the appropriateness of changes in the quantum of executive remuneration in the context of the company overall, including changes in employee remuneration more broadly.
- A relevant and fairly constructed peer universe. It is undesirable simply to use "median" pay as a benchmark since this, if used broadly, can lead to ratcheted increases in remuneration.'

The ABI and NAPF guidance is at odds with most companies, who as a matter of routine will check the competitiveness of their pay every year. Companies will not undertake a fundamental review of remuneration each year. However it is part of prudent risk management to keep an eye on developments elsewhere in the market place.

44.2 Methodologies

Methodologies are important. The choice of methodology can significantly impact on the benchmarking results produced.

In the following sections we cover:

- How to value the pay package
- Internal and external pay comparisons
- How to choose comparators
- Combining pay and performance
- Benchmarking the % of pay at risk, % dilution, gearing of incentives and performance measures.

44.3 How to value the pay package

In order to make comparisons between and within companies, methodologies must be agreed which value the different components and enable the total value of the package to be assessed.

Some parts of remuneration are easier to value than others. Some choices are clear-cut whilst for some pay components there may be several different choices which could be useful, and sometimes only by looking at scenario analysis can the full picture be seen.

Salary is easy to value. Either the current contractual salary, or the amount paid in the year can be used.

For **benefits** (other than pension) the taxable value is used.

Pension is much more complicated. There is potentially a tax free lump sum at retirement of 25% of the HMRC approved fund. If the plan is a defined benefit, then the pension will be paid after retirement for x years, until the executive dies and then the widow(er) will receive the widow(er)'s pension until he/she dies. The defined benefit is calculated as a percentage of the final pensionable salary. It is an option on the final salary, on their expected years of service and the likely longevity of the executive. The value of this depends on how healthy the executive is. His or her perceived value of money that they will not receive for years will vary enormously from individual to individual. The Government's DRRR (see Chapter 28) has a rough rule of thumb of 20 times the increase in accrued benefit in the year and this approach looks likely to become the standard for comparisons.

A defined contribution or money purchase pension (DC) is paid after retirement via draw down or annuity. The value ascribed to it is the value of the contribution paid by the company in the year.

No adjustment is made for the tax effectiveness of pension.

Bonus. Should the comparison be of the actual bonus paid, the target or the maximum opportunity? Should deferred bonus be discounted? If so, how? Should it be the amounts paid in the year, or the amounts awarded in respect of the year, which can be paid in the year after the performance period, deferred for several years, or if awarded in the form of nil cost options may not be exercised for ten years? Also the share price at sale may be different to the share price at award. Which should be used for valuing bonus paid in deferred shares?

If there is a matching bonus award with performance conditions attached, then by convention this is regarded not as bonus, but as a long term incentive award and valued as such.

LTIP and Options

Some questions to consider are:

- Should it be the expected value of award (eg as in IFRS 2, but with no discount for the risk of leaving before vesting) or actual received? Or perhaps the value of the award if the business plan was achieved?
- How to discount future earnings which are high risk and may be subject to many factors outside the executive's control?
- Whether to include previous awards (from earlier years) and if so how to do it?
- Scenario analysis? Should there be a single figure of comparison or a range of figures?

By convention there are three figures which are used.

(i) The expected value of awards made in the year

(ii) The potential value of gains from awards made in the year using scenarios of threshold, target and maximum

(iii) The actual amounts of awards that vest in the year or in the case of share options the notional gain at the date of vesting.

It should be noted that the first and second are useful in assessing the decisions made by the remuneration committee in the year; and the third is useful in reviewing the decisions made in the past and assessing how well the remuneration committee has done its job, and is used in disclosure of remuneration in the DRRR.

The lifetime's earnings model (see **Figure 43** in **Chapter 42**) enables the consideration of previous awards as well as awards made in the year.

The table below summarises the approach MM&K use when comparing remuneration policy.

Table 35: Definitions and measurement of pay

	Definition	**Measurement**
SALARY and FEES	Full salary/fee.	Cash paid in respect of the year.
BENEFITS	All taxable benefits including recruitment and tax payments, dividends received in cash over the vesting period of long term incentives and deferred awards.	Taxable value.
PENSION	All pensions related benefits including: (a) cash in lieu of pension (b) company contributions to funded money purchase schemes (c) benefit achieved in year from participating in a defined benefit pension plan (d) benefit achieved in year from participating in a unfunded retirement schemes (e) benefit achieved in year as a result of participation in unfunded money purchase schemes.	Cash values for (a) and (b). For (c) and (d), the additional value achieved in year calculated using the HMRC methodology for assessing lifetime limits. For (e), the increase in value of the lump sum the director would receive over the reporting period, on the assumption that the scheme provided for a lump sum. See above for more detail.
BONUS	Full bonus awarded in relation to the performance year.	Total cash equivalent including amount deferred. Measure deferred element at expected value on date of award. (plus sometimes scenario analyses of policy, target and maximum are modelled)
LTIP	All other awards where final vesting is determined as a result of the achievement of performance conditions that are measured over a period of greater than one year (eg shares under long term incentives, matching shares under deferred bonus arrangements and share options). Where there are no further performance conditions for long term incentives, awards granted related to current performance year.	Estimated value at date of award. (in addition, scenario analyses of policy, target and maximum are sometimes modelled)

If a figure is for a part year, it is normally annualised to enable valid comparisons.

44.4 Internal comparisons

Pay can be compared either internally, ie within the company, or externally, ie to other companies.

Internal comparisons are much more visible and therefore are more important.

Questions to consider are:

- How much more should the CEO be paid?
- What should the relativities be with:
  - the top team
  - the next tier(s) and
  - the average employee?
- How should this trend over time?
- How should this vary with performance?

Figures 44 and 45 show methodologies which can be used to illustrate these points.

Figure 44: Pay benchmarking of internal relativities

	CEO	Tier 2	Tier 3	Tier 4
Salary	£290,000	£200,000	£	£
Bonus (max % salary)	100%	100%	80%	35%
LTIP award % salary	150%	90%	70%	50%
Pension	6.5%	6.5%	6.5%	6.5%
Other	Recruitment Award (worth c.£2million, so far)	Recruitment Award (worth c£500k, so far)		

Figure 45: Internal relativities of pay and performance

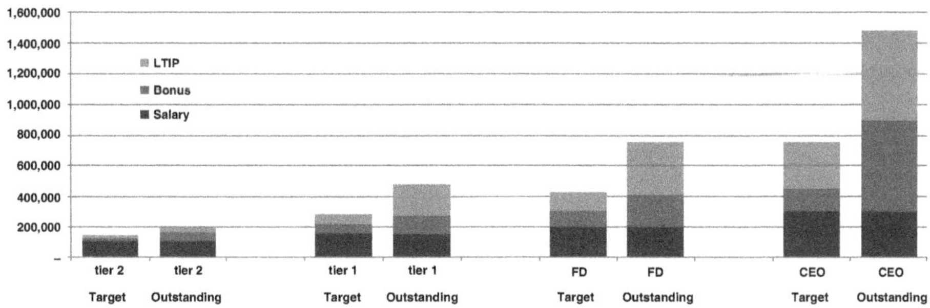

Another model which is useful is the lifetime earnings comparison (see **Sections 40.2** and **42.2**.

44.5 External comparisons

Comparisons to other companies are harder to undertake. Companies and roles are rarely directly comparable. Some companies overdo this aspect in developing reward strategy. It is more relevant if you have lost good people or cannot recruit the calibre you want.

The UK Corporate Governance Code, ABI and NAPF are all very wary of external benchmarking.

However, institutional investors in quoted companies are very keen that remuneration packages are in line with comparator groups. This can be an extremely dangerous practice when it comes to base salaries as the comparator group chosen for a particular organisation will often, at the urging of the CEO, include businesses rather larger than the company itself.

This can result in companies feeling they have to increase the remuneration of their directors to the median level of the comparator group. Effectively you get locked into what might be called an 'upper quartile syndrome' in which everybody is trying to pay slightly higher than their competitors in the comparator group. This is an inevitably inflationary spiral and has led to significant overpayment of Boards in some large quoted plc groups.

44.6 How to choose comparators

Ideally comparators should be in the same sector, in the same business, about the same size, in similar geographies, with similar strategies and are those companies to which executives are recruited from and move to. In practice some sort of compromise has to be made to these criteria.

Good comparators are usually those in a range of half to two times turnover, or if comparing on the basis of market capitalisation or assets, in a range of half to two times that measure.

Sometimes much bigger companies will have a Divisional MD whose roles might be comparable to the CEO.

Likewise sometimes divisional MDs may be comparable to the CEOs of smaller companies.

Table 36: How to choose comparators

Company	Market cap (pound m)	Turnover/Sales (pound m, last reported)	Number of Employees	Sector	Subsector	Position	Salary	Bonus	Deferred Bonus	LTI	Pension and Other Benefits	Total
1	32,930	31,708	19,375			Chief Executive Officer						
2	6,475	4,779	4,833			Chief Executive Officer						
3	5,302	4,307	9,150			Chief Executive Officer						
4	6,602	3,312	3,379			Chief Executive Officer						
5	2,772	2,610	8,007			Chief Executive Officer						
6	2,981	2,023	6,412			Chairman						
7	2,495	1,477	3,408			Chief Executive Officer		too big for CEO comparison but Div MDs may be comparable to your CEO				
8	2,013	1,007	2,589			Managing Director						
9	1,586	823	3,025			Chief Executive Officer						
10	260	792	500			Managing Director						
11	1,031	671	3,127			Managing Director						
12	651	623	3,209			Chief Executive Officer						
13	1,122	588	2,037			Chief Executive Officer						
14	552	476	2,922			Executive Chairman						
15	474	401	1,178			Chief Executive Officer						
16	392	322	500			Managing Director		Good comparators - half to 2 x turnover				
17	305	265	500			Chief Executive Officer						
18	231	250	1,318			Chief Executive Officer						
19	281	238	1,191			Chief Executive Officer						
20	233	208	734			Chief Executive Officer						
21	108	190	809			Chief Executive Officer						
22	218	184	732			Managing Director						
23	128	176	621			Chief Executive Officer						
24	142	175	619			Deputy Chairman						
25	203	170	824			Chief Executive Officer						
26	65	148	732			Chief Executive Officer						
27	113	138	506			Chairman						
28	71	117	413			Chairman						
29	177	115	406			Chairman						
30	4	103	457			Managing Director						
31	69	101	385			Chief Executive Officer						
32	192	96	433			Chief Executive Officer						
33	155	78	274			Chief Executive Officer						
34	121	53	687			Managing Director						
35	147	43	20			Chairman		too small for CEO comparison to your CEO but your Div MDs may be comparable to these CEOs				
36	147	43	25			Chief Executive Officer						
37	147	43	21			Chief Executive Officer						
38	147	43	27			Deputy Chairman						
39	129	40	810			Chairman						
40	129	40	830			Managing Director						
41	129	40	810			Chief Executive Officer						
42	104	36	253			Chairman						

A 'good' robust comparator group will be one where the median size of the comparators is similar to the company, ideally in terms of turnover, market capitalisation, employees, assets, % of turnover overseas, etc.

It is interesting to note that for example in both the oil & gas and basic resources (ie mining, etc) industries, the median CEO's total remuneration is below that of those in companies of a similar market capitalisation in other sectors. However when evaluated across companies of similar turnover they become the highest remunerated. This is because in most sectors, the major determinant of market capitalisation, the current perceived value of the business, is based on current turnover, profits and future growth which are reflected in its P/E ratio. This is also true for established (producing) companies in the oil and gas and basic resources sectors, but for companies where the focus is on exploration, a company's market capitalisation is often made up principally by its perceived future value of income, which might not arise until many years into the future. As a result, a comparison of the remuneration of CEOs based on market capitalisation would be unfair, as other sectors would comprise larger, more developed, more complex companies with greater turnover.

Thus, when looking at this type of analysis, it is important to use the most reflective measure of business 'size' for that industry.

Utilities pay lower total remuneration than other companies. They operate in a highly regulated environment and to pay too much would risk a negative reaction from their regulator.

Many of the sector differences vary for different size companies. For example small start-up fast growth telecoms companies pay much less than similar sized other companies, but mature telecoms companies pay similar rates to most other large companies.

Cautionary notes about using survey data:

The MM&K/Manifest Executive Director Total Remuneration Survey provides a good estimate of the remuneration market and excellent background data. It complements, rather than being a substitute for, detailed individual company benchmarking data.

In all cases judgement is required.

Although sector can be a key driver of pay, the degree of internationalism, the complexity of the business and many other factors impact on pay levels. Consequently size and sector differentials should not be blindly followed in the design of future awards for executives.

Note regarding TSR comparators in performance conditions in LTIPs:

The choice of comparators in TSR performance conditions in LTIPs and options requires different criteria in their choice then remuneration comparisons. As TSR is a percentage, it is normalised for size and much large and smaller companies can be included in such groups.

How to measure and allow for performance

A company which is performing in the upper quartile might expect its pay to also be in the upper quartile. This issue is discussed further below (see **44.8**, **46.7–46.13** and **47.12–47.16**).

44.7 How to compare jobs

Comparing CEO jobs is relatively easy as the CEO role in most companies is similar.

The size of the other roles will be different. The use of some form of job evaluation methodology may be appropriate, such as the Hay Guide Chart and Profiling Method. However such comparisons are not easy for Non-Executive Directors or external shareholders to understand and can be viewed as black box methods. They are time-consuming to do and complicated job evaluation methods are not appropriate in an environment when jobs and job responsibilities are changing quickly.

Alternatively a simple comparison using reporting levels and taking note of the turnover, profits, assets and employees of each of the divisional heads may be sufficient.

A balance has to be struck between the black box methods and the felt fair approaches[1] which are at least transparent.

It should also be noted that clarity of understanding of each role, what it is accountable for, the key performance targets for the coming period(s) and how they will be measured is crucial to performance management and in some cases the effective management of risk. In the bubble period of banking, these aspects of human resource management got lost with consequent huge destruction of shareholder value.

44.8 Combining pay and performance

The usual approach is to compare the actual and the target and maximum opportunity with competitors' actual and expected payments.

---

1 The felt-fair test is derived from the felt-fair principle formulated by Eliot Jaques and used by job evaluators who commonly use it to test the results of a job evaluation. See Michael Armstrong and Angela Baron, *The Job Evaluation Handbook* (1995), p 41 (books.google.co.uk/books?isbn=0852925816).

Figure 46: Comparison of target and maximum with market pay data

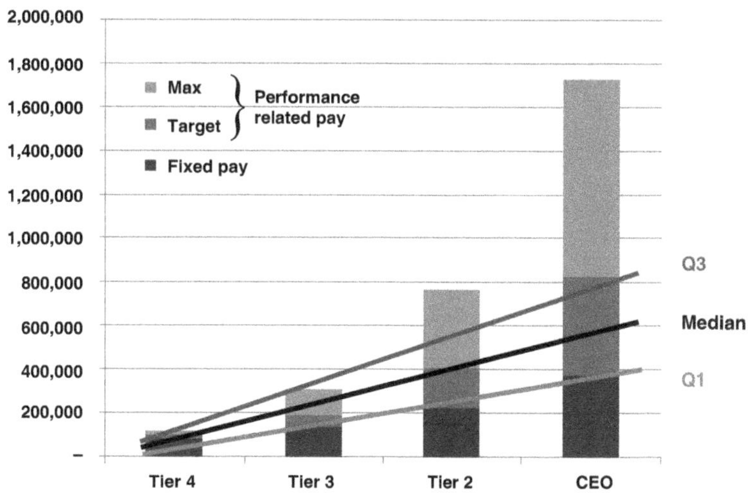

More detailed analysis of each individual comparator company's remuneration under a range of scenarios is very time-consuming to do. They may also be very difficult to do, because companies perform differently and have different starting positions, eg leverage, exposure to different geographies, technological disruptive factors, etc. Consequently these factors can make the results less meaningful.

44.9 Total remuneration – what it is and why it matters

The Remuneration Committee has to make decisions each year about directors' pay. The consequences of these decisions may not be apparent until some years in the future. Nevertheless the Remuneration Committee needs a methodology of evaluating its decisions, including:

(i) best estimate of the net present value of awards made in the year

(ii) scenario analyses of potential value of awards made in the year

(iii) value of awards that vest in the year and options exercised

(iv) value of cash pay received in the year plus taxable value of benefits plus the increase, from the start to the end of the year, in gains to date of deferred bonuses and LTIPs and options.

In making its decisions on executive directors' pay, the Remuneration Committee must also think about previous awards and the degree to which they impact on rewards.

Total Remuneration Levels

The market data tells us that total remuneration is related to size of the company and to sector.

In developing a remuneration strategy a key decision is the proportion of remuneration that is performance related and, within that, the proportion that is linked to annual and longer term incentives.

Data on market practice is in **Chapter 32**, including pay levels, increases, mix and differentials.

45 Salary

45.1 Code and best practice guidance

The UK Corporate Governance Code is not very forthcoming about salaries. It states the Remuneration Committee:

> 'should also be sensitive to pay and employment conditions elsewhere in the group, especially when determining annual salary increases.'

No other explicit guidance is given on salaries but, of course, the comments about total remuneration need to be considered:

> **'D.1 The Level and Components of Remuneration**
>
> Main Principle Levels of remuneration should be sufficient to attract, retain and motivate directors of the quality required to run the company successfully, but a company should avoid paying more than is necessary for this purpose. A significant proportion of executive directors' remuneration should be structured so as to link rewards to corporate and individual performance.
>
> The remuneration committee should judge where to position their company relative to other companies. But they should use such comparisons with caution in view of the risk of an upward ratchet of remuneration levels with no corresponding improvement in performance.'

Best practice guidance

Institutional investors in quoted companies used to be very keen that remuneration packages were in line with comparator groups. However in 2010/11 they changed their stance and recognised that benchmarking salaries every year is potentially inflationary and may lead to a ratcheting of remuneration which is not supported by underling performance.

The NAPF has suggested that in general, for executive directors:

> '**Base pay** increases should be capped at inflation, unless there are sound and compelling reasons for a different approach.'

The ABI guidance on directors' salaries is:

'Base pay should be set at a level which reflects the role and responsibility of the individual, whilst respecting the principle of paying no more than is necessary.

Where Remuneration Committees seek to increase base pay the reasons should be fully disclosed and justified. Salary decisions should not be taken purely on the basis of simple benchmarking against peer companies. If benchmarking is used, the aim should not solely be to match the "median" but to provide a point of reference for determining the appropriate salary for the specific job. The constant chasing of a perceived median has been a major contributor to the spiralling levels of pay.

Remuneration Committees should also be aware of the multiplier effect that increases in base pay have on the overall quantum of remuneration.'

45.2 Considerations in setting salary policy

The annual guaranteed salary is the foundation of the executive remuneration package in the UK. Base salary is often a key factor in determining the level of other elements of the package: defined benefit pension is based on final salary; defined contribution pension is a percentage of salary; annual bonus is usually calculated as a percentage of salary; and the value of awards of LTIPs and options are set as a percentage of salary. Getting the salary right is therefore the most important remuneration issue facing most employers in the UK.

Salary agreements for managers and directors are universally based upon payment monthly in arrears, with the employer being responsible for the necessary deductions of employee and employer's National Insurance and any tax, so that an individual receives a net sum each month from which no further deductions will be made.

45.3 Differentials

Salary differentials should reflect the added value the individual can make, the job responsibilities and the market practice. The MM&K/Manifest 2012 Total Remuneration Survey showed how the differentials are larger in larger companies.

Salary of 2nd highest paid director as % CEO							
	Turnover £ millions						
	<30	**31–100**	**101–300**	**301–1,000**	**1,001–3,000**	**3,001–10,000**	**>10,000**
Q1	62%	65%	61%	62%	60%	56%	63%
Median	72%	71%	69%	68%	66%	61%	67%
Q3	90%	83%	80%	79%	77%	67%	74%

Another way to look at this is the ratio of the CEO pay versus the second highest paid.

Salary of CEO as a multiple of the 2nd highest paid director							
	Turnover £ millions						
	<30	**31–100**	**101–300**	**301–1,000**	**1,001–3,000**	**3,001–10,000**	**>10,000**
Q1	1.11	1.21	1.25	1.26	1.30	1.48	1.35
Median	1.39	1.41	1.44	1.46	1.52	1.63	1.50
Q3	1.62	1.55	1.64	1.62	1.67	1.80	1.59

Aligning other directors' pay to the CEO reflects the personal value add of the director vis-à-vis the CEO and highlights succession issues.

At lower levels, a 30% to 50% premium between subordinate and boss might be typical, although on promotion a rise of 10% to 15% might be awarded as this will allow further progression over time to the market rate. The Remuneration Committee needs to ask why the CEO and other directors should be different to other employees. This can be justified by the extra added value required of the role. The corollary is that there should be clear and tough performance expectations.

The above data shows that in the larger companies, the CEO is generally paid 50% more than the second highest paid director, but in some companies the CEO is paid twice as much as the second highest paid director. If this is a true reflection of the added value of the CEO vis-à-vis other directors, it highlights the gap between these roles and a potential problem of internal succession.

In smaller companies, the differentials between the CEO and other executive directors are lower – the second highest paid director is paid at 75% of the rate of the CEO. This means that the CEO, whilst the boss, is paid only one third more than the others and suggests he/she is more likely to support a team approach.

It should also be noted that in terms of pay, size matters. Bigger companies pay bigger salaries, bigger bonuses, much bigger long term incentives and bigger pensions. Added together this gives them far bigger total remuneration.

Remuneration increases in line with the logarithm of turnover or market capitalisation. For smaller companies this is a straight line relationship. For larger companies, executive directors are on a curve to infinity. **Chart 4** in **Chapter 32** highlights the very different make-up of the package of the largest companies.

In small companies, directors' remuneration packages are a significant cost, which limits the scope to pay more and acts as a control mechanism on the potential total remuneration. In large companies, directors' remuneration is a small proportion of total costs and profits and no such internal constraint exists.

When a CEO achieves superstar status, this may create problems in itself. There are numerous examples of CEOs who have achieved an exalted status (with commensurate power and remuneration packages), where the performance of the company has subsequently faltered, eg Jack Welch at GE, Jeff Skilling at Enron, Conran Black at Hollinger, Feld at Lehmans, Chuck Prince at Citigroup (who left with a $38m package in bonuses, shares and options after multibillion-dollar write-downs), Stan O'Neal at Merrill Lynch (who retired after announcing losses of $8bn, taking a final pay deal worth $161m), and in the UK Lord Browne at BP, Lord Simpson at GEC/Marconi, Asil Nadir at Polly Peck, Sir Fred Goodwin at RBS and Bob Diamond at Barclays.

A large CEO-to-Number-Two gap may hint that there really is no Number Two—at least not in terms of succession planning. It suggests the company does not have a strong candidate for the top spot, so what happens tomorrow if the CEO is gone?

The Remuneration Committee needs to consider very carefully how much extra value the CEO creates and how much he/she should be paid for doing so compared to the next tiers of management. In many companies the development and delivery of the business strategy is a team effort. If one person is taking too big a slice of the pie, then the others will feel their contribution is under-rewarded. Remuneration Committees should not be misled by the often fallacious arguments in the press that a company's performance is the work of just one person. This is press myopia and is convenient for them as it makes the story interesting for their readers and easy for them to write. It is rarely like this in practice.

Even when this is the case (and I argue it should only be the case in far fewer cases than currently occur), the Remuneration Committee needs to be even more vigilant that the risks of over ambitious investment strategies and expensive acquisitions are most carefully managed.

This is why it is so important that the Remuneration Committee understand the business strategy and the drivers of value in the different parts of the business and the relative contribution of the different members of the senior executive team.

A problem facing companies with significant overseas interests is that the key executive cadre running the US, German and maybe Japanese divisions might well earn salaries above those paid for the main Board in the UK. This anomaly is usually overturned in terms of total remuneration, as the main

Board are entitled to higher bonuses and much bigger share or option allocations. Most groups have come to terms with the reality of international trade, when the head office in the UK, not one of the world's highest-salaried executive societies, and it is not unknown for group CEOs to be paid less in salary terms than the US, German and Japanese divisional heads who report to them.

A typical structure might be as follows:

	% of CEO		**% of tier above**	
	Salary	**Total Remuneration**	**Salary**	**Total Remuneration**
CEO	100%	100%		
Tier 2	65%	60%	65%	60%
Tier 3	40%	30%	60%	50%
Tier 4	25%	15%	60%	50%

US relativities

Depending on the industry, the median multiple of the top to the second-highest-paid executive is anywhere from 1.35 to 2.34, according to a recent Conference Board[1] report. Furthermore, the multiple ranges from 2.95 to 4.61 when comparing the first and fifth highest-paid people. (In dollars: $2.5 million, $1.3 million, and $763,000 median compensation for Numbers One, Two, and Five, respectively.)

JP Morgan allegedly wouldn't invest in a company whose CEO earned more than 50 percent above the next officer down. Likewise, GE chief executive Jeffrey Immelt told the *Financial Times* that to motivate staff and avoid excesses, CEO pay should remain a small multiple of that of the most senior twenty-five managers. Immelt asked:

> 'Should the CEO make five times, three times, or twice what this group make? That is debatable, but twenty times is lunacy.'

Immelt's 2010 compensation was $21.4 million, about 1.5 times that of GE's next-highest-paid executive.

Jim Heim, managing director at US compensation consultancy Pearl Meyer & Partners said:

> 'I get concerned when I see that a CEO makes five times more than the Number Two. Some groups of investors get concerned when it's more than three times more.'

---

[1] http://www.conference-board.org

When a company head earns far more than his management team, the logic goes, it indicates that the CEO is king and everyone else a courtier.

High ratios are uncommon. Ratios of CEO to 'Number Two' are smallest in financial and business-service sectors and largest in food and tobacco industries, indicating the extent to which companies in various fields distribute power between the CEO and the executive team—not surprising given the prominence in finance of the CFO, who's often in the second role, making between 40 and 60 percent of the CEO's pay. A 'C-suite' may also wield less power at other, especially smaller, firms, where the CEO wears many hats. At times the CEO is the main strategist, with more value wrapped up in his personality. You can see this at companies in the retail market, like Ralph Lauren, where without that person, the value of the enterprise is reduced.

45.4 Salary levels

As noted above there are considerable differences by sector and there are concerns about the dangers of benchmarking. However a good sense check and starting point for any potential further analyses is to look at similar sized companies in terms of turnover and market capitalisation.

Salary CEO £000							
	Market capitalisation £ millions						
	<30	**31–100**	**101–300**	**301–1,000**	**1,001–3,000**	**3,001–10,000**	**>10,000**
Upper Quartile	250	319	402	519	652	829	1,170
Median	193	244	328	425	525	736	950
Lower Quartile	145	195	253	350	438	644	864

Source MM&K/Manifest Executive Director Total Remuneration Survey 2012

45.5 Annual salary reviews

A salary grid with higher increases for higher performers is the recommended approach for most levels of staff. This leads to progression over time to a salary commensurate with performance. These concepts are illustrated in **Figure 47** below which show progression for A, B and C performers and the salary increase grid which would drive this.

Figure 47: Salary progression and salary increase grids

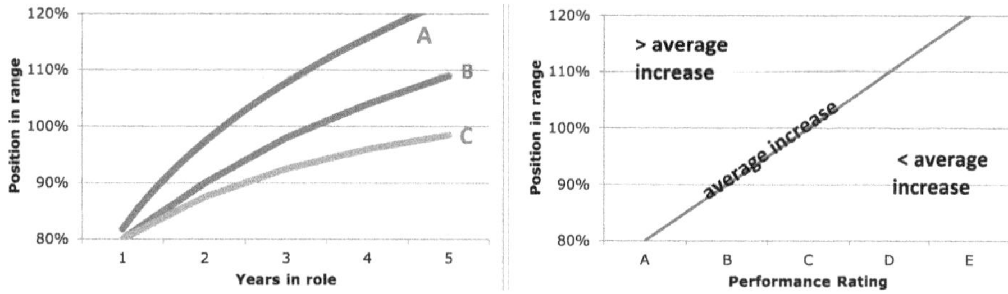

However such concepts do not work for CEOs. Most CEOs think they are outstanding or at least very good and when they see the salary increase grid will want to be given above average increases. This will be inflationary.

Also it is impossible to recruit a new CEO and tell him that he is going to be at the bottom of his range or 90% of the range.

A much better route is to agree upon hire (or on promotion) that the CEO's salary will be fixed and will not increase, or that it will increase only at the same rate as the average employee in the company. This will create the right culture whereby the CEO knows he/she only gets additional rewards if their performance related rewards pay out.

Sometimes, on promotion, a Remuneration Committee may decide to appoint internally and set the new CEO's pay so that it is increased to the full CEO rate over two or even three years. This can avoid the annual report showing a huge increase. It is worth looking at the CEO lifetime rewards analysis (see **Chapter 42**) before making such a decision as it may be quite small in the context of long term rewards. It may be better to trade off a higher salary for a smaller exit compensation terms of say six months rather than 12 months in the event of exit. In view of the age legislation rules, it can be quite difficult to exit a CEO without paying off their contract in their final year, so this point requires careful thought on appointment.

It is however normal for salaries to be reviewed once a year. Main board salaries in quoted companies are reviewed by the Remuneration Committee; other salaries in such groups tend to be reviewed by the CEO, divisional director or head of department. In private companies, senior salaries are normally reviewed by the CEO or Chairman and then approved by the Board, with the same below Board levels as used in fully quoted groups.

Most companies are increasingly using an overall review grid, whereby the Board agrees how much they can afford next year in terms of an increase in salaries, which is a fixed overhead once it has been agreed. The CEO would therefore issue a note to all those reviewing their subordinates' salaries in which he or she makes it clear that the total increase in the salary bill for each department could be no higher than, say, 4% and within this discretion can only be used over half the amount, ie 2%. In practice this means that the best performers could get an increase of 6% and the worst performers could only get an increase of 2%. The use of this system has increased but some companies allow the differential to range from, say, 8% in the case above to 0%. However, people not given a salary review when others in the department have received an increase are likely to be fairly disaffected. If they are not worth a review, it might be better to bite the bullet and allow them to go before the review takes place.

Since 1993, there have been sustained year-on-year increases in directors' salaries among the largest companies. Among the constituents of the FTSE 100, the median base salary for the highest paid director (either the CEO or the Executive Chairman) increased from £301,000 to £850,000 (in 2011), approximately 6% per annum compound, ie 182%. In that time inflation increased by 57% and average wages by 64%.

There are many exceptions to this. Some companies in expanding industries will have paid significantly higher figures than this, whereas other employers in contracting or static industries will have reviewed at the bottom end of these figures.

Because the media tend to highlight high pay increases, there is a danger that Boards are panicked into feeling that they have got to offer much too high a basic salary increase to keep directors happy. Executives do, of course, feed this particular fear.

The UK Corporate Governance Code states:

> 'They should also be sensitive to pay and employment conditions elsewhere in the group, especially when determining annual salary increases.'

The increase in the RPI has traditionally been used as a benchmark for the setting of salaries amongst lower paid and support staff. Any increase that does not match the RPI is likely to mean the employee is slightly worse off in the following year than he or she was in the one just past. Unions and other collective organisations are, of course, extremely keen to use this as the bottom line in any negotiations. Boards setting salaries need to be aware that this is not so commonly used in private sector organisations as it was in the inflationary 1980s and 1990s.

It is fairly easy to review salaries when the company has had a good year. You would probably review at RPI + 4–5% or restrict the increase to the average of all employees. The problem comes when the company has had a bad year and profits barely cover the cost of capital or, even worse, when it is making a loss.

In this situation it is very unlikely any bonuses will be paid and the natural feeling for colleagues who have worked well, despite the lack of corporate success, is that they deserve an increase. This is where independent directors can earn their corn, because it is obviously necessary to put a brake on any increase in fixed central costs, such as salaries. One solution is to phase increases so that you, for instance, give an increase of 2% with a promise of a second review in, say, four to six months if trading starts to improve, at which point you would possibly give another 2% increase. The use of more frequent reviews is one way to take account of turnaround situations when a company simply cannot afford to be as generous as it might wish on the normal review date.

Owner-managed companies

There is a danger in owner-managed companies that the proprietor, probably the Chairman/CEO, earns significant dividends from his or her stake in the company. For this reason they may not maintain their own salary at the level they would need to pay if they hired an outside professional.

The danger is that he or she then tries to preserve normal differentials so that directors on the main Board and subsidiary may be significantly under-salaried because of the depression created by the view of the owner-manager.

In such a situation, the danger is that staff will leave for higher-paid jobs in more traditionally remunerated companies.

The incidence of this type of underpayment is more common than is often supposed. The reason given by the owner-manager is that the company simply cannot afford more, and this may knock on in terms of the business plan, because the company may not be pricing its products at a sufficient level to support a necessary salary structure for the type of skills it needs.

This is one of the areas in which independent directors on private company Boards can play a significant part by suggesting a review of the company's entire business plan, with a principal objective of raising salaries to competitive rates so that key executives and technical staff are not tempted to leave the company for bigger groups.

45.6 Salary increases – market data

CEO salary increases slowed in 2010, in many companies to zero, but the most recent data confirms salaries have started to increase again. The median increases by size category were as follows:

Table 37: CEO median increases

Turnover £millions	**<30**	**31–100**	**101–300**	**301–1,000**	**1,001–3,000**	**3,001–10,000**	**>10,000**
2011[2]	**2%**	**4%**	**4%**	**3%**	**3%**	**2%**	**2%**
2010[3]	3%	2%	0%	0%	1%	0%	2%
2009	4%	5%	5%	5%	4%	3%	5%
2008	5%	7%	7%	7%	8%	8%	9%
2007	6%	5%	7%	7%	7%	7%	8%
2006	4%	5%	5%	6%	6%	7%	6%
2005	5%	6%	7%	5%	8%	9%	7%
2004	3%	6%	6%	6%	8%	5%	7%
2003	3%	4%	6%	6%	6%	8%	7%
Average 2003–2011	4%	5%	5%	5%	6%	6%	6%

About one third of CEOs had no increase in their last reported pay review.

Figure 48: CEO salary increases (2011 data)

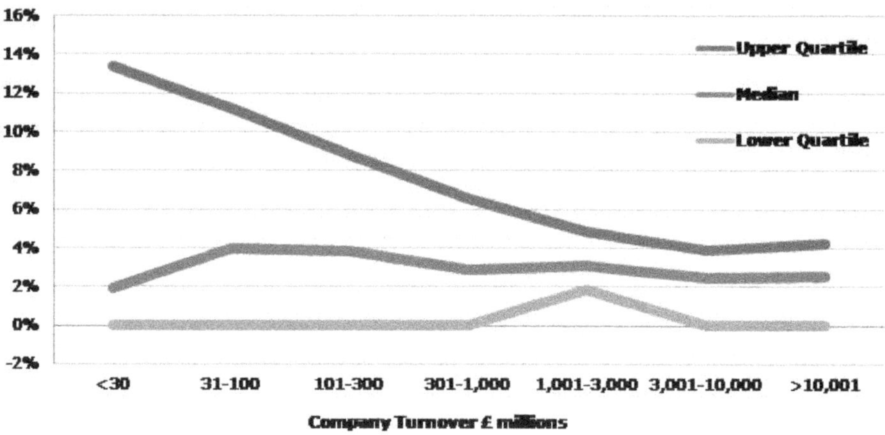

45.7 Future salary increases

A company specific approach is the best approach. Many sectors are different and within them companies are reacting differently and emerging at different speeds from the global recession and liquidity crisis.

[2] This latest data includes companies with year ends March 2011 or December 2011.
[3] 2010 refers to the results from the MM&K/Manifest June 2011 report.

Those companies where there is company-wide restraint on pay increases should set the example at the top. One of David Cameron's first actions as Prime Minister was to reduce Ministers' salaries by 5% and such actions send powerful messages and facilitate strong leadership and tough decisions to come.

Some institutional investors have opined that there should be no catch-up in future salary increases to make up for previous pay freezes. Typically a company in the current environment will review recommendations such as:

- nil increases if the company is struggling and cutting costs, as top management should set an example to staff; or
- 2% to 3% as the general increase but with expectation that around 20% of executives will get 5% to 10%. In this environment you need to ensure that your stars are rewarded as you cannot afford to lose them; or
- some sectors are growing strongly and may wish to give more. It should depend on the company's remuneration strategy and its linkage of pay to performance: a well-structured incentive pay programme should generate rewards in such circumstances and additional salary increases may not be consistent with the remuneration strategy.

Bonuses are usually a better way to reward than salaries, as it keeps fixed costs down. This approach is equally true at all levels. If applied across the whole company, it will give employees comfort that the company can keep more jobs open in any future downturn, even if the scope for salary increases is limited.

46 Bonus (Annual Incentive Pay)

This chapter covers:

- Design process and steps
- Bonus opportunity
  - Target
  - Actual
- Bonus pay-outs
  - As % maximum
  - As % salary
  - In £s
- Deferred bonus awards
  - As % of cash bonus
- Performance measures
- Setting bonus targets, thresholds and maximum
- Claw-back/malus
- Profit sharing.

46.1 Design process and steps

Step 1 is to decide the remuneration strategy, which will decide what % of pay is linked to performance and what part of that is based on annual performance and what the performance measures are.

Each year the Remuneration Committee will review the bonus and decide whether to change it. The figure below shows a logical process for the Remuneration Committee to think through the annual review of bonus.

The bonus paid is a product of the salary, the potential bonus opportunity, how easy/tough the target and maximum are, and the performance of the company/executives against the targets. Each of these is considered below.

Figure 49: Process for annual bonus review

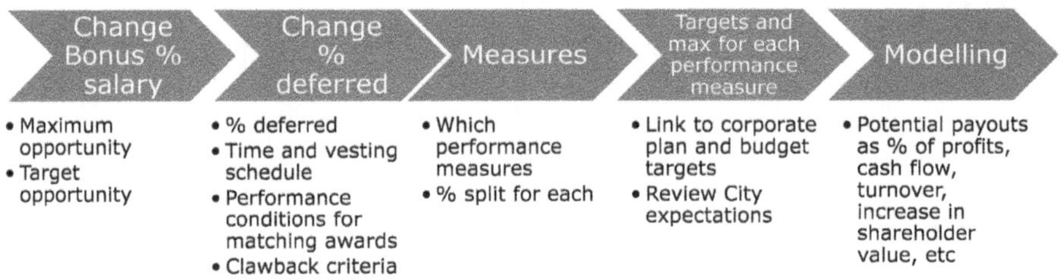

46.2 Background

The maximum that may be earned as an annual bonus is usually set at a proportion of salary. Twenty years ago, the majority of FTSE 100 companies set the upper limit for annual bonuses at between 40% and 60% of salary. By 2010, these ceilings had increased to 175% of salary, with some companies going to 250% or more. So the trend is clearly towards the potential payment of higher percentages, of bigger salaries.

The MM&K/Manifest Executive Director Total Remuneration Survey data show the increase in the average amounts paid to FTSE 100 CEOs. It should be noted that the FTSE dropped in value by 40% over the period 2000–2002 and again in 2007–2008. One would expect therefore that bonus payments were less than the target level, but this was not the case.

Table 38: FTSE 100 average CEO bonus and deferred bonus history (averages)

	Salary £000	Bonus £000	Deferred Bonus £000	Cash Bonus + Deferred Bonus	
				£000	Salary
Latest data 2012/13[1]	**852**	**555**	**717**	**1,272**	**149%**
2012	862	640	805	1,445	168%
2011	850	794	803	1,793	188%
2010	825	857	488	1,345	163%
2009	818	715	462	1,177	144%
2008	810	750	377	1,127	139%
2007	755	828	350	1,178	156%
2006	711	740	249	990	139%
2005	716	623	299	922	129%

1 Latest data 2012/13 is an analysis of companies with year ends mostly in Dec 2012 or March 2013. 2012 refers to an analysis of companies with year ends in 2012.

2004	672	635	224	859	128%
2003	659	581	127	708	108%
2002	620	504	69	573	92%
2001	525	369	3	372	71%
2000	499	345	4	348	70%
1999	444	214	-	214	48%
1998	425	188	-	188	44%

Note: Figures in this table are averages

The increase in total bonus from 44% of salary to 188% is dramatic and reflects a significant cultural shift.

Chart 11: FTSE 100 average CEO salary and bonus in £ millions

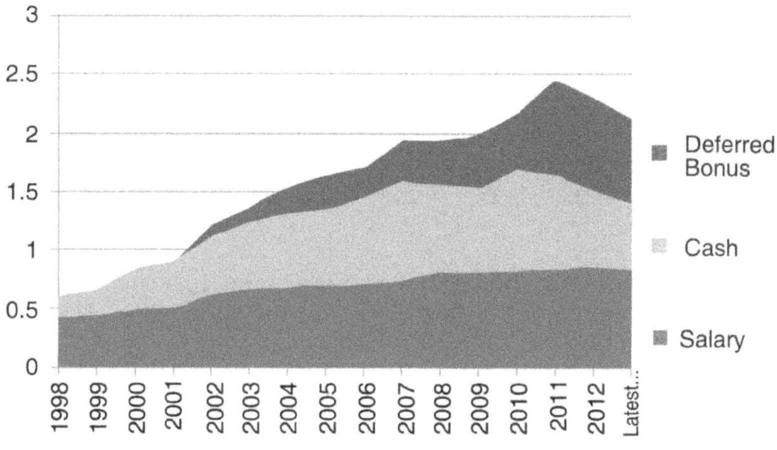

Higher quantums also mean the design of the incentive bonus plan is much more important than it was twenty years ago.

46.3 Code and best practice guidance

The UK Corporate Governance Code in Schedule A says:

> 'The remuneration committee should consider whether the directors should be eligible for annual bonuses. If so, performance conditions should be relevant, stretching and designed to promote the long-term success of the company.
>
> Upper limits should be set and disclosed. There may be a case for part payment in shares to be held for a significant period.

In normal circumstances, shares granted or other forms of deferred remuneration should not vest, and options should not be exercisable, in less than three years. Directors should be encouraged to hold their shares for a further period after vesting or exercise, subject to the need to finance any costs of acquisition and associated tax liabilities.

The total potentially available rewards should not be excessive.

Payouts or grants under all incentive schemes, including new grants under existing share option schemes, should be subject to challenging performance criteria reflecting the company's objectives, including non-financial performance metrics where appropriate. Remuneration incentives should be compatible with risk policies and systems.

Consideration should be given to the use of provisions that permit the company to reclaim variable components in exceptional circumstances of misstatement or misconduct.'

Best practice guidance

The NAPF has suggested that in general, for executive directors **bonuses** should be aligned with profits – thus if profits fall then bonuses also fall.

The NAPF has also said that remuneration practices which would most likely cause concern and may trigger a voting sanction in the absence of sufficient explanation include:

'• Insufficiently demanding or inappropriate performance targets
- Inappropriate use (or lack or use) of discretion
- Guaranteed, pensionable or discretionary annual bonuses
- Insufficient disclosure on the scope of annual bonuses and performance conditions (retrospective disclosure can be acceptable).'

The ABI guidelines state:

'Annual bonuses incentivise performance and reward achievement in line with the agreed corporate strategy.

Annual bonuses exist to reward contribution to the business during the year above the level expected for being in receipt of a salary. They should be clearly linked to business targets, ideally through the KPIs reported in the Strategic Report. Where other measures are chosen, these should be explained and justified. The KPIs can be both financial and non-financial.

The measurements chosen must be quantifiable and the targets set at the start of the year.

Companies should clearly disclose and justify the performance measures chosen and the related targets. Where consideration of commercial sensitivities may prevent a fuller disclosure of specific short-term targets at the start of the performance period, shareholders expect to be informed of the main performance parameters, both corporate and personal, for the financial year being reported on.

Following payment of the bonus, companies should provide a full analysis in the Remuneration Report of the extent to which the relevant targets were actually met.

Maximum participation levels should be disclosed and any increases in the maximum from one year to the next explicitly justified.

Deferring a portion of the bonus into shares can create a greater alignment with shareholders, particularly where there is no long term incentive. However, this should not result in an increase in the overall quantum of the bonus.

Shareholders discourage the payment of annual bonuses to executive directors if the business has suffered an exceptional negative event, even if some specific targets have been met. In such circumstances, shareholders should be consulted on bonus policy and any proposed payments should be carefully explained.

Discretion should be retained to ensure that a payment that is inappropriate in all the company's circumstances is not made. Companies should disclose the range of discretion which can be applied to bonus awards.'

The annual cash bonus is the longest established system of providing additional incentive to staff in the UK. It is the way management specifically rewards those who have made a greater than normal contribution to the results of the year and most directors are very jealous of their right to award such bonuses, which is a critical part of their control/incentive mechanism of their staff.

Whereas 30 years ago bonuses were discretionary within an overall budget figure, so that the boss had the right to discriminate very significantly between people within his department, modern practice is to make some of the bonus specific and linked to the achievement of certain departmental or corporate targets, leaving a rather smaller amount to the managers' discretion.

The GC100 and Investor Group published their view of best practice in September 2013 in relation to the new DRRR. Their document included their view of discretion, which seems to have been accepted as the new model of best practice. It reads as follows:

1.1 Flexibility, discretion and judgement

Background and introduction

The company's remuneration committee's approach to flexibility, discretion and judgement in respect of directors' pay is an important practical issue. Discretion is relevant to many aspects of policy and disclosure, but is not dealt with in any depth by distinct provisions in the Companies Act 2006 or the Regulations. Given their importance, the Group felt that discretion and related concepts should be addressed in this section, before setting out more specific guidance on its use under the Regulations.

Companies and shareholders want directors to be remunerated in a way that reflects their performance in their delivery of the company's strategy. This will need to be reflected in the manner in which the policy is applied and particularly at the end of performance periods. Discretion may be in either an upwards or a downwards direction, but any upwards discretion will inevitably be the subject of considerable shareholder scrutiny and will require careful explanation. For example, the Group recognises that the simple application of arithmetic targets may lead to anomalies such as a maximum bonus being paid when the targets have been met, but for some other reason investors consider that the performance of the company has been below par. Without some discretion, such situations cannot be addressed.

Under the new regime for directors' remuneration, a remuneration committee will prepare a remuneration policy and seek authority from the shareholders in a general meeting for its implementation.

In drafting the policy, the remuneration committee will need to give itself sufficient operational flexibility over pay, some of which may be provided by setting out discretions for the committee to use. The remuneration committee will then need to exercise discretion or judgement in various circumstances when implementing the approved policy. To this extent, the new regime has not altered the role of the committee, but it has set new requirements that must be met before any discretion can be exercised.

The Group's view is that flexibility, discretion and judgement are crucial for the successful design and implementation of a remuneration policy. This is acknowledged by the ABI remuneration principles[2].

Shareholders recognise that one of the tasks of the non-executive directors is the oversight of the performance of the executive directors and of the business as a whole. They, through the remuneration

---

[2] The Association of British Insurers' Principles of Remuneration, dated November 2012. This guidance is available from http://www.ivis.co.uk/ExecutiveRemuneration.aspx.

committee, are best placed to exercise flexibility, discretion or judgement and to ensure a fair outcome in remuneration.

Concepts of flexibility, discretion and judgement

The Group approaches the concepts of flexibility, judgement and discretion, and their relationship, in the following way:

- Flexibility needs to be provided for in drafting the remuneration policy, and this will require some discretion to be included. Flexibility is crucial in the implementation of a three-year approved policy, and its scope needs to be clearly set out within the policy. Once the framework of remuneration has been approved by the shareholders, each year the remuneration committee will need flexibility to determine pay, short-term incentives and the terms of long-term incentives (such as share plan awards).
- Discretion, in an upwards or downwards direction, may be needed to ensure that the outcome of implementation of the remuneration policy is fair to the director and fair to the investors, taking into account the overall performance and position of the company. Other kinds of discretion may also be required, such as the ability to set the level of each component of remuneration within a range from time to time over the life of the policy.
- Judgement also may be needed in respect of features such as the incentive targets used in the annual implementation of the policy. Some will be hard arithmetic targets (for example, EPS and TSR), others may require more judgement and a qualitative assessment by the remuneration committee at the end of the year (for example, the company's reputation). Judgement in this sense will often not involve any exercise of discretion (see *Discretion or judgement?* below).

Discretion or judgement?

There is an important distinction between discretion and judgement, and both have a role to play in pay decisions. In a number of areas, the remuneration committee is routinely asked to apply its judgement to what is appropriate within the bounds of the remuneration policy, or of a particular remuneration award or arrangement. This will not necessarily represent the exercise of "discretion" in the meaning of the Regulations. For example, the assessment of the satisfaction of an annual bonus objective based on progress against an aspect of strategy will be a matter for judgement rather than discretion.

Judgement of this kind, if no discretion is involved, need not be disclosed under the requirements relating to discretion. However, the remuneration committee may wish to consider disclosing the factors taken into account when they have exercised their judgement in determining the extent to which the relevant objective has been satisfied, to provide investors sufficient insight to be able to assess the link between pay and performance. The extent of the explanation that investors generally expect to see will vary depending on the complexity of the case.

Requirements (see paragraphs 12(3) and 24(4) of the Regulations)

The Regulations include two express requirements about discretion, one applying to the annual remuneration report and the other to the remuneration policy, and no express references to flexibility or judgement. The Companies Act 2006 and the Regulations also include provisions with implicit effects in respect of flexibility, judgement and discretion over pay.

Under the new regime, the approval of the remuneration policy will come from a binding vote of the shareholders. The pay of the directors must therefore fall within the terms of the approved remuneration policy. A payment outside the approved remuneration policy, including any use of discretion outside the policy, will require a separate approval by ordinary resolution of the shareholders in general meeting. Failure to do so could impose personal liability on the directors serving on the remuneration committee or on the board more generally.

Where any discretion has been exercised in respect of a short-term or long-term incentive, for example to avoid the application of performance measures or targets resulting in awards that do not fairly reflect investors' experience over the relevant period, companies must include details of how the discretion was exercised and the resulting level of award determined in the annual remuneration report (see *paragraph 12(3)(d) of the Regulations*).

Where the remuneration policy provides for the exercise of discretion over "any aspect of policy", it must also clearly disclose the extent of that discretion in respect of any "such variation, change or amendment". Companies can decide the appropriate manner in which to set out the extent of discretion, as the Regulations do not require this to be done quantitatively (or in any other specified manner). However, companies must make the extent clear in each case, and will want it to be clear so that discretion can be used with confidence (see *paragraph 24(4) of the Regulations*).

The maximum for each component, which is required to be specified in the future policy table (see *4.4: Future policy table*), will constrain the extent of any discretion applicable to that component. The way that each maximum is expressed may also suggest how to express the extent of a discretion over that component (see *paragraph 26(c) of the Regulations*). The remuneration policy must also explain how each component of remuneration "operates", and this will provide the context in which discretion must be described (see *paragraph 26(b) of the Regulations*).

Guidance

Remuneration committees may wish to consider the following two priorities:

- A policy should ensure that investors have sufficient information to be able to approve it, broadly knowing what to expect in terms of directors' remuneration whilst avoiding the risk of unexpected outcomes in future annual remuneration reports.
- The remuneration committee will also need flexibility to tailor the terms of remuneration arrangements for individual directors over the life of the policy, without the policy becoming a "shopping list" of possible components (which could be another way of providing for all reasonable eventualities with less reliance on discretion).

The Group does **not** recommend including in the policy only a general statement that all of the components of remuneration are subject to appropriate adjustment at the complete discretion of the remuneration committee. Investors are likely to have concerns about the way such a broad discretion might be used, and so find it hard to approve the policy. Equally, companies may find such a broad discretion difficult to exercise with confidence if (as will often be the case) there is any doubt that investors will agree. However, given that a policy, expected to last for three years, is the authority under which the company can pay its directors, it may not be unreasonable for the policy to provide for some discretion to be used in genuinely unforeseen and exceptional circumstances.

Remuneration committees, in preparing their remuneration policies, will need to analyse each component of the remuneration package for directors, both executive and non-executive. They will need to consider the flexibility, judgement and discretion that will or may be required, including when hiring or parting company with directors. Having specified as clearly as possible the operational discretions that remuneration committees' reasonably anticipate they may need, it may be appropriate for the policy to provide for an "emergency" discretion for use only in other circumstances, which will be genuinely unforeseen and exceptional.

An example of circumstances requiring such a discretion might be an urgent need to provide a benefit of a type related to changed circumstances or strategy that has not been provided for in a recently approved policy, when it would be disproportionate to seek specific approval from a general meeting. Investors will find it easier to approve policies including such discretions if they are drafted so as to reduce the scope for misuse, for example, by including a specific higher maximum for long-term incentives to be used only in genuinely unforeseen and exceptional circumstances.

Where an exercise of discretion is disclosed in the annual remuneration report, investors expect that companies will report the circumstances leading to that exercise of discretion and why it was required; and also its consequences for the remuneration outcomes.

46.4 Bonus potential

The figure below shows that an annual cap on CEO bonus of 100% of salary is generally median practice except for the larger companies, where the median cap rises to 200% of salary. Many of those companies have bonus potential of 250% or 300% of salary.

Figure 50: Maximum bonus opportunity for CEOs (2011 data)

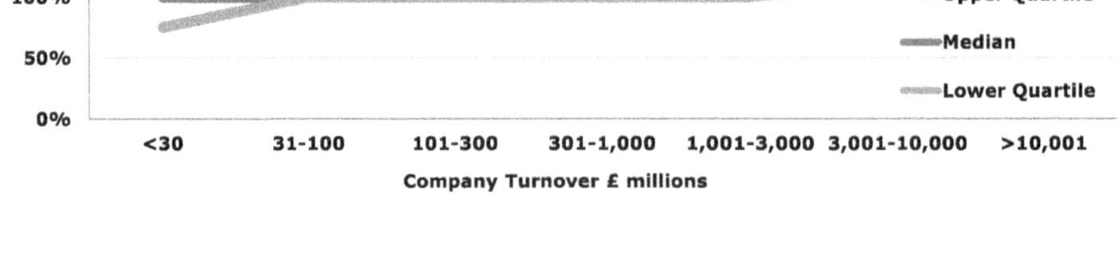

It is interesting to compare the increase in bonus opportunity over the long term. **Figure 51** demonstrates how the magnitude of the bonus opportunity has increased since 2003. The early part of this period is dominated by increases in bonus opportunity, at all levels. The median has stayed at 100% of salary for companies below £1bn turnover but has continued to increase for companies larger than £1bn turnover:

Figure 51: CEO bonus maximum opportunity as % salary

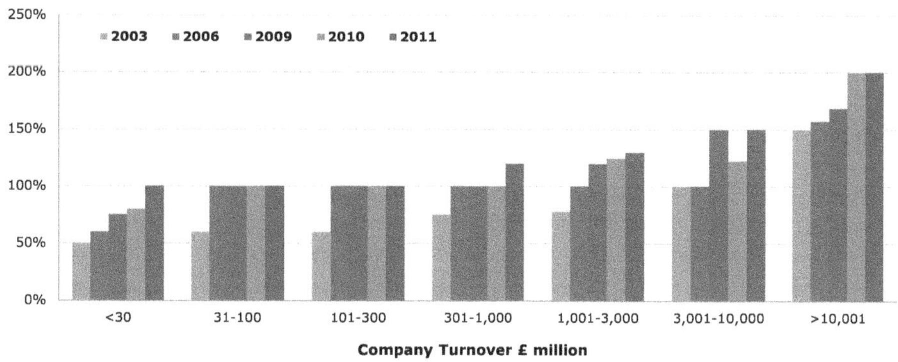

46.5 Deferred bonus

Deferral of bonus has become increasingly common (see **Table 38** above). The Walker[3] Report strongly recommended this for the financial sector. However the practice had already become increasingly prevalent in the non-financial sector well before that. 74% of FTSE 100 companies are estimated to have deferred bonus plans and 52% of FTSE 250 have such plans. Mostly these plans have been introduced at that same time as bonus levels have also been increased, so the impact on executives' cash earnings have been mitigated and over the long run considerably enhanced. Not all these plans have made deferred bonus awards yet, so the figures in the table may reflect previous practice and next year's results are likely to be higher. The figures in the table are noticeably higher than those reported in the May 2011 MM&K/Manifest Executive Director Total Remuneration Survey report.

Table 39: CEO median deferred bonus as % of total bonus paid (2011 data)

Turnover £millions	**<30**	**31–100**	**101–300**	**301–1,000**	**1,001–3,000**	**3,001–10,000**	**>10,000**
Q3	0%	0%	0%	0%	37%	32%	52%
Median	0%	0%	0%	0%	0%	0%	28%
Q1	0%	0%	0%	0%	0%	0%	0%

There are many reasons why deferral is a good idea. It helps retention. It ensures that payment is only made if performance is maintained in the future (if the rules are so written). It can provide malus if future performance declines so providing (some more) alignment with shareholders. It enables

[3] Walker reported on the crisis in 'A review of corporate governance in UK banks and other financial services industry entities, November 2009'

claw-back of bonus in the case of malfeasance (strictly speaking a claw-back clause will allow bonuses that have already been paid to be clawed back from executives. However such clauses will always be open to legal dispute. The benefit of deferral is that is much easier to claw-back that part of bonus that has not already been paid out.) In the 45% taxation regime, the deferral of bonus (and other pay) is potentially attractive if the executive thinks that when she/he ultimately receives the pay he/she will be taxed at a lower tax rate.

Deferral may be mandatory or voluntary. The participant may be given extra shares after three years to encourage him or her to defer the bonus. There may be extra matching shares which vest according to performance over the next three years. This type of bonus creates a long-term incentive and handcuffs for key executives. The downside is that there is no long-term incentive when no bonus is awarded, so such plans are usually combined with options and/or LTIPs to make a cohesive and integrated approach.

Although bonus payments have again seen a significant increase, executives may not have seen more cash in their hands because a large proportion of FTSE 350 companies have a requirement for a significant amount of any annual bonus (typically 33–50%) to be deferred. Deferrals are typically into shares and for a period of three years. Deferred bonus plans now less commonly offer a matching award than in previous years and interestingly this trend is not limited to the financial sector.

The trend is an increase in the number of plans which have deferral of part of the annual bonus but do not provide matching shares.

The following table shows the different types of plan which are currently in operation for the FTSE 100 and the FTSE 250.

Table 40: Type of deferred annual bonus plans in FTSE 350 (live plans – 2011 data)

	Type of match		
	performance related matching shares	**non-performance matching shares**	**no matching shares**
FTSE 100	35%	10%	62%
FTSE 250	25%	12%	72%
	Voluntary deferral (% of plans)	**Compulsory deferral** (% of plans)	**Combination of voluntary and compulsory** (% of plans)
FTSE 100	12%	67%	21%
FTSE 250	15%	72%	13%

	Deferral periods (% of companies)			
	1 year	**2 years**	**3 years**	**>3 years**
FTSE 100	0%	18%	82%	1%
FTSE 250	9%	22%	68%	2%

Matching ratios

The maximum performance-related matching share awards in FTSE 350 companies are:

Share matching ratio	**<1:1**	**1:1**	**1.5:1**	**2:1**	**>2:1**
of FTSE 350 companies	9%	37%	6%	38%	10%

See **Section 47.23** for further information on bonus matching awards.

46.6 Bonus payments[4]

The history of bonus payments as a % of maximum is as follows:

Table 41: CEO median bonus payment as % of maximum opportunity

Turnover £millions	**<30**	**31–100**	**101–300**	**301–1,000**	**1,001–3,000**	**3,001–10,000**	**>10,000**
2011	**35%**	**37%**	**50%**	**50%**	**50%**	**50%**	**46%**
2010	19%	47%	50%	57%	59%	51%	48%
2009	29%	43%	31%	37%	41%	41%	45%
2008	28%	33%	45%	48%	50%	51%	41%
2007	42%	40%	66%	61%	57%	65%	59%
2006	32%	45%	50%	53%	47%	47%	55%
2005	32%	45%	50%	53%	47%	47%	55%
2004	21%	41%	24%	52%	55%	54%	66%
2003	38%	39%	28%	38%	48%	69%	53%
Average 2003–11	33%	42%	43%	50%	50%	53%	53%

The 2012 MM&K/Manifest Executive Director Total Remuneration Survey also shows that bonus plans have higher maxima and are not more difficult to

4 In the tables in this chapter the amounts of bonus paid refer to those amounts paid in the year and exclude deferred bonus. Deferred bonus is included in the long term incentive awards and amounts received in the year in the MM&K/Manifest surveys. The maximum bonus opportunity includes both bonus paid in the year and deferred bonus (but not matching bonus awards).

achieve in larger companies than medium sized ones. Smaller companies set tougher targets. The data is the CEO median value in each turnover range.

Table 42: CEO median bonus payments, maxima and bonus paid as % of maximum opportunity

Turnover £millions	**<30**	**31–100**	**101–300**	**301–1,000**	**1,001–3,000**	**3,001–10,000**	**>10,000**
Cash Bonus £000	-	56	132	288	331	445	902
Cash Bonus as % salary	0%	28%	47%	67%	65%	66%	89%
Bonus Maximum % salary	100%	100%	100%	120%	130%	150%	200%
Cash Bonus as % maximum	35%	37%	50%	50%	50%	46%	45%

Figure 52: CEO median bonus payments & maximum opportunity

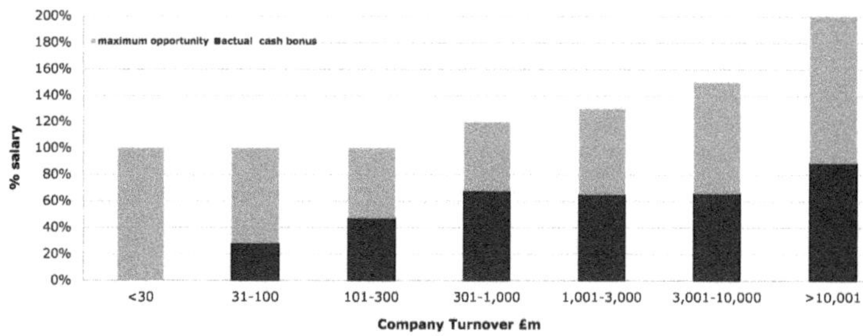

Two patterns emerge. Large companies are more likely to pay bonuses and pay bigger bonuses as a percentage of the maximum opportunity. Large companies tend to use multiple measures, which appear to make it more likely that a high percentage of bonus opportunity will be paid.

Figure 53: Bonus payment as % maximum opportunity (2011 data)

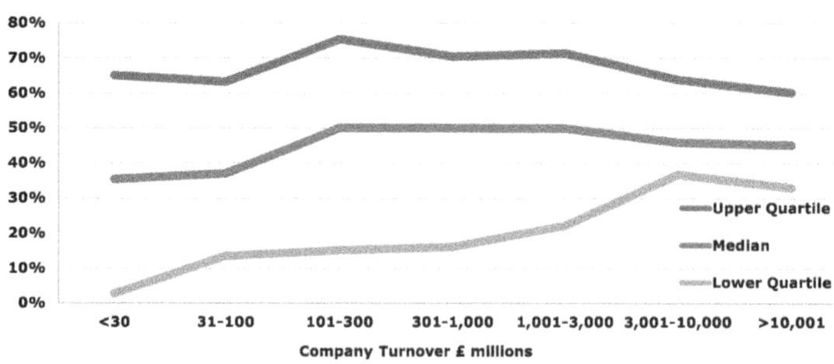

The second pattern is that larger companies have on average increased their bonus opportunities, hence their payments are higher.

On average, cash bonus payments rose by 13% in FTSE 100 and 7% in FTSE 250 companies but were flat in Small Cap and AIM companies. Many CEOs had much bigger increases in their bonuses. Partly this reflected a recovery from the bad years of 2009 and 2008.

Table 43: CEO median increases in bonus payouts

Turnover £millions	<30	31–100	101–300	301–1,000	1,001–3,000	3,001–10,000	>10,000
2011	**0%**	**0%**	**0%**	**0%**	**0%**	**-6%**	**0%**
2010	0%	0%	13%	16%	36%	8%	9%
2009	0%	0%	-15%	-2%	0%	-12%	0%
2008	0%	-1%	0%	0%	2%	-16%	-2%
2007	0%	0%	14%	12%	18%	19%	9%
2006	0%	0%	8%	8%	5%	6%	18%
2005	0%	5%	6%	0%	5%	0%	17%
2004	0%	12%	0%	11%	10%	15%	4%
2003	0%	0%	0%	4%	9%	25%	19%
Average 2003–11	0%	2%	2%	4%	6%	5%	9%

The median increase in 2011 was zero. It is noticeable that despite the trend to defer more bonus, the cash bonus has not decreased.

The pattern of payments in 2011 is complex. CEOs of the very biggest companies were awarded increases in their median bonus in 2010 up to pre credit-crunch levels and in 2012 are at a similar level. Medium sized companies show a long trend of increasing the bonus as a percentage of salary and a bounce from credit-crunch levels. Small companies have much lower bonuses as a percentage of salary; they often do not pay out at all. Many of the smallest companies do not have bonus plans. In addition the trend to defer bonuses also complicates the picture and the figures shown above are significantly less than the expected value of bonus including deferred bonus.

Table 44: CEO median cash bonus paid as % salary

Turnover £millions	<30	31–100	101–300	301–1,000	1,001–3,000	3,001–10,000	>10,000
2011	**0%**	**28%**	**47%**	**67%**	**65%**	**68%**	**89%**
2010	0%	31%	50%	75%	88%	75%	98%
2009	0%	15%	30%	33%	62%	46%	69%
2008	0%	20%	48%	62%	64%	51%	73%

Turnover £millions	<30	31–100	101–300	301–1,000	1,001–3,000	3,001–10,000	>10,000
2007	3%	34%	51%	63%	80%	79%	99%
2006	0%	27%	48%	55%	53%	57%	84%
2005	0%	31%	30%	41%	50%	62%	77%
2004	11%	31%	17%	41%	57%	61%	83%
2003	13%	21%	20%	38%	44%	51%	82%
Average 2003–11	3%	26%	37%	51%	62%	60%	83%

There was a wide spread of actual bonuses. One quarter of CEOs of the largest companies (£10bn + market cap) were paid less than 58% salary and one quarter more than 115% of salary.

Figure 54: CEO cash bonus payments as a % of salary (2011 data)

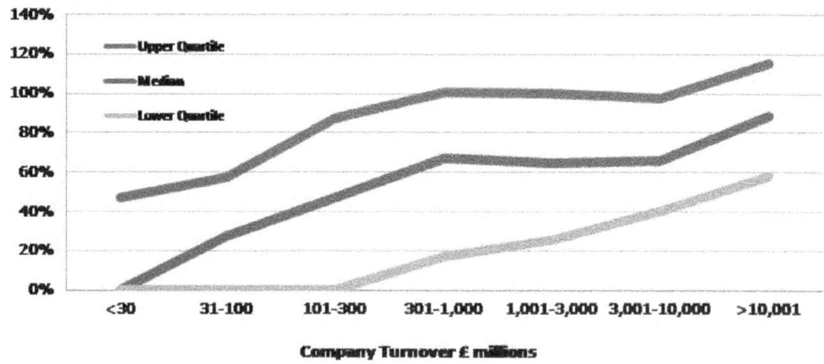

Figure 55: CEO cash bonus payments as a % maximum opportunity (2011 data)

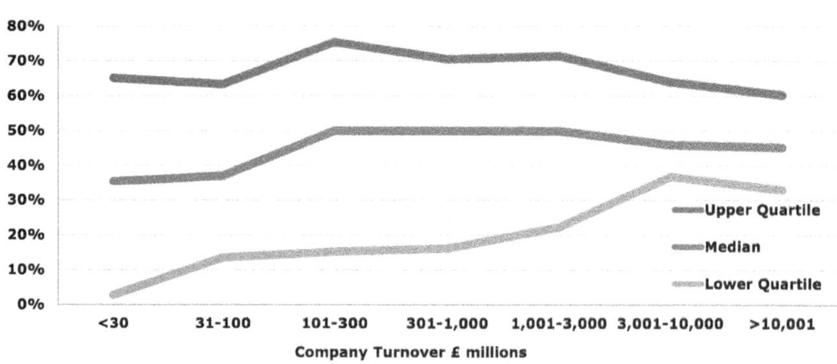

The spread of bonus payments has narrowed considerably in the past decade, particularly in the FTSE 100 companies. Partly, this may be due to the introduction of the balanced scorecard or multiple performance measures which increase the odds that part of the bonus will be achieved. It may be however that when the ABI and others opposed the use of restricted shares with no performance conditions, companies saw the introduction of deferred bonus as a way of awarding restricted shares by the back door, but without the need to go into head to head confrontation with the ABI and key institutional shareholders.

46.7 Bonus design

A classic bonus pattern would be that if the department, division or group achieves 90–95% of the annual target, whether these are profits before tax or some other measure, managers would start to earn a small bonus, which would increase steadily as the results exceed budgets. In most companies the bonus would be capped at about 120% of target.

One example of a bonus plan is the 70/30 model, whereby 70% of a bonus is delivered automatically if the group of which the individual is a member has delivered profits in line with or above the business plan. 30% is left as a discretionary reward so that individuals working extremely effectively can be acknowledged in the discretionary reward which is not linked to salary. The automatic award is nearly always linked to salary so that the higher paid get a higher bonus.

Bonuses are usually linked to the annual appraisal. Good practice indicates that the appraisal interview normally takes place s before the annual bonus announcements are made.

Whether or not annual cash bonuses should be capped is an ongoing argument. Most people are in favour of this system because if a group can exceed their budgets by more than 20%, the chances are there has been very loose budgeting or an unexpected movement not anticipated when the budget was set, ie the cost of some input material has collapsed, one of the competitor's factories has burned down, or the currency in which the company trades has moved favourably against those of competitors.

Another purpose of capping the bonus is to ensure that lucky breaks do not create very large payments, when the management may not have to try very hard to enjoy a windfall bonus.

On the other side there are those who believe that you should always pay for outperformance. There are some companies in which bonus expectations can be 200% of salary or more. These tend to be financial service organisations, for example, dealer teams who often have relatively low salaries, with the whole remuneration package tilted towards the bonus. This approach can be dangerous in many companies as it can lead to managers trying to pack additional profits into the final months of the year so that they earn a higher bonus. The inevitable consequence is under-performance against budgets for the first three months of the next year, but by then several of the beneficiaries of the bonus may have left the company or moved to other departments.

46.8 Performance measures

Profit has traditionally been the favourite performance measure in annual bonus plans. However, it is a lagging indicator of shareholder value and, as has been most dramatically evidenced in the US, capable of accounting manipulation. Statistical studies show that it is poorly correlated to share price movements. Nevertheless, it is an important cornerstone of almost any annual incentive plan. Remuneration committees need to independently check that the profit data they are shown is a fair reflection of the underlying performance of the company.

The choice of performance measures and their relative importance in the delivery of performance-related pay is a window on corporate governance, as they indicate what is felt to be important in the company. The exclusive use of profit in annual bonus plans is a warning sign. The performance measures that determine the remuneration of the management of the company should include those that drive the future business success, for example, customer satisfaction, customer retention, customer growth, average revenue per customer, employee satisfaction, staff turnover and average length of service, environmental and social responsibility measures, health and safety, product development, brand management, effective relationships with regulators, etc. If these measures are not part of the incentive plans, then the company may be saying one thing to its shareholders but internally may be behaving quite differently. Hence, this is a crucial window on what is happening inside the company.

Cash flow, return on capital employed and economic value added (EVA) are also common financial measures. Like profit they are lagging indicators. The Remuneration Committee should also consider using leading indicators of shareholder value. These will often be company or sector specific.

A well-designed plan may have financial, non-financial, operational measures and strategic goals. Evaluation of the bonus award in such plans requires judgment by the Remuneration Committee as well as a good understanding of the business, its strategic challenges and competitors' performance. The use of the balanced scorecard approach is very effective in some circumstances.

Perhaps the best way is to consider the conceptual model of operational and financial measures as discussed in detail in **Section 40.6** (see **Fig 40**).

Key principles

In designing an incentive plan, the critical issue is to identify performance measures which are aligned with business strategy. In doing this, there are certain key principles that should be followed.

The measures should recognise the remuneration strategy and the stage of development of the business; the figure below illustrates measures appropriate for various stages of the business life-cycle:

Figure 56: Lifecycle stages

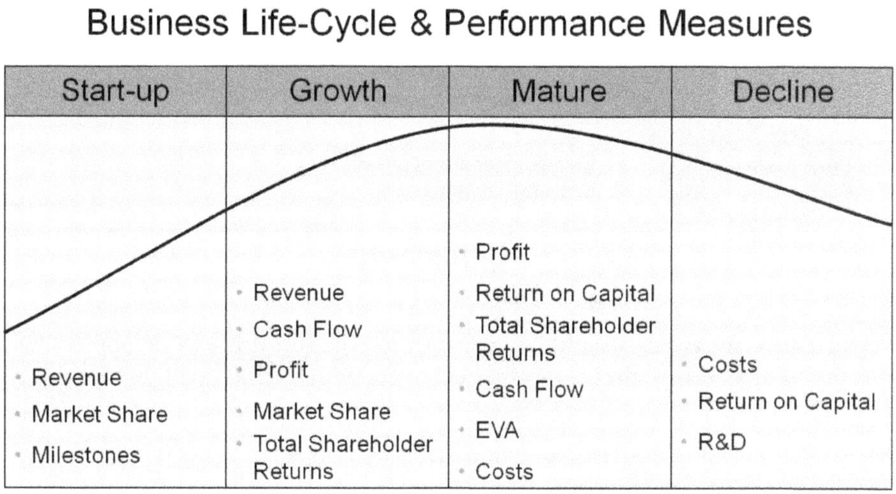

Another consideration in determining the appropriate performance measures is for the executives to understand how their own performance will impact both the business and their reward. A complex incentive system may accurately measure business performance but it may also obscure the 'line-of-sight' and so not be effective in driving the desired management actions.

The figure below illustrates the trade-off between the accuracy of performance measures and complexity.

Figure 57: Performance and complexity trade-off

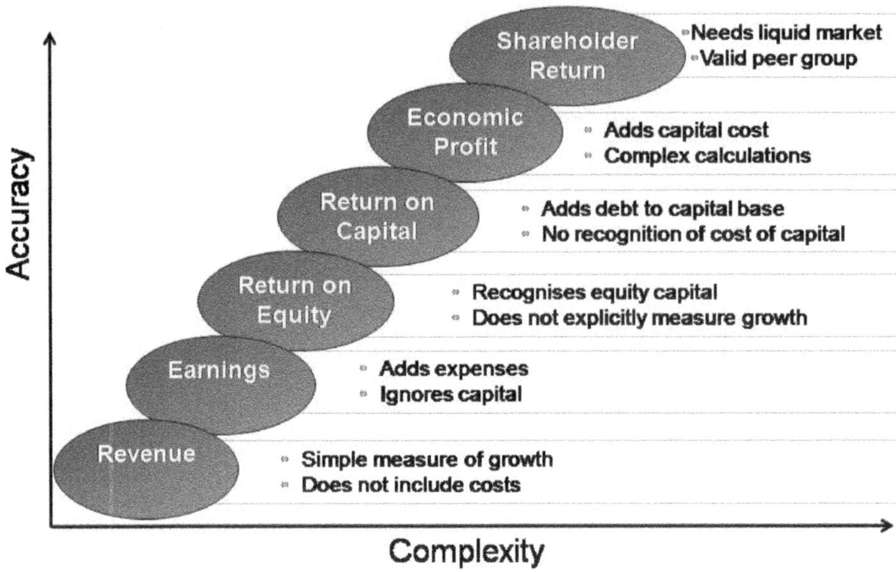

Performance measures should have regard to risk and this can be approached through considering the time frames over which risks will emerge. For example:

- Operational: Ongoing operational risks could be expected to be seen over comparatively short time frames – one year should be sufficient.
- Development: Investing capital in existing businesses will require a longer time to have confidence in outcomes – two or three years should be appropriate.
- Strategic: Major strategic decisions such as entering a new country, making a substantial acquisition or starting new business lines will take even longer to ascertain outcomes and whether they are sustainable – measurement can be over three to five years or, perhaps, longer.

46.9 Combining bonus measures and weightings

Profit (whether measured as EPS, profit after tax, before tax, EBITDA, etc) remains the most common bonus measure. Increasingly other measures are being used. Partly this is to reflect the broader focus of KPIs, and partly it recognises that profits are only a lagging indicator of shareholder value.

The following table shows how different measures can be combined and weighted in a bonus plan. The 2013 Large and Small Companies Regulations require such disclosure, along with the LTI measures. When designing bonus plans and considering performance measures the Remuneration Committee should take account of long term incentive measures and ensure that the rationale for different measures or double counting of some measures make sense.

Table 45: Variable pay additional disclosure of performance conditions and outcomes for latest year

Variable Pay	Details of performance conditions (and weightings)	Targets set	Award achievable	Performance achieved
Bonus	Profit growth (50%)	Threshold = +10% Target = +15% Maximum = +25% Increase on previous year	Nil 50% 100%	75%
	ROCE (20%)	Threshold = 10% Target = +11% Maximum = +13%	Nil 50% 100%	50%
	New Product launches and sales progress (15%)	Threshold Target Maximum Set by remuneration committee and judgment/discretionary assessment at year end	Nil 50% 100%	25%
	International Expansion (15%)	Threshold Target Maximum Set by remuneration committee and judgment/discretionary assessment at year end	Nil 50% 100%	100%
	Overall			**56.5%**
LTI	TSR relative to comparator group (50%)	Median Q3	25% 100%	50%
	EPS growth over 3 years (50%)	Threshold = RPI + 3% per annum Maximum = RPI + 10% per annum	25% 100%	30%
	Overall			**40%**

Where different directors have different goals and/or weightings the above table would have additional rows for each director.

The following diagram can help visualise the debate about what weighting a company should give to the different performance elements and also shows how well the CEO has performed against the various criteria.

Figure 58: Performance Weighting Matrix

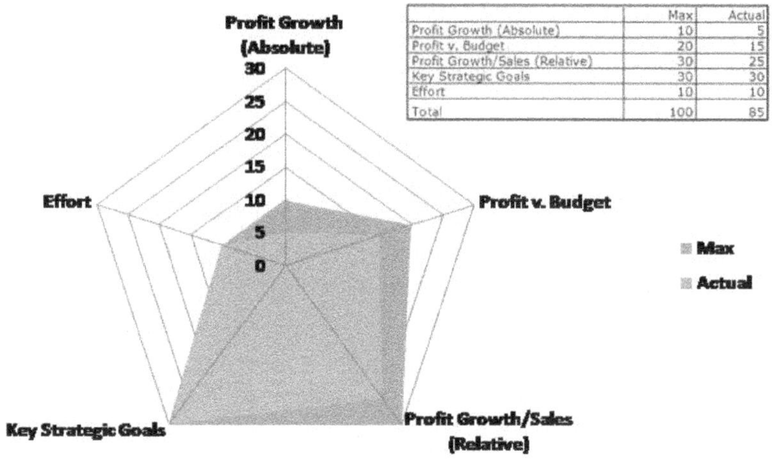

	Max	Actual
Profit Growth (Absolute)	10	5
Profit v. Budget	20	15
Profit Growth/Sales (Relative)	30	25
Key Strategic Goals	30	30
Effort	10	10
Total	100	85

Investors have not been very receptive to requests that executives be rewarded for their hard efforts, preferring that executives are rewarded for outputs (results) rather than inputs (effort).

With the rise in the maximum bonus opportunity the design of the plan and the setting of the targets have become ever more critical. If companies are struggling with setting targets for bonus, companies can:

(i) Make less pay dependent on setting of targets, by decreasing the bonus opportunity and either increasing salary or increasing the amount of long term incentive.[5]

(ii) Lower the gearing of the plan by starting payment at well below target and setting a stretch maximum at well above target.

(iii) Use the Obermatt Bonus Index, which measures financial operating performance relative to peer companies. MM&K have teamed up with Obermatt to provide this service to UK companies.
See www.obermatt.com for more details.

(iv) Split the bonus into a Profits Sharing Plan (see **46.15**) and a short term incentive plan. The nature of Profit Sharing is that it is low geared. The short term incentive plan can he highly performance focused. The combination can be quite effective in both rewarding and motivating.

---

5 Eg by using LTIPs, with market related performance conditions, options or just plain restricted shares.

The challenge for each company is to decide what types of incentive it wants and how much to pay for each type of performance.

46.10 Linkage of EPS and Bonus

Some people think bonus should reduce if profits reduce. So it is interesting to compare below the median increase in bonus with the median % increase in earnings per share over the long term, which shows there is no such relationship.

Increased bonus opportunities are probably the main reason for increased bonus payments. In 2008 and 2009 there was a reduction in cash bonus payments in the largest companies. There is no clear pattern in 2010, although in the £1 to £3 billion turnover category the median increase in bonus was a remarkable 36%. In 2011 bonuses were at similar levels to 2010 although EPS increased in most turnover categories.

Table 46: CEO cash bonus & EPS increase (medians)

	Turnover £m	<30	31–100	101–300	301–1,000	1,001–3,000	3,001–10,000	>10,001
2011	**Bonus % increase**	**0%**	**0%**	**0%**	**0%**	**0%**	**-6%**	**0%**
	EPS % increase	**0%**	**13%**	**8%**	**10%**	**15%**	**11%**	**21%**
2010	Bonus % increase	0%	0%	12%	18%	36%	8%	10%
	EPS % increase	0%	5%	26%	61%	34%	18%	21%
2009	Bonus % increase	0%	0%	-3%	0%	0%	-8%	0%
	EPS % increase	0%	0%	0%	-22%	0%	0%	-13%
2008	Bonus % increase	0%	-1%	0%	0%	2%	-16%	-2%
	EPS % increase	0%	0%	5%	6%	3%	-5%	8%
2007	Bonus % increase	0%	0%	14%	12%	18%	19%	9%
	EPS % increase	46%	27%	23%	26%	28%	6%	13%
2006	Bonus % increase	0%	0%	8%	8%	5%	6%	18%
	EPS % increase	24%	16%	13%	14%	14%	13%	12%
2005	Bonus % increase	0%	5%	6%	0%	5%	0%	17%
	EPS % increase	24%	16%	13%	14%	14%	13%	12%
2004	Bonus % increase	0%	12%	0%	11%	10%	15%	4%
	EPS % increase	21%	16%	12%	13%	13%	18%	19%
2003	Bonus % increase	0%	0%	0%	4%	9%	25%	19%
	EPS % increase	18%	13%	11%	9%	10%	9%	10%

This table, above, is a most interesting comparison, but it is rather hard to understand the long-term trend by inspection. So it is also presented graphically, at least for the largest companies, with the X-axis year, the Y-axis % change, and a line each for EPS and bonus.

Chart 12: CEO cash bonus and EPS relationship for companies > £10 bn turnover (Medians)

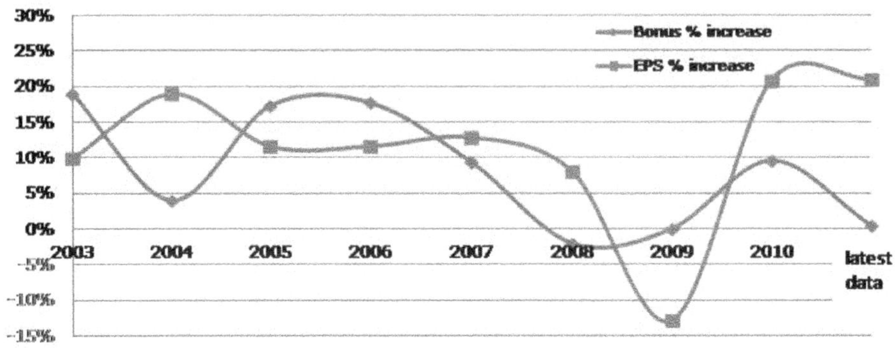

The FTSE 100 index dropped 6% in 2011, having increased by 9% in 2010. Since 31 December the FTSE 100 index has decreased and at 24 May 2012 was 5,350. The median EPS of FTSE 100 companies increased again, by 13% in 2011, having increased also by 21% in 2010.

As noted above, the median increase in annual (cash) bonus for CEOs in 2011 was zero. This was the case for most sizes of companies. In 2010, median annual bonus for CEOs rose by 16% in £1 to 3 billion turnover companies, but by lesser amounts elsewhere.

The reasons for this may include:

- Targets that were set at levels that were easy to hit – in many cases it is felt that targets were lower than market expectations.
- The introduction of measures other than EPS and profit has led to more judgement in setting goals and assessing how well executives have performed.
- A goal of remuneration strategy is to retain and motivate executives. Some Remuneration Committees are loath to upset their CEO and so they permit soft targets.
- It is particularly notable that, despite the increased trend of deferral of part of annual bonus, the figures for the element of annual bonuses paid in cash has not reduced – suggesting that the aim is not to defer bonuses, but to add another long term element – perhaps instead of LTIP grants.

46.11 Setting bonus targets

The remuneration benchmarking will have established an appropriate external market reference points for remuneration levels and developed a set of internally relevant performance measures. In setting bonus targets the Remuneration Committee should calibrate these and assess potential performance pay outcomes from a range of different operating results.

The process involved in calibrating the remuneration structure is summarised as follows:

Figure 59: Bonus threshold, target and outstanding/maximum performance

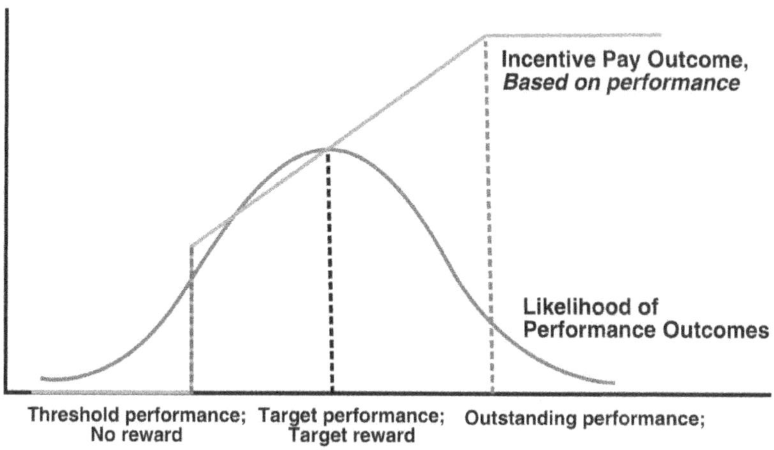

Remuneration Committees should look at a range of potential performance outcomes and develop a mechanism for linking these to payments. This will take into account of:

- market competitive levels of performance pay and how these relate to performance measures.
- existing performance pay arrangements. Prospective payments under a new system should be compared with what would have been paid under the old system.
- whether payments should, at least partially, be deferred.

Target performance can be set in a number of ways and it is best practice to consider all of these to ensure the target set is robust and fair to executives and shareholders:

- budget
- City analyst expectations
- profits growth implied by p/e ratio

- history
- long term growth assumptions in the corporate plan.

In cases where the above are felt not to work satisfactorily, then the assessment of relative operational performance against a peer group of companies should be considered.

In benchmarking bonus plans, Remuneration Committees need to consider carefully whether the targets they set are more stretching, similar or easier than those of their competitors. This is of course very difficult to assess. It might be easier for Company A to achieve 30% EPS growth than Company B to achieve 20% EPS growth.

Are companies setting excessively tough targets for bonus plans? Two recent articles lead us to question this. The first was from the McKinsey Quarterly which concluded that only one third of companies grow revenues by more than 10% and the median was 6%.[6] The second was by Tony Jackson in the FT[7], saying that abnormal rising margins are too good to last forever, which means that for the next few years we should not expect profit growth from higher profit margins (on average or not for more than half of companies).

Multiplying A x B means that most companies will not see profit increases above 6%. This suggests a 6% increase in profits should be a fair target for bonus plans.

6% is consistent with, but slightly less than, the long run return on shares in large companies (eg most pension funds are valued on an assumption of 7.5% returns from equities).

There is a danger that Remuneration Committees set incentive targets that are too tough.[8] Over the long haul, it can overshadow the benefits of patience and discipline: patience to nurture new growth platforms over many years and discipline to uncover the types of growth that will create the most value.

There are other ways to grow profits. See **Section 40.6** for illustrations. These need to be considered when setting incentive goals. This is as much a business strategy issue as an incentive bonus issue. Some actions take more time than others to flow through into bottom line accounting results. If management are being asked on the one hand to undertake various strategic

---

6 See McKinsey on Finance Number 43, Spring 2012

7 http://www.ft.com/cms/s/0/9e1c626a-7f21-11e0-b239-00144feabdc0.html#axzz253iwTLgt

8 For example in the run up to the 2007/08 crisis, many banks had ROE of over 20%. To maintain this ROE created excessive pressure to grow profits at unattainable levels, which could not be done without taking on excessive risk. In 2012 Barclays announced a new reduced target of 13% ROE. However the stock market still does not believe that this is realistic, as was evidenced by the share price and the reluctance of investors to buy Barclays' shares at the price then, or now.

initiatives which will build long term value but impact on short term results, the bonus plan needs to take account of this.

The corollary of this is that if management should not be rewarded for achieving short term incentive targets by taking actions that are not in the business plan and are not in the long term interest of the company (eg cutting R&D expenditure, cutting advertising and other marketing spend, hiring freezes).

Management should be concerned about both creating value and conserving value.

- A company which aims foremost to conserve value will be cautious about investments in new product development, about moves into new territories, about leverage.
- A start-up company or early stage company will seek to grow quickly. Such companies are risky. It is a statistical fact that a company with a volatility of 50% can expect its share price to decline. It is not easy to explain this fact to management, who will be fully committed to their plan. Nor to their Non-Executive Directors who have approved the strategy. But it is a fact; the capital asset pricing model tells us so. **Chart 16** in **Chapter 47.15** shows approximately what might happen.

Companies with high growth potential will have higher p/e ratios as is shown in the graph below.

Figure 60: Theoretical relationship of PE ratio and expected future growth rate

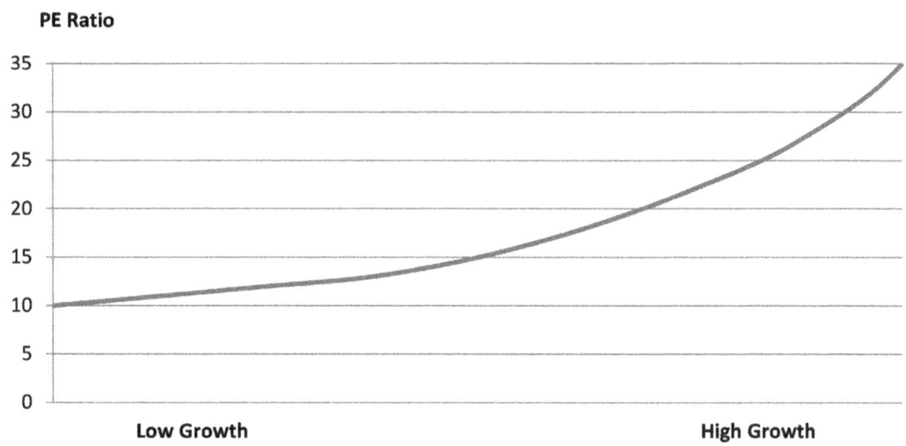

Most mature companies are a mixture of mature and innovation. They need to encourage innovation as otherwise they will decline and die.

To summarise, the steady state rate of increase in profits should be in the 6% to 10% range for most companies. The factors discussed above can justify a lower or higher growth target in a particular year.

46.12 Bonus plan gearing – setting thresholds and maxima

Incentive gearing was discussed in **Chapter 40.12** as was the debate about highly geared and low geared incentive plans and so is not re-examined here. The other challenge is how high to set the maximum or outstanding level of performance, and how low to set the threshold.

To get the maximum incentive and motivational impact it is best for the bonus plan to be 'in-play', so the threshold must not be too tough, nor must the maximum be too easy. It is suggested that you aim for a one in five years' probability of the threshold not being met; and a similar probability that the maximum is achieved.

Looking at the volatility of the share price will give some guidance.

The volatility (the standard deviation of annual share price movements) can be estimated from daily share price movements and is the City's view of how predictable or unpredictable the company's future profits are likely to be. As a rough guideline, you might consider this:

Volatility	20%	30%	50%
1 year profit target should be x% higher than target The probability of achieving this level is about 20% (1 year in 5)	30% (ie if target is 6% then outstanding should be 36%.)	45%	75%
3 year profit target should be x% higher than target The probability of achieving this level is about 20% (1 in 5)	50% (ie if target is 6% per annum then outstanding should be 70%.)	80%	130%

If, however, a company uses a profit measure before exceptional items, then a much narrower scale of incentives might be appropriate. In the author's experience, companies tend to set targets too high and maximum/ outstanding levels that are too low.

Two other issues require consideration:

(i) Payment for achieving threshold

The easiest and best approach is to start from zero payout at threshold performance. Many plans pay more than zero for achieving threshold as it is intended to signify a significant achievement. If there a several measures the best approach is to start from zero as anything else becomes too complex.

(ii) Straight line gearing or other shape

There are strong advocates of increased gearing (some call it accelerated payouts) above target and equally strong advocates of reduced gearing above target (the main arguments being that excessive rewards are windfalls or a result of poor targeting). There are pros and cons for each argument. It is however simpler to have a straight line, particularly if there are several measures.

Once you have understood the above, you will be in a position to develop the remuneration strategy and its incentive plan components.

46.13 Claw-back and Malus

Claw-back is simply the recovery of a bonus or share award where it later transpires that the bonus or award was calculated by reference to overestimated performance. That might be because:

- there was misstatement or misrepresentation in the reported accounts
- the original performance measure was inadequate
- unforeseen developments have come to light since payment of the award which show the performance to be illusory.

How can it be implemented?

Claw-back rules need to be objective for legal and practical reasons.

If claw-back is too widely drafted it will threaten the motivational power of the award, detracting from the whole point of implementing the bonus plan in the first place. From the legal perspective, widely drafted claw-back provisions may also be unenforceable under UK law.

Examples of effective claw-back would be based around:

- uncovering a breach of contract or code of conduct during the bonus period, where such breach did not come to light until after the award had been paid.
- specified falls in company performance or asset levels occurring during the 12 month period following award.

Realistically, claw-back can only be introduced through an amendment to plan rules. Employee consent will be needed unless express provisions in the plan rules allow otherwise, but in the current environment it may be possible to push the changes through and, in the absence of employee objection, rely on implied consent to the changes.

The biggest issue with claw-back is around recovery. Claw-back is only effective if employees can pay the money back and it's that concern that is causing real problems in practice.

A simpler approach is to defer part of bonus and only make the deferred payment if the Remuneration Committee is satisfied with subsequent performance.

Malus

The UBS model was the first well know approach which coined the term 'malus'.

UBS launched a new compensation model in late 2008, which amongst other things, set out its new variable compensation model based on a bonus/malus (good/bad) system.

Their model does not use claw-back per se but replicates claw-back through the use of bonus and malus awards under a cash balance plan. Malus awards are made where there is a financial loss or large balance sheet adjustment within the recipient's group or the recipient has, for instance, committed compliance misconduct or breached risk parameters.

The plan works on a rolling three year basis. At the end of any given year, to the extent the recipient has a positive balance in the cash balance plan, 33% of that balance is paid to them in cash. The remaining 66% is rolled over to the next year as described below:

Example UBS model					
Cash balance	Year 1	Year 2	Year 3	Year 4	Etc.
Previous year balance		100	40	120	60
+ Awarded bonus	150		140		
- Awarded malus		-40		-30	
= Interim balance	150	60	180	90	
x Payout	33%	33%	33%	33%	
= Amount paid out	50	20	60	30	
Balance after payout	100	40	120	60	

Source: UBS Compensation Report, November 17 2008.

This smoothing of payments to executives manages the issue of illusory performance by holding back two-thirds of the annual bonus award. The result is a smoothing of the payout to executives avoiding the enforceability, tax and cash recovery issues referred to above.

46.14 Payment of the bonus and taxation

Traditionally bonuses were paid once the accounts had been published and all the figures were out in the open. They were then paid as a single lump sum with the next month's salary. More sophisticated companies are now paying bonuses on a phased basis, whereby, for example, 25–50% is paid at the end of the year, 25–50% is paid three months later and a final tranche is paid after the end of the year; or in equal thirds over three years. The beauty of this approach is that if there is any creative accounting, it will tend to come out before the second tranche has been paid and, at the same time, it does not encourage key staff to leave after receiving a very big single payment.

With younger staff, it is quite important to ensure that they are not encouraged to start a life-style that can only be supported by continuous high bonuses. Phasing tends to reduce the risk of their over-trading as well as looking for an alternative employer and claiming they think they can meet inflated expectations.

Taxation

Cash bonuses are treated as part of the individual's normal remuneration. Full tax and National Insurance is deducted by the employer before the payment is made to the employee.

Awards to trusts and the use of sub-trusts used to be prudent tax planning. Disguised remuneration legislation was passed by the Government in 2011, which means that once remuneration has been 'earmarked' to an executive there is a tax charge. This is a complex area and is changing rapidly and expert up to date advice should be sought.

Deferred bonus is usually awarded in shares in the form of nil cost options. The tax charge usually arises on exercise of the option but care must be taken so that shares are not earmarked for the potential option exercise as this will trigger a tax charge under the disguised remuneration arrangements.

Claw-back provisions can mean that an executive has already paid tax when the claw-back mechanism comes into effect. This is also a complex area and is also changing rapidly and expert up to date advice should be sought.

46.15 Profit Sharing

A profit share plan, in its strictest sense, is a plan where the payment is based on x% of profits. The term is also used when the design is x% of profits above some threshold.

The nature of both of these is that the payout goes up or down in line with changes in profits. Hence the term profit share as it is a sharing of the profit between employees and owners.

However there is another consequence in that employees benefit when the economy is buoyant and the company does well (and vice versa). This is different to the concept of an incentive scheme whereby participants in the plan are rewarded for achieving goals that are under their control (or at least mainly so).

Small companies often use profit sharing as they reserve x% of profits to be shared between employees. A not unusual arrangement is that 50% of profits are shared with employees, 33% is used to pay dividends to shareholders and the other sixth is used to re-invest in the business. As small companies grow they require more working capital and so this type of arrangement can only fund modest rates of growth. Faster growing companies will often require more capital.

Accountants and lawyers often have a profit pool which is shared amongst partners. Larger firms have developed quite complex arrangements whereby shares are earned and can only reduce slowly over time.

In larger companies, profit sharing is used mostly in the finance sector and in trading jobs, where it is often combined with low salaries as high profit shares are expected. Most companies in industry prefer to have a threshold which has to be achieved. There is also increasing recognition that it is over-simplistic to try to measure performance in a single measure of profit. Most businesses are far too complex to measure using a single figure as the future performance is usually dependent on achieving a variety of goals in a single year.

A profit share is a call on the profits, but only for the time that the person is an employee of the company. In some respects it has similar attributes to being a shareholder, but the rights to profit shares cease when employment ends whereas shareholders rights persist.

The nature of profit sharing is that participants share in the success of the company. If the economy is buoyant and the company is doing well, then the participants profit shares go up. If times are tough then profits drop then so does the profit share. Profit sharing is a reward for success, not a reward for management achieving specific goals.

Splitting bonus into its component parts of sharing in success and incentives to achieve specific targets can greatly add to clarity of what the reward strategy is trying to achieve.

Much of the criticism of remuneration arrangements is that they are too complex and that they should be simplified, with cries for fewer incentive schemes. **In this case, it is the opposite**: the addition of an extra plan can greatly simplify the understanding of what the company is trying to achieve. For example:

Reward item	**Purpose**
Share options and share ownership rules	Rewards long term growth in share price. Share in success for those willing to stay in the company for a considerable time.
Long term incentive plan	Focusses on three to five year goals.
Annual incentive plan	**Motivates to achieve specific short term operational goals**
Profit Sharing	**Share in success**
Pension and benefits	Market competitiveness, security
Salary	Market competitiveness

Company-wide Profit Sharing Schemes

Many companies have company-wide profit sharing schemes, with perhaps the most well known being the John Lewis Partnership.

A key constituent of an ethical pay program is a profit sharing plan for all employees so that all employees know and see that they and the executive directors pay is aligned with profits and share the success and pain together.

The Lib-Lab pact in 1978 introduced the Approved Profit Sharing Scheme and became quite popular. The Share Incentive Plan (SIP) replaced it from 2002, but has not proved to be as popular. The name does not quite have the same ring to it. There is of course no reason why companies cannot call their plans Profit Sharing Schemes, even though the enabling tax effective legislation underpinning it is the SIP.

46.16 Checklist for Bonus

Why is the company doing this?	Eg: Motivation Retention Reward Profit Sharing
Cultural match	What sorts of behaviours will be encouraged by the bonus? What downside risks are there? What risk management steps will be taken?
How much? and affordability	Threshold, target and maximum opportunities (% salary) of profit, cash flow, other key metrics Links to competitive benchmarks [10] year run of CEO bonus (£ and % salary) and company performance against KPIs
Performance criteria and stretch	Is the target level of performance fair? Is it at budget? How tough is the budget? How does it compare with historic performance, and City analyst expectations and implied expectation in the p/e ratio? Are thresholds and maxima fair? Is the gearing too steep or too flat?
Deferral	Is profit subject to mark to market and other significant judgements about future events? If so should bonus be deferred until better view of future outcomes is clear? Will deferral of bonus help retention? deferred similar to competitor practice?
Claw-back and Malus	Are these included in the plan detailed rules?
Discretion	To ensure payments reflect performance. Can targets and payments be revised up and down? Is there a degree of asymmetric adjustments in favour of the executives? Are general rules and reasons for discretion understood and accepted by all parties? And explained to shareholders?

47 Long-Term Incentives

This Chapter covers:

- Process to set and review long term incentives (LTIs)
- Best practice
- Different types of LTI
- Awards (Expected Value)
- Pay-outs (Realised Value)
- Pay-outs compared to Award Levels
- Deferred Bonus Awards
- Mix of Options and LTIPs
- Performance Measures
- Valuation issues
- Liquidity issues.

47.1 Process to set and review long term incentives

New long term incentives schemes in quoted companies will require shareholder approval (see **Chapter 8.3**).

The first step is to decide the remuneration strategy, which will specify:

- Proportion of pay linked to performance
  - fixed and variable
  - annual and longer term
- How performance will be measured
- Gearing of incentive plans
- Types of long term incentive plans, eg:
  - Deferred Bonus
  - LTIP
  - Options

- Share ownership, retention and sale rules.

Each year the Remuneration Committee will review the LTI and decide whether to change it. The figure below shows a logical process for the Remuneration Committee to think through the LTI design review process.

Figure 61: LTI review process and target setting

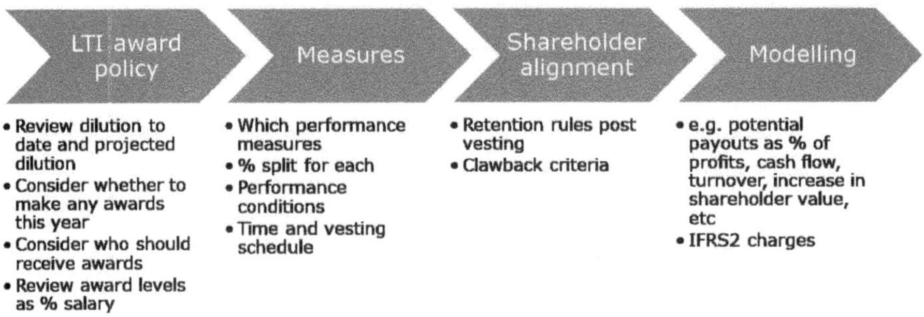

47.2 Code and best practice guidance

The UK Corporate Governance Code in Schedule A says:

> **'D.1 The Level and Components of Remuneration**
>
> Supporting Principles
>
> The performance-related elements of executive directors' remuneration should be stretching and designed to promote the long-term success of the company.
>
> The remuneration committee should judge where to position their company relative to other companies. But they should use such comparisons with caution in view of the risk of an upward ratchet of remuneration levels with no corresponding improvement in performance.'

The UK Corporate Governance Code in Schedule A has much more guidance on LTIs than on other forms of remuneration. It says:

> 'The remuneration committee should consider whether the directors should be eligible for benefits under long-term incentive schemes. Traditional share option schemes should be weighed against other kinds of long-term incentive scheme.
>
> Executive share options should not be offered at a discount save as permitted by the relevant provisions of the Listing Rules.
>
> In normal circumstances, shares granted or other forms of deferred remuneration should not vest, and options should not be exercisable, in

less than three years. Directors should be encouraged to hold their shares for a further period after vesting or exercise, subject to the need to finance any costs of acquisition and associated tax liabilities.

Any new long-term incentive schemes which are proposed should be approved by shareholders and should preferably replace any existing schemes or, at least, form part of a well-considered overall plan incorporating existing schemes.

The total potentially available rewards should not be excessive.

Payouts or grants under all incentive schemes, including new grants under existing share option schemes, should be subject to challenging performance criteria reflecting the company's objectives, including non-financial performance metrics where appropriate. Remuneration incentives should be compatible with risk policies and systems.

Grants under executive share option and other long-term incentive schemes should normally be phased rather than awarded in one large block.

Consideration should be given to the use of provisions that permit the company to reclaim variable components in exceptional circumstances of misstatement or misconduct.'

Best practice guidance

The NAPF has noted that shareholders are likely to oppose:

- 'Layering of new share award schemes on top of existing schemes;
- Inappropriate use (or lack of use) of discretion;
- Insufficiently demanding or inappropriate performance targets;
- Any provision for re-testing of performance conditions;
- Change in control provisions triggering earlier and/or larger payments and rewards.'

The ABI guidelines are quite prescriptive. They state:

'Long term incentives

General

Long-term incentives exist to reward the successful implementation of strategy and the creation of shareholder value over a period appropriate to the strategic objectives of the company. Equity based long-term incentive schemes are the most effective way to align the interests of participants and shareholders.

The performance period should be clearly linked to the timing of the implementation of the strategy of the business, which should be no less than three years and shareholders would generally prefer longer. Committees should consider the use of additional holding periods.

All new incentives or any substantive changes to existing schemes should be subject to prior approval by shareholders by means of a separate and binding resolution. Any change in quantum should be fully explained and justified.

Scheme and individual participation limits must be fully disclosed in share incentive schemes.

The operation of share incentive schemes should not lead to dilution in excess of the limits acceptable to shareholders.

Performance conditions

The widely differing nature of business models and industry characteristics means that the appropriate performance measures and conditions for different companies may vary significantly. Performance measures and vesting conditions should be fully explained and clearly linked to the achievement of appropriately challenging financial performance which will enhance shareholder value.

Whilst other considerations may apply in particular circumstances, for example, restructuring, shareholders will expect that remuneration policies and structures will normally be consistent with the following criteria:

- Shareholders have a clear preference for financial measures linked to value creation. Performance criteria should be linked to the Company's long-term strategy and targets reflect an appropriate balance between the shorter- and longer-term.
- Remuneration Committees will need to consider, and explain, appropriate performance criteria in the light of the specific business characteristics of the group in question. Performance criteria should fully reflect the performance of the business as a whole and should be applied consistently across measurement periods.
- The definition of any performance measurement should be clearly disclosed.
- Retesting of performance conditions is not acceptable.
- Remuneration Committees should ensure that, when using in isolation either comparative or absolute performance metrics, the result does not produce outcomes that are not in line with the

overall performance of the company, its future prospects or the experience of its shareholders over the performance period.

- Comparator groups used for performance purposes should be both relevant and representative. Where only a small number of companies is used for a comparator group, Remuneration Committees should satisfy themselves that the comparative performance will not result in arbitrary outcomes. Awards should not vest for less than median performance.
- Where operational measurements are used, they would generally be expected:
  - To include, subject to business strategy, one or more measures relating to overall business volume or growth
  - To include one or more measures relating to business efficiency or profitability
  - To avoid the risk of providing an implicit incentive to take undue operational or financial risks or, in particular, to adopt an unduly risky capital structure.
- Where Total Shareholder Return (TSR) relative to a relevant index or peer group is used, Remuneration Committees should satisfy themselves prior to vesting that the recorded TSR or other criterion is a genuine reflection of the company's underlying financial performance, and explain their reasoning.
- The calculation of starting and finishing values for TSR should be made by reference to average share prices over a short period of time at the beginning and end of the performance period. Lengthy averaging periods should be avoided. Where TSR is used as a performance criterion and the chosen comparator group includes companies listed in overseas markets, it is essential that TSR be measured on a consistent basis. The standard approach should be for a common currency to be used. Where there are compelling grounds for the calculation to be based on local currency TSR of comparator group companies, then the reasons for choosing this approach should be fully explained.
- Where appropriate, Remuneration Committees should take account of the ABI Guidelines on Responsible Investment Disclosures (http://www.ivis.co.uk/ResponsibleInvestmentDisclosure.aspx).

Vesting

Threshold vesting amounts, reflecting expected performance, should not be significant by comparison with annual base salary.

Awards' structures with a marked 'cliff edge' vesting profile are considered inappropriate. Full vesting should reflect exceptional performance and so be dependent on achievement of significantly greater value creation than that applicable to threshold vesting.

Sliding scales and graduated vesting profiles are a useful way of ensuring that performance conditions are genuinely challenging. They generally provide a better motivator for improving corporate performance than a 'single hurdle'.

Grant Size

Windfall gains may arise if the level of share or option grants expressed as a multiple of salary is maintained after a substantial fall in the share price. Where this risk exists, grants should be scaled back.

Cost

The primary information that should be disclosed includes:

- The potential value of awards due to individual scheme participants on full vesting. This should be expressed by reference to the face value of shares or shares under option at point of grant, and expressed as a multiple of base salary.
- The maximum dilution which may arise through the issue of shares to satisfy entitlements.

Change of control provisions

Scheme rules should state that there will be no automatic waiving of performance conditions either in the event of a change of control or where subsisting options and awards are "rolled over" in the event of a capital reconstruction, and/or the early termination of the participant's employment. Remuneration Committees should use best endeavours to provide meaningful disclosure that quantifies the aggregate payments arising on a change of control.

In the event of a change of control, the key determinant of the level of awards vesting should be underlying financial performance. Also, any such early vesting as a consequence of a change of control should be on a time pro-rata basis i.e. taking into account the vesting period that has elapsed at the time of change of control. Remuneration Committees should satisfy themselves that the measured performance provides genuine evidence of underlying financial achievement over any shorter time period. They should explain their reasoning in the Remuneration Report or other relevant documentation sent to shareholders.

Pricing and timing of awards

The price at which shares are issued under a scheme should not be less than the mid-market price (or similar formula) immediately preceding grant of the shares under the scheme.

Options granted under executive (discretionary) schemes should not be granted at a discount to the prevailing mid-market price.

Repricing or surrender and regrant of awards or 'underwater' share options is not appropriate.

The rules of a scheme should provide that share or option awards should normally be granted within a 42 day period following the publication of the company's results.

Life of schemes and incentive awards

No awards should be made beyond the life of the scheme approved on adoption by shareholders, which should not exceed 10 years.

Shares and options should not vest or be exercisable within three years from the date of grant. In addition, options should not be exercisable more than ten years from the date of grant.

Where individuals choose to terminate their employment before the end of the service period, or in the event that employment is terminated for cause, any unvested options or conditional share-based award should normally lapse.

In other circumstances of cessation of employment,[1] some portion of the award may vest, to the extent of the service period that has been completed, but subject to the achievement of relevant performance criteria. In general, the originally stipulated performance measurement period should continue to apply. However, where in the opinion of the Remuneration Committee, early vesting is appropriate, or where it is otherwise necessary,[2] awards should vest by reference to performance criteria achieved over the period to date.

Where options vest, in the event of death or cessation of employment of the option holder or where a company is taken over (except where arrangements are made for a switch to options of the offeror company), or where they have already vested at the time of such event, they must be exercised (or lapse) within 12 months. Where the performance measurement period applicable to an option extends beyond the point

1 Such circumstances may include disability, ill health, redundancy, retirement or analogous reasons for departure of a 'good leaver' nature.

2 Such circumstances may include death and also occasions such as takeover of the company or sale or transfer of the business undertaking where awards are not being rolled over into equivalent awards in the successor entity or new employer.

of cessation of employment, options must be exercised within 12 months of vesting following the end of the performance measurement period.

Any shares or options that a company may grant in exchange for those released under the schemes of acquired companies should normally be taken into account for the purposes of dilution and individual participation limits determined in accordance with this Guidance.

Dilution

The rules of a scheme must provide that commitments to issue new shares or re-issue treasury shares, when aggregated with awards under all of the company's other schemes, must not exceed 10% of the issued ordinary share capital (adjusted for share issuance and cancellation) in any rolling 10 year period. Remuneration Committees should ensure that appropriate policies regarding flow-rates exist in order to spread the potential issue of new shares over the life of relevant schemes in order to ensure the limit is not breached.

Commitments to issue new shares or re-issue treasury shares under executive (discretionary) schemes should not exceed 5% of the issued ordinary share capital of the company (adjusted for share issuance and cancellation) in any rolling 10 year period. This may be exceeded where vesting is dependent on the achievement of significantly more stretching performance criteria. The implicit dilution commitment should always be provided for at point of grant even where, as in the case of share-settled share appreciation rights, it is recognised that only a proportion of shares may in practice be used.'

There has been a swing away from share options to LTIPs. As noted below, there are good reasons why part of the reward package should be in the form of options, which in most situations can be a desirable and effective reward mechanism. However option awards should not be excessive.[3]

The accounting standard IFRS 2[4] has been cited as a reason to switch away from options. The intellectual rigour of such arguments is dubious, as studies

---

3 The best research is Professor Kees Cools' study of why companies do bad things: 'The dilemma of the successful CEO'. He identified CEOs of 25 major frauds and identified as the major causes Huge Stock Option grants (8 times), Large Press Profile (3 times) and High Growth Targets (6 times). Although huge stock options grants can lead to fraudulent behaviour, but it is illogical to extrapolate that normal size option grants are a bad thing. Grants of sensibly sized options can create a long term incentive in increasing the share price of the company and that this helps to create an identity of interest with shareholders.

4 IFRS 2 requires the value of options and share plans to be shown in the accounts on a fair value basis and then trued up each year for changes in assumptions for non-market related performance conditions (such as EPS), leavers and the expected vesting period.

have shown that the impact of options had already been priced into most shares, as the information to value options was already available in most accounts.

The 50% income tax and penal changes to executive pensions required a fundamental rethink for many companies, and required companies to take a long term perspective.

The banking disasters have led to new rules regarding bonus deferral, claw-back and risk. An increase in the amounts of deferral of bonus is widely agreed as best practice; as is claw-back of incentives in the case of overstated results (although the precise details of how to implement this requires careful drafting). The concept of risk and its adjustment in incentive design is proving complex to implement.

Note to the second edition: there is an emerging trend in best practice to move to five year performance periods or three year performance periods combined with a minimum further two year retention period (meaning the executive has an interest in the shares for five years at least). This is desired by Fidelity and others.

47.3 Awards (expected value)

Larger companies make much larger awards of long term incentives than smaller companies. Not only do they have larger salaries, but their awards as a % salary are much higher. There is also a very wide range of practice:

Chart 13: CEO – median expected value of LTIs (% salary)

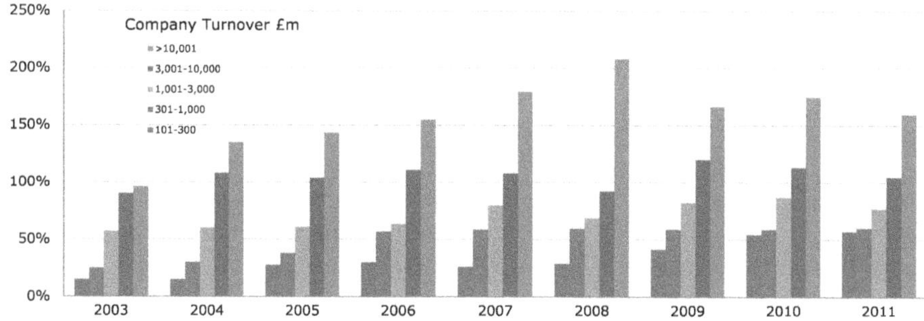

The reduction in LTI awards of the very largest companies (>£10 billion turnover) reflects partly their switch to annual bonus and deferred bonus plans. Their total remuneration has increased despite this drop in LTI awards.

Award levels vary considerably between companies as is shown in the next graph.

Chart 14: CEO – LTIs expected value (% salary) (2011 data)

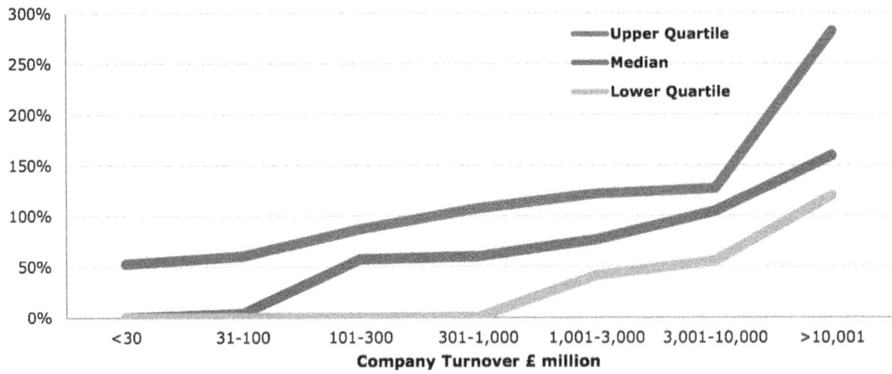

47.4 Amounts realised[5] from LTIPs

Table 47: Median CEO gains from exercised options, vested LTIPs and deferred bonus payouts in £000

Turnover £millions	<30	31–100	101–300	301–1,000	1,001–3,000	3,001–10,000	>10,000
2011	**£0**	**£0**	**£0**	**£0**	**£72**	**£170**	**£1,142**
2010	£0	£0	£0	£12	£127	£346	£1,335
2009	£0	£0	£0	£0	£82	£317	£601
2008	£0	£0	£0	£0	£115	£24	£926
2007	£0	£0	£0	£0	£0	£138	£337
2006	£0	£0	£0	£0	£0	£120	£136
2005	£0	£0	£0	£0	£0	£106	£888
2004	£0	£0	£0	£0	£0	£56	£613
2003	£0	£0	£0	£0	£0	£8	£345

Long term incentives paid out in over half of the largest companies, with no LTI payments in more than half of smaller companies. The increasingly complex combinations of LTIPs, share options and deferred bonus mean that there is a good chance of one or other paying out.

It would appear that more complexity is correlated with more pay.

The introduction of multiple targets into LTIPs will also tend to increase the chances of some pay out. (Smaller companies have much simpler pay

5 The term 'amounts realised' is used to refer to the amount of LTIPs and deferred share schemes that vest in the year, plus gains on options exercised in the year. The amounts realised were from awards made in earlier years.

arrangements, that are much more transparent and their executives' pay has tended to be much more correlated to performance.)

Amounts realised from LTIPs, deferred bonus matching plans and the exercise of options were modest in most cases from 2004 to 2008. Executives 'realised' much less than the 'expected value' of long term incentive awards. The bear markets of 2001–02 and 2007–09 meant many options were underwater[6] or had limited gains. The better stock market performance in 2009 and 2010 has led to increased pay outs.

Executives at larger companies have done relatively better as LTIPs were more prevalent and more likely to pay out than options in this period. The CEO long term incentive pay outs in 2010 were, in 25% of the largest companies (market cap > £10bn), at least £2.9 million, which was only 3.2 times the median of £0.9 million. The move to increase the proportion of performance related pay is not being sufficiently reflected in large differential rewards for the CEOs of these companies.

47.5 Comparison of payouts from awards

It is interesting to compare whether LTIP and option pay outs are in line with award levels or much less or greater.

Table 48: Gains realised £000s from exercised options & vested LTIPs and deferred bonus:

Turnover £ millions	**<30**	**31–100**	**101–300**	**301–1,000**	**1,001–3,000**	**3,001–10,000**	**>10,001**
Lower Quartile	0	0	0	0	0	0	314
Median	0	0	0	0	72	170	1,142
Upper Quartile (Q3)	0	28	37	419	593	1,095	3,032
Q3 gains as a multiple of Median	0.0	0.0	0.0	0.0	8.2	6.4	2.7
Q3 gains as % salary	0%	0%	12%	98%	111%	154%	322%

Source: 2012 MM&K/Manifest Executive Director Total Remuneration Survey

The UK Corporate Governance Code says that performance related pay should be a significant proportion of total remuneration. However the above data suggests that performance related pay, for most companies, is not working the way that shareholders envisage. Instead, most plans are designed to generate the sorts of pay levels sufficient to keep senior executives satisfied, with only limited upside and downside for performance.

6 Options where the exercise price is higher than the current share price.

Note: market data on individual plans is potentially misleading as some companies only award LTIPs, some only options and some a mixture. Thus it is best to review data for the expected value of *all* types of long-term incentive plans. The MM&K/Manifest Executive Director Total Remuneration Survey shows the rapid six fold increase in the importance of this element of the remuneration package as % salary and eleven-fold increase in £ terms since 1998.

Table 49: CEO average pay in FTSE 100 companies (£000s)

Year	**Salary £000**	**Options Fair Value £000**	**LTIP Fair Value £000**	**Total LTI Fair Value £000**	**Total LTI Fair Value as % salary**
1998	425	88	62	150	35%
1999	444	145	128	273	62%
2000	499	209	243	455	91%
2001	525	252	227	483	92%
2002	620	568	336	904	146%
2003	659	433	408	841	128%
2004	672	393	573	966	144%
2005	716	343	696	1,038	145%
2006	711	366	618	983	138%
2007	755	267	1,011	1,278	169%
2008	810	116	1,364	1,856	229%
2009	818	182	985	1,167	143%
2010	825	164	1,333	1,497	181%
2011	850	193	1,455	1,647	194%

Source: 2012 MM&K/Manifest Executive Director Total Remuneration Survey

47.6 Categorisation of LTIs

These can be categorised by type of plan and by payment mechanism.

Types of LTI plan:

(i) LTIP

(ii) Share Options

(iii) Matching bonus awards

(iv) Co-investment plans

(v) Carry plans

(vi) Subsidiary share and long term incentive plans

(vii) Restricted share plans

(viii) Cash long term incentive plans

(ix) Retention incentives.

Payment mechanism:

(i) shares

(ii) share options

(iii) units

(iv) co-co's,[7] etc

(v) cash.

Sections 7.4 to **7.14** described the different types of plan structures and their taxation treatment.

A description of each type of plan follows in **47.9** onwards.

47.7 Dilution and burn rates

The ABI and NAPF guidelines limit dilution to 10% for all schemes and 5% for executive schemes, both over ten years. The limits should be spread over the ten years, so the limit for executive schemes is an average of 0.5% per annum. However, the ABI guidelines then go on to say that the limit for executive schemes may be exceeded where vesting is dependent on the achievement of significantly more stretching performance criteria.

The institutional guidelines[8] suggest 5% dilution over ten years for executive share schemes, but allow more if there are stretching performance targets. Remuneration Committees are meant to plan ahead and make phased grants, so the 5% limit equates to 0.5% a year.

In contrast the median dilution in the US is 1.9% per annum, which creates a problem for any UK employer wishing to compete with US corporations.

There is also a provision for smaller companies to have a 10% dilution limit.

For many of the smaller companies MM&K works with, even 10% is not sufficient to properly incentivise management.

---

7 Contingent convertibles, also known as CoCo bonds, Cocos or contingent convertible notes, are slightly different to regular convertible bonds in that the likelihood of the bonds converting to equity is 'contingent' on a specified event, such as the stock price of the company exceeding a particular level for a certain period of time. Some banks have used this type of vehicle to pay deferred bonuses.

8 The ABI Guidelines are in Appendix 4 and can be downloaded from their website: http://www.abi.org.uk/

This is an area where one should expect there to be greater focus and there will be more analysis on this in the future.

Private Equity investors typically offer up to 20% or even 30% of the equity to managers as their incentive. However these deals are structured so that the equity only has value if there has been an underlying return on the debt. They are also usually highly leveraged. There is therefore a much higher threshold level of performance required, before the equity incentive plan starts to pay out, than in quoted plc incentive plans. So the percentage dilution figures are not comparable, as they measure different things.

The percentages of the total awards that go to the CEO, to the top five and to others are useful statistics to see where the awards are being directed.

47.8 Scheme documentation

Long term incentive schemes for quoted companies have to be approved by shareholders. This requires a set of scheme rules, a shareholder resolution and a letter to shareholders which should explain the proposed scheme and its supporting rationale.

Individuals who receive awards will also be sent award certificates and supporting documentation and explanation.

These are important as in the event of any dispute, the rules together with any supporting documents, letters, emails, etc and minutes of Remuneration Committee meetings will be used to interpret what the intention of the scheme was.

47.9 Change in control

According to the ABI guidelines:

> 'Scheme rules should state that there will be no automatic waiving of performance conditions either in the event of a change of control or where subsisting options and awards are 'rolled over' in the event of a capital reconstruction, and/or the early termination of the participant's employment. Remuneration Committees should use best endeavours to provide meaningful disclosure that quantifies the aggregate payments arising on a change of control.
>
> In the event of a change of control, the key determinant of the level of awards vesting should be underlying financial performance. Also, any such early vesting as a consequence of a change of control should be on a time pro-rata basis i.e. taking into account the vesting period that has elapsed at the time of change of control. Remuneration Committees should satisfy themselves that the measured performance provides

genuine evidence of underlying financial achievement over any shorter time period. They should explain their reasoning in the Remuneration Report or other relevant documentation sent to shareholders.'

However many people argue that there can be circumstances whereby it is appropriate to award full vesting of LTIPs to management. Strictly drafted rules with no Remuneration Committee discretion can create perverse incentives for the management to delay completion of a takeover.

The best practice is to permit Remuneration Committee discretion whilst taking note of shareholder preferences.

47.10 LTIPs (performance restricted stock)

Long-term incentive plans (LTIPs) are a misnomer as mostly they are three years and so are mid-term not long term.

By long term, most organisations mean incentive bonuses measured over three or more years that are then paid in a single or a phased number of payments.

Most quoted companies tend to base a proportion of such payments on shares or share options in line with the UK Corporate Governance Code guidelines. Incentives via shares or options in private companies who do not have a market for their equity will require a formula-based valuation which will need to be agreed with HMRC.

The use of medium to long-term incentives of this kind has been increasing for the past fifteen years, as they tie the management to a shareholder value-based bonus system.

The size of potential payments under long-term incentive plans have created a significant amount of shareholder, media and political comment over the past several years.

It is an area where Remuneration Committees have a particularly important part to play to ensure that:

- the performance triggers for long-term incentives are sufficiently demanding and clearly add shareholder value.
- the payment currency, whether cash, shares or options can only be encashed over time, so that executive beneficiaries are not tempted to leave the company after a significant pay-out.
- creative accountancy (or the use of discretion and judgement in interpreting the terms in incentive plans) has not been used so that the company appears to have exceeded certain trigger targets for very large pay-outs when under strict accounting rules, the targets would not have been met.

- the availability of a long-term performance payment system is usually critical at this level when executives are considering whether or not to join a company. They may well be walking away from options in their existing employer worth several hundred thousand pounds, which is one of the reasons for 'golden hellos' when a recruit is offered a large number of options by his or her new employer to compensate for those he or she would sacrifice.

47.11 LTIPs – Quantum

Since 1996, PIRC has tracked the structure of new share schemes in which directors will participate. Awards of conditional shares and/or share options are usually expressed as a multiple of base salary. In 1997 (the first year after the Greenbury Report became effective), 68% of new conditional share plans made awards worth less than 100% of salary each year. By 2002, only 17% of new schemes awarded less than 100% of salary, with 24% offering more than 145% of salary each year.

The 2012 MM&K/Manifest Executive Director Total Remuneration Survey shows the current levels which are much increased since 2002.

Company turnover £million	**LTIPs: maximum award face value of shares as % salary**						
	<30	**31–100**	**101–300**	**301–1,000**	**1,001–3,000**	**3,001–10,000**	**>10,000**
Q1	100%	100%	100%	100%	106%	125%	200%
Median	**150%**	**150%**	**150%**	**150%**	**200%**	**200%**	**300%**
Q3	200%	200%	200%	200%	200%	250%	493%

Source: MM&K/Manifest

As noted above, this type of market data is potentially misleading as some companies only award LTIPs, some only options and some a mixture. Thus it is best to review data for the expected value of all types of long-term incentive plans.

47.12 LTIPS – Performance measures

Another area attracting much attention is the secondary or underpinning performance measures used to permit vesting.

The usual measure is TSR compared with a comparator group of companies, with a secondary measure of financial performance, usually EPS. There is, however, a wide range of alternatives that might be appropriate to a company's particular circumstances. It is often difficult to find a good comparator group. Acquisitions and mergers deplete comparator groups, so at least 12 and preferably 20 are needed. Sometimes this is not possible; for example, BP compares itself with four oil multi-nationals.

For TSR performance targets, the norm of no payment below median is almost universal. Maximum vesting at upper quartile is increasingly common and has been for the past two or three years.

A typical vesting schedule would be:

Performance	**of award vesting**
Below median	Nothing
Median	25% of target award
Upper quartile	100% of target award
Upper decile or above	100% or 150% or even 200% of target award

There would be a sliding scale of payments between these points. It should be noted that the practice has become to announce an award figure of say 100% of salary, which would be paid at upper quartile performance. However, there may be additional rewards above this level, for example, the upper decile multiplier maximum could be 200% of salary. It should be further noted that these percentages are based on current salary and share price at award. If the share price has gone up, so, probably, will the payout. If upper decile performance is achieved the share price is likely to have grown substantially, for example, if the share price doubled and upper decile performance was achieved, the so-called maximum award of 100% of salary would be worth 400% of salary after three years.

The chart below shows that the upper quartile (ie 25th percentile) is most frequently the maximum vesting position. The conformity of approach suggests that many companies adopt boilerplate approaches rather than thinking through what is right for their strategy.

Figure 62: LTIP relative TSR maximum vesting performance target

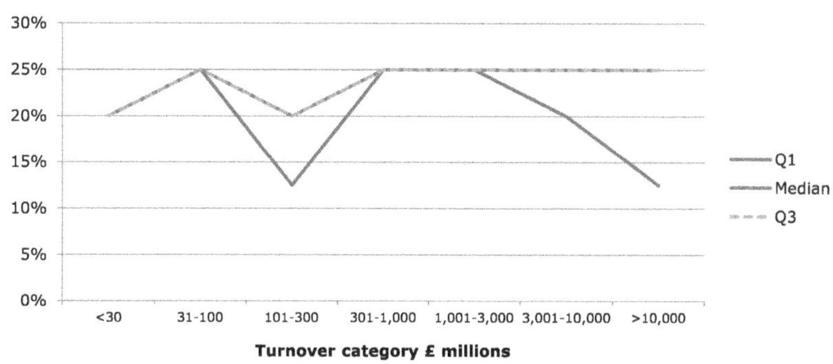

More recent plans have increasingly split the award between two or more measures, for example 50% might be on TSR relative to a comparator group of companies and 50% might be on EPS growth. It is worth noting that such plans are more complex and are rewarding a mixture of (i) relative TSR growth, (ii) growth in EPS and (iii) changes in the share price. Careful modelling is required to ensure the Remuneration Committee and the executives who participate understand what is being rewarded and to what degree over a range of scenarios.

Interestingly, and perhaps reflecting the current economic circumstances, for LTIPs the median point for maximum vesting is EPS growth of RPI+8% per annum (last year it was RPI+8%, the previous year RPI+5% and the year before that it was RPI+10%). With RPI, in 2011, at around 4–5% (last year 4%, the previous year -0.4% and the year before that plus 4%) and a dividend yield of say 3%, this still seems a rather low target for maximum vesting, given the starting points are the somewhat depressed EPS figures of 2008 and 2009.

The market data is as follows:

Figure 63: LTIP EPS (real growth v RPI) threshold and maximum performance targets

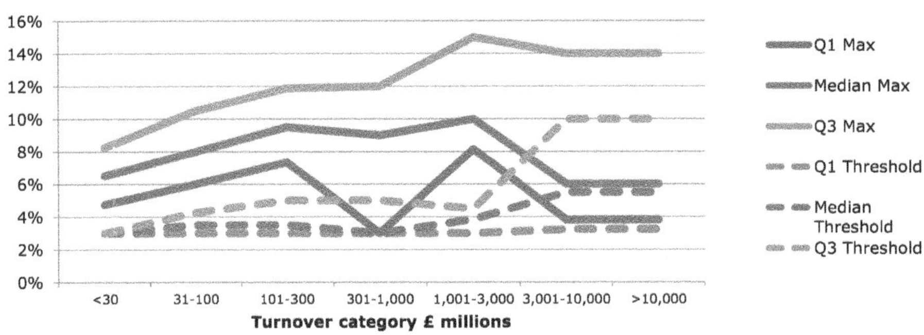

There is little disclosure of the definition of EPS, how exceptional items are treated and how much discretion the Remuneration Committee can apply. It is difficult to see how tough the targets will be in practice.

There is an increasing use of balanced scorecard type measures and discretion in LTIP performance measures. Best practice may be in the process of following this trend, but it is too early to say definitively.

47.13 LTIPs – Modelling the impact of performance measures

The combination of share retention arrangements and LTIPs with relative TSR performance conditions produces the following returns if the shares are held for eight years.

The green line is the share price after eight years and consists of all those companies in the FTSE 100 at end of 2002 that were still quoted at the end of 2010. This graph follows the expected lognormal distribution. A small proportion have achieved returns in excess of 1,000% over the eight year period.

2002–2010 was a period of good returns as the average TSR of this group was 15% per annum and median growth was 13% per annum over this period.

The red line shows the performance vesting schedule and the blue line the value of LTIP awarded at the end of 2002 if kept until the end of 2010.

The chart shows how the TSR performance schedule produces a highly geared incentive. However as noted in **Section 40.4**, much of the performance is beyond the control of the executives and so this is not a good incentive plan.

Chart 15: LTIP payouts if shares held for eight years

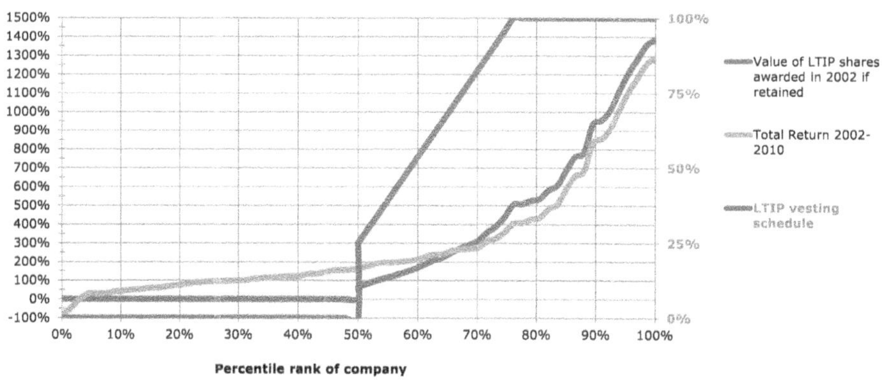

This type of plan encourages short term-ism and rewards risky strategies.

47.14 LTIPs – Retention period

Some plans have a further mandatory retention period after the three-year vesting, with the aim of retention/handcuffs. Others use the retention period to ensure alignment with shareholders, and this can be an alternative to more complicated clawback arrangements. As noted elsewhere the best practice is a two year retention period after a three year performance period (or simply a five year performance period). Some plans require retention up until retirement.

It can be difficult for executive directors to sell shares, particularly in small companies where there is limited liquidity. This has the effect of ensuring retention of shares obtained from LTIPs.

Some plans make awards in the form of nil-price options, which enable the executive to choose when to exercise after the award vests.

Share ownership and share retention programmes are best considered in the context of the whole remuneration strategy, rather than as a component of the LTIP.

47.15 LTIPs – Setting targets

A start-up company or early stage company will seek to grow quickly. Such companies are risky. A company with a share price volatility of 50% can expect its share price to decline. The statistics are not easy to explain to highly committed, motivated managers committed to their growth plan. But it is a fact and **Chart 16** shows the likely outcomes.

Chart 16: Theoretical relationship of volatility and expected future share price

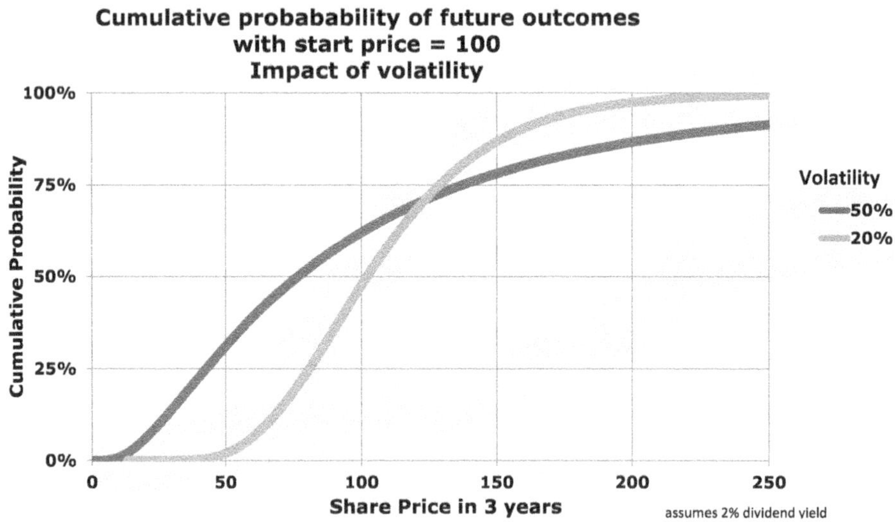

The reason for this result may not be immediately obvious. However with higher volatility there is a higher probability of high value but low probability events. With 20% volatility there is almost nil chance of the share price increasing by more than 200% in three years; but with 50% volatility the probability is about 13%.

The consequence is that whatever performance criteria are chosen, the threshold and maximum performance levels should be much wider in a high volatility and in a low volatility company. This is a very important point when targets are being set for three years ahead.

Much of the discussion in **Sections 46.11** (Setting bonus targets) and **46.12** (Bonus Gearing) is relevant to setting LTIP targets and the reader is advised to read those sections before designing LTIP targets.

47.16 LTIPs – Link to share ownership and share retention

The nature of the incentive will change if the executive cannot cash in after three years, but instead has to hold his/her shares until retirement or at least until several more years have passed.

47.17 Communicating LTIPs

Many employees find it quite complex to understand how well they are doing with their LTIPs. This is less so in the first year of a plan, but when three cycles are running, often with different comparator groups, this can be much less clear than working out the 'in the money' value of options.

With relative TSR it is difficult for executives to keep a precise track of performance. So the company must circulate regular updates on performance as otherwise the plan loses its motivational effect. The old maxim applies here 'what gets measured gets done'.

47.18 Share options

The UK Corporate Governance Code says in Schedule A:

> 'Traditional share option schemes should be weighed against other kinds of long-term incentive scheme.
>
> Executive share options should not be offered at a discount save as permitted by the relevant provisions of the Listing Rules.
>
> In normal circumstances, shares granted or other forms of deferred remuneration should not vest, and options should not be exercisable, in less than three years. Directors should be encouraged to hold their shares for a further period after vesting or exercise, subject to the need to finance any costs of acquisition and associated tax liabilities.

Any new long-term incentive schemes which are proposed should be approved by shareholders and should preferably replace any existing schemes or, at least, form part of a well-considered overall plan incorporating existing schemes.

The total potentially available rewards should not be excessive.

Payouts or grants under all incentive schemes, including new grants under existing share option schemes, should be subject to challenging performance criteria reflecting the company's objectives, including non-financial performance metrics where appropriate. Remuneration incentives should be compatible with risk policies and systems.

Grants under executive share option and other long-term incentive schemes should normally be phased rather than awarded in one large block.

Consideration should be given to the use of provisions that permit the company to reclaim variable components in exceptional circumstances of misstatement or misconduct.'

47.19 EMI and CSOPs

The best scheme of all was introduced in the 2000 Budget and subsequently enhanced in the 2002 Budget. However, Enterprise Management Incentives (EMI) are only available to companies (in a qualifying trade) with a gross asset value of less than £30 million. The maximum option is over £250,000 of shares. EMI options are taxed as capital gains tax. See **Section 7.6** for more details of EMI schemes.

Company Share Option Plans (CSOP) allow a grant of options over shares of up to £30,000 per employee. See **7.5** for more details.

47.20 Share Options – Quantums

Institutional investors have more specific guidance on quantums and performance measures, which are complex and sometimes contradictory. Most of those who have guidelines used to expect that any award of more than one times salary (face value of options) will have tougher performance targets attached and any award above two times salary will have significantly tougher targets.

Prior to 1999, most discretionary option schemes in which directors participated had rules limiting the holding of options to the equivalent of four times a director's remuneration in any ten-year period. One undesirable side-effect of this rule was that an award of the whole amount could be made in one block and then no more options could then be issued until the previous ones were exercised. In 1999, the Association of British Insurers

(ABI) amended its rules by removing this limit and replacing it with guidance that awards should be made annually. It suggested that an equivalent award level would be options with a face value of one times salary.

The result was an immediate change in new schemes. In 2000, PIRC found that 65% of new option schemes used a new-style annual award limit. Initially, one times salary was the most popular limit. However, by 2002, the ceiling had been raised so that 47% of new schemes specified a limit of two times salary[3].

The 2012 MM&K/Manifest Executive Director Total Remuneration Survey showed maximum award face values at that time. The clear continued increase in the ceiling since 2002 is obvious.

	Options: maximum award face value of shares as % salary						
Company turnover £million	**<30**	**31–100**	**101–300**	**301–1,000**	**1,001–3,000**	**3,001–10,000**	**>10,000**
Q1	125%	80%	100%	100%	150%	200%	200%
Median	**150%**	**125%**	**200%**	**200%**	**200%**	**228%**	**300%**
Q3	175%	200%	250%	200%	288%	300%	550%

As with annual bonuses, these higher multiples of salary are themselves based on larger salaries, creating a powerful multiplier effect through executive director remuneration structures.

As noted above, market data is potentially misleading as some companies only award LTIPs, some only options and some a mixture. Thus it is best to review data for the expected value of all types of long-term incentive plans.

47.21 Share Options – Performance measures

Since the share option is meant to reward share price growth over a ten year period, there seems no logic in having a single set of tough EPS performance conditions at year 3.

However best practice guidelines continue to recommend performance measures.

PIRC report that there has been some movement to toughen performance conditions. In 1996, 67% of new share option schemes used a measure of earnings per share (EPS) to determine the exercise of options and of these, 48% of new schemes required EPS growth of 2% in excess of inflation for full vesting. In 2006 EPS was still the most popular performance condition with most new option schemes using it. However, most schemes now have a vesting scale whereby different levels of options become exercisable for gradually tougher performance. In most cases, the required EPS targets are relatively weak compared to market expectations of the company's performance.

Another area attracting much attention is the secondary or underpinning performance measures used to permit vesting.

EPS performance targets for options and LTIPs started to be toughened around 2006, following the pressure from some institutions, but in many cases remain significantly below analysts' estimates of future growth. Such conditions are often window dressing, to meet corporate governance tick box requirements.

There is little disclosure of the definition of EPS, how exceptional items are treated and how much discretion the Remuneration Committee can apply. It is difficult to see how tough the targets will be in practice.

For options the median EPS growth test for maximum vesting it has increased to RPI+8% whereas it was at RPI+5% per annum. In most cases, the option is unlikely to be significantly in the money if such a performance target has not been achieved, so the impact of the EPS performance condition is marginal at best and at worst it merely adds confusion and complexity.

47.22 Deferred Bonus

In these plans part of the bonus is deferred and used to buy shares which vest usually in three years. Deferral may be mandatory or voluntary. The participant may be given extra shares after three years to encourage him or her to defer the bonus. There may be extra matching shares which vest according to performance over the next three years (see **47.23**).

This type of bonus creates a long-term incentive and handcuff for key executives. The downside is that there is no long-term incentive when no bonus is awarded, so such plans are usually combined with options and/or LTIPs to make a cohesive and integrated approach.

More information on deferred bonus is given in **46.5**.

47.23 Matching Bonus Awards

In matching bonus plans the executive can defer part or all of his or her bonus and they will then receive matching shares if performance targets are achieved.

The performance conditions which are attached to Matching Bonus Awards are typically similar to those that are attached to LTIPs which are discussed in **47.12**.

Although usually the targets are similar to the LTIP targets, companies are free to choose whatever targets they feel are appropriate. The main difference between LTIP and matching bonus awards is that the award in the LTIP is not linked to the annual bonus amount, but tends to be a fixed amount.

This is really a special form of an LTIP award, with the size of the award depending on the size of the bonus.

Hence when the award is made it is linked in size to the bonus award, but where there may be extra matching shares which vest according to performance over the next three years.

Usually part of the bonus is paid in shares and a condition of the Matching Bonus Award is that the executive cannot sell his/her (bonus) shares. Thus if the share price decreases the executive may lose part of the value of his/her bonus as the (bonus) shares are worth less and the matching bonus award may not vest.

However if the Matching Bonus Award performance conditions are met and the share price increases the award is worth significantly more.

Matching ratios

The maximum performance-related matching share awards in FTSE 350 companies are:

Share matching ratio	**<1:1**	**1:1**	**1.5:1**	**2:1**	**>2:1**
of FTSE 350 companies	9%	37%	6%	38%	10%

47.24 Restricted Stock

Restricted Stock or restricted shares refer to awards of shares without performance conditions other than time vesting. If the executive leaves he forfeits the restricted stock award.

Restricted stock awards are much more common in the US, which is why the term restricted stock is often used in the UK, rather than restricted shares.

Restricted stock/share awards are frowned upon by UK institutional investors whose guidelines on best practice are that awards of shares should always have performance conditions attached to their vesting.

Restricted shares are particularly useful as retention incentives as the executive sees that he/she should receive value from an award and only needs to complete the necessary service to receive the award.

47.25 Retention incentives ('handcuffs')

When the market for good people is particularly vibrant, it may be necessary to offer retention incentives to ensure that enough good people stay to manage the company. It is usually better to offer performance-related incentives.

If a company is potentially going bust or is going to be sold, then incentives to tie in the key players may be appropriate, especially if the business will be worth less if these people were to leave. In such circumstances, the payment of guaranteed amounts may be more effective in retention than incentives where people are unsure of payments and feel they have little effect on the end results.

If a key executive announces he or she is going to leave, it may be appropriate to negotiate with them and give them a better offer to stay. In such circumstances, payment of guaranteed amounts may be more effective in retention than incentives, although a mixture of both and possibly a salary rise may be the optimum solution. Remuneration Committees should have flexibility in their remuneration policy to manage such situations and can use Rule 9.4.2 of the Listing Rules for a special LTI plan.

47.26 Co-investment plans

Co-investment plans are a more recent development. They are a variation on the typical LTIP. The executive has to buy shares in the company (or use shares he already owns for this purpose) and lodge them with the company. He then receives an award of restricted shares which are contingent on future performance. Most plans of this type have a five-year performance period so create a better alignment with long-term shareholders than the typical LTIP. Also the requirement to invest and hold shares in the company provides some downside alignment.

Matching awards can be as much as five times the investment amount. WPP is an example of a company which has such a plan.

Reinvesting previous awards of shares in a new co-investment plan can be very tax effective as, if structured correctly, it defers the receipt of the previous award and hence the tax liability.

47.27 Carry plans

These plans are most frequently seen in the private equity industry (see **51.1**).

The concept is that the executives receive a share in the increase in the value of the company (or in the case of the asset management industry, of a relevant fund that the executive(s) manage). This is called a carry.

47.28 Subsidiary long term incentive plans

These can either be based around subsidiary shares or cash based. The same design principles apply. The valuation of subsidiary shares is potentially difficult if there is no liquidity in the shares.

However the increased line-of-sight and consequential increased management motivation can mean that such plans are worth constructing. Many shareholders and the ABI guidelines frown upon subsidiary share plans.

Directors of the main Board should generally not have subsidiary share plans as this produces a conflict with their duty to the parent company shareholders.

When real shares cannot be used, a cash long term incentive plan in the subsidiary may be appropriate.

47.29 Cash long term incentive plans

It is difficult to construct an argument for a cash long term incentive. The targets, if achieved, should flow through into improvements in the share price. If they do not, then why should there be a payment to the executives?

Sometimes executives have lost confidence in the value ascribed to the company by the market and say they prefer a cash plan to one based around shares. Before implementing a cash plan it may be better to revisit the business strategy to confirm that it is appropriate, sufficiently challenging and is well understood by shareholders and analysts.

In the few cases that cash long term incentives are appropriate, they normally pay out three years from inception and may be overlapping so each year a new three-year cycle is started or have a focussed single one-off award. They are normally measured against more demanding and wide-ranging targets than annual cash bonuses. A normal range of trigger targets for a three-year bonus would be 'earnings per share' (EPS) plus control of cash flow against three-year budgets and possibly return on capital employed.

One of the purposes of a longer-term bonus is to ensure executives use the assets of the company as well as its revenue to best effect. Schemes often therefore involve specific targets to sell off surplus property, inventory or other non-core assets over the three years of the programme. Remuneration Committees normally insist that any such scheme is self-financing, the bonus becoming a revenue cost.

Private companies sometimes prefer cash long term incentive plans due to difficulties in valuing shares, share liquidity and concerns over dilution, especially of voting rights.

47.30 Checklist for Long Term Incentives

The list below can be used as both a checklist and to develop a term sheet for a new plan.

Item	Comment, questions and examples
Why is the company doing this?	Motivation Retention Reward Alignment with shareholders
Cultural match	What sorts of behaviours will be encouraged by the incentive? How does the long term incentive fit with bonus and other reward components? What downside risks are there? What risk management steps will be taken?
Type of shares	Eg ordinary shares or special shares
Dividends	Are dividend equivalents included? Eg a cash amount equal to dividends prior to vesting paid in cash on vesting; and post vesting a cash payment at the same time as dividends
Form of award	Eg restricted share, conditional share, option, nil cost option
How much? and affordability	Threshold, target and maximum opportunities (% salary) of profit, cash flow, other key metrics Links to competitive benchmarks [10] year run of CEO bonus (£ and % salary) and company performance against KPIs
Performance conditions determining vesting	Conditions Timing Definitions of terms, treatment of exceptionals, impact of acquisitions and disposals, leverage and debt and dividend changes, dividends and Remuneration Committee discretion in determination of outcomes

Item	Comment, questions and examples
Performance conditions stretch	Is the target level of performance fair? Is it at budget/corporate plan level? How tough is the budget/plan? How does it compare with historic performance and City analyst expectations and implied expectation in the p/e ratio? Are thresholds and maxima fair? Is the gearing too steep or too flat?
Deferral	Is profit subject to mark to market and other significant judgements about future events? If so should payout be deferred until better view of future outcomes is clear? Will deferral of payout help retention? Is % deferred similar to competitor practice?
Claw-back and Malus	Are these included in the plan detailed rules?
Share retention and share ownership rules and share sale rules	Have these been considered?
Types of award	Share Options (nil cost, or nominal cost) Conditional Share Awards Restricted Shares 'Phantom' equivalents (ie cash)
Award	A collective term to cover Share Options, Conditional Share Awards or Restricted Shares
Shares used	Eg 'A' ordinary shares in the capital of the Company
Eligibility for grants	All executive directors, senior executives and other employees of the Company and its subsidiaries
Expected participation	Executive directors Other selected senior executives
Timing of grants	Within [42] days of adoption of the plan by shareholders or of the announcement of annual or half-yearly results At other times if there are exceptional circumstances Not during a proscribed period or more than [10] years after adoption date
Decisions on grants	Decisions on participation and size of grants made by Remuneration Committee
Confirmation of grants	Grant notice issued by Company as a deed to each participant with details of terms and conditions
Payment for grants by participants	None

Item	Comment, questions and examples
Share capital limits	Limit to new shares or treasury shares which can be used for all share plans 10% of issued share capital in any 10-year period Limit to new shares or treasury shares which can be used for discretionary share plans 5% of issued share capital in any 10-year period
Individual limits	Maximum 'face value' at grant of shares subject to performance share awards in any financial year of [300%] of participant's annual base salary Initial policy is to award the CEO and FD over shares to the value of [100%] of salary Maximum may be exceeded in exceptional circumstances (eg to attract new hires)
Amount paid for the shares on vesting	Nil
Rights of participants before exercise	Awards not transferable No voting, dividend or other rights over the shares (but see dividend equivalents below)
Timing of vesting	No part of the award may vest before the [eg fifth] anniversary of grant or, if later, the date when the Committee determines the extent that performance conditions have been met. The first Awards will be granted in [month year] or within [42] days of AGM. These Awards will not be capable of vesting in full until [month year].
Cessation of employment	Eg definition of 'good leavers' to include death, injury, redundancy and other reasons (eg retirement) at Committee's discretion 'Good leavers' are entitled to exercise awards which have already vested within 6 months of cessation. Unvested awards will vest according to the performance conditions on the normal vesting date at the end of the [5] year performance period, but reduced pro rata to the proportion of the normal vesting period which had elapsed up to cessation. These must be exercised within [6] months of vesting. Remuneration Committee have discretion to vest more if it deems it appropriate. In the case of death and other 'good leaver' circumstances at the Committee's discretion, a proportion of unvested awards (based on time elapsed and underlying financial performance to date) may vest immediately on cessation and must be exercised within [6]/[12] months 'Bad leavers' forfeit all unexercised awards (even if vested) [may be unfair unless due to misconduct]

Item	Comment, questions and examples
Adjustments to performance conditions	Eg performance conditions for awards already granted may be modified or waived by the Committee if events occur which cause them to be no longer appropriate. Any modifications to conditions should be fair and reasonable and put participants into a broadly comparable position to that in which they were in before the events occurred.
Procedure for delivering shares	On vesting, the Company may issue new shares or deliver treasury shares (within the above share capital limits) or arrange for shares purchased on the market to be delivered through an employee benefit trust [rights may be settled in cash paid either by employing company or EBT]
Tax withholding	Condition of exercise that any employee's tax and social security are deducted
Rights over shares acquired	Participant has full dividend, voting and other shareholder rights from date of delivery of shares.
Bankruptcy	Rights under awards lapse
Change in control	If any person gains control of the Company, a proportion of unvested awards vests, related to time since grant and underlying financial performance to date (determined by the Committee). Alternatively, with agreement of the acquiring company, awards can be exchanged for equivalent awards over shares in that company
Internal reorganisation (including demerger)	Awards are exchanged for equivalent awards over shares in another company, as determined by the Committee
Liquidation of Company	On a voluntary liquidation, a proportion of unvested awards (based on time elapsed and underlying financial performance to date) vests on the resolution being passed On a compulsory liquidation, awards lapse
Variations in share capital	Fair and reasonable adjustments made to the number of shares subject to awards and to share capital limits by the Committee, taking professional advice as necessary. Same would apply to performance conditions.
Amendments to the rules	The board of directors of the Company, acting on recommendations of Committee, may amend the rules at any time Shareholders must approve changes to key features – eg eligibility, share capital and individual limits Changes cannot adversely affect existing awards without participants' consent

Item	Comment, questions and examples
Overseas plans	The Board may establish sub-plans for overseas jurisdictions, modified to take account of local tax provisions and other regulations But these must comply with eligibility criteria and count towards the share capital and individual award limits
Contractual rights	Eg award grants are discretionary and not part of employment contracts. They do not count as remuneration for pension or other benefit purposes Eg no right to compensation for loss of rights on leaving employment for any reason
Governing law	England
Trust (EBT)	[The Company] Employee Share Trust, which may be used in association with this plan to satisfy awards
Trustees	Means the trustee for the time being of the [the Company] Employee Share Trust.
Discretion	Do rules provide for judgement and discretion as recommended by the GC100 and Investor Group?

48 Share Ownership

48.1 Introduction

Share Ownership Guidelines, like other parts of remuneration, have been imported from the US. The idea is that directors must build and hold a substantial stake in shares in the business. Most shareholders like to see directors with significant personal investment in the company. Companies need to consider whether their guidelines are mandatory or advisory and what penalties for non-achievement are to be applied.

The scandals in the US and the global financial crisis will increase the pressure for directors to hold shares for a minimum period of one or two years after exercise, after selling shares to pay taxes.

Some companies expect executives to retain a minimum of shares which vest through share plans so as to build up towards the share ownership target.

Some LTIPs require executives to buy and agree to hold shares for the life of an LTIP award.

48.2 Best practice guidance

The UK Corporate Governance Code barely mentions share ownership. It says in Schedule A:

> 'There may be a case for part payment in shares to be held for a significant period.'

Best practice

The QCA guide is particularly strong on Share Ownership. It says:

'• The principles and culture of long-term share ownership should be encouraged for executive directors, senior management and elsewhere, through establishing share ownership guidelines and other means. This leads to directors and senior managers building their shareholding during their time at the company.

- There should be a formal policy on how share sales may be conducted, including:

  – compliance with the company's share dealing code

  - at a minimum, an agreement that no share sales should be permitted until executive directors have built a meaningful shareholding in the company
  - ideally, an agreement that shares should not normally be sold while directors maintain tenure at the company, except to fund tax obligations relating to awards.
- A long-term focus is achieved through deferral of part of the annual bonus into shares and operating performance periods beyond three years.
- Consideration should be given to the introduction of claw-back provisions in the exceptional events of misstatement and/or misconduct or if a director's employment terminates within three years of an award.
- Remuneration policy can encourage retention of executives through:
  - retention periods being set for vested share awards beyond their normal vesting dates
  - long-term incentive awards being granted subject to stretching but realistic targets
  - a performance culture where apt rewards can be earned through the achievement of transparent but stretching targets.'

48.3 Survey data

Typical requirements for FTSE 100 companies are as follows:

Multiple of salary	CEO	Other Directors
Upper quartile	3	2
Median	**2**	**1.5**
Lower Quartile	1.3	1

Smaller companies either do not have formal guidelines or when they do the multiples are lower. One times salary is typical.

In the US, The median multiple of salary and multiple of retainer requirements are 5X and 4X for executives and directors, respectively. The median value of CEO ownership requirements is $5.7 million and the median time required to achieve such ownership is five years.

MM&K in conjunction with Hanson Green and DirectorBank conduct an annual survey of Life in The Boardroom. In the 2012 survey, 488 directors –

298 Chairmen and 190 Non-Executive Directors – contributed to the survey. They provided data on 1,300 appointments on main market, AIM and private company Boards. There were a number of questions asked about share ownership and the responses were:

> '81% of Chairman and NEDs believe ownership of significant amounts of shares improves the alignment of executive directors and shareholders.
>
> 93% of Chairman and NEDs believe the principles and culture of long-term share ownership should be encouraged for executive directors, so they build their shareholding during their entire tenure at the company.
>
> 93% of Chairman and NEDs believe encouraging a longer term focus by deferring part of the annual bonus into shares is a good idea.
>
> Despite these strongly supportive answers, when asked what the multiple of salary that CEOs should own in shares, the answers were around three times salary. This appears to be in conflict with their other answers about "significant" share ownership.

CEOs should have a target to own shares worth a minimum of 0, 1, 2, 3, 5, 10 times salary	**choosing this answer**
0	6%
1	17%
2	22%
3	24%
5	24%
10	6%

> Only 49% of Chairman and NEDs believe there should be a formal policy restricting share sales by directors (except to fund tax obligations relating to awards) whilst directors still maintain tenure at the company. 27% disagree and 6% disagree strongly with this.
>
> Should pay above a certain amount have to be in shares? The UK Corporate Governance Code says that remuneration should be linked to the long term success of the company, so the survey floated the following question that any pay over £500,000 should be paid in shares that do not vest until retirement or 12 months after the director leaves the company. 5% of NEDs "strongly agreed" with this idea and about 25% "agreed". 18% were neutral. However, the majority disagreed (41%) or strongly disagreed (11%).'

48.4 Institutional Views

Table 50: Institutional views

Investing house or agency	Position on share retention	Source
Legal and General	Shareholding requirements should be meaningful, taking into account the size of the company and potential size of share awards received. A company granting annual awards of shares with a face value of 400% of salary should set a target shareholding of at least 4x salary to be achieved within a 5-year period. Unvested shares do not count.	UK corporate governance policy
M&G	Our preference is for deferred share ownership plans with dividend accrual on shares which vest rather than for share option schemes. We expect directors to have a direct shareholding in the company which is substantial in the context of their remuneration.	Issues arising from share ownership
ABI-IVIS	Executive Directors and senior executives should build up significant shareholdings in companies. Unvested share-based incentives should not count towards these requirements. The performance period of LTI schemes should be clearly linked to the timing of the implementation of the strategy of the business, which should be no less than three years and shareholders would generally prefer longer. Committees should consider the use of additional holding periods.	ABI policy
NAPF, Hermes EOS, BT Pension Scheme, Railpen, USS	Management should make a material long-term investment in shares of the business they manage. The meaning of 'long-term' will differ from company to company but three years, the most commonly used time period for long-term awards, is often not long enough. In many situations it may be appropriate for a material proportion of shares granted to be held for a longer period. Companies should also consider ensuring that executives are exposed to some tail risk once they have left a company.	Joint remunera-tion principles

Investing house or agency	Position on share retention	Source
Threadneedle Investments	Threadneedle expects directors to hold a meaningful share in the companies they manage. LTI awards granted to directors should not vest in less than three years, with an additional two-year holding period. Effectively, managers should hold their shares for a period of 5 years.	http://www.threadneedle.co.uk/media/1392381/en_corporate_governance_policy.pdf
PIRC	PIRC will oppose the introduction of all new long-term incentive plans as part of a significant shift in its analysis of governance issues. Managing Director of PIRC – 'LTIPs are not long term and they do not incentivise. They are also ineffective due to amendments and manipulation by remuneration committees.'	UK Shareholder voting guidelines 2013

48.5 Implementation Issues

It is generally agreed that Share Ownership by executives (and lower level employees) is a good idea and should be encouraged.

However, Share Ownership will not stop a Lehman Brothers'[1] or RBS-type disaster. Those cases needed better, stronger corporate governance in order to control over-powerful CEOs.

Ways to encourage Share Ownership are:

- Paying bonus partly in shares.
- Having a significant proportion of pay in the form of equity based incentives.
- Share retention rules that require the executive to retain, say, 75% of shares acquired through incentive plans, net of tax.
- All-employee share schemes, eg the tax effective SIP, SAYE and CSOP plans in the UK and similar plans in other countries.

---

1 Lehman Brothers employees owned 30% of its shares. However senior executives were able to sell $1.1 billion of shares in the years prior to the company going bust. Deferral, claw-back and rules regarding phased sales can lessen such risks for shareholders.

49 Pension

This chapter has been written by Bhargaw Buddhdev, who is a Partner specialising in Executive Pensions at Barnett Waddingham LLP. He can be contacted at: Decimal Place, Chiltern Avenue, Amersham, HP6 5FG. Telephone 01494 788100, website: www.barnett-waddingham.co.uk

49.1 Introduction

Pension is deferred pay. It is important to think of it as a potentially significant part of the total remuneration package. Although pensions have been an important part of directors' remuneration, historically there has been less focus on this part of the remuneration package.

However, there has been an increasing focus in pension provision in directors' remuneration packages primarily due to the recent changes in pension's tax relief.

49.2 Code and best practice guidance

The UK Corporate Governance Code says in Schedule A:

> 'In general, only basic salary should be pensionable. The Remuneration Committee should consider the pension consequences and associated costs to the company of basic salary increases and any other changes in pensionable remuneration, especially for directors close to retirement.'

Best practice

The guidance on pension provision within the 'ABI Principles of Remuneration' is very helpful:

> 'Pension provision can represent a considerable cost to the company and this should be recognised by the Remuneration Committee when considering total executive remuneration.
>
> Pension related payments should not be used as a mechanism for increasing total remuneration. The pension provision for executives should, where possible, be in line with the general approach to the

employees as a whole. Any differences in pension contribution rates for executives and the general workforce should be disclosed and justified to shareholders.

Payments in lieu of pension scheme participation should be clearly disclosed and treated as a separate non-salary benefit. There should be informative disclosure identifying incremental value accruing to pension scheme participation and any other superannuation arrangements.

Changes in pension benefit entitlements or to transfer values reflecting significant changes in actuarial and other relevant assumptions should be fully identified and explained. Where changes to pension benefit entitlements or transfers are made at the discretion of the Remuneration Committee, these should be made clear and justification should be provided. Pensions paid on early retirement should be subject to abatement.'

The NAPF guidance on remuneration principles for building and reinforcing long-term business success (produced in conjunction with Hermes EOS, the BT Pension Scheme, RPMI Railpen Investments and the Universities Superannuation Scheme) says:

'it is not always clear why some executive directors receive … far more generous pension arrangements – or cash in lieu – than less senior colleagues. Remuneration committees should consider whether they are able credibly to justify any such differentials.'

The transfer value of the accrued pension, and the increase in the transfer value, no longer need to be disclosed in remuneration reports with an effective after 13 December 2013 (this was the date on which the FRC published amendments to the Listing Rules to remove the requirement, slightly earlier than had been proposed through consultation. The requirement had already been removed from the Companies Act for reports with an effective date from 30 September 2013). Instead, there is now a requirement to show an estimate of the value of pension of 20 times the increase in accrued benefit. The true cost of the pension plan over the long-term will no longer need to be disclosed. For transparency, it would be preferable for both figures to be disclosed alongside the NAPF/LAPPF recommended best practice guidance. However, the change in requirements does reduce the risk of distortions in the value of defined benefit (DB) pensions brought about by changes in market conditions.

49.3 Types of pension scheme

There are two main categories of pension plan, defined benefit (DB) and defined contribution (DC – often also referred to as money purchase plans).

The majority of DB plans promise a pension after retirement calculated as a proportion of the final pensionable salary (which can comprise salary plus bonus and benefits, although the UK Corporate Governance Code recommends that only basic salary should be pensionable). The proportion of salary is generally the number of years' service divided by the accrual rate. Most employee pension plans have an accrual rate of 60ths or 80ths. However some directors have 45ths or 30ths, or a guarantee of two-thirds of salary to be earned over the period to normal retirement age. The combination of faster accrual rates and higher than average salary increases means the DB plan is worth much more to directors than it is to the average employee. How much it is worth in practice depends on how long the executive lives after he retires and, if he has a spouse, how long they subsequently live, and therefore how long any widow's pension will be payable. The expected value will depend on:

- final pensionable salary (and hence salary increases before retirement);
- years of service
- retirement date
- accrual rate
- discount rate (the higher the future investment return assumption, the lower the value of assets needed today to meet the cost of benefits when they fall due)
- longevity assumptions
- rules for indexation of pension after leaving the scheme and after retirement
- the dependants' pension allowance.

Changes in the expected value will depend on changes to the above, in particular on salary increases and discount rate.

DC plans are much simpler than DB plans. A sum of money is contributed to the plan on behalf of the participant and this is invested generally in accordance with their wishes. The value on retirement will depend on investment returns.

Hybrid plans are combinations of DB and DC plans.

Top up schemes: Top up schemes above the HMRC limits are typically provided by large UK companies. The simplest format is a cash allowance that the executive can choose to spend or invest as he/she wishes.

49.4 UK government limits on pension tax reliefs

The government sets limits around the amount of pension savings one can make and build up without paying additional tax. These limits are called the annual allowance (AA) and the lifetime allowance (LTA). From 6 April 2014 AA will reduce from £50,000 to £40,000 and the LTA will reduce from £1.5 million to £1.25 million.

Annual allowance

The AA is the maximum amount of pension saving one can have each year, that benefits from tax relief.

For DC schemes, this includes pension savings by both the individual and his employer. If the pension saving is more than the AA, this is taxed at the individual's marginal rate of tax.

For DB schemes each £1 per annum increase in pension entitlement (after allowance for inflation) is valued at £16 to see how much of the AA has been used up.

The AA was introduced on 6 April 2006 (A-Day) at £215,000 and it steadily increased for the next four years to £255,000 from 6 April 2010. It was then reduced from £255,000 to £50,000 from 6 April 2011. Therefore, for the tax years 2011/12, 2012/13 and 2013/14 the AA was £50,000 but will be reduced to £40,000 from 6 April 2014.

Unused allowances from the previous three tax years may be carried forward.

Any excess pension savings above the new allowance will be taxed as income. This is penal because the funds will be subject to tax again when eventually drawn as pension. The amount of tax will be based on how much of the excess savings fall into each income tax band.

Someone who is a member of more than one scheme, or pays additional voluntary contributions (AVCs), will need to be more careful as the limits include contributions to all pension arrangements.

The total amount of tax relief available is restricted to 100% of relevant UK taxable earnings in that year.

Calculation of annual allowance

For final salary benefits, each £1 per annum increase in pension entitlement is valued at £16 to calculate how much of the AA has been used up, and the increase in any cash entitlement is taken at face value. Each £1 of pension built up is net of inflation – the opening value of all final salary benefits can be uprated by an inflation allowance which uses the annual increase in the Consumer Prices Index (CPI).

For DC benefits, all contributions paid during the period for assessment (the pension input period) are added together and there is no adjustment for inflation.

Pension input period

The pension input period (PIP) is the period used to calculate the increase in pension saving each year. Contributions and benefits build-up are measured over this period for assessment against the AA. The PIP does not need to be aligned with tax years.

For someone who is a member of more than one pension arrangement, all PIPs ending in a particular tax year are aggregated when assessing against the AA for that tax year.

Carry forward

If someone has not used all their AA in one or more of the last three years, the unused amount is available for carry forward to the current tax year. This means one can make pension savings above the AA (currently £50,000 but reducing to £40,000 from 6 April 2014) in one year and not have to pay an AA charge if there is sufficient unused AA from the previous three tax years.

Annual allowance tax charge

A tax charge on the amount of your annual pension savings that is greater than the £50,000 AA limit (£40,000 from 1 April 2014) is payable. The tax rate applied to this excess amount will be the same as the individual's highest marginal rate of income tax.

Scheme pays

If the AA tax charge is £2,000 or less, the individual is required to pay it direct to HMRC or, subject to the scheme's agreement it may be paid to HMRC by the scheme with a reduction in accrued annual pension benefits to be paid out in the future.

If the AA tax charge is more than £2,000 the charge may be paid by the individual or, if requested by the individual, the scheme is obliged to pay it through a reduction in the annual pension benefits due to be paid out in future, rather than out of current income. This option is called 'scheme pays'. There are strict time limits for individuals to notify their scheme if the AA tax charge is to be paid by the scheme, by reduction of pension benefits.

Lifetime allowance

The lifetime allowance (LTA) is the maximum level of benefits that you can take from all registered pension schemes without incurring additional tax charges. The LTA was set at £1.5 million for the tax year 2006/07 and increased to £1.8 million for the tax year 2011/12. It then reduced from £1.8 million to £1.5 million from 6 April 2012 and will further reduce to £1.25 million from 6 April 2014. The LTA limit applies to funds and pensions built up in any registered pension schemes. It is assessed each time that benefits start to be paid or are transferred to a qualifying recognised overseas pension scheme (known as 'benefit crystallisation events').

How is LTA calculated?

To value defined benefits, each £1 per annum of pension is multiplied by 20 and added to any cash lump sum taken. The £1.25 million LTA (effective from 6 April 2014) is equivalent to a pension of £62,500 per annum at retirement (or pension of £50,000 per annum together with a cash lump sum of £250,000, for example).

Defined contribution benefits are assessed at face value.

If the LTA is exceeded then the excess value is taxed at 55% if taken as a lump sum, or at 25% if taken as a pension, plus the usual marginal rate of income tax through retirement.

Funds and pensions that have already built up, with a current value below the LTA, may grow to exceed the LTA by retirement, allowing for ongoing build-up of pension, deferred benefit revaluation, or investment gains.

The LTA tax charge is normally paid by the pension scheme on behalf of the member with a consequent reduction in their pension.

Lifetime allowance protection

Enhanced Protection

Enhanced Protection was available until 5 April 2009. Individuals with Enhanced Protection will not have to pay an LTA tax charge, regardless of their pension savings on 5 April 2006. Enhanced Protection is lost if after 5 April 2006: (i) a further contribution is paid to a money purchase arrangement; (ii) pension savings build up in a final salary scheme, in general terms, by the greater of 5% per annum, the rise in the cost of living, or increase in pensionable pay; or (iii) if any savings are made in a new pension arrangement.

Primary Protection

Primary Protection was available if pension savings of at least £1.5 million had been built up as at 5 April 2006. The last day for application to be made was 5 April 2009. A Primary Protection factor was given which is used to calculate the monetary amount of the individual's personal LTA when they take their benefits. An individual's personal LTA would then be increased from A-Day onwards, in the way the standard LTA would increase from A-Day (ie by 20% – using the standard LTA of £1.8 million, which ignores the reductions in LTA after A-Day to £1.5 million and £1.25 million). Primary Protection cannot be given up but it can be lost if an individual's protected pension rights are reduced to a value below £1.5 million because of a pension sharing order on divorce.

Fixed Protection 2012

When the LTA reduced from £1.8 million to £1.5 million (from 6 April 2012), to protect people who have been contributing to pension schemes on the expectation of an LTA of £1.8 million, Fixed Protection 2012 was introduced. Fixed Protection 2012 was available until 5 April 2012. It enabled individuals to register for a personal LTA, fixed at £1.8 million, provided they stopped all pension contributions to money purchase schemes and do not build up savings in a defined benefit scheme by more than the permitted limit in each tax year (ie by no more than the relevant CPI). Fixed Protection 2012 cannot be given up but it can be lost if after 5 April 2012 a further contribution is paid to a money purchase arrangement, pension savings build up in a final salary scheme by more than a permitted limit (revaluation of a deferred member's pension is allowed) or savings are made to a new pension arrangement. If Fixed Protection 2012 is lost, the individual's LTA will revert to the standard level (currently £1.5 million, but reducing to £1.25 million from 6 April 2014).

Lifetime allowance protections from 6 April 2014

The government introduced two new types of LTA protection effective from 6 April 2014.

Fixed Protection 2014 will allow individuals to retain the LTA of £1.5 million, but (as with Fixed Protection 2012) no further pension savings will be allowed after 6 April 2014.

Individual Protection 2014 will only be available to individuals with pension savings in excess of £1.25 million on 5 April 2014. They will then have a personalised LTA equal to the value of their pension savings as at 5 April 2014, but capped at £1.5 million.

Unlike Fixed Protection 2014, individuals will be able to carry on with further pension savings without losing their Individual Protection.

Both these forms of protection allow an individual to have an LTA above the standard LTA of £1.25m which will be effective from 6 April 2014. However, if in the future the standard LTA rises to more than the protected level, then the individual's LTA would move to the standard (higher) amount.

Individual Protection 2014 will be available to individuals with Enhanced Protection. Individual Protection 2014 will allow further pension savings without losing protection. Any pension savings above the individual's 'personalised' LTA are likely to be subject to an LTA charge when the benefits are taken. Registration for Individual Protection 2014 will be available after 6 April 2014 and individuals will have until 5 April 2017 to register.

49.5 Auto-enrolment

All employers will be required at some point during the five years from 1 October 2012 to auto-enrol eligible 'jobholders' automatically into a suitable pension scheme and make at least a minimum pension contribution.

For high earners, the tests which companies use to ensure they meet the minimum level of contributions are met may lead to contributions above the AA, giving rise to a member tax charge. The impact of the AA will need closer consideration still when it reduces to £40,000 from 6 April 2014.

It will also be important to assess the position of executives individually and make sure they have access to appropriate information. Some may have Enhanced or Fixed Protection (from 2012 or 2014), which will be lost if further benefits are accrued. This is likely to place an additional tax liability on the executive. The executive will need to be auto-enrolled if they are eligible (in the same way as other eligible jobholders) but will need to opt out within one month of being automatically enrolled in order to retain the LTA Protection.

49.6 Pension value – market data

Barnett Waddingham carried out research covering the majority of FTSE 100 companies accounts published for the years ending between 1 October 2011 and 30 September 2012. This research shows that although the number of DB pension schemes in the UK is declining, DB schemes are still the most common form of pension provision for FTSE 100 directors with 43% of directors belonging to a DB scheme (including current and past service) and with 27% of FTSE 100 directors continuing to accrue benefits.

This compares with the UK population as a whole where only 28% of private sector employees belong to a DB scheme, with far less continuing to accrue benefits in a DB scheme. Of the FTSE 100 companies, 16 continue to provide DB pensions to all of their directors, a decrease from 24 for the previous year.

Defined benefit

DB schemes have cost FTSE 100 companies approximately £900,000 per director over their last accounting year. The average value of DB pensions earned to date amongst the FTSE 100 directors is £4.1m, up from £3.7m the previous year. The average accrued pension to date with the current employer is £228,000 pa per director.

The breakdown of the value of DB pensions earned to date is shown below.

Defined contribution

Chart 17: DB pension earnings to date

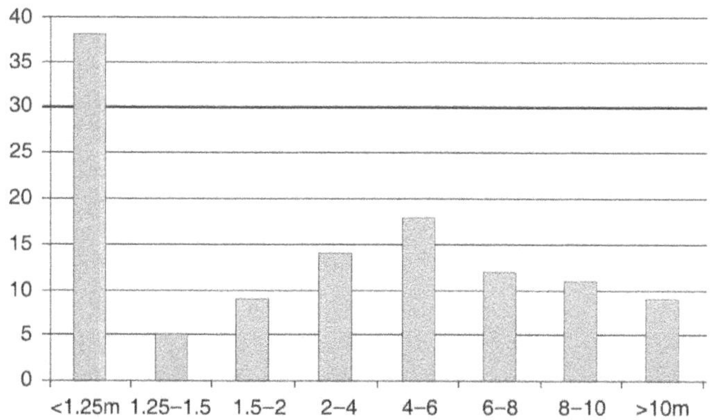

With the ever increasing cost of DB pension provision, companies in the UK have continued to close their DB schemes in favour of DC arrangements.

30% of FTSE 100 directors currently accrue benefits through a DC pension scheme, with 16 of the FTSE 100 companies providing only DC pensions to their directors. For those accruing benefits in a DC scheme, the average employer contribution per director was £147,000, or 25% of salary.

The graph below shows the range of employer contribution rates, as a percentage of basic salary.

Chart 18: DC employer contribution rates

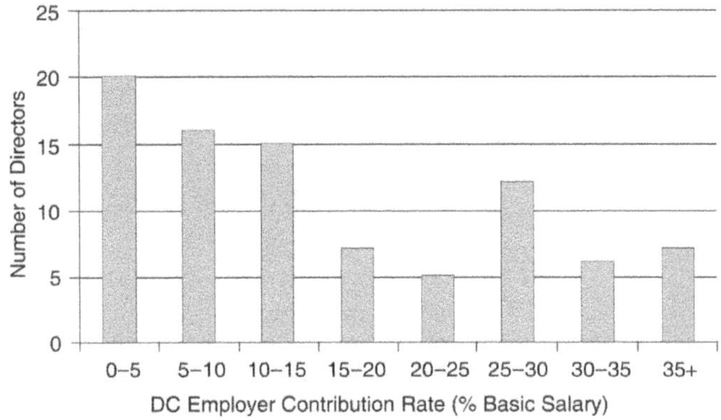

It is worth noting that the average employer contribution of £147,000 per director in a DC arrangement is much less than the average cost of £900,000 per director for DB provision, however it is still three times more than the current AA limit of £50,000 meaning Companies will not be able to maintain contributions at these levels without executives incurring significant AA charges.

Directors themselves make an average contribution of £43,000, or 7% of salary. However a large proportion – 72 out of 90 directors currently accruing DC benefits – do not contribute themselves. Of those who actually contribute, the average is almost £216,000, more than four times the AA limit for 2013/14 and more than five times the AA limit for 2014/15.

Where the main method of providing pensions for a company is through DC arrangements, a flexible combination of DC contributions and cash supplement (or just a cash supplement) is provided for the majority of directors. This allows flexible pension savings making the most of tax allowances available.

Making pension savings in excess of the LTA can still provide value for an executive. Cash supplements will be subject to income tax (at a rate of 45% for individuals with income in excess of £150,000) and 2% employee National Insurance contributions, and most companies are passing onto the executive the additional employer National Insurance contributions, effectively reducing the cash supplement by about a further 12%. This is equivalent to paying approximately 53.4% of the cash in tax and National Insurance contributions.

If benefits in excess of the LTA are taken as cash on retirement, then a one off tax charge of 55% is paid. This is not significantly worse than the effective rate of tax on a cash supplement. In addition savings, within the AA, in a registered pension scheme are not subject to any tax on investment returns before retirement.

Cash in lieu of pension

More and more high earners are finding they are affected by the decrease in the lifetime and annual allowances. With generally strong relationships between directors and the company, and the desire to retain and attract talent, there is a growing trend of companies offering a taxable cash supplement in lieu of some or all pension contributions and accrual.

32% of FTSE 100 directors now receive a cash supplement in lieu of pension accrual or contribution, with 71% of these receiving only cash in lieu of pension.

The remaining 29% who receive a cash supplement in lieu of pension and continue to accrue benefits are evenly split between DB and DC schemes. Those still accruing DB benefits (and receiving cash in lieu) have an average DB cost of £375,000. When we include the cost of cash in lieu of pension this increases to £565,000, still much less than the average cost of £900,000 per director for DB pension provision only. There is a danger that if these high earners do not truly understand what they are giving up, they may not be getting a fair deal.

For those still in a DC scheme and receiving cash in lieu of additional pension contributions, the overall pensions package is on average £179,000 per director with the employer contributing on average £72,000 into the scheme. It is worth noting that whilst this average is higher than the current AA, the majority of directors receive pension contributions of less than the £50,000 limit – this is (most likely) to avoid breaching the AA. It is important for directors to remain up to date with pension legislation to ensure their pension accrual structure remains tax efficient.

It is likely that the numbers being offered cash in lieu of pension will increase following further reductions in pension tax relief. The key question to answer is what is deemed 'fair' for both the employee and the employer. With is a multitude of complicated pension provision structures, especially with DB accrual, it imperative to take into account exactly what is being given up and whether accrual is being limited to a certain level, such as the AA, or foregone completely.

Those who receive cash in lieu of pension provision and do not accrue benefits at all receive on average 32% of salary as cash each year.

The amounts vary by company size as is illustrated overleaf in the data from the MM&K/Manifest September 2013 Executive Director Total Remuneration Survey.

Table 51: MM&K/Manifest September 2013 Executive Director Total Remuneration Survey

Turnover £m	<30			31-100			101-300			301-1,000			1,001-3,000			3,001-10,000			>10,001		
CEO (all figures in £000)	Q1	Median	Q3	Q1	Median	Q3	Q1	Median	Q3	Q1	Median	Q3	Q1	Median	Q3	Q1	Median	Q3	Q1	Median	Q3
Cash allowance in lieu of pension (excl zeroes)	2	4	6	2	10	83	21	66	74	30	79	113	94	147	192	81	151	247	199	255	323
Defined Contribution (excl zeroes)	0	8	30	4	23	35	0	23	48	5	49	63	10	50	111	11	33	50	12	50	123
Defined Benefit (increase in transfer value) (excl zeroes)	19	37	56	0	0	0	0	94	175	6	113	277	65	156	377	46	107	622	346	1,140	1,516
Total Pension (cash allowance + DC + DB) (excl zeroes)	13	26	44	19	29	45	30	50	78	50	91	131	90	148	218	123	225	314	255	365	839
Total Pension (cash allowance + DC + DB)	0	2	25	0	22	36	1	39	63	38	78	126	74	143	214	113	209	312	246	349	817
Total Pension as % salary	0%	2%	11%	0%	10%	13%	0%	10%	18%	10%	18%	25%	16%	25%	31%	19%	29%	39%	28%	35%	87%
Total Remuneration including pension	180	296	607	313	506	761	522	813	1,112	863	1,200	1,945	1,247	1,897	2,427	2,169	2,597	3,373	3,157	4,173	6,200
Pension as % of Total Remuneration	0%	1%	6%	0%	4%	6%	0%	4%	7%	3%	7%	11%	5%	7%	10%	4%	7%	11%	6%	10%	21%
Average of other directors (all figures in £000)																					
Cash allowance in lieu of pension (excl zeroes)	0	26	56	0	0	30	2	27	44	14	38	65	35	65	105	35	72	108	117	153	184
Defined Contribution (excl zeroes)	0	3	15	5	16	24	0	18	33	10	33	50	12	38	50	10	31	50	13	38	94
Defined Benefit (increase in transfer value) (excl zeroes)	0	0	78	0	0	0	0	38	109	20	69	214	4	49	168	17	82	170	195	500	940
Total Pension (cash allowance + DC + DB) (excl zeroes)	6	15	26	14	19	30	18	30	51	30	51	80	46	73	121	59	108	199	149	211	487
Total Pension (cash allowance + DC + DB)	0	0	14	0	15	24	0	23	41	23	45	71	35	67	116	41	97	198	144	207	461
Total Pension as % salary	0%	0%	10%	0%	10%	14%	0%	10%	18%	9%	15%	24%	12%	20%	28%	12%	21%	45%	25%	30%	69%
Total Remuneration including pension	135	197	379	216	357	477	315	450	680	550	777	1,179	718	1,020	1,441	1,080	1,448	1,892	2,147	2,610	3,525
Pension as % of Total Remuneration	0%	0%	5%	0%	5%	7%	0%	4%	8%	2%	6%	11%	4%	7%	9%	3%	6%	13%	6%	8%	15%

Market Capitalisation £m	<30			31-100			101-300			301-1,000			1,001-3,000			3,001-10,000			>10,001		
CEO (all figures in £000)	Q1	Median	Q3	Q1	Median	Q3	Q1	Median	Q3	Q1	Median	Q3	Q1	Median	Q3	Q1	Median	Q3	Q1	Median	Q3
Cash allowance in lieu of pension (excl zeroes)	15	29	90	4	13	40	31	62	96	26	71	111	79	113	169	154	213	270	188	270	333
Defined Contribution (excl zeroes)	0	5	22	3	24	46	3	30	49	4	37	50	12	50	78	10	11	50	9	43	146
Defined Benefit (increase in transfer value) (excl zeroes)	0	0	0	75	167	243	0	59	112	14	136	318	8	109	254	81	96	563	545	1,355	1,681
Total Pension (cash allowance + DC + DB) (excl zeroes)	12	23	30	20	35	64	27	49	80	39	66	131	72	119	193	171	247	313	247	400	1,290
Total Pension (cash allowance + DC + DB)	0	0	20	0	25	53	0	34	60	25	51	118	51	113	190	105	219	309	238	373	1,205
Total Pension as % salary	0%	0%	10%	0%	10%	16%	0%	10%	18%	9%	15%	25%	12%	20%	30%	18%	29%	38%	26%	35%	101%
Total Remuneration including pension	178	247	326	271	425	813	514	679	923	787	1,127	1,445	1,234	1,945	2,418	2,290	3,047	3,678	3,734	5,203	6,643
Pension as % of Total Remuneration	0%	0%	8%	0%	5%	9%	0%	5%	8%	3%	6%	9%	4%	6%	10%	4%	7%	9%	4%	10%	20%
Average of other directors (all figures in £000)																					
Cash allowance in lieu of pension (excl zeroes)	0	0	25	7	27	35	8	32	47	11	28	56	31	63	86	63	98	142	143	173	205
Defined Contribution (excl zeroes)	0	5	13	0	13	28	4	17	34	10	28	47	8	30	50	0	15	71	19	38	75
Defined Benefit (increase in transfer value) (excl zeroes)	0	0	24	55	109	208	0	0	98	0	40	86	19	96	223	3	76	191	271	601	952
Total Pension (cash allowance + DC + DB) (excl zeroes)	6	12	16	14	23	41	15	30	45	26	44	64	37	67	117	71	135	195	125	216	588
Total Pension (cash allowance + DC + DB)	0	3	12	0	15	29	0	17	38	16	36	57	22	60	108	63	121	182	121	214	544
Total Pension as % salary	0%	2%	9%	0%	10%	15%	0%	10%	16%	8%	14%	20%	8%	15%	25%	15%	25%	40%	25%	30%	87%
Total Remuneration including pension	117	155	198	197	317	443	288	431	595	463	687	888	778	1,089	1,536	1,267	1,692	2,047	2,362	2,971	3,807
Pension as % of Total Remuneration	0%	2%	7%	0%	5%	9%	0%	5%	8%	3%	6%	9%	2%	5%	9%	3%	7%	12%	4%	7%	17%

Unfunded pension promise

A non-approved scheme in existence immediately prior to 6 April 2006 (ie a FURBS (funded) or an UURBS (unfunded)) became an Employer Financed Retirement Benefits Scheme (EFRBS) at that date. It has remained possible for a scheme to be established as an EFRBS rather than as a registered pension scheme. The disguised remuneration legislation introduced by Finance Act 2011 means that funded EFRBS have become unviable. However, for unfunded EFRBS (previously known as UURBS) which are a simple promise between the employer and the member, the lack of any third party takes them outside of the disguised remuneration rules. Unfunded EFRBS therefore remain viable and may be appropriate in cases where a substantial additional pension provision is required that cannot be funded through a registered scheme due to annual or lifetime allowance restrictions.

A significant proportion of companies which provide DB pensions are bypassing the tax allowances by providing their executives with pension outside of a tax-registered pension scheme. The provision of future pension through an unfunded and non-registered arrangement avoids annual and lifetime allowance tax charges, but the benefits are payable from the company's resources with no assets earmarked for security on the benefit promised. As there are no assets which have been put aside to provide benefits, there is no guarantee that the pension can be paid in future, and no restrictions on the form of benefits to be provided. It is therefore common for unfunded arrangements to allow the individual flexibility to exchange the pension for a cash lump sum at retirement.

A new duty to notify HMRC under the Disclosure of Tax Avoidance Schemes (DOTAS) regime came into force from 4 November 2013. It may potentially catch some unfunded EFRBS, but not all of these will need to be notified to HMRC. It does not apply to wholly unfunded EFRBS, that is where it does not in any way reduce or eliminate the employment income for tax purposes and where there is no 'relevant step' which is essentially that the employer does not provide a security or earmarking of a sum or asset with a view to paying a pension. A balance sheet liability by itself would not be regarded as earmarking. Employers providing or considering providing future pension through an unfunded EFRBS should seek specialist legal and tax advice regarding whether the arrangement would be required to be notified to HMRC under the DOTAS regime.

No pension provision

Interestingly, 52 FTSE 100 directors received no pension compensation as per companies accounts published for the year ending between 1 October

2011 and 30 September 2012. It is likely that the absence of a pension provision is compensated for when setting salaries and other elements of remuneration.

Many companies provide life assurance benefits through the pension arrangement. If no explicit pension provision is provided, then provision of life assurance benefits should be considered to ensure that executives have sufficient coverage for their needs.

49.7 Pension remuneration checklist

Companies should revisit their reward strategy now. Points to consider include:

(i) How to ensure the HMRC limits are not exceeded.

(ii) Why provide any pension provision above the HMRC limits?

(iii) If executives will be worse off as a result of the new HMRC limits, should there be any compensation for executives?

(iv) Should such compensation be in the form of:

- (a) a supplementary 'pension' cash allowance (currently the most popular method)
- (b) a one off salary increase
- (c) an unfunded pension arrangement providing a pension at retirement, but without the assets being held in trust to provide security
- (d) increased incentive opportunity, either annual bonus or long term incentive
- (e) an award of shares that vest over time, so allowing the executive to build up a substantial stake in the company on top of their £1.5 million HMRC approved pension pot.

(v) Whether, and if so how, to allow tax planning for those individuals who are on the cusp of being taxed at 60% rather than 40% (taxable earnings £100,000 to £113,950) or 45% rather than 40% (taxable earnings over £150,000), via salary sacrifice, bonus sacrifice and related investment guidance on investment bonds, etc?

(vi) Is it appropriate to fund pension savings above the current HMRC limits or would an unfunded arrangement be better? If an unfunded approach is adopted what form of benefits should it provide and what flexibility should be allowed at the individual's retirement.

(vii) Should the company provide a wealth accumulation plan to assist executives to invest any cash allowances awarded in lieu of pension benefits above the HMRC limits? If so should such a plan be optional or obligatory?

(viii) Should the company provide executives with access to independent advice to ensure that the executive is informed about the most appropriate form of benefits for their personal circumstances?

49.8 Directors pension disclosures from 1 October 2013

New Companies Act regulations for the reporting of directors' remuneration have introduced measures proposed and consulted on by the Department for Business, Innovation and Skills. The legislation came into effect from 1 October 2013, but also applies to company years ended on 30 September 2013. The basic principle of the new rules is to disclose a single figure for directors' remuneration from year to year, together with supporting additional information.

The single figure for remuneration will comprise of salary and fees, taxable benefits, short and long term incentives and pensions.

The 'pension' value will comprise cash paid in lieu of pension provision, contributions to money purchase arrangements, and value of pension benefits earned over the year in a DB arrangement which must be calculated in a similar way to that used to assess the liability for tax under the AA rules but using a valuation factor of 20 rather than 16.

50 Other Forms of Remuneration

50.1 Other benefits

Widow's (surviving spouse) pension and life insurance are typically provided as part of the pension plan.

Holidays, private medical and directors' indemnity insurance are also normal benefits.

A company car and for larger companies the use of a chauffeur whilst on company business is also normal.

Larger companies with overseas operations may find it cost effective to have a company plane.

Payment of club membership fees is also a common benefit.

Executives will also be eligible to join all employee share plans, such as SAYE share options and the Share Incentive Plan (SIP).

Housing allowances for executives relocating can be quite a significant benefit in some cases.

50.2 Expenses

CEO expenses are usually signed off by the Chairman of the Remuneration Committee. This is a chore, but occasionally it turns out to be an important chore! There have been cases of inappropriate expenses being submitted. If the CEO does not follow best practice it is difficult for him to ensure the rest of the organisation obeys the rules in spirit as well as to the letter.

50.3 Use of trusts

The use of trusts may previously have been considered by some as best practice or by others as acceptable tax avoidance.

However this has now been stopped by the disguised remuneration legislation; see **Section 7.3**.

Unwinding trusts requires expert advice and assistance.

50.4 Provision of investment advice

Where does remuneration stop and where does the investment of the executives personal wealth management begin?

This is a difficult area as executive remuneration may well impinge on executives' personal investment decisions. Best advice may be for executives to diversify their wealth. However share ownership rules, share retention rules and peer pressure may require executives to retain their shares.

Provision of financial advice falls within the Financial Services Act and companies will not want to give such advice.

However, it can be very time consuming for executives to find out how to get good advice on their personal financial affairs. Their time may be better spent focussing on their day job. For this reason may large companies will adopt one or more advisers who will be able to advise company executives. Companies may pay for some or all of this advice.

Increasingly, with more and bigger cash pension allowances, executives need to consider how to invest their wealth. And hence the provision of investment advice is an area which needs consideration.

51 Directors' Service Contracts

51.1 At a glance

- The UK Corporate Governance Code includes specific provisions on the notice periods and compensation arrangements for directors.
- The ABI and NAPF have jointly issued detailed guidance on contracts.
- A comprehensive service contract for each executive director can help to prevent misunderstandings.
- Each Non-Executive Director will usually have a contract for services. See **Section 53.10**.
- The Large and Medium-sized Companies and Groups (Accounts and Reports) Regulations 2008 (No 410) includes provisions on the retention and location of directors' service contracts (see **Section 5.20**).
- Members of the company are entitled to inspect directors' service contracts. Details have to be disclosed in the remuneration report (see **Section 5.21**).
- Shareholder approval is required for any contract giving a director a right of employment for more than two years, unless the company can give unconditional notice at any time.

51.2 Code and best practice guidance

The UK Corporate Governance Code includes the following provisions:

> 'D.1.4The remuneration committee should carefully consider what compensation commitments (including pension contributions and all other elements) their directors' terms of appointment would entail in the event of early termination. The aim should be to avoid rewarding poor performance. They should take a robust line on reducing compensation to reflect departing directors' obligations to mitigate loss.
>
> D.1.5Notice or contract periods should be set at one year or less. If it is necessary to offer longer notice or contract periods to new directors recruited from outside, such periods should reduce to one year or less after the initial period.'

The Code drafting is quite specific and stronger than previous wording. Large payoffs for failure have consistently attracted negative publicity. In December 2002, in response to continuing concern, the ABI and NAPF issued a joint statement with specific and detailed guidance (see **Appendix 5**). When companies did not follow the new guidance, both the ABI and NAPF were vocal in criticising companies and this led to much negative publicity and some large percentage votes against the remuneration report resolutions at AGMs in 2003. The government responded by issuing another consultation document, 'Rewards for Failure: Directors' Remuneration – Contracts, Performance and Severance' (June 2003). In January 2005 the Department of Trade and Industry announced that it would not legislate at this time but would allow further time to monitor whether the AGM vote on the remuneration report was effective in curtailing rewards for failure.

PIRC first brought shareholders' attention to the potential consequences of long notice periods as far back as 1994 when over 40% of executives in the FTSE 350 had contracts of three years or longer, compared to less than 30% with one year or less.

One-year rolling contracts did not become the most common form of contract in the FTSE 350 until 1998, when just over 50% of directors had one year notice periods compared to approximately 45% on two years' notice. The major change took place in 2001 when 75% of FTSE 350 directors had one year contracts, up from 56% in 2000, and only 23% had a two year contract, down from 42% in the previous year.

The trend towards reducing executive contractual notice periods to one year or less continued during 2002. By the end of 2002, only 16% of executive directors still had a contract with a notice period longer than one year.

In practice nearly all listed companies now (in 2012) follow the UK Corporate Governance Code of one year or less for contracts.

In 2000, whilst contract lengths had been declining the cash value of compensation paid to departing directors had increased for all indices over the previous two years. Average compensation amounts stood at around 120% of salary and 90% of total cash remuneration. In 2001, average compensation amounts stood at around 130% of salary and 90% of total cash remuneration. The explanation for the increase in compensation at a time of shortening notice periods was that compensation was being paid for more elements of a director's emoluments package than simply salary. As the bonus element of packages was increasing, this pushed up compensation relative to salary.

Among FTSE 100 companies, 40% disclosed liquidated damage provisions in 2000, up from 34% in 1999. In FTSE 250 companies, 29% had liquidated damage provisions, up from 23% in 1999. For the Small Cap companies, the percentage had fallen to 11% from 15%.

Chart 19: Notice periods for executive directors 1994–2008 (FTSE 350) (Source: PIRC)

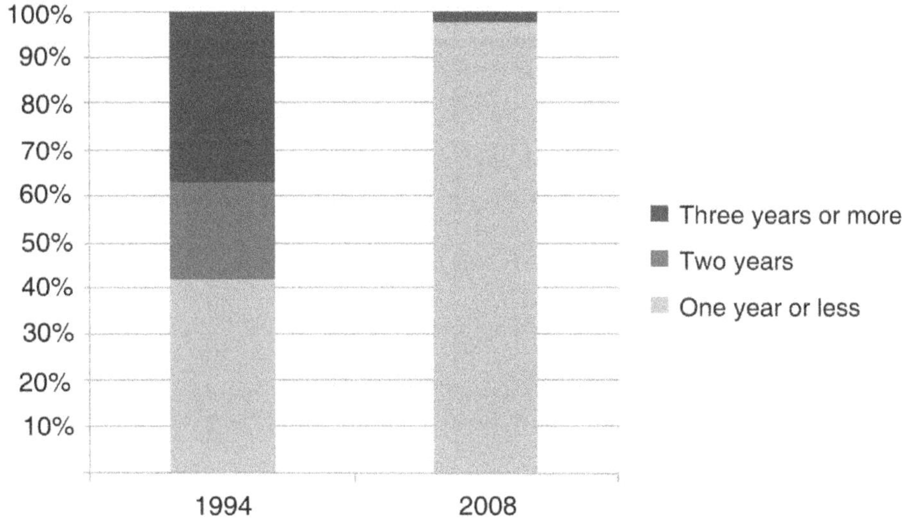

51.3 Service contracts for executive directors

Following years of pressure, most directors' contracts of UK companies do not have notice periods of longer than one year. Around 4% of directors have six-month rolling notice periods. The ABI/NAPF guidance on contracts permits two-year contracts for new recruits, so long as they roll down to one year after 12 months.

An executive director is in effect an employee of the company and it is appropriate that the terms and conditions of his or her appointment should be set out in a written contract of service between the director and the company. A comprehensive service contract can help to prevent misunderstandings and provides a key point of reference if problems arise (side letters, minutes of meetings, meeting notes and emails may also be useful in disputes). A service contract for an executive director should normally include:

- specific duties of the director, including the amount of time to be spent on company activities (this may be particularly important where the individual also holds posts such as Non-Executive directorships in other businesses)
- remuneration, including details of any arrangements involving:
  - benefits in kind (eg private health cover, accommodation, company car)

  - bonus schemes
  - long-term incentive plans
  - share options
- holiday entitlement
- arrangements in the case of prolonged absence through illness
- pension arrangements
- required notice period and procedures in the case of dismissal
- compensation arrangements in the event of early termination of the contract
- clawback and malus provisions (if any)
- compensation and other arrangements in the event of change in control
- confidentiality arrangements
- restrictions after employment.

Other issues may need to be covered, depending on the circumstances.

It should be noted that Non-Executive Directors have a very different role to executive directors and the terms and conditions of their appointment will usually be set out in a contract for services. See **53.10**.

51.4 Liquidated damages and mitigation

Liquidated damages clauses do not comply with the Code, which specifies that companies should take a robust line regarding the departing executive's obligation to mitigate their loss.

The concept of mitigation is that the departing executive is expected to seek and find alternative employment with a similar level of remuneration as soon as possible. It may take several months and the executive may have to accept a lower level of remuneration. Thus an executive on a year's notice might be expected to find similar employment in six to nine months. It will, of course, depend on particular circumstances and the company must take care not to make statements that impact on the executive's reputation and ability to secure another similar job.

An increasingly common practice is to pay termination payments on a monthly basis up until the date the executive is appointed to a new role.

51.5 Claw-back/Deferral of Bonus

The Code says in Appendix 1:

> 'Consideration should be given to the use of provisions that permit the company to reclaim variable components in exceptional circumstances of misstatement or misconduct.'

Strictly speaking a claw-back clause will allow bonuses that have already been paid to be clawed back from executives. However such clauses will always be open to legal dispute. The benefit of deferral is that it is much easier to claw back that part of bonus that has not already been paid out.

The ABI guidance is as follows:

> **'1. Performance Adjustment/Malus and Clawback**
>
> As stated above, structures should include provisions that allow the company, in specified circumstances, to:
>
> – Forfeit all or part of a bonus or long-term incentive award before it has vested and been paid ("performance adjustment" or "malus"); and/or
>
> – Recover sums already paid ("clawback")
>
> Shareholders believe the circumstances in which performance adjustment and clawback can be implemented need to be agreed and documented before awards are made.
>
> The Committee should review the circumstances in which these provisions can apply and ensure that they are appropriate for the company. In general, shareholders accept that performance adjustment will apply to a broader range of circumstances than for clawback. The circumstances should, in each case, be clearly disclosed to shareholders.
>
> The Committee should also consider the enforcement power they have to implement each process.'

This issue is covered in more detail in Chapter **46.13**.

51.6 Conclusions regarding contracts

The issue of compensation associated with notice periods and contracts cannot be looked at in isolation from other elements of directors' remuneration. Salary, bonus, benefits and pension also impact on compensation levels. Therefore, as well as looking at the issue of 'rewards for failure' in relation to contracts, the wider issue of remuneration packages unrelated to any past or future improvements in company performance should also be addressed. The Remuneration Committee needs to consider the total remuneration that may be earned over a number of years under a number of performance scenarios and confirm that the contractual compensation is not an excessive part of this total remuneration.

Shareholder pressure has been successful in reducing notice periods. This suggests that contractual terms are not the outcome of the 'market for executives' but are as much influenced by what is acceptable to shareholders and other interested parties. Shareholders can be expected to be more assertive in enforcing their interests. But in clamping down on one aspect of 'excessive' pay, shareholders should ensure that other payments are not made. In this respect, complexity is a barrier. Shareholders should be analysing remuneration packages in the round, rather than in a fragmentary way, but this is not easy for them to do with complex remuneration structures.

The use of phased payments and/or linking payments to changes in the share price since appointment is generally supported.

Reducing compensation following poor performance is an entirely reasonable concept, though open to considerable legal debate. However, poor performance has wider ramifications than just its impact on compensation levels. One great benefit of Higgs' review is that all Boards should be approaching appraisal and competence issues in a far more professional and consistent way than in the past. If this process is being conducted effectively, poor performance would be identified and dealt with at an earlier stage and should not be an issue for negotiation in a severance situation.

When an executive leaves, he or she may have a significant amount of deferred bonus, LTIPs and options. Often these awards allow the executive some flexibility as to when they choose to exercise the option or 'realise' the deferred bonus or LTIP award. The press usually add up all the amounts the executive will receive and include the pension (the transfer value of the accrued pension) and report this as the 'reward for failure'. With the new DRRR, it will be much clearer in remuneration reports in which year remuneration is awarded and received or receivable. Hopefully, this will avoid the press double counting remuneration in their 'rewards for failure' sums. Of course, it will also be incumbent on companies to be clear and transparent on how much remuneration they have paid executives and when it is or will be paid.

Experience suggests that disclosure of contractual provisions could be improved to build on the new regulations. The simplest solution would be for companies to disclose the maximum compensation payable to each director if their contract was terminated, with a note saying the amount would be subject to mitigation.

Companies can avoid the danger of bad press for 'rewards for failure' by reducing executive contracts to six months' notice and termination payment of six months' salary and benefits. Good executives will be able to find a new job in six months and should not worry about this. Despite the logic of this approach, there seems no enthusiasm for it, which suggests the market for top executives is not an efficient market.

51.7 Service contracts for executive directors

Where a director has a written contract of service with the company, CA 1985, s 318 requires the company to retain a copy of the contract at one of the following locations:

- the company's registered office
- the place where the register of members is kept (if this is not the registered office)
- the company's principal place of business (provided that this is in the part of Great Britain where the company is registered).

If a director does not have a written contract of service, the company must keep a written memorandum of the terms of his or her appointment. The same rules apply to a variation of a director's contract. A parent company is also required to keep copies of service contracts between its subsidiaries and their directors, or a written memorandum of the terms if these contracts are not in writing. Copies of all contracts and memoranda must be kept in the same place. If they are not kept at the registered office, the company must notify the Registrar of Companies of where they are held and of any changes in location. CA 1985, s 318(6) emphasises that these arrangements apply equally in the case of shadow directors. However, there is no formal requirement for a company to retain a copy of a contract, variation or memorandum when the unexpired term is less than 12 months, or where the contract can be terminated by the company within the next 12 months without the payment of compensation.

51.8 Director working outside the UK

Where a director of the company, or of one of its subsidiaries, is required under his or her contract to work wholly or mainly outside the UK, the company is not required to keep a copy of the contract, but it must keep a memorandum giving the director's name and the provisions of the contract relating to its duration. In the case of a contract for a director of a subsidiary, the name and place of incorporation of the subsidiary must also be recorded in the memorandum. These memoranda must be kept in the same place as the contracts and memoranda relating to the other directors.

51.9 Inspection of contracts

Under CA 2006 s 188, any member of the company is entitled to inspect the copies of the directors' contracts of service (or the memoranda where there is no written service contract) without charge. If the company refuses to allow a member to inspect a contract or memorandum, the court can require immediate inspection.

51.10 Shareholder approval for contracts for more than two years

Under CA 2006 s 188, a director cannot be given the right of employment with the company (or, where relevant, with the group) for a period of more than two (previously it was five) years under an agreement which does not allow the company to give unconditional notice at any time, unless this term of the contract has been first approved by the company in general meeting (or, in the case of a private company, by written resolution). Employment is defined as including employment under a contract for services. Where the director is also a director of the company's holding company, prior approval to the arrangement must normally be given by the shareholders of both the subsidiary and the holding company (unless the subsidiary is wholly owned, in which case prior approval of the arrangement by the shareholders of the subsidiary is not required).

A written memorandum setting out the proposed agreement must be available for inspection by the members at the company's registered office for a period of at least 15 days before the meeting and at the meeting itself. In the case of a private company where agreement is to be by written resolution, a copy of the memorandum must be sent to each member before, or at the same time as, the resolution is provided for signature.

A term included in a director's contract in contravention of CA 2006, s 188 is void, and the agreement is deemed to include a term entitling the company to terminate the agreement at any time by the giving of reasonable notice.

51.11 Series of agreements

CA 2006 s 188 includes special provisions to prevent a company entering into a series of shorter agreements with the same director in an attempt to avoid the requirement for shareholder approval of a contract that in effect extends for more than five years.

PART E

CHAIRMAN AND NON-EXECUTIVE DIRECTORS

52 Chairman

52.1 Best practice guidance

The UK Corporate Governance Code gives no guidance about the remuneration of the Chairman. It is strangely silent on the issue.

The UK Corporate Governance Code distinguishes between a Chairman who is independent on appointment and one who is not. The implication is that after some years as a Chairman the issue of independence is not relevant.

The UK Corporate Governance Code does not distinguish between an Executive and a Non-Executive Chairman.

52.2 The role

The Chairman must work closely with the CEO and has to establish an effective working relationship. However, in cases when the CEO is not performing, it is the Chairman who must take the lead in getting the Board to agree to ask the CEO to retire or leave; or in exceptional cases to remove the CEO. This crucial responsibility means that sometimes the relationship of the CEO and Chairman is potentially strained.

Some Non-Executive Chairmen undertake the role as similar to a Non-Executive Director and just requiring some extra time to plan and manage the board meetings. The structure of the remuneration of such a role should be similar to that of other Non-Executive Directors.

Other Non-Executive Chairmen are much more heavily involved in the strategy and leadership of the company. For these, the remuneration needs careful consideration. Their remuneration should be set on the initial appointment when the role needs to be clearly defined. If subsequently, the strategy changes or the executive team changes in a way which impacts on the role of the Chairman, there may be a case for reviewing the Chairman's remuneration.

On appointment there should be a clear understanding of the amount of time that the Chairman is expected to contribute.

See Chapter A2.2 for more information about the role of the Chairman.

52.3 Remuneration

The level of pay of the Chairman should reflect:

- His/her track record and ability to command a rate of remuneration in the market place

- How much he/she is paid in other roles in other companies
- The role and contribution he/she is expected to make and the value this will add to the company
- The time commitment
- The amount that the previous Chairman was paid
- The amount the CEO is paid and how this compares on a per day basis with the Chairman
- Shareholders' views about what is acceptable
- Market data for rates of pay for Chairmen in similar companies.

An Executive Chairman is the most senior executive in the company and should be remunerated like a CEO.

52.4 Types of remuneration structure

Typical practice in quoted companies is that the Chairman is paid a fixed fee and in some cases some of the fee is paid in shares. Sir Derek Higgs, in his Higgs review, recommended that 'innovative' approaches be considered for the Chairman.

The most common types of approach are:

(i) Paid only fees[1]

(ii) Paid a mixture of fees in cash and in shares

(iii) Awarded a number of shares on appointment which vest at a rate of x% per year, plus an annual fee

(iv) Awarded a number of options on appointment plus an annual fee

(v) An annual fee, plus annual awards of options or LTIPs or other types of share awards

(vi) In a turn-round situation a Chairman might be awarded a specific incentive plan as well as his/her annual fees. In such cases the Chairman may become more hands-on.

The use of partly paid shares should be considered as a tax effective way to remunerate Chairmen and Non-Executive Directors.

52.5 Market Data: Fees – Chairman

The following data are taken from the MM&K/Directorbank/Hanson Green 2012 Life in the Boardroom survey which covered 490 Non-Executive Directors and Chairmen with roles in 1,300 companies.

---

1 Annual fees are usually paid monthly.

Fees are usually linked to the time spent, company size, ownership, sector, risk and other company specific factors. The survey shows fee levels broken down by company size and ownership. The first table shows data for UK quoted companies (ie main market listing or AIM). The average fee for the less than £10 million and £10 to £30 million turnover categories are significantly more than the median figures, which indicates that some companies are paying much higher than others and this produces an inconsistent pattern of averages of £51k, £42k and then £63k in the next category. Other than this, the data show quite a consistent pattern.

UK QUOTED companies. Total fees £000 per annum (including shares)	**Turnover £ millions**					
	>10	**10–30**	**30–100**	**100–300**	**300–1,000**	**>1,000**
Upper Quartile	40	49	72	109	173	337
Median	25	26	60	85	133	225
Lower Quartile	16	13	50	58	93	135
Average	51	42	63	88	150	246
Sample Size	25	26	25	22	28	12

50% of companies pay at or above the Median and 50% at or below it. Upper Quartile means 25% of companies are above this. Lower Quartile means 25% of companies are below this.

The next table shows the breakdown for Private Equity and venture capital owned companies. The data has not been smoothed, allowing readers to form their own conclusions. For example, the median figure for the £30 to £100 million turnover category is only £45,000. By looking at the categories on either side, we see that a figure of £60,000 might be a better estimate of the median rate.

PRIVATE EQUITY backed companies. Total fees £000 per annum (including shares)	**Turnover £ millions**						
	<3	**3–10**	**10–30**	**30–100**	**100–300**	**300–1,000**	**>1,000**
Upper Quartile	30	40	49	70	123	114	
Median	23	25	40	45	100	88	300
Lower Quartile	12	20	30	30	65	75	
Average	23	52	50	67	107	116	
Sample Size	17	21	34	25	12	10	1

The data suggest that other UK private companies pay their Chairmen more than Private Equity owned and quoted companies, except in the very smallest category (< £3 million turnover) where fees are about 35% less.

OTHER UK PRIVATE companies*. Total fees £000 per annum (including shares)	**Turnover £ millions**						
	<3	**3–10**	**10–30**	**30–100**	**100–300**	**300–1,000**	**>1,000**
Upper Quartile	30	36	53	85		123	
Median	18	30	40	69	120	120	
Lower Quartile	12	22	29	35		115	
Average	27	33	57	76		118	
Sample Size	68	22	20	14	1	4	0

* Excludes not for Profit, Public Sector and Charities

There are relatively few large private companies and the variations in the survey results reflect this.

The public sector is paying substantially less than listed companies; and for many small public sector organisations no fees are paid. We suspect this is an area for concern – it is difficult to insist on the highest standards of competence, contribution, conduct and performance when directors are not paid a fair reward. If people are paid fairly, then they expect to be held to account. With increasing pressure on costs and value for money in the Public Sector, this problem can only grow.

There is a very wide range of practice in setting fees for Chairmen, particularly in the private sector. The wide variety of practice suggests that fee levels do not reflect a well ordered economic market and that candidates and companies should negotiate hard over fee levels on appointment.

Daily Rates – Chairman

The 'daily rate' is calculated by dividing the total fees (including payments in shares) by the number of days worked in the year.

The data show quite a variation, but indicates that for UK quoted companies the daily rate for a Chairman is around £1,000 for smaller companies, rising to £2,000 for medium sized companies (£30 to £300 million turnover), £3,000 for larger companies and £4,500 for FTSE 100 companies. Some Chairmen are paid a significant amount and this is why the averages and upper quartiles in the smaller turnover categories are much higher than the median figures.

UK QUOTED companies. Daily Rates £ (including shares)	**Turnover £ millions**					
	<10	**10–30**	**30–100**	**100–300**	**300–1,000**	**>1,000**
Upper Quartile	1,633	1,906	3,095	2,875	3,063	4,351
Median	1,277	929	2,200	2,051	2,830	3,555
Lower Quartile	897	583	1,512	1,710	2,155	3,227

The next table shows the breakdown for Private Equity and venture capital backed companies. The analysis across all companies shows that overall daily rates are similar to quoted companies. However, companies which have more than £100 million turnover pay significantly more than those with less than £100 million turnover. The data suggests that those in the £100 million to £300 million turnover range are paid the most per day, however this may be a statistical quirk.

PRIVATE EQUITY backed companies. Daily Rates £ (including shares)	**Turnover £ millions**						
	<3	**3–10**	**10–30**	**30–100**	**100–300**	**300–1,000**	**>1,000**
Upper Quartile	1,406	1,771	1,659	2,333	5,324	3,276	
Median	1,150	1,125	1,228	1,111	3,348	2,728	2,400
Lower Quartile	720	755	839	833	2,027	2,221	

In both Private Equity backed and private companies it is more likely that the Chairman has a stake in the business and will be compensated partly through equity interests.

Other UK private companies pay noticeably less per day.

OTHER UK PRIVATE companies.* Daily Rates £ (including shares)	**Turnover £ millions**						
	<3	**3–10**	**10–30**	**30–100**	**100–300**	**300–1,000**	**>1,000**
Upper Quartile	2,410	1,630	1,485	2,827	2,000		6,000
Median	783	1,250	1,102	1,484	1,591	1,875	3,625
Lower Quartile	625	652	818	980	1,122		1,188

* Excludes not for Profit, Public Sector and Charities

Increases – Chairman

80% of Chairmen did not have a fee increase last year (ie in 2011) and 77% do not expect one next year (2012).

% increases in total annual fees in 2011.	**Turnover £ millions**					
	<10	**10–30**	**30–100**	**100–300**	**300–1,000**	**>1,000**
Upper Quartile	0	0	0	5	4	9
Median	0	0	0	0	0	0
Lower Quartile	0	0	0	0	0	0
Average	1.4	0.2	3.7	5.8	3.2	6.9

expected % Increases in total annual fees in 2012.	**Turnover £ millions**					
	<10	**10–30**	**30–100**	**100–300**	**300–1,000**	**>1,000**
Upper Quartile	0	0	2	2	3	0
Median	0	0	0	0	0	0
Lower Quartile	0	0	0	0	0	0
Average	1.2	3.5	3.8	1.8	1.9	0.6

The average figures are much higher than the medians and in some cases higher than the upper quartile. This is because some Chairmen have had/are expecting significant increases. Quite a number of companies have not made any increases, so it would appear others have given quite substantial increases. In addition new appointees may be able to negotiate higher fees than their predecessors.

Satisfaction rating

26% of Chairmen felt their remuneration is too low, 72% about right and 9% felt it was too high. The results are consistent across all sizes of company.

Other employee surveys consistently report that most employees feel their pay is too low. It is interesting to note that Chairmen are more satisfied about their pay than employees.

Last year (2011) 32% of Chairmen felt their remuneration was too low, 67% about right, and 2% too high. Their views would appear to be changing to reflect the increasing pressure from the ABI, shareholders, politicians and media on remuneration levels.

The average Chairman (if there is such a person) has 1.7 Chairmanships and 1.3 other NED roles where he/she is not Chairman, works about 90 days per year and receives £171,000 in remuneration for and in respect of these roles.

53 Non-Executive Directors (NEDs)

53.1 UK Corporate Governance Code Guidance

'Code Provisions

D.1 The Level and Components of Remuneration …

D.1.3 Where a company releases an executive director to serve as a non-executive director elsewhere, the remuneration report[1] should include a statement as to whether or not the director will retain such earnings and, if so, what the remuneration is.

D.1.4 Levels of remuneration for non-executive directors should reflect the time commitment and responsibilities of the role. Remuneration for non-executive directors should not include share options or other performance-related elements. If, exceptionally, options are granted, shareholder approval should be sought in advance and any shares acquired by exercise of the options should be held until at least one year after the non-executive director leaves the board. Holding of share options could be relevant to the determination of a non-executive director's independence (as set out in provision B.1.1).'

'D.2 Procedure

Main Principle

No director should be involved in deciding his or her own remuneration.'

'Code Provision D.2.3

The board itself or, where required by the Articles of Association, the shareholders should determine the remuneration of the non-executive directors within the limits set in the Articles of Association. Where permitted by the Articles, the board may however delegate this responsibility to a committee, which might include the Chief Executive.'

---

1 As required for UK incorporated companies under the Large and Medium-sized Companies and Groups (Accounts and Reports) Regulations 2008.

53.2 Best practice guidance

The QCA has produced some very useful guidance on fees for NEDs:

- The result of increasing demands on Non-Executives may lead to higher fees. Payment either partly or fully in shares, held during the director's term of office and for a significant period afterwards sends a good signal about the alignment of the director's interests to those of shareholders.
- On the rare occasion Non-Executive Directors participate in performance related remuneration, investors should be consulted and their support obtained.

This guidance is more useful and less restrictive than the ABI and NAPF guidance.

53.3 The role

See **Chapter 2** for more information about the role of directors and NEDs.

Non-Executive Directors have responsibilities in the following areas:

- **Strategy:** Non-Executive Directors should constructively challenge and contribute to the development of strategy.
- **Performance:** Non-Executive Directors should scrutinise the performance of management in meeting agreed goals and objectives and monitoring.
- **Risk:** Non-Executive Directors should satisfy themselves that financial information is accurate and that financial controls and systems of risk management are robust and defensible.
- **People:** Non-Executive Directors are responsible for determining appropriate levels of remuneration of executive directors and have a prime role in appointing, and where necessary removing, senior management and in succession planning.

Non-Executive Directors are the custodians of the governance process. They are not involved in the day-to-day running of business but monitor the executive activity and contribute to the development of strategy.

53.4 Remuneration

The level of pay of the Non-Executive Director should reflect:

- His/her track record and ability to command a rate of remuneration in the market place
- How much he/she is paid in other roles in other companies
- The role and contribution he/she is expected to make and the value this will add to the company

- The time commitment
- The amount that the Chairman and other NEDs are paid
- The amount the CEO is paid and how this compares on a per day basis
- Shareholders views about what is acceptable
- Market data for rates of pay for NEDs in similar companies.

53.5 Types of remuneration structure

Typical practice in quoted companies is that the NED is paid a fixed fee and in some cases some of the fee is paid in shares. The remuneration and types of remuneration structure should reflect the time and nature of the desired role and are usually similar to those of the Chairman, ie:

(i) Paid only fees[2].

(ii) Paid a mixture of fees in cash and in shares.

(iii) Awarded a number of shares on appointment which vest at a rate of x% per year, plus an annual fee.

(iv) Awarded a number of options on appointment plus an annual fee.

(v) An annual fee, plus annual awards of options or LTIPs or other types of share awards.

53.6 Discussion of NED Remuneration Issues

NEDs need to be seen as independent of the company and therefore receive fees, not a salary. Pluralist Non-Executives with several directorships will often have set up a service company to which these fees are paid gross.

Individuals should have their fees paid via the company payroll with National Insurance and tax deducted, unless their fees are paid to a company, but they are still being paid fees, not a salary.

The Chairman and Non-Executive Director Survey, which MM&K produces, shows that 98% of independent directors have a letter of appointment, of which 10% are for one year, 8% are for two years and 80% are for three years.

A NED is always entitled to resign immediately if he or she has a disagreement with the Board or feels there is a point of principle involved.

---

2 Annual fees are usually paid monthly.

In most cases, Non-Executive Directors who lose their appointments following a takeover or merger would be entitled to between three and six months' fees as compensation for loss of office.

It is very important that Non-Executive candidates check the directors' indemnity insurance policy in the light of an increasing number of share-holder and other actions against companies and their Boards; this is probably the most important issue before accepting a Non-Executive Directorship.

In larger groups, with a wider choice of independent directors, many do not sit on any committee and others only sit on one. As a high percentage of governance increasingly takes place in the Audit, Remuneration and Nominations committees, the MM&K survey respondents on large company Boards indicated the fee rates they are now receiving for work on these committees.

MM&K think it is quite likely based on recent assignments that an increase in remuneration over the next year will not necessarily affect base fees, unless corporate performance improves, but there may be a significant increase in subcommittee fees, whether these are paid separately or rolled into a single overall figure.

Shareholders' and pressure group class actions against directors are sharpening candidates' perceptions of the risk as well as the increasing time commitment of ensuring corporate governance compliance and dealing with the increasing tide of Westminster and EU regulators. The fee rate paid to NEDs when calculated on a per day basis is well below the daily rate charged to companies by their professional advisers (eg for tax, audit, legal or other consultancy). In many cases the NED receives up to 50% less than a partner would charge on a per diem basis.

Payment in shares or options

The survey data below shows the percentage of independent directors holding shares or options in their company. Not surprisingly, option holding is much more prevalent among directors of smaller companies where they probably play a greater part in the commercial strategy of the group as well as maintaining a monitoring function in line with independent directors on the Boards of the larger groups.

MM&K has consistently argued for options to be available in certain situations to, particularly, the Chairmen of smaller companies who may well spend two days a week on their responsibilities. Many companies are introduced to the main or AIM markets with independent director option schemes in place but as a number of those directors holding options for some years may well have realised all or part of their holding, directors holding options in quoted companies are likely to decrease. A certain number of companies are now making it clear that they would like independent directors to purchase a shareholding, but very few companies make this a condition.

Recommended make up of fees

The table below shows how the fees for NEDS can be logically made up based on the factors discussed above.

Table 52: An example report showing the construction of fees for NEDs

Chairman and Non-Executive Director Remuneration Report

Recommendations

Company Name: **XYZ plc**

Name	Recommended Fees						Current Fees	Market Data			Recommended % increase	Recommended fees per day	Comment
	Basic Fee	Audit Committee	Remuneration Committee	Nominations Committee	Senior Independent Director	Total Fees		Lower Quartile	Median	Upper Quartile			
Chairman						**101,000**	**101,000** **=95k + 6k car allowance**	**50,000**	**85,000**	**120,000**	**0%**	**2,020**	**Pay is above median**
NED 1	**30,000**	**5,000**	-	**1,000**	**2,000**	**38,000**	**35,000**	**30,000**	**40,000**	**50,000**	**9%**	**1,652**	**MM&K recommend committee fees to reflect time spent**
NED 2	**30,000**	-	**5,000**	**1,000**		**36,000**	**33,000**	**30,000**	**40,000**	**50,000**	**9%**	**1,565**	
NED 3	**30,000**	-	-	**1,000**		**31,000**	**30,000**	**30,000**	**40,000**	**50,000**	**3%**	**1,632**	

The above recommendations are based on
1. Time spent (see table below)
2. Size
3. Complexity and Risk
4. Market Data

from which we conclude

Comparison is based on
£100 - 300m million turnover.
Average complexity and risk.
Days are less than average.

Name	Committees				Estimated Days Spent						
	Audit	Remuneration	Nominations	Senior Independent Director	Board Meetings (incl preparation)	Audit Committee	Remuneration Committee	Nominations Committee	Senior Independent Director	Other	Total Days Spent
Chairman					**32**	**2**	**2**	**2**		**12**	**50**
NED 1	Chair	**member**	**member**	**SID**	**11**	**5**	**2**	**1**	**1**	**3**	**23**
NED 2	**member**	Chair	**member**		**11**	**2**	**6**	**1**		**3**	**23**
NED 3	**member**	**member**	**member**		**11**	**2**	**2**	**1**		**3**	**19**

53.7 Market Data: Fees – Non-Executive Directors

The following data are taken from the MM&K/Directorbank/Hanson Green 2012 Life in the Boardroom survey which covered 490 directors with roles in 1,300 companies.

Fees are usually linked to the time spent, company size, ownership, sector, risk and other company specific factors. The survey shows fee levels broken down by company size and ownership. The first table shows data for UK listed companies (ie main market or AIM).

UK LISTED companies. Total annual fees £000 (including shares)	**Turnover £ millions**						
	<10	**10–30**	**30–100**	**100–300**	**300–1,000**	**1,000–3,000**	**>3,000**
Upper Quartile	30	25	40	45	56	83	108
Median	22	20	34	37	49	59	70
Lower Quartile	17	18	29	25	40	50	60
Average	25	25	34	39	53	68	86
Sample Size	36	22	46	70	57	32	22

PRIVATE EQUITY backed companies. Total annual fees £000 (including shares)	**Turnover £ millions**						
	<3	**3–10**	**10–30**	**30–100**	**100–300**	**300–1,000**	**>1,000**
Upper Quartile	38	23	48	46	40	58	74
Median	22	15	35	40	40	50	60
Lower Quartile	16	6	21	30	30	43	50
Average	62	15	36	43	40	52	64
Sample Size	14	13	10	15	20	7	4

OTHER UK PRIVATE companies.* Total annual fees £000 (including shares)	Turnover £ millions						
	<3	3–10	10–30	30–100	100–300	300–1,000	>1,000
Upper Quartile	15	20	24	44	51	40	65
Median	12	12	17	27	30	35	50
Lower Quartile	10	10	11	24	25	28	45
Average	13	19	20	30	52	36	57
Sample Size	18	22	38	21	18	9	7

* Excludes not for Profit, Public Sector and Charities

It is often argued that the reason that fee rates are substantially higher in listed than private companies is that there is more risk in being a Non-Executive Director of a quoted company. However, in some cases, share ownership and share options in private companies can compensate for lower basic fees.

Median fees for overseas companies are much higher in larger companies than in comparably sized UK companies. Whilst this makes it more attractive from a remuneration point of view to be a director of an overseas company, the burden of Sarbanes-Oxley and the danger of class actions more than compensate for the higher pay. FTSE 100 NED fees have increased faster than smaller companies and comparison with overseas rates of fees may be one reason for this.

When companies come to try and recruit an overseas director, their expectations of fee levels often reflect their home country's typical levels and this in turn creates pressure to increase UK-based directors' fees.

There is a relationship between turnover and fees, but the (statistical) correlation is low, particularly in the private company data. This suggests the market is not a perfect market by any means and potential NEDs should negotiate their remuneration package assertively on appointment.

Daily Rates for Non-Executive Directors

The 'daily rate' has been calculated by dividing the total fees (including payments in shares) by the number of days worked in the year.

In listed companies, the median daily rates are around £1,500 per day for smaller companies and £1,800 per day for larger companies. The figures were about £1,300 and £1,800 respectively for the prior year (2011).

UK LISTED companies. Daily Rates £ (including shares)	Turnover £ millions						
	<10	10–30	30–100	100–300	300–1,000	1,000–3,000	>3,000
Upper Quartile	2,000	1,692	2,079	2,273	2,505	3,333	2,991
Median	1,667	1,423	1,468	1,567	1,863	2,246	2,176
Lower Quartile	1,232	1,022	1,111	1,320	1,504	1,899	1,787

The next table shows the breakdown for Private Equity owned companies. This includes Private Equity and venture capital backed companies.

PRIVATE EQUITY backed companies. Daily Rates £ (including shares)	Turnover £ millions						
	<3	3–10	10–30	30–100	100–300	300–1,000	>1,000
Upper Quartile	1,969	1,000	1,970	2,250	2,589	2,569	3,472
Median	1,031	769	1,464	1,212	1,962	1,719	1,933
Lower Quartile	483	600	902	918	1,313	1,508	1,323

The next table shows the breakdown for other private companies.

OTHER PRIVATE companies. Daily Rates £ (including shares)	Turnover £ millions						
	<3	3–10	10–30	30–100	100–300	300–1,000	>1,000
Upper Quartile	1,575	1,441	1,721	1,750	2,552	1,765	2,000
Median	857	800	950	1,222	1,667	1,320	1,667
Lower Quartile	509	579	667	1,000	1,268	1,267	1,633

Per diem fee rates for Non-Executive Directors and Chairmen have fallen well behind the total remuneration levels of CEOs. The average CEO of a FTSE 100 company receives £4 million total remuneration (source MM&K/Manifest Executive Directors Total Remuneration Survey September 2011 edition). This equates to £18,000 per day – compared to the typical rates of £2,000 to £3,000 for Non-Executive Directors. The average FTSE mid 250 CEO receives approximately £5,000 per day.

Increases – Non-Executive Directors

81% of Non-Executive Directors did not have a fee increase last year (ie in 2011) and 79% do not expect one this year (2012).

increases in total annual fees in 2011.	**Turnover £ millions**					
	<10	**10–30**	**30–100**	**100–300**	**300–1,000**	**>1,000**
Upper Quartile	0	0	0	0	0	2
Median	0	0	0	0	0	0
Lower Quartile	0	0	0	0	0	0
Average	1.2	3.3	1.5	2.2	1.4	2.5

expected increases in total annual fees in 2012.	**Turnover £ millions**					
	<10	**10–30**	**30–100**	**100–300**	**300–1,000**	**>1,000**
Upper Quartile	0	1	0	0	0	2
Median	0	0	0	0	0	0
Lower Quartile	0	0	0	0	0	0
Average	1.1	3.1	1.2	1.4	2.1	1.5

The average figures are much higher than the medians and in some cases higher than the upper quartile. This is because some NEDs have had/are expecting significant increases. Quite a number of companies have not made any increases, so it would appear others have given quite substantial increases. New appointees may be able to negotiate higher fees than their predecessors. There are slightly higher expectations for NED fee increases than for Chairmen.

Satisfaction rating

In 2012, 69% of Non-Executive Directors feel their remuneration is about right, 30% too low and 1% too high. The results were consistent across all sizes of companies.

These results are similar to the previous year. There has been a slight improvement in satisfaction (69% feel about right this year versus 67% last year: 30% feel fees are too low compared to 34% last year).

Non-Executive Directors are more satisfied about their pay than employees.

The average Non-Executive Director has 2.1 roles, works 46 days a year and is paid £85,000 for his/her Non-Executive Director work.

Committee Work and Fees

335 Audit Committee Chairmen and 303 Remuneration Committee Chairmen provided data on time spent and fees in respect of these committees. Data was also received from 366 Audit Committee members and 346 Remuneration Committee members.

In most cases the Chair and members do not receive any additional fees. For those who receive additional fees, the average figures in £ are:

Average fees for specific Committee work in £	Turnover £millions						
	<10	10–30	30–100	100–300	300–1,000	>1,000	All Companies
Audit Chair	3,583	13,500*	4,600	7,792	7,182	12,143	8,382
Audit Member	2,333	7,500*	4,778	3,875	4,667	11,083	6,356
Remuneration Chair	*	*	4,667	5,250	6,313	10,643	7,255
Remuneration Member	*	*	4,800	4,500	5,500	5,556	5,040

* Small sample

Share Ownership, Share Options and Fees Paid in Shares

Share Ownership

84% of Chairmen own part of their company. In companies with less than £10 million turnover, the median Chairman stake is 5%, but this drops to a tiny percentage for big companies. However, there is a very wide range of practices. Interestingly, the median size of the stake, in £s, is similar across different sizes of company.

Chairman: of company owned	Turnover £ millions					
	<10	10–30	30–100	100–300	300–1,000	>1,000
Upper Quartile	10.0%	4.0%	2.1%	1.0%	1.0%	0.2%
Median	5.0%	2.0%	0.8%	0.4%	0.5%	0.1%
Lower Quartile	1.0%	1.0%	0.2%	0.1%	0.1%	0.0%
Average	10.7%	5.2%	3.4%	1.4%	0.6%	0.1%
Shares owned £000 median	100	250	200	175	180	150
with some ownership	78%	88%	87%	75%	90%	88%

60% of Non-Executives own part of their company. For Non-Executive Directors, in companies with less than £10 million turnover, the median stake is 5%, but is a tiny percentage for big companies. There is a very wide range of practice.

In Private Equity owned companies, Chairmen typically have around a 2% stake (more in smaller companies and less in bigger ones, but typically worth several hundred thousand pounds). Some Chairman of private companies own larger percentages: often this is because they are founders or they are family owned firms.

NEDs: of company owned	**Turnover £ millions**					
	<10	**10–30**	**30–100**	**100–300**	**300–1,000**	**>1,000**
Upper Quartile	20.0%	6.0%	2.0%	2.0%	0.1%	3.0%
Median	5.0%	1.3%	0.3%	0.2%	0.1%	0.3%
Lower Quartile	0.8%	0.3%	0.1%	0.1%	0.0%	0.1%
Average	11.3%	4.2%	2.2%	2.2%	0.0%	1.9%
Shares owned £000 median	50	50	68	35	40	73
with some ownership	63%	55%	67%	57%	58%	62%

Share Options

14% of Chairmen have share options in their company. In companies with less than £10 million turnover, the median Chairman option is over 2.5% of the equity, but this drops to a tiny percentage for big companies. However, there is a very wide range of practices.

Chairman: % of company under Option	**Turnover £ millions**					
	<10	**10–30**	**30–100**	**100–300**	**300–1,000**	**>1,000**
Upper Quartile	5.0%	3.0%	2.0%	0.4%	0.2%	
Median	2.5%	3.0%	1.0%	0.3%	0.2%	
Lower Quartile	1.0%	1.0%	0.2%	0.0%	0.0%	
Average	5.7%	2.2%	2.3%	0.3%	0.5%	
Median value of shares under option £000	80	250	400	300	300	
with options	17%	13%	17%	8%	12%	

Where the sample sizes are quite small, results are not presented.

6% of Non-Executives have share options in their company. For Non-Executive Directors, in companies with less than £10 million turnover, the median option is over 1% of the equity, but is a tiny percentage for big companies. There is a very wide range of practice.

NEDs: % of company under Option	**Turnover £ millions**					
	<10	**10–30**	**30–100**	**100–300**	**300–1,000**	**>1,000**
Upper Quartile	2.5%	0.5%	0.8%	1.00%	0.01%	0.01%
Median	1.0%	0.3%	0.5%	0.03%	0.01%	0.01%
Lower Quartile	0.5%	0.1%	0.3%	0.02%	0.01%	0.00%
Average	1.4%	0.6%	0.3%	0.58%	0.03%	0.01%
Median value of shares under option £000	74	40	46	62	50	56
with options	10%	6%	7%	7%	4%	4%

The practices of small companies are very different to larger ones.

The prevalence of options in AIM companies is much higher. The survey found that many NOMADS fail to appreciate companies' previous circumstances when considering a move to AIM and far too often cite the UK Corporate Governance Code principles that options and geared incentives are not appropriate for Non-Executives and that large shareholdings compromise an individual's independence.

However, the survey results show that significant shareholdings and options in AIM and private companies are commonplace. These data can be used by companies to explain that their approach is not uncommon and why they are not compliant with the principles of the Code.

Fees Paid in Shares

Chairman: Fees paid in Shares £000	**Turnover £ millions**					
	<10	**10–30**	**30–100**	**100–300**	**300–1,000**	**>1,000**
Upper Quartile	100	131	350	125		
Median	25	48	50	63	75	255
Lower Quartile	18	39	43	24		
Average	107	123	336	86		
paid partly in shares	8%	4%	8%	7%	2%	7%

Just 6% of Chairmen are paid part of their fees in shares in their company. However, for those that receive shares, the amounts are significant and there is a wide range of practice. The quartiles and sample size numbers relate only to those who are paid partly in shares.

9% of Non-Executives are paid part of their fees in shares in their company. However, for those that receive shares, the amounts are significant and there is a wide range of practice. Nearly all the larger companies which pay part of fees in shares are quoted – 13% of companies with £1 billion plus turnover pay part of their fees in shares, but 15% of quoted companies do so with the median amount being £55,000. Although the UK Corporate Governance Code recommends payment of part of fees in shares, most (85%) do not comply with this part of the Code. If Non-Executive Directors are unwilling to be paid in shares, it makes it difficult for them to insist that executives receive large parts of their rewards in shares.

NEDs: Fees paid in Shares £000	**Turnover £ millions**					
	<10	**10–30**	**30–100**	**100–300**	**300–1,000**	**>1,000**
Upper Quartile	33	33	50	46	23	64
Median	25	28	16	30	13	55
Lower Quartile	14	20	12	20	8	36
Average	33	32	33	38	14	56
paid partly in shares	6%	7%	7%	5%	6%	13%

53.8 Factors that influence Non-Executive Directors' Remuneration

In order to better understand the wide spread of fee levels for Chairmen and NEDs at any particular level of turnover or market capitalisation, we asked some additional questions this year.

We asked what factors influence the fees for NEDs. Again there was quite a variation, with personal contribution, experience and qualifications scoring 42% on average; time spent 27%; payment to reflect risk 24%; and other factors 7%.

Most Chairmen and Non-Executive Directors think personal contribution or experience or qualifications are the major influence on NED fees. Whilst many thought this was the major factor, few thought it was the only factor.

A clear majority agreed with the statement that 'The Board should be willing to pay more than its normal NED fee rate in order to recruit a specific new NED'.

Clearly the majority of participants would be willing to pay more for a higher quality or more experienced recruit if they needed to.

Figure 64: Factors that influence NED fees

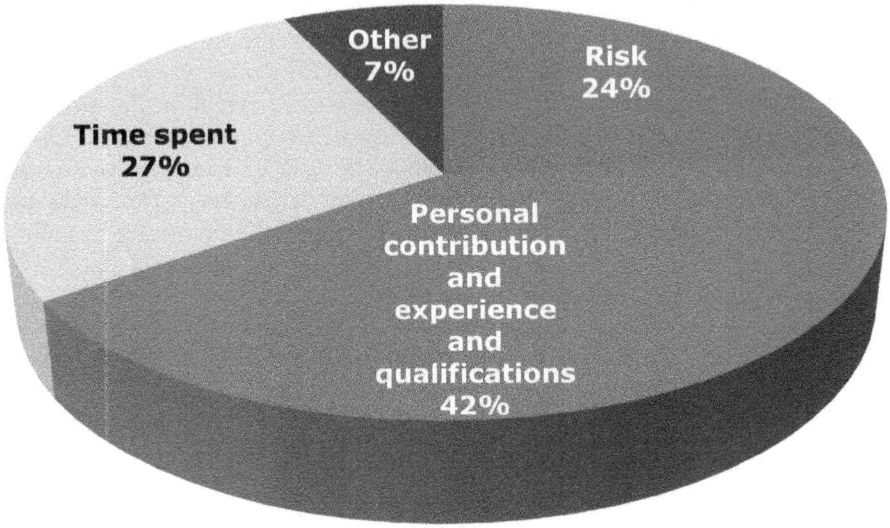

Figure 65: Willingness to pay more for a specific new NED

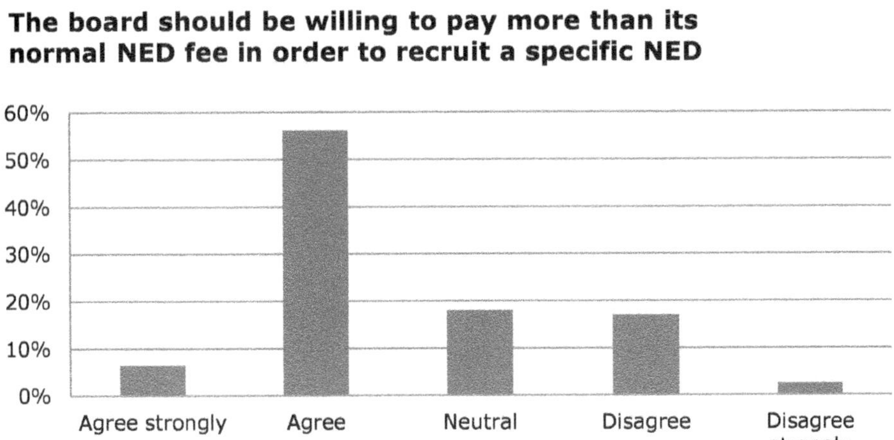

Exploring this further, the hypothesis was tested that Non-Executive fees, and especially Chairmen's fees, might be more a function of the salary in his/her last executive position than a function of the turnover or market capitalisation of the current company: in other words that big and small companies alike might be prepared to pay the amount necessary to secure a candidate with the right experience, because of the potential impact on the business.

The majority did not accept this hypothesis, at least in relation to their own companies.

Figure 66: Are NED fees driven by prior executive position?

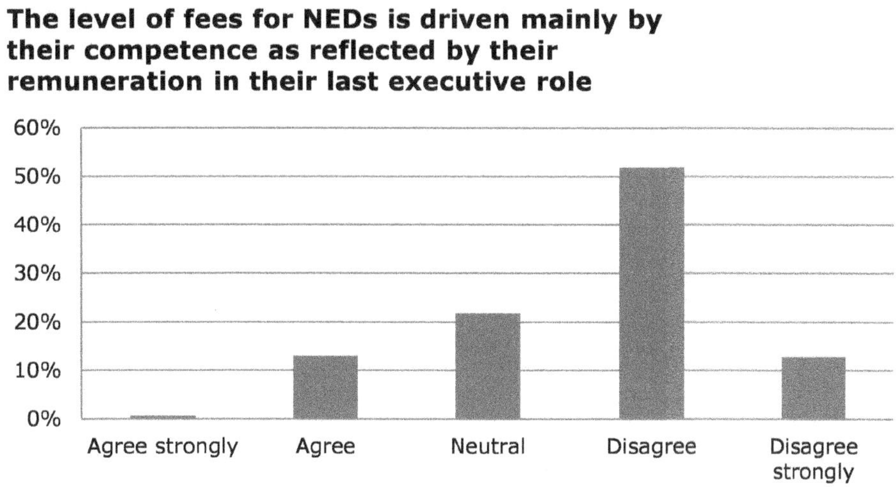

Participants were also asked to give their highest previous pay, and how many years had elapsed since they were full-time executives. A strong correlation between the current fee level and the highest previous executive salary (as a proxy for the level of executive responsibility) would support the hypothesis. In the event a very low correlation was found with last executive salary, both for Chairmen and other NEDs. The view of the majority of participants about the influence of the previous executive salary proved correct. The correlation of the equivalent daily NED fee was no stronger.

The wide spread of fee practice by company size has yet to be explained. Perhaps the answer is that there is only a weak rationale for the fees paid in the first place, and the most important factor (especially with the Chairman) is the ability to negotiate a good fee.

53.9 How should NEDs be paid

A version of this article, by Cliff Weight, first appeared in Boardroom Magazine in 2010.

> 'The UK Corporate Governance Code is strongly against awarding options to Non-Executive Directors and requires prior approval of any award of options. I always thought that the Code in this respect is wrong, so I am greatly pleased to see the new QCA Corporate Governance Guidelines for Smaller Quoted Companies which note

that a Non-Executive Director may not be independent if he/she has a "*significant participation* in the company's share option or performance-related-pay scheme".

The QCA guidelines reflect my own thinking. The question is the size of the options – as it is only when they become excessive that they might lead to a Non-Executive behaving in a way that may not be in the company's best long-term interests. However being able to offer options can help smaller, start-up and fast growth companies to keep costs down and still enable them to attract high-calibre and interested Non-Executive Directors.

Of course, companies do not have to comply with the UK Corporate Governance Code. The requirement is either to comply or to explain non-compliance. I hope that many companies will choose to explain, by saying that they feel the QCA guidelines are more appropriate to them, in respect of the recruitment and remuneration of their Non-Executives.

The role of the Non-Executive has changed. In 1991, the median time spent was 17 days per company. When Tiny Rowland notoriously compared Non-Executives to trinkets on Xmas trees, many Boards would have a Knight and a Lord. Board meetings were amiable in nature and often followed by a jolly good lunch.

The role today is much more professional. Non-Executives must challenge and to do so they must gain a detailed understanding of the company. They must be rigorous, and they must set the pay of the CEO and key executives.

So it is not surprising that the time commitment has nearly doubled to 31 days per year per company.

However their pay has not kept pace with executives' total remuneration as is shown below.

Source: MM&K surveys

What for? And How much?

'We need a debate on "what for?" and "how much?" to pay Non-Executives. I believe we, in the UK, need to pay Non-Executives more, but this should be done in a way that reflects the need for more professionalism, time input and more scrutiny of strategy and risk.

The last 30 years have seen a huge change in the way executive directors are remunerated. There has been a huge growth in performance related elements of remuneration.

Figure 67: NED fees and CEO pay 1991–2011

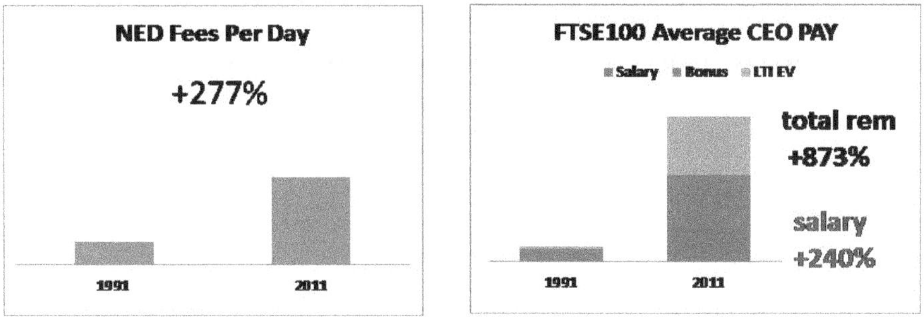

FSTE 100 Non-Executive Directors

	1991	2011	% increase
Fees £	12,500	86,000	588%
Days	17	31	
£ per day	735	2,774	277%

FTSE 100 CEOs

	1991	2011	% increase
Salary	250,000	850,000	240%
Bonus	75,000	1,345,000	
LTI EV	50,000	1,455,000	
Total	375,000	3,650,000	873%

Non-Executive fees (when calculated on a daily basis) have broadly gone up in line with CEO salaries – which is slightly more than average wages. MM&K data for the last 12 years shows average increases of 7% p.a. for CEOs' salaries and NEDs' fees per day and 4% p.a. for average wages.

FTSE 350 Non-Executives are paid differently to those in the US. Exxon, for example, pays its Non-Executives (they call them external directors) each year $100,000 plus 2,500 shares, which at recent share prices were worth slightly less than $200,000. Importantly, their Non-Executives cannot sell these shares until after they retire and there are rules for the phased sale of their shares. This remuneration package is designed to create long term alignment with shareholders.

A mix of fees and shares has, in my view, great merit. I modelled how much a Non-Executive would receive if paid a fee of £50,000 and 10,000 shares a year, assuming:

- the share price when the Non-Executive was appointed was £5,
- 10 year tenure,
- ie a total of £500,000 of fees plus a notional £500,000 of shares as valued at the appointment date;

and compared this to what a typical FTSE 100 Non-Executive would receive (£75,000 a year in fees and no shares or share options).'

Figure 68: NED payment in fees or shares

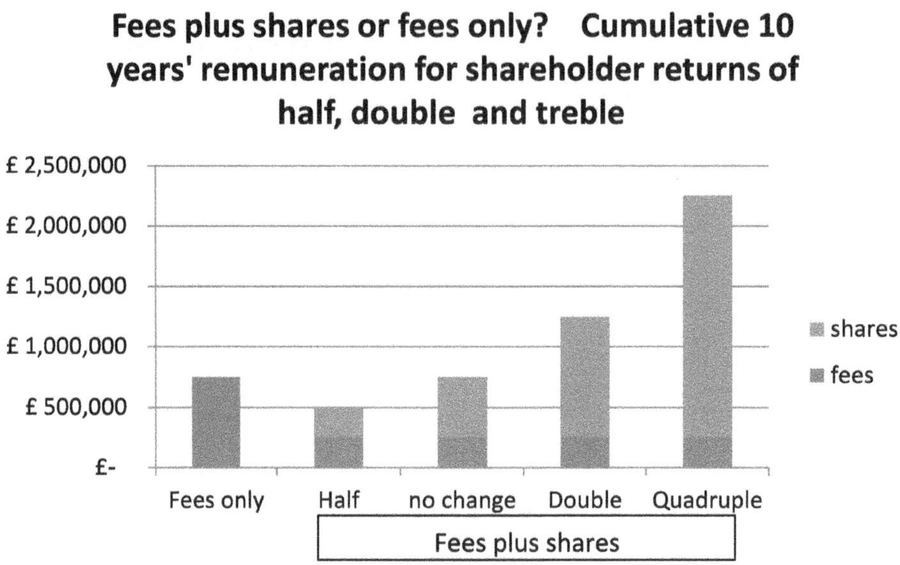

'The outcome depends on what the share price is at the end of the 10 years as the figure illustrates.

For a typical FTSE 100 Non-Executive Director, these are not life-changing amounts. They will not prejudice their independence. However, I do believe this approach will improve the alignment of Non-Executives with long term shareholders, particularly if the shares can only be sold over a number of years, e.g. none for two years, or maximum of 20% a year for each of the first five years after leaving.

Smaller companies may want more performance linkage. For them, a mixture of options and fees may be more appropriate.

In MM&K's annual Chairman and Non-Executive Director survey (2010), we have consistently received comments that Non-Executive Directors should be paid in shares or options.

The survey data shows that only about 17% of companies are paying Non-Executives in shares, but when they do the amounts are typically quite substantial – about half of the total. There is also some evidence that those paid in shares pay more than those paid only in cash.

Only about 20% pay in options. Where options are awarded, they can be very significant. The survey also confirms that options in private and AIM listed companies are a key component of reward in many cases.

At the end of the day companies will get what they pay for and what they deserve. If you want committed Non-Executives thinking carefully about risks, long term strategy and long term success, my suggestions above should help. But always remember that pay by itself is no panacea.'

53.10 Contracts for services of Non-Executive Directors

Higgs provided guidance on the role of the Non-Executive Director and also provided a sample letter of Non-Executive Director appointment, which has subsequently been updated by ICSA (Guidance Note 111214, December 2011), as follows.

ICSA guidance: a sample Non-Executive Director's appointment letter[3]

CONTENTS

i Introduction

ii Sample letter

1 Appointment

2 Time Commitment

3 Duties

4 Remuneration and expenses

5 Independence and outside interests

6 Confidentiality

7 Price sensitive information and dealing in the company's shares

8 Induction

9 Review process

10 Training

11 Insurance and indemnity

12 Independent professional advice

13 Changes to personal details

---

[3] © Institute of Chartered Secretaries & Administrators. Reproduced with the kind permission of ICSA. For the full version of the Guidance Note please visit www.icsaglobal.com/assets/files/pdfs/guidance/Guidance%20Notes%202011/ICSA%20Guidance%20%20sample%20non-executive%20appointment%20letter%20Dec%202011.pdf

i Introduction

This sample letter is not intended to be a prescriptive template. It reflects the various practices of some of the larger companies and aims to provide an initial checklist of the elements a company may wish to cover in its appointment letters. The text and content should be adapted to suit the company's own circumstances.

As well as incorporating standard contract terms, the sample letter covers the reference in the Financial Reporting Council (FRC)'s Guidance on Board Effectiveness to time commitment:

> "Non-executive directors need to make sufficient time available to discharge their responsibilities effectively. The letter of appointment should state the minimum time that the non-executive director will be required to spend on the company's business, and seek the individual's confirmation that he or she can devote that amount of time to the role, consistent with other commitments. The letter should also indicate the possibility of additional time commitment when the company is undergoing a period of particularly increased activity, such as an acquisition or takeover, or as a result of some major difficulty with one or more of its operations."

ii Sample letter

I am pleased to confirm that upon the recommendation of the nomination committee, the Board has approved your appointment as [an independent/a non-independent] non-executive director of [name of company] ("the Company"). This letter sets out the main terms of your appointment.

It is agreed that, on acceptance of this offer, this letter will constitute a contract for services and not a contract of employment.

1 Appointment

1.1 Subject to the remaining provisions of this letter, [your appointment is for an initial term of three years commencing on [date]] [your appointment is for an initial term, from [date] until the conclusion of the Company's Annual General Meeting (AGM) occurring approximately three years from that date], unless terminated earlier by either party giving to the other party [one/three] month['s] [s'] written notice.

1.2 Your appointment is subject to the articles of association. Nothing in this letter shall be taken to exclude or vary the terms of the articles of association as they apply to you as a director of the Company. Your continued appointment as non-executive director is subject to election by the Company's shareholders at the AGM scheduled to be held on [date] and to re-election at any subsequent AGM at which either the articles of association of the Company require, or the Board resolves, that you stand for re-election.

[The Board has resolved to apply Provision B.7.1 of the FRC's UK Corporate Governance Code 2010, whereby all directors will be subject to annual election at the [year] AGM, and expects to do so in subsequent years.]

If the shareholders do not re-elect you as a director, or you are retired from office under the articles of association, your appointment shall terminate automatically, with immediate effect and without compensation.

1.3 Continuation of your contract of appointment is also contingent on satisfactory performance and any relevant statutory provisions relating to the removal of a director.

1.4 Non-Executive Directors are typically expected to serve two three-year terms but may be invited by the Board to serve for an additional period. Any term renewal is subject to Board review and AGM re-election. Notwithstanding any mutual expectation, there is no right to re-nomination by the Board, either annually or after any three-year period.

1.5 You [will/may] be required to serve on one or more committees of the Board. You will be provided with the relevant terms of reference on your appointment to such a committee. [You also [will/may] be asked to serve as a non-executive director on the board of any of the Company's subsidiaries or joint ventures, or as Senior Independent Director.] Any such appointment will be covered in a separate communication.

1.6 Notwithstanding paragraphs 1.1–1.5, we may terminate your appointment with immediate effect if you:

(a) commit a material breach of your obligations under this letter; or

(b) commit any serious or repeated breach or non-observance of your obligations to the Company (which include an obligation not to breach your duties to the Company, whether statutory, fiduciary or common-law); or

(c) are guilty of any fraud or dishonesty or acted in a manner which, in the opinion of the Company acting reasonably, brings or is likely to bring you or the Company into disrepute or is materially adverse to the interests of the Company; or

(d) are convicted of any arrestable criminal offence [other than an offence under road traffic legislation in the UK or elsewhere for which a fine or non-custodial penalty is imposed]; or

(e) are declared bankrupt or have made an arrangement with or for the benefit of your creditors; or

(f) are disqualified from acting as a director.

1.7 On termination of your appointment, you shall at the request of the Company resign from your office as a director of the Company [and all offices held by you in any Group company].

1.8 If there are matters which arise which cause you concern about your role you should discuss them with me [or the Senior Independent Director]. If you have any concerns which cannot be resolved, and you choose to resign for that, or any other, reason, you should provide an appropriate written statement to me [or the Senior Independent Director] for circulation to the Board.

2 Time commitment

2.1 You will be expected to devote such time as is necessary for the proper performance of your duties and you should be prepared to spend at least [number of days] days per [month/year] on company business after the induction phase. This is based on preparation for and attendance at:

- scheduled Board meetings
- [Board dinners]
- [the annual Board strategy away-day(s)]
- the AGM
- [site visits]
- meetings of the non-executive directors
- meetings with shareholders
- updating meetings/training
- meetings as part of the Board evaluation process

[Meetings may involve you in some overseas travel.] Unless urgent and unavoidable circumstances prevent you from doing so, it is expected that you will attend the meetings outlined above.

2.2 The nature of the role makes it impossible to be specific about the maximum time commitment, and there is always the possibility of additional time commitment in respect of preparation time and ad hoc matters which may arise from time to time, and particularly when the Company is undergoing a period of increased activity. At certain times it may be necessary to convene additional Board, committee or shareholder meetings.

2.3 The average time commitment stated in 2.1 will increase should you become a committee member or chair, or if you are given additional responsibilities, such as being appointed the Senior Independent Director, or non-executive director on the boards of any of the Company's subsidiaries. Details of the expected increase in time commitment will be covered in any relevant communication confirming the additional responsibility.

2.4 By accepting this appointment you undertake that, taking into account all other commitments you may have, you are able to, and will, devote sufficient time to your duties as a non-executive director.

3 Duties

3.1 You will be expected to perform your duties, whether statutory, fiduciary or common-law, faithfully, efficiently and diligently to a standard commensurate with both the functions of your role and your knowledge, skills and experience.

3.2 You will exercise your powers in your role as a non-executive director having regard to relevant obligations under prevailing law and regulation, including the Companies Act 2006, the UK Corporate Governance Code and associated guidance[4] and the UK Listing Authority's Listing, Prospectus, and Disclosure and Transparency Rules. [You are also required to comply with the requirements of the [New York Stock Exchange]. You will be advised by the Company Secretary where these differ from requirements in the UK.]

3.3 You will have particular regard to the general duties of directors as set out in Part 10, Chapter 2 of the Companies Act 2006, including the duty to promote the success of the company:

> "A director of a company must act in the way he considers, in good faith, would be most likely to promote the success of the

---

4 The FRC's associated guidance comprises: i. Guidance on Board Effectiveness ii. Going Concern and Liquidity Risk: Guidance for Directors of UK Companies iii. Internal Control: Revised Guidance for Directors iv. Guidance on Audit Committees

company for the benefit of its members as a whole, and in doing so have regard (amongst other matters) to:

(a) the likely consequences of any decision in the long term,

(b) the interests of the company's employees,

(c) the need to foster the company's business relationships with suppliers, customers and others,

(d) the impact of the company's operations on the community and the environment,

(e) the desirability of the company maintaining a reputation for high standards of business conduct, and

(f) the need to act fairly as between members of the company."

3.4 You will have particular regard to the FRC's UK Corporate Governance Code (the "Code") and associated Guidance on Board Effectiveness in respect of the role of the board[5] and the role of the non-executive director.

In your role as non-executive director you will be required to:

- constructively challenge and help develop proposals on strategy;
- scrutinise the performance of management in meeting agreed goals and objectives and monitor the reporting of performance;
- satisfy yourself on the integrity of financial information and that financial controls and systems of risk management are robust and defensible;
- determine appropriate levels of remuneration of executive directors and have a prime role in appointing and, where necessary, removing executive directors, and in succession planning;
- devote time to developing and refreshing your knowledge and skills;
- uphold high standards of integrity and probity and support me and the other directors in instilling the appropriate culture, values and behaviours in the boardroom and beyond;
- insist on receiving high-quality information sufficiently in advance of board meetings; and
- take into account the views of shareholders and other stakeholders where appropriate.

---

5 Excerpts from the Code and Guidance on Board Effectiveness on the role of the board have been appended to this contract in Appendix A

3.5 You will be required to exercise relevant powers under, and abide by, the Company's articles of association.

3.6 You will be required to exercise your powers as a director in accordance with the Company's policies and procedures [and internal control framework].

3.7 You will disclose any direct or indirect interest which you may have in any matter being considered at a board meeting or committee meeting and, save as permitted under the articles of association, you will not vote on any resolution of the Board, or of one of its committees, on any matter where you have any direct or indirect interest.

3.8 You will immediately report to me your own wrongdoing or the wrongdoing or proposed wrongdoing of any employee or director of which you become aware.

3.9 Unless specifically authorised to do so by the Board, you will not enter into any legal or other commitment or contract on behalf of the Company.

4 Remuneration and expenses

4.1 The annual fee rate as at the date of this letter is £[amount] gross per annum, paid [monthly/quarterly] in arrears. This fee covers all duties, including service on any board committee or company subsidiary, with the exception of committee Chairmanships and certain additional responsibilities, such as taking on the role of Senior Independent Director. [In your case, a further fee of £[amount] is payable as at the date of this letter for taking on [chairmanship of the [name of committee] Committee] [./and] [the role of Senior Independent Director].]

4.2 All fees will be paid through PAYE and are subject to income tax and other statutory deductions.

4.3 Fees will be subject to an [annual/periodic] review by the Board.

[4.4 You will comply with the Company's requirements regarding the minimum shareholding level (agreed from time to time by the Board).]

4.5 The Company will reimburse you for all reasonable and properly-documented expenses you incur in performing the duties of your office. The procedure and other guidance in respect of expense claims is set out in [name of document].

4.6 On termination of the appointment you shall only be entitled to such fees as may have accrued to the date of termination, together with reimbursement in the normal way of any expenses properly incurred prior to that date.

5 Independence and outside interests

[5.1 The Board of the Company has determined you to be independent, taking account of the guidance contained in B.1.1 of the UK Corporate Governance Code.]

5.2 You have already disclosed to the Board the significant commitments you have outside this role. You must inform me in advance of any changes to these commitments. In certain circumstances the agreement of the Board may have to be sought before accepting further commitments which either might give rise to a conflict of interest or a conflict of any of your duties to the Company, or which might impact on the time that you are able to devote to your role at the Company.

5.3 It is accepted and acknowledged that you have business interests other than those of the Company and have declared any conflicts that are apparent at present. In the event that you become aware of any further potential or actual conflicts of interest, these should be disclosed to me and the Company Secretary as soon as they become apparent and, again, the agreement of the Board may have to be sought.

6 Confidentiality

6.1 You acknowledge that all information acquired during your appointment is confidential to the Company and should not be released, communicated, nor disclosed either during your appointment or following termination (by whatever means), to third parties without my prior clearance.

6.2 This restriction shall cease to apply to any confidential information which may (other than by reason of your breach) become available to the public generally.

6.3 You acknowledge the need to hold and retain company information (in whatever format you may receive it) under appropriately secure conditions.

6.4 You hereby waive all rights arising by virtue of Chapter IV of Part I of the Copyright Designs and Patents Act 1988 in respect of all copyright works created by you in the course of performing your duties hereunder.

7 Price sensitive information and dealing in the Company's shares

7.1 Your attention is drawn to the requirements under both law and regulation regarding the disclosure of price sensitive information, and in particular to the Disclosure and Transparency Rules of the UK Listing Authority and s52 of the Criminal Justice Act 1993 on insider dealing.

You should avoid making any statements that might risk a breach of these requirements. If in doubt please contact me or the Company Secretary.

7.2 During your period of appointment you are required to comply with the provisions of the Model Code, as annexed to the Listing Rules of the UK Listing Authority, in relation to dealing in the Company's listed securities, and any such other code as the Company may adopt from time to time which sets out the terms for dealings by directors in the Company's listed securities. A copy of the current share dealing code adopted by the Company will be provided to you separately.

8 Induction

8.1 Immediately after appointment, the Company will provide a comprehensive, formal and tailored induction [which will involve travel overseas]. You will be expected to make yourself available during your first year of appointment for not less than an additional [10] days for the purposes of the induction. The Company Secretary will be in touch with further details.

9 Review process

9.1 The performance of individual directors and the whole Board and its committees is evaluated annually.

10 Training

10.1 On an ongoing basis, and further to the annual evaluation process, we will make arrangements for you to develop and refresh your skills and knowledge in areas which we mutually identify as being likely to be required, or of benefit to you, in carrying out your duties effectively. You should endeavour to make yourself available for any relevant training sessions which may be organised for the Board.

11 Insurance and indemnity

11.1 The Company has directors' and officers' liability insurance in place and it is intended to maintain such cover for the full term of your appointment. You have been informed of the current indemnity limit, on which the Board is updated from time to time. Other details of the cover are available from the Company Secretary.

11.2 You will also be granted a deed of indemnity by the Company.

12 Independent professional advice

12.1 Circumstances may occur when it will be appropriate for you to seek advice from independent advisers at the Company's expense. A copy of the Board's agreed procedure under which directors may obtain independent advice will be provided by the Company Secretary. The Company will reimburse the reasonable cost of expenditure incurred by you in accordance with its policy.

13 Changes to personal details

13.1 You shall advise the Company Secretary promptly of any change in address or other personal contact details.

14 Return of property

14.1 Upon termination of your appointment with the Company (for whatever cause), you shall deliver to the Company all documents, records, papers or other company property which may be in your possession or under your control, and which relate in any way to the business affairs of the Company, and you shall not retain any copies thereof.

[15 Non-compete clause

15.1 By countersignature of this letter and in consideration for the fees payable to you under the terms of this letter, you now agree that you will not (without the previous consent in writing of the Company), for the period of six months immediately after the termination of your office, whether as principal or agent and whether alone or jointly with, or as a director, manager, partner, shareholder, employee or consultant of, any other person, carry on or be engaged, concerned or interested in any business which is similar to or competes with any business being carried on by the Company [or any company in the Group.]]

16 Data protection

16.1 By signing this letter you consent to the Company holding and processing information about you for legal, personnel, administrative and management purposes and in particular to the processing of any sensitive personal data (as defined in the Data Protection Act 1998) including, as and when appropriate:

(a) information about your physical or mental health or condition in order to monitor sick leave and take decisions as to your fitness to perform your duties;

(b) information about you that may be relevant to ensuring equality of opportunity and treatment in line with the Company's equal opportunities policy and in compliance with equal opportunities legislation; and

(c) information relating to any criminal proceedings in which you have been involved, for insurance purposes and in order to comply with legal requirements and obligations to third parties.

You consent to the transfer of such personal information to other offices the Company may have [or to a company in the Group] or to other third parties, whether or not outside the European Economic Area, for administration purposes and other purposes in connection with your appointment, where it is necessary or desirable for the Company to do so.

16.2 You will comply at all times with the Company's data protection policy, a copy of which will be provided to you.

17 Rights of third parties

17.1 The Contracts (Rights of Third Parties) Act 1999 shall not apply to this letter. No person other than you and the Company shall have any rights under this letter and the terms of this letter shall not be enforceable by any person other than you and the Company.

18 Law

18.1 Your engagement with the Company is governed by and shall be construed in accordance with the laws of [country] and your engagement shall be subject to the jurisdiction of the courts of [country].

18.2 This letter constitutes the entire terms and conditions of your appointment and no waiver or modification thereof shall be valid unless in writing and signed by the parties hereto.

If you are willing to accept these terms of appointment, please confirm your acceptance by signing and returning to me the enclosed copy of this letter.

Yours sincerely

[name] Chairman

____

I confirm and agree to the terms of my appointment as a non-executive director of [name of company] as set out in this letter.

____

[name]

____

[date]

Appendix A

The UK Corporate Governance Code on the role of the board:

> "A.1 The Role of the Board
>
> Main Principle
>
> Every company should be headed by an effective board which is collectively responsible for the long-term success of the company.
>
> Supporting Principles
>
> The board's role is to provide entrepreneurial leadership of the company within a framework of prudent and effective controls which enables risk to be assessed and managed. The board should set the company's strategic aims, ensure that the necessary financial and human resources are in place for the company to meet its objectives and review management performance. The board should set the company's values and standards and ensure that its obligations to its shareholders and others are understood and met.
>
> All directors must act in what they consider to be the best interests of the company, consistent with their statutory duties."

The FRC Guidance on Board Effectiveness states that an effective board:

- provides direction for management;
- demonstrates ethical leadership, displaying – and promoting throughout the company – behaviours consistent with the culture and values it has defined for the organisation;
- creates a performance culture that drives value creation without exposing the company to excessive risk of value destruction;
- makes well informed and high quality decisions based on a clear line of sight into the business;
- creates the right framework for helping directors meet their statutory duties under the Companies Act 2006, and/or other relevant statutory and regulatory regimes;
- is accountable, particularly to those that provide the company's capital; and
- thinks carefully about its governance arrangements and embraces evaluation of their effectiveness.

Complete versions of the UK Corporate Governance Code and the FRC Guidance on Board Effectiveness can be found at: http://www.frc.org.uk/corporate/ukcgcode.cfm

PART F

54 PE and Hedge Fund Industry Compensation Practice

The comments in this chapter are based on information kindly provided by Nigel Mills, a director of MM&K.

Before considering in detail current market practice in remuneration it is important to consider the typical structure and approach to remuneration within the industries that make up the Alternative Investment space. It is also important to understand the different types of investment firms that exist within these industries.

54.1 Private Equity Industry (including Infrastructure)

Within the Private Equity and Infrastructure Funds ('PE') industry there are three main different types of firm:

- *Wholly independent*, where the fund management entity (typically structured as a limited liability partnership or LLP) is owned entirely by the individual fund managers and other members of the team. Occasionally there is a cornerstone investor (often a previous parent) that has a small – 25% or less – stake in the business.
- *Quasi Captive*, where the fund management entity is owned entirely by a third party bank, insurance company or other asset management business. In these businesses the majority of funds are raised from external investors and the parent entity tends to invest a relatively small proportion of the total PE funds and in some cases none at all.
- *Captive*, where the fund management entity is owned entirely by a third party bank, insurance company or other asset or wealth management business. In these businesses the majority and in many cases all of the funds for PE investing are committed by the parent entity, typically off its own balance sheet.

Another important categorisation within the PE industry relates to the type of investing that the firm does and the main categories are as follows:

- *Direct investing houses.* These would include buy out, growth capital, venture capital and mezzanine.
- *Indirect or fund of fund houses.* These firms invest their funds in direct investing funds (as referred to above), providing their ultimate investors with a broader spread of PE investments than those investing directly. A

sub category of these are secondary fund management entities which tend to invest either in small portfolios of direct investments that may come on the market from a direct investing house which wishes to realise a part of its portfolio in a single transaction, or they may acquire 'secondary' interests in a direct fund which might come on to the market when a fund investor – or limited partner – (whether it be a fund of funds house, a pension scheme or an insurance company) wants to sell down or out its commitment to a particular fund.

Whilst it is important to understand the different types of firm that make up the PE and Infrastructure investing industry, it is equally important to understand that notwithstanding which category a firm or business may fall into, the key elements of Private Equity and Infrastructure remuneration tend to be the same across all categories. These elements comprise:

- Short term compensation
  - Base salary
  - Short term incentive (annual bonus)
  - Partnership profit share/dividends (for partners/shareholders in independent Private Equity firms)
- Long term compensation
  - Participation in a carried interest plan
  - Participation in a co-investment plan (sometimes as an alternative to carry)
- Long term alignment of interest
  - General Partners ('GP') or direct team commitment

There is however some variation in the make-up of and certainly in the levels of remuneration packages within these general headings, and these will be influenced by the ownership structure of the firm as well as by its investment type.

For pure independent houses the structure and levels of the various remuneration elements are directly influenced by the fee arrangements that are in place with the limited partner investors in the firm's funds. In an independent house all of the profits from the management fee and carried interest (performance fee) will typically be shared between the partners and employees of the firm with no need to consider other shareholders.

For pure captive houses there is usually no management fee arrangement and as a result the approach to setting base salary and annual bonus levels tends to differ somewhat from independent houses. However, it is MM&K's experience that all captive houses do consider their competitiveness against the independent houses when determining base salaries and annual bonus awards.

Perhaps the biggest influence over compensation levels at PE firms is driven by the level of funds under management. This is not surprising as those firms with the greater levels of funds under management will naturally have a larger revenue pool generated from their management fees.

Across the industry it has become the expected norm that individuals will receive a base salary and a substantial bonus and, although the level of bonus has declined during the economic downturn, at many PE firms annual bonuses are starting to return to 'historic' levels.

Although short term compensation it important and often significant, more senior investment professionals in the Private Equity industry are even more highly rewarded for long term performance through their participation in the carried interest plan ('CIP').

In independent third party funds, the carried interest is derived from the performance fee that is paid by the limited partner investors in the fund to the fund manager and/or the individual participants in the carry scheme. The performance fee essentially represents a share of the profits made in the underlying fund investments and is usually subject to the fund/investments delivering an annual internal rate of return ('IRR') above a pre-determined hurdle. For the large majority of independent direct investing Private Equity funds in Europe, the carry (or performance fee) is set at 20% with a hurdle IRR of 8%. These figures tend to apply for all types of direct investing funds, whether they are buy-out, growth/development capital, infrastructure or mezzanine. In these houses the partners and other executives in the private equity fund management team will typically share the carried interest amongst themselves although cornerstone investors will sometimes take some of the carry (say 25%) for themselves. Exceptionally a small portion of the carry is retained by the PE house itself and occasionally for the benefit of an employee trust.

Among those firms with an indirect investment strategy the level of carried interest available is generally not so high. As such the carried interest charged on the fund is often around half of that seen in direct investment firms. Results from MM&K's 2010 and 2011 surveys show that 100% of participating firms with indirect investment strategies have some form of long term incentive with 89% of these having a CIP. Among these respondents the median level of carried interest available to the directors and the rest of the team is 9%.

It is also typical for captive houses to have some form of carried interest plan although most typically with smaller levels of carry allocated to the investment team. In captive houses where PE funds are raised from external investors the private equity team will typically receive a proportion of the carried interest, with the parent company and occasionally other cornerstone/institutional investors taking the balance. In these sorts of situations, the private equity team will typically receive around 75% of the carry (which in gross terms would equate to 15% to 18%). In the few captive houses, that still exist that just invest their own balance sheet monies it is more normal for a carried interest plan to exist merely to act as the long term incentive for the PE team. In these cases the carried interest that is made available to the team is usually set at a lower figure than the aforementioned 15% (typically between 10% and 15%).

54.2 Hedge Funds

As in the Private Equity industry, there tends to be three main ownership structures for Hedge Fund businesses; independent, quasi captive and pure captive. Also, in a similar way to Private Equity, Hedge Fund businesses fall either into the category of direct investing firms or indirect investing (basically fund of fund) firms.

As a result, reward structures in the Hedge Fund industry, much like at Private Equity firms, follow a reasonably standardised set pattern.

The remuneration tools available to Hedge Funds are quite specific and are similar to Private Equity firms albeit with one major difference which is discussed below. The components of pay in hedge fund and fund of funds organisations can be broken down as follows:

- Base salary (and draw (advance on profit) for Members in independent houses)
- Discretionary bonus
- Bonuses derived from 'carve outs' – share of management fees and/or performance fees
- Total remuneration linked to fund or firm overall results
- Profit share (for members or partners)
- Dividends for shareholders
- Occasionally, long term incentive structures – real or phantom depending on ownership structure.

As will be evident from the above list, there is no reference to carried interest participation although there is reference to a sharing in performance fees.

Whilst direct investing hedge funds typically do charge a performance fee, the structure of such fee is quite different to a PE fund's performance fee (or carried interest). Whilst Private Equity carried interest plans are typically earned over the long term (over five years or more) and are based on granting the house/participants a share in the cash on cash profits realised by the fund, hedge fund performance fees are typically charged based on performance over a single year with such performance being based on mark to market valuations.

As a consequence of this, hedge fund managers often have no long term incentive arrangements other than in connection with bonus deferral requirements and to the extent relevant, equity ownership in the ultimate parent firm. Occasionally senior hedge fund managers in larger captive entities may participate in some form of long term incentive plan operated by the parent entity but this is not commonplace.

Mandatory deferrals have become increasingly common in larger Hedge Fund organisations over recent years and particularly so in captive hedge fund entities. With the introduction of CRD 3 and the FCA's Remuneration Guidelines it is expected that mandatory deferral of bonuses in hedge fund businesses will become the standard model. This will be further supported by the introduction of the AIFMD in 2013.

The criterion used for determining deferral varies between firms as does the total amount deferred. Many firms only use the total bonus as a criterion with over half applying deferral requirements after a threshold level of bonus is reached. Another method is to look at an individual's total compensation to determine the threshold and then deferring either a percentage of the incumbent's bonus or total compensation.

A further important feature of Hedge Fund remuneration is that, in most cases, where bonuses are required to be deferred, they are typically required to be invested back into the hedge fund or funds managed by the relevant hedge fund manager or by the hedge fund firm generally. This particular feature of Hedge Fund remuneration can be compared with some co-investment plans that are seen in the PE industry.

One other important factor when looking at Private Equity and Hedge Fund remuneration structures revolves around employee benefits. It is generally the case that independent firms (both in the PE industry and the HF industry) do not provide generous benefits packages and in particular typically offer no pension provision at all. This is in contrast to many captive entities where much more generous benefits (notably pension plans) are provided.

Both Private Equity and Hedge Funds are usually structured as LLPs. This is not always the case, eg 3i and Man Group are both listed on the London Stock Exchange. The benefits of LLP structure versus plc structure are discussed in **Chapter 55**.

Table 53 provides a high level summary table which contrasts remuneration practices as between hedge fund managers and executives and private equity fund managers and executives:

Table 53: Comparison of PE and Hedge Fund remuneration structures

Remuneration Element	Investment Type	
	Private Equity	**Hedge Fund**
Base Salary	Higher levels of base salary	Less significant levels of base salary
Annual Bonus	Smaller bonuses but generally considered by all to be an expected and important part of the compensation package	Large bonus is the major incentive component of the HF investment professional compensation package (although deferral applies)
Long Term Incentive	Main focus of reward for PE investment professionals is the Carried Interest Plan. Ties individuals in for the fund duration and directly aligns reward with the performance of the fund.	Long Term Incentive is almost entirely comprised of deferral of short term bonus, invested back into the hedge fund.

54.3 Private Equity investee companies

Remuneration in companies in which Private Equity invest is simpler and more equity based than in quoted companies. There is a higher risk of failure/downside. The pay deal is focused on the initial deal and subsequent liquidity events.

Salaries are set at basic middle class existence levels (enough to pay the groceries and school fees).

The amount of equity for managers is 10 to 20% of the total and the ordinary (sweet) equity will typically be highly leveraged. Equity gains are taxed at capital gains rates with no NIC for the company, which makes equity rewards much more attractive than cash. Capital gains rates are 10% if entrepreneurial relief applies and if not the higher rate is now 28%.

A typical structure might be for the management to own a company which is located in Jersey or Guernsey, which will own a minority percentage of the TopCo with the private equity investor owning the rest. There will then be mezzanine finance, which might be owned by the private equity investor and/or banks and/or other investors. There will also be senior debt.

This type of structure is highly tax efficient for management, as they will only pay UK tax on any income from their management company shares or capital which is remitted back to the UK. If their gains are sufficiently large, then it will be cost-effective to take loans from the management company. When the executive dies, his investments in the management company will be passed to his estate, most probably in trust. As a result of the structure, it is possible for management to pay no UK taxes on their gains.

Managers are closely monitored by investors.

The contrast with a typical quoted UK plc is stark:

Table 54: Comparison of PE backed company and quoted company

Private Equity backed company	**Quoted company**
Pay structure is simple	Pay structure is complex – many plans
Equity is key component	Incentives through annual bonus and long term plans
Equity gains taxed as capital gains	LTIP/share option gains taxed as income plus Employers and Employee NI
Dilution of 10 to 20%	ABI/NAPF guideline of 5% over ten years = 0.5% per annum
Equity awards are front end loaded	ABI/NAPF prefer annual awards of LTIP/share options
No performance conditions on equity	ABI/NAPF prefer stretching performance conditions on both LTIP and Options
Salaries set at basic level	Salaries ratcheted up each year
Lower bonuses	Bonus opportunity typically 100% of salary – more in bigger companies – and trend is rising. Very few CEOs get nil bonus
Risk of failure/downside	Often generous severance terms and good pensions
Highly leveraged	Modest debt/equity leverage
Managers closely monitored by investors	Most shareholders have small (<5%) stakes and need to build consensus over time before they can convey their view to Boards about management performance
Clear strategy and performance drivers	Very bland performance criteria, resulting in blunt instrument

55 PLC versus LLP

The information below is not exhaustive and professional advice should be sought before entering into business and choosing the most suitable corporate vehicle.

Who uses LLP structure?

Private Equity, Hedge Funds, accountants and lawyers all use the LLP structure. Why is this? Firstly, because owners are the directors and partners of the firms. However, there are other reasons why the LLP structure is favoured. The principle of the partnership is that it distributes income to the partners and there is no employers' national insurance. Individual partners are then responsible for income tax and their own national insurance. In contrast, a company accumulates profits. The company has to pay corporation tax. Any dividends which the company pays to shareholders will be subject to income tax by the shareholders, but not national insurance.

What is a partnership?

A partnership is a relatively simple and flexible way for two or more people to own and run a profit-making business together. Social enterprises and other non-profit making organisations should not use this business structure.

Unlike the shareholders in a limited company, the members of a general partnership have no financial protection if the business runs into trouble – each partner is responsible for the debts of the partnership as a whole. This means that each partner's personal assets may be at risk if the business fails.

Disputes between partners can cause difficulties, and the partnership may have to be dissolved if one of its members resigns or dies. It's possible to resolve these issues in advance by drawing up a deed of partnership. It is a good idea for each partner to get legal advice before finalising their level of responsibility in a deed.

Partnerships

There are three forms of 'partnership' currently possible in the UK.

The **ordinary partnership** governed by the Partnerships Act 1890. The majority of firms of lawyers, accountants, chartered surveyors and other professionals are ordinary partnerships.

The **limited partnership** governed by the Limited Partnerships Act 1907 where limited liability is given to the members not involved in the management of the partnership

The **Limited Liability Partnership** governed by the Limited Liability Partnership Act 2000 where '2 or more persons associated for carrying on lawful business with a view to profit must have subscribed their names to an incorporation document' (LLP Act 2002, s 2).

The Limited Liability Partnership and its benefits

Through the process of registration an LLP becomes a legal person distinct from its members. It can therefore:

- enter into contracts in its own name
- sue and be sued in its own name
- buy, sell and lease property in its own name.

The LLP is a hybrid between a limited company and an ordinary partnership offering limited liability to members whilst retaining the flexibility of a partnership and transparency for tax purposes.

Incorporation as a limited liability partnership brings with it a number of advantages, compared to other partnerships, namely:

- Limited liability: The liability of the members is limited to the amount the members agree to contribute on the winding up of the LLP (which can be nothing).
- Perpetual succession: An LLP ceases to exist only if it is formally wound up or struck from the Companies Register by Companies House. Members can leave the LLP for whatever reason and the LLP continues.
- Protection of the name: Incorporation ensures that no other LLP or company can be registered with the same name.

Partners

There are three main types of partner, each of which has different rights and responsibilities.

General partners invest in the business, take part in running it and share in its profits. Each general partner is fully liable for any debts that the partnership may have. This means that they could lose more than their initial investment in the business if it runs into trouble, and that their personal assets could be at risk. Every ordinary and limited partnership must have at least one general partner.

Limited partners are not permitted to participate in the day-to-day running of the business. Their debt is limited to the amount of their initial investment.

Sleeping partners invest money in the business and share in its profits, but do not take part in running it. Like general partners, they are fully liable for the partnership's debts.

Companies and limited liability partnerships (LLPs) as members of partnerships

As well as individuals, other legal entities – such as companies and LLPs – can also be members of partnerships. They have the same rights and responsibilities within the partnership as other partners.

Partnerships whose members are all companies have to prepare 'partnership accounts' and send them to Companies House each year. Members of such partnerships must attach a copy of these documents to their own company accounts when they submit them to Companies House.

Deed of partnership

A deed of partnership is a legally binding agreement between partners who are in business together. It describes how the partnership will be run and the rights and duties of the partners themselves.

It's not necessary to have a deed in order to set up a partnership, but it's a good idea, as it can help to prevent misunderstandings and disputes. It may be a good idea to enlist a solicitor to ensure that each partner understands their responsibilities before the deed is finalised.

As well as giving basic information about the partnership, such as its business name and the names of the partners, the type of business and business address, the deed will usually set out:

- the amount of capital that each partner is to contribute to the business
- the way in which partners will share profits or losses, and whether any of the partners should be paid a salary
- working arrangements, such as how much time each partner should contribute to the business, who does what management tasks and what type of decisions need collective agreement between the partners

- changes to the partnership, such as how new partners can be appointed and what happens if a partner dies or wishes to leave.

If the partnership does not have a deed, it will be governed by the terms of the Partnership Act[1] 1890. This does not offer solutions to many of the problems that can arise and may not suit the way that you and your partners want to work together.

Tax matters of a partnership

The profits and gains of the partnership are shared among the partners. Each is personally responsible for paying tax on their share.

The nominated partner must register the partnership for business taxes with HM Revenue & Customs (HMRC).

Each partner must also register themselves for Self Assessment and National Insurance. The partnership and each partner will each then receive their own Unique Taxpayer Reference for Self Assessment. HMRC will then set up the right tax and National Insurance records for both the partnership and partners.

Every year each individual partner will need to complete a Self Assessment tax return to show the profits they get from the partnership.

The partnership should appoint one of its officers – the nominated partner – to fill in the Self Assessment Partnership Tax Return and send it to HMRC. This includes a Partnership Statement, which shows how profits or losses have been divided among the partners. The nominated partner should also ensure that all other officers are given copies of the Partnership Statement to help them complete their own tax returns. Although the nominated officer has responsibility for the Partnership Tax Return, all the partners are jointly liable for any penalties resulting from it being submitted late or incorrectly.

National Insurance contributions

As well as being responsible for their tax, individual partners are also responsible for paying their own National Insurance contributions (NICs). Partners normally have to pay Class 2 National Insurance contributions. If their annual profits are over a certain amount they also pay Class 4 contributions.

---

[1] For more information about the Partnership Act see http://www.hmrc.gov.uk/manuals/bimmanual/bim72501.htm

Corporation Tax

If partners are companies, they must pay Corporation Tax on their profits from the partnership, and should record the relevant figures on their Corporation Tax return.

LLP v LTD Company – A Comparison

	Limited Company	**Limited Liability Partnership**
Regulations	Companies Act 1985	LLP Act 2000
Liability	Limited to amounts unpaid on shares	Limited to amount of capital agreed to be contributed in the event of winding up
Constitution	Memorandum and articles of association govern the power to act and form the rules of the company – must be filed at Companies House	Agreement between members recommended but not essential. Does not need to be filed on public record
Status	Has a separate legal personality – can own land, sue, be sued etc in its own name	Has a separate legal personality – can own land, sue, be sued etc in its own name
Capital	The minimum share capital of a company is 1p (public company – £50,000) and for a private company, only one share needs to be issued (private companies limited by shares). Shares may be divided into different classes and different denominations with varying rights	No regulations on capital. Capital is not divided into shares
Profits	May pay salaries and dividends from distributable reserves	Members may draw on their profits within the terms of their agreement
Taking out capital	Not generally permitted although companies may be able to purchase or redeem their own shares	Depends on agreement
Management	Private company requires only one director (two for a public company) Directors do not have to be members Directors can be corporations	At least two designated members needed, but all members are treated similar to company directors. Members can be corporations

	Limited Company	**Limited Liability Partnership**
Company Secretary	A Company Secretary is required (in a public company the Company Secretary must be qualified to act)	No Secretary needed
Members	Companies limited by shares or guarantee require only one member. Public and unlimited companies require two	Requires at least two members
Decisions	The Companies Act specifies. Majorities required for many Resolutions	LLP Act sets out some majorities, otherwise unanimous consent required for most decisions unless agreement specifies otherwise
Meetings	The Companies Act requires an AGM (although private companies may elect not to hold one)	No regulations on meetings
Investment	Outside investors may contribute share capital (and take an equity stake without becoming a director) or loans	Outside investors can only contribute loan capital. Only a member can take equity stake
Borrowings	Debentures and fixed and floating charges	Debentures and fixed and floating charges
Written resolutions	Members may pass resolutions by means of written resolutions	Depends on members' agreement
Disclosure	Accounts must be filed at Companies House. Annual return Notice of change of director/secretary/registered office; mortgages; and various other returns	Accounts must be filed at Companies House. Annual return Notice of change of members/registered office; mortgages; and various other returns
Auditors	Need not always have auditors	Need not always have auditors
Taxation	Corporation tax applies	Members taxed as individuals; no Corporation tax
Registration as charity	Possible for a company limited by guarantee	Not possible

The differences of LLP, Company, Limited Partnership and Partnership in terms of tax members and capital gains are summarised as follows.

	LLP	**Company**	**Limited Partnership**	**Partnership**
Tax transparency	Yes	Tax on company and on Shareholders	Yes	Yes
Members	Taxed under Sch D	Directors and employees taxed under Sch E	Taxed under Sch D	Taxed under Sch D
Capital gains	On members (and LLP if insolvency intervenes)	On company and on members	On partners	On partners Class 2 & 4

56 The Pros and Cons of Location Offshore

The footloose nature of large corporations means they can play off one country against another, picking and choosing where to make their legal home as they seek the most generous tax regime.

Even companies whose shares continue to be traded in London can move their legal base elsewhere to reduce their tax burden.

Tax is not the only incentive. Being based abroad can also avoid an enormous amount of red tape and concomitant bureaucracy. Companies value this flexibility.

The downside is that Board meetings have to be held offshore too, and this can involve additional travel and cost and inconvenience. Whilst a trip to Bermuda sounds like a holiday, going for a three hour Board meeting can involve two days of travel time.

Brit Insurance, sponsors of England's Ashes cricket team, is legally based in Amsterdam; advertising giant WPP was technically an Irish company (but gave up and relocated back to the UK). Pharmaceuticals group Shire, global business media firm United Business Media[1], and Experian – which is best known for credit-checks – have all quit Britain. Wolseley, the world's largest supplier of building, heating and plumbing supplies, Glencore and Alliance Boots are based in Switzerland.

Certainly, successive governments have tried to make Britain an attractive home for business. In 1984, the UK levied corporation tax at 52%. By 1996, it had fallen to 33%. It is now 28% and is to be cut to 24%.

But other countries have cut tax too. And in the cold, calculating world of multi-national commerce – in which patriotism counts for nothing – companies will seek out the regime where national exchequers take the smallest slice.

Being located offshore will still require many top executives to be based in the UK if that is where most of the corporate activity actually takes place. Executives based in the UK will still be subject to UK taxation. Some executives, such as those with non-dom status, will find working for a

---

1 On the 18th October 2012 UBM announced 'UBM's Board of Directors has decided to recommend that UBM plc return to a United Kingdom tax domicile, subject to shareholder approval.'

company located offshore particularly tax effective. For those without non-dom status, it is sometimes possible to 'channel' the executive's reward through a family member, who does have non-dom status, such as a spouse. Such payments to non-doms will avoid UK income tax and are highly tax effective.[2]

2 An example is Sir Philip Green, see http://www.ukuncut.org.uk/targets/3

57 Developments in the US and Elsewhere

57.1 US Practices

The main differences are

- Pay is much higher and much more equity based. However it should be noted that US companies tend to be larger than UK ones, so it appears that US pay relative to UK pay is higher than it actually is.
- Disclosure of the top five executives is required and has been so for many years. In contrast in the UK only the pay of directors has to be disclosed (banks now have to disclose the pay of the top eight executives) and as many companies only have two executive directors this is all they have to disclose.
- Disclosure has to include a single figure for total remuneration based on the expected value of long term incentive awards. By contrast, in the UK, the DRRR requirement is for the amounts received.
- Consultants' fees have to be disclosed. This reflects a much greater awareness in the US of the conflicts of interest that remuneration consultants face in advising on executive pay.

57.2 Lessons from America

The following is based on an article by the author Cliff Weight which first appeared in Executive Compensation Briefing in 2011.

> 'The US model of CEO compensation is broken. It has been for years. Enron, WorldCom, Tyco and Hollander are examples of the CEO having too much influence in setting their own pay. This is still the case as is shown by the more recent large payoffs to the CEOs of NYSE, Citigroup, Merrill Lynch, etc. Their Remuneration Committees approved the awards. Why?
>
> Too many CEOs in the US still have the combined Chairman and CEO role. They strongly influence the choice of their Non-Executive Directors and ensure the Remuneration Committee consists of people minded to continue to vote through excessive pay awards. Sarbanes-Oxley did not address this problem. On the positive side, the trend toward separation of the Chairman and CEO roles has increased, with

41 per cent of S&P 500 Boards now splitting the roles, up from 26 per cent in 2001, according to a Nov 2011 Spencer Stuart survey.

Laws and regulations about caps on pay will not work. There is bad precedent in the law of unintended consequences, e.g. s 162 of the US Tax Code[1] which limited pay to $1m p.a. unless it was performance related, which led to a huge increase in the use of options and rise in previously sub-$1m salaries up to the $1m restriction.

Analysts contribute to the excessive pay levels of CEOs. Shares surge on the appointment of a big name CEO. Usually such CEOs command much higher compensation packages than lesser known internal appointments. To justify themselves, new CEOs have to do something. They adopt new strategies, which entail more risk. More risk = higher share price volatility = more chance of a large payout if successful. Academic research (performed by people who do not have a conflict of interest) is conclusive: 70% of acquisitions and mergers do not add value. Nevertheless, CEOs are urged to do deals by investment bankers, strategy consultants, accountants and lawyers, whose fees are paid when the deal is done, irrespective of whether the deal generates superior shareholder returns in the long term.

New hires, not unreasonably, negotiate safety nets[2], in case things don't work out as planned. But they win both ways. The poor shareholder has to suffer the burden and cost of an asymmetric reward package.

But despite these weaknesses, there are lessons to be learnt from America.

US is more long term – better alignment with long term shareholders

The US mix of pay is (on average) 10% salary, 25% bonus and 65% long term incentives. The UK mix is 20% salary, 40% bonus and 40% long term incentives. The US model is more long term and could therefore be considered better than the UK model.

Pay levels in the US are higher than the UK mainly because the companies are bigger. If we were to adjust for size differences, then US pay levels are probably about 20% to 30% higher than the UK in gross terms, but somewhat larger when taxes and cost of living are also taken into account.

Better disclosure

The US disclosure of executive pay is much better than the UK.

---

1 Section 162(m) was added by the Omnibus Budget Reconciliation Act (OBRA) of 1993.

2 It is not the existence of the parachute that is the problem – it is the circumstances in which it can be opened. Once an executive has been in post for three years, surely six months' pay on leaving is adequate – if he is a good performer he will be able to find a new job within six months.

Chart 20: Mix and magnitude of CEO pay in US and UK

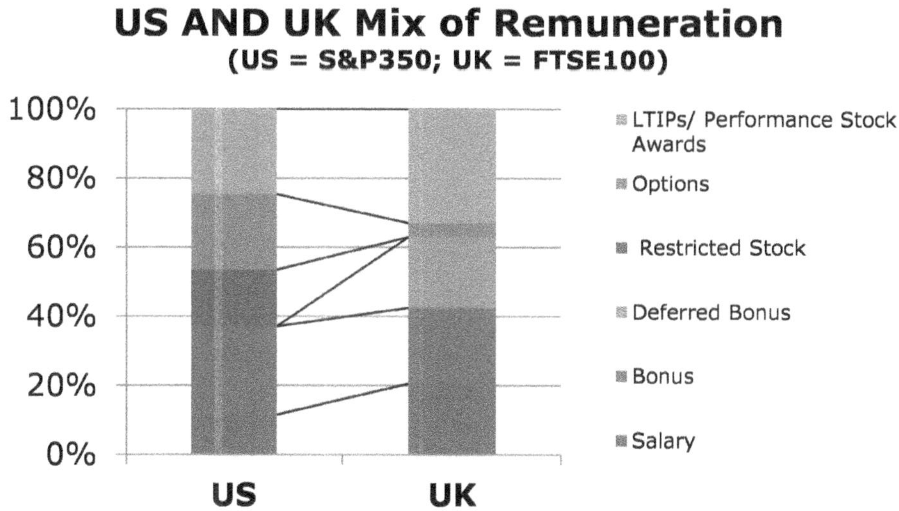

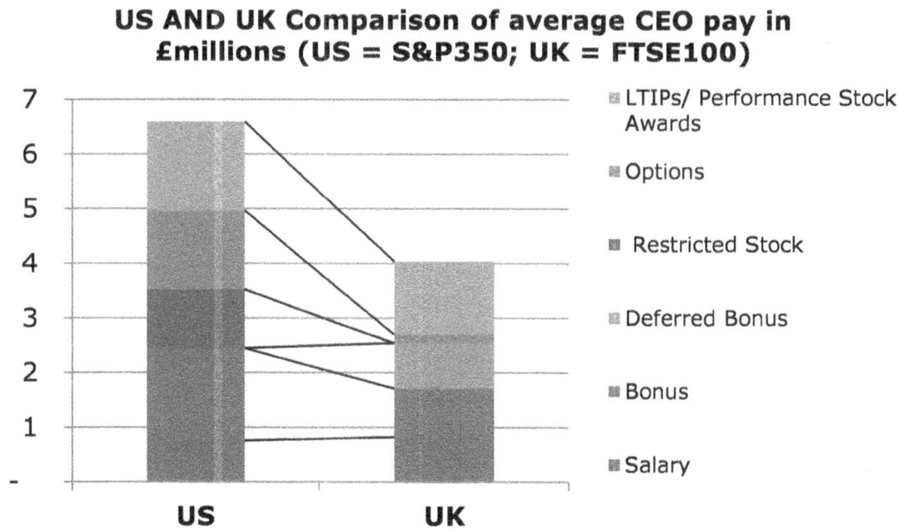

- Most of the data is in XBRL (i.e. a standard format of tables that is easily analysable and makes it easy for users to spot things and quickly see if something is not there. In contrast in the UK there is no proscribed format and so much finding information can be very time consuming – at times it feels like searching for a needle in a haystack).
- Data is shown for the 5 highest paid executives. In the UK companies only have to disclose the directors' data and this creates

an incentive not to promote executives to the Board. Non board pay is hidden from shareholders in the UK.

- There is a total remuneration figure calculated on a standardised agreed format (the expected value of awards made in that year). In contrast, in the UK, there is no requirement to add up total remuneration and the data is often spread over several pages in the annual report and the fair values of share awards are disclosed in a footnote to the accounts which requires further cross referencing.

TARP money repaid early

The US government lent their banks money on favourable terms in 2008, under the Troubled Asset Relief Program (TARP) arrangements. However, banks with TARP loans had severe restrictions on what they could do in terms on executive compensation. This proved to be a very effective incentive for banks to repay their loans as soon as possible.

In contrast, the UK part nationalised RBS and Lloyds and all of Northern Rock, without an effective incentive for these banks to get back to a more normal capital structure.

Executive Consultants Independence

Executive Compensation consultants in the US reached pariah status and have been blamed for the financial crisis. The US politicians have reacted by making it very difficult for consultants to advise the Remuneration Committee and the management. Consequently many executive compensation consultants left their large firms and set up their own independent boutique firms. The SEC now (Dodd Frank) requires the fees paid to executive compensation consultants to be disclosed and this highlights potential conflicts of interest.

Say on Pay and the "Outrage" model

Say on pay not working. The average say on pay vote was 91% in favour in the 2011 AGM season in the US. Just 36 out of 2,200 votes went against the Board resolution. The US corporate governance model of pay has for many years worked on the "outrage" model. In this model, so long as pay is not too outrageous it is approved by shareholders. Such an approach is of course inherently inflationary as anyone who is paid less than the "Outrage" level will try to get their pay increased.

Performance	**High**	√√ ok	√√√ good
	Low	√ ok (-ish)	**OUTRAGE!**
		Low	**High**
		Pay	

The problem is further exacerbated by the proxy adviser Risk Metrics[3] (and their preceding firm ISS) only signalling that pay was worthy of shareholders attention if it was in the top quartile (i.e. top 25% of comparable companies' pay practices). Thus any company who was paid below this knew they could increase their pay without attracting too much negative attention. ISS even offered a service to companies so they could benchmark where they were (which seems to be a bit of a conflict of interest).

Bebchuk and Fried

But perhaps the best lessons are to be learnt (as noted in chapter 31.1) are those from the work of Lucien Bebchuk[4] and Jesse Fried[5], two Harvard professors, who have done extensive research into executive compensation in the US. Their books and research are well worth reading. Some of the points they make include these:

- It is not just a few rotten apples. The problems of executive compensation are widespread, persistent and systemic.
- Executive compensation is not designed to tightly link pay and performance.
- The pay of the top 5 executives accounted for 7.5% of profits last year[6]. This is less than the 10% peak in the period 1998–2002, but remains a significant cost for shareholders.
- The executives' ability to unwind equity positions provides incentives for executives to make short term profits from their shareholdings, which are not available to shareholders. (They are not saying executives trade on inside information – that would be illegal. However executives are better informed that most shareholders about markets, customers and trends: as a result they can come to a decision to reduce their exposure to their company shares earlier than others might do.)
- Non-Executive Directors as not operating as independents. The gift of their continued role is heavily influenceable by the CEO

---

3 Risk Metrics has now reverted to its former name, ISS.

4 Bebchuck and Spamman 'Regulating Bankers' Pay', May 2010

5 Fried and Jackson, 'Pay Without Performance – the unfulfilled promise of executive compensation'; Executive Pensions HBR Discussion Paper 507, March 2005.

6 At the time they were referring to 2009.

and it is usually better not to upset the apple cart by disagreeing about executive compensation issues.

- Pay is not unlimited. But only at a certain level does the outrage factor come into play.
- Companies routinely camouflage their disclosure of executive compensation so as to make if difficult or impossible for readers of the annual reports to see how much executives have been paid and how much they might receive in the future.
- The devil is in the detail, particularly with equity pay and pensions[7]. Executives are often able to persuade their compensation committees to exercise discretion in respect of performance conditions in favour of executives. Executives are able to sell shares when they get wind of information that has not yet been formally assessed or announced to the Board or the market[8].

Conclusions

The UK has, in the main, avoided the worst excesses of egregious pay, whereas there have been numerous (bad) cases in America. America may not be perfect but we should learn from their strengths and their mistakes.

There is a danger that the UK will become too short-termist in its approach to executive compensation and consequently in the way UK companies are managed. The 'best practice' remuneration model that has emerged in the UK is horrendously short-term. The timescale for incentive measurement for bonuses and LTIPs is one to three years. The use of deferred bonus plans has further shortened the timescale of performance measurement. This reflects the systematic short-termism amongst most investors as well as the media. Chief Executives are expected to 'do something' to get results in the short-term.

Share options are now sadly neglected, despite the fact they potentially create an interest in the share price for up to ten years. Rules for retention of shares acquired from incentive plans, together with agreed rules for building up significant stakes in the company are the best way to create alignment with (long-term) shareholders.

---

7 See Executive Pensions Discussion Paper 507, March 2005, Harvard Law School. This paper identified that the median pension value as of total compensation was 34%; and because public firms are not required to disclose the monetary value of pension plans, financial economist and the media alike have generally excluded pension from their pay analyses causing significant distortions in comparison among executive compensation packages and overestimates of the extent to which executive pay is linked to performance.

8 Please note I am not suggesting this is insider trading, but it doesn't seem very ethical!

57.3 EU Developments

The EU has published a directive about disclosure of directors' remuneration and say on pay, but implementation is up to member states and is patchy.

CEBS co-ordinated action on Financial Services and the FSA Remuneration Code for banks and financial organisations reflects this and the G20 FSB (Financial Stability Board) proposals.

The 2012 French election produced a new President, who has promised to increase income tax to 75% for high earners. This is widely predicted to produce an exodus of businessmen.[9]

[9] Update for the 2nd edition: It has! This prediction was correct.

Appendices

Appendix 1 Extracts from Financial Conduct Authority Listing Rules

LR 9.4 Documents requiring prior approval

Employees share schemes and long-term incentive plans

(1) This *rule* applies to the following schemes of a *listed company* incorporated in the *United Kingdom* and of any of its *major subsidiary undertaking* (even if that *major subsidiary undertaking* is incorporated or operates overseas):

(a) an *employees' share scheme* if the scheme involves or may involve the issue of new *shares* or the transfer of *treasury shares*; and

(b) a *long-term incentive scheme* in which one or more *directors* of the *listed company* is eligible to participate.

(2) The *listed company* must ensure that the *employees' share scheme* or *long-term incentive scheme* is approved by an ordinary resolution of the shareholders of the *listed company* in general meeting before it is adopted.

LR 9.4.2 *LR 9.4.1 R* does not apply to the following *long-term incentive schemes*:

(1) an arrangement where participation is offered on similar terms to all or substantially all *employees* of the *listed company* or any of its *subsidiary undertakings* whose *employees* are eligible to participate in the arrangement (provided that all or substantially all *employees* are not *directors* of the *listed company*); and

(2) an arrangement where the only participant is a *director* of the *listed company* (or an individual whose appointment as a *director* of the *listed company* is being contemplated) and the arrangement is established specifically to facilitate, in unusual circumstances, the recruitment or retention of the relevant individual.

LR 9.4.3 For a scheme referred to in *LR 9.4.2 R (2)*, the following information must be disclosed in the first annual report published by the *listed company* after the date on which the relevant individual becomes eligible to participate in the arrangement:

(1) all of the information prescribed in *LR 13.8.11 R*;

(2) the name of the sole participant;

(3) the date on which the participant first became eligible to participate in the arrangement;

(4) an explanation of why the circumstances in which the arrangement was established were unusual;

(5) the conditions to be satisfied under the terms of the arrangement; and

(6) the maximum award(s) under the terms of the arrangement or, if there is no maximum, the basis on which awards will be determined.

Discounted option arrangements

(1) This *rule* applies to the grant to a *director* or *employee* of a *listed company* or of any *subsidiary undertaking* of a *listed company* of an option to subscribe, warrant to subscribe or other similar right to subscribe for *shares* in the capital of the *listed company* or any of its *subsidiary undertakings*.

(2) A *listed company* must not, without the prior approval by an ordinary resolution of the shareholders of the *listed company* in a general meeting, grant the option, warrant or other right if the price per *share* payable on the exercise of the option, warrant or other similar right to subscribe is less than whichever of the following is used to calculate the exercise price:

  (a) the market value of the *share* on the date when the exercise price is determined; or

  (b) the market value of the *share* on the *business day* before that date; or

  (c) the average of the market values for a number of dealing days within a period not exceeding 30 *days* immediately before that date.

LR 9.4.5 *LR 9.4.4 R* does not apply to the grant of an option to subscribe, warrant to subscribe or other similar right to subscribe for *shares* in the capital of a *listed company* or any of its *subsidiary undertakings*:

(1) under an *employees' share scheme* if participation is offered on similar terms to all or substantially all *employees* of the *listed company* or any of its *subsidiary undertakings* whose *employees* are entitled to participate in the scheme; or

(2) following a take-over or reconstruction, in replacement for and on comparable terms with options to subscribe, warrants to subscribe or other similar rights to subscribe held immediately before the take-over or reconstruction for *shares* in either a *company* of which the *listed company* thereby obtains control or in any of that *company's subsidiary undertakings*.

LR 13.8 Other circulars

Employees' share scheme etc

LR 13.8.11 A *circular* to shareholders about the approval of an *employee's share scheme* or *long-term incentive scheme* must:

(1) include either the full text of the scheme or a description of its principal terms;

(2) include, if *directors* of the *listed company* are trustees of the scheme, or have a direct or indirect interest in the trustees, details of the trusteeship or interest;

(3) state that the provisions (if any) relating to:

  (a) the persons to whom, or for whom, *securities*, cash or other benefits are provided under the scheme (the 'participants');

  (b) limitations on the number or amount of the *securities*, cash or other benefits subject to the scheme;

  (c) the maximum entitlement for any one participant; and

  (d) the basis for determining a participant's entitlement to, and the terms of, *securities*, cash or other benefit to be provided and for the adjustment thereof (if any) if there is a capitalisation issue, *rights issue* or *open offer*, sub-division or consolidation of *shares* or reduction of capital or any other variation of capital;

cannot be altered to the advantage of participants without the prior approval of shareholders in general meeting (except for minor amendments to benefit the administration of the scheme, to take account of a change in legislation or to obtain or maintain favourable tax, exchange control or regulatory treatment for participants in the scheme or for the *company* operating the scheme or for members of its group);

(4) state whether benefits under the scheme will be pensionable and, if so, the reasons for this; and

(5) if the scheme is not circulated to shareholders, include a statement that it will be available for inspection:

  (a) from the date of sending the *circular* until the close of the relevant general meeting at a place in or near the City of London or such other place the *FCA* may determine; and

  (b) at the place of the general meeting for at least 15 minutes before and during the meeting.

LR 13.8.12 The resolution contained in the notice of meeting accompanying the *circular* must refer either to:

(1) the scheme itself (if circulated to shareholders); or

(2) the summary of its principal terms included in the *circular*.

LR 13.8.13 The resolution approving the adoption of an *employees' share scheme* or *long-term incentive scheme* may authorise the *directors* to establish further schemes based on any scheme which has previously been approved by shareholders but modified to take account of local tax, exchange control or securities laws in overseas territories, provided that any *shares* made available under such further schemes are treated as counting against any limits on individual or overall participation in the main scheme.

Amendments to employees' share scheme etc

LR 13.8.14 A *circular* to shareholders about proposed amendments to an *employees' share scheme* or a *long-term incentive scheme* must include:

(1) an explanation of the effect of the proposed amendments; and

(2) the full terms of the proposed amendments, or a statement that the full text of the scheme as amended will be available for inspection.

Discounted option arrangements

LR 13.8.15 If shareholders' approval is required by *LR 9.4.4 R*, the *circular* to shareholders must include the following information:

(1) details of the persons to whom the *options*, *warrants* or rights are to be granted; and

(2) a summary of the principal terms of the *options*, *warrants* or rights.

LR 13.8.16 …

  (i) a statement as to whether holders exercising their rights of conversion will retain the next interest payment due on the *securities*.

(2) The *circular* must not contain specific advice as to whether or not to convert the *securities*.

LR 9.8 Annual financial report

[**Note**: *LR 9.8* does not apply to a *listed company* with a financial year ending before 30 September 2013, or to a *listed company* with a financial year ending on or after 30 September 2013 whose annual financial report has been made public on or before 13 December 2013. As set out in *LR TR 11*, a *listed company* with a financial year ending before 30 September 2013, or a *listed company* with a financial year ending on or after 30 September 2013 whose annual financial report has been made public on or before 13 December 2013, must instead comply with the requirements set out in *LR App 2*.]

Information to be included in annual report and accounts

LR 9.8.4 In addition to the requirements set out in *DTR 4.1* a *listed company* must include in its annual financial report, where applicable, the following:

...

(4) details of any long-term incentive schemes as required by *LR 9.4.3 R*;

(5) details of any arrangements under which a *director* of the *company* has waived or agreed to waive any emoluments from the *company* or any *subsidiary undertaking*;

(6) where a *director* has agreed to waive future emoluments, details of such waiver together with those relating to emoluments which were waived during the period under review;

Additional information

LR 9.8.6 In the case of a *listed company* incorporated in the *United Kingdom*, the following additional items must be included in its annual financial report:

(1) a statement setting out all the interests (in respect of which transactions are notifiable to the company under *DTR 3.1.2 R*) of each *person* who is a *director* of the *listed company* as at the end of the period under review including:

  (a) all changes in the interests of each *director* that have occurred between the end of the period under review and a date not more than one month prior to the date of the notice of the annual general meeting; or

(b) if there have been no changes in the period described in paragraph (a), a statement that there have been no changes in the interests of each *director.*

Interests of each *director* includes the interests of *connected persons* of which the *listed company* is, or ought upon reasonable enquiry to become, aware.

(2) a statement showing the interests disclosed to the *listed company* in accordance with *DTR 5* as at the end of the period under review and:

(a) all interests disclosed to the *listed company* in accordance with *DTR 5* that have occurred between the end of the period under review and a date not more than one month prior to the date of the notice of the annual general meeting; or

(b) if no interests have been disclosed to the *listed company* in accordance with *DTR 5* in the period described in (a), a statement that no changes have been disclosed to the *listed company*.

...

(4) a statement setting out:

...

(d) in the case of sales of *treasury shares* for cash made otherwise than through the market, or in connection with an *employees' share scheme*, or otherwise than pursuant to an opportunity which (so far as was practicable) was made available to all holders of the *listed company's securities* (or to all holders of a relevant class of its *securities*) on the same terms, particulars of the names of purchasers of such *shares* sold, or proposed to be sold, by the *company* during the period under review;

(5) a statement of how the *listed company* has applied the Main Principles set out in the *UK Corporate Governance Code*, in a manner that would enable shareholders to evaluate how the principles have been applied;

(6) a statement as to whether the *listed company* has:

(a) complied throughout the accounting period with all relevant provisions set out in the *UK Corporate Governance Code*; or

(b) not complied throughout the accounting period with all relevant provisions set out in the *UK Corporate Governance Code* and if so, setting out:

(i) those provisions, if any it has not complied with;

(ii) in the case of provisions whose requirements are of a

continuing nature, the period within which, if any, it did not comply with some or all of those provisions; and

(iii) the *company's* reasons for non-compliance; and

(7) a report to the shareholders by the Board which contains the information set out in *LR 9.8.8 R*.

LR 9.8.6A

(1) The effect of *LR 9.8.6 R (1)* is that a *listed company* is required to set out a 'snapshot' of the total interests of a *director* and his or her *connected persons*, as at the end of the period under review (including certain information to update it as at a date not more than a month before the date of the notice of the annual general meeting). The interests that need to be set out are limited to those in respect of which transactions fall to be notified under the notification requirement for PDMRs in *DTR 3.1.2 R*. *Persons* who are *directors* during, but not at the end of, the period under review need not be included.

(2) A *listed company* unable to compile the statement in *LR 9.8.6 R (1)* from information already available to it may need to seek the relevant information, or confirmation, from the *director* himself, including that in relation to *connected persons*, but would not be expected to obtain information directly from *connected persons*.

LR 9.8.7 An *overseas company* with a *premium listing* must include in its annual report and accounts the information in *LR 9.8.6R (5)*, *LR 9.8.6R (6)* and *LR 9.8.8 R*.

(1) An *overseas company* with a *premium listing* that is not required to comply with requirements imposed by another *EEA State* that correspond to *DTR 7.2* (Corporate governance statements) must comply with *DTR 7.2* as if it were an *issuer* to which that section applies.

(2) An *overseas company* with a *premium listing* which complies with *LR 9.8.7 R* will be taken to satisfy the requirements of *DTR 7.2.2 R* and *DTR 7.2.3 R*, but (unless it is required to comply with requirements imposed by another *EEA State* that correspond to *DTR 7.2*) must comply with all of the other requirements of *DTR 7.2* as if it were an *issuer* to which that section applies.

Report to shareholders

LR 9.8.8 The report to the shareholders by the Board required by *LR 9.8.6 R (7)* must contain details of the unexpired term of any *director*'s service contract of a *director* proposed for election or re-election at the forthcoming annual general meeting, and, if any *director* proposed for election or re-election does not have a *directors'* service contract, a statement to that effect.

Information required by law

LR 9.8.9 The requirements of *LR 9.8.6R (6)* relating to corporate governance are additional to the information required by law to be included in the *listed company's* annual report and accounts.

Auditors report

LR 9.8.10 A *listed company* must ensure that the auditors review each of the following before the annual report is published:

...

(2) the parts of the statement required by *LR 9.8.6R (6)* (corporate governance) that relate to the following provisions of the *UK Corporate Governance Code*:

  (a) C.1.1;

  (b) C.2.1; and

  (c) C.3.1 to C.3.7.

LR 9 Annex 1 THE MODEL CODE (R) (extracts)

	Definitions		
1	In this code the following definitions, in addition to those contained in the *listing rules*, apply unless the context requires otherwise:		
	(c)	dealing includes:	
		(i)	any acquisition or disposal of, or agreement to acquire or dispose of any of the *securities* of the *company*;
		(ii)	entering into a contract (including a contract for difference) the purpose of which is to secure a profit or avoid a loss by reference to fluctuations in the price of any of the *securities* of the *company*;
		(iii)	the grant, acceptance, acquisition, disposal, exercise or discharge of any option (whether for the call, or put or both) to acquire or dispose of any of the *securities* of the *company*;
	(e)	*prohibited period* means:	
		(i)	any *close period*; or
		(ii)	any period when there exists any matter which constitutes *inside information* in relation to the *company*;
	(f)	*restricted person* means a *person discharging managerial responsibilities*; and	
	Dealings not subject to the provisions of this code		
2	The following dealings are not subject to the provisions of this code:		
	(h)	transfers of *shares* arising out of the operation of an *employees' share scheme* into a savings scheme investing in *securities* of the *company* following:	

	Definitions		
		(i)	exercise of an option under an approved SAYE option scheme; or
		(ii)	release of *shares* from a HM Revenue and Customs approved share incentive plan;
	(i)	with the exception of a disposal of *securities* of the *company* received by a restricted person as a participant, dealings in connection with the following *employees' share schemes*;	
		(i)	an HM Revenue and Customs approved SAYE option scheme or share incentive plan, under which participation is extended on similar terms to all or most employees of the participating *companies* in that scheme; or
		(ii)	a scheme on similar terms to a HM Revenue and Customs approved SAYE option scheme or share incentive plan, under which participation is extended on similar terms to all or most employees of the participating *companies* in that scheme; or
	(j)	the cancellation or surrender of an option under an *employees' share scheme*;	
	(k)	transfers of the *securities* of the *company* by an independent trustee of an *employees' share scheme* to a beneficiary who is not a restricted person;	
	Dealing by restricted persons		
3	A restricted person must not deal in any *securities* of the *company* without obtaining clearance to deal in advance in accordance with paragraph 4 of this code.		
	Awards of securities and options		
12	The grant of options by the board of *directors* under an *employees' share scheme* to individuals who are not restricted persons may be permitted during a prohibited period if such grant could not reasonably be made at another time and failure to make the grant would be likely to indicate that the *company* was in a prohibited period.		
13	The award by the *company* of *securities*, the grant of options and the grant of rights (or other interests) to acquire *securities* of the *company* to restricted persons is permitted in a prohibited period if:		
	(a)	the award or grant is made under the terms of an *employees' share scheme* and the scheme was not introduced or amended during the relevant prohibited period; and	
	(b)	either:	
		(i)	the terms of such *employees' share scheme* set out the timing of the award or grant and such terms have either previously been approved by shareholders or summarised or described in a document sent to shareholders, or
		(ii)	the timing of the award or grant is in accordance with the timing of previous awards or grants under the scheme; and
	(c)	the terms of the *employees' share scheme* set out the amount or value of the award or grant or the basis on which the amount or value of the award or grant is calculated and do not allow the exercise of discretion; and	

	Definitions	
	(d)	the failure to make the award or grant would be likely to indicate that the *company* is in a prohibited period.
	Exercise of options	
14	Where a *company* has been in an exceptionally long prohibited period or the *company* has had a number of consecutive prohibited periods, clearance may be given to allow the exercise of an option or right under an *employees' share scheme*, or the conversion of a convertible security, where the final date for the exercise of such option or right, or conversion of such security, falls during a prohibited period and the restricted person could not reasonably have been expected to exercise it at a time when he was free to deal.	
15	Where the exercise or conversion is permitted pursuant to paragraph 14, clearance may not be given for the sale of the *securities* of the *company* acquired pursuant to such exercise or conversion including the sale of sufficient *securities* of the *company* to fund the costs of the exercise or conversion and/or any tax liability arising from the exercise or conversion unless a binding undertaking to do so was entered into when the *company* was not in a prohibited period.	

Extract from AIM Rules

Restriction on deals

21. An **AIM company** must ensure that its **directors** and **applicable employees** do not **deal** in any of its **AIM securities** during a **close period**. In addition, the purchase or early redemption by an **AIM company** of its **AIM securities** or sale of any **AIM securities** held as **treasury shares** must not be made during a **close period**.

This rule will not apply, however, where such individuals have entered into a binding commitment prior to the **AIM company** being in such a **close period** where it was not reasonably foreseeable at the time such commitment was made that a **close period** was likely and provided that the commitment was **notified** at the time it was made.

The **Exchange** may permit a **director** or **applicable employee** of an **AIM company** to sell its **AIM securities** during a **close period** to alleviate severe personal hardship.

FCA Disclosure Rules and Transparency Rules

DTR 3.1

Purpose

DTR 3.1.1 This chapter sets out the notification obligations of *issuers*, *persons discharging managerial responsibilities* and their *connected persons* in respect of transactions conducted on their own account in *shares* of the *issuer*, or derivatives or any other *financial instrument* relating to those *shares*.

Notification of transactions by persons discharging managerial responsibilities

DTR 3.1.2 *Persons discharging managerial responsibilities* and their *connected persons*, must notify the *issuer* in writing of the occurrence of all transactions conducted on their own account in the *shares* of the *issuer*, or derivatives or any other *financial instruments* relating to those *shares* within four *business days* of the day on which the transaction occurred. [**Note:** Article 6(4) *Market Abuse Directive* and Article 6(1) 2004/72/EC]

(1) The *Act* provides that an individual who is not a *director* can still be a *person discharging managerial responsibilities* in relation to an issuer if they are a 'senior executive of such an issuer' and they meet the criteria set out in the *Act*.

(2) An individual may be a 'senior executive of such an issuer' irrespective of the nature of any contractual arrangements between the individual and the *issuer* and notwithstanding the absence of a contractual arrangement between the individual and the *issuer*, provided the individual has regular access to inside information relating, directly or indirectly, to the *issuer* and has power to make managerial decisions affecting the future development and business prospects of the *issuer*.

DTR 3.1.3 The notification required by *DTR 3.1.2 R* must contain the following information:

(1) the name of the *person discharging managerial responsibilities* within the *issuer*, or, where applicable, the name of the *person connected* with such a *person*;

(2) the reason for responsibility to notify;

(3) the name of the relevant *issuer*;

(4) a description of the *financial instrument*;

(5) the nature of the transaction (e.g. acquisition or disposal);

(6) the date and place of the transaction; and

(7) the price and volume of the transaction. [**Note:** Article 6(3) 2004/72/EC]

Notification of transactions by issuers to a RIS

(1) An *issuer* must notify a *RIS* of any information notified to it in accordance with:

(a) *DTR 3.1.2 R*(Notification of transactions by persons discharging managerial responsibilities);

(b) [deleted]

(c) section 793 of the Companies Act 2006 (Notice requiring information about interests in shares)to the extent that it relates to the interests of a *director* or, as far as the issuer is aware, any *connected person*; and

(d) paragraph 26 of the *Model Code.*

(2) The notification to a *RIS* described in paragraph (1) must be made as soon as possible, and in any event by no later than the end of the *business day* following the receipt of the information by the *issuer.*

DTR 3.1.5 The notification required by *DTR 3.1.4 R* must include the information required by *DTR 3.1.3 R* together with the date on which the notification was made to the *issuer.*

DTR 3.1.6 If an *issuer* makes the appropriate notification to the *RIS* under *DTR 3.1.4 R (1)(a)*, a further notification to an *RIS* is not required in the event of it receiving information regarding the same dealing in a notification under section 793 of the Companies Act 2006.

DTR 3.1.7 An *issuer* may use the form entitled Notification of Transactions of Directors, Persons Discharging Managerial Responsibility or Connected Persons to make the notification required by *DTR 3.1.4 R.*

DTR 3.1.8 An issuer with financial instruments admitted to trading on a regulated market in the United Kingdom that does not fall within)DTR 1.1.1 R (2) or DTR 1.1.1 R (4), must notify equivalent information to that required by DTR 3.1.4 R and DTR 3.1.5 R to a RIS as soon as possible after the issuer becomes aware of the information.

Glossary definitions

long-term incentive scheme

any arrangement (other than a retirement benefit plan, a deferred bonus or any other arrangement that is an element of an executive *director's* remuneration package) which may involve the receipt of any asset (including cash or any security) by a director or employee of the group:

(a) which includes one or more conditions in respect of service and/or performance to be satisfied over more than one financial year; and

(b) pursuant to which the *group* may incur (other than in relation to the establishment and administration of the arrangement) either cost or a liability, whether actual or contingent.

deferred bonus

any arrangement pursuant to the terms of which an *employee* or *director* may receive a bonus (including cash or any security) in respect of service and/or performance in a period not exceeding the length of the relevant financial year notwithstanding that the bonus may, subject only to the *person* remaining a *director* or *employee* of the group, be receivable by the *person* after the end of the period to which the award relates

employees' share scheme

has the same meaning as in section 1166 of the Companies Act 2006.

person discharging managerial responsibilities

(in accordance with section 96B(1) of the *Act*):

(a) a *director* of an *issuer*:

  (i) registered in the *United Kingdom* that has requested or approved admission of its *shares* to trading on a *regulated market*; or

  (ii) not registered in the *United Kingdom* or any other *EEA State* but has requested or approved admission of its shares to trading on a *regulated market* and for whom the *United Kingdom* is its *Home Member State*; or

(b) a senior executive of such an *issuer* who:

  (i) has regular access to *inside information* relating, directly or indirectly, to the *issuer*; and

  (ii) has power to make managerial decisions affecting the future development and business prospects of the *issuer*.

Appendix 2 NAPF Corporate Governance Policy and Voting Guidelines

The Corporate Governance Policy and Voting Guidelines were revised in November 2013.

The NAPF have kindly consented for these to be reproduced in this book.

Those parts that are relevant to remuneration are primarily in Section D and in Appendix 1 Section D of the Guidelines.

The Corporate Governance Policy and Voting Guidelines (November 2013)

Introduction

Members of the National Association of Pension Funds (NAPF) have a clear interest in promoting the success of the companies in which they invest. As a consequence of this, the NAPF has long considered that one of its prime functions is to represent these interests on behalf of pension funds and the investment management firms who manage their assets. The NAPF's efforts are directed towards maximising the long-term returns of its member's assets, irrespective of the potential for short-term discomfort.

The NAPF's Corporate Governance Policy and Voting Guidelines seeks to reflect current market best practice as determined through consultation with its members and aims to assist members in:

- Promoting the success of the companies in which they invest.
- Ensuring that the board and management of these companies are held accountable to shareholders.

In addition to this Policy which is primarily directed towards those companies which report against the UK Corporate Governance Code (the Code), the NAPF also has a Policy and Voting Guidelines for Smaller Companies and another for Investment Companies, both of these can be found on the NAPF website.

In the Preface to the revised UK Corporate Governance Code in September 2012, the Financial Reporting Council (FRC) noted that its two principle conclusions remained: first, that: 'Much more attention needed to be paid to following the spirit of the Code as well as its letter.' Secondly, that: 'The impact of shareholders in monitoring the Code could and should be enhanced by better interaction between the boards of listed companies and their shareholders.'

The above two conclusions present shareholders with a challenge in two respects: firstly, it is harder for them to assess compliance with 'the spirit of the Code' than it is to apply its Principles in a voting policy; and, secondly, 'better interaction' requires a greater understanding of both a company's strategy and shareholders objectives than has often been the case in the past. That said, the NAPF supports these conclusions: it is in both investors' and companies' interests to meet the challenges they pose. Guidance published this year by the Institute of Chartered Secretaries and Administrators (ICSA), *Enhancing Stewardship Dialogue*, is welcome and provides a practical guide to aid an effective dialogue between companies and their shareholders and the Collective Engagement Working Group is also looking at how the environment for engagement between investors and companies can be improved. Effective engagement begins with good-quality reporting and a willingness to listen to shareholder concerns on the one hand and an appreciation of the company's approach to governance on the other. For shareholders and their agents the challenge lies in interpreting companies' application of the Code and developing the skills and resources required for effective engagement. We encourage companies to make efforts to identify their long-term investors – those investing with long-term objectives rather than those involved in short-term trading – to enable regular dialogue with a critical mass of engaged shareholders. In addition, the NAPF coordinates collective meetings and facilitates confidential Case Committees for members who have concerns about particular issues and/or about the strategic direction of companies.

NAPF Corporate Governance Policy remains firmly rooted in the provisions of the UK Corporate Governance Code. Where the views of boards and their shareholders differ on matters of corporate governance, it is to be hoped that constructive discussion will follow, albeit that ultimately shareholders will exercise their rights as owners to do what they see as necessary to protect their interests.

This year sees significant reforms being introduced in the area of executive remuneration, with changes to the way it is to be reported by companies and the introduction of a binding vote alongside an advisory vote on remuneration. The NAPF and Hermes EOS with the BT Pension Scheme, RPMI Railpen Investments and Universities Superannuation Scheme have published 'Remuneration principles for building and reinforcing long-term business success' – we expect companies to be able to articulate how their pay policies meet these principles in a manner which is most appropriate for their company. As the new reforms settle in over the next 12 months, we encourage appropriate and constructive dialogue between issuers and their shareholders.

The main purpose of the NAPF Corporate Governance Policy and Voting Guidelines is to assist investors and their proxy voting agents in their interpretation of the provisions of the Code when assessing a company's compliance with it. While it is particularly focussed on what voting sanctions may be applied at a company meeting, a decision to vote against management can only be taken after proper consideration of the company's explanation for non-compliance and in the light of the particular circumstances at that company.

The Principles of the Code, should be seen in the context of Directors' duties as set out in the Companies Act 2006. To restate, these are to promote the success of the company, while having regard to, amongst other things, the likely consequences of any decision in the long term; the company's impact on its communities and environment, and the desirability of the company to maintain a reputation for high standards of business conduct. This year has seen further examples of different issues impacting upon a company's reputation – including in some cases a business's approach to tax management. We expect boards to explain to shareholders how they approach overseeing and managing these risks. Shareholders may well form judgments on the management of these issues to inform their approach to resolutions at the AGM.

As explained in the NAPF's Responsible Investment Guide (May 2013), the evidence is increasingly robust that extra-financial factors can significantly impact a company's long-term value, reputation, brand growth rate, margins, market share and borrowing costs. The NAPF believes that the management of these factors, which encompass governance and material environmental and social factors, is an integral part of good corporate management. We also believe that effective integration of such factors within investment analyses by investors can moderate against investment risk and potentially improve risk-adjusted returns.

We hope that this Policy will also assist companies and their advisers when they set or review governance practices, by providing guidance as to how shareholders may react to policies which may not comply with the letter of the Code but, in the company's view, are consistent with its spirit.

Joanne Segars
Chief Executive
NAPF
November 2013

UK Corporate Governance Principles

- **The NAPF supports the UK Corporate Governance Code** in its entirety and wishes to add minimal requirements to that body of work.
- **The Remuneration Committee** has a particular responsibility to ensure that executive directors and senior management are appropriately rewarded. This can best be achieved by establishing incentives which are harmonised with the stated long-term objectives of the company. There is increasing concern among shareholders about the asymmetry between remuneration and shareholder returns.

Responsible Investment

Pensions Disclosure

The SRI Pensions Disclosure Regulation 2000 requires 'that trustees of occupational pension funds disclose in the Statement of Investment Principles the extent (if at all) to which social, environmental and ethical considerations are taken into account in their investment strategies'.

In 2009 the NAPF published guidance on Responsible Investing. We see a close link between the more established principles of corporate governance and responsible investing (by both companies and investors) and expect that best practice will develop further in this area especially as pension funds and their investment managers take steps to implement the Principles of the Stewardship Code.

UK Voting Guidelines

For ease of reference, the Guidelines mirror the format of the Code as much as possible.

The general structure is based around a quotation from the Code, followed by a discussion of the relevant Principle and general voting guidance. Detailed voting guidance in support of the Code's Provisions is set out in [NAPF] Appendix 1.

The voting recommendations assume that investors have evaluated explanations for non-compliance, taken account of a company's individual circumstances and engaged as appropriate. They should in no way be interpreted as being prescriptive.

'Comply or explain' confers a dual responsibility: it is the company's duty to avoid 'boiler-plate' explanations, providing instead a thoughtful explanation for areas of non-compliance. Conversely, investors should evaluate explanations, taking care not to adopt a mechanistic approach and should make companies aware of the reasoning behind their votes on contentious issues. An effective 'comply or explain' regime must be based on regular and open dialogue between companies and shareholders, which should extend beyond the voting season.

While recognising the importance of engagement, the NAPF also notes that this may not always be practical where an investor's holding is small and time constraints mean that other governance issues may take priority.

Voting decisions should be made in the context of a company's overall governance arrangements and any trends towards (or away from) improved standards.

Certain governance issues would not generally have voting consequences; an accumulation of minor issues, however, may be indicative of poor governance. A holistic approach should be adopted when assessing governance arrangements.

The use of abstention, together with a clear explanation to the company, may allow an investor to convey a strong signal of concern or dissent with a company's policies.

We note the increase in shareholder resolutions in recent years and encourage their use only where engagement has failed to bring the changes sought by the shareholders concerned.

Finally, shareholders should balance the 'signalling' effect of a voting sanction against the potential for it to exacerbate the situation which they seek to remedy.

SECTION B: Effectiveness

B.1 The board and its committees should have the appropriate balance of skills, experience, independence and knowledge of the company to enable them to discharge their respective duties and responsibilities effectively.

B.2 The board should undertake a formal and rigorous annual evaluation of its own performance and that of its committees and individual directors.

Guidance

Shareholders will look for evidence of implementation of a succession policy.

Given the recognition of the importance of board effectiveness and the widespread acceptance of annual re-election, the NAPF encourages companies to state more fully the skills and experience which a director brings to his/her role. Such a statement should also include other current appointments which might affect his/her ability to make a full contribution to the work of the board (eg an executive role or a potential conflict of interest). In this way shareholders can make a better informed voting decision.

Voting

Absence of a disclosed succession policy or an evaluation process may lead to shareholders abstaining on or opposing the re-election of the chairman of the nominations committee or, where appropriate, the chairman.

SECTION D: Remuneration

D.1. Levels of remuneration should be sufficient to attract, retain and motivate directors of the quality required to run the company successfully, but a company should avoid paying more than is necessary for this purpose. A significant proportion of executive directors' remuneration should be structured so as to link rewards to corporate and individual performance.

D.2. There should be a formal and transparent procedure for developing policy on executive remuneration and for fixing the remuneration packages of individual directors. No director should be involved in deciding his or her own remuneration.

Guidance

The principles set out above are clear and yet remuneration remains one of the key points of dispute between boards and shareholders. We have for some time been concerned that remuneration structures have become too complex and question their effectiveness in motivating management. We believe that remuneration should be proportionate and aligned with shareholder interests and long-term sustainable value creation.

NAPF in its engagement with companies has in recent years been pressing for simpler plans and for executives to be required to hold greater numbers of shares for long periods. On 18 November the NAPF and Hermes EOS with BT Pension Scheme, RPMI Railpen Investments and the Universities Superannuation Scheme published 'Remuneration principles for building and reinforcing long-term business success' – we expect companies to be able to articulate how their pay policies meet these five Principles in a manner which is most appropriate for their company. Investors do not wish to micro-manage businesses and thus will hold the Remuneration Committee accountable for making appropriate judgements.

The NAPF supports the recent reforms to the reporting of executive remuneration introduced by the Government. These reforms give shareholders a binding vote on a company's remuneration policy and require companies to communicate clearly how their policies are being implemented – best practice will evolve over time. The guidance produced by the GC100 and Investor Working Group should assist companies and their investors to implement them successfully and has particular regard for the practical aspects of implementing the directors' remuneration reporting requirements.

We would like to see remuneration policies being designed and put to shareholders with the expectation that they will stand the test of time. As such remuneration policies should on the whole be put to a vote on a triennial rather than an annual basis.

Voting

Remuneration policy is seen by many investors as a litmus test for wider corporate governance practices, it for example encompasses board effectiveness, oversight, strategy and risk management. Shareholders will therefore continue to examine remuneration policies critically, with a view to ensuring that they are closely aligned with their interests.

We expect companies to be able to articulate how their pay policies meet our Principles in a manner which is most appropriate for their company. With the introduction of the new binding vote on remuneration policy shareholders now have several mechanisms through which to express their view on a firm's approach to remuneration; these include:

- A binding vote on remuneration policy
- A binding vote on new share plans
- An advisory vote on the policy's implementation
- A binding vote on the re-election of related directors.

Companies can expect investors to utilise these rights in different manners and as such there will be an onus on investors to communicate their rationale for dissent. On the whole:

- If investors judge that the firm's remuneration policy fails to meet the Principles then they may decide to vote against the policy and potentially the chairman and members of the remuneration committee.
- If investors subsequently judge that the policy has been implemented inappropriately, or the remuneration committee has used its discretion inappropriately then they may decide to vote against the implementation report.

- Additionally, if investors judge that discretion has been used egregiously or consistently inappropriately; or they believe that the policy remains or has become wholly inappropriate for the business they may decide to vote against the remuneration committee chair or even the board chairman.
- Voting sanctions will normally focus on the implementation report and new share scheme proposals, but may from time to time extend to or be escalated to the chairman and members of the remuneration committee.

[NAPF] Appendix 1: Detailed Voting Guidelines

Introduction

In this section we have not repeated the detailed provisions of the Corporate Governance Code, but have sought, under the same headings as the Code, to identify those issues which will be of particular relevance to shareholders when assessing a company's compliance with the Code and deciding what voting sanction, if any, to apply.

A significant number of the Code's provisions relate to disclosure of information about the board or its governance practices, without which it can be very difficult to arrive at an informed opinion about the quality of its compliance. Poor levels of disclosure are likely to lead investors to take a less sympathetic view of explanations of non-compliance.

SECTION D: Remuneration

D.1: The level and components of remuneration

Provisions: performance-related pay/NED pay/early termination/notice periods

Discussion

D.1.1. The NAPF believes that remuneration should be proportionate and aligned with shareholder interests and long-term sustainable value creation.

D.1.2. The Principles for Executive Remuneration – set out below – are intended to provide high-level guidance to companies about investor expectations of their remuneration structures and practices. The Principles deliberately avoid prescribing any specific structures or measures; however, we do expect companies to be able to articulate how their pay policies meet these Principles in a manner which is most appropriate for their company.

1. **Remuneration committees should expect executive management make a material long-term investment in shares of the businesses they manage**

   – The best form of alignment between executives and shareholders is the ownership of shares over the long-term, with ownership obligations increasing with seniority.

   – To the extent this is feasible and appropriate the bulk of variable rewards should flow over time from the benefits of being an equity owner.

2. **Pay should be aligned to long-term strategy and the desired corporate culture throughout the organisation**

   – We encourage remuneration committees to design rewards that encourage the specific behaviours required to drive long-term strategic success. A starting point should be the company's strategic plan and key performance indicators (KPIs).

3. **Pay schemes should be clear, understandable for both investors and executives, and ensure that executive rewards reflect returns to long-term shareholders**

   – Firms should avoid operating multiple long-term schemes – we do not believe that a multiplicity of awards, with varying performance conditions helps to motivate executives.

4. **Remuneration committees should use the discretion afforded them by shareholders to ensure that awards properly reflect business performance**

   – Remuneration committees should exercise their judgement about the overall performance of the company when determining awards. In particular, the committee should consider how the results have been achieved, not just what was achieved.

5. **Companies and investors should have appropriately regular discussions on strategy and long-term performance**

   – Dialogue should be initiated at an early stage of the decision making process and include those investors who are committed to stewardship.

D.1.3. Just as the remuneration committee should adopt a holistic approach when designing and assessing packages, so investors should evaluate remuneration arrangements in their entirety. Shareholders will seek reassurance that there is a clear link between strategy, performance and reward. Total remuneration should be structured to reflect the ambitions and risks inherent in the business. Performance pay should motivate management to deliver results which are both stretching and sustainable.

D.1.4. Remuneration practices which would most likely cause concern and may trigger a voting sanction in the absence of sufficient explanation include:

- Increases in base salary in excess of inflation or that awarded to the rest of the workforce;
- Layering of new share award schemes on top of existing schemes;
- Insufficient alignment with shareholders, e.g. a shareholding requirement of less than 2x salary.
- Inappropriate use (or lack of use) of discretion;
- An awarding of a 'sign-on' bonus without the inclusion of any conditionality and which pays for awards not already vested at previous employer.
- Insufficient disclosure on the scope of annual bonuses and performance conditions (retrospective disclosure can be acceptable);

D.1.5. Remuneration practices which would likely cause concern and may trigger a voting sanction regardless any explanation given include:

- Over frequent re-benchmarking
- Insufficiently demanding or inappropriate performance targets;
- Guaranteed, pensionable, discretionary or 'one-off' annual bonuses;
- Any provision for re-testing of performance conditions;
- Ex-gratia and other non-contractual payments;
- Change in control provisions triggering earlier and/or larger payments and rewards;
- The absence of service contracts for executive directors;

D.1.6. The NAPF, jointly with the ABI, has published guidance on termination payments which is designed to eliminate 'payments for failure'.

D.1.7. The NAPF, jointly with the LAPFF, has published a paper highlighting the importance of the disclosure of pension arrangements for executives.

D.1.8. The checklists above are not exhaustive, particularly as good practice in this area continues to evolve.

D.1.9. Executive pay policy should be clearly aligned with pay policies in the company as a whole. We encourage a coherent remuneration philosophy which is consistent through the organisation. Ever widening pay differentials are often difficult to credibly justify.

Voting

D.1.10. Most individual elements of remuneration policy are likely to be insufficient to trigger a voting sanction in isolation, but might warrant such a measure when coupled with other deviations from good practice. It is also important for investors to be aware of recurring trends in remuneration (for example, a basic salary increase in excess of inflation in a particular year may not cause excessive concern whereas a trend of such increases might well).

D.1.11. The resolutions on the remuneration policy and implementation report will likely be viewed independently by investors. While one does impact the other, a vote for or against one does not necessarily equate to a vote for or against the other. It will be important for both investors and companies to communicate in order to understand the rationale behind voting decisions.

D.1.12. Investors may decide to vote against the re-election of the remuneration committee chair, or in extreme circumstances the Chairman, if there are persistent or severe infringements of good practice; if inappropriate judgement has been exercised or if the policy presented is materially deficient and unaligned with shareholders.

D.2: Procedure

Provisions: Composition of committee/role and responsibilities/role of the board/shareholder approval of long-term incentive schemes

Discussion

D.2.1. The remuneration committee is responsible for the formulation and implementation of executive remuneration packages. While remuneration consultants may act as advisers, they should not involve themselves in the decision-making process, which is the responsibility of the committee members and/or the board. Additionally, it is the responsibility of the remuneration committee chair to lead any engagement with shareholders.

D.2.2. Companies should pay close heed to the GC100 Investor Working Group guidance which provides a framework for the reporting of executive remuneration within the remuneration Report. Companies should avoid boilerplate language and strive to provide meaningful and preferably concise disclosures relevant to the company and its particular circumstances. The report should include a statement from the Remuneration Committee Chairman reflecting the Committee's decisions in that year, including a summary of any discretion applied and stakeholder engagement.

D.2.3. The statement of implementation of remuneration policy should include details on material changes to the remuneration structure (within the pre-approved remuneration policy) and specific details on performance measures and targets for the current financial year (subject to commercial sensitivity), which may not have been determined when the remuneration policy was originally approved. In addition, companies should include a summary of engagement activity with investors during the year, including any significant concerns raised and where appropriate how they've been responded to.

D.2.4. **Consultants to the Remuneration Committee** should be appointed by the committee and be independent of the company's management. Potential conflicts of interest should be scrupulously and demonstrably addressed.

D.2.5. The remuneration committee is exclusively responsible for the selection and appointment of its advisors.

D.2.6. The remuneration committee should disclose whether the Remuneration Consultants Group's 'Code of Conduct' has been taken into consideration when selecting its consultants.

D.2.7. Companies are encouraged to consider submitting the remuneration consultant function to periodic tender and disclose their policy on this matter, including when the consultant was last subject to tender.

D.2.8. If any services are provided by the same remuneration consultants to the company:

- They should be fully disclosed to the remuneration committee and to shareholders.
- The chairman of the remuneration committee should explain to shareholders why it is appropriate for the committee to appoint the same consultants as the company, notwithstanding this conflict of interest.

Voting

D.2.9. Consistently poor disclosure of the procedures set out in the Code may result in a vote against the re-election of the committee chairman and/or against the implementation report.

D.2.10. Companies are encouraged to tailor their long-term incentive schemes to their particular circumstances and to explain those circumstances when seeking approval for a new or amended scheme. While shareholders should be supportive of innovative schemes they will seek assurance that the incentives are aligned with their own interests and may vote against schemes where alignment is seen as poor.

Appendix 3 PIRC Remuneration Guidelines

PIRC have kindly consented for their guidelines that relate to remuneration to be reproduced in this book.

For more information please contact Tom Powdrill on tomp@pirc.co.uk

The following extracts are from PIRC's 'UK SHAREHOLDER VOTING GUIDELINES 2013 – Promoting high standards of business and wealth creation.'

It says:

This document represents PIRC's independent judgement of good corporate practice.

This is the seventeenth edition of PIRC's Shareowner Voting Guidelines, first issued in 1993. It replaces the version published in Spring 2012. Since PIRC launched its Corporate Governance Service in 1991, we have sought continually to update and improve our policies and this document represents the latest expression of PIRC's independent judgement of good corporate practice in accordance with the law, and market best practice.

Adherence to the law is paramount. Of particular relevance to investors, company secretaries and directors are the current significant legal issues in the area of accounting and audit created by the adoption of faulty accounting standards, causing the financial governance – and accountability – model of company law to break down.

The future of comply or explain

PIRC believes that a debate needs to be had as to whether the 'comply or explain' approach of the UK Corporate Governance Code has reached the end of its useful life, or needs to be refocused. The governance of the Code setting process also begs more scrutiny.

In its origination in the Cadbury Code it was meant to be a standard higher than the law, which Cadbury was clearly setting out – or for matters where the law did not specify, e.g. best practice in board structures. (Former PIRC director Jonathan Charkham was Secretary to the Cadbury Committee).

However, 'comply or explain' has become somewhat discredited by being overplayed as if it applied to all areas of governance equally. In retrospect it should have been clearer that it should only ever have been applied in particular areas, and certainly not where it can simply be a cover for abuse where law is a more appropriate basis for investor protection.

In the area of pay in particular, the permissive approach of the Combined Code has failed.

Furthermore, in PIRC's opinion the FRC has in significant areas – accounting and auditing standards – tended to lose sight of the law to the extent that the statutory governance regime breaks down. The Code is then requiring things that are either superfluous or role changing, and failing to address the fundamental problem – i.e. the numbers are wrong. The Cadbury Committee was a response to accounting scandals, to which it was an effective solution. However, post-Enron policy changes did not merely set things back, but have themselves created absolutely unreliable accounting standards.

PIRC notes that particular elements of the Listing Regime had been moved to a 'comply or explain' basis, to permit some things that had previously been prohibited. It is positive that with recent revisions to the Listing Rules an element of realism has struck home and some things are moving away from 'comply or explain' where, comply or explain and disclosure has not worked. One example is its new approach to majority controlled companies.

In the 2013 Guidelines PIRC sets out very clearly where law, practice, indeed accounting standards, have diverged. Particular companies have been very frank about this, certain standards and guidelines do not supplement the law but fundamentally clash with it.

Auditors acting as consultants was almost universally rejected post Enron. However, PIRC has been very disappointed to note that auditors have managed to put themselves into the position of being remuneration consultants, at precisely the time that the remuneration consulting industry is itself discredited and accounting standards, hence investor confidence in the statutory audit has been further undermined.

The key problem the Cadbury Report sought to address was management capture of the auditors, in the case of Maxwell and BCCI. In 2013, it is clear that a large part of the problem is the other way around.

Conscientious directors are having inappropriate accounting forced on them by the auditors and Accounting Standards have been largely created by the auditing profession themselves. This creates problems for conscientious directors but also provides a degree of refuge for precisely the type of director it would be better not to have serving on boards at all.

It does appear that over time significant outputs and strategies of the FRC have been significantly captured by the accounting profession, including by key serving members of the accounting firms having been directly involved in FRC recruitment.

PIRC notes that 'too large to fail' banks were audited by 'too few to fail' auditors.

Fiduciary Duties

> **'The core fiduciary duties are those of loyalty and prudence. Common law defines several facets of the duty of loyalty: 'A fiduciary must act in good faith; he must not profit out of his trust; he must not place himself in a position where his duty and his interest may conflict; he may not act for his benefit or the benefit of a third party without the informed consent of his principal'[1].**

The above quote is from the Kay Review 2012. Given that directors have fiduciary duties, PIRC is very encouraged that John Kay has given a very timely reminder of what fiduciary duties are. In the area of accounting standards and pay, the concepts of prudence and loyalty seem to be consistently lacking.

PIRC notes also that auditors have progressively replaced the concept of their fiduciary duties with one of 'independence', based on their preferred definition, which repeatedly incorporates absolutely unacceptable conflicts of interest.

In PIRC's view, neither serving directors, nor especially auditors are necessarily best placed to consider fiduciary duties given the legal implications in case of breach. That said, defects in the accounting and auditing frameworks would seem to play to the significant disadvantage of directors in general, in order to safeguard the position of the auditor at the directors' – and company's – expense.

Problems with accounting and financial reporting

The banking crisis has revealed systemic problems in accounting standards and hence audited accounts. Accounting standards have become out of step with the law, being contrary to the true and fair view standard of the law. There are extremely serious consequential effects if a company is found to have defective accounts.

---

1 The Kay Review of UK Equity Markets and Long Term Decision Making. July 2012, Department of Business, Innovation and Skills.

In our view there is also confusion in 'Turnbull' type statements, required by the UK Corporate Governance Code, about director duties – vis-a-vis auditor duties – that may operate to the acute disadvantage of directors and also create problems for company secretaries as co-officers of the company.

As a result there is a significant risk that neither the annual statutory reporting obligations of companies – related to the ability to pay lawful dividends – nor the proper accounting records requirement – related to the on-going obligation to be solvent – are being discharged properly by the auditors or the officers of the company.

PIRC notes that neither the FRC, nor the European Commission has legislative powers in setting accounting standards or auditing standards. Both the Commission and the FRC are tasked with applying the law. There are therefore significant problems if their outputs are clashing with, or not properly conforming to, the law.

True and fair view and pay

Given that the true and fair view is a standard that accounts have to comply with in order to show profits that can be distributed, it is also a standard that should validate costs relevant to arriving at profits, including director and executive pay. PIRC notes that IFRS has not merely been delivering profits that fail to give a true and fair view but the distorted profits justify inappropriate pay.

Following standards that are defective, does not escape the fact that the outcome of all of this is accounts that are at best unhelpful, if not misleading.

PIRC is aware of at least one bank where cash bonuses were deferred, and hence not accrued in the accounts as a liability or a charge, due to faults in IFRS. Money was then lent to those employees as a substitute for the cash so that there was no cash flow disadvantage to the employees for the deferral. Taken as a whole the accounting was masking bonus payments even though cash had left the bank.

General meetings

...

Dividends

Distribution policy is fundamental both to the income requirements of investors and to a company's investment and financial planning. Shareowners have a clear financial interest in maintaining and increasing their income from dividends and other distributions, but without compromising the company's long-term future. The directors may be under pressure to increase short-term distributions, but they must exercise their duty to the company as a whole.

For shareowners with long-term liabilities, the key to assessing whether the proposed dividend is consistent with the company's long-term interests, and is sustainable is a full discussion of dividend policy by the directors in the context of the company's strategy and the board's assessment of its prospects. Information on dividend policy in relation to consumer, community or employee benefits is important in assessing whether the company has discharged its responsibilities to all stakeholders in order to maintain long term relationships. Similar information is required when considering other types of distribution or return of capital.

Shareowners should have an annual opportunity to approve the company's dividend policy, or at a minimum any dividend(s) paid or proposed relating to the year under review, whether interim, special or final, and whether or not there is a legal requirement to do so.

Where the company is proposing a scrip dividend, PIRC expects a cash alternative to be proposed in all instances.

In order to support a board that wishes to make changes to its balance sheet to create distributable reserves, PIRC will require an explanation that addresses how the interests of stakeholders have been taken into account. In particular, the board should explain how it is seeking to deal with any pension fund deficit. In order for a company to explain adequately to shareowners how an uncovered distribution can be made, faith in the accounts is paramount and therefore dependent on a totally unqualified auditor statement. In situations where there is a clear discrepancy between company earnings and the level of dividend proposed PIRC may withhold support for the approval of the final dividend. We may, however, apply mitigation if the dividend policy for the year has been discussed adequately and justification has been provided.

As best practice, PIRC believes that companies should provide a clear statement on distribution policy, **setting of the proportionate split between remuneration**, dividends, investment and so on. PIRC would also encourage companies to seek shareholder approval on distribution policy.

Long-term holders

Owners such as pension funds, with long-term liabilities, should in PIRC's view, take a longer term approach to protection of capital value, unlike high-frequency traders and short-term strategic holders such as some hedge funds.

PIRC has welcomed the use of enhanced dividend to reward longer term shareowners. We also encourage longer term incentivisation schemes, including five year targets. We have welcomed recent Government concern in this area through the publication of the BIS consultation on short termism, and, more recently, the establishment of the Kay Review. In addition we believe that companies should consider experimentation in this area and their shareowners should listen to their proposals with an open mind.

Purchase of company's own shares

The economics of share buybacks

PIRC is moving towards a position of regarding buybacks in general negatively and preferring straightforward dividend payments instead. Whilst in theory buybacks should be advantageous to remaining shareowners, in practice this may not be the case for the following reasons:

- directors buy back in the belief that the company's shares are undervalued by the market, when in fact the expiry of time shows that they were not undervalued, i.e. buybacks are being executed on an inaccurate premise, fees accrue to investment banks involved in buyback programmes, which again creates a conflict of interest, further undermining objectivity;
- the fact that buybacks are conducted inherently in a piecemeal fashion – unlike dividends – can make it virtually impossible to properly understand the true performance of a company without considerable 'unpicking' of each buyback tranche;
- Fundamentally, the buyback system is biased to supporting the belief that a company's shares are undervalued, meaning that the least informed and/or most conflicted directors may be prone to conducting buyback programmes which are not at all beneficial to remaining shareowners.

PIRC believes that boards generally may be prone to believing that their shares are undervalued, rather than overvalued. PIRC has yet to observe a chief executive publicly admit that his company's shares were overvalued.

Furthermore, regarding pay, the linkage between buybacks, earnings per share enhancement and remuneration schemes and targets creates a conflict of interest undermining objectivity, it also amplifies complexity already inherent in remuneration schemes. (See later).

Directors' interests

A share repurchase can have the effect of assisting in meeting bonus or incentive scheme targets for executive directors. In these circumstances, we consider that performance targets for annual or longer-term plans should be adjusted to take account of the impact of the buy-back, in much the same way as they would be adjusted to take account of other capital changes, such as rights issues or consolidations. PIRC does not support the use of shareowner funds in buying back existing shares to reward directors where shares are bought at a level other than market price.

Mergers and acquisitions

Many specific corporate activities such as takeovers, mergers, disposals, capital re-organisations and related party transactions are required to be authorised by shareowners, usually at EGMs. These often have significant implications for shareowners and directors. **Shareowners need to be assured those recommendations by management and their corporate finance advisors have been subject to constructive challenge by disinterested directors.** In our own consideration of such corporate actions, PIRC does not aim to duplicate financial analysis undertaken elsewhere. To date, our voting recommendations have typically taken into account:

- The information and justification for such transactions provided by the board
- An assessment of the impact of such transactions on the interests of its employees
- Potential impacts on business relationships with suppliers, customers and others
- Whether standards of business conduct will be maintained during and following the transaction
- Equitable treatment of existing shareowners
- The board structure
- Market reaction to the proposal.

However, PIRC is of the belief that insufficient attention is paid towards the conflicts of interest that can create momentum for ultimately value destructive M&A activity which includes:-

- corporate finance and advisory fees accruing to investment banks advising on deals
- underwriting fees, if M&A requires new capital issues
- directors' remuneration, if successful M&A leads to higher remuneration for running a larger company.

Essentially M&A is creating a one way bet, 'an option' over a successful transaction that long-term shareholders do not benefit from the same optionality in outcomes.

Most of the studies that we have reviewed indicate that a majority of takeovers appear not to add value for shareowners of the acquiring company. PIRC is developing a more detailed and enhanced analysis of M&A proposals that will consider an expanded range of factors that in our view can affect the success of such transactions. This includes the following:

- The rationale behind the proposed transaction – more specifically, if the proposal represents an opportunity for entry to a new market, increased market share, efficiency gains through combining complementary activities or operational cost efficiency.
- The proposed transaction viewed against stated strategy, in particular of the acquirer;
- The acquirer's Mergers and Acquisition (M&A) track record;
- Track record of directors at acquiring or merging companies, or while with other companies, in relation to similar transactions;
- The relative operating performance of acquirer and target;
- Relative size of target to acquirer;
- Executive and non-executive remuneration impacts on both sides;
- The identification of cultural issues and plans to mitigate conflicts;
- Post-deal management structure planning;
- Governance and Corporate Responsibility concerns, in particular at the target company; and
- Acquirer's financing structure for the deal

If the market for corporate control is to operate efficiently, shareowners need to be able to make informed decisions on the merits of differing strategies. While an oppose vote remains the strongest measure for expressing concerns open to institutional shareowners, the importance of pre-deal diligent questioning and active engagement are evident in our view and our enhanced analysis is also being designed to inform clients with respect to these kinds of engagement as well as providing specific voting advice.

Capital raising exercises

...

Share buybacks

PIRC is concerned about share buybacks for a variety of reasons.

The principal reason for buybacks – that directors know when their shares are undervalued, and thus buying back cheaply is a productive use of shareowner funds for the benefit of the remaining shareowners – does not apply in many cases. It is quite clear that often markets have picked up negative information that boards are not aware of and companies undertaking buybacks have in fact been far from undervalued.

Not only may buybacks be motivated by increasing earnings per share for remuneration purposes, but there are other accountability problems with buybacks. It is a difficult task to track the performance of an enterprise at the best of times, particularly with regular changes to and faults with accounting standards. Buybacks change the number of shares in issue and add further complexity on top of the already complex share based remuneration schemes. PIRC believes that there is not only complexity, but inherent circularity in the interaction between buybacks and remuneration schemes without any clarity on whether the performance is deserved.

PIRC would like to see a wider debate on the matter, perhaps in the context of the Kay Review. However, PIRC is increasingly of the view that buybacks do not benefit its clients, and is reserving its position on voting recommendations. On clarity and accountability grounds alone a dividend is more transparent and easier to deal with. Last year PIRC was successful in arguing for the reinstatement of dividend approval at a number of Annual General Meetings. PIRC will continue to monitor any attempts to weaken accountability for distribution policy.

A study in 2007 by Collins Stewart[2] [3] on the UK market analysed the effect of buybacks and found that 'excess returns traditionally associated with buyback stocks had dwindled on average to a negligible level'. The study, in fact, concluded that a substantial number of companies are collectively destroying billions in shareowner value through ill-judged buyback decisions. Similarly in the US, an S&P study found that while buyback activity reached a new record in 2007, only one out of every four of the companies had outperformed the index.

There are numerous reasons for returning capital to shareowners and a buyback will at times be a valid means of doing so. However, management are too often pursuing a buyback authority for the purpose of enhancing EPS results. Therefore, the evidence base suggests that inappropriate buybacks can result in wealth transfer away from continuing shareowners via the triggering

---

2 Collins Stewart. Quest Newsletter, December 2007, UK/Europe Research issue 39.

3 How Rewarding Is Corporate Share Repurchase Activity?, Standard & Poors, November 2007

of executive awards which vest according to performance conditions including EPS, whilst at the same time, cushioning EPS results that largely determine executive bonus payments.

Chapter 06: directors' remuneration

There has been market failure with directors paid more than they are worth.

The current remuneration model is not fit for purpose

PIRC's overall conclusion as a result of the 'shareholder spring' of 2012 is that remuneration committees, particularly in the largest companies, have failed to work.

In recent years PIRC has been consistently recommending voting against the majority of schemes that remuneration committees have commissioned and approved due to weaknesses in the content, the disclosure and weakness in the contractual terms.

During 2012 it has been more widely accepted that there was not only market failure, in paying executives more than they are worth, via opaque and complex schemes, but also basic budgetary control failure in contracting such schemes. Put more fundamentally, a lack of negotiating skills is bound to result in market failure.

Directors have been making promises on behalf of the company that it would be extremely imprudent for the company to make to anyone, let alone to contract for themselves as inherently conflicted parties. Something that is wrong cannot be merely be absolved by following a process.

The problem looked at in the round goes beyond just a conflict of interest. Some boards at the extreme have been signing up to near open ended contingent liabilities – where the beneficiaries are themselves and a broader group of employees – to the extent there has been a misallocation of company resources, potentially a breach of fiduciary duty.

This phenomenon can be seen very clearly in cases of banks having to pay existing bonus commitments out of rescue rights issue proceeds. The need for the latter would under any commonsense view of investment performance always preclude the presence of the former.

Making matters even worse, PIRC has discovered that it is common practice for further bonus payments to be triggered on the basis of the apparently virtuous objective of 'meeting regulatory capital requirements'. However, if one looks through to the overall scheme of things directors are 'taking a cut' from the capital raising itself as part of their remuneration package, including when they have caused the problem that needed it.

That cannot be appropriate. Similarly, the target might also be met merely by cutting the dividend. The outcome is that directors can get more by paying the shareholders less.

Related issues around faulty accounting standards, false accounting, are covered separately. PIRC in 2011 deduced that banks were applying IFRS to the letter, and the spirit of IFRS, such that deferred bonuses for directors and staff, no matter how likely their settlement, were entirely missing from the accounts.

As a result of PIRC intervention, these are now increasingly included by way of note, but the accounts are not giving a true and fair view, because the impact of the note is not being accrued properly as costs and likely liabilities of the company.

The binding shareholder approval model of the law – has been circumvented by other means

PIRC notes that under common law – if the Articles are silent on the point – any amounts paid to directors require shareholder approval at the immediately subsequent AGM on the basis of audited account[4].

This default position of the law recognises the fundamental conflict of interest indirectors deciding their own pay in principle and also requires establishing that the source of that reward is genuine.

However, under most public company Articles, shareholders must approve fees payable for holding office as directors (often Articles prescribe a maximum figure, leaving it to directors to apportion between themselves, and require shareholders' approval for any increase in this figure), but the Articles also provide that the company can enter into service agreements (employment contracts) with executive directors. As such, the entry into a service contract with an executive director does not require shareholders' approval (provided that they have a term that is no longer than two years) and so there are currently no restrictions on the amount that may be paid[5]. And whilst the Articles will prevent a director voting to approve his own service agreement, this would not apply to the other executive directors or the board as a whole. This can be said to amount to self-approval of remuneration.

---

4 See HMRC guidance on director remuneration and dividends. EIM 42320

5 This may change somewhat if shareholder approval is required for remuneration policy pursuant to the Enterprise and Regulatory Reform Bill.

Dilution of the underlying requirement of the law to require absolute shareholder permission has resulted in what might be regarded as predictable outcomes, with the self-approval of pay either being abused deliberately, or simply being handled far too passively (convenient self-interest).

With governance regimes then focussing on 'disclosure' rather than the binding permission envisaged under the common law, the matter of design and disclosure has itself become a matter for opacity.

This is a particular problem in financial services companies, where the business models, assisted by misleading accounting have created a 'black box', with no visibility on cash flows, and no reality or reliability of 'profits', capital and distributable reserves. The FSA Chairman has described them as 'illusory profits'. It is also illusory capital.

Market failure in executive pay has been passing-off under unsound assertions

In PIRC's opinion all three components of the more common schemes; basic salary, LTIP and bonus types of scheme, have resulted in essentially a bypassing of both the balanced market mechanism for paying directors which is the going market rate for the job based on the relevant skills and experience required and those things relevant to the delivery of fiduciary duties.

The market failure is hiding beneath complex disclosure, in some cases no disclosure[6].

Instead of focussing on a going market rate of pay for the job (i.e. the clearing rate) the most common pay schemes have been developed under the more abstract concepts of 'Attract, retain and motivate', which are also endorsed by the UK Corporate Governance Code, together with 'alignment of interests with shareholders'. The net result is a series of devices which have generally justified overpayment, and given reward for failure in particular.

The concept of 'shareholder value' has also been part to the problem. It can result in a distraction away from the primary performance of a company (which is the growth of the capital of the company, or its 'retirement' and the dividend); towards secondary and derivative measures instead.

---

6 Part of the problem derives from importing practice from the USA, where Delaware articles permit the avoidance of liability of directors for breach of duty or breach of trust to the company, i.e. it cannot be assumed that directors are in fact delivering their fiduciary duties as they can contract to escape civil sanctions that exist precisely due to the moral hazard that is created when transacting business within a limited liability company] Problems persist around the choice of language that is prone to spin and solutions that lack substance.

Such derivative measures include the share price, and relative total shareholder return ('TSR'). However, schemes designed using these measures can result in remuneration being 'hedged' against absolute underperformance of the company itself. Relative TSR will always have the inherent capacity to reward absolute investment failure, and share price performance over a particular period in time may merely reward share price volatility.

The code and pay

In PIRC's opinion all three elements of conventional pay schemes have been incorporated into the Code in too much detail, such that the Code is encouraging compliance around an essentially failed model. The terms 'attract', 'retain' and 'motivate' have been attached to discredited and inherently bogus methods of designing schemes. The concept of 'alignment' with shareholders has somewhat eclipsed discharging fiduciary duties in the first instance as part of the basic employment contract.

The lack of attention to basic fiduciary duties is a weakness PIRC notes elsewhere in the FRC regulatory regime, and may well be a product of both auditor and management dominance within the FRC structure. PIRC is pleased to note that the Kay Review raised the point that more attention generally needs to be given to basic fiduciary duties.

> **A significant proportion of executive directors' remuneration should be structured so as to link rewards to corporate and individual performance.**
> Main Principle D.1 Edited Version

> **Levels of remuneration should be sufficient to attract, retain and motivate directors of the quality required to run the company successfully, but a company should avoid paying more than is necessary for this purpose.**
> Main Principle D.1 Edited Version

> **The remuneration committee should judge where to position their company relative to other companies, but they should use such comparisons with caution, in view of the risk of an upward ratchet of remuneration levels with no corresponding improvement in performance.**
> Supporting Principle D.1

> **The performance-related elements of executive directors' remuneration should be stretching and designed to promote the long-term success of the company.**
> Supporting Principle D.1 edited version

Myths of executive remuneration

Attraction

PIRC's interpretation of 'attraction' is that a number of candidates would consider employment, once a role is advertised, thus creating a market in potential candidacy, and hence a reasonably liquid clearing price. The true market dynamic would have demand, supply and competition.

Contrary to that, PIRC notes that a common method of recruitment bypasses advertising. Rather than the job attracting the potential candidates, individuals are approached by head hunters by word of mouth or other non-transparent means.

This process reflects many behavioural biases. One being that in that model the head hunter then is in fact attracted to the person – rather than a wider pool of people attracted to the job. Then the person is asked what their required terms are. The process is inherently prone to self-bidding, and the head hunter too has a vested interest in as high a commission as possible. Such an approach leads to overpayment. This seems in fact to contribute towards 'market failure'. Any market failure is then accentuated by the 'comparative quartile' system of 'benchmarking' executive pay. The 'bench mark' rather than merely measuring executive pay has the wholly pernicious effect of then setting it outside of proper market mechanisms.

Diversity also suffers, because the failure to have open competition for jobs is likely to entrench existing imbalances.

"Retention"

The concept of payment for 'retention' is also creating problems observable in practice. Under market based remuneration, remuneration payments concerned with the objective of retention would be relevant at that point there is a significant risk that retention is actually an issue and it is worth paying to retain that person, and hence retention payments are then necessary.

Instead of applying with those conditionalities, pay schemes are building in a retention element as a matter of course when the additional payment is not demonstrably relevant to the objective of retention. Secondly, new job offers are often buying out the prior employer's remuneration scheme, including the retention element, thus neutering the retention payment precisely when it may be needed.

In PIRC's experience the 'retention' aspect of remuneration schemes now lacks any credibility. Not only are general payments for retention justifying overpayment and contributing to general market failure, but they also make it more expensive to get rid of non-performers. In PIRC's opinion misapplication of the concept of retention has become a significant contributory factor to reward for failure.

During 2012, having already received awards which incorporated retention elements, some high profile CEOs were then ousted by shareholders, thus putting the committee pay policy in direct conflict with shareholder wishes to neither to retain them or pay them off.

Motivation

The motivation aspect of schemes, the bonus element, can all too often be seen to be covering factors that should not only be covered by the job description in the first place, including self-motivation, but are already implicit in the degree of diligence necessary to perform the duties of a director in the first place. Directors have fiduciary duties.

Examples PIRC has seen include; 'The chief executive ...... having good relations with the rest of the board', 'complying with regulatory capital requirements' (superfluous given that solvency is already a fiduciary duty) and 'mitigating the principal risks of the business'.

For such objectives one merely needs to insert the word 'not' in front of the aspiration and the superfluous nature of what is being rewarded then becomes clearly apparent. Putting things the other way round makes it clearer that the target is not only not appropriate to justify additional remuneration, but that failure to do it as a matter of course raises significant questions about whether the person not doing such things should remain employed at all.

A particularly inappropriate target is for any performance award or bonus to be linked to undertaking capital raising. Not only may the capital raising be the result of prior investment failure by the board itself, but the capital that is being raised is actually being put up by shareholders. This can be seen happening in an automotive distributor as well as financial services companies.

Looking at the transaction as a whole, directors rewarding themselves a bonus for a capital raising, amounts to nothing more or less than themselves 'taking their cut' from what the shareholders have only just paid in. It is actually a misapplication of shareholders' funds.

PIRC also notes that such director interest in capital raising is not being disclosed in offer documents as a cost of the fundraising. Such payments represent self-approved yet clandestine 'commissions' paid to directors as a result of capital raising.

If capital is subscribed outside pre-emption, there is the additional problem that shareholders are rewarding directors for having been diluted. The fact that they may have to approve the disapplication of pre-emption is not necessarily an answer.

Alignment of interest with shareholders

This again is a concept being misunderstood to the extent that it is justifying things that in fact represent absolute misalignment of interest.

Firstly, as referred to earlier, directors have fiduciary duties now Codified in the Companies Act 2006, and are accountable to shareholders for doing their job for the company. That does not necessarily require any alignment at all with the capital, merely proper execution of their statutory duties.

Secondly, schemes purporting to 'align' with the interests of shareholders (such as LTIPS) are not actually doing anything of the kind. LTIPs fail to reflect the simple fact that shareholders have placed their capital at risk, and gains are only earnedon the basis of that capital being at risk. LTIPs fail to put capital at risk.

LTIPs are similar to zero cost share options, with elements of 'contracts for difference'. Both in fact are derivatives, not long only shareholding interests.

The 3 year rolling period used for LTIPs can result in substantial rewards for the participant for volatility (down and then up movements in a share price). This can also include volatility of their own creation, such as occurs when a crisis creates a share price fall, and the price then partially recovers. Rewarding any volatility is not an alignment with the interest of the company (the shareholders).

Indeed their ability to compensate management for investment failure due to volatility with rolling performance measurement, award and vesting periods can create what is in fact a hedge against real corporate underperformance. PIRC notes that in Australia holding a hedge against the company is prohibited.

In PIRC's opinion LTIPs are a form of hedge and have probably been designed implicitly for that purpose without being expressed in so many words.

Quite simply, LTIPs are not long-term (3 years is barely even medium term) and they are not aligned with the interest of the body of shareholders, but short-term share traders in fact. In addition LTIPs create a substantial cost in removing underperforming chief executives.

PIRC would therefore expect any genuine attempt to align with shareholders to exclude LTIPs altogether. LTIPs have become as discredited as multi-year rolling director service contracts.

Even if 'alignment with shareholders' is a necessary objective, that alignment is only achieved economically if the directors have in fact acquired the shares at proper market value out of their own financial resources. The description of awards as 'at risk pay' is a deceit.

In the case of one retail banking company, the investment banking arm has over time been subsumed into the same company (i.e. legal entity) as the retail bank, thus the creditors of the investment bank are a claim on the assets of the retail bank. One of the features of the pay scheme was that the investment bank remuneration (but not the retail bank) worked on the basis of return on capital employed of the investment bank. However, one impact of the subsuming of the investment bank into the retail bank – in addition to the risk to the ordinary depositors – was that the capital of the investment bank, no longer being in its own legal entity with its own audited accounts, was no longer apparent.

This creates at least the suspicion that the very purpose of subsuming the investment bank into the retail bank was so that the capital number needed for pay would be less than transparent and could be arbitrarily allocated between the two divisions.

> **Other performance indicators payouts or grants under all incentive schemes, including new grants under existing share option schemes, should be subject to challenging performance criteria reflecting the company's objectives, including non-financial performance metrics where appropriate. Remuneration incentives should be compatible with risk policies and systems.**
> Code Schedule A edited version

> **Non-financial performance metrics should form a significant part of the performance assessment process.**
> FSA Handbook[7].

In PIRCs opinion the use of non-financial performance measures in pay schemes has become a component of reward for investment failure. PIRC believes that non-financial measures should not be invoked unless financial performance itself is satisfactory.

Incomprehensibility

Given all that has been said above about flawed concepts in designing schemes it is not uncommon for the whole thing to then be strung together in a way that is incomprehensible.

---

[7] FSA Remuneration Code 19A.3.37

The Hays 2012 report and accounts states 'the Committee will set EPS targets using market consensus (reflecting the current point in any cycle) being a range of +/- 4% around the consensus forecast EPS as the first year of the three year cycle with a range of RPI plus 4% to RPI plus 12% over the remaining two years of the cycle for threshold and maximum payment respectively'.

PIRC notes that the introduction of a distinct vote on policy could result in post hoc rationalisation of pay by reference to gobbledegook statements that rule nothing out.

<table>
<tr><th>Shareholder value is from:</th><th colspan="4">Some examples of problems with remuneration when compared to the core elements of an investment return</th></tr>
<tr><td>Growth of invested capital (or the eventual return of it by its retirement)</td><td>Relative share price TSR performance measurement still rewards absolute investment non-performance in the company</td><td rowspan="2">Bonus for meeting regulatory capital. Rewards the directors for the shareholders having put new money in, including where capital was depleted.</td><td rowspan="2">Rolling 3 year LTIP performance periods. Whether the measurement is relative or not the LTIP can pay out due to a small rebound from absolute fundamental underperformance.</td><td rowspan="2">EPS growth. Rewards gearing and does not take account of the capital invested (e.g. 10% EPS growth might have been achieved by a 30% increase in capital invested, the return on invested capital has gone down, or by share buy-backs.)</td></tr>
<tr><td>Dividend on invested capital</td><td>Bonus for meeting regulatory capital requirements – a bonus for cutting the dividend</td></tr>
<tr><td>Retirement of capital by its return</td><td>Schemes rarely consider whether the best interests of the company are a limited lifespan, rather than existence into perpetuity</td><td></td><td></td><td>It is beneficial to shrink a company that is returning less than its cost of capital, rather than grow it.</td></tr>
<tr><td>Share price is derived from that.</td><td colspan="4">A share price itself is a derivative of the fundamentals.
A movement in a share price is then a derivative of that.
A relative movement in a share price is a further derivative.</td></tr>
</table>

Voting positions

PIRC will not support new LTIP based schemes, as well as inappropriate existing ones. They are inherently flawed. There is the inherent risk that they are rewarding volatility rather than the performance of the company (creating capital and – lawful – dividends). They are inherently acting as a complex and opaque hedge against absolute company underperformance and long-term share price falls. They are also a significant factor in reward for failure.

PIRC will not support bonus schemes where there are any performance targets that represent things that should be part of fulfilling the role of the job, including fiduciary duties, and are hence superfluous. In the event that the objectives are not clearly disclosed, PIRC will assume that the non-disclosure is obscuring such superfluous targets.

PIRC will not support any pay schemes where 'quartile' type benchmarks are driving the setting of pay. This represents a 'marking to model' method of setting pay – as opposed to managing the cost of pay – and can end up creating a self-referential false market.

PIRC will not support remuneration schemes, or the re-election of a director, where any director receives rewards of any kind as a result of a capital raising. During 2013 PIRC will be looking into more detail as to whether such payments represent inappropriate commissions.

Remuneration consultants

> **'Where remuneration consultants are appointed, they should be identified in the annual report and a statement made as to whether they have any other connection.'**
> New Code Provision D.2.1

PIRC can only conclude that the remuneration consulting industry responsible for the majority of schemes has had a vested interest in creating complex and accommodating outcomes. The performance of the industry actually exhibits many of the features that have been associated with auditors.

Rather than addressing the market failure that is an inherent risk due to self-approval of director pay (with members of remuneration committees tending to be executives elsewhere), the nature of schemes in general has been to create outputs even more dysfunctional than those directors might have come up with by themselves.

PIRC notes that laws have, or still do, prohibit directors from hedging against the performance of the company, or trading in share options due to the inherent conflicts of interest that creates.

The law has recognised the moral hazard of a director holding anything other than a long-only interest in the shares of the company.

PIRC has come across instances where the schemes have been so complex, and contained wholly inappropriate adjustments to numbers and targets, that the directors were unable to explain the scheme themselves and needed to resort to the remuneration consultant explaining matters. In one case neither party was able to provide adequate explanation of what the scheme was about.

PIRC has also been surprised to note the increasing prevalence of remuneration consulting from the company's auditors. This is unacceptable if it:

- puts the auditor in a difficult or conflicting position regarding schemes that are inappropriately affecting the risk appetite, and culture of the organisation, both of which are relevant to going concern and the control environment. There is also the risk that remuneration schemes can create specific incentives for accounting abuses, and,
- make it difficult to envisage how the remuneration consulting side of the audit firm could raise questions about inappropriate accounting practices.

PIRC is continually disappointed to note that whatever rules and guidelines are put in place to prevent audit firm conflicts of interests, conflicts have consistently crept back into the system regardless.

PIRC will not support any remuneration reports, the annual accounts, the reappointment of the auditors, the chair of the remuneration committee or the chair of the audit committee where any audit firm is also the remuneration adviser. PIRC sees no ability to mitigate the conflict of interest. The auditor of any company should never limit his ability to express discontent on any matter privately or publicly. There are so few audit firms, that this adds another complexity, not least in inhibiting rotation. Pay, like tax planning, can have an enduring effect. We note that the EU Commission proposed no non-audit services at all for the largest firms. Irrespective of the outcome of that debate, PIRC wishes to make clear that it regards audit firms being involved in setting remuneration at all is unacceptable.

PIRC will not support any remuneration schemes, remuneration reports, the annual accounts, the reappointment of the auditors, the chair of the remuneration committee or the chair of the audit committee where there is a likely liability, or likely contingent liability, for any element of deferred pay that has not been provided for in the accounts for the year in which it is an appropriation of profits. Under-accruing for any aspect of remuneration is clearly creating budgetary and hence financial risk, is contrary to the true and fair view requirement of the law, and is overstating business margins, as well as making it impossible to assess the remuneration position of executives.

If any directors are being prevented from accruing the likely cost, and disclosing the liability, by the auditors due to problems with faulty accounting standards then PIRC would expect the directors to disclose that fact and invoke the true and fair override. It is positively in the interests of directors to do that, as if the accounts are found to be defective any dividend declare may be unlawful and the directors incur personal liability.

Remuneration committees

There should be a formal and transparent procedure for developing policy on executive remuneration and for fixing the remuneration packages of individual directors. No director should be involved in deciding his or her own remuneration.
Main Principle D.2

Attendance at meetings of remuneration committees

The primary reason for remuneration committees was to ensure that executives were not put in the position of paying themselves. Annual reports do state which remuneration committee members have attended which meetings, however PIRC wishes all attendance to be disclosed. This is particularly relevant if executives and remuneration consultants are also attending.

Close periods and determining the inputs of pay schemes

PIRC notes that whilst there are codified restrictions on director share dealings in close periods. Directors are in fact undertaking economically similar activity, without direct dealing, in setting share based, and target based pay. This would include setting scheme targets at particular times when directors have insider information.

Clawbacks

Consideration should be given to the use of provisions that permit the company to reclaim variable components in exceptional circumstances of misstatement or misconduct.
Code Schedule A edited version

Deferral of long term incentive payments and short term bonus awards and the use of clawback provisions to be used as the means to reclaim amounts if misstatement and misconduct arise.
Walker Recommendation 33

PIRC has been encouraged to see some companies robustly pursuing clawback of prior awards where there have been subsequent events that change the way one looks at the performance of an executive. However, PIRC notes that one reason for needing claw backs is the entirely inappropriate models of profit recognition in the first place, and the permitting of loss exclusion, by imprudent accounting standards. It should not be necessary to claw back what should not have been given in the first place.

Internal comparators

> **(The remuneration committee) should also be sensitive to pay and employment conditions elsewhere in the group, especially when determining annual salary increases.**
> Supporting Principle D.1

Unfortunately this principle is widely ignored by companies, and has been extremely ineffective. Many remuneration committees make little or no reference to it at all in their report; others include a brief statement saying that they have taken pay and conditions of other employees into account, but giving no details of how such considerations have affected their decisions.

In reality, given the ever-widening gap between directors' pay and that of other employees, both within the same companies and throughout the wider economy, we would argue that remuneration committees do not take into account other employees' pay when setting pay for directors. Supporting principle D.1 is routinely ignored by remuneration committees in their decision making as well as in their presentation.

PIRC believes the 'internal comparators' principle should be backed up with additional reporting requirements. Disclosure should be extended to include:

- The ratio between average total annual remuneration of the three highest paid directors (whether executive or non-executive) and average (median) total annual employee remuneration.
- An explanation for any differences between increases in basic pay for directors and those offered to their employees.
- An explanation for any differences in incentive-related pay packages offered to directors compared with those open to all employees in the company.

PIRC can identify no practical reason why regulatory support for internal comparators in the UK should not produce solutions to the difficulties of presenting such data, which is often cited as a reason for avoiding adoption of this principle.

Disclosure

Shareowners have a right to see where their money is going and how much their agents – the directors – are earning from the business. Companies should be aware that investors are concerned at the lack of clarity.

The Directors' Remuneration Report

The Directors' Remuneration Report Regulations (DRRR) require UK companies with a listing in the European Union (EU), and certain other jurisdictions, to publish a remuneration report and to put this to the vote at their annual general meeting[8]. This provides shareowners with important disclosures and an opportunity to hold directors directly accountable for remuneration policies and practices.

Rather than viewing the report as a compliance exercise, companies should recognise that it represents an important opportunity to communicate with shareowners about company strategy and human resource policy. The overall aim should be for a report that is clear, transparent and understandable.

Single Figure Disclosure

One of the ways PIRC believes that this can be achieved is for companies to put a single figure on the whole package for each individual director. This requires transparency in valuing pensions and share based awards, but would be a marked improvement. Currently, there is no requirement for a UK company to provide such a figure, but in the US, the Securities and Exchange Commission (SEC) has implemented a rule to this effect.

The following is not intended to represent full legal disclosure requirements, but highlights certain areas in the DRRR, which PIRC deems particularly relevant when assessing companies' disclosure.

Basic details

– The names of remuneration committee members. This effectively gives legal force to part of Code provision A.1.2.

If a member has joined or left the committee during the year then the relevant dates should be provided.

---

8 Statutory Instrument No. 1986 of 2002 (Northern Ireland Statutory Rule No. 56 of 2005). The 2002 Regulations have been replaced by Regulation 11 and Schedule 8 of the Large and Medium-Sized Companies and Groups (Accounts and Reports) Regulations 2008, following the repeal of Schedule 7A to the Companies Act 1985. The new regulations do not materially differ from the previous DRR regulations

- The name of any remuneration consultants or other person who provided advice of a material nature and fees paid for the services provided. Where consultants are appointed, PIRC considers that a statement should be made on whether they have any other connections with the company or its officers. This basic information is required for accountability.

Policy

- A statement of policy on directors' remuneration for the following and subsequent financial years. Companies are still too often using anodyne references to the need to 'recruit, retain and motivate'. Such statements are of no value to shareowners.

A good policy statement will:

- Describe how the remuneration structure fits with overall corporate strategy and the key drivers behind corporate performance. PIRC seeks concrete evidence for this by evaluating whether the performance targets under executive long-term incentive schemes are linked to KPIs including any non-financial KPIs;
- Emphasise factors specific to the company rather than relying on a general market rationale;
- Explain all elements of fixed and variable pay and their relative – quantitative – importance to include;
- Current base salaries and year on year percentage change;
- Bonus potential and the nature of bonus targets;
- Current policy on incentive awards and performance targets;
- Details of maximum awards under the rules of all existing incentive schemes;
- Justify the choice of performance criteria and the level of targets; and
- Detail and justify any changes to policy from the previous report.

Cash remuneration

- Details of cash remuneration for each individual who was a director at any time during the financial year. The DRRR requires this information in tabular format. PIRC considers it helpful if companies clearly separate the figures for executive and non-executive directors.
- It is unfortunately still common place for companies to circuitously disclose significant one-off payments or compensation payments within

the notes to the pay table. PIRC will view negatively any apparent attempt by a company to smokescreen a significant payment within the small print of a report.

Contract details

– Details of each director's service contract

Each director should have written contractual arrangements that set out a company's liabilities in the event of termination of employment to remove uncertainty.

Details in the remuneration report should include:

– Date of contract;

– Notice period(s); and

– Potential termination payments.

The DRRR provides that sufficient information about contractual provisions should be disclosed, 'such that shareowners can estimate the liability to the company should the director's contract be terminated.' In PIRC's experience the greater part of termination payments arise from non-contractual elements such as allowing options or share awards to be released, pension enhancements or other transfer of shareowners' funds at the discretion of the remuneration committee.

Share based incentives

– Details of each director's holdings of share options, long term incentive schemes or conditional share plans. PIRC considers that for each director, there should be full disclosure of each separate award. The DRRR allows the use of average exercise prices to avoid excessive length. PIRC considers this to be acceptable provided that full details for individual directors are made available on the company's website. If weighted averages are used the DRRR requires options that are 'in the money' or 'underwater' at the company's financial year end to be shown separately.

PIRC considers it best practice to distinguish between awards for which the performance condition has been or is still to be met.

Information required about share based incentives

<table>
<tr><th>Market Value Option</th><th>Share award*</th></tr>
<tr><td colspan="2">Date of grant</td></tr>
<tr><td>Maximum number of options</td><td>Maximum number of shares</td></tr>
<tr><td>Exercise price</td><td>Market price on the date of grant</td></tr>
<tr><td>Date from which the option may be exercised and expiry date</td><td>Date from which shares vest</td></tr>
<tr><td colspan="2">Any additional retention periods</td></tr>
<tr><td colspan="2">Expected value of each outstanding award at time of grant</td></tr>
<tr><td colspan="2">Performance criteria for outstanding awards met since the last annual report or that have yet to be met</td></tr>
<tr><td colspan="2">Details of the vesting scale for varying levels of performance.</td></tr>
<tr><td colspan="2">Performance achieved to date against outstanding targets including ranking where relative or comparative measures are used.</td></tr>
<tr><td>Market price of the shares, at the time of the exercise of any option during the year</td><td>Range of the share price for the reporting period and at the end of the period.</td></tr>
<tr><td colspan="2">Any restatement of targets to account for share buyback impacts.</td></tr>
<tr><td colspan="2">Risk adjustment mechanisms.</td></tr>
<tr><td colspan="2">Inbuilt clawback potential</td></tr>
<tr><td colspan="2">Justification for use of financial or non-financial criteria</td></tr>
<tr><td></td><td>* We include as share awards:
– Conditional share awards – shares that the director becomes entitled to only once the conditions are met
– Restricted share awards – shares to which the director has a delayed beneficial entitlement, but can be forfeit if the conditions are not met; and
– Nil-cost options – director can only exercise the option once the performance conditions are met.
Maximum number of shares/options: some companies quote a figure that can be increased if the company meets a certain performance target e.g., 200% of the maximum award vests if performance conditions are met in full. PIRC considers this to be poor transparency.</td></tr>
</table>

Expected values

– These are not required by DRRR, but are considered best practice to allow shareowners to value the package and make comparisons.

There are three common methods for calculating expected values – the Black Scholes formula, the binomial model and the Monte Carlo simulation. Each model estimates the reward that a participant is likely to receive based on the chances of meeting targets; volatility of the share price and other factors. Companies should disclose the model used and the key assumptions involved. In PIRC's view, this information should be disclosed in the remuneration committee report itself, in addition to the notes to the accounts. Alternatively, it is acceptable for the remuneration committee report to clearly refer the reader to the notes to the accounts to obtain this information.

Termination provisions

– Details of any compensation payments made during the year to past directors.

Any compensation payments made or committed to during the year should be disclosed both at the earliest opportunity via a regulatory announcement and in the annual report and accounts. The basis of the total compensation package needs to be clear, i.e. the individual components of the termination payment should be identified and explained, together with the extent to which mitigation has been applied. This should include any vesting of share incentives for which conditions (whether performance or employment) had not been met.

Performance

– A performance graph showing five-year historic total shareowner return (TSR) performance against an appropriate index. The DRRR prescribes the performance graph that needs to be included in the report and companies therefore have a legal obligation to provide this. However, this may be unsuitable in relation to the company's performance targets and additional graphs may be required to assist shareowners' understanding. Companies should consider carefully the presentation of the graph to provide a fair picture of past performance, including which index is most appropriate for comparison.

Non-executive remuneration

The remuneration report should disclose the level of NED fees, their composition and the process by which they are set. There is an expectation that fees will rise as a more active role is developed for non-executives. This risks repeating the issues with executive excess, and companies need to ensure that they can justify their policies. Market levels for non-executives should not be the sole determining factor. Fees for individual NEDs need to be explained in terms of the time commitment expected, their responsibilities and their skills. Payment of any kind should not continue beyond retirement from the company. We consider it acceptable to pay non-executives partly in shares, but these should not be conditional shares or options, which can lead to too much emphasis on securing short term share price performance. The remuneration of the chairman requires the fullest explanation.

Below-board remuneration

Although executive directors are the overall stewards of the company, often important decisions and responsibility is also allocated to senior managers and other highest paid employees below board level. Such employees may have similar incentives to those at executive level, but this is not always the case. Given the importance of aligning employee incentives with those of shareowners, PIRC considers that companies should disclose the remuneration structures of senior managers, in order to enable shareowners to assess their appropriateness.

In this regard, PIRC supports recommendation 28 of the Walker Review[9] and believes that the recommendation should be applied by all listed companies.

> Walker Review, recommendation 28:
>
> *The remuneration committee should have a sufficient understanding of the company's approach to pay and employment conditions to ensure that it is adopting a coherent approach to remuneration in respect of all employees. The terms of reference of the remuneration committee should accordingly include responsibility for setting the over-arching principles and parameters of remuneration policy on a firm-wide basis.*

There are employees below board level who are both highly paid, in some cases with packages in excess of those of board members, and that are in positions with considerable influence on the direction and risk profile of the company. PIRC thinks that a coherent narrative needs to be set out which describes the relationship between the principle risks and uncertainties explained in the Business Review and the quantum and design of pay for individuals whose roles are not closely linked to these risks.

We believe that improving transparency for senior executives who manage risk will help provide shareholders with more tools to hold senior management to account.

By increasing its knowledge of firm-wide remuneration practice, the Remuneration committee will be able to give greater consideration to the

---

[9] ibid

risk-dimension below board-level and the sensitivities of all employees when designing, monitoring and awarding executive remuneration.

Significant shareholding requirement

Directors should retain a meaningful commitment in the company by way of shares. PIRC considers that a holding equal to one year's salary is generally an appropriate level, and that this holding should be built up within a specified time frame, ideally no more than three years.

Balance of incentive and rewards

Often providing the focal point of company engagement discussions, the balance between incentive and reward section cuts straight to the heart of the debate over 'pay for performance'. While, a chorus of disapproval began over bailed-out banks awarding excessive bonuses, broad based corporate excess has now become very much a point of public concern during recessionary times.

Companies that evidence a clear dislocation between executive reward and company performance are at risk from shareowner revolt and public backlash.

Analysis of remuneration reports 2013

Notwithstanding some elements of pay schemes, such as LTIPs that are fundamentally unacceptable, PIRC provides a remuneration rating for all pay schemes. When analysing remuneration reports PIRC provides a rating of the understandability, quality and depth of disclosure, the balance of performance requirements and potential rewards, directors' pensions and service contract policy. Each rating is based on PIRC's best practice principles in these three areas.

Under this system

A signifies: comes close to or meets PIRC's view of best practice.

E signifies: Particularly poor disclosure or practice, including over complexity and excessiveness.

Ratings between these two points reflect PIRC's assessment based on our proprietary model developed over some 20 years experience analysing directors' pay. PIRC reserves the right to override our general position in exceptional or unusual circumstances. In particular, major concerns over the operation of remuneration policy may have a material effect on our voting advice. Directors' remuneration remains perhaps the most consistently controversial corporate governance issue.

Companies must put remuneration structures in place that properly address the principal-agent problem and do not pose a risk to the invested capital.

The particular flashpoints can be broadly categorised into questions about:

- Pay for performance (long-term incentive schemes, bonuses, salary increases and pension contributions);
- Reward for failure (notice periods and golden parachutes); and
- Inequitable treatment of different stakeholders (employees, shareowners and executives).
- The over complexity of schemes
- Multiple scheme changes subsequent to adoption of 10 year schemes

Specific aspects of remuneration policy

Base salary

In deciding on the balance between fixed and variable pay remuneration committees should take into account the benefits of fixed pay, namely, simplicity and transparency.

Where salaries are significantly higher or lower than the sector average the reasons should be clearly explained. Base salaries should be clearly highlighted and companies should clearly state, and explain, the level of salary increases implemented during the year including a comparison with salaries across the organisation. When describing salary increases disclosure should go beyond describing within-year increases but include absolute increases between fiscal periods.

Remuneration committees should be mindful of the gearing effect that basic cash increases will have on the potential magnitude of the directors' total variable package.

As maximum awards under cash and share incentive schemes are pegged to equivalent salary values, year-on-year salary increases have the effect of disproportionately ratcheting up the total pay package.

Bonuses

Bonuses should never be guaranteed. Bonuses should be designed to encourage and reward executive success, objectively measured rather than viewed as an entitlement. It has become accepted practice at some UK companies to make annual bonus awards in anticipation of future performance. This is the norm for large listed US companies. We do not consider this an appropriate mechanism for incentivising executives as the annual repetition of an expected performance award will over time lead to an expectation that an award is part of the terms and conditions attached to an executives' role.

Potential bonuses should:

- Be offered only as part of a considered package;
- Reward short term performance but this focus should not be to the detriment of longer-term strategy;
- Be capped at a reasonable level; and
- Not be increased without a requirement for better performance.

Amounts paid should:

- Broadly 'fit' with the view of performance in a particular year described in the company's Business Review;
- Be justified with details of performance achieved during the year against sound, credible targets;
- Require prior shareowner approval, if the bonus was not subject to predetermined performance criteria
- Be given back if the indicators upon which the bonus was based are not met due to subsequent restatement of financial or other performance measures upon which they are based.

In PIRC's view, past bonus targets are no longer commercially sensitive. Given the importance of bonuses to the overall remuneration package, and in some cases the multiple of salary represented by these awards alone, it is important that shareowners can assess the performance that triggered any bonus award. This means that companies should at the very least explain the levels of performance achieved against the different bonus measures. Best practice, however, would be to clearly state the precise bonus targets that were in operation in the year under review.

In cases where companies fail to explain the levels of performance achieved against bonus targets during a year in which significant payments have been granted, this will have implications both in terms of the remuneration voting recommendation and our assessment of directors' capabilities and track record.

Rating system for incentive schemes

PIRC uses its proprietary model to rate any proposed scheme and the outcome informs (but does not determine) our voting advice. The rating comprises two letters covering our view of the key performance elements of the scheme and other factors as described in this chapter.

Under this system

A signifies: comes close to or meets best practice in our view

E signifies: there are substantial concerns.

Ratings between these two points reflect PIRC's judgment based on our model. PIRC reserves the right to override our general position in exceptional or unusual circumstances, and where significant improvements have been made during the year.

Shareowner approval

The Listing Rules (LR9.4.1) require that UK companies seek shareowner approval for an employee share scheme or long-term incentive scheme before it is adopted. Exceptions are made for an arrangement where the only participant is a director (current or contemplated) and the arrangement is established specifically to facilitate, in unusual circumstances, the recruitment or retention of the relevant individual (LR9.4.2). Notwithstanding the exemptions allowed in the Listing Rules, PIRC considers that all new share incentive schemes in which any director may participate should be put to the vote; and that non-UK companies should also comply.

Similarly, PIRC believes that substantial amendments to share schemes, such as changing performance conditions and upper award limits, should require shareowner approval. Alterations to share schemes are of fundamental importance to the incentive structure of companies' therefore PIRC believes recourse to a shareowner vote represents the best form accountability.

As it has become common-place for companies to make such amendments without recourse to a vote, PIRC pays particular attention to companies explanations in regard to Code Provision D.2.4 that 'significant changes to existing (share) schemes' should require shareowner approval. In addition, changes made by companies immediately prior to joining the official list may be regarded as an attempt to avoid scrutiny by the company's new owners.

Disclosure

To be able to assess a new incentive scheme, shareowners need adequate information to be able to form a judgement. While it is now commonplace for companies to consult in advance with key shareowners and the representative bodies (including PIRC) this does not diminish the need for transparency when the plan is formally proposed for shareowner approval. The following paragraphs set out what PIRC considers to be necessary disclosure.

Eligibility for participation

Pay structures often seem to be based on the premise that it is only the top executives who are responsible for the success of the business and creating shareowner value. PIRC considers this assumption to be highly questionable. While an individual scheme may be aimed at management at the most senior level, this should be part of a coherent policy.

Administration

Schemes should be administered by the remuneration committee.

Individual participation

A full explanation of the basis on which awards will be made together with the maximum awards permitted under the rules of the scheme. Remuneration structures that offer annual awards in aggregate, in excess of 200% of salary (on an expected value basis) raise concerns for PIRC, and will trigger PIRC's matrix for assessing excessiveness.

Expected value

Although expected values for share based pay will depend on the assumptions used, they provide an estimate of the potential worth to the individual. We consider that all companies should disclose the current expected value of awards under a proposed scheme.

Significant shareholding requirement

A share scheme will not automatically create convergence of interest between directors and shareowners. We believe that companies should require participants in incentive schemes to build up a meaningful holding in the company over a limited time period.

Performance period

Most schemes use a three-year performance period. PIRC believes five years to be better practice to encourage longer term thinking, or at the least, a performance period followed by a further holding period other than the need to finance acquisition costs or upfront tax liabilities. We would encourage remuneration committees to think more imaginatively about performance periods especially if there are business cycles applicable to differing sectors or distinct divisions within a company.

Rolling performance periods are unacceptable.

Performance targets

Full transparency is required including: the composition of and changes to any comparator groups used and the vesting scale. PIRC's position on targets is set out below.

Vesting scales

Vesting scales are important as they provide several levels of payout for levels of performance, which will have a greater probability of encouraging directors to strive for the best performance they can manage than an all-or-nothing pay out point, known as 'cliff vesting'. PIRC considers that schemes should not use incremental vesting scales, whereby performance is measured against the base year every year rather than measuring over the total performance period.

Mechanics of this kind can lead to a payout when no long-term growth has been created, and therefore is not aligned with the interest of shareowners.

Retesting provisions

PIRC does not consider retesting to be acceptable. Any such provisions should be disclosed.

Takeover provisions

Automatic waiving of performance targets on a change in control is unacceptable. Where a company will cease to exist and a director will not go on to work for the enlarged entity, outstanding awards should be pro-rated for time and performance as a matter of course, and there should be no room for remuneration committee discretion on this. Scheme rules should prevent a 'technical' change in control, (e.g., a corporate restructuring using a scheme of arrangement) from triggering vesting. Participants affected should not be allowed to benefit from accelerated vesting if they do not lose their job as a result of the change. Awards should be rolled over into a scheme at the new company.

Scheme limits

PIRC supports the UK institutional consensus on dilution limits. Total awards under all share schemes should not exceed 10% of issued share capital in any ten-year period. In addition, to ensure this allowance is not used exclusively for directors or senior managers, a 5% limit should be placed upon executive schemes.

Companies should disclose the source of the shares to be used to satisfy awards e.g., new issue, treasury shares or bought in the market. PIRC does not support the issue of shares beyond these limits due to the dilutive impact on existing shareowners.

Discretion

However well any scheme is designed there will be the potential for 'perverse' outcomes. Shareowners need to be clearly advised as to the extent of any discretion available to the remuneration committee and how that discretion will be exercised. Where discretion has been applied there should be a clear description of how it has been applied, along with justification for doing so. Prior shareowner approval may be appropriate.

Common performance targets

Earnings per Share (EPS) and Relative Total Shareholder Return (TSR)

EPS and TSR growth are the most common long term incentive scheme targets. With respect to EPS, many schemes previously simply adopted a target of three per cent a year above inflation, which was the minimum acceptable under institutional guidelines.

PIRC has concerns over the use of EPS due to inherent weaknesses in not dealing with return on capital. There is a further problem with adjusted EPS because companies have failed, to date, to disclose the specific accounting items over which they have discretion to strip-out or include as one-time items. This highly discretionary methodology frustrates shareowner accountability.

Companies should provide assurance that where used, any EPS results will be, for the purpose of any incentive awards, adjusted to take account of the effect of any share buybacks enacted during the year.

If relative TSR is selected as a performance criterion, then the remuneration committee should ensure that a suitably large peer group of companies is identified, who should be subject to the effects of similar external factors. If TSR performance is compared against an index, additional information should be disclosed on how this compares performance against the competitor group.

There is growing concern that rewards attached to TSR and EPS performance metrics fail to achieve the desired motivation in recipients. They are increasingly described by board members as lottery tickets on performance over which recipients have no genuine direct control, and, typically, recipients are given little or no line of sight between their performance and reward using these metrics.

Indeed, the use of a performance measure such as relative TSR can leave executives confused over their task. For example, PwC reports one CEO as saying 'I don't know how to manage relative TSR … you don't wake up in the morning trying to manage something relative.'

A growing concern also relates to the belief that TSR can also encourage a strategic herd mentality that leads peers to compete with each other to take on more risk in order to improve the prospects of relative outperformance. Indeed, PIRC notes that as part of engagement with a prominent FTSE100 bank, the company cited the risk of this behaviour as its reason for removing TSR from its LTIP in 2009.

In PIRC's view it does not measure business performance accurately when stock markets are inefficient and can deliver arbitrary awards when M&A activity is high[10].

Moreover, it can reward volatility in stock price performance[11] and handicap companies with high investor expectations. This could mean both that recipients are rewarded less than they deserve or excessively when expectations are set too low against what is achievable.

In regard to EPS there is the concern that it ignores the capital required to generate earnings growth and the cost of that capital. Therefore, in PIRC's view it has only a tenuous link to genuine shareowner value creation. In addition, as noted above in regard to adjusted EPS, it is easily manipulated and therefore lends itself to gaming, which remuneration committees find challenging to police.

PIRC draws attention to the fundamental need to have integrity in accounting outcomes, irrespective of merely applying standards, in order for remuneration schemes to function properly in shareholders' interests. (Section 04, Audit and Reporting).

Contracts

Notice period

The most common notice period for directors' contracts is now one year or less. Contract lengths have reduced substantially over recent years due to investor pressure in response to excessive compensation payments.

---

10 For example, in Nov 2007 Mercer estimated that about one-third of FTSE 100 companies had some bid premium built into their share price in the recent past. See HOW TO: Moving beyond EPS and relative TSR as performance measures. www.mercer.com/referencecontent. jhtml?idContent=1288525.

11 See PricewaterhouseCoopers, Executive compensation: Review of the year 2006 for supporting evidence

A notice period of no longer than one year should be the maximum, which balances the interests of shareowners and the company with those of the director. This should be seen as a ceiling and shorter notice periods may be appropriate. Should it be necessary to reduce an existing notice period of a contract to comply with best practice, we consider that the board should endeavour to minimise the costs involved to shareowners'.

In exceptional circumstances, a longer initial fixed contract period may be acceptable. In such cases, the remuneration committee should explain the circumstances. Fixed initial notice periods should not exceed two years and it should be clear that these reduce to a period of no more than one year after the initial period.

Negotiation and authorisation

A service contract needs to be for services provided to the group of which the director is a board member and to be issued by the board. The review and agreement of the terms, however, needs to be delegated to the remuneration committee. This removes any possibility of the director approving their own remuneration. While each contract is unique to an individual director PIRC believes that it is best practice for the company to regularly review its draft service contract that can be issued as standard terms to all prospective appointees, rather than entering into individual negotiation each time. Should a potential appointee or a current director wish to have the contract reviewed by their own legal representatives, the cost should not be passed on to the company.

Termination provisions

Much of the concern over executive remuneration has been the result of the compensation terms for departing directors, particularly if the company has not performed. Whilst notice periods in contracts have reduced, the resulting compensation payments have not fallen, as provisions have tended to include more elements of remuneration.

Any contractual clauses that imply fixed compensation equivalent to more than one year's salary and benefits will be viewed as a breach of best practice. Such clauses could include change in control provisions that extend a notice period beyond one year, or the inclusion of unearned additional bonus payments in the calculation of compensation.

Termination provisions should include a clause whereby any payment can be reduced in specific circumstances following the failure of a director to perform.

In our view, any benefit in excess of six months' basic salary, whether contractual or not, should be specifically approved by shareowners prior to payment. Given that there are already limitations on the validity of contracts, we see no contradiction with basic contract law. US companies are voluntarily agreeing to shareowner approval of 'golden parachute' arrangements, albeit only when they exceed levels that would be unacceptable in the UK.

Non-Compete arrangements

PIRC recognises that clauses which prevent a director from seeking employment impact on the directors' ability to mitigate a company's loss following termination of the contract. The disclosure of such provisions will assist shareholders in taking a view on the suitability termination payments.

Mitigation

In common law, there is an obligation on the employee to seek work (to 'mitigate' the loss under the contract) and, if the individual secures new employment before the end of the period of notice given by the company, to cease claiming remuneration from the original employer. Companies have the right to enforce this duty to mitigate by negotiating over the level of compensation payable.

Company remuneration reports should confirm that the remuneration committee will seek to apply mitigation rigorously. PIRC supports the use of phased payments to reduce the payments on termination.

Disclosure

To complement shareowners' rights under Section 229 of the Companies Act (the right of members to inspect and request a copy of a director's service contract); we believe that copies of directors' service contracts and letters of appointment should be posted on the company's web page.

Pensions

Pensions tend to be the most opaque elements of directors' packages. In the past the investment community has tended to ignore this aspect of executive pay, but pensions are an increasingly important issue both as part of executive pay and wider employee relations. Company contributions to directors' pensions should take into account:

- Relative importance in the overall package;
- Contribution and accrual rates across the wider group; and
- The funding situation of any Defined Benefit (DB) scheme.

The lack of clarity in relation to pension provision is problematic as this is an area of remuneration that is clearly not performance-related. This raises the possibility of rewards for failure, as was demonstrated in the case of the Royal Bank of Scotland. In addition the preferential provision for directors in place at some companies needs to be scrutinised in reference to the guidance that companies are sensitive to pay and conditions across the group. Therefore it is important that shareowners are provided with sufficient information to review pension arrangements effectively.

There are a number of issues in relation to directors' pensions that PIRC believes that shareowners should be particularly alert to. These include:

- Preferential treatment in respect of accrual in defined benefit schemes. Some directors are provided with accrual rates of 1/40ths or 1/30ths compared to 1/60ths or 1/80ths available to other employees.
- Preferential treatment in respect of contributions to defined contribution schemes. Some directors are provided with exceptionally generous contribution rates that are not available to other staff.
- Large payments 'in lieu of pension'. Some companies provide a cash payment to directors in place of a pension (sometimes called a 'pension allowance'). These are often in 20% to 25% of salary range and are not performance related.
- Other enhancements to benefits that are available to use at the company's discretion, but seem to primarily benefit directors, for example artificially accrued years of service.

In all of these cases, the benefits to shareowners of preferential treatment for directors are not obvious. The problem is compounded because disclosure in this area is poor. Companies are already required to disclose certain information about directors' pensions under the Directors Remuneration Reporting Regulations (DRRR). However many of the more controversial arrangements in place at companies – such as preferential arrangements for directors outlined above – are not captured. Whilst a minority of companies voluntarily make details of such arrangement available in the remuneration report, most do not. This severely hampers the ability of shareowners to take an informed view on the arrangements in place, and whether they adhere to best practice.

There have been some moves to improve disclosure. In 2010 the NAPF and LAPFF issued a joint letter to the FTSE350 seeking improved and standardised disclosure[12]. However in practice it appears that most companies still provide patchy information.

---

[12] http://www.napf.co.uk/PressCentre/Press_releases/0024_061510_Investors_want_greater_transparency_0610.aspx

In order for shareowners to exercise effective oversight, it is important that the market as a whole adheres to best practice in reporting of directors' pensions. PIRC considers that for shareowners to effectively evaluate directors' pensions, in addition to meeting the mandatory disclosure requirements of the DRRR, companies should also meet the following set of best practice questions:

1. Does the company disclose and explain accrual rates attached to defined benefit schemes?
2. Does the company disclose and explain the approximate ongoing cost of defined benefit provisions for directors?
3. Does the company disclose and explain contributions to defined contribution schemes or payments in lieu of pensions?
4. The normal retirement age for directors under all pension schemes is disclosed?
5. Does the company evaluate executive pension arrangements in the context of being sensitive to employment conditions elsewhere in the group?
6. Does the remuneration committee exercise discretion to provide early unreduced pension benefits?

Other practices

A good remuneration policy may be still be undermined by poor practices. These may be indications of how the policy will be implemented in future.

Divergences from an existing remuneration policy

These may include significant discretionary, non-contractual, or ex-gratia payments; failure to apply mitigation; or agreement of new contract terms.

In PIRC's view, any such changes should be subject to prior shareowner approval. Requiring the board to justify itself to shareowners is a useful discipline. Often, the changes appear to shield management from the risks inherent in variable pay – skewing the risk/reward balance.

Controversy can be caused by the committee acting significantly outside a previously stated policy. Remuneration committees should seek to clearly explain the rationale for changes in previous policy e.g., increases in bonus potential or annual incentive rewards; grant of contract with lengthy notice period.

Capital management

Besides the indirect effect a repurchase may have on incentive scheme pay-outs there is also evidence from the US[13] to suggest repurchase activity can combine with heightened levels of insider selling of shares to produce a situation in which it is clear that management is enriching itself at the expense of shareowners.

PIRC therefore considers it imperative that remuneration committees make a statement to the effect that EPS results will be, for the purpose of bonus payments, adjusted to take account of the effect of any buyback during the year.

Recruitment incentives

In the short term, compensating a proposed director for the loss of potential rewards from their previous employer or providing upfront cash or share awards as an enticement to join may appear to be in the interest of the company, if it believes it cannot otherwise attract the executive. However, the practice is not in the company's or investors' long-term interests as it contributes to a general tendency to grant such replacement awards, which in turn devalues the retentive effect of share schemes.

Any such awards, when used, should have challenging performance conditions attached to ensure that the company pays only on the basis of the recruit's delivery rather than apparent potential.

Significant salary increases

Salary increases should be explained as a matter of course, in particular when they reach double digits. PIRC does not consider it appropriate that significant increase be given to simply align with the market, rather it should only be for additional responsibilities.

Large one off share based awards

Share based rewards can produce distorted or unsustainable gains for the individual, unrelated to the company's underlying performance, due to market volatility and other factors.

Best practice is to make smaller awards of options or shares each year, so that rewards are less dependent on market timing. If the company believes that it has a case for making a large award, then this will need to be fully explained and justified.

---

[13] Audit Integrity, Share Repurchases revisited, June 2007

PIRC generally does not look favourably on front-loading of incentive awards.

Option Re-pricing and Replacement

This practice undermines any incentive effect of issuing options in the first place and is not acceptable as a matter of principle. The perceived need to re-price only arises if excessively large awards were made in the first place and are followed by a decline in share price.

Replacement of underwater options with new awards at a lower market price can have the same effective result as re-pricing and will be viewed with scepticism.

Award Re-basing

In response to a sudden decline in performance, a company may consider it appropriate to retroactively alter the performance conditions of awards which have been granted in previous years and are part way through their performance period. Even if the new performance targets are considered to be sufficiently challenging we still consider the re-basing of previously granted awards to be inappropriate as it undermines the use of fixed long-term performance targets in encouraging consistent long-term performance.

PIRC also takes a negative view of companies changing scheme rules specifically to fit tax planning for directors. Designing incentives to fit individual tax arrangements is not a role of the remuneration committee – the job of the committee is to design schemes with appropriate performance conditions, not enable optimal use of international tax laws.

Transaction bonuses

Bonuses for completion of a merger, acquisition, or other transaction assume that the completion of the deal is in itself a measure of success, whereas the value will be in its impact on long-term performance. Transaction bonuses are strongly discouraged.

Appendix 4 ABI Principles of Remuneration

Association of British Insurers

Association of British Insurers
51 Gresham Street
London EC2V 7HQ
Tel: 020 7600 3333
Fax: 020 7696 8999
Direct Tel. 020 7216 7670
E-mail Robert.hingley@abi.org.uk

5 November 2013

Dear Remuneration Committee Chairman,

I write to you at the request of the ABI Investment Committee to outline the main revisions to the ABI's Principles of Remuneration, the updated version of which has been published today. We also outline how the ABI's Institutional Voting Information Service ("IVIS") will approach the new voting and reporting regime.

The ABI's Principles of Remuneration are reviewed annually. Last year, we made significant revisions to the content and structure of the guidance. Given this, we have made only minor amendments and clarifications in 2013. The main changes relate to:

- Performance Adjustment/Malus and Clawback – we provide a clearer definition of performance adjustment and clawback and ask Committees to disclose the circumstances in which performance adjustment or clawback could be used.
- Executive shareholdings – This has been updated to clarify which shares would qualify as meeting the guideline.
- Performance on grant schemes – Whilst many members still retain significant reservations over the use of performance-on-grant schemes. The update provides the conditions shareholders expect these schemes to meet, such as genuinely long holding periods, significant shareholding requirements, lower overall amounts and the disclosure of targets/performance achieved.
- The new Reporting and Voting Regime – Appendix 1 outlines ABI views on various practical aspects of the new reporting arrangements.

With the introduction of the Reporting Regulations and Voting Legislation, the coming year will see significant changes in the way companies report, and shareholders vote, on pay. The Principles should be viewed in conjunction with the guidance on the new reporting regulations produced by the GC 100 and Investor Group. The ABI supports this guidance and encourages companies to adopt the best practice within it.

Under the new voting and reporting regime, IVIS will continue its current approach of assessing companies. IVIS does not issue direct voting recommendations. Instead, in the spirit of comply-or-explain, we highlight key issues and non-compliance with best practice through our Colour Coding system. This gives us flexibility in our dealings with companies and the ability to consider well-reasoned arguments.

When companies seek approval for the Policy Report, IVIS will produce a separate conclusion and status for each of the Policy Report and the Annual Remuneration Report.

The two votes will be colour coded separately. Under our colour coding system, a Blue Top indicates no areas of major concern. The colour showing the strongest concern is Red, followed by Amber.

IVIS's analysis of a company's Policy Report is likely to highlight the following issues on a Red or Amber top:

- *Remuneration structures not aligned to the ABI Principles of Remuneration (including the guidance and appendix)* – As is our current practice, IVIS will highlight remuneration policies or structures which are not in accordance with the ABI Principles of Remuneration.
- *Lack of detail in the Policy Report* – IVIS will highlight where companies fail to provide sufficient detail in the policy report to allow shareholders to make an informed voting decision. ABI members recommend that companies consider the guidance issued by the GC 100 and Investor Group to ensure that they provide sufficient detail in the Policy Report.
- *Use of wide ranging discretion* – Discretion will be an important aspect of the Policy Report, as it will allow Remuneration Committees to ensure their policies will be appropriate over their life. However, IVIS will highlight where policies are drafted with overarching or widely-ranging discretion provisions, particularly without any clear explanation.

If you need any further details on the Principles of Remuneration or IVIS's approach to the forthcoming AGM season, please do not hesitate to contact our Head of Corporate Governance, Andrew Ninian (andrew.ninian@abi.org.uk, 020 7216 7671), or one of the IVIS team (www.ivis.co.uk/contact.aspx).

Yours faithfully,

Robert Hingley

Director of Investment Affairs

Association of British Insurers

ABI Principles of Remuneration

5th November 2013

Foreword

The Principles set out members' views on the role of shareholders and directors in relation to remuneration and the manner in which remuneration should be determined and structured. We believe that these Principles continue to provide a useful guide to shareholder expectations and good practice. As ever, a continued and close dialogue between companies and their shareholders is crucial.

With the introduction of the Reporting Regulations and Voting Legislation which apply to companies with year-ends starting on or after 1 October 2013, the coming year will see significant changes in the way companies report on, and shareholders vote on, executive remuneration. The Principles should be viewed in conjunction with the guidance on the new reporting regulations produced by the GC 100 and Investor Group. The ABI supports this guidance.

This document is designed with a format of over-arching Principles and general Guidance. Appendix 1 covers ABI views on practical aspects of the new reporting arrangements. This document is predominantly for companies with a main market listing but is also relevant to companies on other public markets and other entities.

Members continue to expect that, as a minimum, companies will follow the requirements relating to Remuneration in the UK's Companies Act 2006, Reporting Regulations, the UK Corporate Governance Code and the UK Listing Rules. Where companies are not subject to these regimes they should apply similar high standards.

Robert Talbut
Chief Investment Officer, Royal London Asset Management
Chairman of the Investment Committee of the Association of British Insurers
5th November 2013

ABI PRINCIPLES OF REMUNERATION

i. The Role of Shareholders

a. ABI members as institutional investors are interested in long-term value creation for the benefit of our ultimate clients. We have a fiduciary responsibility to our clients, who are primarily individual savers and pensioners.

b. This responsibility involves ensuring that clients' capital is allocated efficiently and that the companies we own are well governed and run in the interests of their shareholders.

c. As part of this, members seek to ensure that remuneration practices and policies of companies they invest in are aligned with shareholder interests and promote sustainable value creation.

d. ABI members are committed to responsible ownership as outlined in FRC's Stewardship Code, but it is not the role of shareholders to micro-manage companies.

ii. The Role of the Board and Directors

a. Boards of Directors are appointed by shareholders to run companies and act in their interests. They have a fiduciary duty to act in the best interests of their shareholders when determining remuneration. It is their responsibility to promote the long-term success of the company, taking into account the interests of employees, suppliers, customers, community, the environment and society.

b. Executive directors develop and implement strategy for the company. Non-executive directors should constructively challenge and contribute to this process, scrutinise the performance of the executives, and ensure that risk management systems are robust.

c. Non-executive directors, particularly those serving on the Remuneration Committee, should oversee executive remuneration.

iii. Remuneration Committee

a. Shareholders look to the Remuneration Committee to protect and promote their interests in setting executive remuneration. As directors, committee members are accountable to shareholders for the structure and quantum of remuneration.

b. Remuneration Committees should set remuneration within the context of overall corporate performance. Structure should be aligned with strategy and agreed risk appetite, reward success fairly and avoid paying more than is necessary.

c. Remuneration Committees should look at executive remuneration in terms of the pay policy of the company as a whole, pay and conditions elsewhere in the Group, and the overall cost to shareholders.

iv. Remuneration Policies

a. Remuneration policies should be set to promote value creation through transparent alignment with the agreed corporate strategy.

b. Remuneration policies should support performance, encourage the underlying sustainable financial health of the business and promote sound risk management for the benefit of all investors, including shareholders and creditors.

c. Undeserved remuneration undermines the efficient operation of the company. Excessive remuneration adversely affects its reputation and is not aligned with shareholder interests.

d. The board as a whole must consider the aggregate impact of employee remuneration on the finances of the company, its investment and capital needs, and dividends to shareholders.

v. Remuneration Structures

a. The Remuneration Committee should select a remuneration structure which is appropriate for the specific business, and efficient and cost-effective in delivering its longer-term strategy. These Principles do not seek to prescribe or recommend any particular remuneration structure.

b. Complexity is discouraged. Shareholders prefer simple and understandable remuneration structures; simplicity can be improved by limiting variable remuneration to an annual bonus and one long term incentive scheme.

c. Executives and shareholders can have divergent interests, particularly in relation to time horizons and the consequences of failure or corporate underperformance. Incentive structures should have a long-term focus.

d. To avoid payment for failure and promote a long-term focus, remuneration structures should contain a careful balance of fixed and variable pay. They should include a high degree of deferral and measurement of performance over the long-term.

e. Structures should also include provisions that allow the company, in specified circumstances, to:

- Forfeit all or part of a bonus or long-term incentive award before it has vested and been paid ('performance adjustment' or 'malus'); and/or

- Recover sums already paid ('clawback')

f. Executives should build up a high level of personal shareholding to ensure alignment of interest with shareholders.

g. Dilution of shareholders through the issuing of shares to employees represents a significant transfer of value. Dilution limits are an important shareholder protection and should be respected.

GUIDANCE FOR REMUNERATION COMMITTEES

The following guidance is set out to help Remuneration Committees apply the ABI Principles of Remuneration and ensure a proper level of shareholder protection.

SECTION A – GENERAL GUIDANCE

1. Quantum

Quantum of remuneration is a matter of concern to shareholders. Levels of pay that do not reflect corporate performance undermine the ability to reward success and represent excess rent extractions. Undeserved remuneration undermines the efficient operation of the company. Excessive remuneration adversely affects its reputation and is not aligned with shareholder interests. Shareholders are likely to object to levels of pay that do not respect the core principles of paying no more than is necessary and a linkage to sustainable long-term value creation.

Companies must consider the aggregate impact of employee remuneration on the finances of the company, its investment and capital needs, and dividends to shareholders.

The Remuneration Committee should seek specific points of reference against which the appropriateness of quantum can be judged. Useful reference points, which should help avoid unnecessary disagreements with shareholders, include:

– A stated policy that links aggregate remuneration to overall corporate performance. High pay for exceptional performance is consistent with this approach.

– The remuneration policy of the company as a whole. Remuneration Committees should assess the appropriateness of changes in the quantum of executive remuneration in the context of the company overall, including changes in employee remuneration more broadly.

– A relevant and fairly constructed peer universe. It is undesirable simply to use "median" pay as a benchmark since this, if used broadly, can lead to ratcheted increases in remuneration.

2. Executive shareholdings

Executive directors and senior executives should build up significant shareholdings in companies. Unvested share based incentives should not be allowed to count towards the holding requirements and these requirements are not a substitute for performance metrics under share based plans. Shares should only count towards the executive's shareholding guideline if vesting is not subject to any further performance or other conditions such as continued employment. Shares which are vested, but which remain subject to a holding period and/or clawback, may count towards the holding requirement. The use of shareholdings in hedging arrangements or as collateral for loans should be fully disclosed. Shares which are subject to future performance, holding periods, claw-back or shareholding guidelines should not be hedged or used as collateral.

3. Non-executive shareholding

Shareholders encourage non-executive directors to own shares in the company. Chairmen and non-executives may receive part of their fees in shares bought at the market price. However, shareholders consider it inappropriate for chairmen and independent directors to receive incentive awards geared to the share price or corporate performance.

4. Performance Adjustment/Malus and Clawback

As stated above, structures should include provisions that allow the company, in specified circumstances, to:

- Forfeit all or part of a bonus or long-term incentive award before it has vested and been paid ('performance adjustment' or 'malus'); and/or
- Recover sums already paid ('clawback')

Shareholders believe the circumstances in which performance adjustment and clawback can be implemented need to be agreed and documented before awards are made.

The Committee should review the circumstances in which these provisions can apply and ensure that they are appropriate for the company. In general, shareholders accept that performance adjustment will apply to a broader range of circumstances than for clawback. The circumstances should, in each case, be clearly disclosed to shareholders.

The Committee should also consider the enforcement power they have to implement each process.

5. Discretion

Discretion can help Remuneration Committees to ensure that the outcomes of executive pay schemes properly reflect overall corporate performance and the experience of the shareholders in terms of value creation.

Discretion should be exercised diligently and in a manner that is aligned with shareholders' interests. Discretion should only be exercised within the previously agreed boundaries and maxima. If these are exceeded, then shareholders will consider excessive payments to be ex gratia in nature. Remuneration Committees will have to disclose the level of discretion applicable under the Policy Table.

The use of discretion should be clearly disclosed. Remuneration Committees will be held accountable for the way discretion is used.

6. Pay for employees below board level

The Remuneration Committee should be cognisant of pay and conditions elsewhere in the Group and take them into account when determining executive remuneration.

The Committee may have a role in determining pay or having oversight of remuneration at below board level. This is of particular relevance where the levels of remuneration or the risks associated with the activities involved are material to the Group's overall performance.

7. Taxation

Remuneration Committees should not seek to make changes to any element of executive remuneration to compensate participants for changes in their personal tax status.

Remuneration structures that seek to increase tax efficiency should not result in additional costs to the company or an increase in its own tax bill. Remuneration Committees should be aware of the potential damage to the company's and shareholders' reputation from implementing such schemes.

8. Contracts and severance

Companies should follow the Principles and Guidance contained within the ABI and NAPF Statement on Executive Contracts and Severance and the UK Corporate Governance Code. The Statement is available at: http://www.ivis.co.uk/ExecutiveContractsAndSeverance.aspx

9. Recruitment of executive directors

When recruiting Executive Directors, companies should pay no more than is necessary and should fully justify payments to shareholders. Compensating executives for the forfeiture of awards from a previous employer should generally be on a comparable basis, taking account of performance achieved or likely to be achieved, the proportion of performance period remaining and the form of the award.

10. Reward for Failure

It is unacceptable that poor performance by senior executives, which detracts from the value of an enterprise and threatens the livelihood of employees, can result in excessive payments to departing directors. Payment for failure cannot be tolerated. Boards should ensure that this cannot occur, both when negotiating new contracts and when agreeing any payments when contracts are terminated.

11. Special awards and ex gratia payments

Effective remuneration planning involving a balance of short and long term plans, carefully selected and calibrated performance measures and targets, and annual grants, should make exceptional awards unnecessary. A need for special grants, particularly for continuing management, indicates poor planning by the Remuneration Committee.

Special awards may be acceptable when, for example, a new team is brought in to turn around a company. If such awards are made, the Remuneration Committee must justify them.

Shareholders believe that retention awards for main board directors rarely work. Retention concerns on their own are not sufficient grounds for remuneration to increase.

Shareholders do not support the practice of paying transaction related bonuses.

SECTION B – FIXED REMUNERATION

1. Base pay

Base pay should be set at a level which reflects the role and responsibility of the individual, whilst respecting the principle of paying no more than is necessary.

Where Remuneration Committees seek to increase base pay, the reasons should be fully disclosed and justified. Salary decisions should not be taken purely on the basis of simple benchmarking against peer companies. If benchmarking is used, the aim should not solely be to match the "median" but to provide a point of reference for determining the appropriate salary for the specific job. The constant chasing of a perceived median has been a major contributor to the spiralling levels of pay.

Remuneration Committees should also be aware of the multiplier effect that increases in base pay have on the overall quantum of remuneration.

2. Pensions

Pension provision can represent a considerable cost to the company and this should be recognised by the Remuneration Committee when considering total executive remuneration.

Pension related payments should not be used as a mechanism for increasing total remuneration. The pension provision for executives should, where possible, be in line with the general approach to the employees as a whole. Any differences in pension contribution rates for executives and the general workforce should be disclosed and justified to shareholders.

Payments in lieu of pension scheme participation should be clearly disclosed and treated as a separate non-salary benefit. There should be informative disclosure identifying incremental value accruing to pension scheme participation and any other superannuation arrangements.

Changes in pension benefit entitlements or to transfer values reflecting significant changes in actuarial and other relevant assumptions should be fully identified and explained. Where changes to pension benefit entitlements or transfers are made at the discretion of the Remuneration Committee, these should be made clear and justification should be provided. Pensions paid on early retirement should be subject to abatement.

3. Benefits

Benefits should be fully disclosed and, where significant, viewed as an integral component of fixed remuneration.

SECTION C – VARIABLE REMUNERATION

A significant proportion of executive remuneration should be performance related, and tied to the achievement of the agreed corporate strategy and long-term value creation. These Principles do not seek to prescribe or recommend any particular remuneration structure.

Shareholders prefer simple remuneration structures; simplicity can be improved by limiting variable remuneration to an annual bonus and one long term incentive scheme. Remuneration committees may consider non-financial performance criteria in variable remuneration, for example relating to environmental, social and governance (ESG) objectives, or to particular operational objectives. ESG measures should only be used if they are material to the business and quantifiable. In each case, the link to strategy and method of performance measurement should be clearly explained.

No element of variable pay should be pensionable.

1. Annual bonuses

Annual bonuses incentivise performance and reward achievement in line with the agreed corporate strategy.

Annual bonuses exist to reward contribution to the business during the year above the level expected for being in receipt of a salary. They should be clearly linked to business targets, ideally through the KPIs reported in the Strategic Report. Where other measures are chosen, these should be explained and justified. The KPIs can be both financial and non-financial.

The measurements chosen must be quantifiable and the targets set at the start of the year.

Companies should clearly disclose and justify the performance measures chosen and the related targets. Where consideration of commercial sensitivities may prevent a fuller disclosure of specific short-term targets at the start of the performance period, shareholders expect to be informed of the main performance parameters, both corporate and personal, for the financial year being reported on.

Following payment of the bonus, companies should provide a full analysis in the Remuneration Report of the extent to which the relevant targets were actually met.

Maximum participation levels should be disclosed and any increases in the maximum from one year to the next explicitly justified.

Deferring a portion of the bonus into shares can create a greater alignment with shareholders, particularly where there is no long term incentive. However, this should not result in an increase in the overall quantum of the bonus.

Shareholders discourage the payment of annual bonuses to executive directors if the business has suffered an exceptional negative event, even if some specific targets have been met. In such circumstances, shareholders should be consulted on bonus policy and any proposed payments should be carefully explained.

Discretion should be retained to ensure that a payment that is inappropriate in all the company's circumstances is not made. Companies should disclose the range of discretion which can be applied to bonus awards.

2. Long-term incentives

i. General

Long-term incentives exist to reward the successful implementation of strategy and the creation of shareholder value over a period appropriate to the strategic objectives of the company. Equity based long-term incentive schemes are the most effective way to align the interests of participants and shareholders.

The performance period should be clearly linked to the timing of the implementation of the strategy of the business, which should be no less than three years and shareholders would generally prefer longer. Committees should consider the use of additional holding periods.

All new incentives or any substantive changes to existing schemes should be subject to prior approval by shareholders by means of a separate and binding resolution. Any change in quantum should be fully explained and justified.

Scheme and individual participation limits must be fully disclosed in share incentive schemes.

The operation of share incentive schemes should not lead to dilution in excess of the limits acceptable to shareholders.

ii. Performance conditions

The widely differing nature of business models and industry characteristics means that the appropriate performance measures and conditions for different companies may vary significantly. Performance measures and vesting conditions should be fully explained and clearly linked to the achievement of appropriately challenging financial performance which will enhance shareholder value.

Whilst other considerations may apply in particular circumstances, for example, restructuring, shareholders will expect that remuneration policies and structures will normally be consistent with the following criteria:

- Shareholders have a clear preference for financial measures linked to value creation. Performance criteria should be linked to the Company's long-term strategy and targets reflect an appropriate balance between the shorter- and longer-term.

- Remuneration Committees will need to consider, and explain, appropriate performance criteria in the light of the specific business characteristics of the group in question. Performance criteria should fully reflect the performance of the business as a whole and should be applied consistently across measurement periods.
- The definition of any performance measurement should be clearly disclosed.
- Retesting of performance conditions is not acceptable.
- Remuneration Committees should ensure that, when using in isolation either comparative or absolute performance metrics, the result does not produce outcomes that are not in line with the overall performance of the company, its future prospects or the experience of its shareholders over the performance period.
- Comparator groups used for performance purposes should be both relevant and representative. Where only a small number of companies is used for a comparator group, Remuneration Committees should satisfy themselves that the comparative performance will not result in arbitrary outcomes. Awards should not vest for less than median performance.
- Where operational measurements are used, they would generally be expected:
  - To include, subject to business strategy, one or more measures relating to overall business volume or growth
  - To include one or more measures relating to business efficiency or profitability
  - To avoid the risk of providing an implicit incentive to take undue operational or financial risks or, in particular, to adopt an unduly risky capital structure.
- Where Total Shareholder Return (TSR) relative to a relevant index or peer group is used, Remuneration Committees should satisfy themselves prior to vesting that the recorded TSR or other criterion is a genuine reflection of the company's underlying financial performance, and explain their reasoning.
- The calculation of starting and finishing values for TSR should be made by reference to average share prices over a short period of time at the beginning and end of the performance period. Lengthy averaging periods should be avoided. Where TSR is used as a performance criterion and the chosen comparator group includes companies listed in overseas markets, it is essential that TSR be measured on a consistent basis. The standard approach should be for a common currency to be used. Where there are compelling grounds for the calculation to be

based on local currency TSR of comparator group companies, then the reasons for choosing this approach should be fully explained.

- Where appropriate, Remuneration Committees should take account of the ABI Guidelines on Responsible Investment Disclosures (http://www.ivis.co.uk/ResponsibleInvestmentDisclosure.aspx).

iii. Vesting

Threshold vesting amounts, reflecting expected performance, should not be significant by comparison with annual base salary.

Awards' structures with a marked 'cliff edge' vesting profile are considered inappropriate. Full vesting should reflect exceptional performance and so be dependent on achievement of significantly greater value creation than that applicable to threshold vesting.

Sliding scales and graduated vesting profiles are a useful way of ensuring that performance conditions are genuinely challenging. They generally provide a better motivator for improving corporate performance than a 'single hurdle'.

iv. Grant Size

Windfall gains may arise if the level of share or option grants expressed as a multiple of salary is maintained after a substantial fall in the share price. Where this risk exists, grants should be scaled back.

v. Cost

The primary information that should be disclosed includes:

- The potential value of awards due to individual scheme participants on full vesting. This should be expressed by reference to the face value of shares or shares under option at point of grant, and expressed as a multiple of base salary.
- The maximum dilution which may arise through the issue of shares to satisfy entitlements.

vi. Change of control provisions

Scheme rules should state that there will be no automatic waiving of performance conditions either in the event of a change of control or where subsisting options and awards are 'rolled over' in the event of a capital reconstruction, and/or the early termination of the participant's employment. Remuneration Committees should use best endeavours to provide meaningful disclosure that quantifies the aggregate payments arising on a change of control.

In the event of a change of control, the key determinant of the level of awards vesting should be underlying financial performance. Also, any such early vesting as a consequence of a change of control should be on a time pro-rata basis i.e. taking into account the vesting period that has elapsed at the time of change of control. Remuneration Committees should satisfy themselves that the measured performance provides genuine evidence of underlying financial achievement over any shorter time period. They should explain their reasoning in the Remuneration Report or other relevant documentation sent to shareholders.

vii. Pricing and timing of awards

The price at which shares are issued under a scheme should not be less than the mid-market price (or similar formula) immediately preceding grant of the shares under the scheme.

Options granted under executive (discretionary) schemes should not be granted at a discount to the prevailing mid-market price.

Repricing or surrender and regrant of awards or 'underwater' share options is not appropriate.

The rules of a scheme should provide that share or option awards should normally be granted within a 42 day period following the publication of the company's results.

viii. Life of schemes and incentive awards

No awards should be made beyond the life of the scheme approved on adoption by shareholders, which should not exceed 10 years.

Shares and options should not vest or be exercisable within three years from the date of grant. In addition, options should not be exercisable more than ten years from the date of grant.

Where individuals choose to terminate their employment before the end of the service period, or in the event that employment is terminated for cause, any unvested options or conditional share-based award should normally lapse.

In other circumstances of cessation of employment[1], some portion of the award may vest, to the extent of the service period that has been completed, but subject to the achievement of relevant performance criteria. In general, the originally stipulated performance measurement period should continue to apply. However, where in the opinion of the Remuneration Committee,

---

1 Such circumstances may include disability, ill health, redundancy, retirement or analogous reasons for departure of a 'good leaver' nature.

early vesting is appropriate, or where it is otherwise necessary[2], awards should vest by reference to performance criteria achieved over the period to date.

Where options vest, in the event of death or cessation of employment of the option holder or where a company is taken over (except where arrangements are made for a switch to options of the offeror company), or where they have already vested at the time of such event, they must be exercised (or lapse) within 12 months. Where the performance measurement period applicable to an option extends beyond the point of cessation of employment, options must be exercised within 12 months of vesting following the end of the performance measurement period.

Any shares or options that a company may grant in exchange for those released under the schemes of acquired companies should normally be taken into account for the purposes of dilution and individual participation limits determined in accordance with this Guidance.

ix. Dilution

The rules of a scheme must provide that commitments to issue new shares or re-issue treasury shares, when aggregated with awards under all of the company's other schemes, must not exceed 10% of the issued ordinary share capital (adjusted for share issuance and cancellation) in any rolling 10 year period. Remuneration Committees should ensure that appropriate policies regarding flow-rates exist in order to spread the potential issue of new shares over the life of relevant schemes in order to ensure the limit is not breached.

Commitments to issue new shares or re-issue treasury shares under executive (discretionary) schemes should not exceed 5% of the issued ordinary share capital of the company (adjusted for share issuance and cancellation) in any rolling 10 year period. This may be exceeded where vesting is dependent on the achievement of significantly more stretching performance criteria. The implicit dilution commitment should always be provided for at point of grant even where, as in the case of share-settled share appreciation rights, it is recognised that only a proportion of shares may in practice be used.

x. Joint venture companies and subsidiary companies

Shareholders generally consider it undesirable for options and other share-based incentives to be granted over the share capital of a joint venture company.

---

2 Such circumstances may include death and also occasions such as takeover of the company or sale or transfer of the business undertaking where awards are not being rolled over into equivalent awards in the successor entity or new employer.

Discretionary grants over shares of a subsidiary company should be made only in exceptional circumstances. Where companies can justify doing so in terms of contribution to overall value creation, shareholders may consider exceptions, subject to the following:

- Participation in subsidiary company schemes is restricted to those whose time is fully allocated to that subsidiary. Parent company directors should not participate in such schemes.
- There is full disclosure of the accounting treatment used when recognising the cost of option or share awards.
- Grants of options or share awards are subject to appropriately challenging performance criteria.
- Dilution limits relating to the subsidiary company should be disclosed in the context of parent company dilution limits.
- The methodology for valuing the subsidiary company shares and, in the case of option awards, the measurement of volatility of those shares should be disclosed. The party responsible for the valuation process should also be disclosed.
- Any entitlement or obligation to convert subsidiary company shares to parent company shares should be disclosed.

Shareholders may consider further exceptions where the condition of exercise is subject to flotation or sale of the subsidiary company. In such circumstances, grants should be conditional, so that vesting is dependent on a return on investment that exceeds the cost of capital and that the market value of the shares at date of grant is subject to external validation.

Exceptions will apply in the case of an overseas subsidiary company where required by local legislation, or in circumstances where at least 25% of the ordinary share capital of the subsidiary company is listed and held outside the group.

xi. Particular types of scheme

a) Matching schemes

Any matching shares allocated will be considered by shareholders as part of the quantum of total remuneration. The performance conditions should be appropriate to the total amount potentially to be received, including matching shares. Matching schemes may add unnecessary complexity.

b) Option schemes

Dividends should not be paid or accrue in the period prior to exercise, as the shares are not owned by the participant.

c) Performance on grant schemes

Measuring performance achieved prior to the point of grant is generally not favoured. If the Remuneration Committee considers a performance on grant scheme to be appropriate:

- It should be carefully justified, and accompanied with genuinely long holding periods and significant shareholding requirements;
- There should be clear disclosure (in advance) of the performance required, and achieved, to justify grants;
- Given that such schemes are, generally, not subject to future performance or other conditions (other than performance adjustment or clawback), shareholders expect the amounts awarded to be significantly lower than under long-term incentive schemes subject to such conditions;
- The use of a measurable financial performance underpin over the holding period should be considered.

xii. Employee Share Ownership Trusts – ESOTs

ESOTs should not hold more shares at any one time than would be required in practice to match their outstanding liabilities, nor should they be used as an anti-takeover or similar device. Furthermore, an ESOT's deed should provide that any unvested shares held in the ESOT shall not be voted at shareholder meetings. The prior approval of shareholders should be obtained before 5% or more of a company's share capital at any one time may be held within ESOTs.

Where companies have provided for an ESOT to be used to meet scheme requirements, they should disclose the number of shares held by the ESOT in order to assist shareholders with their evaluation of the overall use of shares for remuneration purposes. The company should explain its strategy in this regard.

xiii. All-Employee Schemes

All-Employee schemes, such as SAYE schemes and Share Incentive Plans (SIPs) should operate within an appropriate best practice framework. If newly issued shares are utilised, the overall dilution limits for share schemes should be complied with. The Guidance relating to timing of grants (except for pre-determined regular appropriation of shares under SIPs) applies.

APPENDIX 1 – THE NEW REPORTING AND VOTING REGIME

The ABI supports The Large and Medium-sized Companies and Groups (Accounts and Reports) (Amendment) Regulations 2013 (the "Reporting

Regulations") and voting legislation which apply to companies with year-ends starting on or after 1 October 2013. We also support the GC100 and Investor Group guidance, which has been produced jointly between companies and investors to assist companies in reporting under the new regulations.

The ABI believe that the Principles of Remuneration continue to provide a useful guide to shareholder expectations and good practice under the new remuneration reporting and voting regime. We outline below ABI views on various practical aspects of the new reporting arrangements:

1. Frequency of the vote on the Policy Report – The legislation requires shareholders to vote on a company's Policy Report at least every three years. In normal circumstances, the ABI would expect the Policy Report to be voted on every three years and not on an annual basis; this will help to ensure that the company's remuneration strategy is aligned with the long term business strategy.

2. Policy start date – In normal circumstances shareholders would expect a company's Remuneration Policy to apply immediately after approval. Policies which take effect only at the start of the following financial year may be set too far in advance for meaningful engagement or dialogue with shareholders.

3. Disclosure of the Policy Report – Although not required by the Reporting Regulations, it will be beneficial to shareholders if the Policy Table is disclosed in the Remuneration Report on an annual basis.

4. Commercially sensitive performance targets – Where, in the opinion of the Directors, performance targets are considered to be commercially sensitive, the legislation allows for these targets not to be disclosed. Shareholders recognise that, in some cases, it would be detrimental to the company and shareholders to disclose these targets. However, shareholders consider this provision should generally apply by exception and should be clearly justified to shareholders.

5. Quality of reporting – Companies should seek not just to comply with the Reporting Regulations but should provide a full and clear explanation of the key decisions that the Remuneration Committee has made during the year and the reasons for them.

6. Recruitment of new directors – Companies have to disclose the maximum variable remuneration which can be paid to a new director. This excludes any payments made in compensation for the forfeiture of any award under variable remuneration at a previous employer. Shareholders recognise that companies may need flexibility to allow them to recruit new directors. However, shareholders will not support excessive

limits within their policy and will want any significant differences between the normal policy and the recruitment policy to be clearly justified.

Appendix 5 Joint Statement on Executive Contracts and Severance by the Association of British Insurers (ABI) and the National Association of Pension Funds (NAPF)

ABI

NAPF
Securing the future of pensions

JOINT STATEMENT ON EXECUTIVE CONTRACTS AND SEVERANCE BY THE ASSOCIATION OF BRITISH INSURERS (ABI) AND THE NATIONAL ASSOCIATION OF PENSION FUNDS (NAPF)

---

18 February 2008

1. Introduction

1.1 Our two organisations, whose members are leading institutional investors in UK markets, are publishing an updated statement of best practice on contract and severance policy for directors.

1.2 This statement is aimed at assisting Boards and their Remuneration Committees with the design and application of contractual obligations for senior executives. Shareholders have an expectation that Boards will consider the risks of negotiating inappropriate executive contracts that can lead to situations where failure is rewarded.

1.3 Institutional shareholders believe executives of listed companies should be appropriately rewarded for the value they generate. However, they are also concerned to avoid situations where departing executives are rewarded for under-performance. For many years the ABI and NAPF have considered this to be a matter of good governance and it is clearly addressed in the FRC's Combined Code on Corporate Governance.

2. Principles

2.1 The responsibility for setting directors' contracts lies primarily with the Remuneration Committee.

2.2 In line with the Combined Code, contracts should be set with reasonable notice periods.

2.3 Boards should ensure that executives show leadership by aligning their financial interests with those of the company.

2.4 The level of remuneration received by senior executives already factors in the risk associated with their role. Boards should ensure that contracts do not include any additional financial protection in the event of poor performance leading to termination.

2.5 The Remuneration Committee should carefully consider what commitments (including pension contributions and all other elements) their directors' terms of appointment would entail in the event of early termination.

2.6 Directors' contracts should ensure that severance payments arising from poor corporate performance should not extend beyond basic salary.

2.7 Companies should clearly disclose key elements of directors' contracts on their website and summarise them in the Remuneration Report.

2.8 Companies should fully disclose in their Remuneration Report the constituent parts of any severance payments and justify the total level and elements paid.

3. Guidance

3.1 This Guidance is intended to emphasise certain aspects of the Combined Code and where appropriate provide guidance as to shareholders' expectations.

3.2 Contract policy including terminations and the approach to mitigation should be clearly explained in the Remuneration Report. Also, corporate objectives set for executives by the Board should be clear. The more transparent and understandable the objectives, the easier it is to determine how an executive has performed and therefore prevent payment for failure. Wherever possible, objectives against which performance will be measured should be made public.

Contract Terms

3.3 Remuneration Committees should ensure that the policy and objectives on directors' contracts are clearly stated in the Remuneration Report. Shareholders will take account of contracts and the way they are implemented in considering their vote on the Remuneration Report and the re-election of members of the Remuneration Committee.

3.4 When contracts are being negotiated, boards should consider and avoid the reputational risk of being obliged to make large payments to executives who have failed to perform. Contracts should be reviewed periodically and Remuneration Committees should consider whether the contract provisions are in line with their policy and this Statement.

Notice Periods

3.5 The Combined Code states that under normal circumstances directors should be retained on contracts of one year or less. However we believe that a one-year notice period should not be seen as a floor, and we would strongly encourage boards to consider contracts with shorter notice periods. Compensation for risks run by senior executives is already implicit in the absolute level of remuneration, which mitigates the need for substantial contractual protection.

3.6 If it is necessary to offer executives longer notice periods, for example for incoming executives at companies in difficulties, we would expect the length of the contract to be justified. In that case the termination provisions attached should be fully disclosed and the length of the contract should reduce on a rolling basis in line with the recommendations contained in this Guidance.

Severance Payments

3.7 Remuneration Committees should have the leeway to design a policy appropriate to the needs and objectives of the company, but they must also have a clear understanding of their responsibility to negotiate suitable contracts and be able to justify severance payments to shareholders.

3.8 From the outset, Boards should establish a clear policy to ensure any non-contractual payments are linked to performance. No director should be entitled to discretionary payments in the event of termination of their contract arising from poor corporate performance. Remuneration Committees should consider retaining their discretion to reclaim bonuses if performance achievements are subsequently found to have been significantly mis-stated.

3.9 Contracts should not provide additional compensation for severance as a result of change of control.

3.10 Remuneration Committees should ensure that full benefit of mitigation is obtained. This includes the legal obligation on the part of the outgoing senior executive to mitigate the loss incurred through severance by seeking other employment and reducing the need for compensation. Phased payments are generally appropriate for fulfilling compensation on early termination. The ABI and NAPF are not supportive of the liquidated damages approach which involves agreement at the outset on the amount that will be paid in the event of severance.

Pensions

3.11 Pension entitlement or contributions on severance can represent a large element of cost to shareholders. Remuneration Committees should identify, review and disclose in the Remuneration Report any arrangements that guarantee pensions with limited or no abatement on severance or early retirement. These pension arrangements are no longer regarded as acceptable, except where they are generally available to all employees. Where opportunities arise, existing contracts should be amended. Such conditions should not be included in new contracts.

Inspection Arrangements

3.12 Directors' contracts and any side letters relating to severance terms and pension arrangements should be readily available for shareholder inspection.

4. <u>Conclusion</u>

4.1 It is unacceptable that poor performance by senior executives, which detracts from the value of an enterprise and threatens the livelihood of employees, can result in excessive payments to departing directors. Boards have a responsibility to ensure that this does not occur.

Enquiries to:

<u>ABI</u>
Marc Jobling 020 7216 7541
Patrick Neave 020 7216 7627

<u>NAPF</u>
David Paterson 020 7808 1337

18 February 2008

Appendix 6 Voluntary Code of Conduct in Relation to Executive Remuneration Consulting in the United Kingdom

(January 2014)

Preamble

Executive remuneration consultants are business advisors who provide a valuable service to companies, and in particular remuneration committees, by providing information, analysis and advice on the structure and levels of remuneration for senior executives. In providing this service, the role of consultants is to assist decision makers within the governance structure of the company to make the most informed and appropriate decisions possible having due regard to the organisation's strategy, financial situation, and pay philosophy; the Board's statutory duties: and the views of institutional investors and other stakeholders.

The Code of Conduct (the Code) is the document agreed by the members of the Remuneration Consultants Group Limited (RCG) which was formed in 2009 and represents the overwhelming majority of executive remuneration consultancy firms advising UK listed companies.

This Code clarifies the scope and conduct of the executive remuneration consultants' role, while recognising that all substantive executive remuneration decisions are made by the appropriate governance bodies in the company, primarily Remuneration Committees and their Chairs.

Background, Purpose and Scope

This Code of Conduct sets out the role of executive remuneration consultants, the manner in which they conduct business and the standards of behaviour expected of them.

It is concerned primarily with the way in which remuneration consultants ("Consultants"), whether they be firms or individual practitioners, provide advice to UK listed companies on executive remuneration matters. For the purpose of this Code, these are matters which are recommended by the UK Corporate Governance Code to fall within the terms of reference of a company's Remuneration Committee. By definition, they include all elements of executive directors' remuneration.

It is recognised that in the area of executive remuneration there is the potential for real or perceived conflicts of interest in that:

- executive directors may have personal interests which the Remuneration Committee may consider out of line with the broader interests of shareholders or the company as a whole;
- where advice is provided by Consultants to both the Remuneration Committee and management – whether in the area of executive remuneration or in other areas – it might be considered as being compromised (by the Consultant's own commercial interests or the potentially different interests or perspectives of those to whom the Consultant is providing advice).

This Code sets out ways in which these potential and/or perceived conflicts of interest may be minimised and thereby fosters shareholder and Remuneration Committee confidence in the integrity and objectivity of Consultants.

In this connection it is important to clarify the role that executive remuneration consultants fulfil. Their role is to provide advice and information which they believe to be appropriate and in the best interests of the company. Their input should take fully into account the UK Corporate Governance Code principle that pay should be sufficient, without being excessive, to attract, retain and motivate executives of the right calibre.

The purpose of their input is to support robust and informed decision making by the company on remuneration matters. This is the case regardless of whether these are decisions of the Remuneration Committee or executive directors. Under the UK's unitary board structure, both share a common duty to promote the success of the company.

As far as the scope of this Code is concerned:

- it should be recognised that executive remuneration advice is almost always provided to companies and that client companies will have their own governance codes and processes to assess quality and minimise conflicts;
- this is a voluntary code of conduct and statement of good practice and all Consultants are expected to build it into their terms of business with clients;

The Code was first published in 2009, last reviewed and revised in 2013 and will be reviewed biennially thereafter.

As with the UK Corporate Governance Code, the principles and processes set out in this Code are intended to apply to work carried out for UK premium listed companies and, particularly, the FTSE 350. It is recognised that other organisations (for example AIM companies) may have different governance structures which means that not every aspect of this Code may be relevant. However, it is expected that the same values will be applicable when work is conducted for other organisations which are either not fully listed or do not have a primary listing in the UK.

The authors of this Code recognise that other professional advisors may give advice to Remuneration Committees from time to time (such as solicitors, executive search consultants and actuaries). The Code is not primarily concerned with firms acting in that capacity. This consideration should equally apply to Consultants advising on executive remuneration but not formally appointed by the Remuneration Committee.

Fundamental Principles

Executive remuneration consultants, like other business professionals, should comply with the fundamental principles of transparency, integrity, objectivity, competence, due care and confidentiality. They should also ensure that, whether or not part of a larger consulting group providing a wider range of services, their internal governance structures promote the provision of objective and independent advice. This Code is designed to be complementary to such governance structures and any other codes relating to the professional bodies of which Consultants may be members. Consultants should also offer to brief the Remuneration Committee Chair on the operation of the agreed processes and protocols to minimise or eliminate conflicts of interest.

Where a Remuneration Committee, company or member firm believes that a Consultant has systematically or materially breached the Code, they should report this to the member firm concerned. If the Remuneration Committee or company is dissatisfied with the response, the Chairman of the RCG will be available for consultation. In accordance with the RCG's Articles of Association, membership of the RCG terminates where a member or one or more of its remuneration consultants has failed to meet the standards of behaviour which, in the opinion of the Board it is reasonable to expect.

The rest of this Code expands upon these fundamental principles and contains in the Appendix good practice guidelines on the ways in which these principles should apply.

Transparency

The role of Consultants is not to make decisions for their clients but to assist them in making fully informed decisions. To that end, all substantive advice should be clear and transparent with relevant and appropriate data presented objectively.

Where the Consultant is formally appointed to advise the Remuneration Committee, there should be a clear commitment for the Consultant to make available to the Chair of that Committee an agreed set of disclosures at the outset of the engagement and then annually thereafter. This will include information on the scope and cost of work provided by the Consultant's firm to the company in addition to work provided to the Remuneration Committee. It will also include information on the internal protocols to remove any potential conflicts of interest.

Integrity

Consultants should be straightforward and honest in all professional and business relationships. This implies a duty to deal with matters fairly and openly.

Management of Conflicts to Ensure Objectivity

Consultants should not allow conflict of interest or influence of others to override professional or business judgements and must ensure that they provide the best and most appropriate advice to the client as possible. A key to managing such conflicts is to ensure clarity in identifying to whom within the client the Consultant is providing advice, establishing the role expected of the Consultant and agreeing the processes and protocols to be followed.

When the Consultant is appointed as a principal advisor to the Remuneration Committee, it is important to agree with the Chair of the Remuneration Committee and record, at the outset of the engagement, supporting protocols in order to safeguard objectivity. These are likely to cover information provision and the basis for contact with executive management at the client company ("Client"). The Consultant should also be mindful of the potential conflict arising from other client relationships and draw these to the attention of the Remuneration Committee Chair as appropriate.

In addition, to manage potential conflicts of interest effectively:

- Consultants will not accept fees contingent on the introduction of new remuneration arrangements or the remuneration package (s) agreed for executives

- Consultants will not adopt the role of their firm's client relationship manager for the provision of non-related services on accounts where they are the principal executive remuneration consultant.

These protocols should be reviewed annually to ensure that any perceived or real conflicts of interest are dealt with. The consultant and the Chair of the Remuneration Committee should also discuss whether and how the procedures and protocols in place should be described in the Directors' Remuneration Report.

Competence and Due Care

The principle of competence and due care means that clients are entitled to have confidence in a Consultant's work and imposes an obligation on Consultants to maintain their knowledge at an appropriate level and carry out their work in a careful, thorough and timely manner.

To ensure that all individual consultants within a firm comply with the Code, each firm:

- should have a general code of business conduct which is provided to employees advising in this area;
- should provide training and professional development for all consultants which ensures that they are competent to consult within the framework of this Code.

Confidentiality

Consultants should respect the confidentiality of information acquired as a result of professional and business relationships and should not disclose such information to third parties without proper and specific authority unless there is a legal or professional right or duty to disclose.

Monitoring the effectiveness of the Code

Each year the RCG will carry out a formal review of the effectiveness of the Code. This will be presented and discussed at the RCG's AGM and a summary of the findings will be published on the RCG's website. In carrying out the annual review the RCG will undertake a confidential survey of the individual consultants in the member firms and assess any comments and complaints that have been brought to its attention during the year.

Good Practice Guidelines

These guidelines are provided to illustrate how the Code principles may be followed.

General

1. Consultants should encourage Clients to ensure that pay is properly linked to the long-term performance of the business. Consultants should also encourage Clients to consider the full implications of their decisions. This should include but not be limited to helping Clients reach a rounded and balanced view and to be sensitive to the potentially inflationary impact of market data.
2. Consultants should encourage Clients to consider fully the implications of complex design both on the motivation of executives and on the transparency of arrangements to shareholders and other stakeholders.
3. Where appropriate, Consultants should seek to help Remuneration Committees to take into account talent and succession planning when making decisions on pay.
4. Consultants should make the Remuneration Committee aware of the likely views of shareholders on the Client's executive remuneration with a specific emphasis on major shareholders where appropriate.

Transparency

5. Reports prepared by Consultants should explain the context in which advice is provided and, when advising on potentially significant changes in policy, they should comment on how any proposals compare with best practice and published guidance.
6. Selection of an appropriate comparator group for benchmarking purposes requires careful judgment. Any report should be clear on the types of companies comprised within the comparator group(s) used and the rationale for their selection and summarise the methodology used to value different elements of the remuneration package.
7. Reports and other written documents should identify the sources of information used. It should be made clear where the Consultant is relying on information provided by management or from other consulting firms. Where the Consultant contributes to a joint report with management, it should be clear in the report what is the Consultant's opinion and what is management's opinion.
8. Recognising that internal advice or other Consultants' (e.g. advisors to management) advice may be presented by others to the Remuneration Committee and relied on by it, Consultants should be particularly

careful to ensure that their written advice is capable of being read and understood by the Remuneration Committee without the advisor present.

9. All appointments should be governed by an engagement letter between the Consultant and the Client and should make clear to whom within the Client the Consultant is providing advice, i.e., whether to the Remuneration Committee, CEO or the executive management of the company or otherwise.

10. There should be a clear understanding of the role the Consultant is expected to play when appointed to advise the Remuneration Committee and, specifically, whether the role is to be a principal advisor to the Remuneration Committee on a range of remuneration-related issues (as opposed to providing data or advice on an ad hoc basis or just on specific topics).

11. In order to be aware of and mitigate any potential conflicts of interest, when the Consultant is appointed as principal advisor to the Remuneration Committee, the Committee Chair should agree with the Consultant a set of disclosures at the outset of the engagement and annually thereafter. The precise nature and frequency of the information to be provided should be agreed by the Consultant with the Chair of the Remuneration Committee. Information should be available on:

    - the areas on which the Consultant is engaged to advise the Remuneration Committee and any areas where it has been agreed that the Consultant should not provide advice;
    - the scope and cost of work provided by the Consultant's firm to the company, or senior executives of the company, in addition to work performed directly for the Remuneration Committee. The Consultant should normally report on an annual basis the approximate split of the value of the work done for the Remuneration Committee and for executive management to the Remuneration Committee;
    - The Remuneration Committee should have oversight of all the work that the Consultant carries out for the Company;
    - the safeguards in place to ensure that information provided by the client company are kept confidential and separate both from information of other clients and from other departments within the Consultant's wider firm;
    - the Consultant's code regarding ownership of, and dealing in, the shares of client companies;
    - the way in which the personal remuneration of the principal Consultants engaged in advising on executive remuneration issues is affected, if at all, by the cross-selling of non-related services;

- the process for maintaining quality assurance, ensuring that work covered by this Code is kept independent of any other services provided by the Consultant's firm and for dealing with complaints;

12. Consultants should encourage their Clients to include in their Directors' Remuneration Report a statement of whether they are using Consultants who are members of the RCG.

Integrity

13. When they are appointed as principal advisors to the Remuneration Committee, Consultants should alert the Chair of the Remuneration Committee when they become aware that their advice is being presented in the context of reports, communications or other information where they believe that the information is false or misleading or omits or obscures required information where such omission or obscurity could be misleading.
14. In relation to shareholders' engagement, the Remuneration Committee is responsible for explaining the Company's pay arrangements to shareholders. Where Consultants are involved in this process, their primary responsibility should be to support in the communication process, to set out the Remuneration Committee's proposals to shareholders and to represent fully to the Remuneration Committee all the views expressed to the Consultant in their capacity as agent for the Committee.
15. Consultants should only market their services to both current and prospective clients in a responsible way. Bespoke pay benchmarking reports require Remuneration Committee input into the selection of comparator groups and should not be sent to clients or non-clients on an unsolicited basis.

Objectivity

16. When the Consultant is appointed as principal Remuneration Committee advisor, there are a number of protocols and processes which should be established from the outset to ensure that the Consultant is able to provide best advice in a manner which meets the Remuneration Committee's requirements. These include:

    - agreeing a process to ensure that the Consultant has sufficient information to provide advice in context (which may be achieved by providing for the Consultant to receive copies of all or most Remuneration Committee papers and minutes, not just those relating to matters upon which he or she is specifically being asked for advice);

- an agreement that the Consultant meets at least annually with the Remuneration Committee Chair in order to review remuneration issues and any implications of business strategy development and market change;
- clarity on the extent to which the Consultant should have access to and/or provide advice to management;
- confirmation of the process by which any information and recommendations relating to the Chief Executive Officer and other executives are to be communicated to the Remuneration Committee and the manner and extent to which such information and recommendations should also be communicated to executive management;
- agreement on the flow of papers and, in particular, whether draft papers may be sent to management to check facts and understanding of context prior to being sent to the Remuneration Committee Chair;
- agreement of an annual review of the Consultant's performance and of roles and responsibilities. This should be led by the Chair of the Remuneration Committee but may be initiated by the Consultant. The review of performance should also include an assessment of the extent to which there is a potential conflict of interest which may be perceived to affect the independence and objectivity of the advice provided, where, for example, the Consultant's firm provides other services to the Company or the work provided by the Consultant accounts for a significant proportion of the firm's total revenue.

Competence and Due Care

17. The right for Clients to have confidence in a Consultant's work means that if work which a Consultant considers necessary is precluded by cost or time constraints, then they must either decline to act or qualify the advice.
18. Where a Consultant is aware of any limitations in their advice, they should make their Client aware of such limitation.

Index

[all references are to paragraph number]